ILLINOIS CENTRAL COLLEGE
PN6112.B58 1968
STACKS
Studies in drama
A12900 304834

W9-BXE-577

Studies in Drama

Second Edition

BLAZE ODELL BONAZZA
California State College at Long Beach

EMIL ROY
Northern Illinois University

Harper & Row, Publishers
New York, Evanston, and London

STUDIES IN DRAMA, Second Edition

 For information address Harper & Row, Publishers, Incorporated, 49 East 33rd Street, New York, N.Y. 10016.

Library of Congress Catalog Card Number: 68-11450

Contents

A Structural Approach to Drama

It is a truism of dramatic study that plays are written to be presented on a stage for a particular audience, not to be read by the solitary reader in the restrictive confines of his own room or classroom. One cannot reasonably deny that the best way to appreciate a play properly is to see it, as part of an audience, acted by a group of skilled performers under a perceptive and imaginative director with good scenic and other technical devices at his disposal. Unfortunately one cannot always do this; one frequently has to read a play rather than see it performed or else be denied acquaintance with it. Even if one sees a play presented on stage, it is possible to benefit even more from the performance by having a good knowledge of the play in advance. The more complex the play, of course, the more likely this is to be true. Furthermore, an intelligent reading of a play may excel witnessing a faulty or distorted presentation. Anyone who has carefully read a highly complex play like a Shakespearean tragedy, for example, and then seen it performed ineptly can readily attest to this.

In reading a play, the reader must recreate the work in the theater of his own mind, translating the written word into the imitation of an action intended by the playwright. He has to interpret the meaning of individual lines of dialogue and imagine the intonation of the character's voice, his general appearance and demeanor, even his facial expressions and specific movements to be fully aware of what is going on in the play. He must learn to appreciate the ironies inherent in a dramatic situation when a character says something that has a meaning to the audience other than the one he intends (as when old Cabot in *Desire Under The Elms* boasts about his virility after the birth of the baby) or when he does something which produces a result exactly opposite to the one he intended (as when Lear divides his kingdom to secure a peaceful old age and reaps a harvest of misery and madness instead). Recognizing these dramatic ironies, both verbal and situational, is one of the most important skills the reader can develop; for the full significance of an episode or of an entire play can be missed or misinterpreted if one is insensitive to such deliberate ambiguities of language and reversals of intention in action.

Not only must the reader be alert to subtleties of language and the temporarily hidden significance of certain actions, but he must also be aware of the emotional content of the scene and its relation to the physical setting. In O'Neill's *Desire Under The Elms,* for example, it is not a matter of chance that the critical seduction of Eben by Abbie takes place in the parlor, the room identified with Eben's dead mother, or that in *King Lear* his madness reaches its highest intensity on a barren heath during an earth-shaking storm. Sometimes elements of the setting take on a symbolic meaning, as in *The Glass Menagerie* where the fire escape obviously represents something more than a metal staircase to provide exit in case of a fire.

When a reader engages in this mentally arduous but ultimately rewarding task, he has in a sense produced, directed, and acted out the play and at the same time been his own audience and critic of the play presented. With increasing sophistication in the reading of plays, he can derive a heightened degree of enjoyment from reading plays he may never see acted,

In order to do this with any degree of success, he must take advantage of every clue and hint offered by the playwright in dialogue, action, setting, or stage direction and special effects. Unlike a novel or short story, a play does not usually provide a reader with the kind of psychological analysis or interpretation, implied or explicit, which often serves as a link between the author and the reader of fiction. The playwright assumes his dramatic microcosm will be recreated on stage, unless he is writing *closet* or unperformable drama, and he relies on the dramaturgic devices available to the theater he is writing for to get his meaning and desired emotional effect across. Sophocles' chorus with its ritualized dance patterns and songs relating to the action in *Antigone,* Shakespeare's use of his curtainless stage to produce fluidity of action in *King Lear,* and Williams' use of transparent apartment walls in *The Glass Menagerie* are all examples of such dramaturgic devices. For this reason reading a play is in many ways more difficult than reading most fiction. On the surface a play may look easier because the language and action are more economical and direct, but this apparent simplicity is deceiving. Actually the demands on the reader are such that he needs some method of approach to assist him in coming to grips with this often entertaining but sometimes perplexing art form.

One of the important things the reader must be aware of is the nature of the conventions governing the play he is reading. Plays differ in the way they make demands on the audience's temporary suspension of disbelief. An important convention is the one relating to the nature of the dramatic illusion that is striven for. The reader should ask himself whether the playwright is trying to duplicate literal reality as Ibsen does in *An Enemy of the People* or distorting literal reality, even ignoring it, as Williams does in *The Glass Menagerie* in his attempt to illuminate the human condition. A play is not necessarily more worthwhile intrinsically because it attempts to duplicate "real life," nor is it necessarily more profound because it deals in symbols or uses expressionistic stage devices with things standing for ideas. Playwrights may differ from one another in the techniques they employ because of historical necessity and the physical conditions of their theater as do Sophocles and Shakespeare or because of personal preference as do Shaw and Wilder. Great drama is possible regardless of the type of dramatic illusion exercised by the playwright and participated in by his audience. An intelligent audience will come to accept almost any convention relating to the dramatic illusion as long as it works well with the other elements in the play. We accept the chorus in *Antigone* as observer, actor, and commentator; the soliloquy and aside in *King Lear* as characterization and preparation devices; or the lantern-slide technique in *The Glass Menagerie* for the control of time and mood as contributions to the total effect. We grant the playwright the privilege of using those devices that best suit his particular purpose and idea of the theater. In spite of this concession to him, however, we still have the legitimate right to demand that within the framework of his conventions and physical theater he do his task artistically and honestly and not use things simply for cheap theatrical effect. If he chooses to have a character speak directly to the audience in nonrealistic, rhythmic, even melodic poetic diction replete with imagery, all we ask is that the speech extend characterization, further action, or add beauty to the ideas presented. If he uses his chorus as a character in the action, he must provide it with an appropriate identity and acceptable motivation. If he uses technical gadgetry, it must be for a purpose other than mere clever display.

But conventions are only the scaffolding the dramatic artist uses in his attempt to imitate an action he has selected as being somehow both entertaining and significant, whether he views life tragically as does Sophocles, comically as does Shaw, or with a combined outlook as does Shakespeare. The heart of the play is the action he chooses to represent and the conclusion toward which every incident in the play is directed, as in *Antigone* "to do the will of the gods." One is interested primarily in what happens in a play, to whom it happens, and how and why it does within the limits of dramatic probability and necessity stemming from the playwright's initial situation or *donnée.* The action of most plays, even though superficially complex, is usually reducible to fairly simple elements. In almost any play one character (the *protagonist*) is trying to do something, to gain some goal, which is interfered with by conflict with some other character (the *antagonist*) or with opposing circumstances. In *The Glass Menagerie,* for example, Tom wants freedom to find himself, but this conflicts with Laura's need for understanding companionship and Amanda's desire for the perilous security of a world with genteel illusions. In the struggle that results from any conflict, the protagonist may or may not have allies or people in his confidence, as Lear has in Kent and the Fool; but in his crucial confrontation with his fate, the protagonist usually stands alone. In Synge's *Riders to the Sea* Maurya is trying to reach some accommodation with the harsh circumstances of her life on a barren island surrounded by an unconquerable foe, the sea. She strives to maintain herself in the face of this impersonal hostility and avoid the loss of all her sons, but the relentless sea exacts full payment from her. Antigone, who wants to give her brother a proper burial "to do the will of the gods," works uncompromisingly against the edict of Creon even though she realizes it means her own life is at stake. Creon, in turn, tries to restore political stability in a war-torn land against the will of Antigone associating his own will with that of the gods. This conflict of goals brings about a tragic catastrophe which sheds light on the conditions of human life as Sophocles and his audience saw it. Even when the conflict in a play is not overt, there is one to be found, for drama without conflict is a contradiction in terms. In *Our Town,* for example, the characters are essentially in harmony with one another except for minor confrontations such as those over a boy's responsibility to do his chores or a husband and wife's mild difference over how to spend the money from a small inheritance. But there is a central conflict in the play involving man's attitude toward life, time, and death as exemplified chiefly in the dilemma Emily faces in her desire to revisit the living on an "ordinary" day in the past.

In speaking of plot structure, the term *exposition* is used to refer to the disclosure of information about the past which is necessary to explain what is going on in the present and what may happen as a consequence in the future. In *Antigone* the dialogue in the prologue acquaints us with Antigone's plan of action which brings about Creon's reaction in the play proper. In modern absurdist drama the playwright refuses to enlighten the audience about what has happened prior to present action, or he reveals it in a series of *non sequiturs.* As a result the audience is confused as to what exactly is going on in the play and, by extension, in life—precisely the feeling that the theater of the absurd wants to create about human existence.

Preparation or foreshadowing is the providing of information relating to future action in the play, and this may be done through speech or action. In *An Enemy of the People* the remarks and behavior of the doctor's supposed allies in the newspaper office prepare us for the disastrous outcome of the town meeting which the doctor is pinning his hopes on.

The term *complication* refers to developments in the plot which delay or obstruct the protagonist's attempt to achieve his goal. In *Antigone* Creon's plan to achieve political stability is first complicated by the news that his edict has been violated: a rebel in the recent civil war has been accorded the interdicted burial rites. Further complications occur when the culprit's identity is disclosed and when she refuses to submit to his will; still other complications arise through the resistance Creon encounters in the words and deeds of Haimon, Teiresias, and the chorus. Usually complications are arranged in some kind of sequential, logical pattern suggesting inevitability in an order of increasing importance in the action and growing psychological tension. The most important complication constitutes the *crisis* or turning point, leading to a reversal of fortune or peripety. From this point on, the events lead to a *catastrophe,* which is followed by a *resolution* or *dénouement* or final working-out of things with a return to some emotional plateau. In *Antigone* the action is resolved by Creon's acceptance of guilt and the new wisdom which grows out of the suffering. In some plays the emotionally climactic complication or crisis may result not from action, but from a failure to act. The inability of the characters involved to act decisively to save the orchard in the Chekhov play leads to the catastrophe, the loss of the estate at auction, and to the resolution, the death of illusion in the face of reality, while the disintegrating old order is replaced by dreams of a new order.

But action alone, no matter how well plotted and executed, does not make a truly great play. It may make exciting melodrama or hilarious farce, but it does not make tragedy or true comedy by itself. In order to make bare actions come to life and assume general significance, the playwright must make them the actions of plausibly motivated characters who are somehow representative and still interesting and complex enough in their own right to be worth caring about. Sometimes a playwright succeeds admirably with both his major and minor characters, as Shakespeare does with Lear and Kent in *King Lear;* sometimes he falls short of the ideal as Ibsen does with Dr. Stockmann and Petya in *An Enemy of the People.* The playwright's task is to create suitable characters who could conceivably do the things required of them by the plot and who are, at the same time, not so idiosyncratic that they fail to represent human nature in some universal sense. If Shaw's Captain Shotover in *Heartbreak House* were simply an alcoholic old megalomaniac or Antigone only a perverse adolescent with a martyr complex, they would be of interest only as case studies, not as human beings making decisions of significance to all of us.

The playwright may do his characterizing immediately by showing us a character engaged with another in speech and action as Sophocles does with Antigone in the prologue of his play. Or he may let us learn something about the character by first having someone else in the play comment about him as Kent and Gloucester do about their king in *Lear*. Whenever this latter device is used, the reader should ask himself whether the testimony is coming from a reliable, unprejudiced source or from someone with a special bias. What Goneril says about Lear's "infirmity" to Regan may be true, but it may be incomplete and is probably not unprejudiced. The character may let us know something about himself as Tom does in *The Glass Menagerie* when he tells of his interest in writing poetry or as Lopahin does in referring to his peasant background in *The Cherry Orchard*. Even such self-revelations have to be weighed with other evidence. Whenever there is a conflict between what someone else says about a character, what he says about himself, and what he does in the play, it is generally best to judge the character by the totality of what he does.

Out of the relationship between character and action and the language of the play arises the meaning of the entire work. Of course, the full meaning of any play is the play itself and any attempt to extract its essence like perfume from a flower can never really succeed completely. In fact, any play which can be easily summarized in a simple statement is probably rather thin and superficial to start with. At the same time, however, it is possible to formulate some kind of statement which in some limited way conveys the central emotional and intellectual impact of the play. Very few good plays have been written primarily to convey some message—moral, philosophical, social, or otherwise—but a good play does impart the playwright's attitude toward some important human problem, in comedy as well as tragedy. In *Antigone* Sophocles is certainly saying something about the conflict between the conscience of the individual and the demands of the state as it affects man's relation to a moral universe. In *Lear* Shakespeare is commenting on the tragic destruction which results from the foolish attempt to weigh the imponderable and the redemption made possible by personal suffering and the sacrifice of others. In *The Glass Menagerie* Williams is telling us something about the illusions that shape, distort, and sustain life, and in *Heartbreak House* Shaw is calling our attention to the self-deception and destructive folly mankind constantly engages in.

As you read these plays you will be asked to consider certain questions relating to their structure so that you may better appreciate the artistry of the work and come to a better understanding and a greater enjoyment of it. In an uncritical, unexamined reading some important details may be overlooked and the play thereby lose some of its effect and the meaning obscured. For best results the play should be read in its entirety first and then gone over again with the close scrutiny the questions demand. Synge's *Riders to the Sea* has been provided with a set of answers to the questions raised which could legitimately arise out of the kind of close, thoughtful reading all of these plays richly deserve.

RIDERS TO THE SEA

John Millington Synge

Cast of Characters

MAURYA, *an old woman*
BARTLEY, *her son*
CATHLEEN, *her daughter*
NORA, *a younger daughter*
MEN *and* WOMEN

[*Scene: An island off the west of Ireland. Cottage kitchen, with nets, oil-skins, spinning-wheel, some new boards standing by the wall, etc.* CATHLEEN, *a girl of about twenty, finishes kneading cake, and puts it down in the pot-oven by the fire; then wipes her hands, and begins to spin at the wheel.* NORA, *a young girl, puts her head in at the door.*]

Nora (*in a low voice*). Where is she?

Cathleen: She's lying down, God help her, and may be sleeping, if she's able.

[NORA *comes in softly, and takes a bundle from under her shawl.*]

Cathleen (*spinning the wheel rapidly*). What is it you have?

Nora: The young priest is after bringing them. It's a shirt and a plain stocking were got off a drowned man in Donegal.

[CATHLEEN *stops her wheel with a sudden movement, and leans out to listen.*]

Nora: We're to find out if it's Michael's they are, some time herself will be down looking by the sea.

Cathleen: How would they be Michael's, Nora? How would he go the length of that way to the far north?

Nora: The young priest says he's known the like of it. "If it's Michael's they are," says he, "you can tell herself he's got a clean burial by the grace of God, and if they're not his, let no one say a word about them, for she'll be getting her death," says he, "with crying and lamenting."

[*The door which* NORA *half closed is blown open by a gust of wind.*]

Cathleen (*looking out anxiously*). Did you ask him would he stop Bartley going this day with the horses to the Galway fair?

Nora: "I won't stop him," says he, "but let you not be afraid. Herself does be saying prayers half through the night, and the Almighty God won't leave her destitute," says he, "with no son living."

Cathleen: Is the sea bad by the white rocks, Nora?

Nora: Middling bad, God help us. There's a great roaring in the west, and it's worse it'll be getting when the tide's turned to the wind. (*She goes over to the table with the bundle.*) Shall I open it now?

Cathleen: Maybe she'd wake up on us, and come in before we'd done. (*Coming to the table.*) It's a long time we'll be, and the two of us crying.

Nora (*goes to the inner door and listens*). She's moving about on the bed. She'll be coming in a minute.

Cathleen: Give me the ladder, and I'll put them up in the turf-loft, the way she won't know of them at all, and maybe when the tide turns she'll be going down to see would he be floating from the east.

[*They put the ladder against the gable of the chimney;* CATHLEEN *goes up a few steys and hides the bundle in the turf-loft.* MAURYA *comes from the inner room.*]

Maurya (*looking up at* CATHLEEN *and speaking querulously*). Isn't it turf enough you have for this day and evening?

Cathleen: There's a cake baking at the fire for a short space (*throwing down the turf*) and Bartley will want it when the tide turns if he goes to Connemara.

[NORA *picks up the turf and puts it round the pot-oven.*]

Maurya (*sitting down on a stool at the fire*). He won't go this day with the wind rising from the south and west. He won't go this day, for the young priest will stop him surely.

Nora: He'll not stop him, mother, and I heard Eamon Simon and Stephen Pheetey and Colum Shawn saying he would go.

Maurya: Where is he itself?

Nora: He went down to see would there be another boat sailing in the week, and I'm thinking it won't be long till he's here now, for the tide's turning at the green head, and the hooker's tacking from the east.

Cathleen: I hear some one passing the big stones.

Nora (*looking out*). He's coming now, and he in a hurry.

Bartley (*comes in and looks round the room; speaking sadly and quietly*). Where is the bit of new rope, Cathleen, which was bought in Connemara?

Cathleen (*coming down*). Give it to him, Nora; it's on a nail by the white boards. I hung it up this morning, for the pig with the black feet was eating it.

Nora (*giving him a rope*). Is that it, Bartley?

Maurya: You'd do right to leave that rope, Bartley, hanging by the boards. (BARTLEY *takes the rope.*) It will be wanting in this place, I'm telling you, if Michael is washed up to-morrow morning, or the next morning, or any morning in the week, for it's a deep grave we'll make him by the grace of God.

Bartley (*beginning to work with the rope*). I've no halter the way I can ride down on the mare, and I must go now quickly. This is the one boat going for two weeks or beyond it, and the fair will be a good fair for horses I heard them saying below.

Maurya: It's a hard thing they'll be saying below if the body is washed up and there's no man in it to make the coffin, and I after giving a big price for the finest white boards you'd find in Connemara.

[*She looks round at the boards.*]

Bartley: How would it be washed up, and we after looking each day for nine days, and a strong wind blowing a while back from the west and south?

Maurya: If it wasn't found itself, that wind is raising the sea, and there was a star up against the moon, and it rising in the night. If it was a hundred horses, or a thousand horses you had itself, what is the price of a thousand horses against a son where there is one son only?

Bartley (*working at the halter, to* CATHLEEN). Let you go down each day, and see the sheep aren't jumping in on the rye, and if the jobber comes you can sell the pig with the black feet if there is a good price going.

Maurya: How would the like of her get a good price for a pig?

Bartley (*to* CATHLEEN). If the west wind holds with the last bit of the moon let you and Nora get up weed enough for another cock for the kelp. It's hard set we'll be from this day with no one in it but one man to work.

Maurya: It's hard set we'll be surely the day you're drownd'd with the rest. What way will I live and the girls with me, and I an old woman looking for the grave?

[BARTLEY *lays down the halter, takes off his old coat, and puts on a newer one of the same flannel.*]

Bartley (*to* NORA). Is she coming to the pier?

Nora (*looking out*). She's passing the green head and letting fall her sails.

Bartley (*getting his purse and tobacco*). I'll have half an hour to go down, and you'll see me coming again in two days, or in three days, or maybe in four days if the wind is bad.

Maurya (*turning round to the fire, and putting her shawl over her head*). Isn't it a hard and cruel man won't hear a word from an old woman, and she holding him from the sea?

Cathleen: It's the life of a young man to be going on the sea, and who would listen to an old woman with one thing and she saying it over?

Bartley (*taking the halter*). I must go now quickly. I'll ride down on the red mare, and the gray pony'll run behind me. . . . The blessing of God on you. (*He goes out.*)

Maurya (*crying out as he is in the door*). He's gone now, God spare us, and we'll not see him again. He's gone now, and when the black night is falling I'll have no son left me in the world.

Cathleen: Why wouldn't you give him your blessing and he looking round in the door? Isn't it sorrow enough is on every one in this house without your sending him out with an unlucky word behind him, and a hard word in his ear?

[MAURYA *takes up the tongs and begins raking the fire aimlessly without looking round.*]

Nora (*turning toward her*). You're taking away the turf from the cake.

Cathleen (*crying out*). The Son of God forgive us, Nora, we're after forgetting his bit of bread.

[*She comes over to the fire.*]

Nora: And it's destroyed he'll be going till dark night, and he after eating nothing since the sun went up.

Cathleen (*turning the cake out of the oven*). It's destroyed he'll be, surely. There's no sense left on any person in a house where an old woman will be talking forever.

[MAURYA *sways herself on her stool.*]

Cathleen (*cutting off some of the bread and rolling it in a cloth; to* MAURYA).

Let you go down now to the spring well and give him this and he passing. You'll see him then and the dark word will be broken, and you can say "God speed you," the way he'll be easy in his mind.

Maurya (*taking the bread*). Will I be in it as soon as himself?

Cathleen: If you go now quickly.

Maurya (*standing up unsteadily*). It's hard set I am to walk.

Cathleen (*looking at her anxiously*). Give her the stick, Nora, or maybe she'll slip on the big stones.

Nora: What stick?

Cathleen: The stick Michael brought from Connemara.

Maurya (*taking a stick* NORA *gives her*). In the big world the old people do be leaving things after them for their sons and children, but in this place it is the young men do be leaving things behind for them that do be old.

[*She goes out slowly.* NORA *goes over to the ladder.*]

Cathleen: Wait, Nora, maybe she'd turn back quickly. She's that sorry, God help her, you wouldn't know the thing she'd do.

Nora: Is she gone round by the bush?

Cathleen (*looking out*). She's gone now. Throw it down quickly, for the Lord knows when she'll be out of it again.

Nora (*getting the bundle from the loft*). The young priest said he'd be passing to-morrow, and we might go down and speak to him below if it's Michael's they are surely.

Cathleen (*taking the bundle*). Did he say what way they were found?

Nora (*coming down*). "There were two men," says he, "and they rowing round with poteen before the cocks crowed, and the oar of one of them caught the body, and they passing the black cliffs of the north."

Cathleen (*trying to open the bundle*). Give me a knife, Nora, the string's perished with the salt water, and there's a black knot on it you wouldn't loosen in a week.

Nora (*giving her a knife*). I've heard tell it was a long way to Donegal.

Cathleen (*cutting the string*). It is surely. There was a man in here a while ago—the man sold us that knife—and he said if you set off walking from the rocks beyond, it would be seven days you'd be in Donegal.

Nora: And what time would a man take, and he floating?

[CATHLEEN *opens the bundle and takes out a bit of a stocking. They look at them eagerly.*]

Cathleen (*in a low voice*). The Lord spare us, Nora! isn't it a queer hard thing to say if it's his they are surely?

Nora: I'll get his shirt off the hook the way we can put the one flannel on the other. (*She looks through some clothes hanging in the corner.*) It's not with them, Cathleen, and where will it be?

Cathleen: I'm thinking Bartley put it on him in the morning, for his own shirt was heavy with the salt in it. (*Pointing to the corner.*) There's a bit of a sleeve was of the same stuff. Give me that and it will do.

[NORA *brings it to her and they compare the flannel.*]

Cathleen: It's the same stuff, Nora; but if it is itself aren't there great rolls of it in the shops of Galway, and isn't it many another man may have a shirt of it as well as Michael himself?

Nora (*who has taken up the stocking and counted the stitches, crying out*). It's Michael, Cathleen, it's Michael; God spare his soul, and what will herself say when she hears this story, and Bartley on the sea?

Cathleen (*taking the stocking*). It's a plain stocking.

Nora: It's the second one of the third pair I knitted, and I put up three-score stitches, and I dropped four of them.

Cathleen (*counts the stitches*). It's that number is in it. (*Crying out.*) Ah, Nora, isn't it a bitter thing to think of him floating that way to the far north, and no one to keen him but the black hags that do be flying on the sea?

Nora (*swinging herself round, and throwing out her arms on the clothes*). And isn't it a pitiful thing when there is nothing left of a man who was a great rower and fisher, but a bit of an old shirt and a plain stocking?

Cathleen (*after an instant*). Tell me is herself coming, Nora? I hear a little sound on the path.

Nora (*looking out*). She is, Cathleen. She's coming up to the door.

Cathleen: Put these things away before she'll come in. Maybe it's easier she'll be after giving her blessing to Bartley, and we won't let on we've heard anything the time he's on the sea.

Nora (*helping* CATHLEEN *to close the bundle*). We'll put them here in the corner.

[*They put them into a hole in the chimney corner.* CATHLEEN *goes back to the spinning-wheel.*]

Nora: Will she see it was crying I was?

Cathleen: Keep your back to the door the way the light'll not be on you.

[NORA *sits down at the chimney corner, with her back to the door.* MAURYA *comes in very slowly, without looking at the girls, and goes over to her stool at the other side of the fire. The cloth with the bread is still in her hand. The girls look at each other, and* NORA *points to the bundle of bread.*]

Cathleen (*after spinning for a moment*). You didn't give him his bit of bread?

[MAURYA *begins to keen softly, without turning round.*]

Cathleen: Did you see him riding down? (MAURYA *goes on keening.*)

Cathleen (*a little impatiently*). God forgive you; isn't it a better thing to raise your voice and tell what you seen, than to be making lamentation for a thing that's done? Did you see Bartley, I'm saying to you.

Maurya (*with a weak voice*). My heart's broken from this day.

Cathleen (*as before*). Did you see Bartley?

Maurya: I seen the fearfulest thing.

Cathleen (*leaves her wheel and looks out*). God forgive you; he's riding the mare now over the green head, and the gray pony behind him.

Maurya (*starts, so that her shawl falls back from her head and shows her white tossed hair; with a frightened voice*). The gray pony behind him.

Cathleen (*coming to the fire*). What is it ails you, at all?

Maurya (*speaking very slowly*). I've seen the fearfulest thing any person has seen, since the day Bride Dara seen the dead man with a child in his arms.

Cathleen and ***Nora:*** Uah.

[*They crouch down in front of the old woman at the fire.*]

Nora: Tell us what it is you seen.

Maurya: I went down to the spring well, and I stood there saying a prayer to myself. Then Bartley came along, and he riding on the red mare with the gray pony behind him. (*She puts up her hands, as if to hide something from her eyes.*) The Son of God spare us, Nora!

Cathleen: What is it you seen.

Maurya: I seen Michael himself.

Cathleen (*speaking softly*). You did not, mother; it wasn't Michael you seen, for his body is after being found in the Far North, and he's got a clean burial by the grace of God.

Maurya (*a little defiantly*). I'm after seeing him this day, and he riding and galloping. Bartley came first on the red mare; and I tried to say, "God speed you," but something choked the words in my throat. He went by quickly; and "the blessing of God on you," says he, and I could say nothing. I looked up then, and I crying, at the gray pony, and there was Michael upon it—with fine clothes on him, and new shoes on his feet.

Cathleen (*begins to keen*). It's destroyed we are from this day. It's destroyed, surely.

Nora: Didn't the young priest say the Almighty God wouldn't leave her destitute with no son living?

Maurya (*in a low voice, but clearly*). It's little the like of him knows of the sea. . . . Bartley will be lost now, and let you call in Eamon and make me a good coffin out of the white boards, for I won't live after them. I've had a husband, and a husband's father, and six sons in this house—six fine men, though it was a hard birth I had with every one of them and they coming to the world—and some of them were found and some of them were not found, but they're gone now the lot of them. . . . There were Stephen, and Shawn, were lost in the great wind, and found after in the Bay of Gregory of the Golden Mouth, and carried up the two of them on the one plank, and in by that door.

[*She pauses for a moment; the girls start as if they heard something through the door that is half open behind them.*]

Nora (*in a whisper*). Did you hear that, Cathleen? Did you hear a noise in the northeast?

Cathleen (*in a whisper*). There's some one after crying out by the seashore.

Maurya (*continues without hearing anything*). There was Sheamus and his father, and his own father again, were lost in a dark night, and not a stick or sign was seen of them when the sun went up. There was Patch after was drowned out of a curagh that turned over. I was sitting here with Bartley, and he a baby, lying on my two knees, and I seen two women, and three women, and four women coming in, and they crossing themselves, and not saying a word. I looked out then, and there were men coming after them, and they holding a thing in the half of a red sail, and water dripping out of it—it was a dry day, Nora—and leaving a track to the door.

[*She pauses again with her hand stretched out toward the door. It opens softly and old women begin to come in, crossing themselves on the threshold, and kneeling down in front of the stage with red petticoats over their heads.*]

Maurya (*half in a dream, to* CATHLEEN). Is it Patch, or Michael, or what is it at all?

Cathleen: Michael is after being found in the Far North, and when he is found there how could he be here in this place?

Maurya: There does be a power of young men floating round in the sea, and what way would they know if it was Michael they had, or another man like him, for when a man is nine days in the sea, and the wind blowing, it's hard set his own mother would be to say what man was it.

Cathleen: It's Michael, God spare him, for they're after sending us a bit of his clothes from the Far North.

[*She reaches out and hands* MAURYA *the clothes that belonged to* MICHAEL. MAURYA *stands up slowly, and takes them in her hands.* NORA *looks out.*]

Nora: They're carrying a thing among them and there's a water dripping out of it and leaving a track by the big stones.

Cathleen (*in a whisper to the women who have come in*). Is it Bartley it is?

One of the Women: It is surely, God rest his soul.

[*Two younger women come in and pull out the table. Then men carry in the body of* BARTLEY, *laid on a plank, with a bit of a sail over it, and lay it on the table.*]

Cathleen (*to the women, as they are doing so*). What way was he drowned?

One of the Women: The gray pony knocked him into the sea, and he was washed out where there is a great surf on the white rocks.

[MAURYA *has gone over and knelt down at the head of the table. The women are keening softly and swaying themselves with a slow movement.* CATHLEEN *and* NORA *kneel at the other end of the table. The men kneel near the door.*]

Maurya (*raising her head and speaking as if she did not see the people around her*). They're all gone now, and there isn't anything more the sea can do to me. . . . I'll have no call now to be up crying and praying when the wind breaks from the south, and you can hear the surf is in the east, and the surf is in the west, making a great stir with the two noises, and they hitting one on the other. I'll have no call now to be going down and getting Holy Water in the dark nights after Samhain, and I won't care what way the sea is when the other women will be keening. (*To* NORA.) Give me the Holy Water, Nora; there's a small sup still on the dresser.

[NORA *gives it to her.*]

Maurya (*drops* MICHAEL'S *clothes across* BARTLEY'S *feet, and sprinkles the Holy Water over him*). It isn't that I haven't prayed for you, Bartley, to the Almighty God. It isn't that I haven't said prayers in the dark night till you wouldn't know what I'd be saying; but it's a great rest I'll have now, and it's time surely. It's a great rest I'll have now, and great sleeping in the long nights after Samhain, if it's only a bit of wet flour we do have to eat, and maybe a fish that would be stinking.

[*She kneels down again, crossing herself, and saying prayers under her breath.*]

Cathleen (*to an* OLD MAN). Maybe yourself and Eamon would make a coffin when the sun rises. We have fine white boards herself bought, God help her, thinking Michael would be found, and I have a new cake you can eat while you'll be working.

The Old Man (*looking at the boards*). Are there nails with them?

Cathleen: There are not, Colum; we didn't think of the nails.

Another Man: It's a great wonder she wouldn't think of the nails, and all the coffins she's seen made already.

Cathleen: It's getting old she is, and broken.

[MAURYA *stands up again very slowly and spreads out the pieces of* MICHAEL'S *clothes beside the body, sprinkling them with the last of the Holy Water.*]

Nora (*in a whisper to* CATHLEEN). She's quiet now and easy; but the day Michael was drowned you could hear her crying out from this to the spring well. It's fonder she was of Michael, and would any one have thought that?

Cathleen (*slowly and clearly*). An old woman will be soon tired with anything she will do, and isn't it nine days herself is after crying and keening, and making great sorrow in the house?

Maurya (*puts the empty cup, mouth downwards, on the table, and lays her hands together on* BARTLEY'S *feet*). They're all together this time, and the end is come. May the Almighty God have mercy on Bartley's soul, and on Michael's soul, and on the souls of Sheamus and Patch, and Stephen and Shawn; (*bending her head*) and may He have mercy on my soul, Nora, and on the soul of every one is left living in the world.

[*She pauses, and the keen rises a little more loudly from the women, then sinks away.*]

Maurya (*continuing*). Michael has a clean burial in the Far North, by the grace of the Almighty God. Bartley will have a fine coffin out of the white boards, and a deep grave surely. What more can we want than that? No man at all can be living forever, and we must be satisfied.

[*She kneels down again and the curtain falls slowly.*]

DISCUSSION QUESTIONS AND ANSWERS

Structure

What kind of environment does Maurya exist in and how is it represented?

Maurya and the survivors of her family live in a harsh, inhospitable environment. The island where their small cottage is located is isolated and barren, surrounded by a threatening sea, bleak, and lashed by the winds. While the men go out to sea to fish, transport whiskey, or trade with neighboring islands, the women knit clothing, bake their bread, and mourn the deaths of their men.

In the first segment of the play (before Bartley enters), how does Synge (pr. "Sing") foreshadow the future and build suspense while revealing information about the past (Exposition)?

While a sense of foreboding is supplied by the sight of the new boards, both Cathleen and Nora are under heavy strain: Cathleen stops the wheel suddenly when

Michael's name is mentioned, and they are startled when the wind blows the door open. Both girls are afraid that Maurya should hear about the bundle of clothes; that the bundle confirm their fears that Michael is dead; and that Bartley decide to take his proposed journey.

What kinds of conflict are introduced early in the play?

There is conflict involving the conspiracy to hide the bundle; between the girl's attempt to carry on normal, everyday tasks and the impingements of fear, apprehension, and natural forces (like the wind); and between all their fears that Bartley will meet his death and the young priest's blandly pious reassurances that "the Almighty God won't leave her destitute."

What conflict dominates the action during Bartley's presence?

After Maurya comes in, followed by Bartley, the two engage in a battle of wills. Maurya initiates an attempt, no less desperate for its indirectness, to break her son's resolve to go to sea. He resists her suggestion to stay, aware of the false hope of escape it promises from the rigorous conditions of their life.

How does the third segment (before Bartley's body is brought in) mix the commonplace with the tragic?

Ironically, although the girls are eager to end their uncertainty about Michael's fate, they are also hindered by Maurya's presence, reluctant to confirm their worst suspicions and finally hindered both by the tight knot and the ambiguity of the evidence. Yet the entire action unfolds through commonplace, domestic activity: bread-baking, providing Maurya with a stick to help her over the stones, using a recently purchased knife to cut a stubborn string, and finally seeing the truth through recognizing a detail as mundane as dropped stitches.

How does Synge use exposition and reversal to bring the action to a crisis?

When Maurya re-enters, shocked and entranced, the vision of Michael she has just seen expands in a great lament not only for Michael and Bartley, but for all her family, all islanders, and all men by all mothers. Maurya compresses a whole lifetime of suffering into a few moments. It is ironic that while she is describing an earlier family disaster, the islanders bring in dead the son she had just recalled as a baby. Yet there is no panic or confusion: everyone knows exactly what to do, for they have enacted the same tragic ritual many times before.

What tragic recognition does Maurya achieve?

Maurya finally recognizes the mystery of life and death: when no man can live forever, the best the living can do for them is to provide them a decent burial. When the worst imaginable finally happens, Maurya accepts her fate with poise, calmness, and resignation. Hers is an heroic acceptance.

How is the conclusion of the play ironic?

Although Maurya uses Christian terms and symbols, sprinkling Bartley's body with holy water and phrasing her resignation in prayerful terms, organized Christianity has been of no help to her. The young priest had said God would not leave her destitute with no living son, but she feels that religion is ineffective against the hunger for destruction at the heart of the universe. The terrible dilemma to be faced is that if a woman has, like Maurya, several good providers, she will probably have enough to eat, but she also has unremitting anxiety about their safety. Without sons or men one has no worries, but will probably go short of the necessities of life: "It's a good rest I'll have now . . . if it's only a bit wet flour we do have to eat, and maybe a fish that would be stinking." She now has peace but at a terrible price.

Characterization

How is Maurya characterized?

While Maurya is old enough to have borne, raised, and lost a husband and five sons, and to manifest the querulousness and infirmities of old age, she still possesses a powerful will, a deep sense of resentment against fate, and a religious fervor which emerges both in compelling visions and a Christian faith. Her past trials have inspired great love and respect for her in her children, whose reserve, self-respect, and matter-of-factness she has fostered. Just as Nora and Cathleen refuse to upset her with premature news of Michael's death, Maurya is too proud to beg or order Bartley to stay. She realizes she might upset her daughters and even provoke Bartley into going, especially since other islanders will attempt the trip and since the priest has not forbidden it.

How are Maurya's two daughters differentiated?

Although both of the daughters are apprehensive, affectionate, and hard-working, Nora's youth and inexperience is revealed by her naive, artless questions. Cathleen, who is the older, makes most of the decisions—in hiding the bundle, reprimanding her mother for failing to give Bartley her blessing, and in sending Maurya out with bread for Bartley. At the end, Cathleen assumes responsibility for keeping the home together, now that Maurya is incapable of it: she finds out how Bartley met his death and arranges for his burial.

How is Bartley characterized?

Like his mother, Bartley is sad and quiet. Both of them know he is a doomed man —sooner or later—but he is more vigorous, firm, and business-like than she is. While she is sure he will be going never to return, he ignores her comments, speaking only to his sisters about the jobs to be done. He acts as though his absence will only be temporary, although it is clear he is leaving for good and that he is fully aware of this possibility.

How are the islanders characterized?

The islanders are type-cast as sympathetic mourners, intimately acquainted with Maurya's past sorrows, feeling a close identification with her losses because they have felt the same apprehension and sadness.

Language

How does Synge use language to express a tone of understatement, apprehension, and sadness?

While the characters use vivid, descriptive terms for their tasks, living habits, and natural environment, they also tend to understate their fears and use hyperbole for values. In her attempt to make Bartley stay, for example, Maurya stresses not her real fear that Bartley will go, but her worry that Michael, if washed up, will not get decent burial. Synge also uses aphorisms: "In the big world the old people do be leaving things after them for their sons and children; but in this place it is the young men do be leaving things behind for them that do be old"; metaphorical descriptions, as of the sea birds as "black hags"; and dialect terms such as "hookers" and "curaghs" for the small boats add a sense of elemental simplicity to the setting and actions.

Synge also uses Gaelic syntax as in the unusual use of prepositions ("I after giving a big price"), the placement of verbs first ("It's hard set I am to walk"), use of *present tense* ("my heart's broken from this day"), the use of 'and' ("And it's destroyed he'll be going"), and in the retention of question form in indirect speech ("He went down to see would there be another boat sailing in the week") for the same purpose.

Theme

The meaning of the play arises from a series of thematic suggestions which are far richer and more complex than Maurya's ostensible theme statement at the end: "No man at all can be living forever, and we must be satisfied." Man must accept the conditions of his existence and adapt to them as best he can. He is doomed to defeat in his struggle with nature and fate, but he can face his defeat with heroic acceptance of the inevitable when it happens.

What motifs emerge from the progression of the action?

One of the themes involves the inevitability of man's conflict with nature and the inevitability of man's defeat. Maurya's querulous understatements, Bartley's resigned steadfastness, and finally Cathleen's exasperated interjection, "It's the life of a young man to be going on the sea," all establish this motif.

Another motif is the conflict of dream and illusion: the dream that husbands, fathers, and sons will return safely with love, security, and plenty of food conflicts with the reality that no one can escape the sea. Sooner or later all of them will be drowned.

Yet they must continue dreaming for there are no alternatives but suicide and emigration—neither of which ever even occur to any of the characters.

Yet another motif is the conflict between Christian beneficence and natural malevolence. Although these people use Christian symbols and idioms repeatedly, the depredations of the sea appear irresistible and overwhelming.

Symbolism

The very ineffectiveness of Maurya's struggle, while most of the action has already occurred or happens offstage, should reveal something about the play's symbolism.

What is the significance of the play's title, for instance?

The "riders to the sea" mentioned in the title are the eight men, Maurya's men, who rode down to the sea to sustain life but instead found death. The sea itself is the play's central ironic symbol, representing both a state of barbaric vagueness, disorder, and chaos, as well as a place of purgatorial suffering. Through separation and loss, the characters achieve recognition and resignation. Yet the sea also gives rise to a paradox: those on shore are living but lonely, while those who have drowned belong to the community of the dead.

What other symbols appear in the play?

While all the objects which appear on stage seem to be part of the isolated, wave-washed island existence of Irish fishermen, they are endowed with symbolic overtones through the progression of the action. The clean, white boards standing by the wall foreshadow Bartley's death, for example, while the bundle of Michael's clothes, so trivial and insignificant in itself, symbolizes the truth which Maurya and her daughters find so hard to accept. Ironically, the death of a relative leaves nothing of substance behind. In putting the empty cup mouth downwards on the table after sprinkling Bartley's body, Maurya signifies her empty womb and waiting grave: she has nothing more to look forward to, either of hope or despair.

ANTIGONE

✤ *Sophocles*

An English Version by
DUDLEY FITTS AND ROBERT FITZGERALD

Introductory Comment

Sophocles wrote *Antigone* for one of the most artificial theatres that has ever existed. The actors wore formalized masks and heavy clothing, a chorus provided song and dance which amplified and intensified the action, and the play unfolded within an orchestra or dancing place which was still dedicated, with its altar and temple, to a divinity. The playwright not only wrote the words, but he also trained his amateur actors, composed the music, and choreographed the dance movements for his chorus. *Antigone* was part of a trilogy (the other two parts being lost) which was presented in competition with other works. The audience customarily took a vote on the quality of the plays which they observed.

According to an involved Greek myth, Antigone was one of four children of an incestuous marriage between Oedipus and his mother Iocasta. Although Laïos had tried to circumvent a prophecy that his son would kill him and marry the queen by exposing Oedipus to the elements, the boy was rescued. When he grew to manhood, Oedipus himself tried to escape the prophecy by leaving for another land. But on the road he encountered a king whom he killed in a quarrel. By answering the riddle of the sphinx who was oppressing Thebes, Oedipus became king, married the widowed queen, and ruled prosperously until his attempts to end a plague revealed him as the criminal. His wife-mother Iocasta hanged herself and Oedipus blinded himself and went into self-exile, leaving his throne to his two sons, Polyneices and Eteocles, who were to rule during alternate years. When Eteocles refused to give up the throne, however, Polyneices raised an army in Argos, unsuccessfully attacked Thebes, and died along with his brother in single combat.

Although contemporary Western society no longer stresses the link between a ritualized burial and peace for the dead which dominates Antigone's being, the struggle which results from her sense of personal duty is still timely. She is doomed before the beginning of the play, never marshals common sense at all to support her position, and goes to her death long before the play ends. Ironically, it is Creon as the supremely rational man who through his apparently reasonable resistance to Antigone is lifted to a higher level of wisdom by his tragic experience. Most attempts to apply Aristotelian criteria of tragic stature to Antigone have failed: although she is the victim of fate, she has free will. Yet she has no "tragic flaw," for it is her unambiguous, supra-rational position which is vindicated at the end. Her inner struggle, if it ever existed, had ended before the play ended, and her fate sealed without much external struggle either. Moreover, she undergoes no ironic reversal or recognition. Her death is a straight-line culmination of a directly-intuited decision.

Although the play bears Antigone's name, it is the complex interplay between her and Creon as it draws together their conflicting views of rationality, social order, universal morality, family ties, and the duties of leadership which results in tragedy. Despite the terrible shock which Creon endures, the implications of the play are affirmative: although man can never fully understand the demands of divine justice, the opposing demands of right and wrong are woven into the structure of the universe.

Cast of Characters

ANTIGONE
ISMENE
EURYDICE
CREON
HAIMON
TEIRESIAS
A SENTRY
A MESSENGER
CHORUS

Scene: *Before the palace of Creon, King of Thebes. A central double door, and two lateral doors. A platform extends the length of the façade, and from this platform three steps lead down into the "orchestra," or chorus-ground.* TIME: *Dawn of the day after the repulse of the Argive army from the assault on Thebes.*

PROLOGUE

[ANTIGONE *and* ISMENE *enter from the central door of the Palace.*]

Antigone: Ismene, dear sister,
You would think that we had already suffered enough
For the curse on Oedipus:
I cannot imagine any grief
That you and I have not gone through. And now—
Have they told you of the new decree of our King Creon?

Ismene: I have heard nothing: I know
That two sisters lost two brothers, a double death
In a single hour; and I know that the Argive army
Fled in the night; but beyond this, nothing.

Antigone: I thought so. And that is why I wanted you
To come out here with me. There is something we must do.

Ismene: Why do you speak so strangely.

Antigone: Listen, Ismene:
Creon buried our brother Eteocles
With military honors, gave him a soldier's funeral,
And it was right that he should; but Polyneices,
Who fought as bravely and died as miserably,—
They say that Creon has sworn
No one shall bury him, no one mourn for him,
But his body must lie in the fields, a sweet treasure
For carrion birds to find as they search for food.
That is what they say, and our good Creon is coming here
To announce it publicly; and the penalty—
Stoning to death in the public square!
There it is,
And now you can prove what you are:

A true sister, or a traitor to your family.

Ismene: Antigone, you are mad! What could I possibly do?

Antigone: You must decide whether you will help me or not.

Ismene: I do not understand you. Help you in what?

Antigone: Ismene, I am going to bury him. Will you come?

Ismene: Bury him! You have just said the new law forbids it.

Antigone: He is my brother. And he is your brother, too.

Ismene: But think of the danger! Think what Creon will do!

Antigone: Creon is not strong enough to stand in my way.

Ismene: Ah sister!
Oedipus died, everyone hating him
For what his own search brought to light, his eyes
Ripped out by his own hand; and Iocaste died,
His mother and wife at once: she twisted the cords
That strangled her life; and our two brothers died,
Each killed by the other's sword. And we are left:
But oh, Antigone,
Think how much more terrible than these
Our own death would be if we should go against Creon
And do what he has forbidden; We are only women,
We cannot fight with men, Antigone!
The law is strong, we must give in to the law
In this thing, and in worse. I beg the Dead
To forgive me, but I am helpless: I must yield
To those in authority. And I think it is dangerous business
To be always meddling.

Antigone: If that is what you think,
I should not want you, even if you asked to come.
You have made your choice, you can be what you want to be.
But I will bury him; and if I must die,
I say that this crime is holy: I shall lie down
With him in death, and I shall be as dear
To him as he to me.
It is the dead,
Not the living, who make the longest demands:
We die for ever . . .
You may do as you like.
Since apparently the laws of the gods mean nothing to you.

Ismene: They mean a great deal to me; but I have no strength
To break laws that were made for the public good.

Antigone: That must be your excuse.
I suppose. But as for me,
I will bury the brother I love.

Ismene: Antigonê,
I am so afraid for you!

Antigone: You need not be:
You have yourself to consider, after all.

Ismene: But no one must hear of this, you must tell no one!
I will keep it a secret, I promise!

Antigone: Oh tell it! Tell everyone!
Think how they'll hate you when it all comes out
If they learn that you knew about it all the time!

Ismene: So fiery! You should be cold with fear.

Antigone: Perhaps. But I am doing only what I must.

Ismene: But can you do it? I say that you cannot.

Antigone: Very well: when my strength gives out, I shall do no more.

Ismene: Impossible things should not be tried at all.

Antigone: Go away, Ismene:
I shall be hating you soon, and the dead will too,
For your words are hateful. Leave me my foolish plan:
I am not afraid of the danger; if it means death,
It will not be the worst of deaths—death without honor.

Ismene: Go then, if you feel that you must.
You are unwise,
But a loyal friend indeed to those who love you.

[*Exit into the Palace.* ANTIGONE *goes off, L. Enter the* CHORUS.]

PARODOS

[STROPHE 1]

Chorus: Now the long blade of the sun, lying
Level east to west, touches with glory
Thebes of the Seven Gates. Open, unlidded
Eye of golden day! O marching light
Across the eddy and rush of Dirce's stream,
Striking the white shields of the enemy
Thrown headlong backward from the blaze of morning!

Choragos: Polyneices their commander
Roused them with windy phrases,
He the wild eagle screaming
Insults above our land,
His wings their shields of snow,
His crest their marshalled helms.

[ANTISTROPHE 1]

Chorus: Against our seven gates in a yawning ring
The famished spears came onward in the night;
But before his jaws were sated with our blood,
Or pinefire took the garland of our towers,
He was thrown back; and as he turned, great Thebes—
No tender victim for his noisy power—
Rose like a dragon behind him, shouting war.

Choragos: For God hates utterly
The bray of bragging tongues;
And when he beheld their smiling,
Their swagger of golden helms,
The frown of his thunder blasted
Their first man from our walls.

[STROPHE 2]

Chorus: We heard his shout of triumph high in the air
Turn to a scream; far out in a flaming arc
He fell with his windy torch, and the earth struck him.
And others storming in fury no less than his
Found shock of death in the dusty joy of battle.

Choragos: Seven captains at seven gates
Yielded their clanging arms to the god
That bends the battle-line and breaks it.
These two only, brothers in blood,
Face to face in matchless rage,
Mirroring each the other's death,
Clashed in long combat.

[ANTISTROPHE 2]

Chorus: But now in the beautiful morning of victory
Let Thebes of the many chariots sing for joy!
With hearts for dancing we'll take leave of war:
Our temples shall be sweet with hymns of praise,
And the long night shall echo with our chorus.

SCENE I

Choragos: But now at last our new King is coming:
Creon of Thebes, Menoikeus' son.
In this auspicious dawn of his reign
What are the new complexities
That shifting Fate has woven for him?
What is his counsel? Why has he summoned
The old men to hear him?

[*Enter* CREON *from the Palace, C. He addresses the* CHORUS *from the top step.*]

Creon: Gentlemen: I have the honor to inform you that our Ship of State, which recent storms have threatened to destroy, has come safely to harbor at last, guided by the merciful wisdom of Heaven. I have summoned you here this morning because I know that I can depend upon you: your devotion to King Laïos was absolute; you never hesitated in your duty to our later ruler Oedipus; and when Oedipus died, your loyalty was transferred to his children. Unfortunately, as you know, his two sons, the princes Eteocles and Polyneices, have killed each other in battle; and I, as the next in blood, have succeeded to the full power of the throne.

I am aware, of course, that no Ruler can expect complete loyalty from his subjects until he has been tested in office. Nevertheless, I say to you at the very outset that I have nothing but contempt for the kind of Governor who is afraid, for whatever reason, to follow the course that he knows is best for the State; and as for the man who sets private friendship above the public welfare,—I have no use for him, either. I call God to witness that if I saw my country headed for ruin, I should not be afraid to speak out plainly; and I need hardly remind you that I would never have any dealings with an enemy of the people. No one values friendship more highly than I; but we must remember that friends made at the risk of wrecking our Ship are not real friends at all.

These are my principles, at any rate, and that is why I have made the following decision concerning the sons of Oedipus: Eteocles, who died as a man should die, fighting for his country, is to be buried with full military honors, with all the ceremony that is usual when the greatest heroes die; but his brother Polyneices, who broke his exile to come back with fire and sword against his native city and the shrines of his father's gods, whose one idea was to spill the blood of his blood and sell his own people into slavery—Polyneices, I say, is to have no burial: no man is to touch him or say the least prayer for him; he shall lie on the plain, unburied; and the birds and the scavenging dogs can do with him whatever they like.

This is my command, and you can see the wisdom behind it. As long as I am King, no traitor is going to be honored with the loyal man. But whoever shows by word and deed that he is on the side of the State,—he shall have my respect while he is living, and my reverence when he is dead.

Choragos: If that is your will, Creon son of Menoikeus,
You have the right to enforce it: we are yours.

Creon: That is my will. Take care that you do your part.

Choragos: We are old men: let the younger ones carry it out.

Creon: I do not mean that: the sentries have been appointed.

Choragos: Then what is it that you would have us do?

Creon: You will give no support to whoever breaks this law.

Choragos: Only a crazy man is in love with death!

Creon: And death it is; yet money talks, and the wisest
Have sometimes been known to count a few coins too many.

[*Enter* SENTRY *from L.*]

Sentry: I'll not say that I'm out of breath from running, King, because every time I stopped to think about what I have to tell you, I felt like going back. And all the time a voice kept saying, "You fool, don't you know you're walking straight into trouble?"; and then another voice: "Yes, but if you let somebody else get the news to Creon first, it will be even worse than that for you!" But good sense won out, at least I hope it was good sense, and here I am with a story that makes no sense at all; but I'll tell it anyhow, because, as they say, what's going to happen's going to happen, and—

Creon: Come to the point. What have you to say?

Sentry: I did not do it. I did not see who did it. You must not punish me for what someone else has done.

Creon: A comprehensive defense!
More effective, perhaps,
If I knew its purpose. Come: what is it?

Sentry: A dreadful thing . . . I don't know how to put it—

Creon: Out with it!

Sentry: Well, then;
The dead man—
Polyneices—

[*Pause. The* SENTRY *is overcome, fumbles for words.* CREON *waits impassively.*]

out there—
someone,—
New dust on the slimy flesh!

[*Pause. No sign from* CREON.]

Someone has given it burial that way, and
Gone . . .

[*Long pause.* CREON *finally speaks with deadly control:*]

Creon: And the man who dared do this?

Sentry: I swear I
Do not know! You must believe me!
Listen:
The ground was dry, not a sign of digging, no,
Not a wheeltrack in the dust, no trace of anyone.
It was when they relieved us this morning: and one of them,

The corporal, pointed to it.
There it was,
The strangest—
Look:
The body, just mounded over with light dust: you see?
Not buried really, but as if they'd covered it
Just enough for the ghost's peace. And no sign
Of dogs or any wild animal that had been there.
And then what a scene there was! Every man of us
Accusing the other: we all proved the other man did it,
We all had proof that we could not have done it.
We were ready to take hot iron in our hands,
Walk through fire, swear by all the gods,
It was not I!
I do not know who it was, but it was not I!

[CREON'S *rage has been mounting steadily, but the* SENTRY *is too intent upon his story to notice it.*]

And then, when this came to nothing, someone said
A thing that silenced us and made us stare
Down at the ground: you had to be told the news,
And one of us had to do it! We threw the dice,
And the bad luck fell to me. So here I am,
No happier to be here than you are to have me:
Nobody likes the man who brings bad news.

Choragos: I have been wondering, King: can it be that the gods have done this?

Creon (*furiously*). Stop!
Must you doddering wrecks
Go out of your heads entirely? "The gods!"
Intolerable!
The gods favor this corpse? Why? How had he served them?
Tried to loot their temples, burn their images,
Yes, and the whole State, and its laws with it!
Is it your senile opinion that the gods love to honor bad men?
A pious thought!—
No, from the very beginning
There have been those who have whispered together,
Stiff-necked anarchists, putting their heads together,
Scheming against me in alleys. These are the men,
And they have bribed my own guard to do this thing.
Money! (*Sententiously.*)
There's nothing in the world so demoralizing as money.
Down go your cities,
Homes gone, men gone, honest hearts corrupted,
Crookedness of all kinds, and all for money!

[*To* SENTRY.]

But you—!
I swear by God and by the throne of God,
The man who has done this thing shall pay for it!
Find that man, bring him here to me, or your death
Will be the least of your problems: I'll string you up
Alive, and there will be certain ways to make you
Discover your employer before you die;
And the process may teach you a lesson you seem to have missed:

The dearest profit is sometimes all too dear:
That depends on the source. Do you understand me?
A fortune won is often misfortune.

Sentry: King, may I speak?

Creon: Your very voice distresses me.

Sentry: Are you sure that it is my voice, and not your conscience?

Creon: By God, he wants to analyze me now!

Sentry: It is not what I say, but what has been done, that hurts you.

Creon: You talk too much.

Sentry: Maybe; but I've done nothing.

Creon: Sold your soul for some silver: that's all you've done.

Sentry: How dreadful it is when the right judge judges wrong!

Creon: Your figures of speech
May entertain you now; but unless you bring me the man,
You will get little profit from them in the end.

[*Exit* CREON *into the Palace.*]

Sentry: "Bring me the man"—!
I'd like nothing better than bringing him the man!
But bring him or not, you have seen the last of me here.
At any rate, I am safe!

[*Exit* SENTRY.]

ODE I

[STROPHE 1]

Chorus: Numberless are the world's wonders, but none
More wonderful than man; the stormgray sea
Yields to his prows, the huge crests bear him high;
Earth, holy and inexhaustible, is graven
With shining furrows where his plows have gone
Year after year, the timeless labor of stallions.

[ANTISTROPHE 1]

The lightboned birds and beasts that cling to cover,
The lithe fish lighting their reaches of dim water,
All are taken, tamed in the net of his mind;
The lion on the hill, the wild horse windy-maned,
Resign to him; and his blunt yoke has broken
The sultry shoulders of the mountain bull.

[STROPHE 2]

Words also, and thought as rapid as air,
He fashions to his good use; statecraft is his,
And his the skill that deflects the arrows of snow,
The spears of winter rain: from every wind
He has made himself secure—from all but one:
In the late wind of death he cannot stand.

[ANTISTROPHE 2]

O clear intelligence, force beyond all measure!
O fate of man, working both good and evil!

When the laws are kept, how proudly his city stands!
When the laws are broken, what of his city then?
Never may the anarchic man find rest at my hearth,
Never be it said that my thoughts are his thoughts.

SCENE II

[*Re-enter* SENTRY *leading* ANTIGONE.]

Choragos: What does this mean? Surely this captive woman
Is the Princess, Antigone. Why should she be taken?

Sentry: Here is the one who did it! We caught her
In the very act of burying him.—Where is Creon?

Choragos: Just coming from the house.

[*Enter* CREON, *C.*]

Creon: What has happened?
Why have you come back so soon?

Sentry (*expansively*). O King,
A man should never be too sure of anything:
I would have sworn
That you'd not see me here again: your anger
Frightened me so, and the things you threatened me with;
But how could I tell then
That I'd be able to solve the case so soon?
No dice-throwing this time: I was only too glad to come!
Here is this woman. She is the guilty one:
We found her trying to bury him.
Take her, then; question her; judge her as you will.
I am through with the whole thing now, and glad of it.

Creon: But this is Antigone! Why have you brought her here?

Sentry: She was burying him, I tell you!

Creon (*Severely*). Is this the truth?

Sentry: I saw her with my own eyes. Can I say more?

Creon: The details: come, tell me quickly!

Sentry: It was like this:
After those terrible threats of yours, King,
We went back and brushed the dust away from the body.
The flesh was soft by now, and stinking,
So we sat on a hill to windward and kept guard.
No napping this time! We kept each other awake.
But nothing happened until the white round sun
Whirled in the center of the round sky over us:
Then, suddenly,
A storm of dust roared up from the earth, and the sky
Went out, the plain vanished with all its trees
In the stinging dark. We closed our eyes and endured it.
The whirlwind lasted a long time, but it passed;
And then we looked, and there was Antigone!

I have seen
A mother bird come back to a stripped nest, heard
Her crying bitterly a broken note or two
For the young ones stolen. Just so, when this girl
Found the bare corpse, and all her love's work wasted,
She wept, and cried on heaven to damn the hands
That had done this thing.
And then she brought more dust
And sprinkled wine three times for her brother's ghost.
We ran and took her at once. She was not afraid,
Not even when we charged her with what she had done.
She denied nothing.
And this was a comfort to me,
And some uneasiness: for it is a good thing
To escape from death, but it is no great pleasure
To bring death to a friend.
Yet I always say
There is nothing so comfortable as your own safe skin!

Creon *(slowly, dangerously)*. And you, Antigone,
You with your head hanging,—do you confess this thing?

Antigone: I do. I deny nothing.

Creon *(to* SENTRY*)*. You may go.

[*Exit* SENTRY.]

[*To* ANTIGONE.]

Tell me, tell me briefly:
Had you heard my proclamation touching this matter?

Antigone: It was public. Could I help hearing it?

Creon: And yet you dared defy the the law.

Antigone: I dared.
It was not God's proclamation. That final Justice
That rules the world below makes no such laws.
Your edict, King, was strong,
But all your strength is weakness itself against
The immortal unrecorded laws of God.
They are not merely now: they were, and shall be,
Operative for ever, beyond man utterly.
I knew I must die, even without your decree:
I am only mortal. And if I must die
Now, before it is my time to die,
Surely this is no hardship: can anyone
Living, as I live, with evil all about me,
Think Death less than a friend? This death of mine
Is of no importance; but if I had left my brother
Lying in death unburied, I should have suffered.
Now I do not.
You smile at me. Ah Creon,
Think me a fool, if you like; but it may well be
That a fool convicts me of folly.

Choragos: Like father, like daughter: both headstrong, deaf to reason!
She has never learned to yield.

Creon: She has much to learn.
The inflexible heart breaks first, the toughest iron
Cracks first, and the wildest horses bend their necks
At the pull of the smallest curb.
Pride? In a slave?
This girl is guilty of a double insolence,
Breaking the given laws and boasting of it.
Who is the man here,

She or I, if this crime goes unpunished?
Sister's child, or more than sister's child,
Or closer in blood—she and her sister
Win bitter death for this!

[*To* SERVANTS.]

Go, some of you,
Arrest Ismene. I accuse her equally.
Bring her: you will find her sniffling in the house there.

Her mind's a traitor: crimes kept in the dark
Cry for light, and the guardian brain shudders;
But how much worse than this
Is brazen boasting of barefaced anarchy!

Antigone: Creon, what more do you want than my death?

Creon: Nothing.
That gives me everything.

Antigone: Then I beg you: Kill me.
This talking is a great weariness: your words
Are distasteful to me, and I am sure that mine
Seem so to you. And yet they should not seem so:
I should have praise and honor for what I have done.
All these men here would praise me
Were their lips not frozen shut with fear of you.

[*Bitterly.*]

Ah the good fortune of kings,
Licensed to say and do whatever they please!

Creon: You are alone here in that opinion.

Antigone: No, they are with me. But they keep their tongues in leash.

Creon: Maybe. But you are guilty, and they are not.

Antigone: There is no guilt in reverence for the dead.

Creon: But Eteocles—was he not your brother too?

Antigone: My brother too.

Creon: And you insult his memory?

Antigone (*Softly*). The dead man would not say that I insult it.

Creon: He would: for you honor a traitor as much as him.

Antigone: His own brother, traitor or not, and equal in blood.

Creon: He made war on his country. Eteocles defended it.

Antigone: Nevertheless, there are honors due all the dead.

Creon: But not the same for the wicked as for the just.

Antigone: Ah Creon, Creon,
Which of us can say what the gods hold wicked?

Creon: An enemy is an enemy, even dead.

Antigone: It is my nature to join in love, not hate.

Creon (*finally losing patience*). Go join them, then; if you must have your love,
Find it in hell!

Choragos: But see, Ismene comes:

[*Enter* ISMENE, *guarded.*]

Those tears are sisterly, the cloud
That shadows her eyes rains down gentle sorrow.

Creon: You too, Ismene,
Snake in my ordered house, sucking my blood
Stealthily—and all the time I never knew
That these two sisters were aiming at my throne!

Ismene,
Do you confess your share in this crime, or deny it?

Answer me.

Ismene: Yes, if she will let me say so. I am guilty.

Antigone (*coldly*). No, Ismene. You have no right to say so.
You would not help me, and I will not have you help me.

Ismene: But now I know what you meant; and I am here
To join you, to take my share of punishment.

Antigone: The dead man and the gods who rule the dead
Know whose act this was. Words are not friends.

Ismene: Do you refuse me, Antigonê?
I want to die with you:
I too have a duty that I must discharge to the dead.

Antigone: You shall not lessen my death by sharing it.

Ismene: What do I care for life when you are dead?

Antigone: Ask Creon. You're always hanging on his opinions.

Ismene: You are laughing at me. Why, Antigone?

Antigone: It's a joyless laughter, Ismene.

Ismene: But can I do nothing?

Antigone: Yes. Save yourself. I shall not envy you.
There are those who will praise you; I shall have honor, too.

Ismene: But we are equally guilty!

Antigone: No more, Ismene.
You are alive, but I belong to Death.

Creon (*to the* CHORUS). Gentlemen, I beg you to observe these girls:
One has just now lost her mind; the other,
It seems, has never had a mind at all.

Ismene: Grief teaches the steadiest minds to waver, King.

Creon: Yours certainly did, when you assumed guilt with the guilty!

Ismene: But how could I go on living without her?

Creon: You are.
She is already dead.

Ismene: But your own son's bride!

Creon: There are places enough for him to push his plow.
I want no wicked women for my sons!

Ismene: O dearest Haimon, how your father wrongs you!

Creon: I've had enough of your childish talk of marriage!

Choragos: Do you really intend to steal this girl from your son?

Creon: No; Death will do that for me.

Choragos: Then she must die?

Creon (*ironically*). You dazzle me.
—But enough of this talk!

[*To* GUARDS.]

You, there, take them away and guard them well:
For they are but women, and even brave men run
When they see Death coming.

[*Exeunt* ISMENE, ANTIGONE, *and* GUARDS.]

ODE II

[STROPHE 1]

Chorus: Fortunate is the man who has never tasted God's vengeance!
Where once the anger of heaven has struck, that house is shaken
For ever: damnation rises behind each child
Like a wave cresting out of the black northeast,
When the long darkness under sea roars up
And bursts drumming death upon the wind-whipped sand.

[ANTISTROPHE 1]

I have seen this gathering sorrow from time long past
Loom upon Oedipus' children: generation from generation
Takes the compulsive rage of the enemy god.
So lately this last flower of Oedipus' line
Drank the sunlight! but now a passionate word
And a handful of dust have closed up all its beauty.

[STROPHE 2]

What mortal arrogance
Transcends the wrath of Zeus?
Sleep cannot lull him, nor the effortless long months
Of the timeless gods: but he is young for ever,
And his house is the shining day of high Olympos.
All this is and shall be,
And all the past, is his.
No pride on earth is free of the curse of heaven.

[ANTISTROPHE 2]

The straying dreams of men
May bring them ghosts of joy:
But as they drowse, the waking embers burn them;
Or they walk with fixed eyes, as blind men walk.
But the ancient wisdom speaks for our own time:
Fate works most for woe
With Folly's fairest show.
Man's little pleasure is the spring of sorrow.

SCENE III

Choragos: But here is Haimon, King, the last of all your sons.
Is it grief for Antigonê that brings him here,
And bitterness at being robbed of his bride?

[*Enter* HAIMON.]

Creon: We shall soon see, and no need of diviners. —Son,
You have heard my final judgment on that girl:
Have you come here hating me, or have you come
With deference and with love, whatever I do?

Haimon: I am your son, father. You are my guide.
You make things clear for me, and I obey you.
No marriage means more to me than your continuing wisdom.

Creon: Good. That is the way to behave: subordinate
Everything else, my son, to your father's will.
This is what a man prays for, that he may get
Sons attentive and dutiful in his house,
Each one hating his father's enemies,
Honoring his father's friends. But if his sons
Fail him, if they turn out unprofitably,
What has he fathered but trouble for himself
And amusement for the malicious?
So you are right
Not to lose your head over this woman.
Your pleasure with her would soon grow cold, Haimon,
And then you'd have a hellcat in bed and elsewhere.
Let her find her husband in Hell!
Of all the people in this city, only she
Has had contempt for my law and broken it.

Do you want me to show myself weak before the people?
Or to break my sworn word? No, and I will not.
The woman dies.
I suppose she'll plead "family ties." Well, let her.
If I permit my own family to rebel,
How shall I earn the world's obedience?
Show me the man who keeps his house in hand,
He's fit for public authority.
I'll have no dealings
With law-breakers, critics of the government:
Whoever is chosen to govern should be obeyed—
Must be obeyed, in all things, great and small,
Just and unjust! O Haimon,
The man who knows how to obey, and that man only,
Knows how to give commands when the time comes.
You can depend on him, no matter how fast
The spears come: he's a good soldier, he'll stick it out.
Anarchy, anarchy! Show me a greater evil!
This is why cities tumble and the great houses rain down,
This is what scatters armies!

No, no: good lives are made so by discipline.
We keep the laws then, and the lawmakers,
And no woman shall seduce us. If we must lose,
Let's lose to a man, at least! Is a woman stronger than we?

Choragos: Unless time has rusted my wits,
What you say, King, is said with point and dignity.

Haimon (*boyishly earnest*). Father:
Reason is God's crowning gift to man, and you are right

To warn me against losing mine. I cannot say—
I hope that I shall never want to say!—that you
Have reasoned badly. Yet there are other men
Who can reason, too; and their opinions might be helpful.
You are not in a position to know everything
That people say or do, or what they feel:
Your temper terrifies them—everyone
Will tell you only what you like to hear.
But I, at any rate, can listen; and I have heard them
Muttering and whispering in the dark about this girl.
They say no woman has ever, so unreasonably,
Died so shameful a death for a generous act:
"She covered her brother's body. Is this indecent?
She kept him from dogs and vultures. Is this a crime?
Death?—She should have all the honor that we can give her!"

This is the way they talk out there in the city.

You must believe me:
Nothing is closer to me than your happiness.
What could be closer? Must not any son
Value his father's fortune as his father does his?
I beg you, do not be unchangeable:
Do not believe that you alone can be right.
The man who thinks that,
The man who maintains that only he has the power
To reason correctly, the gift to speak, the soul—
A man like that, when you know him, turns out empty.

It is not reason never to yield to reason!

In flood time you can see how some trees bend,
And because they bend, even their twigs are safe,
While stubborn trees are torn up, roots and all.
And the same thing happens in sailing:
Make your sheet fast, never slacken,—and over you go,
Head over heels and under: and there's your voyage.
Forget you are angry! Let yourself be moved!
I know I am young; but please let me say this:
The ideal condition
Would be, I admit, that men should be right by instinct;
But since we are all too likely to go astray,
The reasonable thing is to learn from those who can teach.

Choragos: You will do well to listen to him, King,
If what he says is sensible. And you, Haimon,
Must listen to your father.—Both speak well.

Creon: You consider it right for a man of my years and experience
To go to school to a boy?

Haimon: It is not right
If I am wrong. But if I am young, and right,
What does my age matter?

Creon: You think it right to stand up for an anarchist?

Haimon: Not at all. I pay no respect to criminals.

Creon: Then she is not a criminal?

Haimon: The City would deny it, to a man.

Creon: And the City proposes to teach me how to rule?

Haimon: Ah. Who is it that's talking like a boy now?

Creon: My voice is the one voice giving orders in this City!

Haimon: It is no City if it takes orders from one voice.

Creon: The State is the King!

Haimon: Yes, if the State is a desert.

[*Pause.*]

Creon: This boy, it seems, has sold out to a woman.

Haimon: If you are a woman: my concern is only for you.

Creon: So? Your "concern"! In a public brawl with your father!

Haimon: How about you, in a public brawl with justice?

Creon: With justice, when all that I do is within my rights?

Haimon: You have no right to trample on God's right.

Creon (*completely out of control*). Fool, adolescent fool! Taken in by a woman!

Haimon: You'll never see me taken in by anything vile.

Creon: Every word you say is for her!

Haimon (*quietly, darkly*). And for you.
And for me. And for the gods under the earth.

Creon: You'll never marry her while she lives.

Haimon: Then she must die.—But her death will cause another.

Creon: Another?
Have you lost your senses? Is this an open threat?

Haimon: There is no threat in speaking to emptiness.

Creon: I swear you'll regret this superior tone of yours!
You are the empty one!

Haimon: If you were not my father, I'd say you were perverse.

Creon: You girlstruck fool, don't play at words with me!

Haimon: I am sorry. You prefer silence.

Creon: Now, by God—!
I swear, by all the gods in heaven above us,
You'll watch it, I swear you shall!

[*To the* SERVANTS.]

Bring her out!
Bring the woman out! Let her die before his eyes!
Here, this instant, with her bridegroom beside her!

Haimon: Not here, no; she will not die here, King.
And you will never see my face again.
Go on raving as long as you've a friend to endure you.

[*Exit* HAIMON.]

Choragos: Gone, gone.
Creon, a young man in a rage is dangerous!

Creon: Let him do, or dream to do, more than a man can.
He shall not save these girls from death.

Choragos: These girls?
You have sentenced them both?

Creon: No, you are right.
I will not kill the one whose hands are clean.

Choragos: But Antigonê?

Creon (*somberly*). I will carry her far away
Out there in the wilderness, and lock her

Living in a vault of stone. She shall have food,
As the custom is, to absolve the State of her death.
And there let her pray to the gods of hell:
They are her only gods:
Perhaps they will show her an escape from death,
Or she may learn,
though late,
That piety shown the dead is pity in vain.

[*Exit* CREON.]

ODE III

[STROPHE]

Chorus: Love, unconquerable
Waster of rich men, keeper
Of warm lights and all-night vigil
In the soft face of a girl:
Sea-wanderer, forest-visitor!
Even the pure Immortals cannot escape you,
And mortal man, in his one day's dusk,
Trembles before your glory.

[ANTISTROPHE]

Surely you swerve upon ruin
The just man's consenting heart,
As here you have made bright anger
Strike between father and son—
And none has conquered but Love!
A girl's glance working the will of heaven:
Pleasure to her alone who mocks us,
Merciless Aphrodite.

SCENE IV

[*As* ANTIGONE *enters guarded.*]

Choragos: But I can no longer stand in awe of this,
Nor, seeing what I see, keep back my tears.
Here is Antigonê, passing to that chamber
Where all find sleep at last.

[STROPHE I]

Antigone: Look upon me, friends, and pity me
Turning back at the night's edge to say
Good-by to the sun that shines for me no longer;
Now sleepy Death
Summons me down to Acheron, that cold shore:
There is no bridesong there, nor any music.

Chorus: Yet not unpraised, not without a kind of honor,
You walk at last into the underworld;
Untouched by sickness, broken by no sword.
What woman has ever found your way to death?

[ANTISTROPHE I]

Antigone: How often I have heard the story of Niobe,
Tantalos' wretched daughter, how the stone

Clung fast about her, ivy-close: and they say
The rain falls endlessly
And sifting soft snow; her tears are never done.
I feel the loneliness of her death in mine.

Chorus: But she was born of heaven, and you
Are woman, woman-born. If her death is yours,
A mortal woman's, is this not for you
Glory in our world and in the world beyond?

[STROPHE 2]

Antigone: You laugh at me. Ah, friends, friends,
Can you not wait until I am dead? O Thebes,
O men many-charioted, in love with Fortune,
Dear springs of Dirce, sacred Theban grove,
Be witnesses for me, denied all pity,
Unjustly judged! and think a word of love
For her whose path turns
Under dark earth, where there are no more tears.

Chorus: You have passed beyond human daring and come at last
Into a place of stone where Justice sits.
I cannot tell
What shape of your father's guilt appears in this.

[ANTISTROPHE 2]

Antigone: You have touched it at last: that bridal bed
Unspeakable, horror of son and mother mingling:
Their crime, infection of all our family!
O Oedipus, father and brother!
Your marriage strikes from the grave to murder mine.
I have been a stranger here in my own land:
All my life
The blasphemy of my birth has followed me.

Chorus: Reverence is a virtue, but strength
Lives in established law: that must prevail.
You have made your choice,
Your death is the doing of your conscious hand.

[EPODE]

Antigone: Then let me go, since all your words are bitter,
And the very light of the sun is cold to me.
Lead me to my vigil, where I must have
Neither love nor lamentation; no song, but silence.

[CREON *interrupts impatiently.*]

Creon: If dirges and planned lamentations could put off death,
Men would be singing for ever.

[*To the* SERVANTS.]

Take her, go!
You know your orders: take her to the vault
And leave her alone there. And if she lives or dies,
That's her affair, not ours: our hands are clean.

Antigone: O tomb, vaulted bride-bed in eternal rock,
Soon I shall be with my own again
Where Persephone welcomes the thin ghosts underground:
And I shall see my father again, and you, mother,
And dearest Polyneices—

dearest indeed
To me, since it was my hand
That washed him clean and poured the ritual wine:
And my reward is death before my time!

And yet, as men's hearts know, I have done no wrong,
I have not sinned before God. Or if I have,
I shall know the truth in death. But if the guilt
Lies upon Creon who judged me, then, I pray,
May his punishment equal my own.

Choragos: O passionate heart,
Unyielding, tormented still by the same winds!

Creon: Her guards shall have good cause to regret their delaying.

Antigone: Ah! That voice is like the voice of death!

Creon: I can give you no reason to think you are mistaken.

Antigone: Thebes, and you my fathers' gods,
And rulers of Thebes, you see me now, the last
Unhappy daughter of a line of kings,
Your kings, led away to death. You will remember
What things I suffer, and at what men's hands,
Because I would not transgress the laws of heaven.

[*To the* GUARDS, *simply.*]

Come: let us wait no longer.

[*Exit* ANTIGONE, *L., guarded.*]

ODE IV

[STROPHE 1]

Chorus: All Danae's beauty was locked away
In a brazen cell where the sunlight could not come:
A small room, still as any grave, enclosed her.
Yet she was a princess too,
And Zeus in a rain of gold poured love upon her.
O child, child,
No power in wealth or war
Or tough sea-blackened ships
Can prevail against untiring Destiny!

[ANTISTROPHE 1]

And Dryas' son also, that furious king,
Bore the god's prisoning anger for his pride:
Sealed up by Dionysos in deaf stone,
His madness died among echoes.
So at the last he learned what dreadful power
His tongue had mocked:
For he had profaned the revels,
And fired the wrath of the nine
Implacable Sisters that love the sound of the flute.

[STROPHE 2]

And old men tell a half-remembered tale
Of horror done where a dark ledge splits the sea
And a double surf beats on the gray shores:
How a king's new woman, sick
With hatred for the queen he had imprisoned,
Ripped out his two sons' eyes with her bloody hands
While grinning Ares watched the shuttle plunge

Four times: four blind wounds crying for revenge,

[ANTISTROPHE 2]

Crying, tears and blood mingled.—Piteously born,
Those sons whose mother was of heavenly birth!
Her father was the god of the North Wind
And she was cradled by gales,
She raced with young colts on the glittering hills
And walked untrammeled in the open light:
But in her marriage deathless Fate found means
To build a tomb like yours for all her joy.

SCENE V

[*Enter blind* TEIRESIAS, *led by a boy. The opening speeches of* TEIRESIAS *should be in singsong contrast to the realistic lines of* CREON.]

Teiresias: This is the way the blind man comes, Princes, Princes,
Lock-step, two heads lit by the eyes of one.

Creon: What new thing have you to tell us, old Teiresias?

Teiresias: I have much to tell you: listen to the prophet, Creon.

Creon: I am not aware that I have ever failed to listen.

Teiresias: Then you have done wisely, King, and ruled well.

Creon: I admit my debt to you. But what have you to say?

Teiresias: This, Creon: you stand once more on the edge of fate.

Creon: What do you mean? Your words are a kind of dread.

Teiresias: Listen, Creon:
I was sitting in my chair of augury, at the place
Where the birds gather about me. They were all a-chatter,
As is their habit, when suddenly I heard
A strange note in their jangling, a scream, a
Whirring fury; I knew that they were fighting,
Tearing each other, dying
In a whirlwind of wings clashing. And I was afraid.
I began the rites of burnt-offering at the altar,
But Hephaistos failed me: instead of bright flame,
There was only the sputtering slime of the fat thigh-flesh
Melting: the entrails dissolved in gray smoke,
The bare bone burst from the welter. And no blaze!

This was a sign from heaven. My boy described it,
Seeing for me as I see for others.

I tell you, Creon, you yourself have brought
This new calamity upon us. Our hearths and altars
Are stained with the corruption of dogs and carrion birds
That glut themselves on the corpse of Oedipus' son.
The gods are deaf when we pray to them, their fire

Recoils from our offering, their birds of omen
Have no cry of comfort, for they are gorged
With the thick blood of the dead.
O my son,
These are no trifles! Think: all men make mistakes,
But a good man yields when he knows his course is wrong,
And repairs the evil. The only crime is pride.

Give in to the dead man, then: do not fight with a corpse—
What glory is it to kill a man who is dead?
Think, I beg you:
It is for your own good that I speak as I do.
You should be able to yield for your own good.

Creon: It seems that prophets have made me their especial province.
All my life long
I have been a kind of butt for the dull arrows
Of doddering fortune-tellers!
No, Teiresias:
If your birds—if the great eagles of God himself
Should carry him stinking bit by bit to heaven,
I would not yield. I am not afraid of pollution:
No man can defile the gods.
Do what you will,
Go into business, make money, speculate
In India gold or that synthetic gold from Sardis,
Get rich otherwise than by my consent to bury him.
Teiresias, it is a sorry thing when a wise man
Sells his wisdom, lets out his words for hire!

Teiresias: Ah Creon! Is there no man left in the world—

Creon: To do what?—Come, let's have the aphorism!

Teiresias: No man who knows that wisdom outweighs any wealth?

Creon: As surely as bribes are baser than any baseness.

Teiresias: You are sick, Creon! You are deathly sick!

Creon: As you say: it is not my place to challenge a prophet.

Teiresias: Yet you have said my prophecy is for sale.

Creon: The generation of prophets has always loved gold.

Teiresias: The generation of kings has always loved brass.

Creon: You forget yourself! You are speaking to your King.

Teiresias: I know it. You are a king because of me.

Creon: You have a certain skill; but you have sold out.

Teiresias: King, you will drive me to words that—

Creon: Say them, say them!
Only remember: I will not pay you for them.

Teiresias: No, you will find them too costly.

Creon: No doubt. Speak:
Whatever you say, you will not change my will.

Teiresias: Then take this, and take it to heart!
The time is not far off when you shall pay back
Corpse for corpse, flesh of your own flesh.
You have thrust the child of this world into living night,
You have kept from the gods below the child that is theirs:
The one in a grave before her death, the other,

Dead, denied the grave. This is your crime:
And the Furies and the dark gods of Hell
Are swift with terrible punishment for you.

Do you want to buy me now, Creon?

Not many days,
And your house will be full of men and women weeping,
And curses will be hurled at you from far
Cities grieving for sons unburied, left to rot
Before the walls of Thebes.

These are my arrows, Creon: they are all for you.

[*To* BOY.]

But come, child: lead me home.
Let him waste his fine anger upon younger men.
Maybe he will learn at last
To control a wiser tongue in a better head.

[*Exit* TEIRESIAS.]

Choragos: The old man has gone, King, but his words
Remain to plague us. I am old, too,
But I cannot remember that he was ever false.

Creon: That is true. . . . It troubles me.
Oh it is hard to give in! but it is worse
To risk everything for stubborn pride.

Choragos: Creon: take my advice.

Creon: What shall I do?

Choragos: Go quickly: free Antigone from her vault
And build a tomb for the body of Polyneices.

Creon: You would have me do this?

Choragos: Creon, yes!
And it must be done at once: God moves
Swiftly to cancel the folly of stubborn men.

Creon: It is hard to deny the heart! But I
Will do it: I will not fight with destiny.

Choragos: You must go yourself, you cannot leave it to others.

Creon: I will go.

—Bring axes, servants:
Come with me to the tomb. I buried her, I
Will set her free.

Oh quickly!
My mind misgives—
The laws of the gods are mighty, and a man must serve them
To the last day of his life!

[*Exit* CREON.]

PAEAN

[STROPHE I]

Choragos: God of many names

Chorus: O Iacchos

son
of Kadmeian Semele

O born of the Thunder!
Guardian of the West

Regent
of Eleusis' plain

O Prince of maenad Thebes
and the Dragon Field by rippling Ismenos

[ANTISTROPHE 1]

Choragos: God of many names

Chorus: the flame of torches
flares on our hills
the nymphs of Iacchos
dance at the spring of Castalia:
from the vine-close mountain
come ah come in ivy:
Evohé evohé! sings through the streets of Thebes

[STROPHE 2]

Choragos: God of many names

Chorus: Iacchos of Thebes
heavenly Child
of Semele bride of the Thunderer!
The shadow of plague is upon us:
come
with clement feet
oh come from Parnasos
down the long slopes
across the lamenting water

[ANTISTROPHE 2]

Choragos: Io Fire! Chorister of the throbbing stars!
O purest among the voices of the night!
Thou son of God, blaze for us!

Chorus: Come with choric rapture of circling Maenads
Who cry *Io Iacche!*
God of many names!

ÉXODOS

[*Enter* MESSENGER, *L.*]

Messenger: Men of the line of Kadmos, you who live
Near Amphion's citadel:
I cannot say
Of any condition of human life, "This is fixed,
This is clearly good, or bad." Fate raises up,
And Fate casts down the happy and unhappy alike:
No man can foretell his Fate.
Take the case of Creon:
Creon was happy once, as I count happiness:
Victorious in battle, sole governor of the land,
Fortunate father of children nobly born.
And now it has all gone from him! Who can say
That a man is still alive when his life's joy fails?
He is a walking dead man. Grant him rich,
Let him live like a king in his great house:
If his pleasure is gone, I would not give
So much as the shadow of smoke for all he owns.

Choragos: Your words hint at sorrow: what is your news for us?

Messenger: They are dead. The living are guilty of their death.

Choragos: Who is guilty? Who is dead? Speak!

Messenger: Haimon.
Haimon is dead; and the hand that killed him
Is his own hand.

Choragos: His father's or his own?

Messenger: His own, driven mad by the murder his father had done.

Choragos: Teiresias, Teiresias, how clearly you saw it all!

Messenger: This is my news: you

must draw what conclusions you can from it.

Choragos: But look: Eurydice, our Queen: Has she overheard us?

[*Enter* EURYDICE *from the Palace, C.*]

Eurydice: I have heard something, friends:
As I was unlocking the gate of Pallas' shrine,
For I needed her help today, I heard a voice
Telling of some new sorrow. And I fainted
There at the temple with all my maidens about me.
But speak again: whatever it is, I can bear it:
Grief and I are no strangers.

Messenger: Dearest Lady,
I will tell you plainly all that I have seen.
I shall not try to comfort you: what is the use,
Since comfort could lie only in what is not true?
The truth is always best.
I went with Creon
To the outer plain where Polyneices was lying,
No friend to pity him, his body shredded by dogs.
We made our prayers in that place to Hecate
And Pluto, that they would be merciful. And we bathed
The corpse with holy water, and we brought
Fresh-broken branches to burn what was left of it,
And upon the urn we heaped up a towering barrow
Of the earth of his own land.
When we were done, we ran
To the vault where Antigonê lay on her couch of stone.
One of the servants had gone ahead,
And while he was yet far off he heard a voice
Grieving within the chamber, and he came back
And told Creon. And as the King went closer,
The air was full of wailing, the words lost,
And he begged us to make all haste. "Am I a prophet?"
He said, weeping, "And must I walk this road,
The saddest of all that I have gone before?
My son's voice calls me on. Oh quickly, quickly!
Look through the crevice there, and tell me
If it is Haimon, or some deception of the gods!"

We obeyed; and in the cavern's farthest corner
We saw her lying:
She had made a noose of her fine linen veil
And hanged herself. Haimon lay beside her,
His arms about her waist, lamenting her,
His love lost under ground, crying out
That his father had stolen her away from him.
When Creon saw him the tears rushed to his eyes
And he called to him: "What have you done, child? Speak to me.
What are you thinking that makes your eyes so strange?
O my son, my son, I come to you on my knees!"
But Haimon spat in his face. He said not a word,
Staring—
And suddenly drew his sword
And lunged. Creon shrank back, the blade missed; and the boy,
Desperate against himself, drove it half its length

Into his own side, and fell. And as he died
He gathered Antigonê close in his arms again,
Choking, his blood bright red on her white cheek.
And now he lies dead with the dead, and she is his
At last, his bride in the houses of the dead.

[*Exit* EURYDICE *into the Palace.*]

Choragos: She has left us without a word. What can this mean?

Messenger: It troubles me, too; yet she knows what is best,
Her grief is too great for public lamentation,
And doubtless she has gone to her chamber to weep
For her dead son, leading her maidens in his dirge.

Choragos: It may be so: but I fear this deep silence.

[*Pause.*]

Messenger: I will see what she is doing. I will go in.

[*Exit* MESSENGER *into the Palace.*]

[*Enter* CREON *with attendants, bearing* HAIMON'S *body.*]

Choragos: But here is the King himself: oh look at him,
Bearing his own damnation in his arms.

Creon: Nothing you say can touch me any more.
My own blind heart has brought me
From darkness to final darkness. Here you see
The father murdering, the murdered son—
And all my civic wisdom!

Haimon my son, so young, so young to die,
I was the fool, not you; and you died for me.

Choragos: That is the truth; but you were late in learning it.

Creon: This truth is hard to bear. Surely a god
Has crushed me beneath the hugest weight of heaven.
And driven me headlong a barbaric way
To trample out the thing I held most dear.

The pains that we will take to come to pain!

[*Enter* MESSENGER *from the Palace.*]

Messenger: The burden you carry in your hands is heavy,
But it is not all: you will find more in your house.

Creon: What burden worse than this shall I find there?

Messenger: The Queen is dead.

Creon: O port of death, deaf world,
Is there no pity for me? And you, Angel of evil,
I was dead, and your words are death again.
Is it true, boy? Can it be true?
Is my wife dead? Has death bred death?

Messenger: You can see for yourself.

[*The doors are opened, and the body of* EURYDICE *is disclosed within.*]

Creon: Oh pity!
All true, all true, and more than I can bear!
O my wife, my son!

Messenger: She stood before the altar, and her heart
Welcomed the knife her own hand guided,
And a great cry burst from her lips for Megareus dead,
And for Haimon dead, her sons; and her last breath
Was a curse for their father, the murderer of her sons.
And she fell, and the dark flowed in through her closing eyes.

Creon: O God, I am sick with fear.
Are there no swords here? Has no one a blow for me?

Messenger: Her curse is upon you for the deaths of both.

Creon: It is right that it should be. I alone am guilty.
I know it, and I say it. Lead me in,
Quickly, friends.
I have neither life nor substance. Lead me in.

Choragos: You are right, if there can be right in so much wrong.
The briefest way is best in a world of sorrow.

Creon: Let it come,
Let death come quickly, and be kind to me.
I would not ever see the sun again.

Choragos: All that will come when it will; but we, meanwhile,
Have much to do. Leave the future to itself.

Creon: All my heart was in that prayer!

Choragos: Then do not pray any more: the sky is deaf.

Creon: Lead me away. I have been rash and foolish.
I have killed my son and my wife.
I look for comfort; my comfort lies here dead.
Whatever my hands have touched has come to nothing.
Fate has brought all my pride to a thought of dust.

[*As* CREON *is being led into the house, the* CHORAGOS *advances and speaks directly to the audience.*]

Choragos: There is no happiness where there is no wisdom;
No wisdom but in submission to the gods.
Big words are always punished,
And proud men in old age learn to be wise.

DISCUSSION QUESTIONS

Prologue

1. While Antigone is technically a law-breaker, doomed by an arbitrary decree made before the play starts, it is Creon her antagonist who is the storm-center of conflict. How is Antigone characterized by her argument with Ismene?
2. How does Ismene serve as Antigone's foil (i.e., a contrasting type)?
3. The religious duty for which Antigone risks death is no longer relevant today. However, are there other issues—political, religious, and social—which have contemporary significance?
4. What view of the after-life is implied by Antigone's words?
5. How do the tone and content of the choral Parodos (Entrance Song) contrast ironically with the preceding argument?

Scene I

1. Creon's speech to the assembled chorus is far more pragmatic, directive, and impersonal than anything which preceded it. What view of political principles motivates Creon?

2. What do we learn about Creon's character here?
3. How does the guard's fear help characterize Creon?
4. How does the suggestion of the Chorus as to who buried Polyneices establish a potential conflict?
5. Is the reluctance of first the Chorus and then the guard to accept Creon's version of danger to the state ironic?
6. The Chorus has already been presented as a loyal supporter of Creon's authority. Is there any way in which their first Ode broadens Creon's view of human nature?

Scene II

1. How is the sentry's second report ironic?
2. How does Antigone justify her apparent treason?
3. What does Creon's suspicion of Ismene tell us about him?
4. What kinds of tensions or conflicting values increase in severity as the play progresses?
5. How is Creon's situation potentially tragic?
6. How does Antigone foreshadow the Chorus's rebellion?
7. How does Antigone's nature contrast with that of all the others in the play?
8. How does Antigone's attitude toward Polyneices differ from Creon's?
9. How does Ismene become more like Antigone?
10. What factors keep Creon from appearing as a villain?
11. Why does Antigone reject Ismene?
12. How is the second Ode related to the preceding action?

Scene III

1. In the third scene, Creon's preoccupation with the law has begun to shift to a concern for untrammeled power. What is ironic about Creon's speech to Haimon, in view of what Haimon is about to say?
2. On what grounds does Haimon attack his father's position?
3. What values clash in the argument between Creon and Haimon?
4. Does Haimon resemble his father in their dispute? How?
5. Why does Creon angrily reject Haimon's advice?
6. According to the Chorus, how are love's powers paradoxical?

Scene IV

1. In this scene, although the play is little more than half over, Antigone makes her last appearance. Has Antigone's character changed?
2. How does the Chorus stress the spiritual benefits of Antigone's death?
3. How does Antigone see her death as ironic?
4. How does Antigone remain uncompromising to the end?
5. How is Creon's haste ironic, in view of action yet to come?

6. How is the Chorus's mention of Danae, Dryas' son (Lycurgus), and a mythical Cleopatra relevant to Antigone's situation?
7. Has the Chorus begun to waver in its loyalty to Creon?

Scene V

1. Teiresias is that suffering seer whom Sophocles also used in *Oedipus* to reveal a truth which other mortals found too hard and uncomfortable to see. How does his appearance with a boy reverse Creon's parent-child situation?
2. How is Creon's characterization furthered by his reaction to Teiresias' appearance?
3. What is ironic about Creon's double crime?
4. What do Creon's mistakes about the motives of his "enemies" reveal about his attitude toward human nature?
5. How does Teiresias extend Creon's "sickness" to an entire society?
6. Why do first the Chorus, and then Creon, accept Teiresias' judgment?
7. In each scene of the play nearly equally matched characters have met, found themselves at cross-purposes, and fought bitterly. But until this time Creon has won each round. How has he learned from defeat in this encounter?

After the Play

1. Is there any resemblance between the appearance of the messenger in this scene and that of the sentry in the Prologue?
2. How had Haimon's death and Creon's near-death been foreshadowed?
3. How does the double suicide of Antigone and Haimon resemble the situation in *Romeo and Juliet?*
4. The source of the play and the attitudes of Haimon and Antigone make their deaths seem inevitable. How has Sophocles still managed to surprise us?
5. What does the failure of Creon to free Antigone first represent?
6. Antigone's tragedy is terrible, but it is foreseen and swift. Creon's grows before our eyes. How do his enlightened virtues correspond to his previous faults?
7. What forces, as they have appeared in the play's action, have been directed against Creon?
8. Although Creon was a wise man with tradition and experience on his side, his judgment was wrong, and Antigone's instinct was right. What have he and the Chorus learned about piety?
9. To justify his treatment of Polyneices and Eteocles, Creon had referred to the concept of poetic justice: the good prosper, and the evil perish—or they should in a rational scheme of things. Does Creon deserve his punishment?
10. What has Creon learned about the structure of the universe?
11. Even though Creon has more than twice Antigone's lines, the play has been given her name. To what extent is the play her tragedy?
12. Can it be argued that Creon is dramatically dominant?
13. How do the tragedies suffered by both main characters depend on their interplay?

KING LEAR

❖ *William Shakespeare*

Introductory Comment

In *King Lear* we have tragic drama in English carried to its highest level. The play is a perfect blending of character-in-depth, multiple but unified action, a theme of universal, lasting significance, and language of consummate beauty and mood-creating power. *King Lear* emerges from this blending as a magnificently structured whole that engages our mind and moves our heart through pity and fear to moral insight and uplift. The folly and greatness of Lear, the honesty and devotion of Cordelia and Kent, the hypocrisy and cruelty of Goneril and Regan, the ruthless amoral sophistry and scheming of Edmund, the fond credulity of Gloucester, the resourcefulness and loyalty of Edgar, and the heart-rending wise folly of the Fool are made manifest in a series of skilfully interwoven events that form a pattern of awesome, tragic significance.

Shakespeare exploits every device of language—vivid imagery, startling because of its singular appropriateness, powerful, emotion-laden rhythms, words and phrases with symbolic overtones and compressed meanings—to create the dramatic world of the play. We are conjured into emotional participation by the elegant language of court, lofty and imperious or hypocritical and scheming; by the simple diction of sincerity of Cordelia and Kent; by the clever word-play and quibbling of Edmund; by the bumbling, vapid utterances of the deceived Gloucester; by the doggerel verse of Edgar and the Fool pitilessly exposing the truth about human folly and evil; and by the heart-searching ravings of a mind unhinged with grief when Lear, an outcast of filial ingratitude, wanders over the symbolically barren and deserted heath swept by a physical storm reflecting a monstrous upheaval in the moral universe.

In order to appreciate fully such a play as this, one must accept the convention that great emotions are best expressed in great poetry. The language of literal reality is too flimsy a vehicle to bear the burden of the great grief and great joy of a Lear, a Cordelia, or a Gloucester. The initial barrier presented by the difficulties of Shakespearean English is one well worth the trouble to surmount. When one makes this effort and overcomes the difficulty, he is well repaid by the grandeur of Shakespeare's dramatic conception. The changes in speech and customs since Shakespeare's day will have little ultimate effect on appreciation of the play if one approaches it with a willingness to relinquish linguistic and dramatic prejudices nourished on tape-recorder language and drab realism pretending to be truth and on wide-screen opulence and empty bombast pretending to be moving entertainment. In *King Lear* one hears the sounds of genuine dramatic eloquence speaking the universal language of overwhelming human emotion against a background of significant action. Seeing a competent performance which emphasizes the language or at least listening to a good reading of the play is almost indispensable to the real understanding and appreciation of this great work.

Cast of Characters

LEAR, *King of Britain*
KING OF FRANCE
DUKE OF BURGUNDY
DUKE OF CORNWALL
DUKE OF ALBANY
EARL OF KENT
EARL OF GLOUCESTER
EDGAR, *son to Gloucester*
EDMUND, *bastard son to Gloucester*
CURAN, *a courtier*
OLD MAN, *tenant to Gloucester*
DOCTOR
FOOL
OSWALD, *steward to Goneril*
A CAPTAIN *in Edmund's command*
GENTLEMAN
A HERALD
SERVANTS *to Cornwall*
GONERIL, REGAN, CORDELIA } *daughters to Lear*
KNIGHTS *attending on Lear,* CAPTAINS, MESSENGERS, SOLDIERS, ATTENDANTS

ACT I

SCENE I

LEAR'S *Palace*

[*Enter* KENT, GLOUCESTER, *and* EDMUND.]

Kent: I thought the King had more affected[1] the Duke of Albany than Cornwall.

Gloucester: It did always seem so to us; but now, in the division of the kingdom, it appears not which of the Dukes he values most, for equalities are so weighed that curiosity[2] in neither can make choice of either's moiety.[3]

Kent: Is not this your son, my lord?

Gloucester: His breeding, sir, hath been at my charge. I have so often blushed to acknowledge him that now I am brazed[4] to't.

Kent: I cannot conceive[5] you.

Gloucester: Sir, this young fellow's mother could; whereupon she grew round-wombed, and had indeed, sir, a son for her cradle ere she had a husband for her bed. Do you smell a fault?

Kent: I cannot wish the fault undone, the issue[6] of it being so proper.[7]

Gloucester: But I have a son, sir, by order of law, some year elder than this, who yet is no dearer in my account. Though this knave came something saucily into the world before he was sent for, yet was his mother fair, there was good sport at his making, and the whoreson must be acknowledged. Do you know this noble gentleman, Edmund?

Edmund: No, my lord.

Gloucester: My Lord of Kent. Re-

I, i, [1] more affected: liked better. [2] curiosity: fastidious choice. [3] moiety: share. [4] brazed: inured, hardened. [5] conceive: understand. [6] issue: outcome, offspring. [7] proper: handsome, attractive.

member him hereafter as my honorable friend.

Edmund: My services to your lordship.

Kent: I must love you, and sue to know you better.

Edmund: Sir, I shall study deserving.[8]

Gloucester: He hath been out nine years, and away he shall again.

[*Sennet.*]

The King is coming.

[*Enter one bearing a coronet,* KING LEAR, ALBANY, CORNWALL, GONERIL, REGAN, CORDELIA, *and* ATTENDANTS.]

Lear: Attend the lords of France and Burgundy, Gloucester.

Gloucester: I shall, my liege.

[*Exeunt* GLOUCESTER *and* EDMUND.]

Lear: Meantime we shall express our darker purpose.[9]
Give me the map there. Know that we have divided
In three our kingdom; and 'tis our fast intent
To shake all cares and business from our age,
Conferring them on younger strengths while we
Unburthened crawl toward death. Our son of Cornwall,
And you, our no less loving son of Albany,
We have this hour a constant will to publish
Our daughters' several dowers, that future strife
May be prevented now. The princes, France and Burgundy,
Great rivals in our youngest daughter's love,
Long in our court have made their amorous sojourn,
And here are to be answered. Tell me, my daughters
Since now we will divest us both of rule,
Interest of territory, cares of state,
Which of you shall we say doth love us most,
That we our largest bounty may extend
Where nature doth with merit challenge.[10] Goneril,
Our eldest-born, speak first.

Goneril: Sir, I love you more than words can wield the matter;
Dearer than eyesight, space, and liberty;
Beyond what can be valued, rich or rare;
No less than life, with grace, health, beauty, honor;
As much as child e'er loved, or father found;
A love that makes breath poor, and speech unable.
Beyond all manner of so much I love you.

Cordelia (*aside*). What shall Cordelia speak? Love, and be silent.

Lear: Of all these bounds, even from this line to this,
With shadowy forests and with champains riched,[11]
With plenteous rivers and wide-skirted meads,[12]
We make thee lady. To thine and Albany's issue
Be this perpetual. What says our second daughter,
Our dearest Regan, wife to Cornwall?

Regan: I am made of the selfsame metal that my sister is,
And prize me[13] at her worth. In my true heart
I find she names my very deed of love,

[8] study deserving: try to merit it. [9] darker purpose: secret intention. [10] Where . . . challenge: where ties of blood and individual worth are combined. [11] champains riched: enriched with fields. [12] wide-skirted meads: wide meadows. [13] prize me: value me.

Only she comes too short, that I profess
Myself an enemy to all other joys
Which the most precious square[14] of sense possesses,
And find I am alone felicitate
In your dear Highness' love.

Cordelia (*aside*). Then poor Cordelia!
And yet not so; since I am sure my love's
More richer than my tongue.

Lear: To thee and thine hereditary ever
Remain this ample third of our fair kingdom,
No less in space, validity,[15] and pleasure
Than that conferred on Goneril. Now, our joy,
Although the last, not least, to whose young love
The vines of France and milk of Burgundy
Strive to be interessed,[16] what can you say to draw
A third more opulent than your sisters? Speak.

Cordelia: Nothing, my lord.

Lear: Nothing?

Cordelia: Nothing.

Lear: Nothing can come of nothing; speak again.

Cordelia: Unhappy that I am, I cannot heave
My heart into my mouth. I love your Majesty
According to my bond, nor more nor less.

Lear: How, how, Cordelia? Mend your speech a little,
Lest it may mar your fortunes.

Cordelia: Good my lord,
You have begot me, bred me, loved me; I
Return those duties back as are right fit,
Obey you, love you, and most honor you.
Why have my sisters husbands, if they say
They love you all? Haply,[17] when I shall wed,
That lord whose hand must take my plight[18] shall carry
Half my love with him, half my care and duty.
Sure I shall never marry like my sisters,
To love my father all.

Lear: But goes thy heart with this?

Cordelia: Ay, good my lord.

Lear: So young, and so untender?

Cordelia: So young, my lord, and true.

Lear: Let it be so! Thy truth then be thy dower!
For, by the sacred radiance of the sun,
The mysteries of Hecate[19] and the night,
By all the operation of the orbs[20]
From whom we do exist and cease to be,
Here I disclaim[21] all my paternal care,
Propinquity[22] and property of blood,
And as a stranger to my heart and me
Hold thee from this for ever. The barbarous Scythian,
Or he that makes his generation[23] messes[24]
To gorge his appetite, shall to my bosom
Be as well neighbored, pitied, and relieved
As thou my sometime daughter.

Kent: Good my liege—

Lear: Peace, Kent!
Come not between the dragon and his wrath.
I loved her most, and thought to set my rest
On her kind nursery.[25] Hence and avoid my sight!
So be my grave my peace as here I give
Her father's heart from her! Call France! Who stirs?
Call Burgundy! Cornwall and Albany,

[14] square: measure, criterion. [15] validity: worth. [16] interessed: attached. [17] haply: eventually. [18] plight: wedding promise. [19] Hecate: goddess of magic. [20] orbs: heavenly bodies. [21] disclaim: renounce. [22] propinquity: blood relationship. [23] generation: offspring, children. [24] messes: meals. [25] nursery: care.

With my two daughters' dowers digest[26] the third;
Let pride, which she calls plainness,[27] marry her.
I do invest you jointly with my power,
Preëminence, and all the large effects
That troop with majesty. Ourself, by monthly course,
With reservation of an hundred knights,
By you to be sustained, shall our abode
Make with you by due turns. Only we still retain
The name, and all the additions[28] to a king; the sway,
Revenue, execution of the rest,
Beloved sons, be yours, which to confirm
This coronet[29] part betwixt you.

Kent: Royal Lear,
Whom I have ever honored as my king,
Loved as my father, as my master followed,
As my great patron thought on in my prayers—

Lear: The bow is bent and drawn; make from the shaft.

Kent: Let it fall rather, though the fork invade
The region of my heart! Be Kent unmannerly
When Lear is mad. What wouldst thou do, old man?
Think'st thou that duty shall have dread to speak
When power to flattery bows? To plainness honor's bound
When majesty stoops to folly. Reserve thy doom,[30]
And in thy best consideration check
This hideous rashness. Answer my life my judgment,
Thy youngest daughter does not love thee least,
Nor are those empty-hearted whose low sound
Reverbs[31] no hollowness.

Lear: Kent, on thy life, no more!

Kent: My life I never held but as a pawn
To wage against thine enemies; nor fear to lose it,
Thy safety being the motive.

Lear: Out of my sight!

Kent: See better, Lear, and let me still remain
The true blank[32] of thine eye.

Lear: Now by Apollo—

Kent: Now by Apollo, King,
Thou swearest thy gods in vain.

Lear: O vassal! miscreant!

[*Laying his hand on his sword.*]

Albany, Cornwall: Dear sir, forbear!

Kent: Kill thy physician, and thy fee bestow
Upon the foul disease. Revoke thy doom,
Or, whilst I can vent clamor[33] from my throat,
I'll tell thee thou dost evil.

Lear: Hear me, recreant!
On thine allegiance, hear me!
Since thou has sought to make us break our vow,
Which we durst never yet, and with strained pride
To come betwixt our sentence and our power,
Which nor our nature nor our place can bear,
Our potency[34] made good, take thy reward.
Five days we do allot thee for provision
To shield thee from diseases of the world,
And on the sixth to turn thy hated back
Upon our kingdom. If, on the tenth day following,

[26] digest: incorporate. [27] plainness: honesty. [28] additions: titles. [29] coronet: ducal crown. [30] doom: sentence. [31] reverbs: echoes. [32] blank: target-center; guide. [33] vent clamor: utter a sound. [34] potency: regal power.

Thy banished trunk[35] be found in our dominions,
The moment is thy death. Away! By Jupiter,
This shall not be revoked.

Kent: Fare thee well, King; sith thus thou wilt appear,
Freedom lives hence, and banishment is here.
(*To* CORDELIA.) The gods to their dear shelter take thee, maid,
That justly think'st and hast most rightly said!
(*To* REGAN *and* GONERIL.) And your large[36] speeches may your deed approve,[37]
That good effects may spring from words of love.
Thus Kent, O princes, bids you all adieu;
He'll shape his old course in a country new.

[*Exit.*]

[*Flourish. Re-enter* GLOUCESTER *with* FRANCE *and* BURGUNDY, *and* ATTENDANTS.]

Gloucester: Here's France and Burgundy, my noble lord.

Lear: My Lord of Burgundy,
We first address toward you, who with this king
Hath rivalled for our daughter. What in the least
Will you require in present dower with her,
Or cease your quest of love?

Burgundy: Most royal Majesty,
I crave no more than hath your Highness offered,
Nor will you tender[38] less.

Lear: Right noble Burgundy,
When she was dear to us, we did hold her so,
But now her price is fallen. Sir, there she stands.
If aught within that little seeming substance,
Or all of it, with our displeasure pieced,[39]
And nothing more, may fitly like[40] your Grace,
She's there, and she is yours.

Burgundy: I know no answer.

Lear: Will you, with those infirmities she owes,[41]
Unfriended, new adopted to our hate,
Dowered with our curse, and strangered with our oath,
Take her, or leave her?

Burgundy: Pardon me, royal sir;
Election makes not up[42] on such conditions.

Lear: Then leave her, sir, for by the power that made me
I tell you all her wealth. (*To* FRANCE.) For you, great King,
I would not from your love make such a stray
To match you where I hate; therefore beseech you
To avert your liking a more worthier way
Than on a wretch whom nature is ashamed
Almost to acknowledge hers.

France: This is most strange,
That she that even but now was your best object,
The argument[43] of your praise, balm of your age,
Most best, most dearest, should in this trice of time
Commit a thing so monstrous to dismantle
So many folds of favor. Sure her offence
Must be of such unnatural degree

[35] trunk: body, person. [36] large: fine-sounding. [37] approve: support, confirm. [38] tender: offer. [39] pieced: added to it. [40] like: please. [41] owes: has, owns. [42] election . . . up: no choice is possible. [43] argument: topic.

That monsters[44] it, or your fore-vouched affection
Fallen into taint; which to believe of her
Must be a faith that reason without miracle
Could never plant in me.

Cordelia: I yet beseech your Majesty,
If for I want that glib and oily art
To speak and purpose not, since what I well intend,
I'll do't before I speak—that you make known
It is no vicious blot, murther, or foulness,
No unchaste action or dishonored step,
That hath deprived me of your grace and favor;
But even for want of that for which I am richer,
A still-soliciting[45] eye, and such a tongue
As I am glad I have not, though not to have it
Hath lost me in your liking.

Lear: Better thou
Hadst not been born than not to have pleased me better.

France: Is it but this—a tardiness in nature
Which often leaves the history unspoke
That it intends to do? My Lord of Burgundy,
What say you to the lady? Love's not love
When it is mingled with regards that stand
Aloof from the entire point.[46] Will you have her?
She is herself a dowry.

Burgundy: Royal Lear,
Give but that portion which yourself proposed,
And here I take Cordelia by the hand,
Duchess of Burgundy.

Lear: Nothing. I have sworn; I am firm.

Burgundy: I am sorry then, you have so lost a father
That you must lose a husband.

Cordelia: Peace be with Burgundy!
Since that respects[47] of fortune are his love,
I shall not be his wife.

France: Fairest Cordelia, that art most rich, being poor;
Most choice, forsaken; and most loved, despised!
Thee and thy virtues here I seize upon.
Be it lawful I take up what's cast away.
God's, gods! 'tis strange that from their coldest neglect
My love should kindle to inflamed respect.
Thy dowerless daughter, King, thrown to my chance,
Is queen of us, of ours, and our fair France.
Not all the dukes of waterish Burgundy
Can buy this unprized precious maid of me.
Bid them farewell, Cordelia, though unkind;
Thou losest here, a better where to find.

Lear: Thou hast her, France; let her be thine; for we
Have no such daughter, nor shall ever see
That face of hers again. Therefore be gone
Without our grace, our love, our benison.[48]
Come, noble Burgundy.

[*Flourish. Exeunt all but* FRANCE, GONERIL, REGAN, *and* CORDELIA.]

France: Bid farewell to your sisters.

Cordelia: The jewels of our father, with washed eyes
Cordelia leaves you. I know you what you are;
And like a sister am most loath to call

[44] that monsters it: that makes it monstrous. [45] still-soliciting: forever-begging. [46] entire point: chief consideration. [47] respects: considerations, matters. [48] benison: blessing.

Your faults as they are named. Use well our father;
To your professed bosoms[49] I commit him;
But yet, alas, stood I within his grace,
I would prefer[50] him to a better place.
So farewell to you both.

Goneril: Prescribe not us our duty.

Regan: Let your study
Be to content your lord, who hath received you
At fortune's alms.[51] You have obedience scanted,[52]
And well are worth the want that you have wanted.[53]

Cordelia: Time shall unfold what plighted[54] cunning hides.
Who cover faults, at last shame them derides.
Well may you prosper!

France: Come, my fair Cordelia.

[*Exeunt* FRANCE *and* CORDELIA.]

Goneril: Sister, it is not little I have to say of what most nearly appertains to us both. I think our father will hence tonight.

Regan: That's most certain, and with you; next month with us.

Goneril: You see how full of changes his age is. The observation we have made of it hath not been little. He always loved our sister most, and with what poor judgment he hath now cast her off appears too grossly.

Regan: 'Tis the infirmity of his age; yet he hath ever but slenderly known himself.

Goneril: The best and soundest of his time hath been but rash; then must we look to receive from his age not alone the imperfections of long-ingraffed condition,[55] but therewithal the unruly waywardness that infirm and choleric years bring with them.

Regan: Such unconstant starts[56] are we like to have from him as this of Kent's banishment.

Goneril: There is further compliment[57] of leave-taking between France and him. Pray you let us hit[58] together. If our father carry authority with such dispositions as he bears, this last surrender of his will but offend us.

Regan: We shall further think of it.

Goneril: We must do something, and i'th'heat.[59]

[*Exeunt.*]

SCENE II

GLOUCESTER'S *Castle*

[*Enter* EDMUND, *with a letter.*]

Edmund: Thou, Nature,[1] art my goddess; to thy law
My services are bound. Wherefore should I
Stand in the plague[2] of custom, and permit
The curiosity of nations to deprive me,
For that I am some twelve or fourteen moonshines
Lag of a brother?[3] Why bastard? wherefore base?
When my dimensions are as well compact,

[49] professed bosoms: hearts that have professed love. [50] prefer: assign, advance. [51] alms: charity. [52] scanted: ignored, slighted. [53] and . . . wanted: and well deserve the lack of love you are guilty of yourself. [54] plighted: pleated, folded; i.e., hidden. [55] long-engraffed condition: confirmed habits. [56] unconstant starts: impetuous rages. [57] compliment: official courtesies. [58] hit: agree, "get together." [59] i'th'heat: immediately.
I, ii, [1] Nature: for Edmund, the principle of self-interest. [2] stand in the plague of: be hampered by. [3] For . . . brother: simply because I am a year or so younger.

My mind as generous, and my shape as true,
As honest madam's issue? Why brand they us
With base? with baseness? bastardy? base, base?
Who, in the lusty stealth of nature, take
More composition and fierce quality
Than doth, within a dull, stale, tired bed,
Go to the creating a whole tribe of fops[4]
Got 'tween asleep and wake? Well then,
Legitimate Edgar, I must have your land.
Our father's love is to the bastard Edmund
As to the legitimate. Fine word "legitimate"!
Well, my legitimate, if this letter speed,[5]
And my invention,[6] thrive, Edmund the base
Shall top the legitimate. I grow, I prosper:
Now, gods, stand up for bastards!

[*Enter* GLOUCESTER.]

Gloucester: Kent banished thus! and France in choler parted.
And the King gone to-night? subscribed[7] his power.
Confined to exhibition![8] All this done
Upon the gad?[9] Edmund, how now? What news?

Edmund: So please your lordship, none. (*Putting up the letter.*)

Gloucester: Why so earnestly seek you to put up that letter?

Edmund: I know no news, my lord.

Gloucester: What paper were you reading?

Edmund: Nothing, my lord.

Gloucester: No? What needed then that terrible dispatch of it into your pocket? The quality of nothing hath not such need to hide itself. Let's see. Come, if it be nothing, I shall not need spectacles.

Edmund: I beseech you, sir, pardon me. It is a letter from my brother that I have not all o'er-read; and for so much as I have perused, I find it not fit for your o'erlooking.[10]

Gloucester: Give me the letter, sir.

Edmund: I shall offend, either to detain or give it. The contents, as in part I understand them, are to blame.

Gloucester: Let's see, let's see.

Edmund: I hope, for my brother's justification, he wrote this but as an essay[11] or taste of my virtue.

Gloucester (*reads*). "This policy and reverence of age makes the world bitter to the best of our times; keeps our fortunes from us till our oldness cannot relish them. I begin to find an idle and fond[12] bondage in the oppression of aged tyranny, who sways, not as it hath power, but as it is suffered.[13] Come to me, that of this I may speak more. If our father would sleep till I waked him, you should enjoy half his revenue for ever, and live the beloved of your brother, Edgar."
Hum! Conspiracy? "Sleep till I waked him, you should enjoy half his revenue." My son Edgar! Had he a hand to write this? a heart and brain to breed it in? When came you to this? Who brought it?

Edmund: It was not brought me, my lord: there's the cunning of it. I found it thrown in at the casement of my closet.[14]

Gloucester: You know the character[15] to be your brother's?

Edmund: If the matter were good, my lord, I durst swear it were his; but in re-

[4] fops: dandified fools. [5] speed: succeed. [6] invention: scheme. [7] subscribed: signed away. [8] exhibition: pension. [9] gad: spur (of the moment). [10] o'erlooking: perusal. [11] essay: trial.

[12] fond: foolish. [13] suffered: endured, put up with. [14] closet: chamber, room. [15] character: handwriting.

spect of that, I would fain think it were not.

Gloucester: It is his?

Edmund: It is his hand, my lord; but I hope his heart is not in the contents.

Gloucester: Has he never before sounded you in this business?

Edmund: Never, my lord. But I have heard him oft maintain it to be fit that, sons at perfect age, and fathers declining, the father should be as ward to the son, and the son manage his revenue.

Gloucester: O villain, villain! His very opinion in the letter! Abhorred villain! Unnatural, detested, brutish villain! worse than brutish! Go, sirrah, seek him; I'll apprehend him. Abominable villain! Where is he?

Edmund: I do not well know, my lord. If it shall please you to suspend your indignation against my brother till you can derive from him better testimony of his intent, you should run a certain course; where, if you violently proceed against him, mistaking his purpose, it would make a great gap in your own honor and shake in pieces the heart of his obedience. I dare pawn down my life for him that he hath writ this to feel[16] my affection to your honor, and to no further pretence of danger.

Gloucester: Think you so?

Edmund: If your honor judge it meet,[17] I will place you where you shall hear us confer of this and by an auricular assurance[18] have your satisfaction, and that without any further delay than this very evening.

Gloucester: He cannot be such a monster.

Edmund: Nor is not, sure.

Gloucester: To his father, that so tenderly and entirely loves him. Heaven and earth! Edmund, seek him out; wind me into him,[19] I pray you; frame the business after your own wisdom. I would unstate myself to be in a due resolution.[20]

Edmund: I will seek him, sir, presently[21] convey[22] the business as I shall find means, and acquaint you withal.

Gloucester: These late eclipses in the sun and moon portend no good to us. Though the wisdom of nature[23] can reason[24] it thus and thus, yet nature finds itself scourged by the sequent[25] effects. Love cools, friendship falls off, brothers divide. In cities, mutinees; in countries, discord; in palaces, treason; and the bond cracked 'twixt son and father. This villain of mine comes under the prediction; there's son against father: the King falls from bias of nature;[26] there's father against child. We have seen the best of our time. Machinations, hollowness, treachery, and all ruinous disorders follow us disquietly to our graves. Find out this villain, Edmund; it shall lose thee nothing; do it carefully. And the noble and true-hearted Kent banished! his offence, honesty! 'Tis strange.

[*Exit.*]

Edmund: This is the excellent foppery[27] of the world, that, when we are sick in fortune, often the surfeit[28] of our own behavior, we make guilty of our disasters the sun, the moon, and the star; as if we were villains on necessity, fools by heavenly compulsion, knaves, thieves, and treachers by spherical predominance,[29]

[16] feel: try, test. [17] meet: appropriate, suitable. [18] auricular assurance: aural proof. [19] wind me into him: find out his intentions for me. [20] I would unstate . . . resolution: I would give up everything to know. [21] presently: right away. [22] convey: handle. [23] wisdom of nature: science. [24] reason: explain. [25] sequent: resulting. [26] bias of nature: normal behavior. [27] foppery: foolishness. [28] surfeit: excess. [29] spherical predominance: astrological influence.

drunkards, liars, and adulterers by an enforced obedience of planetary influence; and all that we are evil in, by a divine thrusting on. An admirable evasion of whoremaster man, to lay his goatish[30] disposition to the charge of a star! My father compounded with my mother under the Dragon's Tail, and my nativity was under Ursa Major, so that it follows I am rough and lecherous. Tut! I should have been that I am, had the maidenliest star in the firmament twinkled on my bastardizing. Edgar—

[*Enter* EDGAR.]

and pat! he comes, like the catastrophe[31] of the old comedy. My cue is villainous melancholy, with a sigh like Tom o' Bedlam.[32] O these eclipses do portend these divisions. Fa, sol, la, mi.

Edgar: How now, brother Edmund? What serious contemplation are you in?

Edmund: I am thinking, brother, of a prediction I read this other day, what should follow these eclipses.

Edgar: Do you busy yourself with that?

Edmund: I promise you, the effects he writes of succeed[33] unhappily, as of unnaturalness between the child and the parent; death, dearth, dissolutions of ancient amities; divisions in state, menaces and maledictions against king and nobles; needless diffidences,[34] banishment of friends, dissipation of cohorts,[35] nuptial breaches, and I know not what.

Edgar: How long have you been a sectary astronomical?[36]

Edmund: Come, come, when saw you my father last?

Edgar: The night gone by.

Edmund: Spake you with him?

Edgar: Ay, two hours together.

Edmund: Parted you in good terms? Found you no displeasure in him by word or countenance?

Edgar: None at all.

Edmund: Bethink yourself wherein you may have offended him; and at my entreaty forbear his presence until some little time hath qualified[37] the heat of his displeasure, which at this instant so rageth in him that with the mischief of[38] your person it would scarcely allay.[39]

Edgar: Some villain hath done me wrong.

Edmund: That's my fear. I pray you have a continent forbearance[40] till the speed of his rage goes slower; and, as I say, retire with me to my lodging, from whence I will fitly bring you to hear my lord speak. Pray ye, go; there's my key. If you do stir abroad, go armed.

Edgar: Armed, brother?

Edmund: Brother, I advise you to the best. Go armed. I am no honest man if there be any good meaning toward you. I have told you what I have seen and heard; but faintly, nothing like the image and horror of it. Pray you, away!

Edgar: Shall I hear from you anon?

Edmund: I do serve you in this business.

[*Exit* EDGAR.]

A credulous father, and a brother noble,
Whose nature is so far from doing harms
That he suspects none; on whose foolish
honesty

[30] goatish: lecherous. [31] catastrophe: final episode. [32] Tom o' Bedlam: discharged lunatic. [33] succeed: occur. [34] diffidences: suspicions. [35] dissipation of cohorts: breaches of friendship.

[36] sectary astronomical: believer in astrology. [37] qualified: cooled off. [38] mischief of: injury to. [39] allay: be lessened or appeased. [40] continent forbearance: self-control.

My practices[41] ride easy! I see the business.
Let me, if not by birth, have lands by wit;
All with me's meet that I can fashion fit.[42]

[*Exit.*]

SCENE III

THE DUKE OF ALBANY'S *Palace*

[*Enter* GONERIL *and* OSWALD, *her* STEWARD.]

Goneril: Did my father strike my gentleman for chiding of his fool?

Oswald: Ay, madam.

Goneril: By day and night he wrongs me. Every hour
He flashes into one gross crime or other
That sets us all at odds; I'll not endure it.
His knights grow riotous, and himself upbraids us
On every trifle. When he returns from hunting
I will not speak with him; say I am sick.
If you come slack of[1] former services,
You shall do well; the fault of it I'll answer.

Oswald: He's coming, madam; I hear him. (*Horns within.*)

Goneril: Put on what weary negligence you please,
You and your fellows; I'd have it come to question.[2]
If he distaste it, let him to our sister,
Whose mind and mine I know in that are one,
Not to be overruled. Idle old man,
That still would manage those authorities
That he hath given away! Now, by my life,
Old fools are babes again, and must be used
With checks as flatteries, when they are seen abused.[3]
Remember what I tell you.

Oswald: Very well, madam.

Goneril: And let his knights have colder looks among you;
What grows of it, no matter. Advise your fellows so.
I would breed from hence occasions,[4] and I shall,
That I may speak. I'll write straight to my sister
To hold my very course. Prepare for dinner.

[*Exeunt.*]

SCENE IV

A HALL IN THE SAME

[*Enter* KENT, *disguised.*]

Kent: If but as well I other accents borrow,
That can my speech defuse,[1] my good intent
May carry through itself to that full issue
For which I razed[2] my likeness. Now, banished Kent,
If thou canst serve where thou dost stand condemned,
So may it come, thy master, whom thou lovest,
Shall find thee full of labors.

[*Horns within. Enter* LEAR, KNIGHTS, *and* ATTENDANTS.]

Lear: Let me not stay[3] a jot for dinner; go get it ready.

[*Exit an* ATTENDANT.]

[41] practices: schemes. [42] All . . . fit: anything will do that will suit my purpose. I, iii, [1] come slack of: fail in. [2] come to question: come to a head (showdown). [3] and must . . . seen abused: must be reprimanded when they are in the wrong. [4] breed . . . occasions: find excuses. I, iv, [1] defuse: disguise. [2] razed: shaved, altered. [3] stay: wait.

How now? What art thou?

Kent: A man, sir.

Lear: What dost thou profess? What wouldst thou with us?

Kent: I do profess to be no less than I seem, to serve him truly that will put me in trust, to love him that is honest, to converse with him that is wise and says little, to fear judgment,[4] to fight when I cannot choose, and to eat no fish.[5]

Lear: What art thou?

Kent: A very honest-hearted fellow, and as poor as the King.

Lear: If thou be'st as poor for a subject as he's for a king, thou art poor enough. What wouldst thou?

Kent: Service.

Lear: Who wouldst thou serve?

Kent: You.

Lear: Dost thou know me, fellow?

Kent: No, sir; but you have that in your countenance which I would fain call master.

Lear: What's that?

Kent: Authority.

Lear: What services canst thou do?

Kent: I can keep honest counsel, ride, run, mar a curious tale in telling it and deliver a plain message bluntly. That which ordinary men are fit for, I am qualified in, and the best of me is diligence.

Lear: How old art thou?

Kent: Not so young, sir, to love a woman for singing, nor so old to dote on her for anything. I have years on my back forty-eight.

Lear: Follow me; thou shalt serve me. If I like thee no worse after dinner, I will not part from thee yet. Dinner, ho, dinner! Where's my knave? my fool? Go you and call my fool hither.

[*Exit an* ATTENDANT.]

[*Enter* OSWALD.]

You, you, sirrah, where's my daughter?

Oswald: So please you—

[*Exit.*]

Lear: What says the fellow there? Call the clotpoll[6] back.

[*Exit a* KNIGHT.]

Where's my fool, ho? I think the world's asleep.

[*Re-enter* KNIGHT.]

How now? Where's that mongrel?

Knight: He says, my lord, your daughter is not well.

Lear: Why came not the slave back to me when I called him?

Knight: Sir, he answered me in the roundest[7] manner, he would not.

Lear: He would not?

Knight: My lord, I know not what the matter is, but to my judgment your Highness is not entertained with that ceremonious affection[8] as you were wont. There's a great abatement of kindness appears as well in the general dependents[9] as in the Duke himself also and your daughter.

Lear: Ha! say'st thou so?

Knight: I beseech you pardon me, my Lord, if I be mistaken; for my duty cannot be silent when I think your Highness wronged.

Lear: Thou but rememberest[10] me of mine own conception. I have perceived a most faint neglect of late, which I have rather blamed as mine own jealous curiosity than as a very pretence[11] and purpose

[4] judgment: judgment day. [5] eat no fish: am not a Catholic. [6] clotpoll: blockhead. [7] roundest: most insolent. [8] entertained . . . affection: treated with proper formality and respect. [9] dependents: servants. [10] rememberest: remind. [11] pretence: deliberate intention.

of unkindness; I will look further into't. But where's my fool? I have not seen him this two days.

Knight: Since my young lady's going into France, sir, the fool hath much pined away.

Lear: No more of that; I have noted it well. Go you and tell my daughter I would speak with her.

[*Exit* KNIGHT.]

Go you, call hither my fool.

[*Exit an* ATTENDANT.]

[*Re-enter* OSWALD.]

O, you, sir, you, come you hither, sir. Who am I, sir?

Oswald: My lady's father.

Lear: "My lady's father"? My lord's knave! You whoreson dog! you slave! you cur!

Oswald: I am none of these, my lord; I beseech your pardon.

Lear: Do you bandy looks with me, you rascal? (*Striking him.*)

Oswald: I'll not be struck, my lord.

Kent: Nor tripped neither, you base football player. (*Tripping up his heels.*)

Lear: I thank thee, fellow. Thou servest me, and I'll love thee.

Kent: Come, sir, arise, away! I'll teach you differences. Away, away! If you will measure your lubber's length again, tarry; but away! Go to! Have you wisdom? So. (*Pushes Oswald out.*)

Lear: Now, my friendly knave, I thank thee. There's earnest[12] of thy service. (*Giving* KENT *money.*)

[*Enter* FOOL.]

Fool: Let me hire him too. Here's my coxcomb.[13] (*Offering* KENT *his cap.*)

Lear: How now, pretty knave? How dost thou?

Fool: Sirrah, you were best take my coxcomb.

Kent: Why, fool?

Fool: Why? For taking one's part that's out of favor. Nay, an thou canst not smile as the wind sits, thou'lt catch cold shortly.[14] There, take my coxcomb! Why, this fellow has banished two on's daughters, and did the third a blessing against his will. If thou follow him, thou must needs wear my coxcomb. How now, nuncle?[15] Would I had two coxcombs and two daughters!

Lear: Why, my boy?

Fool: If I gave them all my living, I'ld keep my coxcombs myself. There's mine! beg another of thy daughters.

Lear: Take heed, sirrah—the whip.

Fool: Truth's a dog must to kennel; he must be whipped out, when Lady the brach[16] may stand by th' fire and stink.

Lear: A pestilent gall to me!

Fool: Sirrah, I'll teach thee a speech.

Lear: Do.

Fool: Mark it, nuncle.

Have more than thou showest,
Speak less than thou knowest,
Lend less than thou owest,
Ride more than thou goest,[17]
Learn more than thou trowest,[18]
Set less than thou throwest,[19]
Leave thy drink and thy whore.
And keep in-a-door,
And thou shalt have more
Than two tens to a score.[20]

Kent: This is nothing, fool.

[12] earnest: payment. [13] coxcomb: fool's cap. [14] Nay . . . shortly: If you don't curry favor with those in power, you'll soon be out in the cold. [15] nuncle: (mine) uncle. [16] brach: hound bitch. [17] goest: walk. [18] trowest: believe. [19] throwest: toss dice. [20] score: twenty.

Fool: Then 'tis like the breath of an unfeed lawyer—you gave me nothing for't. Can you make no use of nothing, nuncle?

Lear: Why, no, boy. Nothing can be made out of nothing.

Fool (*to* KENT). Prithee tell him, so much the rent of his land comes to. He will not believe a fool.

Lear: A bitter fool!

Fool: Dost thou know the difference, my boy, between a bitter fool and a sweet one?

Lear: No, lad; teach me.

Fool: That lord that counselled thee
To give away thy land,
Come place him here by me—
Do thou for him stand.
The sweet and bitter fool
Will presently appear;
The one in motley[21] here,
The other found out there.

Lear: Dost thou call me fool, boy?

Fool: All thy other titles thou hast given away; that thou wast born with.

Kent: This is not altogether fool, my lord.

Fool: No, faith, lords and great men will not let me. If I had a monopoly out, they would have part on't. And ladies too, they will not let me have all the fool to myself; they'll be snatching. Give me an egg, nuncle, and I'll give thee two crowns.

Lear: What two crowns shall they be?

Fool: Why, after I have cut the egg i' th' middle and eat up the meat, the two crowns of the egg. When thou clovest thy crown i' th' middle and gavest away both parts, thou borest thine ass on thy back o'er the dirt. Thou hadst little wit in thy bald crown when thou gavest thy golden one away. If I speak like myself in this, let him be whipped that first finds it so.

(*Sings.*) Fools had ne'er less grace in a year,
For wise men are grown foppish,
And know not how their wits to wear,
Their manners are so apish.

Lear: When were you wont to be so full of songs, sirrah?

Fool: I have used it, nuncle, ever since thou madest thy daughters thy mother, for when thou gavest them the rod, and puttest down thine own breeches,

(*Sings.*) Then they for sudden joy did weep,
And I for sorrow sung,
That such a king should play bo-peep
And go the fools among.

Prithee, nuncle, keep a schoolmaster that can teach thy fool to lie. I would fain learn to lie.

Lear: An[22] you lie, sirrah, we'll have you whipped.

Fool: I marvel what kin thou and thy daughters are. They'll have me whipped for speaking true; thou'lt have me whipped for lying; and sometimes I am whipped for holding my peace. I had rather be any kind o' thing than a fool, and yet I would not be thee, nuncle. Thou hast pared thy wit o' both sides and left nothing i' th' middle. Here comes one o' the parings.

[*Enter* GONERIL.]

Lear: How now, daughter? What makes that frontlet[23] on? Methinks you you are too much o' late i' th' frown.

Fool: Thou wast a pretty fellow when thou hadst no need to care for her frowning; now thou art an O without a figure.

[21] motley: multicolored fool's costume. [22] an: if. [23] frontlet: furrowed brow.

I am better than thou art now; I am a fool, thou art nothing. (*To* GONERIL.) Yes, forsooth, I will hold my tongue. So your face bids me, though you say nothing. Mum, mum!

He that keeps nor crust nor crumb,
Weary of all, shall want some.

(*Points at* LEAR.) That's a shealed peascod.[24]

Goneril: Not only, sir, this your all-licensed fool,
But other of your insolent retinue
Do hourly carp[25] and quarrel, breaking forth
In rank, and not-to-be-endured riots. Sir,
I had thought, by making this well known unto you,
To have found a safe redress, but now grow fearful,
By what yourself, too, late have spoke and done,
That you protect this course, and put it on[26]
By your allowance, which if you should, the fault
Would not scape censure, nor the redresses sleep,
Which, in the tender of a wholesome weal,
Might in their working do you that offence
Which else were shame, that then necessity
Must call discreet proceeding.[27]

Fool: For you know, nuncle,

The hedge-sparrow fed the cuckoo so long
That it had it head bit off by it young.

So out went the candle, and we were left darkling.

Lear: Are you our daughter?

Goneril: I would you would make use of your good wisdom,
Whereof I know you are fraught[28] and put away
These dispositions which of late transform you
From what you rightly are.

Fool: May not an ass know when the cart draws the horse? Whoop, Jug, I love thee!

Lear: Does any here know me? This is not Lear.
Does Lear walk thus? speak thus? Where are his eyes?
Either his notion[29] weakens, his discernings
Are lethargied[30]—Ha! waking? 'Tis not so!
Who is it that can tell me who I am?

Fool: Lear's shadow.

Lear: I would learn that, for by the marks of sovereignty,
Knowledge, and reason, I should be false persuaded
I had daughters.

Fool: Which they will make an obedient father.

Lear: Your name, fair gentlewoman?

Goneril: This admiration,[31] sir, is much o' th' savor
Of other your new pranks. I do beseech you
To understand my purposes aright.
As you are old and reverend, you should be wise.
Here do you keep a hundred knights and squires;
Men so disordered, so deboshed,[32] and bold

[24] shelled peascod: empty peapod, hollow shell. [25] carp: complain. [26] put it on: encourage it. [27] which if you should . . . discreet proceeding: If you don't behave, I'll have to take drastic action in the interests of the common good.

[28] fraught: well-endowed. [29] notion: intelligence. [30] discernings . . . lethargied: senses asleep. [31] admiration: false amazement. [32] deboshed: debauched.

That this our court, infected with their manners,
Shows like a riotous inn. Epicurism[33] and lust
Make it more like a tavern or a brothel
Than a graced palace. The shame itself doth speak
For instant remedy. Be then desired
By her that else will take the thing she begs
A little to disquantity your train,[34]
And the remainder that shall still depend
To be such men as may besort[35] your age,
Which know themselves, and you.

Lear: Darkness and devils!
Saddle my horses; call my train together!
Degenerate bastard, I'll not trouble thee;
Yet have I left a daughter.

Goneril: You strike my people, and your disordered rabble
Make servants of their betters.

[*Enter* ALBANY.]

Lear: Woe that too late repents! O, sir, are you come?
Is it your will? Speak, sir! Prepare my horses.
Ingratitude, thou marble-hearted fiend,
More hideous when thou show'st thee in a child
Than the sea-monster!

Albany: Pray, sir, be patient.

Lear (*to* GONERIL). Detested kite,[36] thou liest!
My train are men of choice and rarest parts,
That all particulars of duty know
And in the most exact regard support
The worships of their name. O most small fault,
How ugly didst thou in Cordelia show,
Which, like an engine,[37] wrenched my frame of nature
From the fixed place, drew from my heart all love
And added to the gall.[38] O Lear, Lear, Lear!
Beat at this gate that let thy folly in (*striking his head*)
And thy dear judgment out! Go, go, my people.

Albany: My lord, I am guiltless, as I am ignorant
Of what hath moved you.

Lear: It may be so, my lord.
Hear, Nature, hear, dear goddess, hear!
Suspend thy purpose, if thou didst intend
To make this creature fruitful.
Into her womb convey sterility.
Dry up in her the organs of increase,
And from her derogate[39] body never spring
A babe to honor her! If she must teem,[40]
Create her child of spleen,[41] that it may live
And be a thwart disnatured[42] torment to her.
Let it stamp wrinkles in her brow of youth,
With cadent[43] tears fret[44] channels in her cheeks,
Turn all her mother's pains and benefits
To laughter and contempt, that she may feel
How sharper than a serpent's tooth it is
To have a thankless child! Away, away!

[*Exit.*]

Albany: Now, gods that we adore, whereof comes this?

[33] Epicurism: wild living. [34] A little . . . train: reduce the number of your knights. [35] besort: befit. [36] kite: carrion crow. [37] engine: torture rack. [38] gall: bitterness. [39] derogate: degenerate. [40] teem: produce offspring. [41] spleen: malice, ill will. [42] thwart disnatured: perverse and unnatural. [43] cadent: falling. [44] fret: wear, erode.

Goneril: Never afflict yourself to know more of it,
But let his disposition have that scope
That dotage gives it.

[*Re-enter* LEAR]

Lear: What, fifty of my followers at a clap?[45]
Within a fortnight?
Albany: What's the matter, sir?
Lear: I'll tell thee. (*To* GONERIL.)
Life and death! I am ashamed
That thou hast power to shake my manhood thus,
That these hot tears, which break from me perforce,
Should make thee worth them. Blasts and fogs upon thee!
Th' untented[46] woundings of a father's curse
Pierce every sense about thee! Old fond eyes,
Beweep this cause again, I'll pluck ye out,
And cast you, with the waters that you lose,
To temper clay. Yea, is it come to this?
Let it be so. Yet have I left a daughter,
Who I am sure is kind and comfortable.[47]
When she shall hear this of thee, with her nails
She'll flay thy wolvish visage. Thou shalt find
That I'll resume the shape which thou dost think
I have cast off for ever.

[*Exeunt* LEAR, KENT, *and* ATTENDANTS.]

Goneril: Do you mark that, my lord?
Albany: I cannot be so partial, Goneril,
To the great love I bear you—
Goneril: Pray you, content. What, Oswald, ho!
(*To the* FOOL.) You sir, more knave than fool, after your master!
Fool: Nuncle Lear, nuncle Lear, tarry!
Take the fool with thee.
A fox, when one has caught her,
And such a daughter,
Should sure to the slaughter,
If my cap would buy a halter.
So the fool follows after.

[*Exit.*]

Goneril: This man hath had good counsel! A hundred knights?
'Tis politic[48] and safe to let him keep
At point[49] a hundred knights; yes, that on every dream,
Each buzz,[50] each fancy, each complaint, dislike,
He may enguard his dotage with their powers
And hold our lives in mercy.—Oswald, I say!
Albany: Well, you may fear too far.
Goneril: Safer than trust too far.
Let me still take away the harms I fear,
Not fear still to be taken. I know his heart.
What he hath uttered I have writ my sister.
If she sustain him and his hundred knights,
When I have showed the unfitness—

[*Re-enter* OSWALD.]

How now, Oswald?
What, have you writ that letter to my sister?
Oswald: Yes, madam.
Goneril: Take you some company, and away to horse!

[45] clap: clap of one's hands. [46] untented woundings: uncovered wounds. [47] comfortable: comfort-giving. [48] politic: wise. [49] at point: fully armed. [50] buzz: rumor.

Inform her full of my particular fear,
And thereto add such reasons of your own
As may compact[51] it more, Get you gone,
And hasten your return.

[*Exit* OSWALD.]

No, no, my lord,
This milky gentleness and course[52] of yours,
Though I condemn it not, yet, under pardon,
You are much more at task[53] for want of wisdom
Than praised for harmful mildness.

Albany: How far your eyes may pierce I cannot tell;
Striving to better, oft we mar what's well.

Goneril: Nay then—

Albany: Well, well; the event.[54]

[*Exeunt.*]

SCENE V

Court before ALBANY'S *Palace*

[*Enter* LEAR, KENT, *and* FOOL.]

Lear: Go you before to Gloucester with these letters. Acquaint my daughter no further with anything you know than comes from her demand out of the letter. If your diligence be not speedy, I shall be there afore you.

Kent: I will not sleep, my lord, till I have delivered your letter.

[*Exit.*]

Fool: If a man's brains were in's heels, were't not in danger of kibes?[1]

Lear: Ay, boy.

Fool: Then I prithee be merry; thy wit shall ne'er go slipshod.[2]

Lear: Ha, ha, ha!

Fool: Shalt see thy other daughter will use thee kindly[3]; for though she's as like this as a crab's[4] like an apple, yet I can tell what I can tell.

Lear: What canst tell, boy?

Fool: She'll taste as like this as a crab does to a crab. Thou canst tell why one's nose stands i'th' middle on's face?

Lear: No.

Fool: Why, to keep one's eyes of either side's nose, that what a man cannot smell out, he may spy into.

Lear: I did her wrong.

Fool: Canst tell how an oyster makes his shell?

Lear: No.

Fool: Nor I neither; but I can tell why a snail has a house.

Lear: Why?

Fool: Why, to put's head in; not to give it away to his daughters, and leave his horns without a case.

Lear: I will forget my nature. So kind a father!—Be my horses ready?

Fool: The asses are gone about 'em. The reason why the seven stars are no more than seven is a pretty reason.

Lear: Because they are not eight?

Fool: Yes indeed. Thou wouldst make a good fool.

Lear: To tak't again perforce![5] Monster ingratitude!

Fool: If thou wert my fool, nuncle, I'ld have thee beaten for being old before thy time.

Lear: How's that?

[51] compact it more: add to it. [52] course: behavior. [53] at task: criticized. [54] event: outcome, "we'll see." I, v, [1] kibes: chilblains. [2] slipshod: clad in slippers. [3] kindly: according to her nature. [4] crab: crabapple (a small tart variety of apple). [5] perforce: by force.

Fool: Thou shouldst not have been old till thou hadst been wise.

Lear: O, let me not be mad, not mad, sweet heaven!
Keep me in temper; I would not be mad!

[*Enter* GENTLEMAN.]

How now? Are the horses ready?

Gentleman: Ready, my lord.

Lear: Come, boy.

Fool: She that's a maid now, and laughs at my departure,
Shall not be a maid long, unless things be cut shorter.

[*Exeunt.*]

ACT II

SCENE I

The EARL OF GLOUCESTER'S *Castle*

[*Enter* EDMUND *and* CURAN, *meeting.*]

Edmund: Save thee,[1] Curan.

Curan: And you, sir. I have been with your father, and given him notice that the Duke of Cornwall and Regan his Duchess will be here with him this night.

Edmund: How comes that?

Curan: Nay, I know not. You have heard of the news abroad—I mean the whispered ones, for they are yet but ear-kissing[2] arguments?

Edmund: Not I. Pray you, what are they?

Curan: Have you heard of no likely wars toward[3] 'twixt the two Dukes of Cornwall and Albany?

Edmund: Not a word.

Curan: You may do, then, in time. Fare you well, sir.

Edmund: The Duke be here to-night? The better! best!

[*Exit.*]

This weaves itself perforce into my business.
My father hath set guard to take my brother;
And I have one thing, of a queasy question,[4]
Which I must act. Briefness and fortune, work!
Brother, a word! Descend! Brother, I say!

[*Enter* EDGAR.]

My father watches. O sir, fly this place;
Intelligence[5] is given where you are hid;
You have now the good advantage of the night.
Have you not spoken 'gainst the Duke of Cornwall?
He's coming hither, now i'th' night, i'th' haste,
And Regan with him. Have you nothing said
Upon his party 'gainst the Duke of Albany?
Advise yourself.

Edgar: I am sure on't, not a word.

Edmund: I hear my father coming. Pardon me;
In cunning[6] I must draw my sword upon you;

II, i, [1] save thee: God save thee (a salutation). [2] ear-kissing arguments: whispered rumors. [3] toward: threatening. [4] of a queasy question: of a delicate nature. [5] intelligence: information. [6] in cunning: as part of our scheme.

Draw, seem to defend yourself; now quit you well.[7]
Yield! Come before my father. Light, ho, here!
Fly, brother.—Torches, torches!—So farewell.

[*Exit* EDGAR.]

Some blood drawn on me would beget opinion[8]
Of my more fierce endeavor. (*Wounds his arm.*) I have seen drunkards
Do more than this in sport.—Father, father!—
Stop, stop! No help?

[*Enter* GLOUCESTER, *and* SERVANTS *with torches.*]

Gloucester: Now, Edmund, where's the villain?

Edmund: Here stood he in the dark, his sharp sword out,
Mumbling of wicked charms, conjuring the moon
To stand auspicious mistress.[9]

Gloucester: But where is he?

Edmund: Look, sir, I bleed.

Gloucester: Where is the villain, Edmund?

Edmund: Fled this way, sir. When by no means he could—

Gloucester: Pursue him, ho! Go after.

[*Exeunt some* SERVANTS.]

By no means what?

Edmund: Persuade me to the murther of your lordship;
But that I told him the revenging gods
'Gainst parricides did all their thunders bend;
Spoke with how manifold and strong a bond
The child was bound to th' father—sir, in fine,[10]
Seeing how loathly opposite[11] I stood
To his unnatural purpose, in fell[12] motion
With his prepared[13] sword he charges home
My unprovided body, lanced mine arm;
And when he saw my best alarumed spirits,
Bold in the quarrel's right, roused to th' encounter,
Or whether gasted[14] by the noise I made,
Full suddenly he fled.

Gloucester: Let him fly far.
Not in this land shall he remain uncaught;
And found—dispatch.[15] The noble Duke my master,
My worthy arch[16] and patron, comes tonight.
By his authority I will proclaim it,
That he which finds him shall deserve our thanks,
Bringing the murderous coward to the stake;
He that conceals him, death.

Edmund: When I dissuaded him from his intent
And found him pight[17] to do it, with curst speech
I threatened to discover[18] him. He replied,
"Thou unpossessing bastard, dost thou think,
If I would stand against thee, would the reposal
Of any trust, virtue, or worth in thee
Make thy words faithed?[19] No. What I should deny

[7] quit you well: defend yourself properly. [8] beget opinion: create the impression. [9] conjuring . . . mistress: invoking witchcraft. [10] in fine: in short. [11] loathy opposite: strongly opposed. [12] fell: evil. [13] prepared: drawn. [14] gasted: terrified. [15] dispatch: punish. [16] arch: superior. [17] pight: determined. [18] discover: expose. [19] faithed: believed.

(As this I would; ay, though thou didst produce
My very character), I'ld turn it all
To thy suggestion, plot, and damned practice;
And thou must make a dullard of the world,
If they not thought the profits of my death
Were very pregnant and potential spurs[20]
To make thee seek it."

Gloucester: O strange and fastened[21] villain,
Would he deny his letter? I never got[22] him.

[*Tucket*[23] *within.*]

Hark, the Duke's trumpets! I know not why he comes.
All ports I'll bar; the villain shall not scape;
The Duke must grant me that. Besides, his picture
I will send far and near, that all the kingdom
May have due note of him, and of my land,
Loyal and natural boy, I'll work the means
To make thee capable.[24]

[*Enter* CORNWALL, REGAN, *and* ATTENDANTS.]

Cornwall: How now, my noble friend? Since I came hither
(Which I can call but now) I have heard strange news.

Regan: If it be true, all vengeance comes too short
Which can pursue the offender. How dost, my lord?

Gloucester: O madam, my old heart is cracked, it's cracked!

Regan: What, did my father's godson seek your life?
He whom my father named, your Edgar?

Gloucester: O lady, lady, shame would have it hid!

Regan: Was he not companion with the riotous knights
That tended upon my father?

Gloucester: I know not, madam. 'Tis too bad, too bad!

Edmund: Yes, madam, he was of that consort.[25]

Regan: No marvel then though he were ill affected.[26]
'Tis they have put him on the old man's death,
To have the expense and waste of his revenues.
I have this present evening from my sister
Been well informed of them, and with such cautions
That, if they come to sojourn at my house,
I'll not be there.

Cornwall: Nor I, assure thee, Regan.
Edmund, I hear that you have shown your father
A childlike[27] office.

Edmund: It was my duty, sir.

Gloucester: He did bewray[28] his practice, and received
This hurt you see, striving to apprehend him.

Cornwall: Is he pursued?

Gloucester: Ay, my good lord.

Cornwall: If he be taken, he shall never more
Be feared of doing harm. Make your own purpose,

[20] pregnant and potential spurs: strong and likely reasons. [21] fastened: confirmed. [22] got: begot, fathered. [23] tucket: trumpet call. [24] capable: legitimate heir. [25] consort: group. [26] ill affected: evilly disposed. [27] childlike office: service worthy of a son. [28] bewray: betray.

How in my strength you please.[29] For
 you, Edmund,
Whose virtue and obedience doth this instant
So much commend itself, you shall be
 ours.
Natures of such deep trust we shall much
 need;
You we first seize on.

Edmund: I shall serve you, sir,
Truly, however else.

Gloucester: For him I thank your Grace.

Cornwall: You know not why we came to visit you—

Regan: Thus out of season, threading
 dark-eyed night.
Occasions, noble Gloucester, of some
 poise,[30]
Wherein we must have use of your advice.
Our father he hath writ, so hath our sister,
Of differences, which I best thought it fit
To answer from[31] our home; the several
 messengers
From hence attend dispatch.[32] Our good
 old friend,
Lay comforts to your bosom, and bestow
Your needful counsel to our businesses,
Which craves the instant use.[33]

Gloucester: I serve you, madam.
Your Graces are right welcome.

[*Exeunt. Flourish.*]

SCENE II

Before GLOUCESTER'S *Castle*

[*Enter* KENT *and* OSWALD, *severally.*[1]]

Oswald: Good dawning to thee, friend; art of this house?

Kent: Ay.

Oswald: Where may we set our horses?

Kent: I'th mire.

Oswald: Prithee, if thou lov'st me, tell me.

Kent: I love thee not.

Oswald: Why then, I care not for thee.

Kent: If I had thee in Lipsbury Pinfold,[2] I would make thee care for me.

Oswald: Why dost thou use me thus? I know thee not.

Kent: Fellow, I know thee.

Oswald: What dost thou know me for?

Kent: A knave, a rascal, an eater of broken meats; a base, proud, shallow, beggarly, three-suited, hundred-pound, filthy worsted-stocking knave; a lily-livered, action-taking,[3] whoreson, glass-gazing, superserviceable,[4] finical rogue; one-trunk-inheriting slave; one that wouldst be a bawd[5] in way of good service, and art nothing but the composition of a knave, beggar, coward, pander, and the son and heir of a mongrel bitch; one whom I will beat into clamorous whining, if thou deny'st the least syllable of thy addition.[6]

Oswald: Why, what a monstrous fellow art thou, thus to rail on one that's neither known of thee nor knows thee!

Kent: What a brazen-faced varlet art thou, to deny thou knowest me! Is it two days ago since I tripped up thy heels and beat thee before the King? (*Draws his sword.*) Draw, you rogue, for though it be night yet the moon shines. I'll make a sop o'th' moonshine of you.[7] Draw, your whoreson cullionly barbermonger,[8] draw!

Oswald: Away! I have nothing to do with thee.

[29] Make . . . please: Use my authority as you see fit. [30] poise: importance. [31] from: away from. [32] attend: are waiting for the return messages. [33] use: action. II, ii, [1] severally: by different entrances. [2] If . . . Pinfold: If I had my hands on you. [3] action-taking: resorting to law. [4] superserviceable: toadying. [5] bawd: pimp. [6] addition: rightful titles. [7] I'll . . . you: I'll mop you up. [8] cullionly barber-monger: despicable fop.

Kent: Draw, you rascal! You come with letters against the King, and take Vanity the puppet's part[9] against the royalty of her father. Draw, you rogue, or I'll so carbonado your shanks;[10] draw, you rascal! Come your ways!

Oswald: Help, ho! murther! help!

Kent: Strike, you slave! Stand, rogue! Stand, you neat slave! Strike! (*Beating him.*)

Oswald: Help, ho! murther! murther!

[*Enter* EDMUND, *with his rapier drawn,* GLOUCESTER, CORNWALL, REGAN, SERVANTS.]

Edmund: How now? What's the matter? Part!

Kent: With you, goodman boy,[11] if you please! Come, I'll flesh[12] ye; come on, young master!

Gloucester: Weapons? arms? What's the matter here?

Cornwall: Keep peace, upon your lives!
He dies that strikes again. What is the matter?

Regan: The messengers from our sister and the King.

Cornwall: What is your difference? Speak!

Oswald: I am scarce in breath, my lord.

Kent: No marvel, you have so bestirred your valor. You cowardly rascal, nature disclaims in thee; a tailor made thee.

Cornwall: Thou art a strange fellow. A tailor make a man?

Kent: A tailor, sir; a stonecutter or a painter could not have made him so ill, though he had been but two years o' the trade.

Cornwall: Speak yet, how grew your quarrel?

Oswald: This ancient ruffian, sir, whose life I have spared
At suit of his gray beard—

Kent: Thou whoreson zed![13] thou unnecessary letter! My lord, if you will give me leave, I will tread this unbolted villain into mortar and daub the walls of a jakes[14] with him. "Spare my gray beard," you wagtail?[15]

Cornwall: Peace, sirrah!
You beastly knave, know you no reverence?

Kent: Yes, sir, but anger hath a privilege.

Cornwall: Why art thou angry?

Kent: That such a slave as this should wear a sword,
Who wears no honesty. Such smiling rogues as these,
Like rats, oft bite the holy cords atwain
Which are too intrinse[16] t' unloose; smooth[17] every passion
That in the natures of their lords rebel,
Bring oil to fire, snow to their colder moods;
Renege, affirm, and turn their halcyon beaks
With every gale and vary of their masters,[18]
Knowing naught (like dogs) but following.
A plague upon your epileptic visage!
Smile you my speeches, as I were a fool?
Goose, an I had you upon Sarum Plain,
I'ld drive ye cackling home to Camelot.

Cornwall: What, art thou mad, old fellow?

[9] and . . . part: play the role of Vanity in a puppet show. [10] carbonado your shanks: slice up your legs. [11] my goodman boy: an insulting reference to Edmund's youth. [12] flesh ye: wound you. [13] zed: the letter Z. [14] jakes: privy, outhouse. [15] wagtail: small strutting bird. [16] intrinse: closely tied (i.e., the bonds of matrimony). [17] smooth: cater to. [18] Renege . . . masters: be their master's stooge in everything.

Gloucester: How fell you out? Say that.

Kent: No contraries hold more antipathy
Than I and such a knave.

Cornwall: Why dost thou call him knave? What is his fault?

Kent: His countenance likes me not.

Cornwall: No more perchance does mine, or his, or hers.

Kent: Sir, 'tis my occupation to be plain;
I have seen better faces in my time
Than stands on any shoulder that I see
Before me at this instant.

Cornwall: This is some fellow
Who, having been praised for bluntness, doth affect
A saucy roughness,[19] and constrains the garb[20]
Quite from his nature. He cannot flatter, he!
An honest mind and plain, he must speak truth!
An they will take it, so; if not, he's plain.
These kind of knaves I know which in this plainness
Harbor more craft and more corrupter ends
Than twenty silly-ducking observants[21]
That stretch their duties nicely.

Kent: Sir, in good faith, in sincere verity,
Under the allowance of your great aspect,
Whose influence, like the wreath of radiant fire
On flickering Phoebus' front—

Cornwall: What mean'st by this?

Kent: To go out of my dialect,[22] which you discommend[23] so much. I know, sir, I am no flatterer. He that beguiled you in a plain accent was a plain knave, which for my part I will not be, though I should win your displeasure to entreat me to't.

Cornwall: What was th' offence you gave him?

Oswald: I never gave him any.
It pleased the King his master very late
To strike at me, upon his misconstruction;[24]
When he, conjunct,[25] and flattering his displeasure,
Tripped me behind; being down, insulted, railed
And put upon him such a deal of man
That worthied[26] him, got praises of the King
For him attempting who was self-subdued,[27]
And, in the fleshment[28] of this dread exploit,
Drew on me here again.

Kent: None of these rogues and cowards
But Ajax[29] is their fool.

Cornwall: Fetch forth the stocks!
You stubborn ancient knave, you reverent[30] braggart,
We'll teach you—

Kent: Sir, I am too old to learn.
Call not your stocks for me; I serve the King,
On whose employment I was sent to you.
You shall do small respect, show too bold malice
Against the grace and person of my master,

[19] saucy roughness: insolent rudeness. [20] constrains . . . nature: assumes an unnatural pose. [21] observants: servants. [22] dialect: normal manner of speaking. [23] discommend: disapprove of. [24] misconstruction: misinterpretation. [25] conjunct: together with. [26] worthied him: increased his value. [27] self-subdued: self-controlled (i.e., Oswald restrained himself). [28] fleshment: annoyance. [29] Ajax: an insulting reference to Cornwall with a pun on the words "a jakes" (privy). [30] reverent: old.

Stocking his messenger.[31]

Cornwall: Fetch forth the stocks! As I have life and honor,
There shall he sit till noon.

Regan: Till noon? Till night, my lord, and all night too!

Kent: Why, madam, if I were your father's dog,
You should not use me so.

Regan: Sir, being his knave, I will.

Cornwall: This is a fellow of the self-same color
Our sister speaks of. Come, bring away[32] the stocks!

[*Stocks brought out.*]

Gloucester: Let me beseech your Grace not to do so.
His fault is much, and the good King his master
Will check him for't. Your purposed low correction
Is such as basest and contemnedest wretches
For pilferings and most common trespasses
Are punished with. The King must take it ill
That he, so slightly valued in his messenger,
Should have him thus restrained.

Cornwall: I'll answer that.

Regan: My sister may receive it much more worse,
To have her gentleman abused, assaulted,
For following her affairs. Put in his legs.

[KENT *is put in the stocks.*]

Come, my good lord, away.

[*Exeunt all but* GLOUCESTER *and* KENT.]

Gloucester: I am sorry for thee, friend; 'tis the Duke's pleasure,
Whose disposition, all the world well knows,
Will not be rubbed[33] nor stopped. I'll entreat for thee.

Kent: Pray do not, sir. I have watched and travelled hard;
Some time I shall sleep out, the rest I'll whistle;
A good man's fortune may grow out at heels.[34]
Give you good morrow!

Gloucester: The Duke's to blame in this; 'twill be ill taken.

[*Exit.*]

Kent: Good King, that must approve the common saw,[35]
Thou out of heaven's benediction comest
To the warm sun!
Approach, thou beacon to this under globe,[36]
That by thy comfortable beams I may
Peruse this letter. Nothing almost sees miracles
But misery. I know 'tis from Cordelia,
Who hath most fortunately been informed
Of my obscured course,[37] and (*reads*) "shall find time
From this enormous state,[38] seeking to give
Losses their remedies." All weary and o'erwatched,[39]
Take vantage, heavy eyes, not to behold
This shameful lodging.
Fortune, good night; smile once more, turn thy wheel.

[*Sleeps.*]

[31] stocking his messenger: putting his messenger in the stocks. [32] away: out. [33] rubbed: turned aside. [34] A . . . heels: misfortune comes to the best of men. [35] that . . . saw: prove the truth of the common proverb. [36] thou . . . underglobe: sun to the earth. [37] obscured course: secret plan. [38] enormous state: wicked state of affairs. [39] o'erwatched: weary with watching.

SCENE III

Near GLOUCESTER'S *Castle*

[*Enter* EDGAR.]

Edgar: I heard myself proclaimed,[1]
And by the happy[2] hollow of a tree
Escaped the hunt. No port is free, no place
That guard and most unusual vigilance
Does not attend my taking.[3] Whiles I may scape,
I will preserve myself; and am bethought[4]
To take the basest and most poorest shape
That ever penury, in contempt of man,
Brought near to beast. My face I'll grime with filth,
Blanket my loins, elf[5] all my hair in knots,
And with presented nakedness outface
The winds and persecutions of the sky.
The country gives me proof and precedent
Of Bedlam[6] beggars, who, with roaring voices,
Strike in their numbed and mortified bare arms
Pins, wooden pricks, nails, sprigs of rosemary;
And with this horrible object, from low[7] farms,
Poor pelting[8] villages, sheepcotes, and mills,
Sometime with lunatic bans, sometime with prayers,
Enforce their charity. "Poor Turlygod! poor Tom!"
That's something yet! Edgar I nothing am.[9]

[*Exit.*]

II, iii, [1] proclaimed: cried out after. [2] happy: happily found. [3] taking: capture. [4] am bethought: intend. [5] elf: mess up. [6] bedlam: insane asylum. [7] low: lowly, humble. [8] pelting: paltry. [9] Edgar . . . am: as Edgar I no longer am anything. II, iv, [1] cruel: pun on "crewel," meaning worsted. [2] nether-stocks: stockings.

SCENE IV

Before GLOUCESTER'S *Castle;* KENT *in the Stocks*

[*Enter* LEAR, FOOL, *and* GENTLEMAN.]

Lear: 'Tis strange that they should so depart from home,
And not send back my messenger.

Gentleman: As I learned,
The night before there was no purpose in them
Of this remove.

Kent: Hail to thee, noble master!

Lear: Ha!
Mak'st thou this shame thy pastime?

Kent: No, my lord.

Fool: Ha, ha! he wears cruel[1] garters. Horses are tied by the head, dogs and bears by the neck, monkeys by the loins, and men by the legs. When a man's over lusty at legs, then he wears wooden nether-stocks.[2]

Lear: What's he that hath so much thy place mistook
To set thee here?

Kent: It is both he and she—
Your son and daughter.

Lear: No.

Kent: Yes.

Lear: No, I say.

Kent: I say yea.

Lear: No, no, they would not!

Kent: Yes, they have.

Lear: By Jupiter, I swear no!

Kent: By Juno, I swear ay!

Lear: They durst not do't;
They could not, would not do't. 'Tis worse than murther

To do upon respect[3] such violent outrage.
Resolve[4] me with all modest haste which way
Thou mightst deserve or they impose this usage,
Coming from us.[5]

Kent: My lord, when at their home
I did commend your Highness' letters to them,
Ere I was risen from the place that showed
My duty kneeling, came there a reeking post,[6]
Stewed in his haste, half breathless, panting forth
From Goneril his mistress salutations;
Delivered letters, spite of intermission,[7]
Which presently they read; on whose contents,
They summoned up their meiny,[8] straight took horse,
Commanded me to follow and attend
The leisure of their answer, gave me cold looks,
And meeting here the other messenger,
Whose welcome I perceived had poisoned mine—
Being the very fellow which of late
Displayed so saucily against your Highness—
Having more man than wit about me, drew;
He raised the house with loud and coward cries.
Your son and daughter found this trespass worth
The shame which here it suffers.

Fool: Winter's not gone yet, if the wild geese fly that way.

Fathers that wear rags
Do make their children blind,
But fathers that bear bags[9]
Shall see their children kind.
Fortune, that arrant whore,
Ne'er turns the key to the poor.

But for all this, thou shalt have as many dolors[10] for thy daughters as thou canst tell in a year.

Lear: O, how this mother[11] swells up toward my heart!
Hysterica passio! Down, thou climbing sorrow!
Thy element's below! Where is this daughter?

Kent: With the Earl, sir, here within.

Lear: Follow me not;
Stay here.

[*Exit.*]

Gentleman: Made you no more offence but what you speak of?

Kent: None.
How chance the King comes with so small a number?

Fool: An thou hadst been set i'th' stocks for that question, thou'dst well deserved it.

Kent: Why, fool?

Fool: We'll set thee to school to an ant, to teach thee there's no laboring i'th' winter. All that follow their noses are led by their eyes but blind men, and there's not a nose among twenty but can smell him that's stinking. Let go thy hold when a great wheel runs down a hill, lest it break thy neck with following it; but the great one that goes upward, let him draw thee after. When a wise man gives thee better counsel, give me mine again. I

[3] respect: the respect owed the king. [4] Resolve: inform. [5] Coming from us: since you were a royal messenger. [6] reeking post: sweating messenger. [7] spite of intermission: even though it meant interrupting me. [8] meiny: followers. [9] bags: purses, bags of gold. [10] dolors: sorrows, with a pun on "dollars." [11] mother: rage.

would have none but knaves follow it, since a fool gives it.

That sir which serves and seeks for gain,
And follows but for form,
Will pack when it begins to rain
And leave thee in the storm.
But I will tarry, the fool will stay,
And let the wise man fly.
The knave turns fool that runs away;
The fool no knave, perdy.[12]

Kent: Where learned you this, fool?
Fool: Not i'th' stocks, fool.

[*Re-enter* LEAR *and* GLOUCESTER.]

Lear: Deny to speak with me? They are sick? they are weary?
They have travelled all the night? Mere fetches,[13]
The images[14] of revolt and flying off!
Fetch me a better answer.
Gloucester: My dear lord,
You know the fiery quality of the Duke,
How unremovable and fixed he is
In his own course.
Lear: Vengeance! plague! death! confusion!
Fiery? What quality? Why, Gloucester, Gloucester,
I'd speak with the Duke of Cornwall and his wife.
Gloucester: Well, my good lord, I have informed them so.
Lear: Informed them? Dost thou understand me, man?
Gloucester: Ay, my good lord.
Lear: The King would speak with Cornwall; the dear father
Would with his daughter speak, commands her service.
Are they informed of this? My breath and blood!
Fiery? the fiery Duke? Tell the hot Duke that—
No, but not yet! May be he is not well;
Infirmity doth still neglect all office
Whereto our health is bound.[15] We are not ourselves
When nature, being oppressed, commands the mind
To suffer with the body. I'll forbear,
And am fallen out with my more headier will,[16]
To take the indisposed and sickly fit
For the sound man.—Death on my state! Wherefore
Should he sit here? This act persuades me
That this remotion[17] of the Duke and her
Is practice only. Give me my servant forth.
Go tell the Duke and's wife I'ld speak with them—
Now, presently. Bid them come forth and hear me,
Or at their chamber door I'll beat the drum
Till it cry sleep to death.
Gloucester: I would have all well betwixt you.

[*Exit.*]

Lear: O me, my heart, my rising heart! But down!
Fool: Cry to it, nuncle, as the cockney did to the eels when she put 'em i'th' paste alive. She knapped[18] em o'th' coxcombs with a stick and cried "Down, wantons, down!" 'Twas her brother that, in pure kindness to his horse, buttered his hay.

[*Re-enter* CORNWALL, REGAN, GLOUCESTER, SERVANTS.]

[12] perdy: by God. [13] fetches: excuses. [14] images: exact duplicates. [15] Infirmity . . . bound: When we are ill, we neglect the duties we perform when we are well. [16] And . . . will: retract my hasty decision. [17] remotion: absence. [18] knapped: struck.

Lear: Good morrow to you both.
Cornwall: Hail to your Grace!

[KENT *here set at liberty.*]

Regan: I am glad to see your Highness.
Lear: Regan, I think you are; I know what reason
I have to think so. If thou shouldst not be glad,
I would divorce me from thy mother's tomb,
Sepulchring an adultress. (*To* KENT.) O, are you free?
Some other time for that.—Beloved Regan,
Thy sister's naught.[19] O Regan, she hath tied
Sharp-toothed unkindness, like a vulture, here!

[*Points to his heart.*]

I can scarce speak to thee. Thou'lt not believe
With how depraved a quality—O Regan!
Regan: I pray you, sir, take patience. I have hope
You less know how to value her desert
Than she to scant her duty.
Lear: Say, how is that?
Regan: I cannot think my sister in the least
Would fail her obligation. If, sir, perchance
She have restrained the riots of your followers,
'Tis on such ground, and to such wholesome end,
As clears her from all blame.
Lear: My curses on her!
Regan: O, sir, you are old!
Nature in you stands on the very verge
Of her confine.[20] You should be ruled, and led
By some discretion that discerns your state
Better than you yourself. Therefore I pray you
That to our sister you do make return;
Say you have wronged her, sir.
Lear: Ask her forgiveness?
Do you but mark how this becomes the house:[21]
"Dear daughter, I confess that I am old; (*Kneels.*)
Age is unnecessary, on my knees I beg
That you'll vouchsafe me raiment, bed, and food."
Regan: Good sir, no more! these are unsightly tricks.
Return you to my sister.
Lear (*rises*). Never, Regan!
She hath abated me of half my train,
Looked black upon me, struck me with her tongue,
Most serpent-like, upon the very heart.
All the stored vengeances of heaven fall
On her ingrateful top; strike her young bones,
You taking airs,[22] with lameness!
Cornwall: Fie, sir, fie!
Lear: You nimble lightnings, dart your blinding flames
Into her scornful eyes; infect her beauty,
You fen-sucked fogs, drawn by the powerful sun,
To fall and blast her pride!
Regan: O the blest gods! so will you wish on me
When the rash mood is on.
Lear: No, Regan, thou shalt never have my curse;

[19] naught: evil, wicked. [20] Nature . . . confine: You are approaching senility. [21] becomes the house: suits my royal position. [22] taking airs: infectious vapors.

Thy tender-hefted[23] nature shall not give
Thee o'er to harshness. Her eyes are fierce, but thine
Do comfort, and not burn. 'Tis not in thee
To grudge my pleasures, to cut off my train,
To bandy hasty words, to scant my sizes,[24]
And, in conclusion, to oppose the bolt[25]
Against my coming in. Thou better know'st
The offices of nature, bond of childhood,
Effects of courtesy, dues of gratitude.
Thy half o'th' kingdom hast thou not forgot,
Wherein I thee endowed.

Regan: Good sir, to the purpose.

[*Tucket within.*]

Lear: Who put my man i'th' stocks?

Cornwall: What trumpet's that?

Regan: I know't—my sister's. This approves[26] her letter,
That she would soon be here.

[*Enter* OSWALD.]

Is your lady come?

Lear: This is a slave, whose easy-borrowed pride
Dwells in the fickle grace of her he follows.
Out, varlet, from my sight!

Cornwall: What means your Grace?

[*Enter* GONERIL.]

Lear: Who stocked my servant? Regan, I have good hope
Thou didst not know on't.—Who comes here? O heavens!
If you do love old men, if your sweet sway
Allow obedience, if you yourselves are old,
Make it your cause! Send down, and take my part!

[23] tender-hefted: kindly disposed. [24] to scant my sizes: to cut my allowance. [25] to oppose the bolt: to lock the door. [26] approves: confirms.

(*To* GONERIL.) Art not ashamed to look upon this beard?—
O Regan, wilt thou take her by the hand?

Goneril: Why not by the hand, sir?
How have I offended?
All's not offence that indiscretion finds
And dotage terms so.

Lear: O sides, you are too tough!
Will you yet hold? How came my man i'th' stocks?

Cornwall: I set him there, sir; but his own disorders
Deserved much less advancement.

Lear: You? Did you?

Regan: I pray you, father, being weak, seem so.
If, till the expiration of your month,
You will return and sojourn with my sister,
Dismissing half your train, come then to me.
I am now from home, and out of that provision
Which shall be needful for your entertainment.[27]

Lear: Return to her, and fifty men dismissed?
No, rather I abjure all roofs, and choose
To wage against the enmity of the air,
To be a comrade with the wolf and owl—
Necessity's sharp pinch! Return with her?
Why the hot-blooded France, that dowerless took
Our youngest born, I could as well be brought
To knee his throne, and squire-like, pension beg
To keep base life afoot. Return with her?
Persuade me rather to be slave and sumpter[28]
To this detested groom. (*Points at* OSWALD.)

[27] entertainment: maintenance, support.
[28] sumpter: pack animal.

Goneril: At your choice, sir.
Lear: I prithee, daughter, do not make me mad.
I will not trouble thee, my child; farewell.
We'll no more meet, no more see one another.
But yet thou art my flesh, my blood, my daughter,
Or rather a disease that's in my flesh,
Which I must needs call mine. Thou art a boil,
A plague sore, an embossed[29] carbuncle
In my corrupted blood. But I'll not chide thee;
Let shame come when it will, I do not call it;
I do not bid the Thunder-bearer shoot
Nor tell tales of thee to high-judging Jove.
Mend when thou canst; be better at thy leisure;
I can be patient, I can stay with Regan,
I and my hundred knights.
Regan: Not altogether so.
I looked not for you yet, nor am provided
For your fit welcome. Give ear, sir to my sister,
For those that mingle reason with your passion
Must be content to think you old, and so—
But she knows what she does.
Lear: Is this well spoken?
Regan: I dare avouch it, sir. What, fifty followers?
Is it not well? What should you need of more?
Yea, or so many, sith that both charge and danger[30]
Speak 'gainst so great a number? How in one house
Should many people, under two commands,
Hold amity? 'Tis hard, almost impossible.
Goneril: Why might not you, my lord, receive attendance
From those that she calls servants, or from mine?
Regan: Why not, my lord? If then they chanced to slack[31] ye,
We could control them. If you will come to me
For now I spy a danger, I entreat you
To bring but five-and-twenty; to no more
Will I give place or notice.
Lear: I gave you all—
Regan: And in good time you gave it!
Lear: Made you my guardians, my depositaries,
But kept a reservation[32] to be followed
With such a number. What, must I come to you
With five-and-twenty? Regan, said you so?
Regan: And speak't again, my lord.
No more with me.
Lear: Those wicked creatures yet do look well-favored[33]
When others are more wicked; not being the worst
Stands in some rank of praise (*To* GONERIL.) I'll go with thee.
Thy fifty yet doth double five-and-twenty,
And thou art twice her love.
Goneril: Hear me my lord;
What need you five-and-twenty, ten, or five,
To follow in a house where twice so many
Have a command to tend you?
Regan: What need one?
Lear: O, reason not the need! Our basest beggars
Are in the poorest thing superflous,[34]
Allow not nature more than nature needs,

[29] embossed: swollen. [30] charge and danger: cost and risk. [31] slack: neglect. [32] reservation: condition. [33] well-favored: pleasant looking.

[34] superfluous: provided beyond the demands of absolute need.

Man's life is cheap as beast's. Thou art a lady;
If only to go warm were gorgeous,
Why, nature needs not what thou gorgeous wear'st,
Which scarcely keeps thee warm. But, for true need—
You heavens, give me that patience, patience I need!
You see me here, you gods, a poor old man,
As full of grief as age, wretched in both;
If it be you that stirs these daughters' hearts
Against their father, fool me not so much
To bear it tamely; touch me with noble anger,
And let not women's weapons, water drops,
Stain my man's cheeks! No, you unnatural hags!
I will have such revenges on you both
That all the world shall—I will do such things—
What they are yet, I know not, but they shall be
The terrors of the earth! You think I'll weep;
No, I'll not weep.
I have full cause of weeping, but this heart

[*Storm and tempest.*]

Shall break into a hundred thousand flaws[35]
Or ere I'll weep. O fool, I shall go mad!

[*Exeunt* LEAR, GLOUCESTER, KENT, *and* FOOL.]

Cornwall: Let us withdraw; 'twill be a storm.

Regan: This house is little; the old man and's people
Cannot be well bestowed.

Goneril: 'Tis his own blame hath put himself from rest
And must needs taste his folly.

Regan: For his particular,[36] I'll re-receive him gladly,
But not one follower.

Goneril: So am I purposed.
Where is my Lord of Gloucester?

Cornwall: Followed the old man forth.

[*Re-enter* GLOUCESTER.]

He is returned.

Gloucester: The king is in high rage.

Cornwall: Whither is he going?

Gloucester: He calls to horse, but will I know not whither.

Cornwall: 'Tis best to give him way; he leads himself.

Goneril: My lord, entreat him by no means to stay.

Gloucester: Alack, the night comes on, and the bleak winds
Do sorely ruffle. For many miles about
There's scarce a bush.

Regan: O, sir, to wilful men
The injuries that they themselves procure
Must be their schoolmasters. Shut up your doors.
He is attended with a desperate train,[37]
And what they may incense him to, being apt[38]
To have his ear abused, wisdom bids fear.

Cornwall: Shut up your doors, my lord; 'tis a wild night.
My Regan counsels well. Come out o'th' storm.

[*Exeunt.*]

[35] flaws: pieces. [36] particular: himself alone. [37] desperate train: Lear's retinue of knights. [38] apt: prone, inclined to.

ACT III

SCENE I

A Heath

[*Storm still. Enter* KENT *and a* GENTLEMAN *severally.*]

Kent: Who's there, besides foul weather?

Gentleman: One minded like the weather, most unquietly.

Kent: I know you; where's the King?

Gentleman: Contending with the fretful elements,
Bids the wind blow the earth into the sea,
Or swell the curléd water 'bove the main,[1]
That things might change or cease, tears his white hair,
Which the impetuous blasts, with eyeless rage,
Catch in their fury and make nothing of,
Strives in his little world of man[2] to outscorn
The to-and-fro-conflicting wind and rain.
This night, wherein the cub-drawn bear[3] would couch,
The lion and the belly-pinched[4] wolf
Keep their fur dry, unbonneted[5] he runs,
And bids what will take all.

Kent: But who is with him?

Gentleman: None but the fool, who labors to outjest
His heart-struck injuries.

Kent: Sir, I do know you,
And dare upon the warrant of my note
Commend a dear thing to you.[6] There is division
(Although as yet the face of it is covered
With mutual cunning) 'twixt Albany and Cornwall,
Who have (as who have not, that their great stars
Throned and set high?) servants, who seem no less,
Which are to France the spies and speculations
Intelligent of our state.[7] What hath been seen,
Either in snuffs and packings[8] of the Dukes,
Or the hard rein which both of them have borne
Against the old kind King, or something deeper,
Whereof, perchance, these are but furnishings[9]—
But, true it is, from France there comes a power[10]
Into this scattered kingdom, who already.
Wise in our negligence, have secret feet
In some of our best ports and are at point
To show their open banner. Now to you:
If on my credit[11] you dare build so far
To make your speed to Dover, you shall find
Some that will thank you, making just report

III, i, [1] main: land. [2] little world of man: (man is a microsom, i.e., a miniature duplicate of the universe). [3] cub-drawn bear: mother bear sucked dry by her cubs; hence hungry. [4] belly-pinched: voracious, empty-stomached. [5] unbonneted: hatless. [6] commend a dear thing to you: entrust you with an important matter. [7] speculations . . . state: spies informed of our affairs. [8] snuffs and packings: disagreements and intrigues. [9] furnishings: pretenses. [10] power: armed force. [11] credit: reliability.

Of how unnatural and bemadding sorrow
The King hath cause to plain.[12]
I am a gentleman of blood and breeding,
And from some knowledge and assurance offer
This office[13] to you.

Gentleman: I will talk further with you.

Kent: No, do not.
For confirmation that I am much more
Than my out-wall,[14] open this purse and take
What it contains. If you shall see Cordelia
As fear not but you shall show her this ring,
And she will tell you who your fellow is
That yet you do not know. Fie on this storm!
I will go seek the King.

Gentleman: Give me your hand. Have you no more to say?

Kent: Few words, but, to effect, more than all yet:
That, when we have found the King in which your pain[15]
That way, I'll this, he that first lights on him
Holla the other.

[*Exeunt severally.*]

SCENE II

Another Part of the Heath

[*Storm still. Enter* LEAR *and* FOOL.]

Lear: Blow, winds, and crack your cheeks! rage, blow,
You cataracts and hurricanoes, spout
Till you have drenched our steeples, drowned the cocks![1]
You sulphurous and thought-executing[2] fires,
Vaunt-couriers[3] of oak-cleaving thunder-bolts,
Singe my white head! And thou, all-shaking thunder,
Strike flat the thick rotundity o'th' world,
Crack Nature's molds, all germains[4] spill at once,
That make ingrateful man!

Fool: O nuncle, court holy water[5] in a dry house is better than this rain water out o'door. Good nuncle, in, and ask thy daughters' blessing! Here's a night pities neither wise men nor fools.

Lear: Rumble thy bellyful! Spit, fire; spout, rain!
Nor rain, wind, thunder, fire are my daughters;
I tax[6] not you, you elements, with unkindness;
I never gave you kingdom, called you children;
You owe me no subscription.[7] Then let fall
Your horrible pleasure. Here I stand your slave,
A poor, infirm, weak, and despised old man;
But yet I call you servile ministers,
That will with two pernicious daughters join
Your high-engendered battles 'gainst a head
So old and white as this. O! O! 'tis foul!

Fool: He that has a house to put's head in has a good head-piece.

The codpiece that will house
Before the head has any,

[12] plain: complain. [13] office: task. [14] out-wall: outward appearance. [15] pain: efforts, services. III, ii, [1] cocks: weather vanes. [2] thought-executing: quick as thought (lightning). [3] vaunt-couriers: forerunners. [4] germains: human semen. [5] court holy water: fulsome praise, abject flattery. [6] tax: arraign, accuse. [7] subscription: loyalty, obedience.

The head and he shall louse:
So beggars marry many.
The man that makes his toe
What he his heart should make
Shall of a corn cry woe,
And turn his sleep to wake.
For there was never yet fair woman but she made mouths in a glass.[8]

[*Enter* KENT.]

Lear: No, I will be the pattern of all patience; I will say nothing.

Kent: Who's there?

Fool: Mary, here's grace and a codpiece; that's a wise man and a fool.

Kent: Alas, sir, are you here? Things that love night
Love not such nights as these. The wrathful skies
Gallow[9] the very wanderers of the dark
And make them keep their caves; since I was man,
Such sheets of fire, such bursts of horrid thunder,
Such groans of roaring wind and rain, I never
Remember to have heard; man's nature cannot carry
The affliction not the fear.

Lear: Let the great gods,
That keep this dreadful pudder[10] o'er our heads,
Find out their enemies now. Tremble, thou wretch,
That hast within thee undivulged crimes
Unwhipped of justice. Hide thee, thou bloody hand,
Thou perjured, and thou simular[11] man of virtue
That are incestuous; caitiff, in pieces shake
That under covert and convenient seeming[12]
Hast practised on man's life. Close pent-up guilts,
Rive your concealing continents,[13] and cry
These dreadful summoners grace.[14] I am a man
More sinned against than sinning.

Kent: Alack, bareheaded?
Gracious my lord, hard by here is a hovel;
Some friendship will it lend you 'gainst the tempest;
Repose you there, while I to this hard house
More harder than the stones whereof 'tis raised,
Which even but now, demanding after you,
Denied me to come in, return, and force
Their scanted courtesy.

Lear: My wits begin to turn.
Come on, my boy. How dost, my boy? Art cold?
I am cold myself. Where is this straw, my fellow?
The art of our necessities is strange,
That can make vile things precious. Come, your hovel.
Poor fool and knave, I have one part in my heart
That's sorry yet for thee.

Fool (*sings*).

He that has and a little tiny wit—
With hey, ho, the wind and the rain—
Must make content with his fortunes fit,[15]
For the rain it raineth every day.

Lear: True, boy. Come bring us to this hovel.

[*Exeunt* LEAR *and* KENT.]

[8] made . . . glass: admired herself in a mirror. [9] gallow: frighten. [10] pudder: upheaval. [11] simular: pretended. [12] seeming: outward appearance. [13] rive . . . continents: split open your protective outer covering. [14] and . . . grace: ask for mercy of these awful accusors—thunder and lightning. [15] Must . . . fit: must be satisfied with what little his intelligence merits.

Fool: This is a brave night to cool a courtesan. I'll speak a prophecy ere I go:

When priests are more in word than matter;
When brewers mar their malt with water;
When nobles are their tailors' tutors,
No heretics burned, but wenches suitors;
When every case in law is right,
No squire in debt nor no poor knight;
When slanders do not live in tongues,
Nor cutpurses[16] come not to throngs;
When usurers tell their gold i'th' field,
And bawds and whores do churches build:
Then shall the realm of Albion
Come to great confusion.
Then comes the time, who lives to see't,
That going shall be used with feet.

This prophecy Merlin shall make, for I live before his time.

[*Exit.*]

SCENE III

GLOUCESTER'S *Castle*

[*Enter* GLOUCESTER *and* EDMUND *with lights.*]

Gloucester: Alack, alack, Edmund, I like not this unnatural dealing. When I desired their leave that I might pity him, they took from me the use of mine own house, charged[1] me on pain of perpetual displeasure neither to speak of him, entreat for him, nor any way sustain[2] him.

Edmund: Most savage and unnatural!

Gloucester: Go to; say you nothing. There is division betwixt the Dukes, and a worse matter than that. I have received a letter this night—'tis dangerous to be spoken—I have locked the letter in my closet. These injuries the King now bears will be revenged home; there is part of a power already footed,[3] we must incline to the King. I will seek him and privily relieve him. Go you and maintain talk with the Duke, that my charity be not of him perceived; if he ask for me, I am ill and gone to bed. If I die for't, as no less is threatened me, the King my old master must be relieved. There is strange things toward, Edmund; pray you be careful.

[*Exit.*]

Edmund: This courtesy, forbid thee, shall the Duke
Instantly know, and of that letter too.
This seems a fair deserving,[4] and must draw me
That which my father loses—no less than all;
The younger rises when the old doth fall.

[*Exit.*]

SCENE IV

The Heath. Before a Hovel

[*Storm still. Enter* LEAR, KENT, *and* FOOL.]

Kent: Here is the place, my lord; good my lord, enter.
The tyranny of the open night's too rough
For nature to endure.

Lear: Let me alone.

Kent: Good my lord, enter here.

Lear: Will break my heart?

Kent: I had rather break mine own; good my lord, enter.

Lear: Thou think'st 'tis much that this contentious storm

[16] cutpurses: thieves who stole by cutting purses and pockets away. III, iii, [1] charged: ordered. [2] sustain: succour, assist. [3] footed: landed. [4] fair deserving: a service worth a good reward.

Invades us to the skin; so 'tis to thee;
But where the greater malady is fixed,
The lesser is scarce felt. Thou'dst shun a bear,
But if thy flight lay toward the raging sea,
Thou'dst meet the bear i'th' mouth. When the mind's free,
The body's delicate; the tempest in my mind
Doth from my senses take all feeling else
Save what beats there. Filial ingratitude!
Is it not as this mouth should tear this hand
For lifting food to't? But I will punish home![1]
No, I will weep no more. In such a night
To shut me out! Pour on; I will endure.
In such a night as this! O Regan, Goneril!
Your old kind father, whose frank heart gave all!
O, that way madness lies; let me shun that!
No more of that.

Kent: Good my lord, enter here.

Lear: Prithee go in thyself, seek thine own ease;
This tempest will not give me leave to ponder
On things would hurt me more. But I'll go in.
(*To the* FOOL.) In boy, go first.—You houseless poverty—
Nay, get thee in; I'll pray, and then I'll sleep.

[*Exit* FOOL.]

Poor naked wretches, wheresoe'er you are,
That bide the pelting of this pitiless storm,
How shall your houseless heads and unfed sides,
Your looped and windowed raggedness,[2] defend you
From seasons such as these? O, I have ta'en
Too little care of this! Take physic, pomp;[3]
Expose thyself to feel what wretches feel,
That thou mayst shake the superflux[4] to them
And show the heavens more just.

Edgar (*within*). Fathom and half, fathom and half! Poor Tom!

[*Reenter* FOOL *from the hovel.*]

Fool: Come not in here, nuncle, here's a spirit. Help me, help me!

Kent: Give me thy hand. Who's there?

Fool: A spirit, a spirit! He says his name's poor Tom.

Kent: What art thou that dost grumble there i'th' straw? Come forth.

[*Enter* EDGAR *disguised as a madman.*]

Edgar: Away, the foul fiend follows me! Through the sharp hawthorn blows the cold wind. Hum; go to thy bed and warm thee.

Lear: Didst thou give all to thy daughters, and art thou come to this?

Edgar: Who gives anything to poor Tom, whom the foul fiend hath led through fire and through flame, through ford and whirlpool, o'er bog and quagmire; that hath laid knives under his pillow and halters in his pew, set ratsbane[5] by his porridge, made him proud of heart, to ride on a bay trotting horse over four-inched bridges, to course[6] his own shadow for a traitor. Bless thy five wits, Tom's acold. O, do de, do de, do de; bless thee from whirlwinds, star-blasting,[7] and taking![8] Do poor Tom some charity,

III, iv, [1] home: to the hilt, thoroughly. [2] looped . . . raggedness: tattered and torn. [3] Take physic, pomp: purge yourself, kings. [4] superflux: excess. [5] ratsbane: rat poison. [6] course: chase after. [7] star-blasting: malignant influence of stars. [8] taking: mischief done by fairies.

whom the foul fiend vexes. There could I have him now—and there—and there again—and there!

[*Storm still.*]

Lear: What, have his daughters brought him to this pass? Couldst thou save nothing? Wouldst thou give 'em all?

Fool: Nay, he reserved a blanket, else we had been all shamed.

Lear: Now all the plagues that in the pendulous air
Hang fated o'er men's faults light on thy daughters!

Kent: He hath no daughters, sir.

Lear: Death, traitor! nothing could have subdued nature
To such a lowness but his unkind daughters.
Is it the fashion that discarded fathers
Should have thus little mercy on their flesh?
Judicious punishment, 'twas this flesh begot
Those pelican[9] daughters.

Edgar: Pillicock sat on Pillicock's Hill. 'Allow, 'allow, loo, loo!

Fool: This cold night will turn us all to fools and madmen.

Edgar: Take heed o'th' foul fiend; obey thy parents; keep thy word justly; swear not; commit not with man's sworn spouse; set not thy sweet heart on proud array. Tom's acold.

Lear: What hast thou been?

Edgar: A servingman, proud in heart and mind; that curled my hair, wore gloves in my cap, served the lust of my mistress' heart and did the act of darkness[10] with her; swore as many oaths as I spake words, and broke them in the sweet face of heaven; one that slept in the contriving of lust, and waked to do it. Wine loved I deeply, dice dearly, and in woman outparamoured[11] the Turk. False of heart, light of ear, bloody of hand, hog in sloth, fox in stealth, wolf in greediness, dog in madness, lion in prey! Let not the creaking of shoes nor the rustling of silks betray thy poor heart to woman. Keep thy foot out of brothels, thy hand out of plackets,[12] thy pen from lender's books, and defy the foul fiend. Still through the hawthorn blows the cold wind; says suum, mun, hey nonny. Dolphin my boy; boy, sessa! let him trot by.

[*Storm still.*]

Lear: Thou wert better in a grave than to answer with thy uncovered body this extremity of the skies. Is man no more than this? Consider him well. Thou owest the worm no silk, the beast no hide, the sheep no wool, the cat[13] no perfume. Ha, here's three on's are sophisticated![14] Thou art the thing itself; unaccommodated[15] man is no more but such a poor, bare, forked animal as thou art. Off, off, you lendings![16] Come, unbutton here.

[*Tears at his clothes.*]

Fool: Prithee, nuncle, be contented; 'tis a naughty night to swim in. Now a little fire in a wild field were like an old lecher's heart—a small spark, all the rest on's body cold. Look, here comes a walking fire.

[*Enter* GLOUCESTER *with a torch.*]

Edgar: This is the foul fiend Flibbertigibbet; he begins at curfew, and walks till the first cock. He gives the web and

[9] pelican: (young pelicans were believed to live on their parents' blood). [10] act of darkness: sex act. [11] outparamoured: carried on with women more. [12] plackets: openings in the sides of dresses and undergarments. [13] cat: civet cat glands. [14] sophisticated: altered by clothing. [15] unaccommodated: natural—without clothes. [16] lendings: borrowed things; here, clothing.

the pin,[17] squints the eye, and makes the harelip; mildews the white wheat, and hurts the poor creature of earth.

Saint Withold footed thrice the 'old;[18]
He met the nightmare, and her nine fold;[19]
Bid her alight
And her troth plight,
And aroint thee, witch, aroint thee![20]

Kent: How fares your Grace?

Lear: What's he?

Kent: Who's there? What is't you seek?

Gloucester: What are you there? Your names?

Edgar: Poor Tom, that eats the swimming frog, the toad, the tadpole, the wall-newt and the water; that in the fury of his heart, when the foul fiend rages, eats cow-dung for sallets,[21] swallows the old rat and the ditch-dog, drinks the green mantle of the standing pool; who is whipped from tithing to tithing,[22] and stock-punished and imprisoned; who hath had three suits to his back, six shirts to his body, horse to ride, and weapon to wear;

But mice and rats, and such small deer,[23]
Have been Tom's food for seven long year.

Beware my follower; peace, Smulkin,[24] peace, thou fiend!

Gloucester: What, hath your Grace no better company?

Edgar: The prince of darkness is a gentleman!
Modo he's called, and Mahu.

Gloucester: Our flesh and blood, my lord, is grown so vile,
That it doth hate what gets[25] it.

Edgar: Poor Tom's acold.

Gloucester: Go in with me; my duty cannot suffer
To obey in all your daughters' hard commands.
Though their injunction be to bar my doors
And let this tyrannous night take hold upon you,
Yet have I ventured to come seek you out
And bring you where both fire and food is ready.

Lear: First let me talk with this philosopher;
What is the cause of thunder?

Kent: Good my lord, take his offer; go into the house.

Lear: I'll talk a word with this same learned Theban.[26]
What is your study?

Edgar: How to prevent the fiend and to kill vermin.

Lear: Let me ask you one word in private.

Kent: Importune him once more to go, my lord.
His wits begin to unsettle.

Gloucester: Canst thou blame him?

[*Storm still.*]

His daughters seek his death. Ah, that good Kent!
He said it would be thus—poor banished man!
Thou sayest the King grows mad: I'll tell thee, friend,
I am almost mad myself. I had a son,
Now outlawed from my blood; he sought my life

[17] web and the pin: eye diseases. [18] 'old: pasture land. [19] nine fold: nine young ones. [20] aroint thee: get out of here. [21] sallets: salads. [22] Tithing to tithing: parish to parish. [23] deer: animals generally. [24] Smulkin, Modo, Mahu: names of demons. [25] gets: begets, sires. [26] Theban: philosopher.

But lately, very late. I loved him, friend,
No father his son dearer; true to tell thee,
The grief hath crazed my wits. What a night 's this!
I do beseech your Grace—

Lear: O, cry you mercy,[27] sir.
Noble philosopher, your company.

Edgar: Tom's acold.

Gloucester: In, fellow, there, into th' hovel; keep thee warm.

Lear: Come, let's in all.

Kent: This way, my lord.

Lear: With him!
I will keep still[28] with my philosopher.

Kent: Good my lord, soothe him; let him take the fellow.

Gloucester: Take him you on.

Kent: Sirrah, come on; go along with us.

Lear: Come, good Athenian.

Gloucester: No words, no words! hush.

Edgar: Child[29] Rowland to the dark tower came;

His word was still
Fie, foh, and fum!
I smell the blood of a British man.

[*Exeunt.*]

SCENE V

GLOUCESTER'S *Castle*

[*Enter* CORNWALL *and* EDMUND.]

Cornwall: I will have my revenge ere I depart his house.

Edmund: How, my lord, I may be censured, that nature[1] thus gives way to loyalty, something fears me to think of.

Cornwall: I now perceive it was not altogether your brother's evil disposition made him seek his death, but a provoking merit, set awork by a reproveable badness in himself.[2]

Edmund: How malicious is my fortune that I must repent to be just! This is the letter he spoke of, which approves him an intelligent party to the advantages of France.[3] O heavens! that this treason were not—or not I the detector!

Cornwall: Go with me to the Duchess.

Edmund: If the matter of this paper be certain, you have mighty business in hand.

Cornwall: True or false, it hath made thee Earl of Gloucester. Seek out where thy father is, that he may be ready for our apprehension.[4]

Edmund (*aside*). If I find him comforting the King, it will stuff his suspicion more fully.—I will persevere in my course of loyalty, though the conflict be sore between that and my blood.

Cornwall: I will lay trust upon thee, and thou shalt find a dearer father in my love.

[*Exeunt.*]

SCENE VI

A Farmhouse near GLOUCESTER'S *Castle*

[*Enter* KENT *and* GLOUCESTER.]

Gloucester: Here is better than the open air; take it thankfully. I will piece out the comfort with what addition I can;[1] I will not be long from you.

Kent: All the power of his wits have

[27] cry you mercy: beg of you. [28] keep still: stay. [29] child: old word for "young warrior." III, v, [1] nature: natural affection, filial love. [2] I now perceive . . . in himself: I realize now your brother may have been provoked into trying to kill your father because of the old man's evil nature. [3] which approves . . . of France: which proves he knew of the French plans to invade England. [4] apprehension: capture. III, vi, [1] I will . . . can: I'll bring whatever else I can to make him comfortable.

given way to his impatience. The gods reward your kindness!

[*Exit* GLOUCESTER.]

[*Enter* LEAR, EDGAR, *and* FOOL.]

Edgar: Frateretto[2] calls me, and tells me Nero is an angler in the lake of darkness. Pray, innocent,[3] and beware the foul fiend.

Fool: Prithee, nuncle, tell me whether a madman be a gentleman or a yeoman.

Lear: A king, a king!

Fool: No, he's a yeoman that has a gentleman to his son, for he's a mad yeoman[4] that sees his son a gentleman before him.

Lear: To have a thousand with red burning spits[5]
Come hizzing in upon 'em—

Edgar: The foul fiend bites my back.

Fool: He's mad that trusts in the tameness of a wolf, a horse's health, a boy's love, or a whore's oath.

Lear: It shall be done; I will arraign them straight.[6]
(*To* EDGAR.) Come, sit thou here, most learned justicer.
(*To the* FOOL.) Thou, sapient sir, sit here. Now, you she-foxes!

Edgar: Look, where he stands and glares! Want'st thou eyes at trial, madam?

Come o'er the bourn,[7] Bessy, to me.

Fool: Her boat hath a leak,
And she must not speak
Why she dares not come over to thee.

Edgar: The foul fiend haunts poor Tom in the voice of a nightingale. Hopdance[8] cries in Tom's belly for two white herring. Croak not, black angel; I have no food for thee.

Kent: How do you, sir? Stand you not so amazed.
Will you lie down and rest upon the cushions?

Lear: I'll see their trial first; bring in their evidence.
(*To* EDGAR.) Thou, robed man of justice, take thy place.
(*To the* FOOL.) And thou, his yokefellow of equity,[9]
Bench[10] by his side. (*To* KENT.) You are o'th' commission,[11]
Sit you too.

Edgar: Let us deal justly.

Sleepest or wakest thou, jolly shepherd?
Thy sheep be in the corn;
And for one blast of thy minikin[12] mouth
Thy sheep shall take no harm.

Purr! the cat is gray.

Lear: Arraign her first; 'tis Goneril. I here take my oath before this honorable assembly, she kicked the poor King her father.

Fool: Come hither, mistress; is your name Goneril?

Lear: She cannot deny it.

Fool: Cry you mercy, I took you for a joint-stool.[13]

Lear: And here's another whose warped[14] looks proclaim
What store[15] her heart is made on. Stop her there!
Arms, arms! sword! fire! Corruption in the place!
False justicer, why hast thou let her scape?

[2] Frateretto: another fiend. [3] innocent: the fool. [4] yeoman: wealthy farmer. [5] spits: meat skewers. [6] straight: immediately. [7] bourn: stream, brook. [8] Hopdance: another fiend. [9] yokefellow of equity: judicial colleague.

[10] bench: sit down. [11] commission: panel of judges. [12] minikin: tiny. [13] joint-stool: ordinary wooden stool. [14] warped: twisted. [15] store: substance.

Edgar: Bless thy five wits!

Kent: O pity, sir, where is the patience now
That you so oft have boasted to retain?

Edgar (*aside*). My tears begin to take his part so much
They mar my counterfeiting.[16]

Lear: The little dogs and all,
Tray, Blanch, and Sweetheart, see, they bark at me.

Edgar: Tom will throw his head at them. Avaunt, you curs!

Be thy mouth or black or white,
Tooth that poisons if it bite;
Mastiff, greyhound, mongrel grim,
Hound or spaniel brach or lym,[17]
Bobtail tyke or trundle-tail—[18]
Tom will make them weep and wail;
For, with throwing thus my head,
Dogs leap the hatch, and all are fled.

Do de, de, de. Sessa! Come, march to wakes[19] and fairs and market towns. Poor Tom, thy horn[20] is dry.

Lear: Then let them anatomize[21]
Regan. See what breeds about her heart. Is there any cause in nature that makes these hard hearts? (*To* EDGAR.) You sir, I entertain[22] for one of my hundred; only I do not like the fashion of your garments. You'll say they are Persian; but let them be changed.

Kent: Now, good my lord, lie here and rest awhile.

Lear: Make no noise, make no noise; draw the curtains.
So, so, we'll go to supper i'th' morning.

Fool: And I'll go to bed at noon.

[*Reenter* GLOUCESTER.]

Gloucester: Come hither, friend; where is the King my master?

Kent: Here, sir, but trouble him not; his wits are gone.

Gloucester: Good friend, I prithee take him in thy arms;
I have o'erheard a plot of death upon him;
There is a litter ready; lay him in't
And drive toward Dover, friend, where thou shalt meet
Both welcome and protection. Take up thy master.
If thou shouldst dally half an hour, his life,
With thine, and all that offer to defend him,
Stand in assured loss. Take up, take up,
And follow me, that will to some provision
Give thee quick conduct.

Kent: Oppressed nature sleeps;
This rest might yet have balmed[23] thy broken senses,
Which, if convenience will not allow,
Stand in hard cure.[24] (*To the* FOOL.) Come, help to bear thy master;
Thou must not stay behind.

Gloucester: Come, come, away!

[*Exeunt all but* EDGAR.]

Edgar: When we our betters see bearing our woes,
We scarcely think our miseries our foes.
Who alone suffers suffers most i'th' mind,
Leaving free things and happy shows behind;
But then the mind much sufferance doth o'erskip
When grief hath mates, and bearing[25] fellowship.
How light and portable my pain seems now,

[16] counterfeiting: pretended madness. [17] lym: bloodhound. [18] trundle-tail: curled tail. [19] wakes: parties. [20] horn: bottle, canteen. [21] anatomize: cut open. [22] entertain: employ, take. [23] balmed: healed. [24] stand in hard cure: will not be cured. [25] bearing: suffering.

When that which makes me bend makes the King bow.
He childed as I fathered! Tom, away!
Mark the high noises,[26] and thyself bewray[27]
When false opinion, whose wrong thought defiles thee,
In thy just proof repeals and reconciles thee.[28]
What will hap more to-night, safe scape the King!
Lurk, lurk.

[*Exit.*]

SCENE VII

GLOUCESTER'S *Castle*

[*Enter* CORNWALL, REGAN, GONERIL, EDMUND, *and* SERVANTS.]

Cornwall (*to* GONERIL). Post speedily to my lord your husband; show him this letter: the army of France is landed.—Seek out the traitor Gloucester.

[*Exeunt some of the* SERVANTS.]

Regan: Hang him instantly.

Goneril: Pluck out his eyes.

Cornwall: Leave him to my displeasure. Edmund, keep you our sister company. The revenges we are bound to take upon your traitorous father are not fit for your beholding. Advise the Duke where you are going, to a most festinate[1] preparation; we are bound to the like. Our posts[2] shall be swift and intelligent betwixt us. Farewell, dear sister; farewell, my Lord of Gloucester.

[*Enter* OSWALD.]

How now? Where's the King?

Oswald: My Lord of Gloucester hath conveyed him hence.
Some five or six and thirty of his knights,
Hot questrists[3] after him, met him at gate,
Who, with some other of the lord's dependents,
Are gone with him toward Dover, where they boast
To have well-armèd friends.

Cornwall: Get horses for your mistress.

Goneril: Farewell, sweet lord, and sister.

Cornwall: Edmund, farewell.

[*Exeunt* GONERIL, EDMUND, *and* OSWALD.]

Go seek the traitor Gloucester,
Pinion him like a thief, bring him before us.

[*Exeunt other* SERVANTS.]

Though well we may not pass[4] upon his life
Without the form of justice, yet our power
Shall do a courtesy to our wrath, which men
May blame, but not control.

[*Enter* GLOUCESTER, *brought in by two or three.*]

Who's there? the traitor?

Regan: Ingrateful fox! 'tis he.

Cornwall: Bind fast his corky[5] arms.

Gloucester: What mean your Graces?
Good my friends, consider
You are my guests. Do me no foul play, friends.

Cornwall: Bind him, I say.

[SERVANTS *bind him.*]

Regan: Hard, hard. O filthy traitor!

Gloucester: Unmerciful lady as you are, I'm none.

[26] mark . . . noises: listen for the hue and cry. [27] thyself bewray: reveal yourself. [28] When . . . thee: when the lies about you are disproved.

III, vii, [1] festinate: rapid. [2] posts: messengers. [3] questrists: searchers. [4] pass: pass judgment. [5] corky: shriveled.

Cornwall: To this chair bind him. Villain, thou shalt find—

[REGAN *plucks his beard.*][6]

Gloucester: By the kind gods, 'tis most ignobly done
To pluck me by the beard.

Regan: So white, and such a traitor!

Gloucester: Naughty lady,
These hairs which thou dost ravish from my chin
Will quicken,[7] and accuse thee. I am your host.
With robber's hands my hospitable favors[8]
You should not ruffle thus. What will you do?

Cornwall: Come, sir, what letters had you late from France?

Regan: Be simple-answered, for we know the truth.

Cornwall: And what confederacy have you with the traitors
Late footed in the kingdom?

Regan: To whose hands have you sent the lunatic King: Speak.

Gloucester: I have a letter guessingly set down,
Which came from one that's of a neutral heart,
And not from one opposed.

Cornwall: Cunning.
And false.

Cornwall: Where hast thou sent the King?

Gloucester: To Dover.

Regan: Wherefore to Dover? Wast thou not charged at peril[9]—

Cornwall: Wherefore to Dover? Let him first answer that.

Gloucester: I am tied to th' stake, and I must stand the course.[10]

Regan: Wherefore to Dover, sir?

Gloucester: Because I would not see thy cruel nails
Pluck out his poor old eyes; nor thy fierce sister
In his anointed flesh stick boarish fangs.
The sea, with such a storm as his bare head
In hell-black night endured, would have buoyed[11] up
And quenched the stelled fires.[12]
Yet, poor old heart, he holp the heavens to rain.
If wolves had at thy gate howled that stern time,
Thou shouldst have said "Good porter, turn the key."
All cruels else subscribed;[13] But I shall see
The winged vengeance overtake such children.

Cornwall: See't shalt thou never. Fellows, hold the chair.
Upon these eyes of thine I'll set my foot.

Gloucester: He that will think to live till he be old,
Give me some help!—O cruel! O you gods!

Regan: One side will mock another.
Th' other too!

Cornwall: If you see vengeance—

First Servant: Hold your hand, my lord!
I have served you ever since I was a child;
But better service have I never done you
Than now to bid you hold.

Regan: How now, you dog?

First Servant: If you did wear a beard upon your chin,
I'ld shake it on this quarrel.

[6] (S. D.) Regan . . . beard: (plucking someone's beard was a gross insult to his dignity). [7] quicken: come to life. [8] favors: features of his face. [9] Wast . . . peril: weren't you ordered under threat of penalty. [10] course: attack by tormenters. [11] buoyed up: swelled. [12] stelled fires: star light. [13] All . . . subscribed: all other cruel things would have shown mercy.

Regan: What do you mean?
Cornwall: My villain!

[*Draw and fight.* CORNWALL *is wounded.*]

First Servant: Nay, then, come on, and take the chance of anger.
Regan: Give me thy sword. A peasant stand up thus?

[*Takes a sword and runs at him behind.*]

First Servant: O, I am slain! My lord, you have one eye left
To see some mischief on him. O! (*Dies.*)
Cornwall: Lest it see more, prevent it. Out, vile jelly!
Where is thy luster now?
Gloucester: All dark and comfortless!
Where's my son Edmund?
Edmund, enkindle all the sparks of nature[14]
To quit[15] this horrid act.
Regan: Out, treacherous villain!
Thou call'st on him that hates thee. It was he
That made the overture[16] of thy treasons to us,
Who is too good to pity thee.
Gloucester: O my follies! Then Edgar was abused.
Kind gods, forgive me that, and prosper him!
Regan: Go thrust him out at gates, and let him smell
His way to Dover.

[*Exit one with* GLOUCESTER.]

How is't, my lord? How look you?
Cornwall: I have received a hurt; follow me, lady.
Turn out that eyeless villain; throw this slave
Upon the dunghill. Regan. I bleed apace;[17]
Untimely comes his hurt. Give me your arm.

[*Exit* CORNWALL, *led by* REGAN.]

Second Servant: I'll never care what wickedness I do,
If this man come to good.
Third Servant: If she live long,
And in the end meet the old course of death,[18]
Women will all turn monsters.
Second Servant: Let's follow the old Earl, and get the bedlam
To lead him where he would. His roguish madness
Allows itself to anything.
Third Servant: Go thou. I'll fetch some flax and whites of eggs
To apply to his bleeding face. Now heaven help him!

[*Exeunt severally.*]

[14] enkindle . . . nature: arouse your filial love. [15] quit: avenge. [16] overture: revelation. [17] apace: severely. [18] old . . . death: natural death from old age.

ACT IV

SCENE I

The Heath

[*Enter* EDGAR.]

Edgar: Yet better thus, and known to be contemned,[1]
Than still[2] contemned and flattered. To be worst,
The lowest and most dejected thing of fortune,
Stands still in esperance,[3] live not in fear.
The lamentable change is from the best;
The worst returns to laughter. Welcome then,
Thou unsubstantial air that I embrace!
The wretch that thou hast blown unto the worst
Owes nothing to thy blasts.

[*Enter* GLOUCESTER, *led by an* OLD MAN.]

But who comes here?
My father, poorly led? World, world, O world!
But that thy strange mutations make us hate thee,
Life would not yield to age.

Old Man: O my good lord,
I have been your tenant, and your father's tenant,
These fourscore years.

Gloucester: Away! Get thee away! Good friend, be gone;
Thy comforts can do me no good at all;
Thee they may hurt.

Old Man: You cannot see your way.

Gloucester: I have no way, and therefore want no eyes;
I stumbled when I saw. Full oft 'tis seen
Our means secure us,[4] and our mere defects
Prove our commodities.[5] Oh dear son Edgar,
The food[6] of thy abusèd father's wrath,
Might I but live to see thee in my touch,
I'ld say I had eyes again!

Old Man: How now? Who's there?

Edgar (*aside*). O gods! who is't can say "I am at the worst"?
I am worse than e'er I was.

Old Man: 'Tis poor mad Tom.

Edgar (*aside*). And worse I may be yet. The worst is not
So long as we can say "This is the worst."

Old Man: Fellow, where goest?

Gloucester: Is it a beggarman?

Old Man: Madman and beggar too.

Gloucester: He has some reason, else he could not beg.
I'th' last night's storm I such a fellow saw,
Which made me think a man a worm. My son
Came then into my mind, and yet my mind
Was then scarce friends with him. I have heard more since.
As flies to wanton boys are we to th' gods.
They kill us for their sport.

IV, i, [1] contemned: despised. [2] still: always. [3] The lowest . . . esperance: the most unfortunate of men still has some hope. [4] Our . . . us: our advantages deceive us. [5] and . . . commodities: our misfortunes are actually blessings. [6] food: source.

Edgar (*aside*). How should this be?
Bad is the trade that must play fool to sorrow,
Angering itself and others.—Bless thee, master!

Gloucester: Is that the naked fellow?

Old Man: Ay, my lord.

Gloucester: Then, prithee, get thee always. If for my sake
Thou wilt o'ertake us hence a mile or twain
I'th' way toward Dover, do it for ancient love,
And bring some covering for this naked soul,
Who I'll entreat to lead me.

Old Man: Alack, sir, he is mad!

Gloucester: 'Tis the time's plague when madmen lead the blind.
Do as I bid thee, or rather do thy pleasure.
Above the rest, be gone.

Old Man: I'll bring him the best 'parel[7] that I have,
Come on't what will.

[*Exit.*]

Gloucester: Sirrah, naked fellow—

Edgar: Poor Tom's acold (*Aside.*) I cannot daub it[8] further.

Gloucester: Come hither, fellow.

Edgar (*aside.*) And yet I must.—Bless thy sweet eyes, they bleed.

Gloucester: Know'st thou the way to Dover?

Edgar: Both stile and gate, horseway and footpath. Poor Tom hath been scared out of his good wits. Bless thee, good man's son, from the foul fiend! Five fiends have been in poor Tom at once: of lust, as Obidicut; Hobbididence, prince of dumbness; Mahu, of stealing; Modo, of murder; Flibbertigibbet, of mopping and mowing,[9] who since possesses chambermaids and waiting women. So, bless thee, master!

Gloucester: Here, take this purse, thou whom the heavens' plagues
Have humbled to all strokes; that I am wretched
Makes thee the happier. Heavens deal so still!
Let the superfluous and lust-dieted man,
That slaves your ordinance,[10] that will not see
Because he does not feel, feel your power quickly;
So distribution should undo excess,
And each man have enough. Dost thou know Dover?

Edgar: Ay, master.

Gloucester: There is a cliff, whose high and bending head
Looks fearfully in the confinèd deep.
Bring me but to the very brim of it,
And I'll repair the misery thou dost bear
With something rich about me. From that place
I shall no leading need.

Edgar: Give me thy arm;
Poor Tom shall lead thee.

[*Exeunt.*]

SCENE II

Before the DUKE OF ALBANY'S *Palace*

[*Enter* GONERIL *and* EDMUND.]

Goneril: Welcome, my lord. I marvel our mild husband
Not met us on the way.

[*Enter* OSWALD.]

Now, where's your master?

7 'parel: apparel, garments. 8 daub it: pretend. 9 mopping and mowing: making faces.

10 That . . . ordinances: that subordinates your laws to his desires.

Oswald: Madam, within, but never man so changed.
I told him of the army that was landed:
He smiled at it. I told him you were coming:
His answer was, "The worse." Of Gloucester's treachery
And of the loyal service of his son
When I informed him, then he called me sot
And told me I had turned the wrong side out.
What most he should dislike seems pleasant to him;
What like, offensive.

Goneril (*to* EDMUND). Then shall you go no further.
It is the cowish terror of his spirit
That dares not undertake;[1] he'll not feel wrongs
Which tie him to an answer. Our wishes on the way
May prove effects.[2] Back, Edmund, to my brother;
Hasten his musters[3] and conduct his powers.
I must change arms at home and give the distaff[4]
Into my husband's hands. This trusty servant
Shall pass between us; ere long you are like to hear
(If you dare venture in your own behalf)
A mistress's[5] command. Wear this;
(*Gives a favor.*)
spare speech;
Decline your head. This kiss, if it durst speak,
Would stretch thy spirits up into the air.
Conceive,[6] and fare thee well.

Edmund: Yours in the ranks of death!

[*Exit.*]

Goneril: My most dear Gloucester!
O, the difference of man and man!
To thee a woman's services are due;
My fool usurps my body.[7]

Oswald: Madam, here comes my lord.

[*Exit.*]

[*Enter* ALBANY.]

Goneril: I have been worth the whistle.

Albany: O Goneril,
You are not worth the dust which the rude wind
Blows in your face; I fear your disposition.
That nature which contemns its origin
Cannot be bordered certain[8] in itself;
She that herself will sliver and disbranch
From her material[9] sap, perforce must wither
And come to deadly use.[10]

Goneril: No more! The text is foolish.[11]

Albany: Wisdom and goodness to the vile seem vile;
Filths savor but themselves. What have you done?
Tigers, not daughters, what have you performed?
A father, and a gracious agèd man,
Whose reverence even the head-lugged bear[12] would lick,

IV, ii, [1] undertake: attempt anything. [2] May prove effects: may come true. [3] Hasten his muster: help recruit his men. [4] distaff: spinning stick. [5] mistress's: lady love's. [6] Conceive: think about it. [7] My fool . . . body: I have foolishly given myself away to the wrong man. [8] bordered certain: contained. [9] material: nourishing. [10] deadly use: no good. [11] The . . . foolish: your moralizing is stupid. [12] head-lugged bear: bear with torn and bleeding head.

Most barbarous, most degenerate, have you madded.
Could my good brother[13] suffer you to do it?
A man, a prince, by him so benefited!
If that the heavens do not their visible spirits
Send quickly down to tame these vile offences,
It will come,
Humanity must perforce prey on itself,
Like monsters of the deep.

Goneril: Milk-livered man!
That bearest a cheek for blows, a head for wrongs,
Who hast not in thy brows an eye discerning
Thine honor from thy suffering; that not knowest
Fools do those villains pity who are punished
Ere they have done their mischief. Where's thy drum?
France spreads his banners in our noiseless[14] land,
With plumèd helm thy state begins to threat,
Whiles thou, a moral fool, sit'st still, and criest
"Alack, why does he so?"

Albany: Thou changèd and self-cov-
Proper deformity seems not in the fiend
So horrid as in woman.

Goneril: O vain fool!

Albany: Thou changèd and self-cov. ered[15] thing, for shame!
Bemonster not thy feature! Were't my fitness
To let these hands obey my blood,[16]
They are apt enough to dislocate and tear
Thy flesh and bones. Howe'er thou art a fiend,
A woman's shape doth shield thee.

Goneril: Marry, your manhood mew![17]

[*Enter a* GENTLEMAN.]

Albany: What news?

Gentleman: O, my good lord, the Duke of Cornwall's dead,
Slain by his servant, going to put out
The other eye of Gloucester.

Albany: Gloucester's eyes?

Gentleman: A servant that he bred, thrilled[18] with remorse,
Opposed against the act, bending his sword
To his great master, who thereat enraged,
Flew on him, and amongst them felled him dead;
But not without that harmful stroke which since
Hath plucked him after.

Albany: This shows you are above,
You justicers, that these our nether[19] crimes
So speedily can venge! But O poor Gloucester!
Lost he his other eye?

Gentleman: Both, both, my lord.
This letter, madam, craves a speedy answer.
'Tis from your sister.

Goneril (*aside*). One way I like this well;
But being widow, and my Gloucester with her,
May all the building in my fancy pluck[20]
Upon my hateful life. Another way

[13] brother: Cornwall. [14] noiseless: tranquil. [15] self-covered: deceitful. [16] blood: rage. [17] Marry . . . mew: (a contemptuous expression calling Albany's manhood into question).

[18] thrilled: overcome. [19] nether: lower, i.e., on earth below. [20] May . . . pluck: she may ruin all my plans.

The news is not so tart.—I'll read, and answer.

[*Exit.*]

Albany: Where was his son when they did take his eyes?

Gentleman: Come with my lady hither.

Albany: He is not here.

Gentleman: No, my good lord, I met him back again.[21]

Albany: Knows he the wickedness?

Gentleman: Ay, my good lord; 'twas he informed against him,
And quit the house on purpose, that their punishment
Might have the freer course.

Albany: Gloucester, I live
To thank thee for the love thou showedst the King,
And to revenge thine eyes. Come hither, friend.
Tell me what more thou knowest.

[*Exeunt.*]

SCENE III

A French Camp near Dover

[*Enter* KENT *and a* GENTLEMAN.]

Kent: Why the King of France is so suddenly gone back know you no reason?

Gentleman: Something he left imperfect in the state, which since his coming forth is thought of, which imports to the kingdom so much fear and danger that his personal return was most required and necessary.

Kent: Who hath he left behind him general?

Gentleman: The Marshal of France, Monsieur la Far.

Kent: Did your letters pierce[1] the Queen to any demonstration of grief?

Gentleman: Ay, sir; she took them, read them in my presence,
And now and then an ample tear trilled down
Her delicate cheek. It seemed she was a queen
Over her passion,[2] who, most rebel-like,
Sought to be king o'er her.

Kent: O, then it moved her?

Gentleman: Not to a rage; patience and sorrow strove
Who should express her goodliest. You have seen
Sunshine and rain at once: her smiles and tears
Were like a better way.[3] Those happy smilets
That played on her ripe lip seemed not to know
What guests were in her eyes, which parted thence
As pearls from diamonds dropped. In brief,
Sorrow would be a rarity most beloved,
If all could so become it.

Kent: Made she no verbal question?

Gentleman: Faith, once or twice she heaved the name of father.
Pantingly forth, as if it pressed her heart,
Cried "Sisters, sisters! Shame of ladies! Sisters!
Kent! father! sisters! What, i'th' storm? i'th' night?
Let pity not be believed!" There she shook
The holy water from her heavenly eyes,
And clamor moistened.[4] Then away she started
To deal with grief alone.

[21] back again: on the way back. IV, iii, [1] pierce: arouse. [2] passion: grief. [3] Were . . . way: were similar but even prettier. [4] And . . . moistened: added tears to her cries.

Kent: It is the stars,
The stars above us, govern our conditions,
Else one self mate and mate[5] could not beget
Such different issues. You spoke not with her since?

Gentleman: No.

Kent: Was this before the King returned?

Gentleman: No, since.

Kent: Well, sir, the poor distressèd Lear's i'th' town,
Who sometime, in his better tune, remembers
What we are come about, and by no means
Will yield to see his daughter.

Gentleman: Why, good sir?

Kent: A sovereign shame so elbows[6] him; his own unkindness
That stripped her from his benediction, turned her
To foreign casualties,[7] gave her dear rights
To his dog-hearted daughters—these things sting
His mind so venomously that burning shame
Detains him from Cordelia.

Gentleman: Alack, poor gentleman!

Kent: Of Albany's and Cornwall's powers you heard not?

Gentleman: 'Tis so; they are afoot.

Kent: Well, sir, I'll bring you to our master Lear
And leave you to attend him. Some dear cause[8]
Will in concealment wrap me up awhile.
When I am known aright, you shall not grieve
Lending me this acquaintance. I pray you go
Along with me.

[*Exeunt.*]

[5] self . . . mate: one set of parents. [6] elbows: prods. [7] casualties: circumstances. [8] dear cause: important business. IV, iv, [1] rank fumiter . . . darnel: varieties of English weeds and wild flowers [2] century: a group of one hundred.

SCENE IV

The French Camp. A Tent

[*Enter, with drum and colors,* CORDELIA, DOCTOR, *and* SOLDIERS.]

Cordelia: Alack, 'tis he! Why, he was met even now
As mad as the vexed sea, singing aloud,
Crowned with rank fumiter and furrow weeds,
With hardocks, hemlock, nettles, cuckoo flowers,
Darnel,[1] and all the idle weeds that grow
In our sustaining corn. A century[2] send forth;
Search every acre in the high-grown field
And bring him to our eye.

[*Exit an* OFFICER.]

What can man's wisdom
In the restoring his bereavèd sense?
He that helps him take all my outward worth.[3]

Doctor: There is means, madam.
Our foster nurse of nature is repose,
The which he lacks. That to provoke in him
Are many simples operative,[4] whose power
Will close the eye of anguish.

Cordelia: All blest secrets,
All you unpublished virtues[5] of the earth,
Spring with my tears! be aidant and remediate[6]
In the good man's distress! Seek, seek for him!

[3] outward worth: material possessions. [4] simples operative: curative herbs. [5] unpublished virtues: hidden remedies. [6] aident and remediate: helpful and curative.

Lest his ungoverned rage dissolve the life
That wants the means to lead it.

[*Enter* MESSENGER.]

Messenger: News, madam.
The British powers are marching hitherward.

Cordelia: 'Tis known before. Our preparation stands
In expectation of them. O dear father,
It is thy business that I go about.
Therefore great France
My mourning and importuned tears hath pitied.
No blown ambition doth our arms incite,
But love, dear love, and our aged father's right.
Soon may I hear and see him!

[*Exeunt.*]

SCENE V

GLOUCESTER'S *Castle*

[*Enter* REGAN *and* OSWALD.]

Regan: But are my brother's powers set forth?

Oswald: Ay, madam.

Regan: Himself in person there?

Oswald: Madam, with much ado.
Your sister is the better soldier.

Regan: Lord Edmund spake not with your lord at home?

Oswald: No, madam.

Regan: What might import my sister's letter to him?

Oswald: I know not, lady.

Regan: Faith, he is posted hence on serious matter.
It was great ignorance, Gloucester's eyes being out,
To let him live; where he arrives he moves
All hearts against us. Edmund, I think, is gone,
In pity of his misery, to dispatch
His nighted[1] life; moreover, to descry
The strength o'th' enemy.

Oswald: I must needs after him, madam, with my letter.

Regan: Our troops set forth to-morrow. Stay with us;
The ways are dangerous.

Oswald: I may not, madam.
My lady charged my duty in this business.

Regan: Why should she write to Edmund? Might not you
Transport her purposes by word? Belike,
Something—I know not what—I'll love thee much—
Let me unseal the letter.

Oswald: Madam, I had rather—

Regan: I know your lady does not love her husband;
I am sure of that; and at her later being here
She gave strange oeliads[2] and most speaking looks
To noble Edmund. I know you are of her bosom.

Oswald: I, madam?

Regan: I speak in understanding. Y'are; I know't,
Therefore I do advise you take this note.[3]
My lord is dead; Edmund and I have talked,
And more convenient is he for my hand
Than for your lady's. You may gather more.
If you do find him, pray you give him this;
And when your mistress hears thus much from you,
I pray desire her call her wisdom to her.
So fare you well.
If you do chance to hear of that blind traitor,
Preferment[4] falls on him that cuts him off.

IV, v, [1] nighted: darkened, i.e., blinded. [2] oeliads: wanton glances. [3] take this note: heed this. [4] preferment: advancement.

Oswald: Would I could meet him, madam; I should show
What party I do follow.

Regan: Fare thee well.

[*Exeunt.*]

SCENE VI

The Country near Dover

[*Enter* GLOUCESTER, *and* EDGAR *dressed like a peasant.*]

Gloucester: When shall I come to the top of that same hill?

Edgar: You do climb up it now. Look how we labor.

Gloucester: Methinks the ground is even.

Edgar: Horrible steep.
Hark, do you hear the sea?

Gloucester: No, truly.

Edgar: Why, then, your other senses grow imperfect
By your eyes' anguish.

Gloucester: So may it be indeed.
Methinks thy voice is altered, and thou speakest
In better phrase and matter than thou didst.

Edgar: Y'are much deceived. In nothing am I changed
But in my garments.

Gloucester: Methinks y'are better spoken.

Edgar: Come on, sir, here's the place; stand still. How fearful
And dizzy 'tis to cast one's eyes so low!
The crows and choughs that wing the midway air
Show scarce so gross as beetles. Halfway down
Hangs one that gathers sampire[1]—dreadful trade!
Methinks he seems no bigger than his head.
The fishermen that walk upon the beach
Appear like mice; and yond tall anchoring bark,
Diminished to her cock;[2] her cock, a buoy
Almost too small for sight. The murmuring surge
That on th'unnumbered idle pebble chafes
Cannot be heard so high. I'll look no more,
Lest my brain turn, and the deficient sight
Topple down headlong.

Gloucester: Set me where you stand.

Edgar: Give me your hand. You are now within a foot
Of th'extreme verge. For all beneath the moon
Would I not leap upright.

Gloucester: Let go my hand.
Here, friend, 's another purse; in it a jewel
Well worth a poor man's taking. Fairies and gods
Prosper it with thee! Go thou further off;
Bid me farewell, and let me hear thee going.

Edgar: Now fare ye well, good sir.

Gloucester: With all my heart.

Edgar (*aside*). Why I do trifle thus with his despair
Is done to cure it.

Gloucester: O you mighty gods! (*He kneels.*)
This world I do renounce, and, in your sights,
Shake patiently my great affliction off.
If I could bear it longer and not fall
To quarrel with your great opposeless wills,
My snuff[3] and loathed part of nature should
Burn itself out. If Edgar live, O, bless him!
Now, fellow, fare thee well. (*He falls forward.*)

IV, vi, [1] sampire: plant of the carrot family. [2] cock: rowboat. [3] snuff: burnt-out candle end.

Edgar: Gone, sir, farewell—
And yet I know not how conceit[4] may rob
The treasury of life when life itself
Yields to the theft. Had he been where he thought,
By this had thought been past.—Alive or dead?
Ho you, sir! friend! Hear you, sir? Speak!—
Thus might he pass[5] indeed; yet he revives.
What are you, sir?

Gloucester: Away, and let me die.

Edgar: Hadst thou been aught but gossamer, feathers, air,
So many fathom down precipitating,
Thou'dst shivered like an egg; but thou dost breathe,
Hast heavy substance, bleed'st not, speak'st, art sound;
Ten masts at each[6] make not the altitude
Which thou hast perpendicularly fell;
Thy life's a miracle. Speak yet again.

Gloucester: But have I fallen, or no?

Edgar: From the dread summit of this chalky bourn.
Look up a-height; the shrill-gorged[7] lark so far
Cannot be seen or heard. Do but look up.

Gloucester: Alack, I have no eyes.
Is wretchedness deprived that benefit
To end itself by death? 'Twas yet some comfort
When misery could beguile the tyrant's rage
And frustrate his proud will.

Edgar: Give me your arm.
Up—so. How is't? Feel you your legs? You stand.

Gloucester: Too well, too well.

Edgar: This is above all strangeness.
Upon the crown o'th' cliff what thing was that
Which parted from you?

Gloucester: A poor unfortunate beggar.

Edgar: As I stood here below, methought his eyes
Were two full moons; he had a thousand noses,
Horns whelked[8] and waved like the enridgèd sea;
It was some fiend. Therefore, thou happy father,
Think that the clearest gods, who make them honors
Of men's impossibilities,[9] have preserved thee.

Gloucester: I do remember now. Henceforth I'll bear
Affliction till it do cry out itself.
"Enough, enough," and die. That thing you speak of,
I took it for a man. Often 'twould say
"The fiend, the fiend"—he led me to that place.

Edgar: Bear free and patient thoughts.
[*Enter* LEAR, *mad.*]
But who comes here?
The safer[10] sense will ne'er accommodate[11]
His master thus.

Lear: No, they cannot touch me for coining;
I am the King himself.

Edgar: O thou side-piercing sight!

Lear: Nature's above art in that respect. There's your press money.[12] That fellow handles his bow like a crow-keeper.[13] Draw me a clothier's yard.[14]

[4] conceit: imagination. [5] pass: die, pass away. [6] at each: piled on top one another. [7] shrill-gorged: shrill-voiced. [8] whelked: twisted. [9] who make . . . impossibilities: who win honor by doing things impossible for men to do. [10] safer: normal. [11] accommodate: attire, dress. [12] press money: payment to soldier for being drafted into service. [13] crow-keeper: scare-crow. [14] draw . . . yard: draw the bow full length.

Look, look, a mouse! Peace, peace, this piece of toasted cheese will do't. There's my gauntlet; I'll prove it on a giant. Bring up the brown bills.[15] O, well flown,[16] bird! i'th' clout,[17] i'th' clout! Hewgh! Give the word.

Edgar: Sweet marjoram.

Lear: Pass.

Gloucester: I know that voice.

Lear: Ha! Goneril with a white beard? They flattered me like a dog, and told me I had white hairs in my beard ere the black ones were there. To say "ay" and "no" to everything I said! "Ay" and "no" too was no good divinity.[18] When the rain came to wet me once, and the wind to make me chatter, when the thunder would not peace at my bidding, there I found 'em, there I smelt 'em out. Go to, they are not men o' their words! they told me I was everything. 'Tis a lie—I am not ague-proof.

Gloucester: The trick[19] of that voice I do well remember.
Is't not the King?

Lear: Ay, every inch a king!
When I do stare, see how the subject quakes.
I pardon that man's life. What was thy cause?
Adultery?
Thou shalt not die. Die for adultery? No.
The wren goes to't, and the small gilded fly
Does lecher[20] in my sight.
Let copulation thrive; for Gloucester's bastard son
Was kinder to his father than my daughters
Got 'tween the lawful sheets.
To't, luxury,[21] pell-mell! for I lack soldiers.
Behold yond simpering dame,
Whose face between her forks[22] presages snow,[23]
That minces virtue, and does shake the head
To hear of pleasure's name
The fitchew[24] nor the soilèd[25] horse goes to't
With a more riotous appetite.
Down from the waist they are Centaurs,
Though women all above.
But to the girdle do the gods inherit,
Beneath is all the fiend's.
There's hell, there's darkness, there is the sulphurous pit; burning, scalding, stench, consumption. Fie, fie, fie! pah, pah! Give me an ounce of civet, good apothecary, to sweeten my imagination. There's money for thee.

Gloucester: O, let me kiss that hand!

Lear: Let me wipe it first, it smells of mortality.

Gloucester: O ruined piece of nature! This great world
Shall so wear out to naught. Dost thou know me?

Lear: I remember thine eyes well enough. Dost thou squiny[26] at me? No, do thy worst, blind Cupid! I'll not love. Read thou this challenge; mark but the penning of it.

Gloucester: Were all the letters suns,
I could not see.

Edgar (*aside*). I would not take this from report. It is,
And my heart breaks at it.

Lear: Read.

Gloucester: What, with the case[27] of eyes?

[15] brown bills: infantrymen. [16] well flown: well shot (of an arrow). [17] i'th clout: in the bull's eye. [18] was . . . divinity: was not true. [19] trick: sound. [20] Lecher: fornicate. [21] luxury: sexual appetite. [22] forks: legs. [23] presages snow: suggests chasteness. [24] fitchew: polecat (an oversexed animal). [25] soiled: grass fed; hence, lively. [26] squiny: ogle. [27] case: empty sockets.

Lear: O, ho, are you there with me? No eyes in your head, nor no money in your purse? Your eyes are in a heavy case, your purse in a light. Yet you see how this world goes.

Gloucester: I see it feelingly.

Lear: What, art mad? A man may see how this world goes with no eyes. Look with thine ears. See how yond justice rails upon yond simple thief. Hark in thine ear; change places and, handy-dandy, which is the justice, which is the thief? Thou hast seen a farmer's dog bark at a beggar?

Gloucester: Ay, sir.

Lear: And the creature run from the cur? There thou mightst behold the great image of authority: a dog's obeyed in office.
Thou rascal beadle,[28] hold thy bloody hand!
Why dost thou lash that whore? Strip thine own back.
Thou hotly lusts to use her in that kind[29]
For which thou whip'st her. The usurer hangs the cozener.[30]
Through tattered clothes small vices do appear;
Robes and furred gowns hide all. Plate sin with gold,
And the strong lance of justice hurtless breaks;
Arm it in rags, a pygmy's straw does pierce it.
None does offend, none—I say none! I'll able[31] 'em.
Take that of me, my friend, who have the power
To seal th'accuser's lips. Get thee glass eyes
And, like a scurvy politician, seem
To see the things thou dost not. Now, now, now, now!
Pull off my boots. Harder, harder! So.

Edgar: O, matter and impertinency[32] mixed!
Reason in madness!

Lear: If thou wilt weep my fortunes, take my eyes.
I know thee well enough; thy name is Gloucester.
Thou must be patient. We came crying hither;
Thou knowest, the first time that we smell the air
We wawl and cry. I will preach to thee. Mark.

Gloucester: Alack, alack the day!

Lear: When we are born, we cry that we are come
To this great stage of fools. This' a good block.[33]
It were a delicate stratagem to shoe
A troop of horse with felt. I'll put't in proof,[34]
And when I have stolen upon these sons-in-law,
Then kill, kill, kill, kill, kill, kill!

[*Enter a* GENTLEMAN *with* ATTENDANTS.]

Gentleman: O, here he is! Lay hand upon him.—Sir,
Your most dear daughter—

Lear: No rescue? What, a prisoner? I am even
The natural fool of fortune. Use me well;
You shall have ransom. Let me have a surgeon;
I am cut to th' brains.

Gentleman: You shall have anything.

Lear: No seconds?[35] All myself?
Why, this would make a man a man of salt,[36]

[28] beadle: parish official. [29] in that kind: for the same reason. [30] cozener: swindler. [31] able: show. [32] matter and impertinency: sense and nonsense. [33] block: hat. [34] I'll . . . proof: I'll put it to the test. [35] seconds: supporters, allies. [36] salt: tears.

To use his eyes for garden waterpots,
Ay, and laying autumn's dust.

Gentleman: Good sir—

Lear: I will die bravely, like a smug bridegroom. What!
I will be jovial. Come, come, I am a king;
My masters, know you that?

Gentleman: You are a royal one, and we obey you.

Lear: Then there's life in't. Come, an you get it, you shall get it by running. Sa, sa, sa, sa!

[*Exit running.* ATTENDANTS *follow.*]

Gentleman: A sight most pitiful in the meanest wretch.
Past speaking of in a king! Thou hast one daughter
Who redeems nature from the general curse
Which twain[37] have brought her to.

Edgar: Hail, gentle sir.

Gentleman: Sir, speed you. What's your will?

Edgar: Do you hear aught, sir, of a battle toward?

Gentleman: Most sure and vulgar.[38] Every one hears that
Which can distinguish sound.

Edgar: But, by your favor,
How near's the other army?

Gentleman: Near and on speedy foot; the main descry
Stands on the hourly thought.[39]

Edgar: I thank you, sir. That's all.

Gentleman: Though that the Queen on special cause is here,
Her army is moved on.

Edgar: I thank you, sir.

[*Exit* GENTLEMAN.]

[37] twain: two (Goneril and Regan). [38] vulgar: commonly known. [39] the main . . . thought: the main enemy forces will appear shortly. [40] art: experiencing. [41] pregnant: receptive.

Gloucester: You ever-gentle gods, take my breath from me;
Let not my worser spirit tempt me again
To die before you please!

Edgar: Well pray you, father.

Gloucester: Now, good sir, what are you?

Edgar: A most poor man, made tame to fortune's blows,
Who, by the art[40] of known and feeling sorrows,
Am pregnant[41] to good pity. Give me your hand;
I'll lead you to some biding.[42]

Gloucester: Hearty thanks.
The bounty and the benison of heaven
To boot, and boot!

[*Enter* OSWALD.]

Oswald: A proclaimed prize! Most happy!
That eyeless head of thine was first framed flesh
To raise my fortunes. Thou old unhappy traitor,
Briefly thyself remember,[43] the sword is out
That must destroy thee.

Gloucester: Now let thy friendly hand
Put strength enough to't.

[EDGAR *interposes.*]

Oswald: Wherefore, bold peasant,
Darest thou support a published traitor? Hence,
Lest that the infection of his fortune take
Like hold on thee. Let go his arm.

Edgar: Chill[44] not let go, zir, without vurther 'cagion.

Oswald: Let go, slave, or thou diest!

Edgar: Good gentleman, go your gait,[45] and let poor voke pass.

[42] biding: safe haven. [43] thyself remember: confess your sins. [44] Chill: I will (Edgar assumes a peasant dialect). [45] go your gait: go your own way.

An chud ha' bin zwaggered out of my life, 'twould not ha' bin zo long as 'tis by a vortnight. Nay, come not near the old man.
Keep out, che vore ye,[46] or Ise try whether your costard[47] or my ballow[48] be the harder. Chill be plain with you.

Oswald: Out, dunghill! (*They fight.*)

Edgar: Chill pick your teeth, zir. Come, no matter vor your foins.[49]

[OSWALD *falls.*]

Oswald: Slave, thou hast slain me. Villain, take my purse.
If ever thou wilt thrive, bury my body,
And give the letters which thou findest about me
To Edmund Earl of Gloucester. Seek him out
Upon the British party. O, untimely death! Death! (*Dies.*)

Edgar: I know thee well. A serviceable villain,
As duteous to the vices of thy mistress
As badness would desire.

Gloucester: What, is he dead?

Edgar: Sit you down, father; rest you.
Let's see his pockets; these letters that he speaks of
May be my friends. He's dead; I am only sorry
He had no other deathsman. Let us see.
Leave, gentle wax,[50] and, manners, blame us not.
To know our enemies' minds, we'ld rip their hearts;
Their papers, is more lawful.

(*Reads.*)

Let our reciprocal vows be remembered. You have many opportunities to cut him off. If your will want not,[51] time and place will be fruitfully offered. There is nothing done, if he return the conqueror. Then am I the prisoner, and his bed my jail, from the loathed warmth whereof deliver me, and supply the place for your labor.

Your (wife, so I would say) affectionate servant,

GONERIL.

O indistinguished[52] space of woman's will!
A plot upon her virtuous husband's life,
And the exchange, my brother! Here in the sands
Thee I'll rake up,[53] the post unsanctified
Of murtherous lechers; and in the mature time
With this ungracious paper strike the sight
Of the death-practised Duke.[54] For him 'tis well
That of thy death and business I can tell.

Gloucester: The King is mad. How stiff[55] is my vile sense,
That I stand up, and have ingenious[56] feeling
Of my huge sorrows! Better I were distract.[57]
So should my thoughts be severed from my griefs,
And woes by wrong imaginations lose
The knowledge of themselves.

[*A drum afar off.*]

Edgar: Give me your hand.
Far off methinks I hear the beaten drum.
Come, father, I'll bestow you with a friend.

[*Exeunt.*]

46 che vore ye: I warn you. 47 costard: head. 48 ballow: staff, cudgel. 49 foins: sword thrusts. 50 wax: sealing wax on the letter. 51 If . . . not: if you really desire it. 52 indistinguished: limitless. 53 rake up: dig up ground for burial. 54 death-practised Duke: Albany. 55 stiff: resistant. 56 ingenious: acute. 57 distract: insane.

SCENE VII

A Tent in the French Camp

[*Enter* CORDELIA, KENT, DOCTOR, *and* GENTLEMAN.]

Cordelia: O thou good Kent, how shall I live and work
To match thy goodness? My life will be too short
And every measure fail me.

Kent: To be acknowledged, madam, is o'erpaid.
All my reports go with the modest truth;
Nor more nor clipped, but so.

Cordelia: Be better suited;[1]
These weeds[2] are memories of those worser hours.
I prithee put them off.

Kent: Pardon, dear madam,
Yet to be known shortens my made intent.[3]
My boon I make it that you know me not
Till time and I think meet.

Cordelia: Then be't so, my good lord.
(*To the* DOCTOR). How does the King?

Doctor: Madam, sleeps still.

Cordelia: O you kind gods,
Cure this great breach in his abusèd nature!
The untuned and jarring senses, O, wind up
Of this child-changèd father!

Doctor: So please your Majesty
That we may wake the King? He hath slept long.

Cordelia: Be governed by your knowledge, and proceed
I'th' sway of your own will.[4] Is he arrayed?

[*Enter* LEAR *in a chair carried by* SERVANTS.]

Gentleman: Ay, madam. In the heaviness of sleep
We put fresh garments on him.

Doctor: Be by, good madam, when we do awake him.
I doubt not of his temperance.[5]

Cordelia: Very well.

[*Music.*]

Doctor: Please you draw near. Louder the music there!

Cordelia: O my dear father, restoration hang
Thy medicine on my lips, and let this kiss
Repair those violent harms that my two sisters
Have in thy reverence made!

Kent: Kind and dear princess!

Cordelia: Had you not been their father, these white flakes
Had challenged pity of them. Was this a face
To be opposed against the warring winds,
To stand against the deep dread-bolted thunder
In the most terrible and nimble stroke
Of quick cross lightning? to watch—poor perdu![6]—
With this thin helm? Mine enemy's dog,
Though he had bit me, should have stood that night
Against my fire; and wast thou fain, poor father,
To hovel thee with swine and rogues forlorn,
In short and musty straw? Alack, alack!
'Tis wonder that thy life and wits at once
Had not concluded all.—He wakes. Speak to him.

V, vii, [1] Be better suited: don more suitable clothing. [2] weeds: garments. [3] Yet . . . intent: to disclose my identity now would interfere with my plan. [4] and proceed . . . will: do whatever you consider necessary. [5] temperance: sanity. [6] perdu: a sentinel in an exposed position.

Doctor: Madam, do you; 'tis fittest.

Cordelia: How does my royal lord? How fares your Majesty?

Lear: You do me wrong to take me out o'th' grave.
Thou art a soul in bliss; but I am bound
Upon a wheel of fire, that mine own tears
Do scald like molten lead.

Cordelia: Sir, do you know me?

Lear: You are a spirit, I know. When did you die?

Cordelia: Still, still, far wide!

Doctor: He's scarce awake. Let him alone awhile.

Lear: Where have I been? Where am I? Fair daylight?
I am mightily abused. I should e'en die with pity,
To see another thus. I know not what to say;
I will not swear these are my hands. Let's see.
I feel this pin prick. Would I were assured
Of my condition!

Cordelia: O, look upon me, sir,
And hold your hands in benediction o'er me.
No, sir, you must not kneel.

Lear: Pray, do not mock me.
I am a very foolish fond old man,
Fourscore and upward, not an hour more nor less;
And, to deal plainly,
I fear I am not in my perfect mind.
Methinks I should know you, and know this man,
Yet I am doubtful, for I am mainly ignorant
What place this is, and all the skill I have
Remembers not these garments; nor I know not
Where I did lodge last night. Do not laugh at me;
For as I am a man I think this lady
To be my child Cordelia.

Cordelia: And so I am! I am!

Lear: Be your tears wet? Yes, faith. I pray weep not.
If you have poison for me, I will drink it.
I know you do not love me, for your sisters
Have, as I do remember, done me wrong.
You have some cause, they have not.

Cordelia: No cause, no cause.

Lear: Am I in France?

Kent: In your kingdom, sir.

Lear: Do not abuse me.

Doctor: Be comforted, good madam. The great rage
You see is killed in him; and yet it is danger
To make him even o'er[7] the time he has lost.
Desire him to go in. Trouble him no more
Till further settling.

Cordelia: Will't please your Highness walk?

Lear: You must bear with me.
Pray you now, forget and forgive. I am old and foolish.

[*Exeunt all but* KENT *and* GENTLEMAN.]

Gentleman: Holds it true, sir, that the Duke of Cornwall was so slain?

Kent: Most certain, sir.

Gentleman: Who is conductor of his people?

Kent: As 'tis said, the bastard son of Gloucester.

Gentleman: They say Edgar, his banished son, is with the Earl of Kent in Germany.

Kent: Report is changeable. 'Tis time to look about; the powers of the kingdom approach apace.

[7] To . . . o'er: to make him retrace.

Gentleman: The arbitrement[8] is like to be bloody.
Fare you well, sir.

[*Exit.*]

Kent: My point and period[9] will be throughly wrought,
Or well or ill, as this day's battle's fought.

[*Exit.*]

ACT V

SCENE I

The British Camp near Dover

[*Enter, with drum and colors,* EDMUND, REGAN, GENTLEMAN, *and* SOLDIERS.]

Edmund: Know of the Duke if his last purpose hold,
Or whether since he is advised by aught
To change the course. He's full of alteration
And self-reproving. Bring his constant pleasure.[1]

[*Exit an* OFFICER.]

Regan: Our sister's man is certainly miscarried.

Edmund: Tis to be doubted,[2] madam.

Regan: Now, sweet lord,
You know the goodness I intend upon you.
Tell me—but truly—but then speak the truth—
Do you not love my sister?

Edmund: In honored love.

Regan: But have you never found my brother's way
To the forfended[3] place?

Edmund: That thought abuses[4] you.

Regan: I am doubtful that you have been conjunct[5]
And bosomed with her, as far as we call hers.

Edmund: No, by mine honor, madam.

Regan: I never shall endure her. Dear my lord,
Be not familiar with her.

Edmund: Fear me not.
She and the Duke her husband!

[*Enter, with drum and colors,* ALBANY, GONERIL, SOLDIERS.]

Goneril (*aside*). I had rather lose the battle than that sister
Should loosen him and me.

Albany: Our very loving sister, well bemet.
Sir, this I hear: the King is come to his daughter,
With others whom the rigor of our state[6]
Forced to cry out. Where I could not be honest,
I never yet was valiant. For this business,
It touches us as France invades our land,
Not bolds[7] the King, with others whom, I fear,
Most just and heavy causes make oppose.

Edmund: Sir, you speak nobly.

Regan: Why is this reasoned?[8]

Goneril: Combine together 'gainst the enemy;

[8] arbitrement: settlement of the issue. [9] point and period: conclusion of my story. V, i, [1] constant pleasure: final decision. [2] doubted: feared. [3] forfended: forbidden (i.e., Goneril's bed).

[4] abuses: does you wrong. [5] I . . . conjunct: I fear you have been intimate with her. [6] rigor of our state: harsh rule. [7] bolds: supports. [8] reasoned: quibbled.

For these domestic and particular[9] broils
Are not the question here.

Albany: Let's then determine
With th'ancient of war[10] on our proceeding.

Edmund: I shall attend you presently at your tent.

Regan: Sister, you'll go with us?

Goneril: No.

Regan: 'Tis most convenient. Pray you go with us.

Goneril (*aside*). O, ho, I know the riddle.— I will go.

[*As they are going out, enter* EDGAR *disguised.*]

Edgar: If e'er your Grace had speech with man so poor,
Hear me one word.

Albany: I'll overtake you—Speak.

[*Exeunt all but* ALBANY *and* EDGAR.]

Edgar: Before you fight the battle, ope this letter.
If you have victory, let the trumpet sound
For him that brought it. Wretched though I seem,
I can produce a champion that will prove
What is avouchèd there. If you miscarry,
Your business of the world hath so an end,
And machination ceases. Fortune love you!

Albany: Stay till I have read the letter.

Edgar: I was forbid it.
When time shall serve, let but the herald cry,
And I'll appear again.

Albany: Why, fare thee well. I will o'er look thy paper.

[*Exit* EDGAR.]

[*Reenter* EDMUND.]

Edmund: The enemy's in view; draw up your powers.
Here is the guess of their true strength and forces
By diligent discovery; but your haste
Is now urged on you.

Albany: We will greet the time.

[*Exit.*]

Edmund: To both these sisters have I sworn my love;
Each jealous of the other, as the stung
Are of the adder. Which of them shall I take?
Both? one? or neither? Neither can be enjoyed,
If both remain alive. To take the widow
Exasperates, makes mad her sister Goneril,
And hardly shall I carry out my side,[11]
Her husband being alive. Now then, we'll use
His countenance[12] for the battle, which being done,
Let her who would be rid of him devise
His speedy taking off. As for the mercy
Which he intends to Lear and to Cordelia—
The battle done, and they within our power,
Shall never see his pardon; for my state
Stands on[13] me to defend, not to debate.

[*Exit.*]

SCENE II

A Field between the Two Camps

[*Alarum within. Enter, with drum and colors,* CORDELIA *and* LEAR *with French forces; and exeunt.*]

[*Enter* EDGAR *and* GLOUCESTER.]

Edgar: Here, father, take the shadow of this tree

[9] particular: personal. [10] ancient of war: seasoned soldiers. [11] my side: my part of the bargain. [12] countenance: approval. [13] stands on: forces.

For your good host; pray that the right may thrive.
If ever I return to you again,
I'll bring you comfort.

Gloucester: Grace go with you, sir!

[*Exit* EDGAR.]

[*Alarum and retreat within. Reenter* EDGAR.]

Edgar: Away, old man! give my thy hand, away!
King Lear hath lost, he and his daughter ta'en.
Give me thy hand; come on!

Gloucester: No further, sir. A man may rot even here.

Edgar: What, in ill thoughts again? Men must endure
Their going hence, even as their coming hither;
Ripeness is all. Come on.

Gloucester: And that's true too.

[*Exeunt.*]

SCENE III

The British Camp near Dover

[*Enter, in conquest, with drum and colors,* EDMUND; LEAR *and* CORDELIA *as prisoners;* SOLDIERS, CAPTAIN.]

Edmund: Some officers take them away. Good guard
Until their greater pleasures[1] first be known
That are to censure them.

Cordelia: We are not the first
Who with best meaning have incurred the worst.
For thee, oppressèd king, I am cast down;
Myself could else outfrown false Fortune's frown.
Shall we not see these daughters and these sisters?

Lear: No, no, no, no! Come, let's away to prison.
We two alone will sing like birds i'th' cage.
When thou dost ask me blessing, I'll kneel down
And ask of thee forgiveness. So we'll live,
And pray, and sing, and tell old tales, and laugh
At gilded butterflies, and hear poor rogues
Talk of court news; and we'll talk with them too—
Who loses and who wins; who's in, who's out—
And take upon's the mystery of things,
As if we were gods' spies; and we'll wear out,
In a walled prison, packs and sects of great ones
That ebb and flow by the moon.

Edmund: Take them away.

Lear: Upon such sacrifices, my Cordelia,
The gods themselves throw incense. Have I caught thee?
He that parts us shall bring a brand from heaven
And fire us hence[2] like foxes. Wipe thine eyes.
The goodyears[3] shall devour 'em, flesh and fell,[4]
Ere they shall make us weep! We'll see 'em starved first.
Come.

[*Exeunt* LEAR *and* CORDELIA, *guarded.*]

Edmund: Come hither, Captain; hark.
Take thou this note. Go follow them to prison.

V, iii, [1] greater pleasures: the desires of those in authority. [2] fire us hence: chase us with fire. [3] good-years: evil times. [4] fell: skin, hide.

One step I have advanced thee; if thou dost
As this instructs thee, thou dost make thy way
To noble fortunes. Know thou this, that men
Are as the time is; to be tender-minded
Does not become a sword. Thy great employment
Will not bear question. Either say thou'lt do't,
Or thrive by other means.

Captain: I'll do't, my lord.

Edmund: About it! and write happy when thou hast done.
Mark: I say instantly, and carry it so
As I have set it down.

Captain: I cannot draw a cart, nor eat dried oats;
If it be man's work, I'll do't.

[*Exit.*]

[*Flourish. Enter* ALBANY, GONERIL, REGAN, SOLDIERS.]

Albany: Sir, you have showed to-day your valiant strain,[5]
And fortune led you well. You have the captives
Who were the opposites[6] of this day's strife;
I do require them of you, so to use them
As we shall find their merits and our safety
May equally determine.

Edmund: Sir, I thought it fit
To send the old and miserable King
To some retention and appointed guard;
Whose age has charms in it, whose title more,
To pluck the common bosom[7] on his side
And turn our impressed lances[8] in our eyes
Which do command them. With him I sent the Queen,
My reason all the same; and they are ready
To-morrow, or at further space, to appear
Where you shall hold your session. At this time
We sweat and bleed; the friend hath lost his friend,
And the best quarrels in the heat are cursed
By those that feel their sharpness.
The question of Cordelia and her father
Requires a fitter place.

Albany: Sir, by your patience,
I hold you but a subject of this war,
Not as a brother.

Regan: That's as we list to grace him.
Methinks our pleasure might have been demanded
Ere you had spoke so far. He led our powers,
Bore the commission of my place and person,
The which immediacy[9] may well stand up
And call itself your brother.

Goneril: Not so hot!
In his own grace he doth exalt himself
More than in your addition.[10]

Regan: In my rights
By me invested, he compeers[11] the best.

Goneril: That were the most if he should husband you.

Regan: Jesters do oft prove prophets.

Goneril: Holla, holla!
That eye that told you so looked but asquint.

Regan: Lady, I am not well, else I should answer
From a full-flowing stomach. General,

[5] strain: mettle. [6] opposites: enemies. [7] Common bosom: sympathy of the common people. [8] impressed lances: spears of conscripted soldiers. [9] immediacy: direct connection (with me). [10] addition: titles. [11] compeers: equals.

Take thou my soldiers, prisoners, patrimony;
Dispose of them, of me; the walls are thine.
Witness the world that I create thee here
My lord and master.

Goneril: Mean you to enjoy him?

Albany: The let-alone[12] lies not in your good will.

Edmund: Nor in thine, lord.

Albany: Half-blooded[13] fellow, yes.

Regan (*to* EDMUND). Let the drum strike, prove my title thine.

Albany: Stay yet; hear reason. Edmund, I arrest thee
On capital treason; and, in thine attaint,[14]
This gilded serpent (*points to* GONERIL).
For your claim, fair sister,
I bar it in the interest of my wife.
'Tis she is subcontracted[15] to this lord,
And I, her husband, contradict your banns.
If you will marry, make your loves to me;
My lady is bespoke.

Goneril: An interlude![16]

Albany: Thou are armed, Gloucester. Let the trumpet sound.
If none appear to prove upon thy person
Thy heinous, manifest, and many treasons,
There is my pledge (*throws down a glove*). I'll prove it on thy heart,
Ere I taste bread, thou art in nothing less
Than I have here proclaimed thee.

Regan: Sick, O, sick!

Goneril (*aside*). If not, I'll ne'er trust medicine.

Edmund: There's my exchange (*throws down a glove*). What in the world he is
That names me traitor, villain-like he lies.
Call by thy trumpet. He that dares approach,
On him, on you, who not? I will maintain
My truth and honor firmly.

Albany: A herald, ho!

Edmund: A herald, ho, a herald!

[*Enter a* HERALD.]

Albany: Trust to thy single virtue,[17] for thy soldiers,
All levied in my name, have in my name
Took their discharge.

Regan: My sickness grows upon me.

Albany: She is not well. Convey her to my tent.

[*Exit* REGAN, *led.*]

Come hither, herald. Let the trumpet sound,
And read out this.

Captain: Sound, trumpet! (*A trumpet sounds.*)

Herald (*reads*). If any man of quality or degree within the lists of the army will maintain upon Edmund, supposed Earl of Gloucester, that he is a manifold traitor, let him appear by the third sound of the trumpet. He is bold in his defence.

Edmund: Sound! (*First trumpet.*)

Herald: Again! (*Second trumpet.*)

Herald: Again! (*Third trumpet.*)

(*Trumpet answers within.*)

[*Enter* EDGAR, *armed, a trumpet before him.*]

Albany: Ask him his purposes, why he appears
Upon this call o'th' trumpet.

Herald: What are you?
Your name, your quality? and why you answer
This present summons?

[12] let-alone: permission. [13] half-blooded: illegitimate. [14] in thine attaint: involved with you.

[15] subcontracted: pledged. [16] interlude: farcical skit. [17] single virtue: own prowess.

Edgar: Know my name is lost,
By treason's tooth bare-gnawn and canker-bit.[18]
Yet am I noble as the adversary
I come to cope.[19]

Albany: Which is that adversary?

Edgar: What's he that speaks for Edmund Earl of Gloucester?

Edmund: Himself. What say'st thou to him?

Edgar: Draw thy sword,
That, if my speech offend a noble heart,
Thy arm may do thee justice. Here is mine.
Behold, it is the privilege of mine honors,
My oath, and my profession. I protest,
Maugre[20] thy strength, place, youth, and eminence,
Despite thy victor sword and fire-new fortune,
Thy valor and thy heart, thou art a traitor,
False to thy gods, thy brother, and thy father,
Conspirant 'gainst this high illustrious prince,
And from th'extremest upward of thy head
To the descent and dust beneath thy foot,
A most toad-spotted traitor. Say thou "no,"
This sword, this arm, and my best spirits are bent
To prove upon thy heart, whereto I speak,
Thou liest.

Edmund: In wisdom I should ask thy name;
But since thy outside looks so fair and war-like,
And that thy tongue some say[21] of breeding breathes,
What safe and nicely[22] I might well delay
By rule of knighthood, I disdain and spurn.
Back do I toss those treasons to thy head;
With the hell-hated lie o'erwhelm thy heart;
Which, for they yet glance by and scarcely bruise,
This sword of mine shall give them instant way
Where they shall rest for ever. Trumpets, speak!

[*Alarums. Fight.* EDMUND *falls.*]

Albany: Save him, save him!

Goneril: This is mere practice,[23] Gloucester.
By th' law of arms thou wast not bound to answer
An unknown opposite. Thou art not vanquished,
But cozened and beguiled.

Albany: Shut your mouth, dame,
Or with this paper shall I stop it. (*Shows her letter to* EDMUND.)—(*To* EDMUND.) Hold, sir.
(*To* GONERIL.) Thou worse than any name, read thine own evil.
No tearing, lady! I perceive you know it.

Goneril: Say if I do—the laws are mine, not thine.
Who can arraign me for't?

Albany: Most monstrous!
Know'st thou this paper?

Goneril: Ask me not what I know.

[*Exit.*]

Albany: Go after her. She's desperate; govern[24] her.

[*Exit an* OFFICER.]

Edmund: What you have charged me with, that have I done,

[18] canker-bit: chewed to pieces. [19] cope: do battle with. [20] Maugre: in spite of. [21] say: indication. [22] nicely: according to strict rules. [23] mere practice: trickery. [24] govern: restrain.

And more, much more; the time will bring it out.
'Tis past, and so am I—But what art thou
That hast this fortune on me? If thou'rt noble,
I do forgive thee.

Edgar: Let's exchange charity.
I am no less in blood than thou art, Edmund;
If more, the more th' hast wronged me.
My name is Edgar and thy father's son.
The gods are just, and of our pleasant vices
Make instruments to plague us.
The dark and vicious place where thee he got[25]
Cost him his eyes.

Edmund: Th' hast spoken right, 'tis true;
The wheel is come full circle, I am here.

Albany: Methought thy very gait did prophesy
A royal nobleness; I must embrace thee.
Let sorrow split my heart if ever I
Did hate thee, or thy father!

Edgar: Worthy prince, I know't.

Albany: Where have you hid yourself?
How have you known the miseries of your father?

Edgar: By nursing them, my lord. List a brief tale,
And when 'tis told, O that my heart would burst!
The bloody proclamation to escape
That followed me so near (O, our lives' sweetness!
That we the pain of death would hourly die
Rather than die at once!) taught me to shift
Into a madman's rags, t'assume a semblance
That very dogs disdained, and in this habit
Met I my father with his bleeding rings,
Their precious stones new lost; became his guide,
Led him, begged for him, saved him from despair;
Never—O fault—revealed myself unto him
Until some half hour past, when I was armed,
Not sure, though hoping of this good success,
I asked his blessing, and from first to last
Told him my pilgrimage. But his flawed heart
Alack, too weak the conflict to support
'Twixt two extremes of passion, joy and grief,
Burst smilingly.

Edmund: This speech of yours hath moved me,
And shall perchance do good; but speak you on;
You look as you had something more to say.

Albany: If there be more, more woeful, hold it in;
For I am almost ready to dissolve,
Hearing of this.

Edgar: This would have seemed a period
To such as love not sorrow; but another,
To amplify too much, would make much more,
And top extremity.[26]
Whilst I was big in clamor,[27] came there a man,
Who, having seen me in my worst estate,
Shunned my abhorred society; but then, finding

[25] The dark . . . got: the adulterous way in which he sired you. [26] top extremity: be too much. [27] big in clamor: loudly lamenting.

Who 'twas that so endured, with his strong arms
He fastened on my neck, and bellowed out
As he'd burst heaven; threw him on my father;
Told the most piteous tale of Lear and him
That ever ear received; which in recounting
His grief grew puissant,[28] and the strings of life
Began to crack. Twice then the trumpets sounded,
And there I left him tranced.[29]

Albany: But who was this?

Edgar: Kent, sir, the banished Kent, who in disguise
Followed his enemy king and did him service
Improper for a slave.

[*Enter a* GENTLEMAN *with a bloody knife.*]

Gentleman: Help, help, O, help!

Edgar: What kind of help?

Albany: Speak, man.

Edgar: What means that bloody knife?

Gentleman: 'Tis hot, it smokes.
It came even from the heart of—O, she's dead!

Albany: Who dead? Speak, man.

Gentleman: Your lady, sir, your lady! and her sister
By her is poisoned; she confesses it.

Edmund: I was contracted[30] to them both. All three
Now marry in an instant.

[*Enter* KENT.]

Edgar: Here comes Kent.

Albany: Produce their bodies, be they alive or dead.

[*Exit* GENTLEMAN.]

This judgment of the heavens, that makes us tremble,
Touches us not with pity. Oh, is this he?
The time will not allow the compliment[31]
That very manners urges.

Kent: I am come
To bid my king and master aye good night.
Is he not here?

Albany: Great thing of us forgot!
Speak, Edmund, where's the King? and where's Cordelia? (*The bodies of* GONERIL *and* REGAN *are brought in.*)
Seest thou this object, Kent?

Kent: Alack, why thus?

Edmund: Yet Edmund was beloved.
The one the other poisoned for my sake,
And after slew herself.

Albany: Even so. Cover their faces.

Edmund: I pant for life. Some good I mean to do,
Despite of mine own nature. Quickly send
(Be brief in it) to the castle, for my writ
Is on the life of Lear and on Cordelia.
Nay, send in time.

Albany: Run, run, O, run!

Edgar: To who, my lord? Who has the office? Send
Thy token of reprieve.

Edmund: Well thought on. Take my sword;
Give it the Captain.

Albany: Haste thee for thy life.

[*Exit* EDGAR.]

Edmund: He hath commission from thy wife and me
To hang Cordelia in the prison and
To lay the blame upon her own despair
That she fordid[32] herself.

Edmund: The gods defend her! Bear him hence awhile. (EDMUND *is borne off.*)

[28] puissant: powerful. [29] tranced: in a trance. [30] contracted: pledged. [31] compliment: formal courtesies. [32] fordid: committed suicide.

[*Enter* LEAR, *with* CORDELIA *dead in his arms,* EDGAR, GENTLEMAN, *and others following.*]

Lear: Howl, howl, howl, howl, O, you are men of stones.
Had I your tongues and eyes, I'ld use them so
That heaven's vault should crack. She's gone for ever!
I know when one is dead, and when one lives;
She's dead as earth. Lend me a looking glass;
If that her breath will mist or stain the stone,[33]
Why, then she lives.

Kent: Is this the promised end?[34]

Edgar: Or image of that horror?

Albany: Fall and cease![35]

Lear: This feather stirs; she lives! If it be so,
It is a chance which does redeem all sorrows
That ever I have felt.

Kent: O my good master!

Lear: Prithee away!

Edgar: 'Tis noble Kent, your friend.

Lear: A plague upon you, murderers, traitors all!
I might have saved her; now she's gone for ever.
Cordelia, Cordelia, stay a little. Ha!
What is't thou say'st? Her voice was ever soft,
Gentle, and low—an excellent thing in women.
I killed the slave that was a-hanging thee.

Captain: 'Tis true, my lords, he did.

Lear: Did I not, fellow?
I have seen the day, with my good biting falchion[36]
I would have made them skip. I am old now,
And these same crosses[37] spoil me. Who are you?
Mine eyes are not o'th' best. I'll tell you straight.

Kent: If fortune brag of two she loved and hated,
One of them we behold.

Lear: This is a dull sight. Are you not Kent?

Kent: The same—
Your servant Kent. Where is your servant Caius?

Lear: He's a good fellow. I can tell you that.
He'll strike, and quickly too. He's dead and rotten.

Kent: No, my good lord, I am the very man—

Lear: I'll see that straight.

Kent: That from your first of difference[38] and decay
Have followed you sad steps.

Lear: You are welcome hither.

Kent: Nor no man else! All's cheerless, dark, and deadly.
Your eldest daughters have fordone themselves,
And desperately are dead.

Lear: Ay, so I think.

Albany: He knows not what he says, and vain is it
That we present us to him.

Edgar: Very bootless.

[*Enter a* CAPTAIN.]

Captain: Edmund is dead, my lord.

Albany: That's but a trifle here.
You lords and noble friends, know our intent.

[33] stone: mirror. [34] promised end: end of the world. [35] Fall and cease: Let the end of the world come. [36] falchion: sword. [37] crosses: misfortunes. [38] difference: changed status.

What comfort to this great decay may come
Shall be applied. For us, we will resign,
During the life of this old Majesty,
To him our absolute power; (*To* EDGAR *and* KENT.) you to your rights,
With boot, and such addition as your honors
Have more than merited. All friends shall taste
The wages of their virtue, and all foes
The cup of their deservings,—O, see, see!

Lear: And my poor fool[39] is hanged! No, no, no life!
Why should a dog, a horse, a rat, have life,
And thou no breath at all? Thou'lt come to more,
Never, never, never, never, never!
Pray you undo this button. Thank you, sir.
Do you see this? Look on her! look! her lips!
Look there, look there! (*Dies.*)

Edgar: He faints! My lord, my lord!

Kent: Break, heart, I prithee break!

Edgar: Look up, my lord.

Kent: Vex not his ghost; O let him pass! He hates him
That would upon the rack[40] of this tough world
Stretch him out longer.

Edgar: He is gone indeed.

Kent: The wonder is, he hath endured so long.
He but usurped his life.

Albany: Bear them from hence. Our present business
Is general woe. (*To* KENT *and* EDGAR.) Friends of my soul, you twain
Rule in this realm, and the gored state sustain.

Kent: I have a journey, sir, shortly to go.
My master calls me; I must not say no.

Albany: The weight of this sad time we must obey,
Speak what we feel, not what we ought to say.
The oldest hath borne most; we that are young
Shall never see so much, nor live so long.

[*Exeunt with a dead march.*]

[39] fool: (here used as a term of affection referring to Cordelia). [40] rack: torture rack.

DISCUSSION QUESTIONS

Act I, Scene i

1. What exposition is provided by the opening speeches of Kent and Gloucester?
2. What shift in tone occurs after the entrance speeches of Kent and Gloucester?
3. How does it serve the structure of the play to have Gloucester absent during the actual abdication scene?
4. Lear's plan of present division of his kingdom to prevent future strife has superficial elements of reasonableness in it, but it is marred by what crucial error of judgment?
5. What is gained dramatically by having Cordelia unmarried (insofar as characterization, forward movement of the plot, and theme are concerned)?

6. How does Goneril's speech characterize her?
7. What purpose is served by the asides spoken by Cordelia?
8. What are Lear's feelings toward Cordelia? How are they important to the action?
9. What is ironic (in the light of subsequent action) about Lear's remark to Cordelia, "Nothing will come of nothing"?
10. How is Cordelia characterized by her speech?
11. How is Lear characterized throughout this scene?
12. What symbolic and structural role does Kent serve in this scene?
13. How does what Kent says further the characterization of Cordelia?
14. What effect does the use of rhyme have in Kent's farewell speech?
15. To what other characters does France serve as a foil? How?
16. How does it serve the purposes of plot complication and conflict to have Cordelia leave England?
17. What preparation is given in Cordelia's farewell speech?
18. What preparation is contained in the closing remarks of Goneril and Regan?
19. What conflicts have been established in this scene? What is ironic about them?
20. What significant action has taken place in this scene? What reversals of intention and irony are inherent in them?
21. If this were sentimental melodrama instead of tragedy, how might these various actions and conflicts turn out?
22. Since the main plot is that of a tragedy (which assumes that man must pay the consequences of the evil he does through suffering), what is the likely outcome of the forces set into operation?

Act I, Scenes ii, iii, iv, and v

1. What self-characterization is provided in Edmund's soliloquy?
2. What do Lear and Gloucester have in common that acts as a motive force in the play?
3. What is ironic about the intrigue in this scene?
4. If this were a morality play, i.e., one in which the characters represent abstract virtues or vices, what might Edmund be portraying?
5. How is Edgar characterized in this scene (directly or indirectly)?
6. Why is it important that this characterization of Edgar be established early?
7. What is the tone of this scene—somber and tragic, or ironic and melodramatic?
8. How does this scene counterbalance Scene i thematically?
9. What exposition is provided in Scene iii?
10. What preparation is provided?
11. What further characterization of Goneril is provided in this scene?
12. How are Goneril and Edmund similar?
13. What is the chief purpose of this scene—exposition, action, characterization, or preparation?
14. What stage convention must we be willing to accept to make the conversation between Kent and Lear in Scene iv seem credible?

15. What comparisons and contrasts are there between the actions of Edmund in Scene ii and Kent in this scene?
16. What purpose does the Lear-Fool interchange serve, and how does it contrast with Kent's prophecy in Scene i as to tone?
17. What is ironic about this exchange between Lear and the Fool?
18. What purpose is served by the encounter between Lear and Goneril?
19. Is Lear a static or developing character up to this point? Explain.
20. What dramatic irony and what preparation are provided by Lear's decision to leave Goneril's for Regan's castle?
21. How has this scene progressed from deception to truth? (Consider the actions of Kent, the Fool, and Goneril.)
22. What purpose does the Fool's banter serve in Scene v?
23. What is the first indication of Lear's gaining any insight at all into his folly and the evil it has engendered?
24. What preparation does Lear's last remark provide for as to what may happen to him?

Act II

1. What is the importance of the expository details provided by the opening remarks of Curan and Edmund?
2. How does the duel subordinate character to incident to forward the action in the counterplot? (Consider the role played by Edgar.)
3. Why does Edmund speak of the mumbling of wicked charms and conjuring of the moon by Edgar when he talks to Gloucester?
4. What is ironic about Edmund's mention of his illegitimacy?
5. What is ironic about Regan's attitude toward Edgar?
6. How does Edmund's role link the counterplot with the main plot?
7. What dramatic purposes are served by this scene?
8. What is the tone of this scene—tragic or melodramatic? Explain.
9. On what tone does Scene ii begin, and what purpose does the shift in tone serve?
10. How does the encounter between Kent and Cornwall change the initial tone of the scene and further the action?
11. How is Cornwall characterized in this scene (by his own words and actions and by the comments of others)?
12. What is revealed about Regan's character?
13. What preparation for retribution against the villains is provided in this scene?
14. What is the chief purpose of Scene iii and what new force does it put into operation?
15. What is the dramatic purpose of the stychomythia (dialogue in single alternate lines) between Lear and Kent in Scene iv?
16. What exposition is provided to explain ambiguities in the preceding scene?
17. What is the import of the Fool's "winter song"?
18. What is the gist of the Fool's retort to Kent?

19. What role is played by Gloucester in this and in the preceding scene? What does this prepare for?
20. What delusion does Lear still labor under that causes him to fly into a rage at Goneril's words?
21. What stubborn fact persistently interferes with Lear's attempts to ignore reality and find excuses for the refusal of Cornwall and Regan to see him on his arrival at the castle?
22. How does Regan's attitude in the scene further the action?
23. Why is it important for Goneril to be present in this scene?
24. What is the mood or atmosphere of this scene?

Act III

1. How does Scene i provide atmosphere, exposition, and preparation?
2. What symbols are inherent in the atmosphere of the storm and the setting on the heath?
3. What symbolism is inherent in the fact that Lear is accompanied by the Fool?
4. What is the theme (in Scene ii) of Lear's invocation to the storm?
5. What is the import of the Fool's cryptic "codpiece" song?
6. What is Kent's function in this scene?
7. What important character development does Lear go through in this scene that changes our attitude toward him? What emotions does it arouse?
8. Some of the Fool's comments are directly related to the structure of the play; some are primarily addenda for the sake of audience entertainment by providing general or topical observations on life. Which type of comment does the Fool's prophecy seem to be? (Consider the possibility of both elements being in it.)
9. What exposition and preparation does Scene iii provide and how are they important?
10. What tonal contrast is there between Scene iii and Scene ii? How is this achieved?
11. Of what is the severity of the storm a measure? (Scene iv.)
12. How does Lear's central obsession with ingratitude become expanded in this scene? What does this tell about his progress toward madness?
13. In what way is the effect of the storm on Lear ironic?
14. What insight does Lear gain from his suffering?
15. What purpose does Edgar serve in this scene (ironically, structurally, imagistically, and thematically)?
16. Of what is Lear's disrobing symbolic?
17. How does Gloucester's presence in this scene relate to the main plot and to the counterplot?
18. What is the tone of this scene and how has it been brought about?
19. What exposition and preparation are provided in Scene v?
20. What is the dominant obsession of Lear's madness in Scene vi?
21. How is the mock trial scene an ironic counterpart to the "trial scene" in Act I,

Scene i, where Lear attempted to adjudicate the measure of love possessed by his three daughters?

22. How is the mock trial scene kept from becoming comic and burlesque?
23. How has the role of the Fool changed in the course of the action and why?
24. What elements of the melodramatic are there in Scene vii?
25. What elements of the tragic does the scene possess?

Act IV

1. What is ironic about Edgar's opening remarks in Scene i?
2. What is the ironic symbolism of Gloucester's blindness?
3. In what way is he a tragic figure now rather than merely a pathetic one?
4. In what way is he similar to Lear in his suffering?
5. What is ironic about the fate that is meted out to Gloucester?
6. What ironic conflicts does Scene ii prepare for?
7. What is gained by having Cordelia characterized indirectly (by the Gentleman's speech) in Scene iii?
8. What ironic outcome to the Lear-Cordelia conflict set up in Act I does this characterization provide for?
9. What preparation does Scene iv provide?
10. What exposition, action, and preparation does Scene v provide?
11. What is the purpose of the cliff episode in Scene vi?
12. How does this scene between Edgar and Gloucester contrast ironically with the earlier scenes between Gloucester and Edmund?
13. What injustices and sins does Lear rave about and how do they relate to characters and events in the play?
14. What purpose does Oswald's death serve in tying together the two plots?
15. What is the main action in Scene vii? Of what earlier scenes is this scene an ironic counterpart? Wherein lies the irony?
16. What prevents the reconciliation scene from becoming maudlin?
17. What is the purpose of the closing conversation between Kent and the Gentleman?

Act V

1. What preparation is provided in Scene i as to the outcome of the various conflicts and complications set up earlier in the plot?
2. How is the short scene between Edgar and Albany important to the resolution of the play's action?
3. What development in Albany's character has taken place, and how is this important to the structure of the play?
4. What is ironic about the dilemma Edmund finds himself in as expressed in his soliloquy at the end of Scene i?
5. Why is the progress of the battle merely reported in Scene ii rather than being enacted?

6. What characterization of the principal figures is provided in this scene? (Scene iii.)
7. What action takes place in the scene?
8. What adverse criticism might be made about the tone of this scene?
9. What adverse criticism might be made about the credibility of Edmund's characterization in this scene?
10. What adverse criticism might be made of the resolution of the various conflicts?
11. What adverse criticism could be made of the total dramatic effect of the scene?
12. Formulate a statement of the meaning of the play and apply it to the various characters.

THE SCHOOL FOR SCANDAL

Richard Brinsley Sheridan

Introductory Comment

The School for Scandal represents an admirable blend of the satiric and the sentimental so that the total effect is closer to pure, genial laughter than it is to punitive derision or lachrymose empathy. Although the title is derived from the satiric element, this is not really the dominant motif and the satire is not cruel and vicious. Lady Sneerwell's circle of clever backbiters engaged in their absurd preoccupation is clearly intended to be the butt of the playwright's scornfully disapproving laughter. Yet they emerge as being more amusing and entertaining than disgusting and revolting. The tone of Sheridan's satire is a far cry from that of a determined moralist like Ben Jonson who unmercifully excoriates his dramatic embodiments of human folly and vice in such plays as *Volpone* and *The Alchemist.* Actually, the members of the "school for scandal" are given most of the best lines in the play; whereas the characters the playwright obviously approves of speak quite blandly and prosaically for the most part, but they compensate for their lack of brilliance by the good deeds they perform.

Although the play has the outward form of a "comedy of manners," that is, one depicting the manners and foibles of a fashionable, highly sophisticated society, there is nothing brittle and cynical about it. The worth of a character in this play is not determined by how clever and witty he may be but by how spontaneously good, generous, and tolerant he is. In a true comedy of manners, Sir Peter might easily have been made the target of ridicule through the clever hero's successful conquest of his young and willing wife. He is the stuff that cuckolds are made of—an old man married to a beautiful young wife with too much time on her hands. He escapes this fate not through his cleverness and wit but through his magnanimous and understanding nature which converts his errant wife to dutiful and appreciative ways. This, along with Charles's defeat of Joseph, constitutes the sentimental element in the play and it is neatly and cleverly balanced against the satirical. In a true comedy of manners Joseph would better qualify as the hero, with his witty conversation and shrewd intrigues, and Charles would become the rather foolish, easily duped provincial relative aspiring beyond his level and saved from the consequences of his bungling by the timely intervention of one of the tolerant, clever ones.

Part of the appeal of the play still resides in its cleverness of language, one of its strongest points with its original audience. It is the ordinary speech of highly intelligent, educated people of its days raised to its wittiest level by the skilful use of paradox, antithesis, parallelisms, and the choice of the precise words combined with a graceful economy of expression. In creating his dialogue Sheridan was following a tradition of his day which placed a high premium on witty, well-phrased conversation. What he has done is to mine the most productive veins of conversation in high society London of 1777 and sort and polish the brightest gems he has garnered to embellish his play with the sparkle and glitter of language adroitly and imaginatively used.

The situation he deals with is a highly artificial one dependent on the elaborate social structure of a small segment of society, and the theme he deals with, the triumph of virtue over hypocrisy and malice is certainly not a novel one. But in spite of what might have been limitations in subject matter and theme, Sheridan rises above them and his play becomes a laughing comment on human nature in a much more general sense than a mere satirical attack on scandal and hypocrisy might have easily become without his genial comic view and felicity of expression.

Cast of Characters

Men

SIR PETER TEAZLE
SIR OLIVER SURFACE
JOSEPH SURFACE
CHARLES SURFACE
CRABTREE
SIR BENJAMIN BACKBITE
ROWLEY
TRIP
MOSES
SNAKE
CARELESS

and other Companions to CHARLES [SURFACE], *Servants, etc.*

Women

LADY TEAZLE
MARIA
LADY SNEERWELL
MRS. CANDOUR

[SCENE*: London*]

ACT I

SCENE I

LADY SNEERWELL'S *house*

[LADY SNEERWELL *at the dressing-table* —SNAKE *drinking chocolate.*]

Lady Sneer: The paragraphs, you say, Mr. Snake, were all inserted?

Snake: They were, madam, and as I copied them myself in a feigned hand, there can be no suspicion whence they came.

Lady Sneer: Did you circulate the reports of Lady *Brittle's* intrigue with Captain *Boastall?*

Snake: That is in as fine a train as your ladyship could wish,—in the common course of things, I think it must reach Mrs. *Clackit's* ears within four-and-twenty hours; and then, you know, the business is as good as done.

Lady Sneer: Why, truly, Mrs. *Clackit* has a very pretty talent, and a great deal of industry.

Snake: True, madam, and has been tolerably successful in her day:—to my knowledge, she has been the cause of six matches being broken off, and three sons being disinherited, of four forced elopements, as many close confinements, nine separate maintenances, and two divorces;—nay, I have more than once traced her causing a *Tête-à-Tête* in the *Town and Country Magazine,* when the parties perhaps had never seen each other's faces before in the course of their lives.

Lady Sneer: She certainly has talents, but her manner is gross.

Snake: 'Tis very true,—she generally designs well, has a free tongue, and a bold invention; but her coloring is too dark, and her outline often extravagant. She *wants* that *delicacy* of *hint,* and *mellowness* of *sneer,* which distinguish your ladyship's scandal.

Lady Sneer: Ah! you are partial, Snake.

Snake: Not in the least; everybody allows that Lady *Sneerwell* can do more with a *word* or a *look* than many can with the most labored detail, even when they happen to have a little truth on their side to support it.

Lady Sneer: Yes, my dear Snake; and I am no hypocrite to deny the satisfaction I reap from the success of my efforts. Wounded myself, in the early part of my life, by the envenomed tongue of slander, I confess I have since known no pleasure equal to the reducing others to the level of my own injured reputation.

Snake: Nothing can be more natural. But, Lady Sneerwell, there is one affair in which you have lately employed me, wherein, I confess, I am at a loss to guess your motives.

Lady Sneer: I conceive you mean with respect to my neighbor, Sir Peter Teazle, and his family?

Snake: I do; here are two young men, to whom Sir Peter has acted as a kind of guardian since their father's death; the elder possessing the most amiable character, and universally well spoken of; the youngest, the most dissipated and extravagant young fellow in the kingdom, without friends or character,—the former an avowed admirer of your ladyship, and apparently your favorite; the latter attached to Maria, Sir Peter's ward, and confessedly beloved by her. Now, on the face of these circumstances, it is utterly unaccountable to me, why you, the widow of a city knight, with a good jointure, should not close with the passion of a man of such character and expectations as Mr. *Surface;* and more so why you should be so uncommonly earnest to destroy the mutual attachment subsisting between his brother *Charles* and *Maria.*

Lady Sneer: Then, at once to unravel this mystery, I must inform you that love has no share whatever in the intercourse between Mr. *Surface* and me.

Snake: No!

Lady Sneer: His real attachment is to *Maria,* or her fortune; but, finding in his brother a favored rival, he has been obliged to mask his pretensions, and profit by my assistance.

Snake: Yet still I am more puzzled why you should interest yourself in his success.

Lady Sneer: Heav'ns! how dull you are! Cannot you surmise the weakness which I hitherto, through shame, have concealed even from *you?* Must I confess that *Charles*—that libertine, that extravagant, that bankrupt in fortune and reputation—that he it is for whom I am thus anxious and malicious, and to gain whom I would sacrifice everything?

Snake: Now, indeed, your conduct appears consistent; but how came you and Mr. *Surface* so confidential?

Lady Sneer For our mutual interest. I have found him out a long time since —I know him to be artful, selfish, and malicious—in short, a sentimental knave.

Snake: Yet, Sir Peter vows he has not his equal in England—and, above all, he praises him as a man of sentiment.

Lady Sneer: True; and with the assistance of his sentiment and hypocrisy he has brought him [Sir Peter] entirely into his interest with regard to *Maria.*

[*Enter Servant.*]

Serv: Mr. Surface.

Lady Sneer: Show him up.

[*Exit Servant.*]

He generally calls about this time. I don't wonder at people's giving him to me for a lover.

[*Enter* JOSEPH SURFACE.]

Jos. Surf: My dear Lady Sneerwell, how do you do to-day? Mr. Snake, your most obedient.

Lady Sneer: Snake has just been arraigning me on our mutual attachment, but I have informed him of our real views; you know how useful he has been to us; and, believe me, the confidence is not ill placed.

Jos. Surf: Madam, it is impossible for me to suspect a man of Mr. *Snake's* sensibility and discernment.

Lady Sneer: Well, well, no compliments now;—but tell me when you saw your mistress, *Maria*—or, what is more material to me, your brother.

Jos. Surf: I have not seen either since I left you; but I can inform you that they never meet. Some of your stories have taken a good effect on Maria.

Lady Sneer: Ah, my dear Snake! the merit of this belongs to you. But do your brother's distresses increase?

Jos. Surf: Every hour;—I am told he has had another execution in the house yesterday; in short, his dissipation and extravagance exceed any thing I ever heard of.

Lady Sneer: Poor Charles!

Jos. Surf: True, madam;—notwithstanding his vices, one can't help feeling for him.—Aye, poor Charles! I'm sure I wish it was in *my* power to be of any essential service to him.—For the man who does not share in the distresses of a brother, even though merited by his own misconduct, deserves——

Lady Sneer: O lud! you are going to be moral, and forget that you are among friends.

Jos. Surf: Egad, that's true!—I'll keep that sentiment till I see Sir Peter. However, it is certainly a charity to rescue Maria from such a libertine, who, if he is to be reclaimed, can be so only by a person of your ladyship's superior accomplishments and understanding.

Snake: I believe, Lady Sneerwell, here's company coming,—I'll go and copy the letter I mentioned to you.—Mr. Surface, your most obedient.

[*Exit* SNAKE.]

Jos. Surf: Sir, your very devoted.—Lady Sneerwell, I am very sorry you have put any further confidence in that fellow.

Lady Sneer: Why so?

Jos. Surf: I have lately detected him in frequent conference with old *Rowley,* who was formerly my father's steward, and has never, you know, been a friend of mine.

Lady Sneer: And do you think he would betray us?

Jos. Surf: Nothing more likely: take my word for't, Lady Sneerwell, that fellow hasn't virtue enough to be faithful even to his own villainy.—Hah! Maria!

[*Enter* MARIA.]

Lady Sneer: Maria, my dear, how do you do?—What's the matter?

Maria: Oh! there is that disagreeable lover of mine, Sir *Benjamin Backbite,* has just called at my guardian's, with his odious uncle, *Crabtree;* so I slipped out, and run hither to avoid them.

Lady Sneer: Is that all?

Jos. Surf: If my brother *Charles* had been of the party, ma'am, perhaps you would not have been so much alarmed.

Lady Sneer: Nay, now you are severe; for I dare swear the truth of the matter is, Maria heard *you* were here;—but, my dear, what has Sir Benjamin done, that you should avoid him so?

Maria: Oh, he has done nothing—but 'tis for what he has said,—his conversation is a perpetual libel on all his acquaintance.

Jos. Surf: Aye, and the worst of it is, there is no advantage in not knowing him; for he'll abuse a stranger just as soon as his best friend—and his uncle's as bad.

Lady Sneer: Nay, but we should make allowance; Sir Benjamin is a wit and a poet.

Maria: For my part, I own, madam, wit loses its respect with me, when I see it in company with malice.—What do you think, Mr. Surface?

Jos. Surf: Certainly, madam; to smile at the jest which plants a thorn in another's breast is to become a principal in the mischief.

Lady Sneer: Pshaw! there's no possibility of being witty without a little ill nature: the malice of a good thing is the barb that makes it stick.—What's your opinion, Mr. Surface?

Jos. Surf: To be sure, madam, that conversation, where the spirit of raillery is suppressed, will ever appear tedious and insipid.

Maria: Well, I'll not debate how far scandal may be allowable; but in a man, I am sure, it is always contemptible.—We have pride, envy, rivalship, and a thousand motives to depreciate each other; but the male slanderer must have the cowardice of a woman before he can traduce one.

[*Enter* SERVANT.]

Serv: Madam, Mrs. Candour is below, and, if your ladyship's at leisure, will leave her carriage.

Lady Sneer: Beg her to walk in.

[*Exit* SERVANT.]

Now Maria, however here is a character to your taste; for, though Mrs. Candour is a little talkative, everybody allows her to be the best-natured and best sort of woman.

Maria: Yes, with a very gross affectation of good nature and benevolence, she does more mischief than the direct malice of old Crabtree.

Jos. Surf: I'faith 'tis very true, Lady Sneerwell; whenever I hear the current running against the characters of my friends, I never think them in such danger as when Candour undertakes their defence.

Lady Sneer: Hush!—here she is!

[*Enter* MRS. CANDOUR.]

Mrs. Can: My dear Lady Sneerwell, how have you been this century?—Mr. Surface, what news do you hear?—though indeed it is no matter, for I think one hears nothing else but scandal.

Jos. Surf: Just so, indeed, madam.

Mrs. Can: Ah, Maria! child,—what, is the whole affair off between you and Charles? His extravagance, I presume—the town talks of nothing else.

Maria: I am very sorry, ma'am, the town has so little to do.

Mrs. Can: True, true, child: but there is no stopping people's tongues.—I own I was hurt to hear it, as indeed I was to learn, from the same quarter, that your guardian, Sir Peter, and Lady Teazle have not agreed lately so well as could be wished.

Maria: 'Tis strangely impertinent for people to busy themselves so.

Mrs. Can: Very true, child, but what's to be done? People will talk—there's no preventing it.—Why, it was but yesterday I was told that Miss Gadabout had eloped with Sir Filigree Flirt.—But, Lord! there's no minding what one hears—though, to be sure, I had this from very good authority.

Maria: Such reports are highly scandalous.

Mrs. Can: So they are, child—shameful, shameful! But the world is so censorious, no character escapes.—Lord, now who would have suspected your friend, Miss Prim, of an indiscretion? Yet such is the ill-nature of people, that they say her uncle stopped her last week, just as she was stepping into the York Diligence with her dancing-master.

Maria: I'll answer for't there are no grounds for the report.

Mrs. Can: Oh, no foundation in the world, I dare swear; no more, probably, than for the story circulated last month, of Mrs. Festino's affair with Colonel Cassino;—though, to be sure, that matter was never rightly cleared up.

Jos. Surf: The license of invention some people take is monstrous indeed.

Mara: 'Tis so.—But, in my opinion, those who report such things are equally culpable.

Mrs. Can: To be sure they are; tale-bearers are as bad as the tale-makers—'tis an old observation, and a very true one—but what's to be done, as I said before? how will you prevent people from talking?—To-day, Mrs. Clackit assured me Mr. and Mrs. Honeymoon were at last become mere man and wife, like the rest of their acquaintances.—She likewise hinted that a certain widow, in the next street, had got rid of her dropsy and recovered her shape in a most surprising manner. And at the same time Miss Tattle, who was by, affirmed that Lord Buffalo had discovered his lady at a house of no extraordinary fame—and that Sir Harry Bouquet and Tom Saunter were to measure swords on a similar provocation. But, Lord, do you think I would report these things! No, no! tale-bearers, as I said before, are just as bad as tale-makers.

Jos. Surf: Ah! Mrs. Candour, if everybody had your forbearance and good nature!

Mrs. Can: I confess, Mr. Surface, I cannot bear to hear people attacked behind their backs, and when ugly circumstances come out against one's acquaintance I own I always love to think the best.—By the bye, I hope it is not true that your brother is absolutely ruined?

Jos. Surf: I am afraid his circumstances are very bad indeed, ma'am.

Mrs. Can: Ah!—I heard so—but you must tell him to keep up his spirits—everybody almost is in the same way! Lord Spindle, Sir Thomas Splint, Captain Quinze, and Mr. Nickit—all up, I hear, within this week; so, if Charles is undone, he'll find half his acquaintances ruined too—and that, you know, is a consolation.

Jos. Surf: Doubtless, ma'am—a very great one.

[*Enter* SERVANT.]

Serv: Mr. Crabtree and Sir Benjamin Backbite.

[*Exit* SERVANT.]

Lady Sneer: So, Maria, you see your lover pursues you; positively you shan't escape.

[*Enter* CRABTREE *and* SIR BENJAMIN BACKBITE.]

Crab: Lady Sneerwell, I kiss your hands. Mrs. Candour, I don't believe you are acquainted with my nephew, Sir Benjamin Backbite? Egad, ma'am, he has a pretty wit, and is a pretty poet too; isn't he, Lady Sneerwell?

Sir Ben: O fie, uncle!

Crab: Nay, egad it's true—I'll back him at a rebus or a charade against the best rhymer in the kingdom. Has your ladyship heard the epigram he wrote last week on Lady Frizzle's feather catching fire?—Do, Benjamin, repeat it—or the charade you made last night *extempore* at Mrs. Drowzie's *conversazione.*—Come now; your *first* is the name of a fish, your *second* a great naval commander, and——

Sir Ben: Uncle, now—prithee——

Crab: I'faith, ma'am, 'twould surprise you to hear how ready he is at these things.

Lady Sneer: I wonder, Sir Benjamin, you never publish anything.

Sir Ben: To say truth, ma'am, 'tis very vulgar to print; and, as my little productions are mostly satires and lampoons on particular people, I find they circulate more by giving copies in confidence to the friends of the parties—however, I have some love elegies, which, when favored with this lady's smiles, I mean to give to the public.

Crab: 'Fore heav'n, ma'am, they'll immortalize you!—you'll be handed down to posterity like Petrarch's Laura, or Waller's Sacharissa.

Sir Ben: Yes, madam, I think you will like them, when you shall see them on a beautiful quarto page, where a neat rivulet of text shall murmur through a meadow of margin. 'Fore gad, they will be the most elegant things of their kind!

Crab: But, ladies, that's true—have you heard the news?

Mrs. Can: What, sir, do you mean the report of—

Crab: No, ma'am, that's not it.—Miss Nicely is going to be married to her own footman.

Mrs. Can: Impossible!

Crab: Ask Sir Benjamin.

Sir Ben: 'Tis very true, ma'am—everything is fixed, and the wedding liveries bespoke.

Crab: Yes—and they do say there were pressing reasons for it.

Lady Sneer: Why, I *have* heard something of this before.

Mrs. Can: It can't be—and I wonder any one should believe such a story of so prudent a lady as Miss Nicely.

Sir Ben: O lud! ma'am, that's the very reason 'twas believed at once. She has always been so *cautious* and so *reserved,* that everybody was sure there was some reason for it at bottom.

Mrs. Can: Why, to be sure, a tale of scandal is as fatal to the credit of a prudent lady of her stamp as a fever is generally to those of the strongest constitutions; but there is a sort of puny, sickly reputation that is always ailing, yet will outlive the robuster characters of a hundred prudes.

Sir Ben: True, madam, there are valetudinarians in reputation as well as constitution, who, being conscious of their weak part, avoid the least breath of air, and supply their want of stamina by care and circumspection.

Mrs. Can: Well, but this may be all a mistake. You know, Sir Benjamin, very trifling circumstances often give rise to the most injurious tales.

Crab: That they do, I'll be sworn, ma'am. Did you ever hear how Miss

Piper came to lose her lover and her character last summer at Tunbridge?—Sir Benjamin, you remember it?

Sir Ben: Oh, to be sure!—the most whimsical circumstance—

Lady Sneer: How was it, pray?

Crab: Why, one evening, at Mrs. Ponto's assembly, the conversation happened to turn on the difficulty of breeding Nova Scotia sheep in this country. Says a young lady in company, 'I have known instances of it; for Miss Letitia Piper, a first cousin of mine, had a Nova Scotia sheep that produced her twins.' 'What!' cries the old Dowager Lady Dundizzy (who you know is as deaf as a post), 'has Miss Piper had twins?' This mistake, as you may imagine, threw the whole company into a fit of laughing. However, 'twas the next morning everywhere reported, and in a few days believed by the whole town, that Miss Letitia Piper had actually been brought to bed of a fine boy and a girl—and in less than a week there were people who could name the father, and the farm-house where the babies were put out to nurse!

Lady Sneer: Strange, indeed!

Crab: Matter of fact, I assure you. —O lud! Mr. Surface, pray is it true that your uncle, Sir Oliver, is coming home?

Jos. Surf: Not that I know of, indeed, sir.

Crab: He has been in the East Indies a long time. You can scarcely remember him, I believe.—Sad comfort, whenever he returns, to hear how your brother has gone on!

Jos. Surf: Charles has been imprudent, sir, to be sure; but I hope no busy people have already prejudiced Sir Oliver against him,—he may reform.

Sir Ben: To be sure he may—for my part I never believed him to be so utterly void of principle as people say—and though he has lost all his friends, I am told nobody is better spoken of by the Jews.

Crab: That's true, egad, nephew. If the old Jewry were a ward, I believe Charles would be an alderman; no man more popular there, 'fore gad! I hear he pays as many annuities as the Irish tontine; and that, whenever he's sick, they have prayers for the recovery of his health in the Synagogue.

Sir Ben: Yet no man lives in greater splendor.—They tell me, when he entertains his friends, he can sit down to dinner with a dozen of his own securities; have a score [of] tradesmen waiting in the antechamber, and an officer behind every guest's chair.

Jos. Surf: This may be entertainment to you, gentlemen, but you pay very little regard to the feelings of a brother.

Maria (*aside*). Their malice is intolerable!—Lady Sneerwell, I must wish you a good morning—I'm not very well.

[*Exit* MARIA.]

Mrs. Can: O dear! she changes color very much!

Lady Sneer: Do, Mrs. Candour, follow her—she may want assistance.

Mrs. Can: That I will, with all my soul, ma'am.— Poor dear girl! who knows what her situation may be!

[*Exit* MRS. CANDOUR.]

Lady Sneer: 'Twas nothing but that she could not bear to hear Charles reflected on, notwithstanding their difference.

Sir Ben: The young lady's *penchant* is obvious.

Crab: But, Benjamin, you mustn't give up the pursuit for that; follow her, and put her into good humor. Repeat her some of your own verses.—Come, I'll assist you.

Sir Ben: Mr. Surface, I did not mean to hurt you; but depend upon't your brother is utterly undone. (*Going.*)

Crab: O lud, aye! undone as ever man was—can't raise a guinea. (*Going.*)

Sir Ben: And everything sold, I'm told, that was movable. (*Going.*)

Crab: I have seen one that was at his house—not a thing left but some empty bottles that were overlooked and the family pictures, which I believe are framed in the wainscot. (*Going.*)

Sir Ben: And I am very sorry to hear also some bad stories against him. (*Going.*)

Crab: Oh, he has done many mean things, that's certain. (*Going.*)

Sir Ben: But, however, as he's your brother—(*Going.*)

Crab: We'll tell you all, another opportunity.

[*Exeunt* CRABTREE *and* SIR BENJAMIN.]

Lady Sneer: Ha, ha! ha! 'tis very hard for them to leave a subject they have not quite run down.

Jos. Surf. And I believe the abuse was no more acceptable to your ladyship than to Maria.

Lady Sneer: I doubt her affections are farther engaged than we imagined; but the family are to be here this evening, so you may as well dine where you are, and we shall have an opportunity of observing farther;—in the meantime, I'll go and plot mischief, and you shall study sentiments.

[*Exeunt.*]

SCENE II

SIR PETER TEAZLE'S *house*

[*Enter* SIR PETER.]

Sir Peter: When an old bachelor takes a young wife, what is he to expect?—'Tis now six months since Lady Teazle made me the happiest of men—and I have been the miserablest dog ever since that ever committed wedlock! We tift a little going to church, and came to a quarrel before the bells were done ringing. I was more than once nearly choked with gall during the honeymoon, and had lost all comfort in life before my friends had done wishing me joy! Yet I chose with caution—a girl bred wholly in the country, who never knew luxury beyond one silk gown, nor dissipation above the annual gala of a race ball. Yet now she plays her part in all the extravagant fopperies of the fashion and the town, with as ready a grace as if she had never seen a bush nor a grass-plat out of Grosvenor Square! I am sneered at by my old acquaintance—paragraphed in the newspapers. She dissipates my fortune, and contradicts all my humors; yet the worst of it is, I doubt I love her, or I should never bear all this. However, I'll never be weak enough to own it.

[*Enter* ROWLEY.]

Row: Oh! Sir Peter, your servant,—how is it with you, sir?

Sir Pet: Very bad, Master Rowley, very bad;—I meet with nothing but crosses and vexations.

Row: What can have happened to trouble you since yesterday?

Sir Pet: A good question to a married man!

Row: Nay, I'm sure your lady, Sir

Peter, can't be the cause of your uneasiness.

Sir Pet: Why, has anyone told you she was dead?

Row: Come, come, Sir Peter, you love her, notwithstanding your tempers don't exactly agree.

Sir Pet: But the fault is entirely hers, Master Rowley. I am, myself, the sweetest-tempered man alive, and hate a teasing temper—and so I tell her a hundred times a day.

Row: Indeed!

Sir Pet: Aye; and what is very extraordinary, in all our disputes she is always in the wrong! But Lady Sneerwell, and the set she meets at her house, encourage the perverseness of her disposition. Then, to complete my vexations, Maria, my ward, whom I ought to have the power of a father over, is determined to turn rebel too, and absolutely refuses the man whom I have long resolved on for her husband;—meaning, I suppose, to bestow herself on his profligate brother.

Row: You know, Sir Peter, I have always taken the liberty to differ with you on the subject of these two young gentlemen. I only wish you may not be deceived in your opinion of the elder. For Charles, my life on't! he will retrieve his errors yet. Their worthy father, once my honored master, was, at his years, nearly as wild a spark; yet, when he died, he did not leave a more benevolent heart to lament his loss.

Sir Pet: You are wrong, Master Rowley. On their father's death, you know, I acted as a kind of guardian to them both, till their uncle Sir Oliver's Eastern liberality gave them an early independence; of course, no person could have more opportunities of judging of their hearts, and I was never mistaken in my life. Joseph is indeed a model for the young men of the age. He is a man of sentiment, and acts up to the sentiments he professes; but, for the other, take my word for't, if he had any grains of virtue by descent, he has dissipated them with the rest of his inheritance. Ah! my old friend, Sir Oliver, will be deeply mortified when he finds how part of his bounty has been misapplied.

Row: I am sorry to find you so violent against the young man, because this may be the most critical period of his fortune. I came hither with news that will surprise you.

Sir Pet: What! let me hear.

Row: Sir Oliver *is* arrived, and at this moment in town.

Sir Pet: How! you astonish me! I thought you did not expect him this month.

Row: I did not; but his passage has been remarkably quick.

Sir Pet: Egad, I shall rejoice to see my old friend,—'tis sixteen years since we met—we have had many a day together; but does he still enjoin us not to inform his nephews of his arrival?

Row: Most strictly. He means, before it is known, to make some trial of their dispositions.

Sir Pet: Ah! There needs no art to discover their merits—however, he shall have his way; but, pray, does he know I am married?

Row: Yes, and will soon wish you joy.

Sir Pet: What, as we drink health to a friend in a consumption! Ah, Oliver will laugh at me—we used to rail at matrimony together—but he has been steady to his text. Well, he must be at my house, though—I'll instantly give orders for his reception. But, Master Rowley, don't drop a word that Lady Teazle and I ever disagree.

Row: By no means.

Sir Pet: For I should never be able to stand Noll's jokes; so I'd have him think, Lord forgive me! that we are a very happy couple.

Row: I understand you—but then you must be very careful not to differ while he's in the house with you.

Sir Pet: Egad, and so we must—and that's impossible. Ah! Master Rowley, when an old bachelor marries a young wife, he deserves—no—the crime carries the punishment along with it.

[*Exeunt.*]

ACT II

SCENE I

SIR PETER TEAZLE'S *house*

[*Enter* SIR PETER *and* LADY TEAZLE.]

Sir Pet: Lady Teazle, Lady Teazle, I'll not bear it!

Lady Teaz: Sir Peter, Sir Peter, you may bear it or not, as you please; but I ought to have my own way in everything, and what's more, I *will* too.—What! though I was educated in the country, I know very well that women of fashion in London are accountable to nobody after they are married.

Sir Pet: Very well, ma'am, very well, —so a husband is to have no influence, no authority?

Lady Teaz: Authority! No, to be sure—if you wanted authority over me, you should have adopted me, and not married me; I am sure you were old enough.

Sir Pet: Old enough!—aye, there it is!—Well, well, Lady Teazle, though my life may be made unhappy by your temper, I'll not be ruined by your extravagance.

Lady Teaz: My extravagance! I'm sure I'm not more extravagant than a woman of fashion ought to be.

Sir Pet: No, no, madam, you shall throw away no more sums on such unmeaning luxury. 'Slife! to spend as much to furnish your dressing-room with flowers in winter as would suffice to turn the Pantheon into a greenhouse, and give a *fête champêtre* at Christmas!

Lady Teaz: Lord, Sir Peter, am I to blame because flowers are dear in cold weather? You should find fault with the climate, and not with me. For my part, I am sure I wish it was spring all the year round, and that roses grew under one's feet!

Sir Pet: Oons! madam—if you had been born to this, I shouldn't wonder at your talking thus.—But you forget what your situation was when I married you.

Lady Teaz: No, no, I don't; 'twas a very disagreeable one, or I should never have married *you.*

Sir Pet: Yes, yes, madam, you were then in somewhat an humbler style—the daughter of a plain country squire. Recollect, Lady Teazle, when I saw you first, sitting at your tambour, in a pretty figured linen gown, with a bunch of keys by your side, your hair combed smooth over a roll, and your apartment hung round with fruits in worsted, of your own working.

Lady Teaz: O, yes! I remember it very well, and a curious life I led—my daily occupation to inspect the dairy, superintend the poultry, make extracts from the family receipt-book, and comb my aunt Deborah's lapdog.

Sir Pet: Yes, yes, ma'am, 'twas so indeed.

Lady Teaz: And then, you know, my evening amusements! To draw patterns for ruffles, which I had not the materials to make; to play Pope Joan with the curate; to read a novel to my aunt; or to be stuck down to an old spinet to strum my father to sleep after a fox-chase.

Sir Pet: I am glad you have so good a memory. Yes, madam, these were the recreations I took you from; but now you must have your coach—*vis-à-vis*—and three powdered footmen before your chair and, in summer, a pair of white cats to draw you to Kensington Gardens.—No recollection, I suppose, when you were content to ride double, behind the butler, on a docked coach-horse?

Lady Teaz: No—I swear I never did that—I deny the butler and the coach-horse.

Sir Pet: This, madam, was your situation—and what have I not done for you? I have made you a woman of fashion, of fortune, of rank—in short, I have made you my wife.

Lady Teaz: Well, then, and there is but one thing more you can make me to add to the obligation—and that is——

Sir Pet: My widow, I suppose?

Lady Teaz: Hem! hem!

Sir Pet: Thank you, madam—but don't flatter yourself; for though your ill-conduct may disturb my peace, it shall never break my heart, I promise you: however, I am equally obliged to you for the hint.

Lady Teaz: Then why will you endeavor to make yourself so disagreeable to me, and thwart me in every little elegant expense?

Sir Pet: 'Slife, madam, I say, had you any of these elegant expenses when you married me?

Lady Teaz: Lud, Sir Peter! would you have me be out of the fashion?

Sir Pet: The fashion, indeed! what had you to do with the fashion before you married me?

Lady Teaz: For my part, I should think you would like to have your wife thought a woman of taste.

Sir Pet: Aye—there again—taste! Zounds! madam, you had no taste when you married *me!*

Lady Teaz: That's very true, indeed, Sir Peter! and, *after* having married you, I am sure I should never pretend to taste again! But now, Sir Peter, if we have finished our daily jangle, I presume I may go to my engagement of [at] Lady Sneerwell's?

Sir Pet: Aye—there's another precious circumstance!—a charming set of acquaintance you have made there!

Lady Teaz: Nay, Sir Peter, they are people of rank and fortune, and remarkably tenacious of reputation.

Sir Pet: Yes, egad, they are tenacious of reputation with a vengeance; for they don't choose anybody should have a character but themselves! Such a crew! Ah! many a wretch has rid on a hurdle who has done less mischief than those utterers of forged tales, coiners of scandal,—and clippers of reputation.

Lady Teaz: What! would you restrain the freedom of speech?

Sir Pet: Oh! they have made you just as bad as any one of the society.

Lady Teaz: Why, I believe I do bear a part with a tolerable grace. But I vow I have no malice against the people I abuse; when I say an ill-natured thing, 'tis out of pure good humor—and I take it for granted they deal exactly in the same manner with me. But, Sir Peter, you know you promised to come to Lady Sneerwell's too.

Sir Pet: Well, well, I'll call in just to look after my own character.

Lady Teaz: Then, indeed, you must make haste after me or you'll be too late. —So good-bye to ye.

[*Exit* LADY TEAZLE.]

Sir Pet: So—I have gained much by my intended expostulations! Yet with what a charming air she contradicts everything I say, and how pleasingly she shows her contempt of my authority. Well, though I can't make her love me, there is a great satisfaction in quarreling with her; and I think she never appears to such advantage as when she's doing everything in her power to plague me.

[*Exit.*]

SCENE II

LADY SNEERWELL'S

[LADY SNEERWELL, MRS. CANDOUR, CRABTREE, SIR BENJAMIN BACKBITE, *and* JOSEPH SURFACE.]

Lady Sneer: Nay, positively, we will hear it.

Jos. Surf. Yes, yes, the epigram, by all means.

Sir Ben: Plague on't, uncle! 'tis mere nonsense.

Crab: No, no; 'fore gad, very clever for an *extempore!*

Sir Ben: But, ladies, you should be acquainted with the circumstance,—you must know, that one day last week, as Lady Betty Curricle was taking the dust in Hyde Park, in a sort of duodecimo phaëton, she desired me to write some verses on her ponies; upon which, I took out my pocket-book, and in one moment produced the following:

'Sure never were seen two such beautiful ponies!
Other horses are clowns, and these macaronies!
Nay, to give 'em this title I'm sure isn't wrong—
Their legs are so slim, and their tails are so long.'

Crab: There, ladies—done in the smack of a whip, and on horseback too!

Jos. Surf: A very Phœbus, mounted—indeed, Sir Benjamin.

Sir Ben: O dear sir—trifles—trifles.

[*Enter* LADY TEAZLE *and* MARIA.]

Mrs. Can: I must have a copy.

Lady Sneer: Lady Teazle, I hope we shall see Sir Peter.

Lady Teaz: I believe he'll wait on your ladyship presently.

Lady Sneer: Maria, my love, you look grave. Come, you shall sit down to cards with Mr. Surface.

Maria: I take very little pleasure in cards—however, I'll do as your ladyship pleases.

Lady Teaz (*aside*). I am surprised Mr. Surface should sit down with *her.*—I thought he would have embraced this opportunity of speaking to me before Sir Peter came.

Mrs. Can: Now, I'll die but you are so scandalous, I'll forswear your society.

Lady Teaz: What's the matter, Mrs. Candour?

Mrs. Can: They'll not allow our friend Miss Vermilion to be handsome.

Lady Sneer: Oh, surely, she's a pretty woman.

Crab: I am very glad you think so, ma'am.

Mrs. Can: She has a charming fresh color.

Lady Teaz: Yes, when it is fresh put on.

Mrs. Can: O fie! I'll swear her color is natural—I have seen it come and go.

Lady Teaz: I dare swear you have, ma'am—it goes of a night, and comes again in the morning.

Mrs. Can: Ha! ha! ha! how I hate to hear you talk so! But surely, now, her sister *is,* or *was,* very handsome.

Crab: Who? Mrs. Evergreen?—O Lord! she's six-and-fifty if she's an hour!

Mrs. Can: Now positively you wrong her; fifty-two or fifty-three is the utmost—and I don't think she looks more.

Sir Ben: Ah! there is no judging by her looks, unless one could see her face.

Lady Sneer: Well, well, if Mrs. Evergreen *does* take some pains to repair the ravages of time, you must allow she effects it with great ingenuity; and surely that's better than the careless manner in which the widow Ochre caulks her wrinkles.

Sir Ben: Nay, now, Lady Sneerwell, you are severe upon the widow. Come, come, it is not that she paints so ill—but, when she has finished her face, she joins it on so badly to her neck, that she looks like a mended statue, in which the connoisseur may see at once that the head's modern, though the trunk's antique!

Crab: Ha! ha! ha! Well said, nephew!

Mrs. Can: Ha! ha! ha! Well, you make me laugh, but I vow I hate you for't. —What do you think of Miss Simper?

Sir Ben: Why, she has very pretty teeth.

Lady Teaz: Yes; and on that account, when she is neither speaking nor laughing (which very seldom happens), she never absolutely shuts her mouth, but leaves it always on a jar, as it were.

Mrs. Can: How can you be so ill-natured?

Lady Teaz: Nay, I allow even that's better than the pains Mrs. Prim takes to conceal her losses in front. She draws her mouth till it positively resembles the aperture of a poor's-box, and all her words appear to slide out edgeways.

Lady Sneer: Very well, Lady Teazle; I see you can be a little severe.

Lady Teaz: In defence of a friend it is but justice;—but here comes Sir Peter to spoil our pleasantry.

[*Enter* SIR PETER TEAZLE.]

Sir Pet: Ladies, your most obedient —Mercy on me, here is the whole set! a character dead at every word, I suppose. (*Aside.*)

Mrs. Can: I am rejoiced you are come, Sir Peter. They have been *so* censorious. They will allow good qualities to nobody —not even good nature to our friend Mrs. Pursy.

Lady Teaz: What, the fat dowager who was at Mrs. Codille's last night?

Mrs. Can: Nay, her bulk is her misfortune; and, when she takes such pains to get rid of it, you ought not to reflect on her.

Lady Sneer: That's very true, indeed.

Lady Teaz: Yes, I know she almost lives on acids and small whey; laces herself by pulleys; and often, in the hottest noon of summer, you may see her on a little squat pony, with her hair platted up behind like a drummer's, and puffing round the Ring on a full trot.

Mrs. Can: I thank you, Lady Teazle, for defending her.

Sir Pet: Yes, a good defence, truly.

Mrs. Can: But Sir Benjamin is as censorious as Miss Sallow.

Crab: Yes, and she is a curious being to pretend to be censorious!—an awkward gawky, without any one good point under heaven.

Mrs. Can: Positively you shall not be so very severe. Miss Sallow is a relation of mine by marriage, and, as for her person, great allowance is to be made; for, let me tell you, a woman labors under many disadvantages who tries to pass for a girl at six-and-thirty.

Lady Sneer: Though, surely, she is handsome still—and for the weakness in her eyes, considering how much she reads by candle-light, it is not to be wondered at.

Mrs. Can: True; and then as to her manner, upon my word I think it is particularly graceful, considering she never had the least education; for you know her mother was a Welch milliner, and her father a sugar-baker at Bristol.

Sir Ben: Ah! you are both of you too good-natured!

Sir Pet: Yes, damned good-natured! This their own relation! mercy on me! (*Aside.*)

Sir Ben: And Mrs. Candour is of so moral a turn she can sit for an hour to hear Lady Stucco talk sentiment.

Lady Teaz: Nay, I vow Lady Stucco is very well with the dessert after dinner; for she's just like the French fruit one cracks for mottoes—made up of paint and proverb.

Mrs. Can: Well, I never will join in ridiculing a friend; and so I constantly tell my cousin Ogle, and you all know what pretensions she has to be critical in beauty.

Crab: Oh, to be sure! she has herself the oddest countenance that ever was seen; 'tis a collection of features from all the different countries of the globe.

Sir Ben: So she has, indeed—an Irish front!

Crab: Caledonian locks!

Sir Ben: Dutch nose!

Crab: Austrian lip!

Sir Ben: Complexion of a Spaniard!

Crab: And teeth *à la Chinoise!*

Sir Ben: In short, her face resembles a *table d'hôte* at Spa—where no two guests are of a nation——

Crab: Or a congress at the close of a general war—wherein all the members, even to her eyes, appear to have a different interest, and her nose and chin are the only parties likely to join issue.

Mrs. Can: Ha! ha! ha!

Sir Pet: Mercy on my life!—a person they dine with twice a week! (*Aside.*)

Lady Sneer: Go—go—you are a couple of provoking toads.

Mrs. Can: Nay, but I vow you shall not carry the laugh off so—for give me leave to say, that Mrs. Ogle—

Sir Pet: Madam, madam, I beg your pardon—there's no stopping these good gentlemen's tongues. But when I tell *you,* Mrs. Candour, that the lady they are abusing is a particular friend of mine—I hope you'll not take her part.

Lady Sneer: Well said, Sir Peter! but you are a cruel creature—too phelgmatic yourself for a jest, and too peevish to allow wit on others.

Sir Pet: Ah, madam, true wit is more nearly allied to good nature than your ladyship is aware of.

Lady Teaz: True, Sir Peter; I believe they are so near akin that they can never be united.

Sir Ben: Or rather, madam, suppose them man and wife, because one so seldom sees them together.

Lady Teaz: But Sir Peter is such an enemy to scandal, I believe he would have it put down by parliament.

Sir Pet: 'Fore heaven, madam, if they were to consider the sporting with reputation of as much importance as poaching on manors, and pass *An Act for the Preservation of Fame,* I believe many would thank them for the bill.

Lady Sneer: O lud! Sir Peter; would you deprive us of our privileges?

Sir Pet: Aye, madam; and then no person should be permitted to kill characters or run down reputations, but qualified old maids and disappointed widows.

Lady Sneer: Go, you monster!

Mrs. Can: But sure you would not be quite so severe on those who only report what they hear.

Sir Pet: Yes, madam, I would have law merchant for them too; and in all cases of slander currency, whenever the drawer of the lie was not to be found, the injured parties should have a right to come on any of the indorsers.

Crab: Well, for my part, I believe there never was a scandalous tale without some foundation.

Lady Sneer: Come, ladies, shall we sit down to cards in the next room?

[*Enter* SERVANT *and whispers* SIR PETER.]

Sir Pet: I'll be with them directly.—(*Aside.*) I'll get away unperceived.

[*Exit* SERVANT.]

Lady Sneer: Sir Peter, you are not leaving us?

Sir Pet: Your ladyship must excuse me; I'm called away by particular business —but I leave my character behind me.

[*Exit* SIR PETER.]

Sir Ben: Well certainly, Lady Teazle, that lord of yours is a strange being; I could tell you some stories of him would make you laugh heartily, if he wasn't your husband.

Lady Teaz: O pray don't mind that—come, do let's hear them.

[*They join the rest of the company, all talking as they are going into the next room.*]

Jos. Surf (*rising with* MARIA). Maria, I see you have no satisfaction in this society.

Maria: How is it possible I should? If to raise malicious smiles at the infirmities and misfortunes of those who have never injured us be the province of wit or humor, heaven grant me a double portion of dulness!

Jos. Surf: Yet they appear more ill-natured than they are; they have no malice at heart.

Maria: Then is their conduct still more contemptible; for, in my opinion, nothing could excuse the intemperance of their tongues but a natural and ungovernable bitterness of mind.

Jos. Surf: But can you, Maria, feel thus for others, and be unkind to me alone? Is hope to be denied the tenderest passion?

Maria: Why will you distress me by renewing this subject?

Jos. Surf: Ah, Maria! you would not treat me thus, and oppose your guardian, Sir Peter's will, but that I see that profligate *Charles* is still a favored rival.

Maria: Ungenerously urged! But,

whatever my sentiments of that unfortunate young man are, be assured I shall not feel more bound to give him up, because his distresses have lost him the regard even of a brother.

[LADY TEAZLE *returns.*]

Jos. Surf: Nay, but, Maria, do not leave me with a frown—by all that's honest, I swear—Gad's life, here's Lady Teazle. (*Aside.*)—You must not—no, you shall not—for, though I have the greatest regard for Lady Teazle——

Maria: Lady Teazle!

Jos. Surf: Yet were Sir Peter to suspect——

Lady Teaz (*coming forward*). What's this, pray? Do you take her for me?—Child, you are wanted in the next room.—

[*Exit* MARIA.]

What is all this, pray?

Jos. Surf: Oh, the most unlucky circumstance in nature! Maria has somehow suspected the tender concern I have for your happiness, and threatened to acquaint Sir Peter with her suspicions, and I was just endeavoring to reason with her when you came.

Lady Teaz: Indeed! but you seemed to adopt a very tender mode of reasoning—do you *usually* argue on your knees?

Jos. Surf: Oh, she's a child—and I thought a little bombast——but, Lady Teazle, when are you to give me your judgment on my library, as you promised?

Lady Teaz: No, no,—I begin to think it would be imprudent, and you know I admit you as a lover no further than *fashion* requires.

Jos. Surf: True—a mere Platonic cicisbeo, what every London wife is *entitled* to.

Lady Teaz: Certainly, one must not be out of the fashion; however, I have so many of my country prejudices left, that, though Sir Peter's ill humor may vex me ever so, it never shall provoke me to——

Jos. Surf: The only revenge in your power. Well, I applaud your moderation.

Lady Teaz: Go—you are an insinuating wretch! But we shall be missed—let us join the company.

Jos. Surf: But we had best not return together.

Lady Teaz: Well, don't stay—for Maria shan't come to hear any more of your *reasoning,* I promise you.

[*Exit* LADY TEAZLE.]

Jos. Surf: A curious dilemma, truly, my politics have run me into! I wanted, at first, only to ingratiate myself with Lady Teazle, that she might not be my enemy with Maria; and I have, I don't know how, become her serious lover. Sincerely I begin to wish I had never made such a point of gaining so *very good* a character, for it has led me into so many cursed rogueries that I doubt I shall be exposed at last.

[*Exit.*]

SCENE III

SIR PETER'S

[*Enter* SIR OLIVER SURFACE *and* ROWLEY.]

Sir Oliv: Ha! ha! ha! and so my old friend is married, hey?—a young wife out of the country.—Ha! ha! ha!—that he should have stood bluff to old bachelor so long, and sink into a husband at last!

Row: But you must not rally him on the subject, Sir Oliver; 'tis a tender point,

I assure you, though he has been married only seven months.

Sir Oliv: Then he has been just half a year on the stool of repentance!—Poor Peter! But you say he has entirely given up Charles—never sees him, hey?

Row: His prejudice against him is astonishing, and I am sure greatly increased by a jealousy of him with Lady Teazle, which he has been industriously led into by a scandalous society in the neighborhood, who have contributed not a little to Charles's ill name; whereas the truth is, I believe, if the lady is partial to either of them, his brother is the favorite.

Sir Oliv: Aye,—I know there are a set of malicious, prating, prudent gossips, both male and female, who murder characters to kill time, and will rob a young fellow of his good name before he has years to know the value of it,—but I am not to be prejudiced against my nephew by such, I promise you! No, no;—if Charles has done nothing false or mean, I shall compound for his extravagance.

Row: Then, my life on't, you will reclaim him.—Ah, sir, it gives me new life to find that *your* heart is not turned against him, and that the son of my good old master has one friend, however, left.

Sir Oliv: What! shall I forget, Master Rowley, when I was at his years myself? Egad, my brother and I were neither of us very *prudent* youths—and yet, I believe, you have not seen many better men than your old master was?

Row: Sir, 'tis this reflection gives me assurance that Charles may yet be a credit to his family.—But here comes Sir Peter.

Sir. Oliv: Egad, so he does!—Mercy on me, he's greatly altered, and seems to have a settled married look! One may read husband in his face at this distance!

[*Enter* SIR PETER TEAZLE.]

Sir Pet: Hah! Sir Oliver—my old friend! Welcome to England a thousand times!

Sir Oliv: Thank you, thank you, Sir Peter! and i'faith I am glad to find you well, believe me!

Sir Pet: Ah! 'tis a long time since we met—sixteen years, I doubt, Sir Oliver, and many a cross accident in the time.

Sir Oliv: Aye, I have had my share—but, what! I find you are married, hey, my old boy?—Well, well, it can't be helped—and so I wish you joy with all my heart!

Sir Pet: Thank you, thank you, Sir Oliver.—Yes, I have entered into the happy state—but we'll not talk of that now.

Sir Oliv: True, true, Sir Peter; old friends should not begin on grievances at first meeting. No, no, no.

Row: (*to* SIR OLIVER). Take care, pray, sir.

Sir Oliv: Well, so one of my nephews is a wild rogue, hey?

Sir Pet: Wild! Ah! my old friend, I grieve for your disappointment there—he's a lost young man, indeed; however, his brother will make you amends; *Joseph* is, indeed, what a youth should be—everybody in the world speaks well of him.

Sir Oliv: I am sorry to hear it—he has too good a character to be an honest fellow.—Everybody speaks well of him! Psha! then he has bowed as low to knaves and fools as to the honest dignity of genius or virtue.

Sir Pet: What, Sir Oliver! do you blame him for not making enemies?

Sir Oliv: Yes, if he has merit enough to deserve them.

Sir Pet: Well, well—you'll be convinced when you know him. 'Tis edification to hear him converse—he professes the noblest sentiments.

Sir Oliv: Ah, plague of his sentiments! If he salutes me with a scrap of morality in his mouth, I shall be sick directly. But, however, don't mistake me, Sir Peter; I don't mean to defend Charles's errors—but, before I form my judgment of either of them, I intend to make a trial of their hearts—and my friend Rowley and I have planned something for the purpose.

Row: And Sir Peter shall own for once he has been mistaken.

Sir Pet: Oh, my life on Joseph's honor!

Sir Oliv: Well, come, give us a bottle of good wine, and we'll drink the lad's health, and tell you our scheme.

Sir Pet: *Allons,* then!

Sir Oliv: And don't, Sir Peter, be so severe against your old friend's son. Odds my life! I am not sorry that he has run out of the course a little; for my part, I hate to see prudence clinging to the green succors of youth; 'tis like ivy round a sapling, and spoils the growth of the tree.

[*Exeunt.*]

ACT III

SCENE I

SIR PETER'S

[SIR PETER TEAZLE, SIR OLIVER SURFACE, *and* ROWLEY.]

Sir Pet: Well, then—we will see this fellow first, and have our wine afterwards. But how is this, Master Rowley? I don't see the jet of your scheme.

Row: Why, sir, this Mr. Stanley, whom I was speaking of, is nearly related to them, by their mother; he was once a merchant in Dublin, but has been ruined by a series of undeserved misfortunes. He has applied, by letter, since his confinement, both to Mr. *Surface* and *Charles* —from the former he has received nothing but evasive promises of future service, while Charles has done all that his extravagance has left him power to do; and he is, at this time, endeavoring to raise a sum of money, part of which, in the midst of his own distresses, I know he intends for the service of poor Stanley.

Sir Oliv: Ah! he is my brother's son.

Sir Pet: Well, but how is Sir Oliver personally to——

Row: Why, sir, I will inform Charles and his brother that Stanley has obtained permission to apply in person to his friends, and, as they have neither of them ever seen him, let Sir Oliver assume his character, and he will have a fair opportunity of judging at least of the benevolence of their dispositions; and believe me, sir, you will find in the youngest brother one who, in the midst of folly and dissipation, has still, as our immortal bard expresses it,—

'a tear for pity, and a hand
Open as day, for melting charity'

Sir Pet: Psha! What signifies his

having an open hand or purse either, when he has nothing left to give? Well, well, make the trial, if you please; but where is the fellow whom you brought for Sir Oliver to examine, relative to Charles's affairs?

Row: Below, waiting his commands, and no one can give him better intelligence.—This, Sir Oliver, is a friendly Jew, who, to do him justice, has done everything in his power to bring your nephew to a proper sense of his extravagance.

Sir Pet: Pray let us have him in.

Row: Desire Mr. Moses to walk upstairs.

Sir Pet: But why should you suppose he will speak the truth?

Row: Oh, I have convinced him that he has no chance of recovering certain sums advanced to Charles but through the bounty of Sir Oliver, who he knows is arrived; so that you may depend on his fidelity to his interest. I have also another evidence in my power, one Snake, whom I have detected in a matter little short of forgery, and shall shortly produce to remove some of *your* prejudices, Sir Peter, relative to Charles and Lady Teazle.

Sir Pet: I have heard too much on that subject.

Row: Here comes the honest Israelite.

[*Enter* MOSES.]

—This is Sir Oliver.

Sir Oliv: Sir, I understand you have latey had great dealings with my nephew Charles.

Mos: Yes, Sir Oliver—I have done all I could for him, but he was ruined before he came to me for assistance.

Sir Oliv: That was unlucky, truly—for you have had no opportunity of showing your talents.

Mos: None at all—I hadn't the pleasure of knowing his distresses—till he was some thousands worse than nothing.

Sir Oliv: Unfortunate, indeed! But I suppose you have done all in your power for him, honest Moses?

Mos: Yes, he knows that. This very evening I was to have brought him a gentleman from the city, who doesn't know him, and will, I believe, advance him some money.

Sir Pet: What, one Charles has never had money from before?

Mos: Yes; Mr. Premium, of Crutched Friars—formerly a broker.

Sir Pet: Egad, Sir Oliver, a thought strikes me!—Charles, you say, doesn't know Mr. Premium?

Mos: Not at all.

Sir Pet: Now then, Sir Oliver, you may have a better opportunity of satisfying yourself than by an old romancing tale of a poor relation;—go with my friend Moses, and represent Mr. *Premium,* and then, I'll answer for't, you will see your nephew in all his glory.

Sir Oliv: Egad, I like this idea better than the other, and I may visit *Joseph* afterwards, as old *Stanley.*

Sir Pet: True—so you may.

Row: Well, this is taking Charles rather at a disadvantage, to be sure. However, Moses—you understand Sir Peter, and will be faithful?

Mos: You may depend upon me,—this is near the time I was to have gone.

Sir Oliv: I'll accompany you as soon as you please, Moses; but hold! I have forgot one thing—how the plague shall I be able to pass for a Jew?

Mos: There's no need—the principal is Christian.

Sir Oliv: Is he?—I'm sorry to hear

it—but, then again, an't I rather too smartly dressed to look like a money-lender?

Sir Pet: Not at all; 'twould not be out of character, if you went in your own carriage—would it, Moses?

Mos: Not in the least.

Sir Oliv: Well, but how must I talk? there's certainly some cant of usury, and mode of treating, that I ought to know.

Sir Pet: Oh, there's not much to learn—the great point, as I take it, is to be exorbitant enough in your demands—hey, Moses?

Mos: Yes, that's a very great point.

Sir Oliv: I'll answer for't I'll not be wanting in that. I'll ask him eight or ten per cent on the loan, at least.

Mos: If you ask him no more than that, you'll be discovered immediately.

Sir Oliv: Hey! what the plague! how much then?

Mos: That depends upon the circumstances. If he appears not very anxious for the supply, you should require only forty or fifty per cent; but if you find him in great distress, and want the moneys very bad—you may ask double.

Sir Pet: A good honest trade you're learning, Sir Oliver!

Sir Oliv: Truly I think so—and not unprofitable.

Mos: Then, you know, you haven't the moneys yourself, but are forced to borrow them for him of a friend.

Sir Oliv: Oh! I borrow it of a friend, do I?

Mos: Yes, and your friend is an unconscionable dog, but you can't help it.

Sir Oliv: My friend is an unconscionable dog, is he?

Mos: Yes, and he himself has not the moneys by him—but is forced to sell stock at a great loss.

Sir Oliv: He is forced to sell stock, is he, at a great loss, is he? Well, that's very kind of him.

Sir Pet: I'faith, Sir Oliver—Mr. Premium, I mean—you'll soon be master of the trade. But, Moses! wouldn't you have him run out a little against the Annuity Bill? That would be in character, I should think.

Mos: Very much.

Row: And lament that a young man now must be at years of discretion before he is suffered to ruin himself?

Mos: Aye, great pity!

Sir Pet: And abuse the public for allowing merit to an act whose only object is to snatch misfortune and imprudence from the rapacious relief of usury, and give the minor a chance of inheriting his estate without being undone by coming into possession.

Sir Oliv: So, so—Moses shall give me further instructions as we go together.

Sir Pet: You will not have much time, for your nephew lives hard by.

Sir Oliv: Oh, never fear! my tutor appears so able, that though Charles lived in the next street, it must be my own fault if I am not a complete rogue before I turn the corner.

[*Exeunt* SIR OLIVER *and* MOSES.]

Sir Pet: So now I think Sir Oliver will be convinced;—you are partial, Rowley, and would have prepared Charles for the other plot.

Row: No, upon my word, Sir Peter.

Sir Pet: Well, go bring me this Snake, and I'll hear what he has to say presently.—I see Maria, and want to speak with her.—[*Exit* ROWLEY.] I should be glad to be convinced my suspicions of Lady Teazle and Charles were unjust. I have never yet opened my mind on this subject to my friend *Joseph*—I'm determined I will do it—*he* will give me his opinion sincerely.

[*Enter* MARIA.]

So, child, has Mr. Surface returned with you?

Maria: No, sir—he was engaged.

Sir Pet: Well, Maria, do you not reflect, the more you converse with that amiable young man, what return his partiality for you deserves?

Maria: Indeed, Sir Peter, your frequent importunity on this subject distresses me extremely—you compel me to declare, that I know no man who has ever paid me a particular attention whom I would not prefer to Mr. Surface.

Sir Pet: So—here's perverseness! No, no, Maria, 'tis Charles only whom you would prefer—'tis evident his vices and follies have won your heart.

Maria: This is unkind, sir—you know I have obeyed you in neither seeing nor corresponding with him; I have heard enough to convince me that he is unworthy my regard. Yet I cannot think it culpable, if, while my understanding severely condemns his vices, my heart suggests some pity for his distresses.

Sir Pet: Well, well, pity him as much as you please, but give your heart and hand to a worthier object.

Maria: Never to his brother!

Sir Pet: Go, perverse and obstinate! But take care, madam; you have never yet known what the authority of a guardian is—don't compel me to inform you of it.

Maria: I can only say, you shall not have *just* reason. 'Tis true, by my father's will, I am for a short period bound to regard you as his substitute, but must cease to think you so, when you would compel me to be miserable.

[*Exit* MARIA.]

Sir Pet: Was ever man so crossed as I am! everything conspiring to fret me!—I had not been involved in matrimony a fortnight, before her father, a hale and hearty man, died—on purpose, I believe, for the pleasure of plaguing me with the care of his daughter. But here comes my helpmate! She appears in great good humor. How happy I should be if I could tease her into loving me, though but a little!

[*Enter* LADY TEAZLE.]

Lady Teaz: Lud! Sir Peter, I hope you haven't been quarreling with Maria—it isn't using me well to be ill humored when I am not by.

Sir Pet: Ah, Lady Teazle, you might have the power to make me good humored at all times.

Lady Teaz: I am sure I wish I had—for I want you to be a charming sweet temper at this moment. Do be good humored now, and let me have two hundred pounds, will you?

Sir Pet: Two hundred pounds! what, an't I to be in a good humor without paying for it! But speak to me thus, and i'faith there's nothing I could refuse you. You shall have it; but seal me a bond for the repayment.

Lady Teaz: O, no—there—my note of hand will do as well.

Sir Pet (*kissing her hand*). And you shall no longer reproach me with not giving you an independent settlement,—I mean shortly to surprise you; but shall we always live thus, hey?

Lady Teaz: If you please. I'm sure I don't care how soon we leave off quarrelling, provided you'll own *you* were tired first.

Sir Pet: Well—then let our future contest be, who shall be most obliging.

Lady Teaz: I assure you, Sir Peter,

good nature becomes you. You look now as you did before we were married!—when you used to walk with me under the elms, and tell me stories of what a gallant you were in your youth, and chuck me under the chin, you would, and ask me if I thought I could love an old fellow, who would deny me nothing—didn't you?

Sir Pet: Yes, yes, and you were as kind and attentive.

Lady Teaz: Aye, so I was, and would always take your part, when my acquaintance used to abuse you, and turn you into ridicule.

Sir Pet: Indeed!

Lady Teaz: Aye, and when my cousin Sophy has called you a stiff, peevish old bachelor, and laughed at me for thinking of marrying one who might be my father, I have always defended you—and said, I didn't think you so ugly by any means, and that I dared say you'd make a very good sort of a husband.

Sir Pet: And you prophesied right—and we shall certainly now be the happiest couple——

Lady Teaz: And never differ again!

Sir Pet: No, never!—though at the same time, indeed, my dear Lady Teazle, you must watch your temper very narrowly; for in all our little quarrels, my dear, if you recollect, my love, you always began first.

Lady Teaz: I beg your pardon, my dear Sir Peter: indeed, you always gave the provocation.

Sir Pet: Now, see, my angel! take care—*contradicting* isn't the way to keep friends.

Lady Teaz: Then, don't *you* begin it, my love!

Sir Pet: There, now! you—you are going on—you don't perceive, my life, that you are just doing the very thing which you know always makes me angry.

Lady Teaz: Nay, you know if you will be angry without any reason——

Sir Pet: There now! you want to quarrel again.

Lady Teaz: No, I am sure I don't—but, if you will be so peevish——

Sir Pet: There now! who begins first?

Lady Teaz: Why, you, to be sure. I said nothing—but there's no bearing your temper.

Sir Pet: No, no, madam, the fault's in your own temper.

Lady Teaz: Aye, you are just what my cousin Sophy said you would be.

Sir Pet: Your cousin Sophy is a forward, impertinent gipsy.

Lady Teaz: You are a great bear, I'm sure, to abuse my relations.

Sir Pet: Now may all the plagues of marriage be doubled on me, if ever I try to be friends with you any more!

Lady Teaz: So much the better.

Sir Pet: No, no, madam; 'tis evident you never cared a pin for me, and I was a madman to marry you—a pert, rural coquette, that had refused half the honest squires in the neighborhood!

Lady Teaz: And I am sure I was a fool to marry you—an old dangling bachelor, who was single at fifty, only because he never could meet with any one who would have him.

Sir Pet: Aye, aye, madam; but you were pleased enough to listen to me—*you* never had such an offer before.

Lady Teaz: No! didn't I refuse Sir Twivy Tarrier, who everybody said would have been a better match—for his estate is just as good as yours—and he has broke his neck since we have been married.

Sir Pet: I have done with you, madam! You are an unfeeling, ungrateful—but there's an end of everything. I believe you capable of anything that's bad. Yes, madam, I now believe the reports relative to you and Charles, madam—yes, madam, you and Charles—are not without grounds——

Lady Teaz: Take care, Sir Peter! you had better not insinuate any such thing! I'll not be suspected *without cause,* I promise you.

Sir Pet: Very well, madam! very well! a separate maintenance as soon as you please. Yes, madam, or a divorce! I'll make an example of myself for the benefit of all old bachelors. Let us separate, madam.

Lady Teaz: Agreed! agreed! And now, my dear Sir Peter, we are of a mind once more, we may be the *happiest couple,* and *never differ again,* you know: ha! ha! Well, you are going to be in a passion, I see, and I shall only interrupt you—so, bye! bye!

[*Exit.*]

Sir Pet: Plagues and tortures! can't I make her angry neither? Oh, I am the miserablest fellow! But I'll not bear her presuming to keep her temper—no! she may break my heart, but she shan't keep her temper.

[*Exit.*]

SCENE II

CHARLES'S *house*

[*Enter* TRIP, MOSES, *and* SIR OLIVER SURFACE.]

Trip: Here, Master Moses! if you'll stay a moment, I'll try whether—what's the gentleman's name?

Sir Oliv: Mr. Moses, what *is* my name? (*Aside.*)

Mos: Mr. Premium.

Trip: Premium—very well.

[*Exit* TRIP, *taking snuff.*]

Sir Oliv: To judge by the servants one wouldn't believe the master was ruined. But what!—sure, this was my brother's house?

Mos: Yes, sir; Mr. Charles bought it of Mr. Joseph, with the furniture, pictures, &c., just as the old gentleman left it—Sir Peter thought it a great piece of extravagance in him.

Sir Oliv: In my mind, the other's economy in *selling* it to him was more reprehensible by half.

[*Re-enter* TRIP.]

Trip: My master says you must wait, gentlemen; he has company, and can't speak with you yet.

Sir Oliv: If he knew *who* it was wanted to see him, perhaps he wouldn't have sent such a message?

Trip: Yes, yes, sir; he knows *you* are here—I didn't forget little Premium—no, no, no.

Sir Oliv: Very well—and I pray, sir, what may be your name?

Trip: Trip, sir—my name is Trip, at your service.

Sir Oliv: Well, then, Mr. Trip, you have a pleasant sort of a place here, I guess.

Trip: Why, yes—here are three or four of us pass out time agreeably enough; but then our wages are sometimes a little in arrear—and not very great either—but fifty pounds a year, and find our own bags and bouquets.

Sir Oliv (*aside*). Bags and bouquets! halters and bastinadoes!

Trip: But *à propos,* Moses, have you been able to get me that little bill discounted?

Sir Oliv (*aside*). Wants to raise money, too!—mercy on me! Has his distresses, I warrant, like a lord,—and affects creditors and duns.

Mos: 'Twas not to be done, indeed, Mr. Trip. (*Gives the note.*)

Trip: Good lack, you surprise me! My friend *Brush* has indorsed it, and I thought when he put his mark on the back of a bill 'twas as good as cash.

Mos: No, 'twouldn't do.

Trip: A small sum—but twenty pounds. Hark'ee, Moses, do you think you couldn't get it me by way of annuity?

Sir Oliv (*aside*). An annuity! ha! ha! ha! a footman raise money by way of annuity! Well done, luxury, egad!

Mos: But you must insure your place.

Trip: Oh, with all my heart! I'll insure my place, and my life too, if you please.

Sir Oliv (*aside*). It's more than I would your neck.

Trip: But then, Moses, it must be done before this d—d register takes place—one wouldn't like to have one's name made public, you know.

Mos: No, certainly. But is there nothing you could deposit?

Trip: Why, nothing capital of my master's wardrobe has dropped lately; but I could give you a mortgage on some of his winter clothes, with equity of redemption before November—or you shall have the reversion of the French velvet, or a post-obit on the blue and silver;—these, I should think, Moses, with a few pair of point ruffles, as a collateral security—hey, my little fellow?

Mos: Well, well.

[*Bell rings.*]

Trip: Gad, I heard the bell! I believe, gentlemen, I can now introduce you. Don't forget the annuity, little Moses! This way, gentlemen, insure my place, you know.

Sir Oliv (*aside*). If the man be a shadow of his master, this is the temple of dissipation indeed!

[*Exeunt.*]

SCENE III

[CHARLES SURFACE, CARELESS, &c., &c. *at a table with wine, &c.*]

Chas. Surf: 'Fore heaven, 'tis true!—there's the great degeneracy of the age. Many of our acquaintance have taste, spirit, and politeness; but, plague on't, they won't drink.

Care: It is so, indeed, Charles! they give in to all the substantial luxuries of the table, and abstain from nothing but wine and wit.

Chas. Surf: Oh, certainly society suffers by it intolerably! for now, instead of the social spirit of raillery that used to mantle over a glass of bright Burgundy, their conversation is become just like the Spa-water they drink, which has all the pertness and flatulence of champagne, without its spirit or flavor.

1 Gent: But what are *they* to do who love play better than wine?

Care: True, there's Harry diets himself for gaming, and is now under a hazard regimen.

Chas. Surf: Then he'll have the worst of it. What! you wouldn't train a horse for the course by keeping him from corn! For my part, egad, I am now never so successful as when I am a little merry—let me throw on a bottle of champagne, and

I never lose—at least I never feel my losses, which is exactly the same thing.

2 Gent: Aye, that I believe.

Chas. Surf: And, then, what man can pretend to be a believer in love, who is an abjurer of wine? 'Tis the test by which the lover knows his own heart. Fill a dozen bumpers to a dozen beauties, and she that floats at top is the maid that has bewitched you.

Care: Now then, Charles, be honest, and give us your real favorite.

Chas. Surf: Why, I have withheld her only in compassion to you. If I toast her, you must give a round of her peers—which is impossible—on earth.

Care: Oh, then we'll find some canonised vestals or heathen goddesses that will do, I warrant!

Chas. Surf: Here then, bumpers, you rogues! bumpers! Maria! Maria—(*Drink.*)

1 Gent: Maria who?

Chas Surf: O, damn the surname!—'tis too formal to be registered in Love's calendar—but now, Sir Toby Bumper, beware—we must have beauty superlative.

Care: Nay, never study, Sir Toby: we'll stand to the toast, though your mistress should want an eye—and you know you have a song will excuse you.

Sir Toby: Egad, so I have! and I'll give him the song instead of the lady.

[*Sings.*]

SONG AND CHORUS

Here's to the maiden of bashful fifteen;
Here's to the widow of fifty;
Here's to the flaunting extravagant quean,
And here's to the housewife that's thrifty.
[*Chorus.*] Let the toast pass—
Drink to the lass—
I'll warrant she'll prove an excuse for the glass.

Here's to the charmer whose dimples we prize;
Now to the maid who has none, sir;
Here's to the girl with a pair of blue eyes,
And here's to the nymph with but one, sir.
[*Chorus.*] Let the toast pass, &c.

Here's to the maid with a bosom of snow:
Now to *her* that's as brown as a berry:
Here's to the wife with a face full of woe,
And now for the damsel that's merry.
[*Chorus.*] Let the toast pass, &c.

For let 'em be clumsy, or let 'em be slim,
Young or ancient, I care not a feather:
So fill a pint bumper quite up to the brim,
—And let us e'en toast 'em together.
[*Chorus.*] Let the toast pass, &c.

All: Bravo! Bravo!

[*Enter* TRIP, *and whispers* CHARLES SURFACE.]

Chas. Surf: Gentlemen, you must excuse me a little.—Careless, take the chair, will you?

Care: Nay, prithee, Charles, what now? This is one of your peerless beauties, I suppose, has dropped in by chance?

Chas. Surf: No, faith! To tell you the truth, 'tis a Jew and a broker, who are come by appointment.

Care: Oh, damn it! let's have the Jew in—

1 Gent: Aye, and the broker too, by all means.

2 Gent: Yes, yes, the Jew and the broker.

Chas. Surf: Egad, with all my heart! —Trip bid the gentlemen walk in.—

[*Exit* TRIP.]

Though there's one of them a stranger, I can tell you.

Care: Charles, let us give them some generous Burgundy, and perhaps they'll grow conscientious.

Chas. Surf: Oh, hang 'em, no! wine does but draw forth a man's *natural* qualities; and to make *them* drink would only be to whet their knavery.

[*Enter* TRIP, SIR OLIVER SURFACE, *and* MOSES.]

Chas. Surf: So, honest Moses; walk in, pray, Mr. Premium—that's the gentleman's name, isn't it, Moses?

Mos: Yes, sir.

Chas. Surf: Set chairs, Trip.—Sit down, Mr. Premium.—Glasses, Trip.—Sit down, Moses.—Come, Mr. Premium, I'll give you a sentiment; here's 'Success to usury!'—Moses, fill the gentleman a bumper.

Mos: Success to usury!

Care: Right, Moses—usury is prudence and industry, and deserves to succeed.

Sir Oliv: Then here's—All the success it deserves!

Care: No, no, that won't do! Mr. Premium, you have demurred to the toast, and must drink it in a pint bumper.

1 Gent: A pint bumper, at least.

Mos: Oh, pray, sir, consider—Mr. Premium's a gentleman.

Care: And therefore loves good wine.

2 Gent: Give Moses a quart glass—this is mutiny, and a high contempt of the chair.

Care: Here, now for't! I'll see justice done, to the last drop of my bottle.

Sir Oliv: Nay, pray, gentlemen—I did not expect this usage.

Chas. Surf: No, hang it, Careless, you shan't; Mr. Premium's a stranger.

Sir Oliv (*aside*). Odd! I wish I was well out of this company.

Care: Plague on 'em then! if they won't drink, we'll not sit down with 'em. Come, Harry, the dice are in the next room.—Charles, you'll join us—when you have finished your business with these gentlemen?

Chas. Surf: I will! I will!—

[*Exeunt Gentlemen.*]

Careless!

Care: Well!

Chas. Surf: Perhaps I may want *you.*

Care: Oh, you know I am always ready—word, note, or bond, 'tis all the same to me.

[*Exit.*]

Mos: Sir, this is Mr. Premium, a gentleman of the strictest honor and secrecy; and always performs what he undertakes. Mr. Premium, this is——

Chas. Surf: Pshaw! have done! Sir, my friend Moses is a very honest fellow, but a little slow at expression; he'll be an hour giving us our titles. Mr. Premium, the plain state of the matter is this—I am an extravagant young fellow who want[s] money to borrow; you I take to be a prudent old fellow, who ha[s] got money to lend. I am blockhead enough to give fifty per cent sooner than not have it; and you, I presume, are rogue enough to take a hundred if you could get it. Now, sir, you see we are acquainted at once, and may proceed to business without farther ceremony.

Sir Oliv: Exceeding frank, upon my word. I see, sir, you are not a man of many compliments.

Chas. Surf: Oh, no, sir! plain dealing in business I always think best.

Sir Oliv: Sir, I like you the better for't. However, you are mistaken in one thing—I have no money to lend, but I believe I could procure some of a friend; but then he's an unconscionable dog—isn't he, Moses? And must sell stock to accommodate you—mustn't he, Moses?

Mos: Yes, indeed! You know I always speak the truth, and scorn to tell a lie!

Chas. Surf: Right! People that expect truth generally do. But these are trifles, Mr. Premium. What! I know money isn't to be bought without paying for't!

Sir Oliv: Well, but what security could you give? You have no land, I suppose?

Chas. Surf: Not a mole-hill, nor a twig, but what's in beau-pots out at the window!

Sir Oliv: Nor any stock, I presume?

Chas. Surf: Nothing but live stock—and that's only a few pointers and ponies. But pray, Mr. Premium, are you acquainted at all with any of my connections?

Sir Oliv: Why, to say truth, I am.

Chas. Surf: Then you must know that I have a devilish rich uncle in the East Indies, Sir *Oliver Surface,* from whom I have the greatest expectations.

Sir Oliv: That you have a wealthy uncle, I have heard—but how your expectations will turn out is more, I believe, than you can tell.

Chas. Surf: Oh, no!—there can be no doubt—they tell me I'm a prodigious favorite—and that he talks of leaving me everything.

Sir Oliv: Indeed! this is the first I've heard on't.

Chas. Surf: Yes, yes, 'tis just so.—Moses knows 'tis true; don't you, Moses?

Mos: Oh, yes! I'll swear to't.

Sir Oliv (*aside*). Egad, they'll persuade me presently I'm at Bengal.

Chas. Surf: Now I propose, Mr. Premium, if it's agreeable to you, a post-obit on Sir Oliver's life; though at the same time the old fellow has been so liberal to me that I give you my word I should be very sorry to hear anything had happened to him.

Sir Oliv: Not more than *I* should, I assure you. But the bond you mention happens to be just the worst security you could offer me—for I might live to a hundred and never recover the principal.

Chas. Surf: Oh, yes, you would!—the moment Sir Oliver dies, you know, you'd come on me for the money.

Sir Oliv: Then I believe I should be the most unwelcome dun you ever had in your life.

Chas. Surf: What! I suppose you are afraid now that Sir Oliver is too good a life?

Sir Oliv: No, indeed I am not—though I have heard he is as hale and healthy as any man of his years in Christendom.

Chas. Surf: There again you are misinformed. No, no, the climate has hurt him considerably, poor uncle Oliver. Yes, he breaks apace, I'm told—and so much altered lately that his nearest relations don't know him.

Sir Oliv: No! Ha! ha! ha! so much altered lately that his relations don't know him! Ha! ha! ha! that's droll, egad—ha! ha! ha!

Chas. Surf: Ha! ha!—you're glad to hear that, little Premium.

Sir Oliv: No, no, I'm not.

Chas Surf: Yes, yes, you are—ha! ha! ha!—you know that mends your chance.

Sir Oliv: But I'm told Sir Oliver is coming over—nay, some say he is actually arrived.

Chas. Surf: Pshaw! sure I must know better than you whether he's come or not. No, no, rely on't, he is at this moment at Calcutta, isn't he, Moses?

Mos: Oh, yes, certainly.

Sir Oliv: Very true, as you say, you must know better than I, though I have it from pretty good authority—haven't I, Moses?

Mos: Yes, most undoubted!

Sir Oliv: But, sir, as I understand you want a few hundreds immediately, is there nothing you would dispose of?

Chas. Surf: How do you mean?

Sir Oliv: For instance, now—I have heard—that your father left behind him a great quantity of massy old plate.

Chas. Surf: O lud! that's gone long ago—Moses can tell you how better than I can.

Sir Oliv: Good lack! all the family race-cups and corporation-bowls! (*Aside.*) —Then it was also supposed that his library was one of the most valuable and complete.

Chas. Surf: Yes, yes, so it was—vastly too much so for a private gentleman—for my part, I was always of a communicative disposition, so I thought it a shame to keep so much knowledge to myself.

Sir Oliv (*aside*). Mercy on me! learning that had run in the family like an heirloom!—(*Aloud.*) Pray, what are become of the books?

Chas. Surf: You must inquire of the auctioneer, Master Premium, for I don't believe even Moses can direct you there.

Mos: I never meddle with books.

Sir Oliv: So, so, nothing of the family property left, I suppose?

Chas. Surf: Not much, indeed; unless you have a mind to the family pictures. I have got a room full of ancestors above —and if you have a taste for old paintings, egad, you shall have 'em a bargain!

Sir Oliv: Hey! and the devil! sure, you wouldn't sell your forefathers, would you?

Chas. Surf: Every man of'em, to the best bidder.

Sir Oliv: What! your great-uncles and aunts?

Chas. Surf: Aye, and my great-grandfathers and grandmothers too.

Sir Oliv: Now I give him up!—(*Aside.*)—What the plague, have you no bowels for your own kindred? Odd's life! do you take me for Shylock in the play, that you would raise money of me on your own flesh and blood?

Chas. Surf: Nay, my little broker, don't be angry: what need *you* care, if you have your money's worth?

Sir Oliv: Well, I'll be the purchaser—I think I can dispose of the family.—(*Aside.*) Oh, I'll never forgive him this! never!

[*Enter* CARELESS.]

Care: Come, Charles, what keeps you?

Chas. Surf: I can't come yet. I'faith! we are going to have a sale above—here's little Premium will buy all my ancestors!

Care: Oh, burn your ancestors!

Chas. Surf: No, he may do that afterwards, if he pleases. Stay, Careless, we want you; egad, you shall be auctioneer—so come along with us.

Care: Oh, have with you, if that's the case.—I can handle a hammer as well as a dice box!

Sir Oliv (*aside*). Oh, the profligates!

Chas. Surf: Come, Moses, you shall be appraiser, if we want one.—Gad's life, little Premium, you don't seem to like the business.

Sir Oliv: Oh, yes, I do, vastly! Ha! ha! yes, yes, I think it a rare joke to sell one's family by auction—ha! ha!—(*Aside.*) Oh, the prodigal!

Chas. Surf: To be sure! when a man wants money, where the plague should he get assistance, if he can't make free with his own relations?

[*Exeunt.*]

ACT IV

SCENE I

Picture-room at CHARLES'S

[*Enter* CHARLES SURFACE, SIR OLIVER SURFACE, MOSES, *and* CARELESS.]

Chas. Surf: Walk in, gentlemen, pray walk in!—here they are, the family of the Surfaces, up to the Conquest.

Sir Oliv: And, in my opinion, a goodly collection.

Chas. Surf: Aye, aye, these are done in true spirit of portrait-painting—no volunteer grace or expression—not like the works of your modern Raphael, who gives you the strongest resemblance, yet contrives to make your own portrait independent of you; so that you may sink the original and not hurt the picture. No, no; the merit of these is the inveterate likeness—all stiff and awkward as the originals, and like nothing in human nature beside!

Sir Oliv: Ah! we shall never see such figures of men again.

Chas. Surf: I hope not. Well, you see, Master Premium, what a domestic character I am—here I sit of an evening surrounded by my family. But come, get to your pulpit, Mr. Auctioneer—here's an old gouty chair of my grandfather's will answer the puprose.

Care: Aye, aye, this will do. But, Charles, I have ne'er a hammer; and what's an auctioneer without his hammer?

Chas. Surf: Egad, that's true. What parchment have we here? (*Take down a roll.*) *'Richard, heir to Thomas'*—our genealogy in full. Here, Careless, you shall have no common bit of mahogany—here's the family tree for you, you rogue—this shall be your hammer, and now you may knock down my ancestors with their own pedigree.

Sir Oliv (*aside*). What an unnatural rogue!—an *ex post facto* parricide!

Care: Yes, yes, here's a list of your generation indeed;—faith, Charles, this is the most convenient thing you could have found for the business, for 'twill serve not only as a hammer, but a catalogue into the bargain.—But come, begin—A-going, a-going, a-going!

Chas. Surf: Bravo, Careless! Well, here's my great uncle, Sir Richard Raviline, a marvellous good general in his day, I assure you. He served in all the Duke of Marlborough's wars, and got that cut over his eye at the battle of Malplaquet. What say you, Mr. Premium? look at him—there's a hero for you! not cut out of his feathers, as your modern clipped captains are, but enveloped in wig and regimentals, as a general should be. What do you bid?

Mos: Mr. Premium would have you speak.

Chas. Surf: Why, then, he shall have him for ten pounds, and I am sure that's not dear for a staff-officer.

Sir Oliv (*aside*). Heaven deliver me! his famous uncle Richard for ten pounds! —Very well, sir, I take him at that.

Chas. Surf: Careless, knock down my uncle Richard.—Here, now, is a maiden sister of his, my great-aunt Deborah, done by Kneller, thought to be in his best manner, and a very formidable likeness. There she is, you see, a shepherdress feeding her flock. You shall have her for five pounds ten—the sheep are worth the money.

Sir Oliv (*aside*). Ah! poor Deborah! a woman who set such a value on herself! —Five pound ten—she's mine.

Chas. Surf: Knock down my aunt Deborah! Here, now, are two that were a sort of cousins of theirs.—You see, Moses, these pictures were done some time ago, when beaux wore wigs, and the ladies wore their own hair.

Sir Oliv: Yes, truly, head-dresses appear to have been a little lower in those days.

Chas. Surf: Well, take that couple for the same.

Mos: 'Tis [a] good bargain.

Chas. Surf: Careless!—This, now, is a grandfather of my mother's, a learned judge, well known on the western circuit. —What do you rate him at, Moses?

Mos: Four guineas.

Chas. Surf: Four guineas! Gad's life, you don't bid me the price of his wig.—Mr. Premium, *you* have more respect for the woolsack; do let us knock his lordship down at fifteen.

Sir Oliv: By all means.

Care: Gone!

Chas. Surf: And there are two brothers of his, William and Walter Blunt, Esquires, both members of Parliament, and noted speakers; and, what's very extraordinary, I believe this is the first time they were ever bought and sold.

Sir Oliv: That's very extraordinary, indeed! I'll take them at your own price, for the honor of Parliament.

Care: Well said, little Premium! I'll knock 'em down at forty.

Chas. Surf: Here's a jolly fellow—I don't know what relation, but he was mayor of Manchester; take him at eight pounds.

Sir Oliv: No, no—six will do for the mayor.

Chas. Surf: Come, make it guineas, and I'll throw you the two alderman there into the bargain.

Sir Oliv: They're mine.

Chas. Surf: Careless, knock down the mayor and aldermen. But, plague on't! we shall be all day retailing in this manner; do let us deal wholesale—what say you, little Premium? Give me three hundred pounds for the rest of the family in the lump.

Care: Aye, aye, that will be the best way.

Sir Oliv: Well, well, anything to accommodate you; they are mine. But there is one portrait which you have always passed over.

Care: What, that ill-looking little fellow over the settee?

Sir Oliv: Yes, sir, I mean that; though I don't think him so ill-looking a little fellow, by any means.

Chas. Surf: What, that? Oh, that's my uncle Oliver! 'Twas done before he went to India.

Care: Your uncle Oliver! Gad, then you'll never be friends, Charles. That, now, to me, is as stern a looking rogue as ever I saw—an unforgiving eye, and a damned disinheriting countenance! an inveterate knave, depend on't. Don't you think so, little Premium?

Sir Oliv: Upon my soul, sir, I do not; I think it is as honest a looking face as any in the room, dead or alive. But I suppose your uncle Oliver goes with the rest of the lumber?

Chas. Surf: No, hang it! I'll not part with poor Noll. The old fellow has been very good to me, and, egad, I'll keep his picture while I've a room to put it in.

Sir Oliv: The rogue's my nephew after all! (*Aside.*)—But, sir, I have somehow taken a fancy to that picture.

Chas. Surf: I'm sorry for't, for you certainly will not have it. Oons! haven't you got enough of 'em?

Sir Oliv: I forgive him everything! (*Aside.*)—But, sir, when I take a whim in my head, I don't value money. I'll give you as much for that as for all the rest.

Chas. Surf: Don't tease me, master broker; I tell you I'll not part with it, and there's an end on't.

Sir Oliv: How like his father the dog is!—(*Aloud.*) Well, well, I have done. —I did not perceive it before, but I think I never saw such a resemblance.—Well, sir—here is a draught for your sum.

Chas. Surf: Why, 'tis for eight hundred pounds!

Sir Oliv: You will not let Sir Oliver go?

Chas. Surf: Zounds! no! I tell you, once more.

Sir Oliv: Then never mind the difference; we'll balance another time. But give me your hand on the bargain; you are an honest fellow, Charles—I beg pardon, sir, for being so free.—Come, Moses.

Chas. Surf: Egad, this is a whimsical old fellow!—but hark'ee, Premium, you'll prepare lodgings for these gentlemen.

Sir Oliv: Yes, yes, I'll send for them in a day or two.

Chas. Surf: But hold—do now—send a genteel conveyance for them, for, I assure you, they were most of them used to ride in their own carriages.

Sir Oliv: I will, I will, for all but—Oliver.

Chas. Surf: Aye, all but the little honest nabob.

Sir Oliv: You're fixed on that?

Chas. Surf: Peremptorily.

Sir Oliv: A dear extravagant rogue! —Good day!—Come, Moses,—Let me hear now who dares call him profligate!

[*Exeunt* SIR OLIVER *and* MOSES.]

Care: Why, this is the oddest genius of the sort I ever saw!

Chas. Surf: Egad, he's the prince of brokers, I think. I wonder how the devil Moses got acquainted with so honest a fellow.—Ha! here's Rowley.—Do, Careless, say I'll join the company in a moment.

Care: I will—but don't let that old blockhead persuade you to squander any of that money on old musty debts, or any such nonsense; for tradesmen, Charles, are the most exorbitant fellows!

Chas. Surf: Very true, and paying them is only encouraging them.

Care: Nothing else.

Chas. Surf: Aye, aye, never fear.—

[*Exit* CARELESS.]

So! this was an odd old fellow, indeed; Let me see, two-thirds of this is mine by right—five hundred and thirty pounds. 'Fore heaven! I find one's ancestors are more valuable relations than I took 'em for!—Ladies and gentlemen, your most obedient and very grateful humble servant.

[*Enter* ROWLEY.]

Ha! old Rowley! egad, you are just come in time to take leave of your old acquaintance.

Row: Yes, I heard they were going. But I wonder you can have such spirits under so many distresses.

Chas. Surf: Why, there's the point—my distresses are so many, that I can't afford to part with my spirits; but I shall be rich and splenetic, all in good time. However, I suppose you are surprised that I am not more sorrowful at parting with so many near relations; to be sure, 'tis very affecting; but, rot 'em, you see they never move a muscle, so why should I?

Row: There's no making you serious a moment.

Chas. Surf: Yes, faith: I am so now. Here, my honest Rowley, here, get me this changed, and take a hundred pounds of it immediately to old Stanley.

Row: A hundred pounds! Consider only——

Chas. Surf: Gad's life, don't talk about it! poor Stanley's wants are pressing, and, if you don't make haste, we shall have some one call that has a better right to the money.

Row: Ah! there's the point! I never will cease dunning you with the old proverb——

Chas. Surf: 'Be *just* before you're *generous*,' hey!—Why, so I would if I could; but Justice is an old lame hobbling beldame, and I can't get her to keep pace with Generosity, for the soul of me.

Row: Yet, Charles, believe me, one hour's reflection——

Chas. Surf: Aye, aye, it's all very true; but, hark'ee, Rowley, while I have, by heaven I'll give—so, damn your economy! and now for hazard.

[*Exit.*]

SCENE II

The parlor

[*Enter* SIR OLIVER SURFACE *and* MOSES.]

Mos: Well, sir, I think, as Sir Peter said, you have seen Mr. Charles in high glory; 'tis great pity he's so extravagant.

Sir Oliv: True, but he wouldn't sell my picture.

Mos: And loves wine and women so much.

Sir Oliv: But he wouldn't sell my picture!

Mos: And game[s] so deep.

Sir Oliv: But he wouldn't sell my picture. Oh, here's Rowley.

[*Enter* ROWLEY.]

Row: So, Sir Oliver, I find you have made a purchase——

Sir Oliv: Yes, yes, our young rake has parted with his ancestors like old tapestry.

Row: And here has he commissioned me to redeliver you part of the purchase-money—I mean, though, in your necessitous character of old Stanley.

Mos: Ah! there is the pity of all: he is so damned charitable.

Row: And I left a hosier and two tailors in the hall, who, I'm sure, won't be paid, and this hundred would satisfy 'em.

Sir Oliv: Well, well, I'll pay his debts—and his benevolence too; but now I am no more a broker, and you shall introduce me to the elder brother as old Stanley.

Row: Not yet awhile; Sir Peter, I know, means to call there about this time.

[*Enter* TRIP.]

Trip: O gentlemen, I beg pardon for not showing you out; this way—Moses, a word.

[*Exeunt* TRIP *and* MOSES.]

Sir Oliv: There's a fellow for you! Would you believe it, that puppy intercepted the Jew on our coming, and wanted to raise money before he got to his master!

Row: Indeed!

Sir Oliv: Yes, they are now planning an annuity business. Ah, Master Rowley, in my days, servants were content with the follies of their masters, when they were worn a little threadbare—but now they have their vices, like their birthday clothes, with the gloss on.

[*Exeunt.*]

SCENE III

A library in JOSEPH SURFACE'S *house*

[JOSEPH SURFACE *and* SERVANT.]

Jos. Surf: No letter from Lady Teazle?

Serv: No, sir.

Jos. Surf (*Aside*). I am surprised she hasn't sent, if she is prevented from coming. Sir Peter certainly does not suspect me. Yet I wish I may not lose the heiress, through the scrape I have drawn myself in with the wife; however, Charles's imprudence and bad character are great points in my favor. (*Knocking.*)

Serv: Sir, I believe that must be Lady Teazle.

Jos. Surf: Hold! See whether it is or not, before you go to the door—I have a particular message for you, if it should be my brother.

Serv: 'Tis her ladyship, sir; she always leaves her chair at the milliner's in the next street.

Jos. Surf: Stay, stay—draw that screen before the window—that will do;—my opposite neighbor is a maiden lady of so curious a temper.—(*Servant draws the screen, and exits.*) I have a difficult hand to play in this affair. Lady Teazle has lately suspected my views on Maria; but she must by no means be let into that secret,—at least, not till I have her more in my power.

[*Enter* LADY TEAZLE.]

Lady Teaz: What, sentiment in soliloquy! Have you been very impatient now? O lud! don't pretend to look grave. I vow I couldn't come before.

Jos. Surf: O madam, punctuality is a species of constancy, a very unfashionable quality in a lady.

Lady Teaz: Upon my word, you ought to pity me. Do you know that Sir Peter is grown so ill-tempered to me of late, and so jealous of Charles too—that's the best of the story, isn't it?

Jos. Surf (*aside*). I am glad my scandalous friends keep that up.

Lady Teaz: I am sure I wish he would let Maria marry him, and then perhaps he would be convinced; don't you, Mr. Surface?

Jos. Surf (*aside*). Indeed I do not.—Oh, certainly I do! for then my dear Lady Teazle would also be convinced how wrong her suspicions were of my having any design on the silly girl.

Lady Teaz: Well, well, I'm inclined to believe you. But isn't it provoking, to have the most ill-natured things said to one? And there's my friend Lady Sneerwell has circulated I don't know how many scandalous tales of me! and all without any foundation, too—that's what vexes me.

Jos. Surf: Aye, madam, to be sure,

that *is* the provoking circumstance—without foundation! yes, yes, there's the mortification, indeed; for, when a scandalous story is believed against one, there certainly is no comfort like the consciousness of having deserved it.

Lady Teaz: No, to be sure—then I'd forgive their malice; but to attack me, who am really so innocent, and who never say an ill-natured thing of anybody—that is, of any friend—and then Sir Peter, too, to have him so peevish, and so suspicious, when I know the integrity of my own heart—indeed 'tis monstrous!

Jos. Surf: But, my dear Lady Teazle, 'tis your own fault if you suffer it. When a husband entertains a groundless suspicion of his wife, and withdraws his confidence from her, the original compact is broke, and she owes it to the honor of her sex to endeavor to outwit him.

Lady Teaz: Indeed! So that, if he suspects me without cause, it follows that the best way of curing his jealousy is to give him reason for't?

Jos. Surf: Undoubtedly—for your husband should never be deceived in you: and in that case it becomes *you* to be frail in compliment to *his* discernment.

Lady Teaz: To be sure, what you say is very reasonable, and when the consciousness of my own innocence——

Jos. Surf: Ah, my dear madam, there is the great mistake; 'tis this very conscious innocence that is of the greatest prejudice to you. What is it makes you negligent of forms, and careless of the world's opinion? why, the *consciousness* of your innocence. What makes you thoughtless in your conduct, and apt to run into a thousand little imprudences? why, the *consciousness* of your innocence. What makes you impatient of Sir Peter's temper and outrageous at his suspicions? why, the *consciousness* of your own innocence!

Lady Teaz: 'Tis very true!

Jos Surf: Now, my dear Lady Teazle, if you would but once make a trifling *faux pas,* you can't conceive how cautious you would grow—and how ready to humor and agree with your husband.

Lady Teaz: Do you think so?

Jos. Surf: Oh, I'm sure on't; and then you would find all scandal would cease at once, for—in short, your character at present is like a person in a plethora, absolutely dying of too much health.

Lady Teaz: So, so; then I perceive your prescription is, that I must sin in my own defence, and part with my virtue to preserve my reputation?

Jos. Surf: Exactly so, upon my credit, ma'am.

Lady Teaz: Well, certainly this is the oddest doctrine, and the newest receipt for avoiding calumny?

Jos. Surf: An infallible one, believe me. *Prudence,* like *experience,* must be paid for.

Lady Teaz: Why, if my understanding were once convinced——

Jos. Surf: Oh, certainly, madam, your understanding *should* be convinced. Yes, yes—heaven forbid I should persuade you to do anything you *thought* wrong. No, no, I have too much honor to desire it.

Lady Teaz: Don't you think we may as well leave honor out of the argument?

Jos. Surf: Ah, the ill effects of your country education, I see, still remain with you.

Lady Teaz: I doubt they do, indeed; and I will fairly own to you, that if I could be persuaded to do wrong, it would be by Sir Peter's ill-usage sooner than your honorable logic, after all.

Jos. Surf: Then, by this hand, which he is unworthy of——(*Taking her hand.*)

[*Re-enter Servant.*]

'Sdeath, you blockhead—what do you want?

Serv: I beg pardon, sir, but I thought you wouldn't choose Sir Peter to come up without announcing him.

Jos. Surf: Sir Peter!—Oons—the devil!

Lady Teaz: Sir Peter! O lud! I'm ruined! I'm ruined!

Serv: Sir, 'twasn't I let him in.

Lady Teaz: Oh! I'm undone! What will become of me, now, Mr. Logic?—Oh! mercy, he's on the stairs—I'll get behind here—and if ever I'm so imprudent again——(*Goes behind the screen.*)

Jos. Surf: Give me that book. (*Sits down. Servant pretends to adjust his hair.*)

[*Enter* SIR PETER TEAZLE.]

Sir Pet: Aye, ever improving himself! —Mr. Surface, Mr. Surface——

Jos. Surf: Oh, my dear Sir Peter, I beg your pardon. (*Gaping, and throws away the book.*) I have been dozing over a stupid book. Well, I am much obliged to you for this call. You haven't been here, I believe, since I fitted up this room. Books, you know, are the only things I am a coxcomb in.

Sir Pet: 'Tis very neat indeed. Well, well, that's proper; and you make even your screen a source of knowledge—hung, I perceive, with maps.

Jos. Surf: Oh, yes, I find great use in that screen.

Sir Pet: I dare say you must—certainly—when you want to find anything in a hurry.

Jos. Surf (*aside*). Aye, or to hide anything in a hurry either.

Sir Pet: Well, I have a little private business——

Jos. Surf: You needn't stay. (*To Servant.*)

Serv: No, sir.

[*Exit.*]

Jos. Surf: Here's a chair, Sir Peter—I beg——

Sir Pet: Well, now we are alone, there is a subject, my dear friend, on which I wish to unburden my mind to you—a point of the greatest moment to my peace: in short, my good friend, Lady Teazle's conduct of late has made me extremely unhappy.

Jos. Surf: Indeed! I am very sorry to hear it.

Sir Pet: Yes, 'tis but too plain she has not the least regard for me; but, what's worse, I have pretty good authority to suspect she must have formed an attachment to another.

Jos. Surf: You astonish me!

Sir Pet: Yes! and, between ourselves, I think I have discovered the person.

Jos. Surf: How! you alarm me exceedingly.

Sir Pet: Aye, my dear friend, I knew you would sympathize with me!

Jos. Surf: Yes, believe me, Sir Peter, such a discovery would hurt me just as much as it would you.

Sir Pet: I am convinced of it.—Ah! it is a happiness to have a friend whom one can trust even with one's family secrets. But have you no guess who I mean?

Jos. Surf: I haven't the most distant idea. It can't be Sir Benjamin Backbite!

Sir Pet: O, no! What say you to Charles?

Jos. Surf: My brother! impossible!

Sir Pet: Ah, my dear friend, the goodness of your own heart misleads you

—you judge of others by yourself.

Jos. Surf: Certainly, Sir Peter, the heart that is conscious of its own integrity is ever slow to credit another's treachery.

Sir Pet: True; but your brother has no sentiment—you never hear him talk so.

Jos. Surf: Yet I can't but think Lady Teazle herself has too much principle——

Sir Pet: Aye; but what's her principle against the flattery of a handsome, lively young fellow?

Jos. Surf: That's very true.

Sir Pet: And then, you know, the difference of our ages makes it very improbable that she should have any great affection for me; and if she were to be frail, and I were to make it public, why the town would only laugh at me, the foolish old bachelor who had married a girl.

Jos. Surf: That's true, to be sure—they *would* laugh.

Sir Pet: Laugh! aye, and make ballads, and paragraphs, and the devil knows what of me.

Jos. Surf: No, you must never make it public.

Sir Pet: But then again—that the nephew of my old friend, Sir Oliver, should be the person to attempt such a wrong, hurts me more nearly.

Jos. Surf: Aye, there's the point. When ingratitude barbs the dart of injury, the wound has double danger in it.

Sir Pet: Aye—I, that was, in a manner, left his guardian—in whose house he had been so often entertained—who never in my life denied him—my advice!

Jos. Surf: Oh, 'tis not to be credited! There *may* be a man capable of such baseness, to be sure; but, for my part, till you can give me positive proofs, I cannot but doubt it. However, if it should be proved on him, he is no longer a brother of mine! I disclaim kindred with him—for the man who can break through the laws of hospitality, and attempt the wife of his friend, deserves to be branded as the pest of society.

Sir Pet: What a difference there is between you! What noble sentiments!

Jos. Surf: Yet I cannot suspect Lady Teazle's honor.

Sir Pet: I am sure I wish to think well of her, and to remove all ground of quarrel between us. She has lately reproached me more than once with having made no settlement on her; and, in our last quarrel, she almost hinted that she should not break her heart if I was dead. Now, as we seem to differ in our ideas of expense, I have resolved she shall be her own mistress in that respect for the future; and, if I *were* to die, she shall find that I have not been inattentive to her interest while living. Here, my friend, are the drafts of two deeds, which I wish to have your opinion on. By one, she will enjoy eight hundred a year independent while I live; and, by the other, the bulk of my fortune after my death.

Jos. Surf: This conduct, Sir Peter, is indeed truly generous.— (*Aside.*) I wish it may not corrupt my pupil.

Sir Pet: Yes, I am determined she shall have no cause to complain, though I would not have her acquainted with the latter instance of my affection yet awhile.

Jos. Surf: Nor I, if I could help it. (*Aside.*)

Sir Pet: And now, my dear friend, if you please, we will talk over the situation of your hopes with Maria.

Jos. Surf (*softly*). No, no, Sir Peter; another time, if you please.

Sir Pet: I am sensibly chagrined at the little progress you seem to make in her affection.

Jos. Surf: I beg you will not mention it. What are my disappointments when your happiness is in debate! (*Softly.*)—

'Sdeath, I shall be ruined every way! (*Aside.*)

Sir Pet: And though you are so averse to my acquainting Lady Teazle with your passion, I am sure she's not your enemy in the affair.

Jos. Surf: Pray, Sir Peter, now oblige me. I am really too much affected by the subject we have been speaking on to bestow a thought on my own concerns. The man who is entrusted with his friend's distresses can never——

[*Enter Servant.*]

Well, sir?

Serv: Your brother, sir, is speaking to a gentleman in the street, and says he knows you are within.

Jos. Surf: 'Sdeath, blockhead—I'm not within—I'm out for the day.

Sir Pet: Stay—hold—a thought has struck me—you shall be at home.

Jos. Surf: Well, well, let him up.—[*Exit Servant.*] He'll interrupt Sir Peter—however—

Sir Pet: Now, my good friend, oblige me, I entreat you. Before Charles comes, let me conceal myself somewhere; then do you tax him on the point we have been talking on, and his answers may satisfy me at once.

Jos. Surf: O, fie, Sir Peter! would you have me join in so mean a trick?—to trepan my brother too?

Sir Pet: Nay, you tell me you are *sure* he is innocent; if so, you do him the greatest service by giving him an opportunity to clear himself, and you will set my heart at rest. Come, you shall not refuse me; here, behind the screen will be (*Goes to the screen.*)—Hey! what the devil! there seems to be *one* listener here already—I'll swear I saw a petticoat!

Jos. Surf: Ha! ha! ha! Well, this is ridiculous enough. I'll tell you, Sir Peter, though I hold a man of intrigue to be a most despicable character, yet you know, it doesn't follow that one is to be an absolute Joseph either! Hark'ee! 'tis a little French milliner, a silly rogue that plagues me—and having some character—on your coming, she ran behind the screen.

Sir Pet: Ah, you rogue!—But, egad, she has overheard all I have been saying of my wife.

Jos. Surf: Oh, 'twill never go any further, you may depend on't!

Sir Pet: No! then, i'faith, let her hear it out.—Here's a closet will do as well.

Jos. Surf: Well, go in then.

Sir Pet: Sly rogue! sly rogue! (*Goes into the closet.*)

Jos. Surf: A very narrow escape, indeed! and a curious situation I'm in, to part man and wife in this manner.

Lady Teaz: (*peeping from the screen*). Couldn't I steal off?

Jos. Surf: Keep close, my angel!

Sir Pet (*peeping out*). Joseph, tax him home.

Jos. Surf: Back, my dear friend!

Lady Teaz: (*peeping*). Couldn't you lock Sir Peter in?

Jos. Surf: Be still, my life!

Sir Pet (*peeping*). You're sure the little milliner won't blab?

Jos. Surf: In, in, my dear Sir Peter! —'Fore gad, I wish I had a key to the door.

[*Enter* CHARLES SURFACE.]

Chas. Surf: Hollo! brother, what has been the matter? Your fellow would not let me up at first. What! have you had a Jew or a wench with you?

Jos. Surf: Neither, brother, I assure you.

Chas. Surf: But what has made Sir

Peter steal off? I thought he had been with you.

Jos. Surf: He was, brother; but, hearing *you* were coming, he did not choose to stay.

Chas. Surf: What! was the old gentleman afraid I wanted to borrow money of him!

Jos. Surf: No, sir, but I am sorry to find, Charles, that you have lately given that worthy man grounds for great uneasiness.

Chas. Surf: Yes, they tell me I do that to a great many worthy men. But how so, pray?

Jos. Surf: To be plain with you, brother, he thinks you are endeavoring to gain Lady Teazle's affections from him.

Chas. Surf: Who, I? O lud! not I, upon my word.—Ha! ha! ha! so the old fellow has found out that he has got a young wife, has he?—or, what's worse, has her ladyship discovered that she has an old husband?

Jos. Surf: This is no subject to jest on, brother.—He who can laugh——

Chas. Surf: True, true, as you were going to say—then, seriously, I never had the least idea of what you charge me with, upon my honor.

Jos. Surf: Well, it will give Sir Peter great satisfaction to hear this. (*Aloud.*)

Chas. Surf: To be sure, I once thought the lady seemed to have taken a fancy to me; but, upon my soul, I never gave her the least encouragement. Besides, you know my attachment to Maria.

Jos. Surf: But sure, brother, even if Lady Teazle had betrayed the fondest partiality for you——

Chas. Surf: Why, look'ee, Joseph, I hope I shall never deliberately do a dishonorable action—but if a pretty woman were purposely to throw herself in my way—and that pretty woman married to a man old enough to be her father——

Jos. Surf: Well!

Chas. Surf: Why, I believe I should be obliged to borrow a little of your morality, that's all.—But, brother, do you know now that you surprise me exceedingly, by naming *me* with Lady Teazle; for, faith, I alway[s] understood *you* were her favorite.

Jos. Surf: Oh, for shame, Charles! This retort is foolish.

Chas. Surf: Nay, I swear I have seen you exchange such significant glances——

Jos. Surf: Nay, nay, sir, this is no jest——

Chas. Surf: Egad, I'm serious! Don't you remember—one day, when I called here——

Jos. Surf: Nay, prithee, Charles——

Chas. Surf: And found you together——

Jos. Surf: Zounds, sir, I insist——

Chas. Surf: And another time, when your servant——

Jos. Surf: Brother, brother, a word with you!—(*Aside.*) Gad, I must stop him.

Chas. Surf: Informed me, I say, that——

Jos. Surf: Hush! I beg your pardon, but Sir Peter has overheard all we have been saying—I knew you would clear yourself, or I should not have consented.

Chas. Surf: How, Sir Peter! Where is he?

Jos. Surf: Softly, there! (*Points to the closet.*)

Chas. Surf: Oh, 'fore heaven, I'll have him out.—Sir Peter, come forth!

Jos. Surf: No, no——

Chas. Surf: I say, Sir Peter, come into court.—(*Pulls in* SIR PETER.) What! my old guardian!—What—turn inquisitor, and take evidence, incog.?

Sir Pet: Give me your hand, Charles

—I believe I have suspected you wrongfully—but you mustn't be angry with Joseph—'twas my plan!

Chas. Surf: Indeed!

Sir Pet: But I acquit you. I promise you I don't think near so ill of you as I did. What I have heard has given me great satisfaction.

Chas. Surf: Egad, then, 'twas lucky you didn't hear any more. Wasn't it, Joseph? (*Half aside.*)

Sir Pet: Ah! you would have retorted on him.

Chas. Surf: Aye, aye, that was a joke.

Sir Pet: Yes, yes, I know his honor too well.

Chas. Surf: But you might as well have suspected him as me in this matter, for all that. Mightn't he, Joseph? (*Half aside.*)

Sir Pet: Well, well, I believe you.

Jos. Surf (*aside*). Would they were both out of the room!

Sir Pet: And in future, perhaps, we may not be such strangers.

[*Enter Servant who whispers to* JOSEPH SURFACE.]

Jos. Surf: Lady Sneerwell!—stop her by all means—[*Exit Servant.*] Gentlemen—I beg pardon—I must wait on you downstairs—here's a person come on particular business.

Chas. Surf: Well, you can see him in another room. Sir Peter and I haven't met a long time, and I have something to say to him.

Jos. Surf: They must not be left together.—I'll send Lady Sneerwell away, and return directly.—(*Aside.*) Sir Peter, not a word of the French milliner.

[*Exit* JOSEPH SURFACE.]

Sir Pet: Oh! not for the world!—Ah, Charles, if you associated more with your brother, one might indeed hope for your reformation. He is a man of sentiment.—Well, there is nothing in the world so noble as a man of sentiment!

Chas. Surf: Pshaw! he is too moral by half, and so apprehensive of his good name, as he calls it, that I suppose he would as soon let a priest into his house as a girl.

Sir Pet: No, no,—come, come,—you wrong him. No, no, Joseph is no rake, but he is not such a saint in that respect either,—I have a great mind to tell him—we should have a laugh! (*Aside.*)

Chas. Surf: Oh, hang him! he's a very anchorite, a young hermit!

Sir Pet: Hark'ee—you must not abuse him; he may chance to hear of it again, I promise you.

Chas. Surf: Why, you won't tell him?

Sir Pet: No — but — this way. — (*Aside.*) Egad, I'll tell him.—Hark'ee, have you a mind to have a good laugh at Joseph?

Chas. Surf: I should like it of all things.

Sir Pet: Then, i'faith, we will!—I'll be quit with him for discovering me. (*Aside.*)—He had a girl with him when I called.

Chas. Surf: What! Joseph? you jest.

Sir Pet: Hush!—a little—French milliner—and the best of the jest is—she's in the room now.

Chas. Surf: The devil she is!

Sir Pet: Hush! I tell you. (*Points to the screen.*)

Chas. Surf: Behind the screen! 'Slife, let's unveil her!

Sir Pet: No, no, he's coming:—you shan't, indeed!

Chas. Surf: Oh, egad, we'll have a peep at the little milliner!

Sir Pet: Not for the world!—Joseph will never forgive me.

Chas. Surf: I'll stand by you——

Sir Pet (*struggling with Charles*). Odds, here he is!

[JOSEPH SURFACE *enters just as* CHARLES *throws down the screen.*]

Chas. Surf: Lady Teazle, by all that's wonderful!

Sir Pet: Lady Teazle, by all that's horrible!

Chas. Surf: Sir Peter, this is one of the smartest French milliners I ever saw. Egad, you seem all to have been diverting yourselves here at hide and seek—and I don't see who is out of the secret. Shall I beg your ladyship to inform me?—Not a word!—Brother, will you please to explain this matter? What! Morality dumb too!—Sir Peter, though I *found* you in the dark, perhaps you are not so now! All mute! Well—though *I* can make nothing of the affair, I suppose you perfectly understand one another; so I'll leave you to yourselves.—(*Going.*) Brother, I'm sorry to find you *have given that worthy man so much uneasiness,*—Sir Peter! there's nothing *in the world so noble as a man of sentiment!*

[*Exit* CHARLES.]

(*They stand for some time looking at each other.*)

Jos. Surf: Sir Peter—notwithstanding I confess that appearances are against me—if you will afford me your patience—I make no doubt but I shall explain everything to your satisfaction.

Sir Pet: If you please—

Jos. Surf: The fact is, sir, Lady Teazle, knowing my pretensions to your ward Maria—I say, sir, Lady Teazle, being apprehensive of the jealousy of your temper—and knowing my friendship to the family—she, sir, I say—called here—in order that—I might explain those pretensions—but on your coming—being apprehensive—as I said—of your jealousy—she withdrew—and this, you may depend on't is the whole truth of the matter.

Sir Pet: A very clear account, upon my word; and I dare swear the lady will vouch for every article of it.

Lady Teaz (*coming forward*). For not one word of it, Sir Peter!

Sir Pet: How! don't you think it worth while to agree in the lie?

Lady Teaz: There is not one syllable of truth in what that gentleman has told you.

Sir Pet: I believe you, upon my soul, ma'am!

Jos. Surf (*aside*). 'Sdeath, madam, will you betray me?

Lady Teaz: Good Mr. Hypocrite, by your leave, I will speak for myself.

Sir Pet: Aye, let her alone, sir; you'll find she'll make out a better story than *you,* without prompting.

Lady Teaz: Hear me, Sir Peter!—I came here on no matter relating to your ward, and even ignorant of this gentleman's pretensions to her—but I came, seduced by his insidious arguments, at least to listen to his pretended passion, if not to sacrifice *your* honor to his baseness.

Sir Pet: Now, I believe, the truth *is* coming, indeed!

Jos. Surf: The woman's mad!

Lady Teaz: No, sir; she has recovered her senses, and your own arts have furnished her with the means.—Sir Peter, I do not expect you to credit me—but the tenderness you expressed for me, when I am sure you could not think I was a witness to it, has penetrated to my heart, and had I left the place without the shame of this discovery, my future life should have spoke[n] the sincerity of my gratitude. As for that smooth-tongue hypocrite, who would have seduced the wife of his too credulous friend, while he affected honorable addresses to his ward—I behold him now in a light so truly despicable, that I shall never again respect myself for having listened to him.

[*Exit.*]

Jos. Surf: Notwithstanding all this, Sir Peter, heaven knows——

Sir Pet: That you are a villain!—and so I leave you to your conscience.

Jos. Surf: You are too rash, Sir Peter; you shall hear me. The man who shuts out conviction by refusing to——

Sir Pet: Oh!—

[*Exeunt,* JOSEPH SURFACE *following and speaking.*]

ACT V

SCENE I

The library in JOSEPH SURFACE'S *house*

[*Enter* JOSEPH SURFACE *and* SERVANT.]

Jos. Surf: Mr. Stanley! why should you think I would see him? you *must* know he comes to ask something.

Serv: Sir, I should not have let him in, but that Mr. Rowley came to the door with him.

Jos. Surf: Pshaw! blockhead! to suppose that I should *now* be in a temper to receive visits from poor relations!—Well, why don't you show the fellow up?

Serv: I will, sir.—Why, sir, it was not my fault that Sir Peter discovered my lady——

Jos. Surf: Go, fool!

[*Exit* SERVANT.]

Sure, Fortune never played a man of my policy such a trick before! My character with Sir Peter, my hopes with Maria, destroyed in a moment! I'm in a rare humor to listen to other people's distresses! I shan't be able to bestow even a benevolent sentiment on Stanley.—So! here he comes, and Rowley with him. I must try to recover myself—and put a little charity into my face, however.

[*Exit.*]

[*Enter* SIR OLIVER SURFACE *and* ROWLEY.]

Sir Oliv: What! does he avoid us? That was he, was it not?

Row: It was, sir—but I doubt you are come a little too abruptly—his nerves are so weak, that the sight of a poor relation may be too much for him.—I should have gone first to break you to him.

Sir Oliv: A plague of his nerves!—Yet this is he whom Sir Peter extols as a man of the most benevolent way of thinking!

Row: As to his way of thinking, I cannot pretend to decide; for, to do him justice, he appears to have as much speculative benevolence as any private gentleman in the kingdom, though he is seldom so sensual as to indulge himself in the exercise of it.

Sir Oliv: Yet has a string of charitable sentiments, I suppose, at his fingers' ends!

Row: Or, rather, at his tongue's end, Sir Oliver; for I believe there is no sentiment he has more faith in than that 'Charity begins at home.'

Sir Oliv: And his, I presume, is of that domestic sort which never stirs abroad at all.

Row: I doubt you'll find it so;—but he's coming—I mustn't seem to interrupt you; and you know, immediately as you leave him, I come in to announce your arrival in your real character.

Sir Oliv: True; and afterwards you'll meet me at Sir Peter's.

Row: Without losing a moment.

[*Exit* ROWLEY.]

Sir Oliv: So! I don't like the complaisance of his features.

[*Re-enter* JOSEPH SURFACE.]

Jos. Surf: Sir, I beg you ten thousand pardons for keeping you a moment waiting—Mr. Stanley, I presume.

Sir Oliv. At your service.

Jos. Surf: Sir, I beg you will do me the honor to sit down—I entreat you, sir.

Sir Oliv: Dear sir—there's no occasion.—Too civil by half! (*Aside.*)

Jos. Surf: I have not the pleasure of knowing you, Mr. Stanley; but I am extremely happy to see you look so well. You were nearly related to my mother, I think, Mr. Stanley?

Sir Oliv: I was, sir—so nearly that my present poverty, I fear, may do discredit to her wealthy children—else I should not have presumed to trouble you.

Jos. Surf: Dear sir, there needs no apology: he that is in distress, though a stranger, has a right to claim kindred with the wealthy;—I am sure I wish *I* was one of that class, and had it in my power to offer you even a small relief.

Sir Oliv: If your uncle, Sir Oliver, were here, I should have a friend.

Jos. Surf: I wish he were, sir, with all my heart: you should not want an advocate with him, believe me, sir.

Sir Oliv: I should not *need* one—my distresses would recommend me; but I imagined his bounty had enabled *you* to become the agent of his charity.

Jos. Surf: My dear sir, you were strangely misinformed. Sir Oliver is a worthy man, a very worthy sort of man; but—avarice, Mr. Stanley, is the vice of age. I will tell you, my good sir, in confidence, what he has done for me has been a mere nothing; though people, I know, have thought otherwise, and, for my part, I never chose to contradict the report.

Sir Oliv: What! has he never transmitted you bullion! rupees! pagodas!

Jos. Surf: O dear sir, nothing of the kind! No, no; a few presents now and then—china—shawls—Congo tea—avadavats and Indian crackers—little more, believe me.

Sir Oliv (*aside*). Here's gratitude for twelve thousand pounds!—Avadavats and Indian crackers!

Jos. Surf: Then, my dear sir, you have heard, I doubt not, of the extravagance of my brother; there are very few would credit what I have done for that unfortunate young man.

Sir Oliv: Not I, for one! (*Aside.*)

Jos. Surf: The sums I have lent him! Indeed I have been exceedingly to blame—it was an amiable weakness: however, I don't pretend to defend it—and now I feel it doubly culpable, since it has deprived me of the pleasure of serving *you,* Mr. Stanley, as my heart dictates.

Sir Oliv (*aside*). Dissembler!—Then, sir, you cannot assist me?

Jos. Surf: At present, it grieves me to say, I cannot; but, whenever I have the ability, you may depend upon hearing from me.

Sir Oliv: I am extremely sorry——

Jos. Surf: Not more than I am, believe me; to pity, without the power to relieve, is still more painful than to ask and be denied.

Sir Oliv: Kind sir, your most obedient humble servant.

Jos. Surf: You leave me deeply affected, Mr. Stanley.—William, be ready to open the door.

Sir Oliv: O dear sir, no ceremony.

Jos. Surf: Your very obedient.

Sir Oliv: Sir, your most obsequious.

Jos. Surf: You may depend upon hearing from me, whenever I can be of service.

Sir Oliv: Sweet sir, you are too good.

Jos. Surf: In the meantime I wish you health and spirits.

Sir Oliv: Your ever grateful and perpetual humble servant.

Jos. Surf: Sir, yours as sincerely.

Sir Oliv: Now I am satisfied!

[*Exit.*]

Jos. Surf (*solus*). This is one bad effect of a good character; it invites applications from the unfortunate, and there needs no small degree of address to gain the reputation of benevolence without incurring the expense. The silver ore of pure charity is an expensive article in the catalogue of a man's good qualities; whereas the sentimental French plate I use instead of it makes just as good a show, and pays no tax.

[*Enter* ROWLEY.]

Row: Mr. Surface, your servant—I was apprehensive of interrupting you—though my business demands immediate attention—as this note will inform you.

Jos. Surf: Always happy to see Mr. Rowley.—(*Reads.*) How! *'Oliver—Surface!'*—My uncle arrived!

Row: He is, indeed—we have just parted—quite well, after a speedy voyage, and impatient to embrace his worthy nephew.

Jos. Surf: I am astonished!—William! stop Mr. Stanley, if he's not gone.

Row: Oh! he's out of reach, I believe.

Jos. Surf: Why didn't you let me know this when you came in together?

Row: I thought you had particular business. But I must be gone to inform your brother, and appoint him here to meet his uncle. He will be with you in a quarter of an hour.

Jos. Surf: So he says. Well, I am strangely overjoyed at his coming.—(*Aside.*) Never, to be sure, was anything so damned unlucky!

Row: You will be delighted to see how well he looks.

Jos. Surf: Oh! I'm rejoiced to hear it.—(*Aside.*) Just at this time!

Row: I'll tell him how impatiently you expect him.

Jos. Surf: Do, do; pray give my best duty and affection. Indeed, I cannot express the sensations I feel at the thought of seeing him.—[*Exit* ROWLEY.] Certainly his coming just at this time is the cruellest piece of ill fortune.

[*Exit.*]

SCENE II

At SIR PETER'S

[*Enter* MRS. CANDOUR *and* MAID.]

Maid: Indeed, ma'am, my lady will see nobody at present.

Mrs. Can: Did you tell her it was her friend Mrs. Candour?

Maid: Yes, madam; but she begs you will excuse her.

Mrs. Can: Do go again; I shall be glad to see her, if it be only for a moment, for I am sure she must be in great distress.—

[*Exit* MAID.]

Dear heart, how provoking; I'm not mistress of half the circumstances! We shall have the whole affair in the newspapers, with the names of the parties at length, before I have dropped the story at a dozen houses.

[*Enter* SIR BENJAMIN BACKBITE.]

O dear Sir Benjamin! you have heard, I suppose——

Sir Ben: Of Lady Teazle and Mr. Surface——

Mrs. Can: And Sir Peter's discovery——

Sir Ben: Oh, the strangest piece of business, to be sure!

Mrs. Can: Well, I never was so surprised in my life. I am so sorry for all parties, indeed I am.

Sir Ben: Now, I don't pity Sir Peter at all—he was so extravagantly partial to Mr. Surface.

Mrs. Can: Mr. Surface! Why, 'twas with Charles Lady Teazle was detected.

Sir Ben: No such thing—Mr. Surface is the gallant.

Mrs. Can: No, no—Charles is the man. 'Twas Mr. Surface brought Sir Peter on purpose to discover them.

Sir Ben: I tell you I have it from one——

Mrs. Can: And I have it from one——

Sir Ben: Who had it from one, who had it——

Mrs. Can: From one immediately—— But here's Lady Sneerwell; perhaps she knows the whole affair.

[*Enter* LADY SNEERWELL.]

Lady Sneer: So, my dear Mrs. Candour, here's a sad affair of our friend Lady Teazle!

Mrs. Can: Aye, my dear friend, who could have thought it——

Lady Sneer: Well, there's no trusting appearances; though, indeed, she was always too lively for me.

Mrs. Can: To be sure, her manners were a little too free—but she was very young!

Lady Sneer: And had, indeed, some good qualities.

Mrs. Can: So she had, indeed. But have you heard the particulars?

Lady Sneer: No; but everybody says that Mr. Surface——

Sir Ben: Aye, there, I told you—Mr. Surface was the man.

Mrs. Can: No, no, indeed—the assignation was with Charles.

Lady Sneer: With Charles! You alarm me, Mrs. Candour.

Mrs. Can: Yes, yes, he was the lover. Mr. Surface—do him justice—was only the informer.

Sir Ben: Well, I'll not dispute with you, Mrs. Candour; but, be it which it may, I hope that Sir Peter's wound will not——

Mrs. Can: Sir Peter's wound! Oh, mercy! I didn't hear a word of their fighting.

Lady Sneer: Nor I, a syllable.

Sir Ben: No! what, no mention of the duel?

Mrs. Can: Not a word.

Sir Ben: O Lord—yes, yes—they fought before they left the room.

Lady Sneer: Pray let us hear.

Mrs. Can: Aye, do oblige us with the duel.

Sir Ben: 'Sir,' says Sir Peter—immediately after the discovery—'you are a most ungrateful fellow.'

Mrs. Can: Aye, to Charles——

Sir Ben: No, no—to Mr. Surface—'a most ungrateful fellow; and old as I am, sir,' says he, 'I insist on immediate satisfaction.'

Mrs. Can: Aye, that must have been to Charles; for 'tis very unlikely Mr. Surface should go to fight in his house.

Sir Ben: 'Gad's life, ma'am, not at all—'giving me immediate satisfaction.'—On this, madam, Lady Teazle, seeing Sir Peter in such danger, ran out of the room in strong hysterics, and Charles after her, calling out for hartshorn and water! Then, madam, they began to fight with swords——

[*Enter* CRABTREE.]

Crab: With pistols, nephew—I have it from undoubted authority.

Mrs. Can: O Mr. Crabtree, then it is all true!

Crab: Too true, indeed, ma'am, and Sir Peter's dangerously wounded——

Sir Ben: By a thrust of *in seconde* quite through his left side——

Crab: By a bullet lodged in the thorax.

Mrs. Can: Mercy on me! Poor Sir Peter!

Crab: Yes, ma'am—though Charles would have avoided the matter, if he could.

Mrs. Can: I knew Charles was the person.

Sir Ben: Oh, my uncle, I see, knows nothing of the matter.

Crab: But Sir Peter taxed him with the basest ingratitude——

Sir Ben: That I told you, you know.

Crab: Do, nephew, let me speak!—and insisted on an immediate——

Sir Ben: Just as I said.

Crab: Odds life, nephew, allow others to know something too! A pair of pistols lay on the bureau (for Mr. Surface, it seems, had come the night before late from Salt-Hill, where he had been to see the Montem with a friend, who has a son at Eton), so, unluckily, the pistols were left charged.

Sir Ben: I heard nothing of this.

Crab: Sir Peter forced Charles to take one, and they fired, it seems, pretty nearly together. Charles's shot took place, as I told you, and Sir Peter's missed; but, what is very extraordinary, the ball struck against a little bronze Pliny that stood over the chimney-piece, grazed out of the window at a right angle, and wounded the postman, who was just coming to the door with a double letter from Northamptonshire.

Sir Ben: My uncle's account is more circumstantial, I must confess; but I believe mine is the true one, for all that.

Lady Sneer (*aside*). I am more interested in this affair than they imagine, and must have better information.

[*Exit* LADY SNEERWELL.]

Sir Ben (*after a pause looking at each other*). Ah! Lady Sneerwell's alarm is very easily accounted for.

Crab: Yes, yes, they certainly *do* say—but that's neither here nor there.

Mrs. Can: But, pray, where is Sir Peter at present?

Crab: Oh! they brought him home, and he is now in the house, though the servants are ordered to deny it.

Mrs. Can: I believe so, and Lady Teazle, I suppose, attending him.

Crab: Yes, yes; I saw one of the faculty enter just before me.

Sir Ben: Hey! who comes here?

Crab: Oh, this is he—the physician, depend on't.

Mrs. Can: Oh, certainly! it must be the physician; and now we shall know.

[*Enter* SIR OLIVER SURFACE.]

Crab: Well, doctor, what hopes?

Mrs. Can: Aye, doctor, how's your patient?

Sir Ben: Now, doctor, isn't it a wound with a small-sword?

Crab: A bullet lodged in the thorax, for a hundred!

Sir Oliv: Doctor! a wound with a small-sword! and a bullet in the thorax? —Oons! are you mad, good people?

Sir Ben: Perhaps, sir, you are not a doctor?

Sir Oliv: Truly, I am to thank you for my degree, if I am.

Crab: Only a friend of Sir Peter's, then, I presume. But, sir, you must have heard of this accident?

Sir Oliv: Not a word!

Crab: Not of his being dangerously wounded?

Sir Oliv: The devil he is!

Sir Ben: Run through the body——

Crab: Shot in the breast——

Sir Ben: By one Mr. Surface——

Crab: Aye, the younger.

Sir Oliv: Hey! what the plague! you seem to differ strangely in your accounts —however, you agree that Sir Peter is dangerously wounded.

Sir Ben: Oh, yes, we agree there.

Crab: Yes, yes, I believe there can be no doubt of that.

Sir Oliv: Then, upon my word, for a person in that situation, he is the most imprudent man alive—for here he comes, walking as if nothing at all were the matter.

[*Enter* SIR PETER TEAZLE.]

Odds heart, Sir Peter! you are come in good time, I promise you; for we had just *given you over.*

Sir Ben: Egad, uncle, this is the most sudden recovery!

Sir Oliv: Why, man! what do you do out of bed with a small-sword through your body, and a bullet lodged in your thorax?

Sir Pet: A small-sword and a bullet?

Sir Oliv: Aye; these gentlemen would have killed you without law or physic, and wanted to dub me a doctor—to make me an accomplice.

Sir Pet: Why, what is all this?

Sir Ben: We rejoice, Sir Peter, that the story of the duel is not true, and are sincerely sorry for your other misfortunes.

Sir Pet: So, so; all over the town already. (*Aside.*)

Crab: Though, Sir Peter, you were certainly vastly to blame to marry at all, at your years.

Sir Pet: Sir, what business is that of yours?

Mrs. Can: Though, indeed, as Sir Peter made so good a husband, he's very much to be pitied.

Sir Pet: Plague on your pity, ma'am! I desire none of it.

Sir Ben: However, Sir Peter, you must not mind the laughing and jests you will meet with on this occasion.

Sir Pet: Sir, I desire to be master in my own house.

Crab: 'Tis no uncommon case, that's one comfort.

Sir Pet: I insist on being left to myself: without ceremony, I insist on your leaving my house directly!

Mrs. Can: Well, well, we are going; and depend on't, we'll make the best report of you we can.

Sir Pet: Leave my house!

Crab: And tell how hardly you have been treated.

Sir Pet: Leave my house!

Sir Ben: And how patiently you bear it.

Sir Pet: Fiends! vipers! furies! Oh! that their own venom would choke them!

[*Exeunt* MRS. CANDOUR, SIR BENJAMIN BACKBITE, CRABTREE, &C.]

Sir Oliv: They are very provoking indeed, Sir Peter.

[*Enter* ROWLEY.]

Row: I heard high words—what has ruffled you, Sir Peter?

Sir Pet: Pshaw! what signifies asking? Do I ever pass a day without my vexations?

Sir Oliv: Well, I'm not inquisitive—I come only to tell you that I have seen both my nephews in the manner we proposed.

Sir Pet: A precious couple they are!

Row: Yes, and Sir Oliver is convinced that your judgment was right, Sir Peter.

Sir Oliv: Yes, I find *Joseph* is indeed the man, after all.

Row: Yes, as Sir Peter says, he's a man of sentiment.

Sir Oliv: And acts up to the sentiments he professes.

Row: It certainly is edification to hear him talk.

Sir Oliv: Oh, he's a model for the young men of the age! But how's this, Sir Peter? you don't join in your friend Joseph's praise, as I expected.

Sir Pet: Sir Oliver, we live in a damned wicked world, and the fewer we praise the better.

Row: What! do *you* say so, Sir Peter, who were never mistaken in your life?

Sir Pet: Pshaw! plague on you both! I see by your sneering you have heard the whole affair. I shall go mad among you!

Row: Then, to fret you no longer, Sir Peter, we are indeed acquainted with it all. I met Lady Teazle coming from Mr. Surface's, so humbled that she deigned to request me to be her advocate with you.

Sir Pet: And does Sir Oliver know all too?

Sir Oliv: Every circumstance.

Sir Pet: What, of the closet—and the screen, hey?

Sir Oliv: Yes, yes, and the little French milliner. Oh, I have been vastly diverted with the story! ha! ha!

Sir Pet: 'Twas very pleasant.

Sir Oliv: I never laughed more in my life, I assure you: ha! ha!

Sir Pet: O, vastly diverting! ha! ha!

Row: To be sure, Joseph with his sentiments! ha! ha!

Sir Pet: Yes, yes, his sentiments! ha! ha! A hypocritical villain!

Sir Oliv: Aye, and that rogue Charles to pull Sir Peter out of the closet: ha! ha!

Sir Pet: Ha! ha! 'twas devilish entertaining, to be sure!

Sir Oliv: Ha! ha! Egad, Sir Peter, I should like to have seen your face when the screen was thrown down: ha! ha!

Sir Pet: Yes, yes, my face when the screen was thrown down: ha! ha! Oh, I must never show my head again!

Sir Oliv: But come, come, it isn't fair to laugh at you neither, my old friend—though, upon my soul, I can't help it.

Sir Pet: Oh, pray don't restrain your mirth on my account—it does not hurt me at all! I laugh at the whole affair myself.

Yes, yes, I think being a standing jest for all one's acquaintances a very happy situation. O yes, and then of a morning to read the paragraphs about Mr. S——, Lady T——, and Sir P——, will be so entertaining!

Row: Without affectation, Sir Peter, you may despise the ridicule of fools. But I see Lady Teazle going towards the next room; I am sure you must desire a reconciliation as earnestly as she does.

Sir Oliv: Perhaps my being here prevents her coming to you. Well, I'll leave honest Rowley to mediate between you; but he must bring you all presently to Mr. Surface's, where I am now returning, if not to reclaim a libertine, at least to expose hypocrisy.

Sir Pet: Ah! I'll be present at your discovering yourself there with all my heart—though 'tis a vile unlucky place for discoveries!

Row: We'll follow.

[*Exit* SIR OLIVER SURFACE.]

Sir Pet: She is not coming here, you see, Rowley.

Row: No, but she has left the door of that room open, you perceive. See, she is in tears!

Sir Pet: Certainly a little mortification appears very becoming in a wife! Don't you think it will do her good to let her pine a little?

Row: Oh, this is ungenerous in you!

Sir Pet: Well, I know not what to think. You remember, Rowley, the letter I found of hers, evidently intended for Charles!

Row: A mere forgery, Sir Peter! laid in your way on purpose. This is one of the points which I intend Snake shall give you conviction on.

Sir Pet: I wish I were once satisfied of that. She looks this way. What a remarkably elegant turn of the head she has! Rowley, I'll go to her.

Row: Certainly.

Sir Pet: Though, when it is known that we are reconciled, people will laugh at me ten times more!

Row: Let them laugh, and retort their malice only by showing them you are happy in spite of it.

Sir Pet: I'faith, so I will! and, if I'm not mistaken, we may yet be the happiest couple in the country.

Row: Nay, Sir Peter—he who once lays aside suspicion——

Sir Pet: Hold, my dear Rowley! if you have any regard for me, never let me hear you utter anything like a sentiment—I have had enough of them to serve me the rest of my life.

[*Exeunt.*]

SCENE III

The library in JOSEPH SURFACE'S *house*

[JOSEPH SURFACE *and* LADY SNEERWELL.]

Lady Sneer: Impossible! Will not Sir Peter immediately be reconciled to Charles, and of consequence no longer oppose his union with Maria? The thought is distraction to me!

Jos. Surf: Can passion furnish a remedy?

Lady Sneer: No, nor cunning either. Oh, I was a fool, an idiot, to league with such a blunderer!

Jos. Surf: Sure, Lady Sneerwell, *I* am the greatest sufferer; yet you see I bear the accident with calmness.

Lady Sneer: Because the disappointmen doesn't reach your *heart;* your *interest* only attached you to Maria. Had you felt for *her* what *I* have for that ungrateful libertine, neither your temper nor hypocrisy could prevent your showing the sharpness of your vexation.

Jos. Surf: But why should your reproaches fall on *me* for this disappointment?

Lady Sneer: Are you not the cause of it? What had you to do to bate in your pursuit of Maria to pervert Lady Teazle by the way? Had you not a sufficient field for your roguery in blinding Sir Peter, and supplanting your brother? I hate such an avarice of crimes; 'tis an unfair monopoly, and never prospers.

Jos. Surf: Well, I admit I have been to blame. I confess I deviated from the direct road of wrong, but I don't think we're so totally defeated neither.

Lady Sneer: No!

Jos. Surf: You tell me you have made a trial of Snake since we met, and that you still believe him faithful to us—

Lady Sneer: I do believe so.

Jos. Surf: And that he has undertaken, should it be necessary, to swear and prove that Charles is at this time contracted by vows and honor to your ladyship—which some of his former letters to you will serve to support?

Lady Sneer: This, indeed, might have assisted.

Jos. Surf: Come, come; it is not too late yet.—(*Knocking at the door.*) But hark! this is probably my uncle, Sir Oliver: retire to that room; we'll consult farther when he's gone.

Lady Sneer: Well! but if *he* should find you out too—

Jos. Surf: Oh, I have no fear of that. Sir Peter will hold his tongue for his own credit['s] sake—and you may depend on't I shall soon discover Sir Oliver's weak side!

Lady Sneer: I have no diffidence of your abilities—only be constant to one roguery at a time.

[*Exit.*]

Jos. Surf: I will, I will! So! 'tis confounded hard, after such bad fortune, to be baited by one's confederate in evil. Well, at all events, my character is so much better than Charles's, that I certainly — hey! — what! — this is not Sir Oliver, but old Stanley again! Plague on't! that he should return to tease me just now! We shall have Sir Oliver come and find him here—and——

[*Enter* SIR OLIVER SURFACE.]

Gad's life, Mr. Stanley, why have you come back to plague me just at this time? You must not stay now, upon my word.

Sir Oliv: Sir, I hear your uncle Oliver is expected here, and though he has been so penurious to *you,* I'll try what he'll do for *me.*

Jos. Surf: Sir, 'tis impossible for you to stay now, so I must beg—— Come any other time, and I promise you, you shall be assisted.

Sir Oliv: No: Sir Oliver and I must be acquainted.

Jos. Surf: Zounds, sir! then I insist on your quitting the room directly.

Sir Oliv: Nay, sir!

Jos. Surf: Sir, I insist on't!—Here, William! show this gentleman out. Since you compel me, sir—not one moment—this is such insolence! (*Going to push him out.*)

[*Enter* CHARLES SURFACE.]

Chas. Surf: Heyday! what's the matter now? What the devil, have you got hold of my little broker here? Zounds, brother, don't hurt little Premium. What's the matter, my little fellow?

Jos. Surf: So! he has been with you, too, has he?

Chas. Surf: To be sure he has! Why, 'tis as honest a little—— But sure, Joseph, you have not been borrowing money too, have you?

Jos. Surf: Borrowing! no! But, brother, you know here we expect Sir Oliver every——

Chas. Surf: O gad, that's true! Noll mustn't find the little broker here, to be sure.

Jos. Surf: Yet, Mr. Stanley insists——

Chas. Surf: Stanley! why his name is *Premium.*

Jos. Surf: No, no, *Stanley.*

Chas. Surf: No, no, *Premium.*

Jos. Surf: Well, no matter which—but——

Chas. Surf: Aye, aye, Stanley or Premium, 'tis the same thing, as you say; for I suppose he goes by half [a] hundred names, besides A.B.'s at the coffee-houses.

Jos. Surf: Death! here's Sir Oliver at the door. (*Knocking again.*) Now I beg, Mr. Stanley——

Chas. Surf: Aye, and I beg, Mr. Premium——

Sir Oliv: Gentlemen——

Jos. Surf: Sir, by heaven you shall go!

Chas. Surf: Aye, out with him, certainly.

Sir Oliv: This violence——

Jos. Surf: 'Tis your own fault.

Chas. Surf: Out with him, to be sure.

[*Both forcing* SIR OLIVER *out.*]

[*Enter* SIR PETER *and* LADY TEAZLE, MARIA, *and* ROWLEY.]

Sir Pet: My old friend, Sir Oliver—hey! What in the name of wonder!—Here are dutiful nephews!—assault their uncle at the first visit!

Lady Teaz: Indeed, Sir Oliver, 'twas well we came in to rescue you.

Row: Truly it was; for I perceive, Sir Oliver, the character of old Stanley was no protection to you.

Sir Oliv: Nor of Premium either: the necessities of the *former* could not extort a shilling from *that* benevolent gentleman; and now, egad, I stood a chance of faring worse than my ancestors, and being knocked down without being bid for. (*After a pause,* JOSEPH *and* CHARLES *turning to each other.*)

Jos. Surf: Charles!

Chas. Surf: Joseph!

Jos. Surf: 'Tis now complete!

Chas. Surf: Very!

Sir Oliv: Sir Peter, my friend, and Rowley too—look on that elder nephew of mine. You know what he has already received from my bounty; and you know also how gladly I would have regarded half my fortune as held in trust for him—judge, then, my disappointment in discovering him to be destitute of truth—charity—and gratitude!

Sir Pet: Sir Oliver, I should be more surprised at this declaration, if I had not myself found him selfish, treacherous, and hypocritical!

Lady Teaz: And if the gentleman pleads not guilty to these, pray let him call *me* to his character.

Sir Pet: Then, I believe, we need add no more.—if he knows himself, he will consider it as the most perfect punishment that he is known to the world.

Chas. Surf (*aside*). If they talk this way to *Honesty,* what will they say to *me,* by and by?

[SIR PETER, LADY TEAZLE, *and* MARIA *retire.*]

Sir Oliv: As for that prodigal, his brother, there——

Chas. Surf (*aside*). Aye, now comes my turn: the damned family pictures will ruin me!

Jos. Surf: Sir Oliver—uncle!—will you honor me with a hearing?

Chas Surf (*aside*). Now if Joseph would make one of his long speeches, I might recollect myself a little.

Sir Oliv (*to* JOSEPH SURFACE). I suppose you would undertake to justify yourself entirely?

Jos. Surf: I trust I could.

Sir Oliv: Pshaw!—Well, sir! and *you* (*to* CHARLES) could justify yourself too, I suppose?

Chas. Surf: Not that I know of, Sir Oliver.

Sir Oliv: What!—Little Premium has been let too much into the secret, I presume?

Chas. Surf: True, sir; but they were family secrets, and should never be mentioned again, you know.

Row: Come, Sir Oliver, I know you cannot speak of Charles's follies with anger.

Sir Oliv: Odd's heart, no more I can —nor with gravity either. Sir Peter, do you know the rogue bargained with me for all his ancestors—sold me judges and generals by the foot—and maiden aunts as cheap as broken china.

Chas. Surf: To be sure, Sir Oliver, I did make a little free with the family canvas, that's the truth on't. My ancestors may certainly rise in evidence against me, there's no denying it; but believe me sincere when I tell you—and upon my soul I would not say it if I was not—that if I do not appear mortified at the exposure of my follies, it is because I feel at this moment the warmest satisfaction in seeing you, my liberal benefactor.

Sir Oliv: Charles, I believe you. Give me your hand again; the ill-looking little fellow over the settee has made your peace.

Chas. Surf: Then, sir, my gratitude to the original is still increased.

Lady Teaz (*pointing to* MARIA). Yet, I believe, Sir Oliver, here is one whom Charles is still more anxious to be reconciled to.

Sir Oliv: Oh, I have heard of his attachment there; and, with the young lady's pardon, if I construe right—that blush——

Sir Pet: Well, child, speak your sentiments.

Maria: Sir, I have little to say, but that I shall rejoice to hear that he is happy; for me, whatever claim I had to his affection, I willingly resign it to one who has a better title.

Chas. Surf: How, Maria!

Sir Pet: Heyday! what's the mystery now? While he appeared an incorrigible rake, you would give your hand to no one else; and now that he is likely to reform, I warrant you won't have him.

Maria: His own heart—and Lady Sneerwell know the cause.

Chas. Surf: Lady Sneerwell!

Jos. Surf: Brother, it is with great concern I am obliged to speak on this point, but my regard to justice compels me, and Lady Sneerwell's injuries can no longer be concealed. (*Goes to the door.*)

[*Enter* LADY SNEERWELL.]

Sir Pet: So! another French milliner! —Egad, he has one in every room in the house, I suppose!

Lady Sneer: Ungrateful Charles! Well may you be surprised, and feel for the indelicate situation which your perfidy has forced me into.

Chas. Surf: Pray, uncle, is this another

plot of yours? For, as I have life, I don't understand it.

Jos. Surf: I believe, sir, there is but the evidence of one person more necessary to make it extremely clear.

Sir Pet: And that person, I imagine, is Mr. Snake.—Rowley, you were perfectly right to bring him with us, and pray let him appear.

Row: Walk in, Mr. Snake.

[*Enter* SNAKE.]

I thought his testimony might be wanted; however, it happens unluckily, that he comes to confront Lady Sneerwell, and not to support her.

Lady Sneer: Villain! Treacherous to me at last! (*Aside.*)—Speak, fellow, have *you* too conspired against me?

Snake: I beg your ladyship ten thousand pardons: you paid me extremely liberally for the lie in question; but I have unfortunately been offered double to speak the truth.

Sir Pet: Plot and counterplot, egad—I wish your ladyship joy of the success of your negotiation.

Lady Sneer: The torments of shame and disappointment on you all!

Lady Teaz: Hold, Lady Sneerwell—before you go, let me thank you for the trouble you and that gentleman have taken, in writing letters to me from Charles, and answering them yourself; and let me also request you to make my respects to the Scandalous College, of which you are president, and inform them, that Lady Teazle, licentiate, begs leave to return the diploma they granted her, as she leaves off practice, and kills characters no longer.

Lady Sneer: You too, madam!—provoking—insolent! May your husband live these fifty years!

[*Exit.*]

Sir Pet: Oons! what a fury!

Lady Teaz: A malicious creature, indeed!

Sir Pet: Hey! not for her last wish?

Lady Teaz: Oh, no!

Sir Oliv: Well, sir, and what have you to say now?

Jos. Surf: Sir, I am so confounded, to find that Lady Sneerwell could be guilty of suborning Mr. Snake in this manner, to impose on us all, that I know not what to say; however, lest her revengeful spirit should prompt her to injure my brother, I had certainly better follow her directly.

[*Exit.*]

Sir Pet: Moral to the last drop!

Sir Oliv: Aye, and marry her, Joseph, if you can.—Oil and vinegar, egad! you'll do very well together.

Row: I believe we have no more occasion for Mr. Snake at present.

Snake: Before I go, I beg pardon once for all, for whatever uneasiness I have been the humble instrument of causing to the parties present.

Sir Pet: Well, well, you have made atonement by a good deed at last.

Snake: But I must request of the company, that it shall never be known.

Sir Pet: Hey! what the plague! are you ashamed of having done a right thing once in your life?

Snake: Ah, sir,—consider I live by the badness of my character—I have nothing but my infamy to depend on! and, if it were once known that I had been betrayed into an honest action, I should lose every friend I have in the world.

Sir Oliv: Well, well—we'll not traduce you by saying anything in your praise, never fear.

[*Exit* SNAKE.]

Sir Pet: There's a precious rogue! yet that fellow is a writer and a critic!

Lady Teaz: See, Sir Oliver, there needs no persuasion now to reconcile your nephew and Maria.

[CHARLES *and* MARIA *apart.*]

Sir Oliv: Aye, aye, that's as it should be, and, egad, we'll have the wedding to-morrow morning.

Chas. Surf: Thank you, my dear uncle.

Sir Pet: What, you rogue! don't you ask the girl's consent first?

Chas. Surf: Oh, I have done that a long time—above a minute ago—and she has looked yes.

Maria: For shame, Charles!—I protest, Sir Peter, there has not been a word——

Sir Oliv: Well, then, the fewer the better—may your love for each other never know abatement.

Sir Pet: And may you live as happily together as Lady Teazle and I—intend to do!

Chas. Surf: Rowley, my old friend, I am sure you congratulate me; and I suspect that I owe you much.

Sir Oliv: You do, indeed, Charles.

Row: If my efforts to serve you had not succeeded you would have been in my debt for the attempt—but deserve to be happy—and you overpay me.

Sir Pet: Aye, honest Rowley always said you would reform.

Chas. Surf: Why as to reforming, Sir Peter, I'll make no promises, and that I take to be a proof that I intend to set about it.—But here shall be my monitor—my gentle guide.—Ah! can I leave the virtuous path those eyes illumine?

Though thou, dear maid, shouldst wa[i]ve thy *beauty's* sway,
Thou still must rule, because I *will* obey:
An humbled fugitive from Folly view,
No sanctuary near but *Love* and—YOU;

(*To the audience.*)

You can, indeed, each anxious fear remove,
For even *Scandal* dies, if *you* approve.

DISCUSSION QUESTIONS

1. What three lines of action are contained in the plot?
2. How does Sheridan contrast and balance his characters?
3. How does Sheridan introduce melodrama into the conflicts between groups of characters?
4. How are the Surface brothers contrasted through their characteristic actions?
5. How successful has Sheridan been in his attempts to complicate the characters of the brothers?
6. What complications and side-interests in the play tend to shift the play's focus away from the conflict between the brothers?
7. To what extent is the conflict between the brothers resolved by the device of a rich uncle rather than by direct clashes between them?

8. How important is the revelation of concealed facts and identities to the comic effect of the play?
9. How does Sheridan use Sir Oliver as more than a plot device?
10. How does Rowley function in the play?
11. What kinds of exaggeration does Sheridan utilize in his entanglements, foibles, and devices?
12. How is Maria characterized?
13. How is Lady Teazle characterized, especially in terms of actual danger to her virtue?
14. How villainous is Joseph?
15. In what ways does Charles differ from the sinful, careless, eighteenth-century rake?
16. What kinds of foils or illuminating contrasts does Sheridan create for his villains?
17. How does Sheridan's treatment of Charles tend to focus on virtues of sentiment rather than on the foibles and shortcomings of social rigidity?
18. What is the source of Charles's good actions?
19. What commentary on the powers of unaided reason does Sheridan's approval of Charles suggest?
20. Are there any inconsistencies in Sir Oliver's behavior?
21. Are there any inconsistencies in the behavior of Joseph, the cool-headed, prudent man?
22. Why does Sheridan stress Joseph's cleverness in his attempt to seduce Lady Teazle (IV, iii)?
23. To what extent does the effect of the screen scene (IV, iii) depend on coincidence?
24. Why is the scene so effective?
25. Does the scene have any symbolic value?
26. To what extent does forward movement within the scene depend on the direct interaction of characters, rather than on a third person's plotting?
27. What ironies emerge from the screen scene?
28. How does the final gossip scene (V, ii) ameliorate the villainy of the participants?
29. How does Sheridan use dramatic irony to heighten the effect of the gossip scene?
30. How does the conclusion of the play bring the characters to consistent actions?
31. What effect arises from Sheridan's tendency to deal with moral concerns, mostly as they center around hypocrisy, in terms of monetary loss and gain?

AN ENEMY OF THE PEOPLE

✤ *Henrik Ibsen*

Introductory Comment

An Enemy of the People offers us a good example of the "problem play" from the standpoint of theme and of the "well-made play" from the standpoint of structure. The playwright's primary concern in a "problem play" is with a theme of general social importance rather than with one of primarily moral or psychological significance as in *Lear* or *Desire under the Elms.* Ibsen, who helped develop the form, is here concerned with the social problem of an idealistic, impractical reformer striving energetically but futilely, and somewhat foolishly, to correct the hidden evil hypocritically glossed over by a smug, well-satisfied group of men who control the society of the play. To a considerable extent the characters, although they are not simply stereotypes, are intended as typical and their individuality is developed to the extent that they can carry the theme effectively. Here, the protagonist or hero, Dr. Stockmann, is a high-principled social reformer pitted against a group of shrewd practical men benefiting materially from the *status quo.* Stockmann has temporary allies in those who seek to gain something from his attack on the establishment but who abandon him with no compunction when they see that his attack will end in disaster. He fails in his attempt at social reformation partly as a result of the hypocrisy and self-interest of others but also because of his own errors in judgment. It is this latter point which brings the play closer to the traditional concept of tragedy and away from drama used as social propaganda.

To present this confrontation between opposing social forces Ibsen uses the structure of the "well-made play," a nineteenth-century dramatic form created in France by Eugene Scribe and others. In this type of drama the playwright carefully arranges the incidents on the basis of logical and inevitable progression. One event leads inexorably to the next, and the crisis and catastrophe are well prepared for, with anticipation being a large part of whatever dramatic suspense is engendered.

The language and setting in such a play are completely realistic and even drab. Any symbolism employed is quite elementary and limited in its application. In *An Enemy of the People* one might assign symbolic value to a few props, articles of wear, and certain actions, but any such significance would be purely conventional and not thoroughly integrated into the entire structure and theme of the play as is the case in *The Cherry Orchard* and *The Glass Menagerie.*

When it is well executed and when it deals with a significant issue of lasting importance and universal scope a "problem play" can be a great play. It may not rise above melodrama if the issue dealt with is interesting primarily because of its sensational nature or if the dramatic opponents are rendered all-good or all-bad. Or it may become merely dramatized journalism if the theme is too narrow and the characters involved are flat and devoid of dramatic life apart from the issues involved as in some of the proletarian drama of the 1930s.

Through the writing of such plays as *An Enemy of the People* and *A Doll's House* Ibsen has exerted a very strong influence on a number of modern American playwrights, most notably Arthur Miller (*The Crucible, All My Sons,* and *Death of a Salesman*). Ibsen's influence can also be seen in many of the plays of George Bernard Shaw (*Candida, Pygmalion,* and *Major Barbara*); but here the issues, characters, and events are treated with a satirically comic rather than with a heavy-handedly serious tone.

Cast of Characters

DR. THOMAS STOCKMANN, *Medical Officer of the Municipal Baths*

MRS. STOCKMANN, *his wife*

PETRA, *their daughter, a teacher*

EJLIF } *their sons (aged 13 and 10 respectively)*
MORTEN }

PETER STOCKMANN, *the Doctor's elder brother; Mayor of the Town and Chief Constable, Chairman of the Baths' Committee, etc., etc*

MORTEN KIIL, *a tanner (Mrs. Stockmann's adoptive father)*

HOVSTAD, *editor of the "People's Messenger"*

BILLING, *sub-editor*

CAPTAIN HORSTER

ASLAKSEN, *a printer*

Men of various conditions and occupations, some few women, and a troop of schoolboys—the audience at a public meeting

Scene: *The action takes place in a coast town in southern Norway.*

ACT I

Scene: DR. STOCKMANN'S *sitting-room. It is evening. The room is plainly but neatly appointed and furnished. In the right-hand wall are two doors; the farther leads out to the hall, the nearer to the doctor's study. In the left-hand wall, opposite the door leading to the hall, is a door leading to the other rooms occupied by the family. In the middle of the same wall stands the stove, and, further forward, a couch with a looking-glass hanging over it and an oval table in front of it. On the table, a lighted lamp, with a lampshade. At the back of the room, an open door leads to the dining-room.* BILLING *is seen sitting at the dining table, on which a lamp is burning. He has a napkin tucked under his chin, and* MRS. STOCKMANN *is standing by the table handing him a large plateful of roast beef. The other places at the table are empty, and the table somewhat in disorder, a meal having evidently recently been finished.*]

Mrs. Stockmann: You see, if you come an hour late, Mr. Billing, you have to put up with cold meat.

Billing (*as he eats*). It is uncommonly good, thank you—remarkably good.

Mrs. Stockmann: My husband makes such a point of having his meals punctually, you know—

Billing: That doesn't affect me a bit. Indeed, I almost think I enjoy a meal all the better when I can sit down and eat all by myself and undisturbed.

Mrs. Stockmann: Oh well, as long as you are enjoying it—. (*Turns to the hall* *door, listening.*) I expect that is Mr. Hovstad coming too.

Billing: Very likely.

[PETER STOCKMANN *comes in. He wears an overcoat and his official hat, and carries a stick.*]

Peter Stockmann: Good evening, Katherine.

Mrs. Stockmann (*coming forward into the sitting-room*). Ah, good evening—is it you? How good of you to come up and see us!

Peter Stockmann: I happened to be passing, and so—(*looks into the dining-room*). But you have company with you, I see.

Mrs. Stockmann (*a little embarrassed*). Oh, no—it was quite by chance he came in. (*Hurriedly.*) Won't you come in and have something, too?

Peter Stockmann: I! No, thank you. Good gracious—hot meat at night! Not with my digestion.

Mrs. Stockmann: Oh, but just once in a way—

Peter Stockmann: No, no, my dear lady; I stick to my tea and bread and butter. It is much more wholesome in the long run—and a little more economical, too.

Mrs. Stockmann (*smiling*). Now you mustn't think that Thomas and I are spendthrifts.

Peter Stockmann: Not you, my dear; I would never think that of you. (*Points to the Doctor's study.*) Is he not at home?

Mrs. Stockmann: No, he went out for a little turn after supper—he and the boys.

Peter Stockmann: I doubt if that is a wise thing to do. (*Listens.*) I fancy I hear him coming now.

Mrs. Stockmann: No, I don't think it is he. (*A knock is heard at the door*). Come in! (HOVSTAD *comes in from the hall.*) Oh, it is you, Mr. Hovstad!

Hovstad: Yes, I hope you will forgive me, but I was delayed at the printer's. Good evening, Mr. Mayor.

Peter Stockmann (*bowing a little distantly*). Good evening. You have come on business, no doubt.

Hovstad: Partly. It's about an article for the paper.

Peter Stockmann: So I imagined. I hear my brother has become a prolific contributor to the *People's Messenger.*

Hovstad: Yes, he is good enough to write in the *People's Messenger* when he has any home truths to tell.

Mrs. Stockmann (*to* HOVSTAD). But won't you—? (*Points to the dining-room.*)

Peter Stockmann: Quite so, quite so, I don't blame him in the least, as a writer, for addressing himself to the quarters where he will find the readiest sympathy. And, besides that, I personally have no reason to bear any ill will to your paper, Mr. Hovstad.

Hovstad: I quite agree with you.

Peter Stockmann: Taking one thing with another, there is an excellent spirit of toleration in the town—an admirable municipal spirit. And it all springs from the fact of our having a great common interest to unite us—an interest that is in an equally high degree the concern of every right-minded citizen—

Hovstad: The Baths, yes.

Peter Stockmann: Exactly—our fine, new, handsome Baths. Mark my words, Mr. Hovstad—the Baths will become the focus of our municipal life! Not a doubt of it!

Mrs. Stockmann: That is just what Thomas says.

Peter Stockmann: Think how extraordinarily the place has developed within the last year or two! Money has been flowing in, and there is some life and some business doing in the town. Houses and landed property are rising in value every day.

Hovstad: And unemployment is diminishing.

Peter Stockmann: Yes, that is another thing. The burden of the poor rates has been lightened, to the great relief of the propertied classes; and that relief will be even greater if only we get a really good summer this year, and lots of visitors—plenty of invalids, who will make the Baths talked about.

Hovstad: And there is a good prospect of that, I hear.

Peter Stockmann: It looks very promising. Enquiries about apartments and that sort of thing are reaching us every day.

Hovstad: Well, the doctor's article will come in very suitably.

Peter Stockmann: Has he been writing something just lately?

Hovstad: This is something he wrote in the winter; a recommendation of the Baths—an account of the excellent sanitary conditions here. But I held the article over, temporarily.

Peter Stockmann: Ah,—some little difficulty about it, I suppose?

Hovstad: No, not at all; I thought it would be better to wait till the spring, because it is just at this time that people begin to think seriously about their summer quarters.

Peter Stockmann: Quite right; you were perfectly right, Mr. Hovstad.

Hovstad: Yes, Thomas is really indefatigable when it is a question of the Baths.

Peter Stockmann: Well—remember, he is the Medical Officer to the Baths.

Hovstad: Yes, and what is more, they owe their existence to him.

Peter Stockmann: To him? Indeed! It is true I have heard from time to time that some people are of that opinion. At the same time I must say I imagined that I took a modest part in the enterprise.

Mrs. Stockmann: Yes, that is what Thomas is always saying.

Hovstad: But who denies it, Mr. Stockmann? You set the thing going and made a practical concern of it; we all know that. I only meant that the idea of it came first from the doctor.

Peter Stockmann: Oh, ideas—yes! My brother has had plenty of them in his time—unfortunately. But when it is a question of putting an idea into practical shape, you have to apply to a man of different mettle, Mr. Hovstad. And I certainly should have thought that in this house at least—

Mrs. Stockmann: My dear Peter—

Hovstad: How can you think that—?

Mrs. Stockmann: Won't you go in and have something, Mr. Hovstad? My husband is sure to be back directly.

Hovstad: Thank you, perhaps just a morsel. (*Goes into the dining-room.*)

Peter Stockmann (*lowering his voice a little*). It is a curious thing that these farmer's sons never seem to lose their want of tact.

Mrs. Stockmann: Surely it is not worth bothering about! Cannot you and Thomas share the credit as brothers?

Peter Stockmann: I should have thought so; but apparently some people are not satisfied with a share.

Mrs. Stockmann: What nonsense! You and Thomas get on so capitally together. (*Listens.*) There he is at last, I think. (*Goes out and opens the door leading to the hall.*)

Dr. Stockmann (*laughing and talking outside*). Look here—here is another guest for you, Katherine. Isn't that jolly! Come in, Captain Horster; hang your coat up on this peg. Ah, you don't wear an overcoat. Just think, Katherine; I met him in the street and could hardly persuade him to come up! (CAPTAIN HORSTER *comes into the room and greets* MRS. STOCKMANN. *He is followed by* DR. STOCKMANN.) Come along in, boys. They are ravenously hungry again, you know. Come along, Captain Horster; you must have a slice of beef. (*Pushes* HORSTER *into the dining-room.* EJLIF *and* MORTEN *go in after them.*)

Mrs. Stockmann: But, Thomas, don't you see—?

Dr. Stockmann (*turning in the doorway*). Oh, is it you, Peter? (*Shakes hands with him.*) Now that is very delightful.

Peter Stockmann: Unfortunately I must go in a moment—

Dr. Stockmann: Rubbish! There is some toddy just coming in. You haven't forgotten the toddy, Katherine?

Mrs. Stockmann: Of course not; the water is boiling now. (*Goes into the dining-room.*)

Peter Stockmann: Toddy too!

Dr. Stockmann: Yes, sit down and we will have it comfortably.

Peter Stockmann: Thanks, I never care about an evening's drinking.

Dr. Stockmann: But this isn't an evening's drinking.

Peter Stockmann: It seems to me—. (*Looks towards the dining-room.*) It is extraordinary how they can put away all that food.

Dr. Stockmann (*rubbing his hands*). Yes, isn't it splendid to see young people eat? They have always got an appetite, you know! That's as it should be. Lots of food—to build up their strength! They are the people who are going to stir up the fermenting forces of the future, Peter.

Peter Stockmann: May I ask what they will find here to "stir up," as you put it?

Dr. Stockmann: Ah, you must ask the young people that—when the time comes. We shan't be able to see it, of course. That stands to reason—two old fogies, like us—

Peter Stockmann: Really, really! I must say that is an extremely odd expression to—

Dr. Stockmann: Oh, you mustn't take me too literally, Peter. I am so heartily happy and contented, you know. I think it is such an extraordinary piece of good fortune to be in the middle of all this growing, germinating life. It is a splendid time to live in! It is as if a whole new world were being created around one.

Peter Stockmann: Do you really think so?

Dr. Stockmann: Ah, naturally you can't appreciate it as keenly as I. You have lived all your life in these surroundings, and your impressions have got blunted. But I, who have been buried all these years in my little corner up north, almost without ever seeing a stranger who might bring new ideas with him—well, in my case it has just the same effect as if I had been transported into the middle of a crowded city.

Peter Stockmann: Oh, a city—!

Dr. Stockmann: I know, I know; it is all cramped enough here, compared with many other places. But there is life here—there is promise—there are innumerable things to work for and fight for; and that is the main thing. (*Calls.*) Katherine, hasn't the postman been here?

Mrs. Stockman (*from the dining-room*). No.

Dr. Stockmann: And then to be comfortably off, Peter! That is something one learns to value, when one has been on the brink of starvation, as we have.

Peter Stockmann: Oh, surely—

Dr. Stockmann: Indeed I can assure you we have often been very hard put to it, up there. And now to be able to live like a lord! To-day, for instance, we had roast beef for dinner—and, what is more, for supper too. Won't you come and have a little bit? Or let me show it you, at any rate? Come here—

Peter Stockmann: No, no—not for worlds!

Dr. Stockmann: Well, but just come here then. Do you see, we have got a table-cover?

Peter Stockmann: Yes, I noticed it.

Dr. Stockmann: And we have got a lampshade too. Do you see? All out of Katherine's savings! It makes the room so cosy. Don't you think so? Just stand here for a moment—no, no, not there—just here, that's it! Look now, when you get the light on it altogether—I really think it looks very nice, doesn't it?

Peter Stockmann: Oh, if you can afford luxuries of this kind—

Dr. Stockmann: Yes, I can afford it now. Katherine tells me I earn almost as much as we spend.

Peter Stockmann: Almost—yes!

Dr. Stockmann: But a scientific man must live in a little bit of style. I am quite sure an ordinary civil servant spends more in a year than I do.

Peter Stockmann: I daresay. A civil servant—a man in a well-paid position—

Dr. Stockmann: Well, any ordinary merchant, then! A man in that position spends two or three times as much as—

Peter Stockmann: It just depends on circumstances.

Dr. Stockmann: At all events I assure you I don't waste money unprofitably. But I can't find it in my heart to deny myself the pleasure of entertaining my friends. I need that sort of thing, you know. I have lived for so long shut out of it all, that it is a necessity of life to me to mix with young, eager, ambitious men, men of liberal and active minds; and that describes every one of those fellows who are enjoying their supper in there. I wish you knew more of Hovstad—

Peter Stockmann: By the way, Hovstad was telling me he was going to print another article of yours.

Dr. Stockmann: An article of mine?

Peter Stockmann: Yes, about the Baths. An article you wrote in the winter.

Dr. Stockmann: Oh, that one! No, I don't intend that to appear just for the present.

Peter Stockmann: Why not? It seems to me that this would be the most opportune moment.

Dr. Stockmann: Yes, very likely—under normal conditions. (*Crosses the room.*)

Peter Stockmann (*following him with his eyes.*) Is there anything abnormal about the present conditions?

Dr. Stockmann (*standing still*). To tell you the truth, Peter, I can't say just at this moment—at all events not to-night. There may be much that is very abnormal about the present conditions—and it is possible there may be nothing abnormal about them at all. It is quite possible it may be merely my imagination.

Peter Stockmann: I must say it all sounds most mysterious. Is there something going on that I am to be kept in ignorance of? I should have imagined that I, as Chairman of the governing body of the Baths—

Dr. Stockman: And I should have imagined that I—. Oh, come, don't let us fly out at one another, Peter.

Peter Stockmann: Heaven forbid! I am not in the habit of flying out at people, as you call it. But I am entitled to request most emphatically that all arrangements shall be made in a business-like manner, through the proper channels, and shall be dealt with by the legally constituted authorities. I can allow no going behind our backs by any roundabout means.

Dr. Stockmann: Have I ever at any time tried to go behind your backs!

Peter Stockmann: You have an ingrained tendency to take your own way, at all events; and that is almost equally inadmissible in a well-ordered community. The individual ought undoubtedly to acquiesce in subordinating himself to the community—or, to speak more accurately, to the authorities who have the care of the community's welfare.

Dr. Stockmann: Very likely. But what the deuce has all this got to do with me?

Peter Stockmann: That is exactly what you never appear to be willing to learn, my dear Thomas. But, mark my words, some day you will have to suffer for it—sooner or later. Now I have told you. Good-bye.

Dr. Stockmann: Have you taken leave of your senses? You are on the wrong scent altogether.

Peter Stockmann: I am not usually that. You must excuse me now if I—(*calls into the dining-room*). Good night, Katherine. Good night, gentlemen. (*Goes out.*)

Mrs. Stockmann (*coming from the dining-room*). Has he gone?

Dr. Stockmann: Yes, and in such a bad temper.

Mrs. Stockmann: But, dear Thomas, what have you been doing to him again?

Dr. Stockmann: Nothing at all. And, anyhow, he can't oblige me to make my report before the proper time.

Mrs. Stockmann: What have you got to make a report to him about?

Dr. Stockmann: Hm! Leave that to me, Katherine.—It is an extraordinary thing that the postman doesn't come.

[HOVSTAD, BILLING *and* HORSTER *have got up from the table and come into the sitting-room.* EJLIF *and* MORTEN *come in after them.*]

Billing (*stretching himseslf*) Ah!—one feels a new man after a meal like that.

Hovstad: The mayor wasn't in a very sweet temper tonight, then.

Dr. Stockmann: It is his stomach; he has a wretched digestion.

Hovstad: I rather think it was us two of the *People's Messenger* that he couldn't digest.

Mrs. Stockmann: I though you came out of it pretty well with him.

Hovstad: Oh yes; but it isn't anything more than a sort of truce.

Billing: That is just what it is! That word sums up the situation.

Dr. Stockmann: We must remember that Peter is a lonely man, poor chap. He has no home comforts of any kind; nothing but everlasting business. And all that infernal weak tea wash that he pours into himself! Now then, my boys, bring chairs up to the table. Aren't we going to have that toddy, Katherine?

Mrs. Stockmann (*going into the dining-room*). I am just getting it.

Dr. Stockmann: Sit down here on the couch beside me, Captain Horster. We so seldom see you—. Please sit down, my friends. (*They sit down at the table.* MRS.

STOCKMANN *brings a tray, with a spirit-lamp, glasses, bottles, etc., upon it.*)

Mrs. Stockmann: There you are! This is arrack, and this is rum, and this one is the brandy. Now every one must help himself.

Dr. Stockmann (*taking a glass*). We will. (*They all mix themselves some toddy.*) And let us have the cigars. Ejlif, you know where the box is. And you, Morten, can fetch my pipe. (*The two boys go into the room on the right.*) I have a suspicion that Ejlif pockets a cigar now and then!—but I take no notice of it. (*Calls out.*) And my smoking-cap too, Morten. Katherine, you can tell him where I left it. Ah, he has got it. (*The boys bring the various things.*) Now, my friends. I stick to my pipe, you know. This one has seen plenty of bad weather with me up north. (*Touches glasses with them.*) Your good health! Ah, it is good to be sitting snug and warm here.

Mrs. Stockmann (*who sits knitting*). Do you sail soon, Captain Horster?

Horster: I expect to be ready to sail next week.

Mrs. Stockmann: I suppose you are going to America?

Horster: Yes, that is the plan.

Mrs. Stockmann: Then you won't be able to take part in the coming election.

Horster: Is there going to be an election?

Billing: Didn't you know?

Horster: No, I don't mix myself up with those things.

Billing: But do you not take an interest in public affairs?

Horster: No, I don't know anything about politics.

Billing: All the same, one ought to vote, at any rate.

Horster: Even if one doesn't know anything about what is going on?

Billing: Doesn't know! What do you mean by that? A community is like a ship; every one ought to be prepared to take the helm.

Horster: Maybe that is all very well on shore; but on board ship it wouldn't work.

Hovstad: It is astonishing how little most sailors care about what goes on on shore.

Billing: Very extraordinary.

Dr. Stockmann: Sailors are like birds of passage; they feel equally at home in any latitude. And that is only an additional reason for our being all the more keen, Hovstad. Is there to be anything of public interest in to-morrow's Messenger?

Hovstad: Nothing about municipal affairs. But the day after to-morrow I was thinking of printing your article—

Dr. Stockmann: Ah, devil take it—my article! Look here, that must wait a bit.

Hovstad: Really? We had just got convenient space for it, and I thought it was just the opportune moment—

Dr. Stockmann: Yes, yes, very likely you are right; but it must wait all the same. I will explain to you later. (PETRA comes *in from the hall, in hat and cloak and with a bundle of exercise books under her arm.*)

Petra: Good evening.

Dr. Stockmann: Good evening, Petra; come along.

[*Mutual greetings;* PETRA *takes off her things and puts them down on a chair by the door.*]

Petra: And you have all been sitting here enjoying yourselves, while I have been out slaving!

Dr. Stockmann: Well, come and enjoy yourself too!

Billing: May I mix a glass for you?

Petra (*coming to the table*). Thanks,

I would rather do it; you always mix it too strong. But I forgot, father—I have a letter for you. (*Goes to the chair where she has laid her things.*)

Dr. Stockmann: A letter? From whom?

Petra (*looking in her coat pocket*). The postman gave it to me just as I was going out—

Dr. Stockmann (*getting up and going to her*). And you only give it to me now!

Petra: I really had not time to run up again. There it is!

Dr Stockmann (*seizing the letter*). Let's see, let's see, child! (*Looks at the address.*) Yes, that's all right!

Mrs. Stockmann: Is it the one you have been expecting so anxiously, Thomas?

Dr. Stockmann: Yes, it is. I must go to my room now and—. Where shall I get a light, Katherine? Is there no lamp in my room again?

Mrs. Stockmann: Yes, your lamp is all ready lit on your desk.

Dr. Stockmann: Good, good. Excuse me for a moment—. (*Goes into his study.*)

Petra: What do you suppose it is, mother?

Mrs. Stockmann: I don't know; for the last day or two he has always been asking if the postman has not been.

Billing: Probably some country patient.

Petra: Poor old dad!—he will overwork himself soon. (*Mixes a glass for herself.*) There, that will taste good!

Hovstad: Have you been teaching in the evening school again to-day?

Petra (*sipping from her glass*). Two hours.

Billing: And four hours of school in the morning—

Petra: Five hours.

Mrs. Stockmann: And you have still got exercises to correct, I see.

Petra: A whole heap, yes.

Horster: You are pretty full up with work too, it seems to me.

Petra: Yes—but that is good. One is so delightfully tired after it.

Billing: Do you like that?

Petra: Yes, because one sleeps so well, then.

Morten: You must be dreadfully wicked, Petra.

Petra: Wicked?

Morten: Yes, because you work so much. Mr. Rörlund says work is a punishment for our sins.

Ejlif: Pooh, what a duffer you are, to believe a thing like that!

Mrs. Stockmann: Come, come Ejlif!

Billing (*laughing*). That's capital!

Hovstad: Don't you want to work as hard as that, Morten?

Morten: No, indeed I don't.

Hovstad: What do you want to be, then?

Morten: I should like best to be a Viking.

Ejlif: You would have to be a pagan then.

Morten: Well, I could become a pagan, couldn't I?

Billing: I agree with, Morten! My sentiments, exactly.

Mrs. Stockmann (*signalling to him*). I am sure that is not true, Mr. Billing.

Billing: Yes, I swear it is! I am a pagan, and I am proud of it. Believe me, before long we shall all be pagans.

Morten: And then shall be allowed to do anything we like?

Billing: Well, you see, Morten—.

Mrs. Stockmann: You must go to your room now, boys; I am sure you have some lessons to learn for to-morrow.

Ejlif: I should like so much to stay a little longer—

Mrs. Stockmann: No, no; away you go, both of you.

[*The boys say good night and go into the room on the left.*]

Hovstad: Do you really think it can do the boys any harm to hear such things?

Mrs. Stockmann: I don't know, but I don't like it.

Petra: But you know, mother, I think you really are wrong about it.

Mrs. Stockmann: Maybe, but I don't like it—not in our own home.

Petra: There is so much falsehood both at home and at school. At home one must not speak, and at school we have to stand and tell lies to the children.

Horster: Tell lies?

Petra: Yes, don't you suppose we have to teach them all sorts of things that we don't believe?

Billing: That is perfectly true.

Petra: If only I had the means I would start a school of my own, and it would be conducted on very different lines.

Billing: Oh, bother the means—!

Horster: Well, if you are thinking of that, Miss Stockmann, I shall be delighted to provide you with a schoolroom. The great big old house my father left me is standing almost empty; there is an immense dining-room downstairs—

Petra (*laughing*). Thank you very much; but I am afraid nothing will come of it.

Hovstad: No, Miss Petra is much more likely to take to journalism, I expect. By the way, have you had time to do anything with that English story you promised to translate for us?

Petra: No, not yet; but you shall have it in good time.

[DR. STOCKMANN *comes in from his room with an open letter in his hand.*]

Dr. Stockmann (*waving the letter*). Well, now the town will have something new to talk about, I can tell you!

Billing: Something new?

Mrs. Stockmann: What is this?

Dr. Stockmann: A great discovery, Katherine.

Hovstad: Really?

Mrs. Stockmann: A discovery of yours?

Dr. Stockmann: A discovery of mine. (*Walks up and down*). Just let them come saying, as usual, that it is all fancy and a crazy man's imagination! But they will be careful what they say this time, I can tell you!

Petra: But, father, tell us what it is.

Dr. Stockmann: Yes, yes—only give me time, and you shall know all about it. If only I had Peter here now! It just shows how we men can go about forming our judgments, when in reality we are as blind as any moles—

Hovstad: What are you driving at, Doctor?

Dr. Stockmann (*standing still by the table*). Isn't it the universal opinion that our town is a healthy spot?

Hovstad: Certainly.

Dr. Stockmann: Quite an unusually healthy spot, in fact—a place that deserves to be recommended in the warmest possible manner either for invalids or for people who are well—

Mrs. Stockmann: Yes, but my dear Thomas—

Dr. Stockmann: And we have been recommending it and praising it—I have written and written, both in the *Messenger* and in pamphlets—

Hovstad: Well, what then?

Dr. Stockmann: And the Baths—we have called them the "main artery of the town's life-blood," the "nerve-center of our town," and the devil knows what else—

Billing: "The town's pulsating heart" was the expression I once used on an important occasion—

Dr. Stockmann: Quite so. Well, do you know what they really are, these great, splendid, much-praised Baths, that have cost so much money—do you know what they are?

Hovstad: No, what are they?

Mrs. Stockmann: Yes, what are they?

Dr. Stockmann: The whole place is a pesthouse!

Petra: The Baths, father?

Mrs. Stockmann (*at the same time*). Our Baths!

Hovstad: But, Doctor—

Billing: Absolutely incredible!

Dr. Stockmann: The whole Bath establishment is a whited, poisoned sepulcher, I tell you—the gravest possible danger to the public health! All the nastiness up at Mölledal, all that stinking filth, is infecting the water in the conduit-pipes leading to the reservoir; and the same cursed, filthy poison oozes out on the shore too—

Horster: Where the bathing-place is?

Dr. Stockmann: Just there.

Hovstad: How do you come to be so certain of all this, Doctor?

Dr. Stockmann: I have investigated the matter most conscientiously. For a long time past I have suspected something of the kind. Last year we had some very strange cases of illness among the visitors—typhoid cases, and cases of gastric fever—

Mrs. Stockmann: Yes, that is quite true.

Dr. Stockmann: At the time we supposed the visitors had been infected before they came; but later on, in the winter, I began to have a different opinion; and so I set myself to examine the water, as well as I could.

Mrs. Stockmann: Then that is what you have been so busy with?

Dr. Stockmann: Indeed I have been busy, Katherine. But here I had none of the necessary scientific apparatus; so I sent samples, both of the drinking-water and of the sea-water, up to the University, to have an accurate analysis made by a chemist.

Hovstad: And have you got that?

Dr. Stockmann (*showing him the letter*). Here it is! It proves the presence of decomposing organic matter in the water—it is full of infusoria. The water is absolutely dangerous to use, either internally or externally.

Mrs. Stockmann: What a mercy you discovered it in time.

Dr. Stockmann: You may well say so.

Hovstad: And what do you propose to do now, Doctor?

Dr. Stockmann: To see the matter put right—naturally.

Hovstad: Can that be done?

Dr. Stockmann: It must be done. Otherwise the Baths will be absolutely useless and wasted. But we need not anticipate that; I have a very clear idea what we shall have to do.

Mrs. Stockmann: But why have you kept this all so secret, dear?

Dr. Stockmann: Do you suppose I was going to run about the town gossiping about it, before I had absolute proof? No, thank you. I am not such a fool.

Petra: Still, you might have told us—

Dr. Stockmann: Not a living soul. But tomorrow you may run round to the old Badger—

Mrs. Stockmann: Oh, Thomas! Thomas!

Dr. Stockmann: Well, to your grandfather, then. The old boy will have something to be astonished at! I know he thinks I am cracked—and there are lots of other people think so too, I have noticed. But now these good folks shall see—they shall just see—! (*Walks about, rubbing his hands.*) There will be a nice upset in the town, Katherine; you can't imagine what it will be. All the conduit-pipes will have to be relaid.

Hovstad (*getting up*). All the conduit-pipes—?

Dr. Stockmann: Yes, of course. The intake is too low down; it will have to be lifted to a position much higher up.

Petra: Then you were right after all.

Dr. Stockmann: Ah, you remember, Petra—I wrote opposing the plans before the work was begun. But at that time no one would listen to me. Well, I am going to let them have it, now! Of course I have prepared a report for the Baths Committee; I have had it ready for a week, and was only waiting for this to come. (*Shows the letter.*) Now it shall go off at once. (*Goes into his room and comes back with some papers.*) Look at that! Four closely written sheets!—and the letter shall go with them. Give me a bit of paper, Katherine—something to wrap them up in. That will do! Now give it to—to—(*stamps his foot*)—what the deuce is her name?—give it to the maid, and tell her to take it at once to the Mayor.

[MRS. STOCKMANN *takes the packet and goes out through the dining-room.*]

Petra: What do you think uncle Peter will say, father?

Dr. Stockmann: What is there for him to say? I should think he would be very glad that such an important truth has been brought to light.

Hovstad: Will you let me print a short note about your discovery in the *Messenger?*

Dr. Stockmann: I shall be very much obliged if you will.

Hovstad: It is very desirable that the public should be informed of it without delay.

Dr. Stockmann: Certainly.

Mrs. Stockmann (*coming back*). She has just gone with it.

Billing: Upon my soul, Doctor, you are going to be the foremost man in the town!

Dr. Stockmann (*walking about happily*). Nonsense! As a matter of fact I have done nothing more than my duty. I have only made a lucky find—that's all. Still, all the same—

Billing: Hovstad, don't you think the town ought to give Dr. Stockmann some sort of testimonial?

Hovstad: I will suggest it, anyway.

Billing: And I will speak to Aslaksen about it.

Dr. Stockmann: No, my good friends, don't let us have any of that nonsense. I won't hear of anything of the kind. And if the Baths Committee should think of voting me an increase of salary, I will not accept it. Do you hear, Katherine?—I won't accept it.

Mrs. Stockmann: You are quite right, Thomas.

Petra (*lifting her glass*). Your health, father!

Hovstad and Billing: Your health, Doctor! Good health!

Horster (*touches glasses with* DR. STOCKMANN). I hope it will bring you nothing but good luck.

Dr. Stockmann: Thank you, thank you, my dear fellows! I feel tremendously happy! It is a splendid thing for a man to be able to feel that he has done a service to his native town and to his fellow-citizens. Hurrah, Katherine! (*He puts his arms round her and whirls her round and round, while she protests with laughing cries. They all laugh, clap their hands, and cheer the doctor. The boys put their heads in at the door to see what is going on.*)

ACT II

Scene: *The same. The door into the dining-room is shut. It is morning.* MRS. STOCKMANN, *with a sealed letter in her hand, comes in from the dining-room, goes to the door of the* DOCTOR'S *study, and peeps in.*

Mrs. Stockmann: Are you in, Thomas?

Dr. Stockmann (*from within his room*). Yes, I have just come in. (*Comes into the room.*) What is it?

Mrs. Stockmann: A letter from your brother.

Dr. Stockmann: Aha, let us see! (*Opens the letter and reads:*) "I return herewith the manuscript you sent me"— (*Reads on in a low murmur.*) Hm!—

Mrs. Stockmann: What does he say?

Dr Stockmann (*putting the papers in his pocket*). Oh, he only writes that he will come up here himself about midday.

Mrs. Stockmann: Well, try and remember to be at home this time.

Dr. Stockmann: That will be all right; I have got through all my morning visits.

Mrs. Stockmann: I am extremely curious to know how he takes it.

Dr. Stockmann: You will see he won't like its having been I, and not he, that made the discovery.

Mrs. Stockmann: Aren't you a little nervous about that?

Dr. Stockmann: Oh, he really will be pleased enough, you know. But, at the same time, Peter is so confoundedly afraid of anyone's doing any service to the town except himself.

Mrs. Stockmann: I will tell you what, Thomas—you should be good natured, and share the credit of this with him. Couldn't you make out that it was he who set you on the scent of this discovery?

Dr. Stockmann: I am quite willing. If only I can get the thing set right. I—

[MORTEN KIIL *puts his head in through the door leading from the hall, looks round in an enquiring manner, and chuckles.*]

Morten Kiil (*slyly*). Is it—is it true?

Mrs. Stockmann (*going to the door*). Father!—is it you?

Dr. Stockmann: Ah, Mr. Kiil—good morning, good morning!

Mrs. Stockmann: But come along in.

Morten Kiil: If it is true, I will; if not, I am off.

Dr. Stockmann: If what is true?

Morten Kiil: This tale about the water supply. Is it true?

Dr. Stockmann: Certainly it is true. But how did you come to hear it?

Morten Kiil (*coming in*). Petra ran in on her way to the school—

Dr. Stockmann: Did she?

Morten Kiil: Yes; and she declares that—. I thought she was only making a fool of me, but it isn't like Petra to do that.

Dr. Stockmann: Of course not. How could you imagine such a thing!

Morten Kiil: Oh well, it is better never to trust anybody; you may find you have been made a fool of before you know where you are. But it is really true, all the same?

Dr. Stockmann: You can depend upon it that it is true. Won't you sit down? (*Settles him on the couch.*) Isn't it a real bit of luck for the town—

Morten Kiil (*suppressing his laughter*). A bit of luck for the town?

Dr. Stockmann: Yes, that I made the discovery in good time.

Morten Kiil (*as before*). Yes, yes, yes!—But I should never have thought you the sort of man to pull your own brother's leg like this!

Dr. Stockmann: Pull his leg!

Mrs. Stockmann: Really, father dear—

Morten Kiil (*resting his hands and his chin on the handle of his stick and winking slyly at the* DOCTOR). Let me see, what was the story? Some kind of beast that had got into the water-pipes, wasn't it?

Dr. Stockmann: Infusoria—yes.

Morten Kiil: And a lot of these beasts had got in, according to Petra—a tremendous lot.

Dr. Stockmann: Certainly; hundreds of thousands of them, probably.

Morten Kiil: But no one can see them —isn't that so?

Dr. Stockmann: Yes; you can't see them.

Morten Kiil (*with a quiet chuckle*). Damme—it's the finest story I have ever heard!

Dr. Stockmann: What do you mean?

Morten Kiil: But you will never get the Mayor to believe a thing like that.

Dr. Stockmann: We shall see.

Morten Kiil: Do you think he will be fool enough to—?

Dr. Stockmann: I hope the whole town will be fools enough.

Morten Kiil: The whole town! Well, it wouldn't be a bad thing. It would just serve them right, and teach them a lesson. They think themselves so much cleverer than we old fellows. They hounded me out of the council; they did, I tell you—they hounded me out. Now they shall pay for it. You pull their legs too, Thomas!

Dr. Stockmann: Really, I—

Morten Kiil: You pull their legs! (*Gets up.*) If you can work it so that the Mayor and his friends all swallow the same bait, I will give ten pounds to a charity—like a shot!

Dr. Stockmann: That is very kind of you.

Morten Kiil: Yes, I haven't got much money to throw away, I can tell you; but if you can work this, I will give five pounds to a charity at Christmas.

[HOVSTAD *comes in by the hall door.*]

Hovstad: Good morning! (*Stops.*) Oh, I beg your pardon—

Dr. Stockmann: Not at all; come in.

Morten Kiil (*with another chuckle*). Oho!—is he in this too?

Hovstad: What do you mean?

Dr. Stockmann: Certainly he is.

Morten Kiil: I might have known it! It must get into the papers. You know how to do it, Thomas! Set your wits to work. Now I must go.

Dr. Stockmann: Won't you stay a little while?

Morten Kiil: No, I must be off now.

You keep up this game for all it is worth; you won't repent it, I'm damned if you will!

[*He goes out;* MRS. STOCKMANN *follows him into the hall.*]

Dr. Stockmann (*laughing*). Just imagine—the old chap doesn't believe a word of all this about the water supply.

Hovstad: Oh, that was it, then?

Dr. Stockmann: Yes, that was what we were talking about. Perhaps it is the same thing that brings you here?

Hovstad: Yes, it is. Can you spare me a few minutes, Doctor?

Dr. Stockmann: As long as you like, my dear fellow.

Hovstad: Have you heard from the Mayor yet?

Dr. Stockmann: Not yet. He is coming here later.

Hovstad: I have given the matter a great deal of thought since last night.

Dr. Stockmann: Well?

Hovstad: From your point of view, as a doctor and a man of science, this affair of the water-supply is an isolated matter. I mean, you do not realize that it involves a great many other things.

Dr. Stockmann: How do you mean? —Let us sit down, my dear fellow. No, sit here on the couch. (HOVSTAD *sits down on the couch,* DR. STOCKMANN *on a chair on the other side of the table.*) Now then. You mean that—?

Hovstad: You said yesterday that the pollution of the water was due to impurities in the soil.

Dr. Stockmann: Yes, unquestionably it is due to that poisonous morass up at Mölledal.

Hovstad: Begging your pardon, doctor, I fancy it is due to quite another morass altogether.

Dr. Stockmann: What morass?

Hovstad: The morass that the whole life of our town is built on and is rotting in.

Dr. Stockmann: What the deuce are you driving at, Hovstad?

Hovstad: The whole of the town's interests have, little by little, got into the hands of a pack of officials.

Dr. Stockmann: Oh, come!—they are not all officials.

Hovstad: No, but those that are not officials are at any rate the officials' friends and adherents; it is the wealthy folk, the old families in the town, that have got us entirely in their hands.

Dr. Stockmann: Yes, but after all they are men of ability and knowledge.

Hovstad: Did they show any ability or knowledge when they laid the conduit-pipes where they are now?

Dr. Stockmann: No, of course that was a great piece of stupidity on their part. But that is going to be set right now.

Hovstad: Do you think that will be all such plain sailing?

Dr. Stockmann: Plain sailing or no, it has got to be done, anyway.

Hovstad: Yes, provided the press takes up the question.

Dr. Stockmann: I don't think that will be necessary, my dear fellow, I am certain my brother—

Hovstad: Excuse me, doctor; I feel bound to tell you I am inclined to take the matter up.

Dr. Stockmann: In the paper?

Hovstad: Yes. When I took over the *People's Messenger* my idea was to break up this ring of self-opinionated old fossils who had got hold of all the influence.

Dr. Stockmann: But you know you told me yourself what the result had been; you nearly ruined your paper.

Hovstad: Yes, at the time we were obliged to climb down a peg or two, it is quite true; because there was a danger of the whole project of the Baths coming to nothing if they failed us. But now the scheme has been carried through, and we can dispense with these grand gentlemen.

Dr. Stockmann: Dispense with them, yes; but we owe them a great debt of gratitude.

Hovstad: That shall be recognized ungrudgingly. But a journalist of my democratic tendencies cannot let such an opportunity as this slip. The bubble of official infallibility must be pricked. This superstition must be destroyed, like any other.

Dr. Stockmann: I am whole-heartedly with you in that, Mr. Hovstad; if it is a superstition, away with it!

Hovstad: I should be very reluctant to bring the Mayor into it, because he is your brother. But I am sure you will agree with me that truth should be the first consideration.

Dr. Stockmann: That goes without saying. (*With sudden emphasis.*) Yes, but —but—

Hovstad: You must not misjudge me. I am neither more self-interested nor more ambitious than most men.

Dr. Stockmann: My dear fellow— who suggests anything of the kind?

Hovstad: I am of humble origin, as you know; and that has given me opportunities of knowing what is the most crying need in the humbler ranks of life. It is that they should be allowed some part in the direction of public affairs, Doctor. That is what will develop their faculties and intelligence and self-respect—

Dr. Stockmann: I quite appreciate that.

Hovstad: Yes—and in my opinion a journalist incurs a heavy responsibility if he neglects a favorable opportunity of emancipating the masses—the humble and oppressed. I knew well enough that in exalted circles I shall be called an agitator, and all that sort of thing; but they may call what they like. If only my conscience doesn't reproach me, then—

Dr. Stockmann: Quite right! Quite right, Mr. Hovstad. But all the same— devil take it! (*A knock is heard at the door.*) Come in!

[ASLAKSEN *appears at the door. He is poorly but decently dressed, in black, with a slightly crumpled white neckcloth; he wears gloves and has a felt hat in his hand.*]

Aslaksen (*bowing*). Excuse my taking the liberty, Doctor—

Dr. Stockmann (*getting up*). Ah, it is you, Aslaksen!

Aslaksen: Yes, Doctor.

Hovstad (*standing up*). Is it me you want, Aslaksen?

Aslaksen: No; I didn't know I should find you here. No, it was the Doctor I—

Dr. Stockmann: I am quite at your service. What is it?

Aslaksen: Is what I heard from Mr. Billing true, sir—that you mean to improve our water-supply?

Dr. Stockmann: Yes, for the Baths.

Aslaksen: Quite so, I understand. Well, I have come to say that I will back that up by every means in my power.

Hovstad (*to the* DOCTOR). You see!

Dr. Stockmann: I shall be very grateful to you, but—

Aslaksen: Because it may be no bad thing to have us small tradesmen at your back. We form, as it were, a compact majority in the town—if we choose. And it is always a good thing to have the majority with you, Doctor.

Dr. Stockmann: That is undeniably true; but I confess I don't see why such unusual precautions should be necessary in this case. It seems to me that such a plain, straight-forward thing—

Aslaksen: Oh, it may be very desirable, all the same. I know our local authorities so well; officials are not generally very ready to act on proposals that come from other people. That is why I think it would not be at all amiss if we made a little demonstration.

Hovstad: That's right.

Dr. Stockmann: Demonstration, did you say? What on earth are you going to make a demonstration about?

Aslaksen: We shall proceed with the greatest moderation, Doctor. Moderation is always my aim; it is the greatest virtue in a citizen—at least, I think so.

Dr. Stockmann: It is well known to be a characteristic of yours, Mr. Aslaksen.

Aslaksen: Yes, I think I may pride myself on that. And this matter of the water-supply is of the greatest importance to us small tradesmen. The Baths promise to be a regular gold-mine for the town. We shall all make our living out of them, especially those of us who are householders. That is why we will back up the project as strongly as possible. And as I am at present Chairman of the Householders' Association—

Dr. Stockmann: Yes—?

Aslaksen: And, what is more, local secretary of the Temperance Society—you know, sir, I suppose, that I am a worker in the temperance cause?

Dr. Stockmann: Of course, of course.

Aslaksen: Well, you can understand that I come into contact with a great many people. And as I have the reputation of a temperate and law-abiding citizen—like yourself Doctor—I have a certain influence in the town, a little bit of power, if I may be allowed to say so.

Dr. Stockmann: I know that quite well, Mr. Aslaksen.

Aslaksen: So you see it would be an easy matter for me to set on foot some testimonial, if necessary.

Dr. Stockmann: A testimonial?

Aslaksen: Yes, some kind of an address of thanks from the townsmen for your share in a matter of such importance to the community. I need scarcely say that it would have to be drawn up with the greatest regard to moderation, so as not to offend the authorities—who, after all, have the reins in their hands. If we pay strict attention to that, no one can take it amiss, I should think!

Hovstad: Well, and even supposing they didn't like it—

Aslaksen: No, no, no; there must be no discourtesy to the authorities, Mr. Hovstad. It is no use falling foul of those upon whom our welfare so closely depends. I have done that in my time, and no good ever comes of it. But no one can take exception to a reasonable and frank expression of a citizen's views.

Dr. Stockmann (*shaking him by the hand*). I can't tell you, dear Mr. Aslaksen, how extremely pleased I am to find such hearty support among my fellow-citizens. I am delighted—delighted! Now, you will take a small glass of sherry, eh?

Aslaksen: No, thank you; I never drink alcohol of that kind.

Dr. Stockmann: Well, what do you say to a glass of beer, then?

Aslaksen: Nor that either, thank you, Doctor. I never drink anything as early as this. I am going into town now to talk this over with one or two householders, and prepare the ground.

Dr. Stockmann: It is tremendously

kind of you, Mr. Aslaksen; but I really cannot understand the necessity for all these precautions. It seems to me that the thing should go of itself.

Aslaksen: The authorities are somewhat slow to move, Doctor. Far be it from me to seem to blame them—

Hovstad: We are going to stir them up in the paper tomorrow, Aslaksen.

Aslaksen: But not violently, I trust, Mr. Hovstad. Proceed with moderation, or you will do nothing with them. You may take my advice; I have gathered my experience in the school of life. Well, I must say good-bye, Doctor. You know now that we small tradesmen are at your back at all events, like a solid wall. You have the compact majority on your side, Doctor.

Dr. Stockmann: I am very much obliged, dear Mr. Aslaksen. (*Shakes hands with him.*) Good-bye, good-bye.

Aslaksen: Are you going my way, towards the printing-office, Mr. Hovstad?

Hovstad: I will come later; I have something to settle up first.

Aslaksen: Very well. (*Bows and goes out;* STOCKMANN *follows him into the hall.*)

Hovstad (*as* STOCKMANN *comes in again*). Well, what do you think of that, Doctor? Don't you think it is high time we stirred a little life into all this slackness and vacillation and cowardice?

Dr. Stockmann: Are you referring to Aslaksen?

Hovstad: Yes, I am. He is one of those who are floundering in a bog—decent enough fellow though he may be, otherwise. And most of the people here are in just the same case—see-sawing and edging first to one side and then to the other, so overcome with caution and scruple that they never dare to take any decided step.

Dr. Stockmann: Yes, but Aslaksen seemed to me so thoroughly well-intentioned.

Hovstad: There is one thing I esteem higher than that; and that is for a man to be self-reliant and sure of himself.

Dr. Stockmann: I think you are perfectly right there.

Hovstad: That is why I want to seize this opportunity, and try if I cannot manage to put a little virility into these well-intentioned people for once. The idol of Authority must be shattered in this town. This gross and inexcusable blunder about the water-supply must be brought home to the mind of every municipal voter.

Dr. Stockmann: Very well; if you are of the opinion that it is for the good of the community, so be it. But not until I have had a talk with my brother.

Hovstad: Anyway, I will get a leading article ready; and if the Mayor refuses to take the matter up—

Dr. Stockmann: How can you suppose such a thing possible?

Hovstad: It is conceivable. And in that case—

Dr. Stockmann: In that case I promise you—. Look here, in that case you may print my report—every word of it.

Hovstad: May I? Have I your word for it?

Dr. Stockmann (*giving him the MS.*). Here it is; take it with you. It can do no harm for you to read it through, and you can give it me back later on.

Hovstad: Good, good! That is what I will do. And now good-bye, Doctor.

Dr. Stockmann: Good-bye, good-bye. You will see everything will run quite smoothly, Mr. Hovstad—quite smoothly.

Hovstad: H'm!—we shall see. (*Bows and goes out.*)

Dr. Stockmann (*opens the dining-room door and looks in*). Katherine! Oh, you are back, Petra?

Petra (*coming in*). Yes, I have just come from the school.

Mrs. Stockmann (*coming in*). Has he not been here yet?

Dr. Stockmann: Peter? No. But I have had a long talk with Hovstad. He is quite excited about my discovery. I find it has a much wider bearing than I at first imagined. And he has put his paper at my disposal if necessity should arise.

Mrs. Stockmann: Do you think it will?

Dr. Stockmann: Not for a moment. But at all events it makes me feel proud to know that I have the liberal-minded independent press on my side. Yes, and—just imagine—I have had a visit from the Chairman of the Householders' Association!

Mrs. Stockmann: Oh! What did he want?

Dr. Stockmann: To offer me his support too. They will support me in a body if it should be necessary. Katherine—do you know what I have got behind me?

Mrs. Stockmann: Behind you? No, what have you got behind you?

Dr. Stockmann: The compact majority.

Mrs. Stockmann: Really? Is that a good thing for you, Thomas?

Dr. Stockmann: I should think it was a good thing. (*Walks up and down rubbing his hands.*) By Jove, it's a fine thing to feel this bond of brotherhood between oneself and one's fellow citizens!

Petra: And to be able to do so much that is good and useful, father!

Dr. Stockmann: And for one's own native town into the bargain, my child!

Mrs. Stockmann: That was a ring at the bell.

Dr. Stockmann: It must be he, then. (*A knock is heard at the door.*) Come in!

Peter Stockmann (*comes in from the hall*). Good morning.

Dr. Stockmann: Glad to see you, Peter!

Mrs. Stockmann: Good morning, Peter. How are you?

Peter Stockmann: So so, thank you. (*To* DR. STOCKMANN.) I received from you yesterday, after office hours, a report dealing with the condition of the water at the Baths.

Dr. Stockmann: Yes. Have you read it?

Peter Stockmann: Yes, I have.

Dr. Stockmann: And what have you to say to it?

Peter Stockmann (*with a sidelong glance*). Hm!—

Mrs. Stockmann: Come along, Petra. (*She and* PETRA *go into the room on the left.*)

Peter Stockmann (*after a pause*). Was it necessary to make all these investigations behind my back?

Dr. Stockmann: Yes, because until I was absolutely certain about it—

Peter Stockmann: Then you mean that you are absolutely certain now?

Dr. Stockmann: Surely you are convinced of that.

Peter Stockmann: Is it your intention to bring this document before the Baths Committee as a sort of official communication?

Dr. Stockmann: Certainly. Something must be done in the matter—and that quickly.

Peter Stockmann: As usual, you employ violent expressions in your report. You say, amongst other things, that what we offer visitors in our Baths is a permanent supply of poison.

Dr. Stockmann: Well, can you describe it any other way, Peter! Just think—

water that is poisonous, whether you drink it or bathe in it! And this we offer to the poor sick folk who come to us trustfully and pay us at an exorbitant rate to be made well again!

Peter Stockmann: And your reasoning leads you to this conclusion, that we must build a sewer to draw off the alleged impurities from Mölledal and must relay the water-conduits.

Dr. Stockmann: Yes. Do you see any other way out of it? I don't.

Peter Stockmann: I made a pretext this morning to go and see the town engineer, and, as if only half seriously, broached the subject of these proposals as a thing we might perhaps have to take under consideration some time later on.

Dr. Stockmann: Some time later on!

Peter Stockmann: He smiled at what he considered to be my extravagance, naturally. Have you taken the trouble to consider what your proposed alterations would cost? According to the information I obtained, the expenses would probably mount up to fifteen or twenty thousand pounds.

Dr. Stockmann: Would it cost so much?

Peter Stockmann: Yes; and the worst part of it would be that the work would take at least two years.

Dr. Stockmann: Two years? Two whole years?

Peter Stockmann: At least. And what are we to do with the Baths in the meantime? Close them? Indeed we should be obliged to. And do you suppose any one would come near the place after it had got about that the water was dangerous?

Dr. Stockmann: Yes, but, Peter, that is what it is.

Peter Stockmann: And all this at this juncture—just as the Baths are beginning to be known. There are other towns in the neighborhood with qualifications to attract visitors for bathing purposes. Don't you suppose they would immediately strain every nerve to divert the entire stream of strangers to themselves? Unquestionably they would; and then where should we be? We should probably have to abandon the whole thing, which has cost us so much money—and then you would have ruined your native town.

Dr. Stockmann: I—should have ruined—!

Peter Stockmann: It is simply and solely through the Baths that the town has before it any future worth mentioning. You know that just as well as I.

Dr. Stockmann: But what do you think ought to be done, then?

Peter Stockmann: Your report has not convinced me that the condition of the water at the Baths is as bad as you represent it to be.

Dr. Stockmann: I tell you it is even worse!—or at all events it will be in summer, when the warm weather comes.

Peter Stockmann: As I said, I believe you exaggerate the matter considerably. A capable physician ought to know what measures to take—he ought to be capable of preventing injurious influences or of remedying them if they become obviously persistent.

Dr. Stockmann: Well? What more?

Peter Stockmann: The water supply for the Baths is now an established fact, and in consequence must be treated as such. But probably the Committee, at its discretion, will not be disinclined to consider the question of how far it might be possible to introduce certain improvements consistently with a reasonable expenditure.

Dr. Stockmann: And do you suppose

that I will have anything to do with such a piece of trickery as that?

Peter Stockmann: Trickery!

Dr. Stockmann: Yes, it would be a trick—a fraud, a lie, a downright crime towards the public, towards the whole community!

Peter Stockmann: I have not, as I remarked before, been able to convince myself that there is actually any imminent danger.

Dr. Stockmann: You have! It is impossible that you should not be convinced. I know I have represented the facts absolutely truthfully and fairly. And you know it very well, Peter, only you won't acknowledge it. It was owing to your action that both the Baths and the water-conduits were built where they are; and that is what you won't acknowledge—that damnable blunder of yours. Pooh!—do you suppose I don't see through you?

Peter Stockmann: And even if that were true? If I perhaps guard my reputation somewhat anxiously, it is in the interests of the town. Without moral authority I am powerless to direct public affairs as seems, to my judgment, to be best for the common good. And on that account—and for various other reasons too—it appears to me to be a matter of importance that your report should not be delivered to the Committee. In the interests of the public, you must withhold it. Then, later on, I will raise the question and we will do our best, privately; but nothing of this unfortunate affair—not a single word of it—must come to the ears of the public.

Dr. Stockmann: I am afraid you will not be able to prevent that now, my dear Peter.

Peter Stockmann: It must and shall be prevented.

Dr. Stockmann: It is no use, I tell you. There are too many people that know about it.

Peter Stockmann: That know about it? Who? Surely you don't mean those fellows on the *People's Messenger?*

Dr. Stockmann: Yes, they know. The liberal-minded independent press is going to see that you do your duty.

Peter Stockmann (*after a short pause*). You are an extraordinarily independent man, Thomas. Have you given no thoughts to the consequences this may have for yourself?

Dr. Stockmann: Consequences?—for me?

Peter Stockmann: For you and yours, yes.

Dr. Stockmann: What the deuce do you mean?

Peter Stockmann: I believe I have always behaved in a brotherly way to you—have always been ready to oblige or to help you?

Dr. Stockmann: Yes, you have, and I am grateful to you for it.

Peter Stockmann: There is no need. Indeed, to some extent I was forced to do so—for my own sake. I always hoped that, if I helped to improve your financial position, I should be able to keep some check on you.

Dr. Stockmann: What!! Then it was only for your own sake—!

Peter Stockmann: Up to a certain point, yes. It is painful for a man in an official position to have his nearest relative compromising himself time after time.

Dr. Stockmann: And do you consider that I do that?

Peter Stockmann: Yes, unfortunately, you do, without even being aware of it. You have a restless, pugnacious, rebellious disposition. And then there is that disastrous propensity of yours to want to write about every sort of possible and impossible thing. The moment an idea comes into your head, you must needs go and write a newspaper article or a whole pamphlet about it.

Dr. Stockmann: Well, but is it not the duty of a citizen to let the public share in any new ideas he may have?

Peter Stockmann: Oh, the public doesn't require any new ideas. The public is best served by the good, old-established ideas it already has.

Dr. Stockmann: And that is your honest opinion?

Peter Stockmann: Yes, and for once I must talk frankly to you. Hitherto I have tried to avoid doing so, because I know how irritable you are; but now I must tell you the truth, Thomas. You have no conception what an amount of harm you do yourself by your impetuosity. You complain of the authorities, you even complain of the government—you are always pulling them to pieces; you insist that you have been neglected and persecuted. But what else can such a cantankerous man as you expect?

Dr. Stockmann: What next! Cantankerous, am I?

Peter Stockmann: Yes, Thomas, you are an extremely cantankerous man to work with—I know that to my cost. You disregard everything that you ought to have consideration for. You seem completely to forget that it is me you have to thank for your appointment here as medical officer to the Baths—

Dr. Stockmann: I was entitled to it as a matter of course!—I and nobody else! I was the first person to see that the town could be made into a flourishing watering-place, and I was the only one who saw it at that time. I had to fight single-handed in support of the idea for many years; and I wrote and wrote—

Peter Stockmann: Undoubtedly. But things were not ripe for the scheme then—though, of course, you could not judge of that in your out-of-the-way corner up north. But as soon as the opportune moment came I—and the others—took the matter into our hands—

Dr. Stockmann: Yes, and made this mess of all my beautiful plan. It is pretty obvious now what clever fellows you were!

Peter Stockmann: To my mind the whole thing only seems to mean that you are seeking another outlet for your combativeness. You want to pick a quarrel with your superiors—an old habit of yours. You cannot put up with any authority over you. You look askance at anyone who occupies a superior official position; you regard him as a personal enemy, and then any stick is good enough to beat him with. But now I have called your attention to the fact that the town's interests are at stake—and, incidentally, my own too. And therefore I must tell you, Thomas, that you will find me inexorable with regard to what I am about to require you to do.

Dr. Stockmann: And what is that?

Peter Stockmann: As you have been so indiscreet as to speak of this delicate matter to outsiders, despite the fact that you ought to have treated it as entirely official and confidential, it is obviously impossible to hush it up now. All sorts of rumors will get about directly, and everybody who has a grudge against us will take care to embellish these rumors. So it will be necessary for you to refute them publicly.

Dr. Stockmann: I! How? I don't understand.

Peter Stockmann: What we shall expect is that, after making further investigations, you will come to the conclusion that the matter is not by any means as dangerous or as critical as you imagined in the first instance.

Dr. Stockmann: Oho!—so that is what you expect!

Peter Stockmann: And, what is more, we shall expect you to make public profession of your confidence in the Committee and in their readiness to consider fully and conscientiously what steps may be necessary to remedy any possible defects.

Dr. Stockmann: But you will never be able to do that by patching and tinkering at it—never! Take my word for it, Peter; I mean what I say, as deliberately and emphatically as possible.

Peter Stockmann: As an officer under the Committee, you have no right to any individual opinion.

Dr. Stockmann (*amazed*). No right?

Peter Stockmann: In your official capacity, no. As a private person, it is quite another matter. But as a subordinate member of the staff of the Baths, you have no right to express any opinion which runs contrary to that of your superiors.

Dr. Stockmann: This is too much! I, a doctor, a man of science, have no right to—!

Peter Stockmann: The matter in hand is not simply a scientific one. It is a complicated matter, and has its economic as well as its technical side.

Dr. Stockmann: I don't care what it is! I intend to be free to express my opinion on any subject under the sun.

Peter Stockmann: As you please—but not on any subject concerning the Baths. That we forbid.

Dr. Stockmann (*shouting*). You forbid—! You! A pack of—

Peter Stockmann: *I* forbid it—I, your chief; and if I forbid it, you have to obey.

Dr. Stockmann (*controlling himself*). Peter—if you were not my brother—

Petra (*throwing open the door*). Father, you shan't stand this!

Mrs. Stockmann (*coming in after her*). Petra, Petra!

Peter Stockmann: Oh, so you have been eavesdropping.

Mrs. Stockmann: You were talking so loud, we couldn't help—

Petra: Yes, I was listening.

Peter Stockmann: Well, after all, I am very glad—

Dr. Stockmann (*going up to him*). You were saying something about forbidding and obeying?

Peter Stockmann: You obliged me to take that tone with you.

Dr. Stockmann: And so I am to give myself the lie, publicly?

Peter Stockmann: We consider it absolutely necessary that you should make some such public statement as I have asked for.

Dr. Stockmann: And if I do not—obey?

Peter Stockmann: Then we shall publish a statement ourselves to reassure the public.

Dr. Stockmann: Very well; but in that case I shall use my pen against you. I stick to what I have said; I will show that I am right and that you are wrong. And what will you do then?

Peter Stockmann: Then I shall not be able to prevent your being dismissed.

Dr. Stockmann: What—?

Petra: Father—dismissed!

Mrs. Stockmann: Dismissed!

Peter Stockmann: Dismissed from the staff of the Baths. I shall be obliged to propose that you shall immediately be given notice, and shall not be allowed any further participation in the Baths' affairs.

Dr. Stockmann: You would dare to do that!

Peter Stockmann: It is you that are playing the daring game.

Petra: Uncle, that is a shameful way to treat a man like father!

Mrs. Stockmann: Do hold your tongue, Petra!

Peter Stockmann (*looking at* PETRA). Oh, so we volunteer our opinions already, do we? Of course. (*To* MRS. STOCKMANN.) Katherine, I imagine you are the most sensible person in this house. Use any influence you may have over your husband, and make him see what this will entail for his family as well as—

Dr. Stockmann: My family is my own concern and nobody else's!

Peter Stockmann: —for his own family, as I was saying, as well as for the town he lives in.

Dr. Stockmann: It is I who have the real good of the town at heart! I want to lay bare the defects that sooner or later must come to the light of day. I will show whether I love my native town.

Peter Stockmann: You, who in your blind obstinacy want to cut off the most important source of the town's welfare?

Dr. Stockmann: The source is poisoned, man! Are you mad? We are making our living by retailing filth and corruption! The whole of our flourishing municipal life derives its sustenance from a lie!

Peter Stockmann: All imagination—or something even worse. The man who can throw out such offensive insinuations about his native town must be an enemy to our community.

Dr. Stockmann (*going up to him*). Do you dare to—!

Mrs. Stockmann (*throwing herself between them*). Thomas!

Petra (*catching her father by the arm*). Don't lose your temper, father!

Peter Stockmann: I will not expose myself to violence. Now you have had a warning; so reflect on what you owe to yourself and your family. Good-bye. (*Goes out.*)

Dr. Stockmann: (*walking up and down*). Am I to put up with such treatment as this? In my own house, Katherine! What do you think of that!

Mrs. Stockmann: Indeed it is both shameful and absurd. Thomas—

Petra: If only I could give uncle a piece of my mind—

Dr. Stockmann: It is my own fault. I ought to have flown out at him long ago!—shown my teeth!—bitten! To hear him call me an enemy to our community! Me! *I* shall not take that lying down, upon my soul!

Mrs. Stockmann: But, dear Thomas, your brother has power on his side—

Dr. Stockmann: Yes, but I have right on mine, I tell you.

Mrs. Stockmann: Oh yes, right—right. What is the use of having right on your side if you have not got might?

Petra: Oh, mother!—how can you say such a thing!

Dr. Stockmann: Do you imagine that in a free country it is no use having right on your side? You are absurd, Katherine. Besides, haven't I got the liberal-minded, independent press to lead the way, and the compact majority behind me? That is might enough, I should think!

Mrs. Stockmann: But, good heavens, Thomas, you don't mean to—?

Dr. Stockmann: Don't mean to what?

Mrs. Stockmann: To set yourself up in opposition to your brother.

Dr. Stockmann: In God's name, what else do you suppose I should do but take my stand on right and truth?

Petra: Yes, I was just going to say that.

Mrs. Stockmann: But it won't do you any earthly good. If they won't do it, they won't.

Dr. Stockmann: Oho, Katherine! Just give me time, and you will see how I will carry the war into their camp.

Mrs. Stockmann: Yes, you carry the war into their camp, and you get your dismissal—that is what you will do.

Dr. Stockmann: In any case I shall have done my duty towards the public—towards the community. I, who am called its enemy!

Mrs. Stockmann: But towards your family, Thomas? Towards your own home! Do you think that is doing your duty towards those you have to provide for?

Petra: Ah, don't always think first of us, mother.

Mrs. Stockmann: Oh, it is easy for you to talk; you are able to shift for yourself, if need be. But remember the boys, Thomas; and think a little too of yourself, and of me—

Dr. Stockmann: I think you are out of your senses, Katherine! If I were to be such a miserable coward as to go on my knees to Peter and his damned crew, do you suppose I should ever know an hour's peace of mind all my life afterwards?

Mrs. Stockmann: I don't know anything about that; but God preserve us from the peace of mind we shall have, all the same, if you go on defying him! You will find yourself again without the means of subsistence, with no income to count upon. I should think we had had enough of that in the old days. Remember that, Thomas; think what that means.

Dr. Stockmann (*collecting himself with a struggle and clenching his fists*). And this is what this slavery can bring upon a free, honorable man! Isn't it horrible, Katherine?

Mrs. Stockmann: Yes, it is sinful to treat you so, it is perfectly true. But, good heavens, one has to put up with so much injustice in this world.—There are the boys, Thomas! Look at them! What is to become of them? Oh, no, no, you can never have the heart—.

[EJLIF *and* MORTEN *have come in while she was speaking, with their school books in their hands.*]

Dr. Stockmann: The boys—! (*Recovers himself suddenly.*) No, even if the whole world goes to pieces, I will never bow my neck to this yoke! (*Goes towards his room.*)

Mrs. Stockmann (*following him*). Thomas—what are you going to do!

Dr. Stockmann (*at his door*). I mean to have the right to look my sons in the face when they are grown men. (*Goes into his room.*)

Mrs. Stockmann (*bursting into tears*). God help us all!

Petra: Father is splendid! He will not give in.

[*The boys look on in amazement;* PETRA *signs to them not to speak.*]

ACT III

Scene: *The editorial office of the* People's Messenger. *The entrance door is on the left-hand side of the back wall; on the right-hand side is another door with glass panels through which the printing-room can be seen. Another door in the right-hand wall. In the middle of the room is a large table covered with papers, newspapers and books. In the foreground on the left a window, before which stand a desk and a high stool. There are a couple of easy chairs by the table, and other chairs standing along the wall. The room is dingy and uncomfortable; the furniture is old, the chairs stained and torn. In the printing-room the compositors are seen at work, and a printer is working a hand-press.* HOVSTAD *is sitting at the desk, writing.* BILLING *comes in from the right with* DR. STOCKMANN'S *manuscript in his hand.*

Billing: Well, I must say!

Hovstad (*still writing*). Have you read it through?

Billing (*laying the MS. on the desk*). Yes, indeed I have.

Hovstad: Don't you think the Doctor hits them pretty hard?

Billing: Hard? Bless my soul, he's crushing! Every word falls like—how shall I put it?—like the blow of a sledge-hammer.

Hovstad: Yes, but they are not the people to throw up the sponge at the first blow.

Billing: That is true; and for that reason we must strike blow upon blow until the whole of this aristocracy tumbles to pieces. As I sat in there reading this, I almost seemed to see a revolution in being.

Hovstad (*turning round*). Hush!—Speak so that Aslaksen cannot hear you.

Billing (*lowering his voice*). Aslaksen is a chicken-hearted chap, a coward; there is nothing of the man in him. But this time you will insist on your own way, won't you? You will put the Doctor's article in?

Hovstad: Yes, and if the Mayor doesn't like it—

Billing: That will be the devil of a nuisance.

Hovstad: Well, fortunately we can turn the situation to good account, whatever happens. If the Mayor will not fall in with the Doctor's project, he will have all the small tradesmen down on him—the whole of the Householders' Association and the rest of them. And if he does fall in with it, he will fall out with the whole crowd of large shareholders in the Baths, who up to now have been his most valuable supporters—

Billing: Yes, because they will certainly have to fork out a pretty penny—

Hovstad: Yes, you may be sure they will. And in this way the ring will be broken up, you see, and then in every issue of the paper we will enlighten the public on the Mayor's incapability on one point and another, and make it clear that all the positions of trust in the town, the whole control of municipal affairs, ought to be put in the hands of the Liberals.

Billing: That is perfectly true! I see it coming—I see it coming; we are on the threshold of a revolution!

[*A knock is heard at the door.*]

Hovstad: Hush! (*Calls out.*) Come in! (DR. STOCKMANN *comes in by the street door.* HOVSTAD *goes to meet him.*) Ah, it is you, Doctor! Well?

Dr. Stockmann: You may set to work and print it, Mr. Hovstad!

Hovstad: Has it come to that, then?

Billing: Hurrah!

Dr. Stockmann: Yes, print away. Undoubtedly it has come to that. Now they must take what they get. There is going to be a fight in the town, Mr. Billing!

Billing: War to the knife, I hope! We will get our knives to their throats, Doctor!

Dr. Stockmann: This article is only a beginning. I have already got four or five more sketched out in my head. Where is Aslaksen?

Billing (*calls into the printing-room*). Aslaksen, just come here for a minute!

Hovstad: Four or five more articles, did you say? On the same subject?

Dr. Stockmann: No—far from it, my dear fellow. No, they are about quite another matter. But they all spring from the question of the water-supply and the drainage. One thing leads to another, you know. It is like beginning to pull down an old house, exactly.

Billing: Upon my soul, it's true; you find you are not done till you have pulled all the old rubbish down.

Aslaksen (*coming in*). Pulled down? You are not thinking of pulling down the Baths surely, Doctor?

Hovstad: Far from it, don't be afraid.

Dr. Stockmann: No, we meant something quite different. Well, what do you think of my article, Mr. Hovstad?

Hovstad: I think it is simply a masterpiece—

Dr. Stockmann: Do you really think so? Well, I am very pleased, very pleased.

Hovstad: It is so clear and intelligible. One need have no special knowledge to understand the bearing of it. You will have every enlightened man on your side.

Aslaksen: And every prudent man too, I hope?

Billing: The prudent and the imprudent—almost the whole town.

Aslaksen: In that case we may venture to print it.

Dr. Stockmann: I should think so!

Hovstad: We will put it in to-morrow morning.

Dr. Stockmann: Of course—you must not lose a single day. What I wanted to ask you, Mr. Aslaksen, was if you would supervise the printing of it yourself.

Aslaksen: With pleasure.

Dr. Stockmann: Take care of it as if it were a treasure! No misprints—every word is important. I will look in again a little later; perhaps you will be able to let me see a proof. I can't tell you how eager I am to see it in print, and see it burst upon the public—

Billing: Burst upon them—yes, like a flash of lightning!

Dr. Stockmann: —and to have it submitted to the judgment of my intelligent fellow-townsmen. You cannot imagine what I have gone through to-day. I have been threatened first with one thing and with another; they have tried to rob me of my most elementary rights as a man—

Billing: What! Your rights as a man!

Dr. Stockmann: —they have tried to degrade me, to make a coward of me, to force me to put personal interests before my most sacred convictions—

Billing: That is too much—I'm damned if it isn't.

Hovstad: Oh, you mustn't be surprised at anything from that quarter.

Dr. Stockmann: Well, they will get the worst of it with me; they may assure themselves of that. I shall consider the *People's Messenger* my sheet-anchor now, and every single day I will bombard them with one article after another, like bombshells—

Aslaksen: Yes, but—

Billing: Hurrah!—it is war, it is war!

Dr. Stockmann: I shall smite them to the ground—I shall crush them—I shall break down all their defenses, before the eyes of the honest public! That is what I shall do!

Aslaksen: Yes, but in moderation, Doctor—proceed with moderation—

Billing: Not a bit of it, not a bit of it! Don't spare the dynamite!

Dr. Stockmann: Because it is not merely a question of water-supply and drains now, you know. No—it is the whole of our social life that we have got to purify and disinfect—

Billing: Spoken like a deliverer!

Dr. Stockmann: All the incapables must be turned out, you understand—and that in every walk of life! Endless vistas have opened themselves to my mind's eye to-day. I cannot see it all quite clearly yet, but I shall in time. Young and vigorous standard-bearers—those are what we need and must seek, my friends; we must have new men in command at all our outposts.

Billing: Hear, hear!

Dr. Stockmann: We only need to stand by one another, and it will all be perfectly easy. The revolution will be launched like a ship that runs smoothly off the stocks. Don't you think so?

Hovstad: For my part I think we have now a prospect of getting the municipal authority into the hands where it should lie.

Aslaksen: And if only we proceed with moderation, I cannot imagine that there will be any risk.

Dr. Stockmann: Who the devil cares whether there *is* any risk or not! What I am doing, I am doing in the name of truth and for the sake of my conscience.

Hovstad: You are a man who deserves to be supported, Doctor.

Aslaksen: Yes, there is no denying that the Doctor is a true friend to the town —a real friend to the community, that he is.

Billing: Take my word for it. Aslaksen, Dr. Stockmann is a friend of the people.

Aslaksen: I fancy the Householders' Association will make use of that expression before long.

Dr. Stockmann (*affected, grasps their hands*). Thank you, thank you, my dear staunch friends. It is very refreshing to me to hear you say that; my brother called me something quite different. By Jove, he shall have it back, with interest! But now I must be off to see a poor devil—. I will come back, as I said. Keep a very careful eye on the manuscript, Aslaksen, and don't for worlds leave out any of my notes of exclamation! Rather put one or two more in! Capital, capital! Well, good-bye for the present—good-bye, good-bye!

[*They show him to the door, and bow him out.*]

Hovstad: He may prove an invaluably useful man to us.

Aslaksen: Yes, so long as he confines

himself to this matter of the Baths. But if he goes farther afield, I don't think it would be advisable to follow him.

Hovstad: Hm!—that all depends—

Billing: You are so infernally timid, Aslaksen!

Aslaksen: Timid? Yes, when it is a question of the local authorities, I am timid, Mr. Billing; it is a lesson I have learnt in the school of experience, let me tell you. But try me in higher politics in matters that concern the government itself, and then see if I am timid.

Billing: No, you aren't, I admit. But this is simply contradicting yourself.

Aslaksen: I am a man with a conscience, and that is the whole matter. If you attack the government, you don't do the community any harm, anyway; those fellows pay no attention to attacks, you see—they go on just as they are, in spite of them. But *local* authorities are different; they *can* be turned out, and then perhaps you may get an ignorant lot into office who may do irreparable harm to the householders and everybody else.

Hovstad: But what of the education of citizens by self-government—don't you attach any importance to that?

Aslaksen: When a man has interests of his own to protect, he cannot think of everything, Mr. Hovstad.

Hovstad: Then I hope I shall never have interests of my own to protect!

Billing: Hear, hear!

Aslaksen (*with a smile*). Hm! (*Points to the desk.*) Mr. Sheriff Stensgaard was your predecessor at that editorial desk.

Billing (*spitting*). Bah! That turncoat.

Hovstad: I am not a weathercock—and never will be.

Aslaksen: A politician should never be too certain of anything, Mr. Hovstad. And as for you, Mr. Billing, I should think it is time for you to be taking in a reef or two in your sails, seeing that you are applying for the post of secretary to the Bench.

Billing: I—!

Hovstad: Are you, Billing?

Billing: Well, yes—but you must clearly understand I am doing it only to annoy the bigwigs.

Aslaksen: Anyhow, it is no business of mine. But if I am to be accused of timidity and of inconsistency in my principles, this is what I want to point out: my political past is an open book. I have never changed, except perhaps to become a little more moderate, you see. My heart is still with the people; but I don't deny that my reason has a certain bias towards the authorities—the local ones, I mean. (*Goes into the printing-room.*)

Billing: Oughtn't we to try and get rid of him, Hovstad?

Hovstad: Do you know anyone else who will advance the money for our paper and printing bill?

Billing: It is an infernal nuisance that we don't possess some capital to trade on.

Hovstad (*sitting down at his desk*). Yes, if we only had that, then—

Billing: Suppose you were to apply to Dr. Stockmann?

Hovstad (*turning over some papers*). What is the use? He has got nothing.

Billing: No, but he has got a warm man in the background, old Morten Kiil—"the Badger," as they call him.

Hovstad (*writing*). Are you so sure *he* has got anything?

Billing: Good Lord, of course he has! And some of it must come to the Stockmanns. Most probably he will do something for the children, at all events.

Hovstad (*turning half round*). Are you counting on that?

Billing: Counting on it? Of course I am not counting on anything.

Hovstad: That is right. And I should not count on the secretaryship to the Bench either, if I were you; for I can assure you—you won't get it.

Billing: Do you think I am not quite aware of that? My object is precisely *not* to get it. A slight of that kind stimulates a man's fighting power—it is like getting a supply of fresh bile—and I am sure one needs that badly enough in a hole-and-corner place like this, where it is so seldom anything happens to stir one up.

Hovstad (*writing*). Quite so, quite so.

Billing: Ah, I shall be heard of yet!—Now I shall go and write the appeal to the Householders' Association. (*Goes into the room on the right.*)

Hovstad (*sitting at his desk, biting his pen-holder, says slowly*). Hm!—that's it, is it? (*A knock is heard.*) Come in! (PETRA *comes in by the outer door.* HOVSTAD *gets up.*) What, you!—here?

Petra: Yes, you must forgive me—

Hovstad (*pulling a chair forward*). Won't you sit down?

Petra: No, thank you; I must go again in a moment.

Hovstad: Have you come with a message from your father, by any chance?

Petra: No, I have come on my own account. (*Takes a book out of her coat pocket.*) Here is the English story.

Hovstad: Why have you brought it back?

Petra: Because I am not going to translate it.

Hovstad: But you promised me faithfully—

Petra: Yes, but then I had not read it. I don't suppose you have read it either?

Hovstad: No, you know quite well I don't understand English; but—

Petra: Quite so. That is why I wanted to tell you that you must find something else. (*Lays the book on the table.*) You can't use this for the *People's Messenger.*

Hovstad: Why not?

Petra: Because it conflicts with all your opinions.

Hovstad: Oh, for that matter—

Petra: You don't understand me. The burden of this story is that there is a supernatural power that looks after the so-called good people in this world and makes everything happen for the best in their case—while all the so-called bad people are punished.

Hovstad: Well, but that is all right. That is just what our readers want.

Petra: And are you going to be the one to give it to them? For myself, I do not believe a word of it. You know quite well that things do not happen so in reality.

Hovstad: You are perfectly right; but an editor cannot always act as he would prefer. He is often obliged to bow to the wishes of the public in unimportant matters. Politics are the most important thing in life—for a newspaper, anyway; and if I want to carry my public with me on the path that leads to liberty and progress, I must not frighten them away. If they find a moral tale of this sort in the serial at the bottom of the page, they will be all the more ready to read what is printed above it; they feel more secure, as it were.

Petra: For shame! You would never go and set a snare like that for your readers; you are not a spider!

Hovstad (*smiling*). Thank you for having such a good opinion of me. No; as a matter of fact that is Billing's idea and not mine.

Petra: Billing's!

Hovstad: Yes; anyway he propounded that theory here one day. And it is Billing who is so anxious to have that story in the paper; I don't know anything about the book.

Petra: But how can Billing, with his emancipated views—

Hovstad: Oh, Billing is a many-sided man. He is applying for the post of secretary to the Bench, too, I hear.

Petra: I don't believe it, Mr. Hovstad. How could he possibly bring himself to do such a thing?

Hovstad: Ah, you must ask him that.

Petra: I should never have thought it of him.

Hovstad (*looking more closely at her*). No? Does it really surprise you so much?

Petra: Yes. Or perhaps not altogether. Really, I don't quite know—

Hovstad: We journalists are not much worth, Miss Stockmann.

Petra: Do you really mean that?

Hovstad: I think so sometimes.

Petra: Yes, in the ordinary affairs of everyday life, perhaps; I can understand that. But now, when you have taken a weighty matter in hand—

Hovstad: This matter of your father's, you mean?

Petra: Exactly. It seems to me that now you must feel you are a man worth more than most.

Hovstad: Yes, to-day I do feel something of that sort.

Petra: Of course you do, don't you? It is a splendid vocation you have chosen—to smooth the way for the march of unappreciated truths, and new and courageous lines of thought. If it were nothing more than because you stand fearlessly in the open and take up the cause of an injured man—

Hovstad: Especially when that injured man is—ahem!—I don't rightly know how to—

Petra: When that man is so upright and so honest, you mean?

Hovstad (*more gently*). Especially when he is your father, I meant.

Petra (*suddenly checked*). *That?*

Hovstad: Yes, Petra—Miss Petra.

Petra: Is it *that,* that is first and foremost with you? Not the matter itself? Not the truth?—not my father's big generous heart?

Hovstad: Certainly—of course—that too.

Petra: No, thank you; you have betrayed yourself, Mr. Hovstad, and now I shall never trust you again in anything.

Hovstad: Can you really take it so amiss in me that it is mostly for your sake—?

Petra: What I am angry with you for, is for not having been honest with my father. You talked to him as if the truth and the good of the community were what lay nearest to your heart. You have made fools of both my father and me. You are not the man you made yourself out to be. And that I shall never forgive you—never!

Hovstad: You ought not to speak so bitterly, Miss Petra—least of all now.

Petra: Why not now, especially?

Hovstad: Because your father cannot do without my help.

Petra (*looking him up and down*). Are you that sort of man too? For shame!

Hovstad: No, no, I am not. This came upon me so unexpectedly—you must believe that.

Petra: I know what to believe. Goodbye.

Aslaksen (*coming from the printing-room, hurriedly and with an air of mystery*). Damnation, Hovstad!—(*Sees* PETRA.) Oh, this is awkward—

Petra: There is the book; you must

give it to some one else. (*Goes towards the door.*)

Hovstad (*following her*). But, Miss Stockmann—

Petra: Good-bye. (*Goes out.*)

Aslaksen: I say—Mr. Hovstad—

Hovstad: Well, well!—what is it?

Aslaksen: The Mayor is outside in the printing-room.

Hovstad: The Mayor, did you say?

Aslaksen: Yes, he wants to speak to you. He came in by the back door—didn't want to be seen, you understand.

Hovstad: What can he want? Wait a bit—I will go myself. (*Goes to the door of the printing-room, opens it, bows and invites* PETER STOCKMANN *in.*) Just see, Aslaksen, that no one—

Aslaksen: Quite so. (*Goes into the printing-room.*)

Peter Stockmann: You did not expect to see me here, Mr. Hovstad?

Hovstad: No, I confess I did not.

Peter Stockmann (*looking round*). You are very snug in here—very nice indeed.

Hovstad: Oh—

Peter Stockmann: And here I come, without any notice, to take up your time!

Hovstad: By all means, Mr. Mayor. I am at your service. But let me relieve you of your—(*takes* STOCKMANN'S *hat and stick and puts them on a chair*). Won't you sit down?

Peter Stockmann (*sitting down by the table*). Thank you. (HOVSTAD *sits down.*) I have had an extremely annoying experience to-day, Mr. Hovstad.

Hovstad: Really? Ah well, I expect with all the various business you have to attend to—

Peter Stockmann: The Medical Officer of the Baths is responsible for what happened to-day.

Hovstad: Indeed? The Doctor?

Peter Stockmann: He has addressed a kind of report to the Baths Committee on the subject of certain supposed defects in the Baths.

Hovstad: Has he indeed?

Peter Stockmann: Yes—has he not told you? I thought he said—

Hovstad: Ah, yes—it is true he did mention something about—

Aslaksen (*coming from the printing-room*). I ought to have that copy—

Hovstad (*angrily*). Ahem!—there it is on the desk.

Aslaksen (*taking it*). Right.

Peter Stockmann: But look there—that is the thing I was speaking of!

Aslaksen: Yes, that is the Doctor's article, Mr. Mayor.

Hovstad: Oh, is *that* what you were speaking about?

Peter Stockmann: Yes, that is it. What do you think of it?

Hovstad: Oh, I am only a layman—and I have only taken a very cursory glance at it.

Peter Stockmann: But you are going to print it?

Hovstad: I cannot very well refuse a distinguished man—

Aslaksen: I have nothing to do with editing the paper, Mr. Mayor—

Peter Stockmann: I understand.

Aslaksen: I merely print what is put into my hands.

Peter Stockmann: Quite so.

Aslaksen: And so I must—(*moves off towards the printing-room*).

Peter Stockmann: No, but wait a moment, Mr. Aslaksen. You will allow me, Mr. Hovstad?

Hovstad: If you please, Mr. Mayor.

Peter Stockmann: You are a discreet and thoughtful man, Mr. Aslaksen.

Aslaksen: I am delighted to hear you think so, sir.

Peter Stockmann: And a man of very considerable influence.

Aslaksen: Chiefly among the small tradesman, sir.

Peter Stockmann: The small taxpayers are the majority—here as everywhere else.

Aslaksen: That is true.

Peter Stockmann: And I have no doubt you know the general trend of opinion among them, don't you?

Aslaksen: Yes, I think I may say I do, Mr. Mayor.

Peter Stockmann: Yes. Well, since there is such a praiseworthy spirit of self-sacrifice among the less wealthy citizens of our town—

Aslaksen: What?

Hovstad: Self-sacrifice?

Peter Stockmann: It is pleasing evidence of a public-spirited feeling, extremely pleasing evidence. I might almost say I hardly expected it. But you have a closer knowledge of public opinion than I.

Aslaksen: But, Mr. Mayor—

Peter Stockmann: And indeed it is no small sacrifice that the town is going to make.

Hovstad: The town?

Aslaksen: But I don't understand. Is it the Baths—?

Peter Stockmann: At a provisional estimate, the alterations that the Medical Officer asserts to be desirable will cost somewhere about twenty thousand pounds.

Aslaksen: That is a lot of money, but—

Peter Stockmann: Of course it will be necessary to raise a municipal loan.

Hovstad (*getting up*). Surely you never mean that the town must pay—?

Aslaksen: Do you mean that it must come out of the municipal funds?—out of the ill-filled pockets of the small tradesmen?

Peter Stockmann: Well, my dear Mr. Aslaksen, where else is the money to come from?

Aslaksen: The gentlemen who own the Baths ought to provide that.

Peter Stockmann: The proprietors of the Baths are not in a position to incur any further expense.

Aslaksen: Is that absolutely certain, Mr. Mayor?

Peter Stockmann: I have satisfied myself that it is so. If the town wants these very extensive alterations, it will have to pay for them.

Aslaksen: But, damn it all—I beg your pardon—this is quite another matter, Mr. Hovstad!

Hovstad: It is, indeed.

Peter Stockmann: The most fatal part of it is that we shall be obliged to shut the Baths for a couple of years.

Hovstad: Shut them? Shut them altogether?

Aslaksen: For two years?

Peter Stockmann: Yes, the work will take as long as that—at least.

Aslaksen: I'm damned if we will stand that, Mr. Mayor! What are we householders to live upon in the meantime?

Peter Stockmann: Unfortunately that is an extremely difficult question to answer, Mr. Aslaksen. But what would you have us do? Do you suppose we shall have a single visitor in the town, if we go about proclaiming that our water is polluted, that we are living over a plague spot, that the entire town—

Aslaksen: And the whole this is merely imagination?

Peter Stockmann: With the best will in the world, I have not been able to come to any other conclusion.

Aslaksen: Well then I must say it is absolutely unjustifiable of Dr. Stockmann —I beg your pardon, Mr. Mayor—

Peter Stockmann: What you say is lamentably true, Mr. Aslaksen. My brother has unfortunately always been a head-strong man.

Aslaksen: After this, do you mean to give him your support, Mr. Hovstad?

Hovstad: Can you suppose for a moment that I—?

Peter Stockmann: I have drawn up a short *résumé* of the situation as it appears from a reasonable man's point of view. In it I have indicated how certain possible defects might suitably be remedied without out-running the resources of the Baths Committee.

Hovstad: Have you got it with you, Mr. Mayor.

Peter Stockmann (*fumbling in his pocket*). Yes, I brought it with me in case you should—

Aslaksen: Good Lord, there he is!

Peter Stockmann: Who? My brother?

Hovstad: Where? Where?

Aslaksen: He had just gone through the printing-room.

Peter Stockmann: How unlucky! I don't want to meet him here, and I had still several things to speak to you about.

Hovstad (*pointing to the door on the right*). Go in there for the present.

Peter Stockmann: But—?

Hovstad: You will only find Billing in there.

Aslaksen: Quick, quick, Mr. Mayor—he is just coming.

Peter Stockmann: Yes, very well; but see that you get rid of him quickly. (*Goes out through the door on the right, which* ASLAKSEN *opens for him and shuts after him.*)

Hovstad: Pretend to be doing something, Aslaksen. (*Sits down and writes.* ASLAKSEN *begins foraging among a heap of newspapers that are lying on a chair.*)

Dr. Stockmann (*coming in from the printing-room*). Here I am again. (*Puts down his hat and stick.*)

Hovstad (*writing*). Already, Doctor? Hurry up with what we were speaking about, Aslaksen. We are very pressed for time to-day.

Dr. Stockmann (*to* ASLAKSEN). No proof for me to see yet, I hear.

Aslaksen (*without turning round*). You couldn't expect it yet, Doctor.

Dr. Stockmann: No, no; but I am impatient, as you can understand. I shall not know a moment's peace of mind till I see it in print.

Hovstad: H'm!—It will take a good while yet, won't it, Aslaksen?

Aslaksen: Yes, I am almost afraid it will.

Dr. Stockmann: All right, my dear friends; I will come back. I do not mind coming back twice if necessary. A matter of such great importance—the welfare of the town at stake—it is no time to shirk trouble. (*Is just going, but stops and comes back.*) Look here—there is one thing more I want to speak to you about.

Hovstad: Excuse me, but could it not wait till some other time?

Dr. Stockmann: I can tell you in half a dozen words. It is only this. When my article is read to-morrow and it is realized that I have been quietly working the whole winter for the welfare of the town—

Hovstad: Yes, but, Doctor—

Dr. Stockmann: I know what you are going to say. You don't see how on earth it was any more than my duty—my obvious duty as a citizen. Of course it wasn't; I know that as well as you. But my fellow citizens, you know—! Good Lord, think of all the good souls who think so highly of me—!

Aslaksen: Yes, our townsfolk have had a very high opinion of you so far, Doctor.

Dr. Stockmann: Yes, and that is just why I am afraid they—. Well, this is the point; when this reaches them, especially the poorer classes, and sounds in their ears like a summons to take the town's affairs into their own hands for the future—

Hovstad (*getting up*). Ahem! Doctor, I won't conceal from you the fact—

Dr. Stockmann: Ah!—I knew there was something in the wind! But I won't hear a word of it. If anything of that sort is being set on foot—

Hovstad: Of what sort?

Dr. Stockmann: Well, whatever it is —whether it is a demonstration in my honor, or a banquet, or a subscription list for some presentation to me—whatever it is, you must promise me solemnly and faithfully to put a stop to it. You too, Mr. Aslaksen; do you understand?

Hovstad: You must forgive me, Doctor, but sooner or later we must tell you the plain truth—

[*He is interrupted by the entrance of* MRS. STOCKMANN, *who comes in from the street door.*]

Mrs. Stockmann (*seeing her husband*). Just as I thought!

Hovstad (*going towards her*). You too, Mrs. Stockmann?

Dr. Stockmann: What on earth do *you* want here, Katherine?

Mrs. Stockmann: I should think you know very well what I want.

Hovstad: Won't you sit down? Or perhaps—

Mrs. Stockmann: No, thank you; don't trouble. And you must not be offended at my coming to fetch my husband; I am the mother of three children, you know.

Dr. Stockmann: Nonsense!—we know all about that.

Mrs. Stockmann: Well, one would not give you credit for much thought for your wife and children to-day; if you had had that, you would not have gone and dragged us all into misfortune.

Dr. Stockmann: Are you out of your senses, Katherine! Because a man has a wife and children, is he not to be allowed to proclaim the truth—is he not to be allowed to be an actively useful citizen—is he not to be allowed to do a service to his native town!

Mrs. Stockmann: Yes, Thomas—in reason.

Aslaksen: Just what I say. Moderation is everything.

Mrs. Stockmann: And that is why you wrong us, Mr. Hovstad, in enticing my husband away from his home and making a dupe of him in all this.

Hovstad: I certainly am making a dupe of no one—

Dr. Stockmann: Making a dupe of me! Do you suppose *I* should allow myself to be duped!

Mrs. Stockmann: It is just what you do. I know quite well you have more brains than anyone in the town, but you are extremely easily duped, Thomas. (*To* HOVSTAD.) Please to realize that he loses his post at the Baths if you print what he has written—

Aslaksen: What!

Hovstad: Look here, Doctor—

Dr. Stockmann (*laughing*). Ha—ha! —just let them try! No, no—they will take good care not to. I have got the compact majority behind me, let me tell you!

Mrs. Stockmann: Yes, that is just the worst of it—your having any such horrid thing behind you.

Dr. Stockmann: Rubbish, Katherine!

—Go home and look after your house and leave me to look after the community. How can you be so afraid, when I am so confident and happy? (*Walks up and down, rubbing his hands.*) Truth and the People will win the fight, you may be certain! I see the whole of the broadminded middle class marching like a victorious army—! (*Stops beside a chair.*) What the deuce is that lying there?

Aslaksen: Good Lord!

Hovstad: Ahem!

Dr. Stockmann: Here we have the topmost pinnacle of authority! (*Takes the Mayor's official hat carefully between his finger-tips and holds it up in the air.*)

Mrs. Stockmann: The Mayor's hat!

Dr. Stockmann: And here is the staff of office too. How in the name of all that's wonderful—?

Havstad: Well, you see—

Dr. Stockmann: Oh, I understand. He has been here trying to talk you over. Ha—ha!—he made rather a mistake there! And as soon as he caught sight of me in the printing-room—. (*Bursts out laughing.*) Did he run away, Mr. Aslaksen?

Aslaksen (*hurriedly*). Yes, he ran away, Doctor.

Dr. Stockmann: Ran away without his stick or his—Fiddlesticks! Peter doesn't run away and leave his belongings behind him. But what the deuce have you done with him? Ah!—in there, of course. Now you shall see, Katherine!

Mrs. Stockmann: Thomas—please don't—!

Aslaksen: Don't be rash, Doctor.

[DR. STOCKMANN *has put on the Mayor's hat and taken his stick in his hand. He goes up to the door, opens it, and stands with his hand to his hat at the salute.* PETER STOCKMANN *comes in, red with anger.* BILLING *follows him.*]

Peter Stockmann: What does this tomfoolery mean?

Dr. Stockmann: Be respectful, my good Peter. I am the chief authority in the town now. (*Walks up and down.*)

Mrs. Stockmann (*almost in tears*). Really, Thomas!

Peter Stockmann (*following him about*). Give me my hat and stick.

Dr. Stockmann (*in the same tone as before*). If you are chief constable, let me tell you that I am the Mayor—I am the master of the whole town, please understand!

Peter Stockmann: Take off my hat, I tell you. Remember it is part of an official uniform.

Dr. Stockmann: Pooh! Do you think the newly awakened lion-hearted people are going to be frightened by an official hat? There is going to be a revolution in the town to-morrow, let me tell you. You thought you could turn me out; but now I shall turn you out—turn you out of all your various offices. Do you think I cannot? Listen to me. I have triumphant social forces behind me. Hovstad and Billing will thunder in the *People's Messenger,* and Aslaksen will take the field at the head of the whole Householders' Association—

Aslaksen: That I won't, Doctor.

Dr. Stockmann: Of course you will—

Peter Stockmann: Ah!—may I ask then if Mr. Hovstad intends to join this agitation?

Hovstad: No, Mr. Mayor.

Aslaksen: No, Mr. Hovstad is not such a fool as to go and ruin his paper and himself for the sake of an imaginary grievance.

Dr. Stockmann (*looking round him*). What does this mean?

Hovstad: You have represented your case in a false light, Doctor, and therefore I am unable to give you my support.

Billing: And after what the Mayor was so kind as to tell me just now, I—

Dr. Stockmann: A false light! Leave that part of it to me. Only print my article; I am quite capable of defending it.

Hovstad: I am not going to print it. I cannot and will not and dare not print it.

Dr. Stockmann: You dare not? What nonsense!—you are the editor; and an editor controls his paper, I suppose!

Aslaksen: No, it is the subscribers, Doctor.

Peter Stockmann: Fortunately, yes.

Aslaksen: It is public opinion—the enlightened public—householders and people of that kind; they control the newspapers.

Dr. Stockmann (*composedly*). And I have all these influences against me?

Aslaksen: Yes, you have. It would mean the absolute ruin of the community if your article were to appear.

Dr. Stockmann: Indeed.

Peter Stockmann: My hat and stick, if you please. (DR. STOCKMANN *takes off the hat and lays it on the table with the stick.* PETER STOCKMANN *takes them up.*) Your authority as mayor has come to an untimely end.

Dr. Stockmann: We have not got to the end yet. (*To* HOVSTAD.) Then it is quite impossible for you to print my article in the *People's Messenger*?

Hovstad: Quite impossible—out of regard for your family as well.

Mrs. Stockmann: You need not concern yourself about his family, thank you, Mr. Hovstad.

Peter Stockmann (*taking a paper from his pocket.*) It will be sufficient, for the guidance of the public, if this appears. It is an official statement. May I trouble you?

Hovstad (*taking the paper*). Certainly; I will see that it is printed.

Dr. Stockmann: But not mine. Do you imagine that you can silence me and stifle the truth! You will not find it so easy as you suppose. Mr. Aslaksen, kindly take my manuscript at once and print it as a pamphlet—at my expense. I will have four hundred copies—no, five—six hundred.

Aslaksen: If you offered me its weight in gold, I could not lend my press for any such purpose, Doctor. It would be flying in the face of public opinion. You will not get it printed anywhere in the town.

Dr. Stockmann: Then give it me back.

Hovstad (*giving him the MS.*). Here it is.

Dr. Stockmann (*taking his hat and stick*). It shall be made public all the same. I will read it out at a mass meeting of the townspeople. All my fellow-citizens shall hear the voice of truth!

Peter Stockmann: You will not find any public body in the town that will give you the use of their hall for such a purpose.

Aslaksen: Not a single one, I am certain.

Billing: No, I'm damned if you will find one.

Mrs. Stockmann: But this is too shameful! Why should every one turn against you like that?

Dr. Stockmann (*angrily*). I will tell you why. It is because all the men in this town are old women—like you; they all think of nothing but their families, and never of the community.

Mrs. Stockmann (*putting her arm into his*). Then I will show them that an—an old woman can be a man for once. I am going to stand by you, Thomas!

Dr. Stockmann: Bravely said, Katherine! It shall be made public—as I am a living soul! If I can't hire a hall, I shall hire a drum, and parade the town with it and read it at every street-corner.

Peter Stockmann: You are surely not such an arrant fool as that!

Dr. Stockmann: Yes, I am.

Aslaksen: You won't find a single man in the whole town to go with you.

Billing: No, I'm damned if you will.

Mrs. Stockmann: Don't give in, Thomas. I will tell the boys to go with you.

Dr. Stockmann: That is a splendid idea!

Mrs. Stockmann: Morten will be delighted; and Ejlif will do whatever he does.

Dr. Stockmann: Yes, and Petra!—and you too, Katherine!

Mrs. Stockmann: No, I won't do that; but I will stand at the window and watch you, that's what I will do.

Dr. Stockmann (*puts his arms round her and kisses her*). Thank you, my dear! Now you and I are going to try a fall, my fine gentlemen! I am going to see whether a pack of cowards can succeed in gagging a patriot who wants to purify society! (*He and his wife go out by the street door.*)

Peter Stockmann (*shaking his head seriously*). Now he has sent *her* out of her senses, too.

ACT IV

Scene: *A big old-fashioned room in* CAPTAIN HORSTER'S *house. At the back folding doors, which are standing open, lead to an ante-room. Three windows in the left-hand wall. In the middle of the opposite wall a platform has been erected. On this is a small table with two candles, a water-bottle and glass, and a bell. The room is lit by lamps placed between the windows. In the fore-ground on the left there is a table with candles and a chair. To the right is a door and some chairs standing near it. The room is nearly filled with a crowd of townspeople of all sorts, a few women and schoolboys being amongst them. People are still streaming in from the back, and the room is soon filled.*

1st Citizen (*meeting another*). Hullo, Lamstad! You here too?

2nd Citizen: I go to every public meeting, I do.

3rd Citizen: Brought your whistle too, I expect!

2nd Citizen: I should think so. Haven't you?

3rd Citizen: Rather! And old Evensen said he was going to bring a cow-horn, he did.

2nd Citizen: Good old Evensen! (*Laughter among the crowd.*)

4th Citizen (*coming up to them*). I say, tell me what is going on here to-night.

2nd Citizen: Dr. Stockmann is going to deliver an address attacking the Mayor.

4th Citizen: But the Mayor is his brother.

1st Citizen: That doesn't matter; Dr. Stockmann's not the chap to be afraid.

3rd Citizen: But he is in the wrong; it said so in the *People's Messenger.*

2nd Citizen: Yes, I expect he must be in the wrong this time, because neither the Householders' Association nor the Citizens' Club would lend him their hall for his meeting.

1st Citizen: He couldn't even get the loan of the hall at the Baths.

2nd Citizen: No, I should think not.

A Man in another part of the crowd: I say—who are we to back up in this?

Another Man, beside him: Watch Aslaksen, and do as he does.

Billing (*pushing his way through the crowd, with a writing-case under his arm*). Excuse me, gentlemen—do you mind letting me through? I am reporting for the *People's Messenger.* Thank you very much! (*He sits down at the table on the left.*)

A Workman: Who was that?

Second Workman: Don't you know him? It's Billing, who writes for Aslaksen's paper.

[CAPTAIN HORSTER *brings in* MRS. STOCKMANN *and* PETRA *through the door on the right.* EJLIF *and* MORTEN *follow them in.*]

Horster: I thought you might all sit here; you can slip out easily from here, if things get too lively.

Mrs. Stockmann: Do you think there will be a disturbance?

Horster: One can never tell—with such a crowd. But sit down, and don't be uneasy.

Mrs. Stockmann (*sitting down*). It was extremely kind of you to offer my husband the room.

Horster: Well, if nobody else would—

Petra (*who has sat down beside her mother*). And it was a plucky thing to do, Captain Horster.

Horster: Oh, it is not such a great matter as all that.

[HOVSTAD *and* ASLAKSEN *make their way through the crowd.*]

Aslaksen (*going up to* HORSTER). Has the Doctor not come yet?

Horster: He is waiting in the next room. (*Movement in the crowd by the door at the back.*)

Hovstad: Look—here comes the Mayor!

Billing: Yes, I'm damned if he hasn't come after all!

[PETER STOCKMANN *makes his way gradually through the crowd, bows courteously, and takes up a position by the wall on the left. Shortly afterwards* DR. STOCKMANN *comes in by the right-hand door. He is dressed in a black frock-coat, with a white tie. There is a little feeble applause, which is hushed down. Silence is obtained.*]

Dr. Stockmann (*in an undertone*). How do you feel, Katherine?

Mrs. Stockmann: All right, thank you. (*Lowering her voice.*) Be sure not to lose your temper, Thomas.

Dr. Stockmann: Oh, I know how to control myself. (*Looks at his watch, steps on to the platform, and bows.*) It is a quarter past—so I will begin. (*Takes his MS. out of his pocket.*)

Aslaksen: I think we ought to elect a chairman first.

Dr. Stockmann: No, it is quite unnecessary.

Some of the Crowd: Yes—yes!

Peter Stockmann: I certainly think too that we ought to have a chairman.

Dr. Stockmann: But I have called this meeting to deliver a lecture, Peter.

Peter Stockmann: Dr. Stockmann's

lecture may possibly lead to a considerable conflict of opinion.

Voices in the Crowd: A chairman! A chairman!

Hovstad: The general wish of the meeting seems to be that a chairman should be elected.

Dr. Stockmann (*restraining himself*). Very well—let the meeting have its way.

Aslaksen: Will the Mayor be good enough to undertake the task?

Three Men (*clapping their hands*). Bravo! Bravo!

Peter Stockmann: For various reasons, which you will easily understand, I must beg to be excused. But fortunately we have amongst us a man who I think will be acceptable to you all. I refer to the President of the Householders' Association, Mr. Aslaksen.

Several Voices: Yes — Aslaksen! Bravo Aslaksen!

[DR. STOCKMANN *takes up his MS. and walks up and down the platform.*]

Aslaksen: Since my fellow-citizens choose to entrust me with this duty, I cannot refuse.

[*Loud applause.* ASLAKSEN *mounts the platform.*]

Billing (*writing*). "Mr. Aslaksen was elected with enthusiasm."

Aslaksen: And now, as I am in this position, I should like to say a few brief words. I am a quiet and peaceable man, who believes in discreet moderation, and —and—in moderate discretion. All my friends can bear witness to that.

Several Voices: That's right! That's right, Aslaksen!

Aslaksen: I have learnt in the school of life and experience that moderation is the most valuable virtue a citizen can possess—

Peter Stockmann: Hear, hear!

Aslaksen: —And moreover that discretion and moderation are what enable a man to be of most service to the community. I would therefore suggest to our esteemed fellow-citizen, who has called this meeting, that he should strive to keep strictly within the bounds of moderation.

A Man by the door: Three cheers for the Moderation Society!

A Voice: Shame!

Several Voices: Sh!—Sh!

Aslaksen: No interruptions, gentlemen, please! Does anyone wish to make any remarks?

Peter Stockmann: Mr. Chairman.

Aslaksen: The Mayor will address the meeting.

Peter Stockmann: In consideration of the close relationship in which, as you all know, I stand to the present Medical Officer of the Baths, I should have preferred not to speak this evening. But my official position with regard to the Baths and my solicitude for the vital interests of the town compel me to bring forward a motion. I venture to presume that there is not a single one of our citizens present who considers it desirable that unreliable and exaggerated accounts of the sanitary condition of the Baths and the town should be spread abroad.

Several Voices: No, no! Certainly not! We protest against it!

Peter Stockmann: Therefore I should like to propose that the meeting should not permit the Medical Officer either to read or to comment on his proposed lecture.

Dr. Stockmann (*impatiently*). Not permit—! What the devil—!

Mrs. Stockmann (*coughing*). Ahem! —ahem!

Dr. Stockmann (*collecting himself*). Very well. Go ahead!

Peter Stockmann: In my communication to the *People's Messenger,* I have put the essential facts before the public in such a way that every fair-minded citizen can easily form his own opinion. From it you will see that the main result of the Medical Officer's proposals—apart from their constituting a vote of censure on the leading men of the own—would be to saddle the ratepayers with an unnecessary expenditure of at least some thousands of pounds.

[*Sounds of disapproval among the audience, and some cat-calls.*]

Aslaksen (*ringing his bell*). Silence, please, gentlemen! I beg to support the Mayor's motion. I quite agree with him that there is something behind this agitation started by the Doctor. He talks about the Baths; but it is a revolution he is aiming at—he wants to get the administration of the town put into new hands. No one doubts the honesty of the Doctor's intentions—no one will suggest that there can be any two opinions as to that. I myself am a believer in self-government for the people, provided it does not fall too heavily on the ratepayers. But that would be the case here; and that is why I will see Dr. Stockmann damned—I beg your pardon—before I go with him in the matter. You can pay too dearly for a thing sometimes; that is my opinion.

[*Loud applause on all sides.*]

Hovstad: I, too, feel called upon to explain my position. Dr. Stockmann's agitation appeared to be gaining a certain amount of sympathy at first, so I supported it as impartially as I could. But presently we had reason to suspect that we had allowed ourselves to be misled by misrepresentation of the state of affairs—

Dr. Stockmann: Misrepresentation—!

Hovstad: Well, let us say a not entirely trustworthy representation. The Mayor's statement has proved that. I hope no one here has any doubt as to my liberal principles; the attitude of the *People's Messenger* towards important political questions is well known to every one. But the advice of experienced and thoughtful men has convinced me that in purely local matters a newspaper ought to proceed with a certain caution.

Aslaksen: I entirely agree with the speaker.

Hovstad: And, in the matter before us, it is now an undoubted fact that Dr. Stockmann has public opinion against him. Now, what is an editor's first and most obvious duty, gentlemen? Is it not to work in harmony with his readers? Has he not received a sort of tacit mandate to work persistently and assiduously for the welfare of those whose opinions he represents? Or is it possible I am mistaken in that?

Voices from the crowd: No, no! You are quite right!

Hovstad: It has cost me a severe struggle to break with a man in whose house I have been lately a frequent guest —a man who till to-day has been able to pride himself on the undivided goodwill of his fellow-citizens—a man whose only, or at all events whose essential failing is that he is swayed by his heart rather than his head.

A few scattered voices: That is true! Bravo, Stockmann!

Hovstad: But my duty to the community obliged me to break with him.

And there is another consideration that impels me to oppose him, and, as far as possible, to arrest him on the perilous course he has adopted; that is, consideration for his family—

Dr. Stockmann: Please stick to the water-supply and drainage!

Hovstad: —consideration, I repeat, for his wife and his children for whom he has made no provision.

Morten: Is that us, mother?

Mrs. Stockmann: Hush!

Aslaksen: I will now put the Mayor's proposition to the vote.

Dr. Stockmann: There is no necessity! To-night I have no intention of dealing with all that filth down at the Baths. No; I have something quite different to say to you.

Peter Stockmann (*aside*). What is coming now?

A Drunken Man (*by the entrance door*). I am a ratepayer! And therefore I have a right to speak too! And my entire—firm—inconceivable opinion is—

A number of voices: Be quiet, at the back there!

Others: He is drunk! Turn him out! (*They turn him out.*)

Dr. Stockmann: Am I allowed to speak?

Aslaksen (*ringing his bell*). Dr. Stockmann will address the meeting.

Dr. Stockmann: I should like to have seen anyone, a few days ago, dare to attempt to silence me as has been done to-night! I would have defended my sacred rights as a man, like a lion! But now it is all one to me; I have something of even weightier importance to say to you.

[*The crowd presses near to him,* MORTEN KIIL *conspicuous among them.*]

Dr. Stockmann (*continuing*). I have thought and pondered a great deal, these last few days—pondered over such a variety of things that in the end my head seemed too full to hold them—

Peter Stockmann (*with a cough*). Ahem!

Dr. Stockmann: —but I got them clear in my mind at last, and then I saw the whole situation lucidly. And that is why I am standing here to-night. I have a great revelation to make to you, my fellow-citizens! I will impart to you a discovery of a far wider scope than the trifling matter that our water-supply is poisoned and our medicinal Baths are standing on pestiferous soil.

A number of voices (*shouting*). Don't talk about the Baths! We won't hear you! None of that!

Dr. Stockmann: I have already told you that what I want to speak about is the great discovery I have made lately—the discovery that all the sources of our *moral* life are poisoned and that the whole fabric of our civic community is founded on the pestiferous soil of falsehood.

Voices of disconcerted Citizens: What is that he says?

Peter Stockmann: Such an insinuation—!

Aslaksen (*with his hand on his bell*). I call upon the speaker to moderate his language.

Dr. Stockmann: I have always loved my native town as a man only can love the home of his youthful days. I was not old when I went away from here; and exile, longing and memories cast as it were an additional halo over both the town and its inhabitants. (*Some clapping and applause.*) And there I stayed, for many years, in a horrible hole far away up north. When I came into contact with some of the people that lived scattered about among the rocks, I often thought it would have been more service to the poor half-starved creatures if a veterinary doctor had been sent up there, instead of a man like me. (*Murmurs among the crowd.*)

Billing (*laying down his pen*). I'm damned if I have ever heard—!

Hovstad: It is an insult to a respectable population!

Dr. Stockmann: Wait a bit! I do not think anyone will charge me with having forgotten my native town up there. I was like one of the eider-ducks brooding on its nest, and what I hatched was—the plans for these Baths. (*Applause and protests.*) And then when fate at last decreed for me the great happiness of coming home again—I assure you, gentlemen, I thought I had nothing more in the world to wish for. Or rather, there was one thing I wished for—eagerly, untiringly, ardently—and that was to be able to be of service to my native town and the good of the community.

Peter Stockmann (*looking at the ceiling*). You chose a strange way of doing it—ahem!

Dr. Stockmann: And so, with my eyes blinded to the real facts, I revelled in happiness. But yesterday morning—no, to be precise, it was yesterday afternoon—the eyes of my mind were opened wide, and the first thing I realized was the colossal stupidity of the authorities—. (*Uproar, shouts and laughter.* MRS. STOCKMANN *coughs persistently.*)

Peter Stockmann: Mr. Chairman!

Aslaksen (*ringing his bell*). By virtue of my authority—!

Dr. Stockmann: It is a petty thing to catch me up on a word, Mr. Aslaksen. What I mean is only that I got scent of the unbelievable piggishness our leading men had been responsible for down at the Baths. I can't stand leading men at any price!—I have had enough of such people in my time. They are like billy-goats in a young plantation; they do mischief everywhere. They stand in a free man's way, whichever way he turns, and what I should like best would be to see them exterminated like any other vermin—. (*Uproar.*)

Peter Stockmann: Mr. Chairman, can we allow such expressions to pass?

Aslaksen (*with his hand on his bell*). Doctor—!

Dr. Stockmann: I cannot understand how it is that I have only now acquired a clear conception of what these gentry are, when I had almost daily before my eyes in this town such an excellent specimen of them—my brother Peter—slow-witted and hide-bound in prejudice—. (*Laughter, uproar and hisses.* MRS. STOCKMANN *sits coughing assiduously.* ASLAKSEN *rings his bell violently.*)

The Drunken Man (*who has got in again*). Is it me he is talking about? My name's Petersen, all right—but devil take me if I—

Angry Voices: Turn out that drunken man! Turn him out. (*He is turned out again.*)

Peter Stockmann: Who was that person?

1st Citizen: I don't know who he is, Mr. Mayor.

2nd Citizen: He doesn't belong here.

3rd Citizen: I expect he is a navvy from over at (*the rest is inaudible*).

Aslaksen: He had obviously had too much beer.—Proceed, Doctor; but please strive to be moderate in your language.

Dr. Stockmann: Very well, gentlemen, I will say no more about our leading men. And if anyone imagines, from what

I have just said, that my object is to attack these people this evening, he is wrong—absolutely wide of the mark. For I cherish the comforting conviction that these parasites—all these venerable relics of a dying school of thought—are most admirably paving the way for their own extinction; they need no doctor's help to hasten their end. Nor is it folk of that kind who constitute the most pressing danger to the community. It is not they who are most instrumental in poisoning the sources of our moral life and infecting the ground on which we stand. It is not they who are the most dangerous enemies of truth and freedom amongst us.

Shouts from all sides: Who then? Who is it? Name! Name!

Dr. Stockmann: You may depend upon it I shall name them! That is precisely the great discovery I made yesterday. (*Raises his voice.*) The most dangerous enemy of truth and freedom amongst us is the compact majority—yes, the damned compact Liberal majority—that is it! Now you know! (*Tremendous uproar. Most of the crowd are shouting, stamping and hissing. Some of the older men among them exchange stolen glances and seem to be enjoying themselves.* MRS. STOCKMANN *gets up, looking anxious.* EJLIF *and* MORTEN *advance threateningly upon some schoolboys who are playing pranks.* ASLAKSEN *rings his bell and begs for silence.* HOVSTAD *and* BILLING *both talk at once, but are inaudible. At last quiet is restored.*)

Aslaksen: As chairman, I call upon the speaker to withdraw the ill-considered expressions he has just used.

Dr. Stockmann: Never, Mr. Aslaksen! It is the majority in our community that denies me my freedom and seeks to prevent my speaking the truth.

Hovstad: The majority always has right on its side.

Billing: And truth too, by God!

Dr. Stockmann: The majority *never* has right on its side. Never, I say! That is one of these social lies against which an independent, intelligent man must wage war. Who is it that constitute the majority of the population in a country? Is it the clever folk or the stupid? I don't imagine you will dispute the fact that at present the stupid people are in an absolutely overwhelming majority all the world over. But, good Lord!—you can never pretend that it is right that the stupid folk should govern the clever ones! (*Uproar and cries.*) Oh, yes—you can shout me down, I know! but you cannot answer me. The majority has *might* on its side—unfortunately; but *right* it has *not.* I am in the right—I and a few other scattered individuals. The minority is always in the right. (*Renewed uproar.*)

Hovstad: Aha!—so Dr. Stockmann has become an aristocrat since the day before yesterday!

Dr. Stockmann: I have already said that I don't intend to waste a word on the puny, narrow-chested, short-winded crew whom we are leaving astern. Pulsating life no longer concerns itself with them. I am thinking of the few, the scattered few amongst us, who have absorbed new and vigorous truths. Such men stand, as it were, at the outposts, so far ahead that the compact majority has not yet been able to come up with them; and there they are fighting for truths that are too newly-born into the world of consciousness to have any considerable number of people on their side as yet.

Hovstad: So the Doctor is a revolutionary now!

Dr. Stockmann: Good heavens—of

course I am, Mr. Hovstad! I propose to raise a revolution against the lie that the majority has the monopoly of the truth. What sort of truths are they that the majority usually supports? They are truths that are of such advanced age that they are beginning to break up. And if a truth is as old as that, it is also in a fair way to become a lie, gentlemen. (*Laughter and mocking cries.*) Yes, believe me or not, as you like; but truths are by no means as long-lived as Methuselah—as some folk imagine. A normally constituted truth lives, let us say, as a rule seventeen or eighteen, or at most twenty years; seldom longer. But truths as aged as that are always worn frightfully thin, and nevertheless it is only then that the majority recognizes them and recommends them to the community as wholesome moral nourishment. There is no great nutritive value in that sort of fare, I can assure you; and, as a doctor, I ought to know. These "majority truths" are like last year's cured meat—like rancid, tainted ham; and they are the origin of the moral scurvy that is rampant in our communities.

Aslaksen: It appears to me that the speaker is wandering a long way from his subject.

Peter Stockmann: I quite agree with the Chairman.

Dr. Stockmann: Have you gone clean out of your senses, Peter? I am sticking as closely to my subject as I can; for my subject is precisely this, that it is the masses, the majority—this infernal compact majority—that poisons the sources of our moral life and infects the ground we stand on.

Hovstad: And all this because the great, broad-minded majority of the people is prudent enough to show deference only to well-ascertained and well-approved truths?

Dr. Stockmann: Ah, my good Mr. Hovstad, don't talk nonsense about well-ascertained truths! The truths of which the masses now approve are the very truths that the fighters at the outposts held to in the days of our grandfathers. We fighters at the outposts nowadays no longer approve of them; and I do not believe there is any other well-ascertained truth except this, that no community can live a healthy life if it is nourished only on such old marrowless truths.

Hovstad: But instead of standing there using vague generalities, it would be interesting if you would tell us what these old marrowless truths are, that we are nourished on.

[*Applause from many quarters.*]

Dr. Stockmann: Oh, I could give you a whole string of such abominations; but to begin with I will confine myself to one well-approved truth, which at bottom is a foul lie, but upon which nevertheless Mr. Hovstad and the *People's Messenger* and all the *Messenger's* supporters are nourished.

Hovstad: And that is—?

Dr. Stockmann: That is, the doctrine you have inherited from your forefathers and proclaim thoughtlessly far and wide—the doctrine that the public, the crowd, the masses, are the essential part of the population—that they constitute the People—that the common folk, the ignorant and incomplete element in the community, have the same right to pronounce judgment and to approve, to direct and to govern, as the isolated, intellectually superior personalities in it.

Billing: Well, damn me if ever I—

Hovstad (*at the same time, shouting out*). Fellow-citizens, take good note of that!

A number of voices (*angrily*). Oho!

—we are not the People! Only the superior folk are to govern, are they!

A Workman: Turn the fellow out, for talking such rubbish!

Another: Out with him!

Another (*calling out*). Blow your horn, Evensen!

[*A horn is blown loudly, amidst hisses and an angry uproar.*]

Dr. Stockmann (*when the noise has somewhat abated*). Be reasonable! Can't you stand hearing the voice of truth for once? I don't in the least expect you to agree with me all at once; but I must say I did expect Mr. Hovstad to admit I was right, when he had recovered his composure a little. He claims to be a freethinker—

Voices (*in murmurs of astonishment*). Freethinker, did he say? Is Hovstad a freethinker?

Hovstad (*shouting*). Prove it, Dr. Stockmann! When have I said so in print?

Dr. Stockmann (*reflecting*). No, confound it, you are right!—you have never had the courage to. Well, I won't put you in a hole, Mr. Hovstad. Let us say it is I that am the freethinker, then. I am going to prove to you, scientifically, that the *People's Messenger* leads you by the nose in a shameful manner when it tells you that you—that the common people, the crowd, the masses, are the real essence of the People. That is only a newspaper lie, I tell you! The common people are nothing more than the raw material of which a People is made. (*Groans, laughter and uproar.*) Well, isn't that the case? Isn't there an enormous difference between a well-bred and an ill-bred strain of animals? Take, for instance, a common barndoor hen. What sort of eating do you get from a shrivelled up old scrag of a fowl like that? Not much, do you! And what sort of eggs does it lay? A fairly good crow or a raven can lay pretty nearly as good an egg. But take a well-bred Spanish or Japanese hen, or a good pheasant or a turkey—then you will see the difference. Or take the case of dogs, with whom we humans are on such intimate terms. Think first of an ordinary common cur—I mean one of the horrible, coarse-haired, lowbred curs that do nothing but run about the streets and befoul the walls of the houses. Compare one of these curs with a poodle whose sires for many generations have been bred in a gentleman's house, where they have had the best of food and had the opportunity of hearing soft voices and music. Do you not think that the poodle's brain is developed to quite a different degree from that of the cur? Of course it is. It is puppies of well-bred poodles like that, that showmen train to do incredibly clever tricks—things that a common cur could never learn to do even if it stood on its head. (*Uproar and mocking cries.*)

A Citizen (*calls out*). Are you going to make out we are dogs, now?

Another Citizen: We are not animals, Doctor!

Dr. Stockmann: Yes, but, bless my soul, we *are,* my friend! It is true we are the finest animals anyone could wish for; but, even amongst us, exceptionally fine animals are rare. There is a tremendous difference between poodle-men and curmen. And the amusing part of it is, that Mr. Hovstad quite agrees with me as long as it is a question of four-footed animals—

Hovstad: Yes, it is true enough as far as they are concerned.

Dr. Stockmann: Very well. But as soon as I extend the principle and apply it to two-legged animals, Mr. Hovstad stops short. He no longer dares to think independently, or to pursue his ideas to their logical conclusion; so he turns the whole theory upside down and proclaims in the *People's Messenger* that it is the barn-door hens and street curs that are the finest specimens in the menagerie. But that is always the way, as long as a man retains the traces of common origin and has not worked his way up to intellectual distinction.

Hovstad: I lay no claim to any sort of distinction. I am the son of humble country-folk, and I am proud that the stock I come from is rooted deep among the common people he insults!

Voices: Bravo, Hovstad! Bravo! Bravo!

Dr. Stockmann: The kind of common people I mean are not only to be found low down in the social scale; they crawl and swarm all around us—even in the highest social positions. You have only to look at your own fine, distinguished Mayor! My brother Peter is every bit as plebeian as anyone that walks in two shoes —(*laughter and hisses*).

Peter Stockmann: I protest against personal allusions of this kind.

Dr. Stockmann (*imperturbably*). —and that not because he is, like myself, descended from some old rascal of a pirate from Pomerania or thereabouts—because that is who we are descended from—

Peter Stockmann: An absurd legend. I deny it!

Dr. Stockmann: —but because he thinks what his superiors think and holds the same opinions as they. People who do that are, intellectually speaking, common people; and that is why my magnificent brother Peter is in reality so very far from any distinction—and consequently also so far from being liberal-minded.

Peter Stockmann: Mr. Chairman—!

Hovstad: So it is only the distinguished men that are liberal-minded in this country? We are learning something quite new! (*Laughter.*)

Dr. Stockmann: Yes, that is part of my new discovery too. And another part of it is that broad-mindedness is almost precisely the same thing as morality. That is why I maintain that it is absolutely inexcusable in the *People's Messenger* to proclaim, day in and day out, the false doctrine that it is the masses, the crowd, the compact majority, that have the monopoly of broad-mindedness and morality —and that vice and corruption and every kind of intellectual depravity are the result of culture, just as all the filth that is draining into our Baths is the result of the tanneries up at Mölledal! (*Uproar and interruptions.* DR. STOCKMANN *is undisturbed, and goes on, carried away by his ardor, with a smile.*) And yet this same *People's Messenger* can go on preaching that the masses ought to be elevated to higher conditions of life! But, bless my soul, if the *Messenger's* teaching is to be depended upon, this very raising up the masses would mean nothing more or less than setting them straightway upon the paths of depravity! Happily the theory that culture demoralizes is only an old falsehood that our forefathers believed in and we have inherited. No, it is ignorance, poverty, ugly conditions of life, that do the devil's work! In a house which does not get aired and swept every day —my wife Katherine maintains that the floor ought to be scrubbed as well, but that is a debatable question—in such a house, let me tell you, people will lose within two or three years the power of thinking or acting in a moral manner. Lack of oxygen weakens the conscience. And there must be a plentiful lack of oxygen in very many houses in this town, I should think, judging from the fact that the whole compact majority can be unconscientious enough to wish to build the town's prosperity on a quagmire of falsehood and deceit.

Aslaksen: We cannot allow such a grave accusation to be flung at a citizen community.

A Citizen: I move that the Chairman direct the speaker to sit down.

Voices (*angrily*). Hear, hear! Quite right! Make him sit down!

Dr. Stockmann (*losing his self-control*). Then I will go and shout the truth at every street corner! I will write it in other towns' newspapers! The whole country shall know what is going on here!

Hovstad: It almost seems as if Dr. Stockmann's intention were to ruin the town.

Dr. Stockmann: Yes, my native town is so dear to me that I would rather ruin it than see it flourishing upon a lie.

Aslaksen: This is really serious. (*Uproar and cat-calls.* MRS. STOCKMANN *coughs, but to no purpose; her husband does not listen to her any longer.*)

Hovstad (*shouting above the din*). A man must be a public enemy to wish to ruin a whole community!

Dr. Stockmann (*with growing fervor*). What does the destruction of a community matter, if it lives on lies! It ought to be razed to the ground, I tell you! All who live by lies ought to be exterminated like vermin! You will end by infecting the whole country; you will bring about such a state of things that the whole country will deserve to be ruined. And if things come to that pass, I shall say from the bottom of my heart: Let the whole country perish, let all these people be exterminated!

Voices from the crowd: That is talking like an out-and-out enemy of the people!

Billing: There sounded the voice of the people, by all that's holy!

The whole crowd (*shouting*). Yes, yes! He is an enemy of the people! He hates his country! He hates his own people!

Aslaksen: Both as a citizen and as an individual, I am profoundly disturbed by what we have had to listen to. Dr. Stockmann has shown himself in a light I should never have dreamed of. I am unhappily obliged to subscribe to the opinion which I have just heard my estimable fellow-citizens utter; and I propose that we should give expression to that opinion in a resolution. I propose a resolution as follows: "This meeting declares that it considers Dr. Thomas Stockmann, Medical Officer of the Baths, to be an enemy of the people." (*A storm of cheers and applause. A number of men surround the* DOCTOR *and hiss him.* MRS. STOCKMANN *and* PETRA *have got up from their* seats. MORTEN *and* EJLIF *are fighting the other schoolboys for hissing; some of their elders separate them.*)

Dr. Stockmann (*to the men who are hissing him*). Oh, you fools! I tell you that—

Aslaksen (*ringing his bell*). We cannot hear you now, Doctor. A formal vote is about to be taken; but, out of regard for personal feelings, it shall be by ballot and not verbal. Have you any clean paper, Mr. Billing?

Billing: I have both blue and white here.

Aslaksen (*going to him*). That will do nicely; we shall get on more quickly that way. Cut it up into small strips—yes, that's it. (*To the meeting.*) Blue means no; white means yes. I will come round myself and collect votes. (PETER STOCKMANN *leaves the hall.* ASLAKSEN *and one or two others go round the room with the slips of paper in their hats.*)

1st Citizen (*to* HOVSTAD). I say, what has come to the Doctor? What are we to think of it?

Hovstad: Oh, you know how head-strong he is.

2nd Citizen (*to* BILLING). Billing, you go to their house—have you ever noticed if the fellow drinks?

Billing: Well, I'm hanged if I know what to say. There are always spirits on the table when you go.

3rd Citizen: I rather think he goes quite off his head sometimes.

1st Citizen: I wonder if there is any madness in his family?

Billing: I shouldn't wonder if there were.

4th Citizen: No, it is nothing more than sheer malice; he wants to get even with somebody for something or other.

Billing: Well, certainly he suggested a rise in his salary on one occasion lately, and did not get it.

The Citizens (*together*). Ah!—then it is easy to understand how it is!

The Drunken Man (*who has got amongst the audience again*). I want a blue one, I do! And I want a white one too!

Voices: It's that drunken chap again! Turn him out!

Morten Kiil (*going up to* DR. STOCKMANN). Well, Stockmann, do you see what these monkey tricks of yours lead to?

Dr. Stockmann: I have done my duty.

Morten Kiil: What was that you said about the tanneries at Mölledal?

Dr. Stockmann: You heard well enough. I said they were the source of all the filth.

Morten Kiil: My tannery too?

Dr. Stockmann: Unfortunately your tannery is by far the worst.

Morten Kiil: Are you going to put that in the papers?

Dr. Stockmann: I shall conceal nothing.

Morten Kiil: That may cost you dear, Stockmann. (*Goes out.*)

A Stout Man (*going up to* CAPTAIN HORSTER, *without taking any notice of the ladies*). Well, Captain, so you lend your house to enemies of the people?

Horster: I imagine I can do what I like with my own possessions, Mr. Vik.

The Stout Man: Then you can have no objection to my doing the same with mine.

Horster: What do you mean, sir?

The Stout Man: You shall hear from me in the morning. (*Turns his back on him and moves off*).

Petra: Was that not your owner, Captain Horster?

Horster: Yes, that was Mr. Vik the ship-owner.

Aslaksen (*with the voting-papers in his hands, gets up on to the platform and rings his bell*). Gentlemen, allow me to announce the result. By the votes of every one here except one person—

A Young Man: That is the drunk chap!

Aslaksen: By the votes of every one here except a tipsy man, this meeting of citizens declares Dr. Thomas Stockmann to be an enemy of the people. (*Shouts and applause.*) Three cheers for our ancient and honorable citizen community! (*Renewed applause.*) Three cheers for our able and energetic Mayor, who has so loyally suppressed the promptings of family feeling! (*Cheers.*) The meeting is dissolved. (*Gets down.*)

Billing: Three cheers for the Chairman!

The Whole Crowd: Three cheers for Aslaksen! Hurrah!

Dr. Stockmann: My hat and coat, Petra! Captain, have you room on your ship for passengers to the New World?

Horster: For you and yours we will make room, Doctor.

Dr. Stockmann (*as* PETRA *helps him into his coat*). Good. Come, Katherine! Come, boys!

Mrs. Stockmann (*in an undertone*). Thomas, dear, let us go out by the back way.

Dr. Stockmann: No back ways for me, Katherine. (*Raising his voice.*) You will hear more of this enemy of the people, before he shakes the dust off his shoes upon you! I am not so forgiving as a certain Person; I do not say: "I forgive you, for ye know not what ye do."

Aslaksen (*shouting*). That is a blasphemous comparison, Dr. Stockmann!

Billing: It is, by God! It's dreadful for an earnest man to listen to.

A Coarse Voice: Threatens us now, does he!

Other Voices (*excitedly*). Let's go and break his windows! Duck him in the fjord!

Another Voice: Blow your horn, Evensen. Pip, pip!

[*Horn-blowing, hisses, and wild cries.* DR. STOCKMANN *goes out through the hall with his family,* HORSTER *elbowing a way for them.*]

The Whole Crowd (*howling after them as they go*). Enemy of the People! Enemy of the People!

Billing (*as he puts his papers together*). Well, I'm damned if I go and drink toddy with the Stockmanns tonight!

[*The crowd press towards the exit. The uproar continues outside; shouts of* "Enemy of the People!" *are heard from without.*]

ACT V

Scene: DR. STOCKMANN'S *study. Bookcases, and cabinets containing specimens, line the walls. At the back is a door leading to the hall; in the foreground on the left, a door leading to the sitting-room. In the right-hand wall are two windows, of which all the panes are broken. The* DOCTOR'S *desk, littered with books and papers, stands in the middle of the room, which is in disorder. It is morning.* DR. STOCKMANN *in dressing-gown, slippers and a smoking-cap, is bending down and raking with an umbrella under one of the cabinets. After a little while he rakes out a stone.*

Dr. Stockmann (*calling through the open sitting-room door*). Katherine, I have found another one.

Mrs. Stockmann (*from the sitting-room*). Oh, you will find a lot more yet, I expect.

Dr. Stockmann (*adding the stone to a heap of others on the table*). I shall treasure these stones as relics. Ejlif and Morten shall look at them every day, and when they are grown up they shall inherit them as heirlooms. (*Rakes about under a bookcase.*) Hasn't—what the deuce is her name?—the girl, you know—hasn't she been to fetch the glazier, yet?

Mrs. Stockmann (*coming in*). Yes, but he said he didn't know if he would be able to come to-day.

Dr. Stockmann: You will see he won't dare to come.

Mrs. Stockmann: Well, that is just what Randine thought—that he didn't dare to, on account of the neighbors. (*Calls into the sitting-room.*) What is it you want, Randine? Give it to me. (*Goes in, and comes out again directly.*) Here is a letter for you, Thomas.

Dr. Stockmann: Let me see it. (*Opens and reads it.*) Ah!—of course.

Mrs. Stockmann: Who is it from?

Dr. Stockmann: From the landlord. Notice to quit.

Mrs. Stockmann: Is it possible? Such a nice man—

Dr. Stockmann (*looking at the letter*). Does not dare do otherwise he says. Doesn't like doing it, but dare not do otherwise—on account of his fellow-citizens—out of regard for public opinion. Is in a dependent position—dare not offend certain influential men—

Mrs. Stockmann: There, you see, Thomas!

Dr. Stockmann: Yes, yes, I see well enough; the whole lot of them in the town are cowards; not a man among them dares do anything for fear of the others. (*Throws the letter on to the table.*) But it doesn't matter to us, Katherine. We are going to sail away to the New World, and—

Mrs. Stockmann: But, Thomas, are you sure we are well advised to take this step?

Dr. Stockmann: Are you suggesting that I should stay here, where they have pilloried me as an enemy of the people—branded me—broken my windows! And just look here, Katherine—they have torn a great rent in my black trousers too!

Mrs. Stockmann: Oh, dear!—and they are the best pair you have got!

Dr. Stockmann: You should never wear your best trousers when you go out to fight for freedom and truth. It is not that I care so much about the trousers, you know; you can always sew them up again for me. But that the common herd should dare to make this attack on me, as if they were my equals—that is what I cannot, for the life of me, swallow!

Mrs. Stockmann: There is no doubt they have behaved very ill to you, Thomas; but is that sufficient reason for our leaving our native country for good and all?

Dr. Stockmann: If we went to another town, do you suppose we should not find the common people just as insolent as they are here? Depend upon it, there is not much to choose between them. Oh, well, let the curs snap—that is not the worst part of it. The worst is that, from one end of this country to the other, every man is the slave of his Party. Although, as far as that goes, I dare say it is not much better in the free West either; the compact majority, and liberal public opinion, and all that infernal old bag of tricks are probably rampant there too. But there things are done on a larger scale, you see. They may kill you, but they won't put you to death by slow torture. They don't squeeze a free man's soul in a vise, as they do here. And, if need be, one can live in solitude. (*Walks up and down.*) If only I knew where there was a virgin forest or a small South Sea island for sale, cheap—

Mrs. Stockmann: But think of the boys, Thomas.

Dr. Stockmann (*standing still*). What a strange woman you are, Katherine! Would you prefer to have the boys grow up in a society like this? You saw for yourself last night that half the population are out of their minds; and if the other half have not lost their senses, it is because they are mere brutes, with no sense to lose.

Mrs. Stockmann: But, Thomas dear, the imprudent things you said had something to do with it, you know.

Dr. Stockmann: Well, isn't what I said perfectly true? Don't they turn every idea topsy-turvy? Don't they make a regular hotch-potch of right and wrong? Don't they say that the things I know are true, are lies? The craziest part of it all is the fact of these "liberals," men of full age, going about in crowds imagining that they are the broadminded party! Did you ever hear anything like it, Katherine!

Mrs. Stockmann: Yes, yes, it's mad enough of them, certainly; but—(PETRA *comes in from the sitting-room*). Back from school already?

Petra: Yes. I have been given notice of dismissal.

Mrs. Stockmann: Dismissal?

Dr. Stockmann: You too?

Petra: Mrs. Busk gave me my notice; so I thought it was best to go at once.

Dr. Stockmann: You were perfectly right, too!

Mrs. Stockmann: Who would have thought Mrs. Busk was a woman like that!

Petra: Mrs. Busk isn't a bit like that, mother; I saw quite plainly how it hurt her to do it. But she didn't dare do otherwise, she said; and so I got my notice.

Dr. Stockmann (*laughing and rubbing his hands*). She didn't dare do otherwise, either! It's delicious!

Mrs. Stockmann: Well, after the dreadful scenes last night—

Petra: It was not only that. Just listen to this, father!

Dr. Stockmann: Well?

Petra: Mrs. Busk showed me no less than three letters she received this morning—

Dr. Stockmann: Anonymous, I suppose?

Petra: Yes.

Dr. Stockmann: Yes, because they didn't dare to risk signing their names, Katherine!

Petra: And two of them were to the effect that a man, who has been our guest here, was declaring last night at the Club that my views on various subjects are extremely emancipated—

Dr. Stockmann: You did not deny that, I hope?

Petra: No, you know I wouldn't. Mrs. Busk's own views are tolerably emancipated, when we are alone together; but now that this report about me is being spread, she dare not keep me on any longer.

Mrs. Stockmann: And some one who had been a guest of ours! That shows you the return you get for your hospitality, Thomas!

Dr. Stockmann: We won't live in such a disgusting hole any longer. Pack up as quickly as you can, Katherine; the sooner we can get away, the better.

Mrs. Stockmann: Be quiet—I think I hear some one in the hall. See who it is, Petra.

Petra (*opening the door*). Oh, it's you, Captain Horster! Do come in.

Horster (*coming in*). Good morning.

I thought I would just come in and see how you were.

Dr. Stockmann (*shaking his hand*). Thanks—that is really kind of you.

Mrs. Stockmann: And thank you, too, for helping us through the crowd, Captain Horster.

Petra: How did you manage to get home again?

Horster: Oh, somehow or other. I am fairly strong, and there is more sound than fury about these folk.

Dr. Stockmann: Yes, isn't their swinish cowardice astonishing? Look here, I will show you something! There are all the stones they have thrown through my windows. Just look at them! I'm hanged if there are more than two decently large bits of hardstone in the whole heap; the rest are nothing but gravel—wretched little things. And yet they stood out there bawling and swearing that they would do me some violence; but as for *doing* anything—you don't see much of that in this town.

Horster: Just as well for you this time, doctor!

Dr. Stockmann: True enough. But it makes one angry all the same; because if some day it should be a question of a national fight in real earnest, you will see that public opinion will be in favor of taking to one's heels, and the compact majority will turn tail like a flock of sheep, Captain Horster. That is what is so mournful to think of; it gives me so much concern, that—. No, devil take it, it is ridiculous to care about it! They have called me an enemy of the people, so an enemy of the people let me be!

Mrs. Stockmann: You will never be that, Thomas.

Dr. Stockmann: Don't swear to that, Katherine. To be called an ugly name may have the same effect as a pin-scratch in the lung. And that hateful name—I can't get quit of it. It is sticking here in the pit of my stomach, eating into me like a corrosive acid. And no magnesia will remove it.

Petra: Bah!—you should only laugh at them, father.

Horster: They will change their minds some day, Doctor.

Mrs. Stockmann: Yes, Thomas, as sure as you are standing here.

Dr. Stockmann: Perhaps, when it is too late. Much good may it do them! They may wallow in their filth then and rue the day when they drove a patriot into exile. When do you sail, Captain Horster?

Horster: Hm!—that was just what I had come to speak about—

Dr. Stockmann: Why, has anything gone wrong with the ship?

Horster: No; but what has happened is that I am not to sail in it.

Petra: Do you mean that you have been dismissed from your command?

Horster (*smiling*). Yes, that's just it.

Petra: You too.

Mrs. Stockmann: There, you see, Thomas!

Dr. Stockmann: And that for the truth's sake! Oh, if I had thought such a thing possible—

Horster: You mustn't take it to heart; I shall be sure to find a job with some ship-owner or other, elsewhere.

Dr. Stockmann: And that is this man Vik—a wealthy man, independent of every one and everything—! Shame on him!

Horster: He is quite an excellent fellow otherwise; he told me himself he would willingly have kept me on, if only he had dared—

Dr. Stockmann: But he didn't dare? No, of course not.

Horster: It is not such an easy matter, he said, for a party man—

Dr. Stockmann: The worthy man spoke the truth. A party is like a sausage machine; it mashes up all sorts of heads together into the same mincemeat—fatheads and blockheads, all in one mash!

Mrs. Stockmann: Come, come, Thomas dear!

Petra (*to* HORSTER). If only you had not come home with us, things might not have come to this pass.

Horster: I do not regret it.

Petra (*holding out her hand to him*). Thank you for that!

Horster (*to* DR. STOCKMANN). And so what I came to say was that if you are determined to go away, I have thought of another plan—

Dr. Stockmann: That's splendid!—if only we can get away at once.

Mrs. Stockmann: Hush!—wasn't that some one knocking?

Petra: That is uncle, surely.

Dr. Stockmann: Aha! (*Calls out.*) Come in!

Mrs. Stockmann: Dear Thomas, promise me definitely—

[PETER STOCKMANN *comes in from the hall.*]

Peter Stockmann: Oh, you are engaged. In that case, I will—

Dr. Stockmann: No, no, come in.

Peter Stockmann: But I wanted to speak to you alone.

Mrs. Stockmann: We will go into the sitting-room in the meanwhile.

Horster: And I will look in again later.

Dr. Stockmann: No, go in there with them, Captain Horster; I want to hear more about—

Horster: Very well, I will wait, then. (*He follows* MRS. STOCKMANN *and* PETRA *into the sitting-room.*)

Dr. Stockmann: I daresay you find it rather draughty here to-day. Put your hat on.

Peter Stockmann: Thank you, if I may. (*Does so.*) I think I caught cold last night; I stood and shivered—

Dr. Stockmann: Really? I found it warm enough.

Peter Stockmann: I regret that it was not in my power to prevent those excesses last night.

Dr. Stockmann: Have you anything particular to say to me besides that?

Peter Stockmann (*taking a big letter from his pocket*). I have this document for you, from the Baths Committee.

Dr. Stockmann: My dismissal?

Peter Stockmann: Yes, dating from to-day. (*Lays the letter on the table.*) It gives us pain to do it; but, to speak frankly, we dared not do otherwise on account of public opinion.

Dr. Stockmann (*smiling*). Dared not? I seem to have heard that word before, to-day.

Peter Stockmann: I must beg you to understand your position clearly. For the future you must not count on any practice whatever in the town.

Dr. Stockmann: Devil take the practice! But why are you so sure of that?

Peter Stockmann: The Householders' Association is circulating a list from house to house. All right-minded citizens are being called upon to give up employing you; and I can assure you that not a single head of a family will risk refusing his signature. They simply dare not.

Dr. Stockmann: No, no; I don't doubt it. But what then?

Peter Stockmann: If I might advise you, it would be best to leave the place for a little while—

Dr. Stockmann: Yes, the propriety of leaving the place *has* occurred to me.

Peter Stockmann: Good. And then, when you have had six months to think things over, if, after mature consideration, you can persuade yourself to write a few words of regret, acknowledging your error—

Dr. Stockmann: I might have my appointment restored to me, do you mean?

Peter Stockmann: Perhaps. It is not at all impossible.

Dr. Stockmann: But what about public opinion, then? Surely you would not dare to do it on account of public feeling.

Peter Stockmann: Public opinion is an extremely mutable thing. And, to be quite candid with you, it is a matter of great importance to us to have some admission of that sort from you in writing.

Dr. Stockmann: Oh, that's what you are after, is it! I will just trouble you to remember what I said to you lately about foxy tricks of that sort!

Peter Stockmann: Your position was quite different then. At that time you had reason to suppose you had the whole town at your back—

Dr. Stockmann: Yes, and now I feel I have the whole town *on* my back—(*flaring up*). I would not do it if I had the devil and his dam on my back—! Never—never, I tell you!

Peter Stockmann: A man with a family has no right to behave as you do. You have no right to do it, Thomas.

Dr. Stockmann: I have no right! There is only one single thing in the world a free man has no right to do. Do you know what that is?

Peter Stockmann: No.

Dr. Stockmann: Of course you don't, but I will tell you. A free man has no right to soil himself with filth; he has no right to behave in a way that would justify his spitting in his own face.

Peter Stockmann: This sort of thing sounds extremely plausible, of course; and if there were no other explanation for your obstinacy—. But as it happens that there is—

Dr. Stockmann: What do you mean?

Peter Stockmann: You understand very well what I mean. But, as your brother and as a man of discretion, I advise you not to build too much upon expectations and prospects that may so very easily fail you.

Dr. Stockmann: What in the world is all this about?

Peter Stockmann: Do you really ask me to believe that you are ignorant of the terms of Mr. Kiil's will?

Dr. Stockmann: I know that the small amount he possesses is to go to an institution for indigent old workpeople. How does that concern me?

Peter Stockmann: In the first place, it is by no means a small amount that is in question. Mr. Kiil is a fairly wealthy man.

Dr. Stockmann: I had no notion of that!

Peter Stockmann: Hm!—hadn't you really? Then I suppose you had no notion, either, that a considerable portion of his wealth will come to your children, you and your wife having a life-rent of the capital. Has he never told you so?

Dr. Stockmann: Never, on my honor! Quite the reverse; he has consistently done nothing but fume at being so unconscionably heavily taxed. But are you perfectly certain of this, Peter?

Peter Stockmann: I have it from an absolutely reliable source.

Dr. Stockmann: Then, thank God, Katherine is provided for—and the children too! I must tell her this at once—(*calls out*) Katherine, Katherine!

Peter Stockmann (*restraining him*). Hush, don't say a word yet!

Mrs. Stockmann (*opening the door*). What is the matter?

Dr. Stockmann: Oh, nothing, nothing; you can go back. (*She shuts the door.* DR. STOCKMANN *walks up and down in his excitement.*) Provided for!—Just think of it, we are all provided for. And for life! What a blessed feeling it is to know one is provided for!

Peter Stockmann: Yes, but that is just exactly what you are not. Mr. Kiil can alter his will any day he likes.

Dr. Stockmann: But he won't do that, my dear Peter. The "Badger" is much too delighted at my attack on you and your wise friends.

Peter Stockmann (*starts and looks intently at him*). Ah, that throws a light on various things.

Dr. Stockmann: What things?

Peter Stockmann: I see that the whole thing was a combined maneuver on your part and his. These violent, reckless attacks that you have made against the leading men of the town, under the pretence that it was in the name of truth—

Dr. Stockmann: What about them?

Peter Stockmann: I see that they were nothing else than the stipulated price for that vindictive old man's will.

Dr. Stockmann (*almost speechless.*) Peter—you are the most disgusting plebeian I have ever met in all my life.

Peter Stockmann: All is over between us. Your dismissal is irrevocable—we have a weapon against you now. (*Goes out.*)

Dr. Stockmann: For shame! For shame! (*Calls out.*) Katherine, you must have the floor scrubbed after him! Let—what's her name—devil take it, the girl who has always got soot on her nose—

Mrs. Stockmann (*in the sitting-room*). Hush, Thomas, be quiet!

Petra (*coming to the door*). Father, grandfather is here, asking if he may speak to you alone.

Dr. Stockmann: Certainly he may. (*Going to the door.*) Come in, Mr. Kiil. (MORTEN KIIL *comes in.* DR. STOCKMANN *shuts the door after him.*) What can I do for you? Won't you sit down?

Morten Kill: I won't sit. (*Looks around.*) You look very comfortable here to-day, Thomas.

Dr. Stockmann: Yes, don't we!

Morten Kiil: Very comfortable—plenty of fresh air. I should think you have got enough to-day of that oxygen you were talking about yesterday. Your conscience must be in splendid order to-day, I should think.

Dr. Stockmann: It is.

Morten Kiil: So I should think. (*Taps his chest.*) Do you know what I have got here?

Dr. Stockmann: A good conscience, too, I hope.

Morten Kill: Bah!—No, it is something better than that.

[*He takes a thick pocket-book from his breast-pocket, opens it and displays a packet of papers.*]

Dr. Stockmann (*looking at him in astonishment*). Shares in the Baths?

Morten Kiil: They were not difficult to get to-day.

Dr. Stockmann: And you have been buying—?

Morten Kiil: As many as I could pay for.

Dr. Stockmann: But, my dear Mr. Kiil—consider the state of the Baths' affairs!

Morten Kiil: If you behave like a reasonable man, you can soon set the Baths on their feet again.

Dr. Stockmann: Well, you can see for yourself that I have done all I can, but—. They are all mad in this town!

Morten Kiil: You said yesterday that the worst of this pollution came from my tannery. If that is true, then my grandfather and my father before me, and I myself, for many years past, have been poisoning the town like three destroying angels. Do you think I am going to sit quiet under that reproach?

Dr. Stockmann: Unfortunately I am afraid you will have to.

Morten Kiil: No, thank you. I am jealous of my name and reputation. They call me "the Badger," I am told. A badger is a kind of pig, I believe; but I am not going to give them the right to call me that. I mean to live and die a clean man.

Dr. Stockmann: And how are you going to set about it?

Morten Kiil: You shall cleanse me, Thomas.

Dr. Stockmann: I!

Morten Kiil: Do you know what money I have bought these shares with? No, of course you can't know—but I will tell you. It is the money that Katherine and Petra and the boys will have when I am gone. Because I have been able to save a little bit after all, you know.

Dr. Stockmann (*flaring up*). And you have gone and taken Katherine's money for *this!*

Morten Kiil: Yes, the whole of the money is invested in the Baths now. And now I just want to see whether you are quite stark, staring mad, Thomas! If you still make out that these animals and other nasty things of that sort come from my tannery, it will be exactly as if you were to flay broad strips of skin from Katherine's body, and Petra's, and the boys'; and no decent man would do that—unless he were mad.

Dr. Stockmann (*walking up and down*). Yes, but I *am* mad; I *am* mad!

Morten Kiil: You cannot be so absurdly mad as all that, when it is a question of your wife and children.

Dr. Stockmann (*standing still in front of him*). Why couldn't you consult me about it, before you went and bought all that trash?

Morten Kiil: What is done cannot be undone.

Dr. Stockmann (*walks about uneasily*). If only I were not so certain about it—! But I am absolutely convinced that I am right.

Morten Kiil (*weighing the pocket-book in his hand*). If you stick to your mad idea, this won't be worth much, you know. (*Puts the pocket-book in his pocket.*)

Dr. Stockmann: But, hang it all! it might be possible for science to discover some prophylactic, I should think—or some antidote of some kind—

Morten Kiil: To kill these animals, do you mean?

Dr. Stockmann: Yes, or to make them innocuous.

Morten Kiil: Couldn't you try some rat's-bane?

Dr. Stockmann: Don't talk nonsense! They all say it is only imagination, you know. Well, let it go at that! Let them have their own way about it! Haven't the ignorant, narrow-minded curs reviled me as an enemy of the people?—and haven't they been ready to tear the clothes off my back too?

Morten Kiil: And broken all your windows to pieces!

Dr. Stockmann: And then there is my duty to my family. I must talk it over with Katherine; she is great on those things.

Morten Kiil: That is right; be guided by a reasonable woman's advice.

Dr. Stockmann (*advancing towards him*). To think you could do such a preposterous thing! Risking Katherine's money in this way, and putting me in such a horribly painful dilemma! When I look at you, I think I see the devil himself—.

Morten Kiil: Then I had better go. But I must have an answer from you before two o'clock—yes or no. If it is no, the shares go to a charity, and that this very day.

Dr. Stockmann: And what does Katherine get?

Morten Kiil: Not a halfpenny. (*The door leading to the hall opens and* HOVSTAD *and* ASLAKSEN *make their appearance.*) Look at those two!

Dr. Stockmann (*staring at them*). What the devil!—have *you* actually the face to come into my house?

Hovstad: Certainly.

Aslaksen: We have something to say to you, you see.

Morten Kiil (*in a whisper*). Yes or no—before two o'clock.

Aslaksen (*glancing at* HOVSTAD). Aha! (MORTEN KIIL *goes out.*)

Dr. Stockmann: Well, what do you want with me? Be brief.

Hovstad: I can quite understand that you are annoyed with us for our attitude at the meeting yesterday—

Dr. Stockmann: Attitude, do you call it? Yes, it was a charming attitude! I call it weak, womanish—damnably shameful!

Hovstad: Call it what you like, we could not do otherwise.

Dr. Stockmann: You *dared* not do otherwise—isn't that it?

Hovstad: Well, if you like to put it that way.

Aslaksen: But why did you not let us have word of it beforehand?—just a hint to Mr. Hovstad or to me?

Dr. Stockmann: A hint? Of what?

Aslaksen: Of what was behind it all.

Dr. Stockmann: I don't understand you in the least.

Aslaksen (*with a confidential nod*). Oh yes, you do, Dr. Stockmann.

Hovstad: It is no good making a mystery of it any longer.

Dr. Stockmann (*looking first at one of them and then at the other*). What the devil do you both mean?

Aslaksen: May I ask if your father-in-law is not going round the town buying up all the shares in the Baths?

Dr. Stockmann: Yes, he has been buying Bath shares to-day; but—

Aslaksen: It would have been more prudent to get some one else to do it—some one less nearly related to you.

Hovstad: And you should not have let your name appear in the affair. There was no need for anyone to know that the attack on the Baths came from you. You ought to have consulted me, Dr. Stockmann.

Dr. Stockmann (*looks in front of him; then a light seems to dawn on him and he says in amazement*). Are such things conceivable? Are such things possible?

Aslaksen (*with a smile*). Evidently they are. But it is better to use a little *finesse,* you know.

Hovstad: And it is much better to

have several persons in a thing of that sort; because the responsibility of each individual is lessened, when there are others with him.

Dr. Stockmann (*composedly*). Come to the point, gentlemen. What do you want?

Aslaksen: Perhaps Mr. Hovstad had better—

Hovstad: No, you tell him, Aslaksen.

Aslaksen: Well, the fact is that, now we know the bearings of the whole affair, we think we might venture to put the *People's Messenger* at your disposal.

Dr. Stockmann: Do you dare do that now? What about public opinion? Are you not afraid of a storm breaking upon our heads?

Hovstad: We will try to weather it.

Aslaksen: And you must be ready to go off quickly on a new tack, Doctor. As soon as your invective has done its work—

Dr. Stockmann: Do you mean, as soon as my father-in-law and I have got hold of the shares at a low figure?

Hovstad: Your reasons for wishing to get the control of the Baths are mainly scientific, I take it.

Dr. Stockmann: Of course; it was for scientific reasons that I persuaded the old "Badger" to stand in with me in the matter. So we will tinker at the conduit-pipes a little, and dig up a little bit of the shore, and it shan't cost the town a sixpence. That will be all right—eh?

Hovstad: I think so—if you have the *People's Messenger* behind you.

Aslaksen: The Press is a power in a free community, Doctor.

Dr. Stockmann: Quite so. And so is public opinion. And you, Mr. Aslaksen—I suppose you will be answerable for the Householders' Association?

Aslaksen: Yes, and for the Temperance Society. You may rely on that.

Dr. Stockmann: But, gentlemen—I really am ashamed to ask the question—but, what return do you—?

Hovstad: We should prefer to help you without any return whatever, believe me. But the *People's Messenger* is in rather a shaky condition; it doesn't go really well; and I should be very unwilling to suspend the paper now, when there is so much work to do here in the political way.

Dr. Stockmann: Quite so; that would be a great trial to such a friend of the people as you are. (*Flares up.*) But I am an enemy of the people, remember! (*Walks about the room.*) Where have I put my stick? Where the devil is my stick?

Hovstad: What's that?

Aslaksen: Surely you never mean—?

Dr. Stockmann (*standing still*). And suppose I don't give you a single penny of all I get out of it? Money is not very easy to get out of us rich folk, please to remember!

Hovstad: And you please to remember that this affair of the shares can be represented in two ways!

Dr. Stockmann: Yes, and you are just the man to do it. If I don't come to the rescue of the *People's Messenger,* you will certainly take an evil view of the affair; you will hunt me down, I can well imagine—pursue me—try to throttle me as a dog does a hare.

Hovstad: It is a natural law; every animal must fight for its own livelihood.

Aslaksen: And get its food where it can, you know.

Dr. Stockmann (*walking about the room*). Then you go and look for yours in the gutter; because I am going to show you which is the strongest animal of us three! (*Finds an umbrella and brandishes it above his head.*) Ah, now—!

Hovstad: You are surely not going to use violence!

Aslaksen: Take care what you are doing with that umbrella.

Dr. Stockmann: Out of the window with you, Mr. Hovstad!

Hovstad (*edging to the door*). Are you quite mad!

Dr. Stockmann: Out of the window, Mr. Aslaksen! Jump, I tell you! You will have to do it, sooner or later.

Aslaksen (*running round the writing-table*). Moderation, Doctor—I am a delicate man—I can stand so little—(*calls out*) help, help!

[MRS. STOCKMANN, PETRA *and* HORSTER *come in from the sitting-room.*]

Mrs. Stockmann: Good gracious, Thomas! What is happening?

Dr. Stockmann (*brandishing the umbrella*). Jump out, I tell you! Out into the gutter!

Hovstad: An assault on an unoffending man! I call you to witness, Captain Horster. (*Hurries out through the hall.*)

Aslaksen (*irresolutely*). If only I knew the way about here—. (*Steals out through the sitting-room.*)

Mrs. Stockmann (*holding her husband back*). Control yourself, Thomas!

Dr. Stockmann (*throwing down the umbrella*). Upon my soul, they have escaped after all.

Mrs. Stockmann: What did they want you to do?

Dr. Stockmann: I will tell you later on; I have something else to think about now. (*Goes to the table and writes something on a calling-card.*) Look there, Katherine; what is written there?

Mrs. Stockmann: Three big No's; what does that mean?

Dr. Stockmann: I will tell you that too, later on. (*Holds out the card to* PETRA.) There, Petra; tell sooty-face to run over to "the Badger's" with that, as quickly as she can. Hurry up! (PETRA *takes the card and goes out to the hall.*)

Dr. Stockmann: Well, I think I have had a visit from every one of the devil's messengers to-day! But now I am going to sharpen my pen till they can feel its point; I shall dip it in venom and gall; I shall hurl my ink-pot at their heads!

Mrs. Stockmann: Yes, but we are going away, you know, Thomas.

[PETRA *comes back.*]

Dr. Stockmann: Well?

Petra: She has gone with it.

Dr. Stockmann: Good.—Going away, did you say? No, I'll be hanged if we are going away! We are going to stay where we are, Katherine!

Petra: Stay here?

Mrs. Stockmann: Here, in the town?

Dr. Stockmann: Yes, here. This is the field of battle—this is where the fight will be. This is where I shall triumph! As soon as I have had my trousers sewn up I shall go out and look for another house. We must have a roof over our heads for the winter.

Horster: That you shall have in my house.

Dr. Stockmann: Can I?

Horster: Yes, quite well. I have plenty of room, and I am almost never at home.

Mrs. Stockmann: How good of you, Captain Horster!

Petra: Thank you!

Dr. Stockmann (*grasping his hand*). Thank you, thank you! That is one trouble over! Now I can set to work in earnest at once. There is an endless amount of things to look through here, Katherine! Luckily I shall have all my time at my disposal; because I have been dismissed from the Baths, you know.

Mrs. Stockmann (*with a sigh*). Oh yes, I expected that.

Dr. Stockmann: And they want to take my practice away from me too. Let them! I have got the poor people to fall back upon, anyway—those that don't pay anything; and, after all, they need me most, too. But, by Jove, they will have to listen to me; I shall preach to them in season and out of season, as it says somewhere.

Mrs, Stockmann: But, dear Thomas, I should have thought events had showed you what use it is to preach.

Dr. Stockmann: You are really ridiculous, Katherine. Do you want me to let myself be beaten off the field by public opinion and the compact majority and all that devilry? No, thank you! And what I want to do is so simple and clear and straightforward. I only want to drum into the heads of these curs the fact that the liberals are the most insidious enemies of freedom—that party programmes strangle every young and vigorous truth—that considerations of expediency turn morality and justice upside down—and that they will end by making life here unbearable. Don't you think, Captain Horster, that I ought to be able to make people understand that?

Horster: Very likely; I don't know much about such things myself.

Dr. Stockmann: Well, look here—I will explain! It is the party leaders that must be exterminated. A party leader is like a wolf, you see—like a voracious wolf. He requires a certain number of smaller victims to prey upon every year, if he is to live. Just look at Hovstad and Aslaksen! How many smaller victims have they not put an end to—or at any rate maimed and mangled until they are fit for nothing except to be householders or subscribers to the *People's Messenger!* (*Sits down on the edge of the table.*) Come here, Katherine—look how beautifully the sun shines to-day! And this lovely spring air I am drinking in!

Mrs. Stockmann: Yes, if only we could live on sunshine and spring air, Thomas.

Dr. Stockmann: Oh, you will have to pinch and save a bit—then we shall get along. That gives me very little concern. What is much worse is, that I know of no one who is liberal-minded and high-minded enough to venture to take up my work after me.

Petra: Don't think about that, father; you have plenty of time before you.—Hullo, here are the boys already!

[EJLIF *and* MORTEN *come in from the sitting-room.*]

Mrs. Stockmann: Have you got a holiday?

Morten: No; but we were fighting with the other boys between lessons—

Ejlif: That isn't true; it was the other boys were fighting with us.

Morten: Well, and then Mr. Rörlund said we had better stay at home for a day or two.

Dr. Stockmann (*snapping his fingers and getting up from the table*). I have it! I have it, by Jove! You shall never set foot in the school again!

The Boys: No more school!

Mrs. Stockmann: But, Thomas—

Dr. Stockmann: Never, I say. I will educate you myself; that is to say, you shan't learn a blessed thing—

Morten: Hooray!

Dr. Stockmann: —but I will make liberal-minded and high-minded men of you. You must help me with that, Petra.

Petra: Yes, father, you may be sure I will.

Dr. Stockmann: And my school shall be in the room where they insulted me and called me an enemy of the people. But we are too few as we are; I must have at least twelve boys to begin with.

Mrs. Stockmann: You will certainly never get them in this town.

Dr. Stockmann: We shall. (*To the boys.*) Don't you know any street urchins —regular ragamuffins—?

Morten: Yes, father, I know lots!

Dr. Stockmann: That's capital! Bring me some specimens of them. I am going to experiment with curs, just for once; there may be some exceptional heads amongst them.

Morten: And what are we going to do, when you have made liberal-minded and high-minded men of us?

Dr. Stockmann: Then you shall drive all the wolves out of the country, my boys!

[EJLIF *looks rather doubtful about it;* MORTEN *jumps about crying* "Hurrah!"]

Mrs. Stockmann: Let us hope it won't be the wolves that will drive you out of the country, Thomas.

Dr. Stockmann: Are you out of your mind, Katherine? Drive me out! Now— when I am the strongest man in the town!

Mrs. Stockmann: The strongest— now?

Dr. Stockmann: Yes, and I will go so far as to say that now I am the strongest man in the whole world.

Morten: I say!

Dr. Stockmann (*lowering his voice*). Hush! You mustn't say anything about it yet; but I have made a great discovery.

Mrs. Stockmann: Another one?

Dr. Stockmann: Yes. (*Gathers them round him, and says confidentially*). It is this, let me tell you—that the strongest man in the world is he who stands most alone.

Mrs. Stockmann (*smiling and shaking her head*). Oh, Thomas, Thomas!

Petra (*encouragingly, as she grasps her father's hands*). Father!

DISCUSSION QUESTIONS

Act I

1. What is the symbolic significance of the stick that Peter Stockmann carries (in terms of his character and his role in the play)?
2. How is Peter Stockmann characterized as to (1) his health, (2) his spending habits, and (3) his relationship to other people?
3. Why is it ironic that the Baths are the common interest which unites the citizens of the town?
4. What exposition provided in the dialogue between Peter and Dr. Stockmann sets the stage for the conflict between the two?
5. The weapon or tool to set up conflict is introduced early in the "well-made play." What is it here?
6. What corollary conflict already exists between Peter and Dr. Stockmann and what is ironic about it?

7. What characterization polarity is established between Peter and Dr. Stockmann?
8. How does Dr. Stockmann's entry help to characterize him?
9. How does the controversy over the toddy further establish the character differences between Peter and Dr. Stockmann?
10. What is the dramatic significance of Dr. Stockmann's inquiry about the arrival of the postman?
11. What is the dramatic reason for postponing the publication of Dr. Stockmann's article concerning the healthfulness of the baths?
12. Why is it important that Peter Stockmann leave the scene before the arrival of the letter?
13. Why is it important dramatically that Petra give her father the letter instead of having him receive it from the mailman?
14. What is ironic about the expectations of the doctor and his friends in the concluding portion of this act?

Act II

1. How does the sealed letter in Mrs. Stockmann's hand function in the play?
2. How does Dr. Stockmann's failure to anticipate the mayor's reaction to his discovery help to characterize him?
3. How does Mrs. Stockmann serve partly as a foil (a character with contrasting traits) to her husband and partly as an echo?
4. The scene with Morton Kiil contrasts the cynical point of view with the naïve and optimistic. How do the remarks "a bit of luck for the town," "But no one can see them," and "Is he in this too?" create an ironic paradox?
5. How is the cynical, practical-minded attitude of Kiil contrasted with the radical, zealous one of Hovstad?
6. What shibboleths and socialistic jargon used by Hovstad characterize him as slightly ridiculous and insincere?
7. What is ironic about Aslaksen's proposal to hold a "demonstration"?
8. What is comic about Dr. Stockmann's response to Kiil, Hovstad, and Aslaksen?
9. How does the agreement between Dr. Stockmann and Hovstad concerning the printing of the report prepare for the outcome of the interview between Dr. Stockmann and the mayor? What dramatic irony is created, i.e., what contrast is there between what the character expects to happen and what actually will happen?
10. Why is it important that the manuscript be given to Hovstad instead of remaining in Dr. Stockmann's possession?
11. What is ironic about Dr. Stockmann's remark, "Hovstad has put the paper at my disposal if necessity should arise"?
12. What is the purpose of the short scene involving Dr. Stockmann, Mrs. Stockmann, and Petra before the mayor's arrival? What part do the terms "independent liberal press" and "compact majority" play in this scene?

Act III

1. What tonal contrast is established by shifting the action from Dr. Stockmann's home to the office of the *People's Messenger*?
2. What preparatory information is provided by Dr. Stockmann's remark, "This article is only the beginning. I have four or five others sketched out already"?
3. What further characterization of the doctor is provided by his response to Hovstad's praise of the manuscript?
4. How is Dr. Stockmann's remark, "I am not quite clear about everything yet, but I shall see my way presently," indicative of his tragicomic flaw?
5. What is ironic about Dr. Stockmann's remark, "If only we hold together, it will go smoothly, so smoothly"?
6. How does the mention of Billing's aspiration to be secretary of the town council serve as preparatory information?
7. How does the encounter between Hovstad and Petra disclose his true interests? What does it reveal about her?
8. Why is it important that the scene between Hovstad and Petra precede the one between Hovstad and the mayor?
9. What is the symbolic significance of the mayor's coming in by the back door? How does it reveal character?
10. What is ironic about the doctor's reaction to the attitude of Hovstad and Aslaksen after they have been approached by the mayor?
11. Why is it important dramatically that Dr. Stockmann be aware of the defection of Hovstad and Aslaksen? How does his decision to continue alone further characterize him as tragic, comic, or pathetic?
12. If this act contains the crisis in the action, as is the practice in the "well-made play," which episode represents the turning point in the fortune of Dr. Stockmann, and is there a feeling of inevitability about the outcome? Why?
13. What is ironic about the mayor's charge that Dr. Stockmann is an enemy of the people?
14. The tragic hero is characterized by his uncompromising attitude toward what he considers a noble goal. He is willing to sacrifice everything to achieve this goal, even his life, if need be. What is Dr. Stockmann's "noble goal" and what is he willing to sacrifice for it?
15. The comic hero frequently pursues an ignoble, trivial, or impossible-to-achieve goal. What elements of the comic are there about Dr. Stockmann's behavior?

Act IV

1. What expository information is provided by the conversation between the various citizens?
2. What preparatory information provided by this conversation suggests the outcome of the meeting?

3. What does Captain Horster's action reveal about his character? How is he used as a foil?
4. What is the significance of Hovstad and Aslaksen entering the room at the same moment, but making their way through the crowd separately?
5. What is the dramatic purpose of having the mayor present at the meeting?
6. What is ironic about Aslaksen being appointed chairman?
7. What is the significance of the drunkard's presence and remarks at the meeting? How does he serve as a foil? As a parodying echo?
8. How does the Doctor's speech serve to illustrate his naiveté, his intellectual arrogance, and his sense of moral superiority?
9. What is ironic and paradoxical about Dr. Stockmann's speech?
10. How do Hovstad's remarks at the meeting about his humble origins further reveal his character?
11. What is the significance of the remarks made by Morton Kiil and Mr. Vik in relation to dramatic preparation?
12. Compare the tone at the end of this act with that at the end of Act III.

Act V

1. What do the stones and broken windows symbolize?
2. How do the torn trousers add a note of comic incongruity?
3. What do the "primeval forest" and "little South Sea Island" symbolize? Does Dr. Stockmann's desire to go to these places affect his status as a tragic or a comic figure? How?
4. What contrast related to heroic stature is established between the characters of Horster and Dr. Stockmann?
5. What do we learn of Dr. Stockmann's character from his reaction to Horster's dismissal?
6. What is the irony in the mayor's excuse that the dismissal of Dr. Stockmann is necessitated by the pressure of public opinion?
7. What is ironic about the mayor's interpretation of the doctor's motives in discrediting the healthfulness of the Baths?
8. What purpose is served by having the doctor continually forget the maidservant's name?
9. What does the scene with Morton Kiil establish?
10. What is ironic about Kiil's purchase of the stock?
11. How does this purchase create a dilemma for Dr. Stockmann?
12. What is ironic about the role of Hovstad and Aslaksen in their scene with the doctor? What reversal of roles occurs here?
13. Which of Dr. Stockmann's acts and statements render him comic instead of tragic?
14. What irony is there about his final "great discovery"?

MISS JULIE
A Naturalistic Tragedy

✤ *August Strindberg*

Translated by
EVERT SPRINCHORN

Introductory Comment

In an author's preface to *Miss Julie* Strindberg explains the purpose and method behind his writing the play. He says that he had been captured by a theme outside the particular and controversial issues of his day which dealt with a subject of enduring interest—the problem of social rise and downfall. His story, he goes on to say, was chosen from an incident in real life he had heard about and which had moved him deeply because it had the ingredients of tragic drama in it: "When we see an individual on whom fortune has heaped an abundance of gifts go to her ruin and destruction, we are overcome with a tragic feeling." What this superabundance of natural gifts Miss Julie has been endowed with by fortune Strindberg never elaborates on in his prefatory comments although he has much to say about those influences which lead her to ruin.

Rather paradoxically in view of the preceding remarks, but in line with his current belief in social Darwinism—the survival of the strong and fit in society and the necessary extinction of the weak—, scientific objectivity, and Zolaist naturalism, he adds that perhaps a time will come when we will be so enlightened that we will view with indifference the brutal, cynical, heartless spectacle that life has to offer. In these remarks, of course, we recognize the would-be scientific observer speaking rather than the artist, but the play itself is the product of the artist rather than the amateur social psychologist.

In discussing the motivation for his characters' behavior, Strindberg postulates a theory of multiple causation. He sees the behavior of Miss Julie as the result of a combination of circumstances: her reaction to her mother's feminist dogma and practice, her misguided upbringing at the hands of her well-meaning father, her own perverse nature, the negative influence of her fiancé, the festive mood of Midsummer Eve, her father's absence from the manor, her menstrual indisposition, her abnormal preoccupation with animals, the physical excitement of the dancing, the long twilight, the aphrodisiac scent of the flowers, and finally the physical intimacy provided by the heroine being secluded in a bedroom with an aggressive, predatory male.

He also mentions that he has made his characters "characterless," that is, vacillating and disjointed to suit them better to the times. Miss Julie is a victim of her heredity and upbringing, of the discord a mother's crime produces in a family, of the delusions and deceptions of her time, of the circumstances of her own defective constitution. This is what leads her to her untimely and tragic end. Jean, the servant, is "characterless" in the sense that he has a dual character, says Strindberg. He vacillates between love of power and glory and hatred for those who have it. He is polished on the surface, but the inside is uncouth and vulgar. His masculinity makes him the natural aristocrat in his sexual relationship with Miss Julie, the social aristocrat.

One of the questions the play raises in view of Strindberg's professed beliefs and intentions is how much is the play limited by his espousal of the tenets of naturalistic determinism and scientific "objectivity." Or putting the question another way, does the dramatic artist in Strindberg, as in Brecht, rise above the rigid, doctrinaire theories he advances as the basis of his work? Does he create genuine tragic drama or has he merely dramatized some narrow aesthetic and philosophical concepts that limit the play's ultimate value as a work of art?

Characters

MISS JULIE, *twenty-five years old*
JEAN, *valet, thirty years old*
CHRISTINE, *the cook, thirty-five years old*

[*The action of the play takes place in the kitchen of the Count's manor house on Midsummer Eve in Sweden in the 1880s.*]

The scene is a large kitchen. The walls and ceiling are masked by the tormentors and borders. The rear wall runs obliquely upstage from the left. On this wall to the left are two shelves with pots and pans of copper, iron, and pewter. The shelves are decorated with goffered paper. A little to the right can be seen three-fourths of a deep arched doorway with two glass doors, and through them can be seen a fountain with a statue of Cupid, lilac bushes in bloom, and the tops of some Lombardy poplars. From the left of the stage the corner of a large, Dutch-tile kitchen stove protrudes with part of the hood showing. Projecting from the right side of the stage is one end of the servants' dining table of white pine, with a few chairs around it. The stove is decorated with branches of birch leaves; the floor is strewn with juniper twigs. On the end of the table is a large Japanese spice jar filled with lilacs. An icebox, a sink, a wash basin. Over the door a big, old-fashioned bell; and to the left of the door the gaping mouth of a speaking tube.

[CHRISTINE *is standing at the stove, frying something. She is wearing a light-colored cotton dress and an apron.* JEAN *enters, dressed in livery and carrying a pair of high-top boots with spurs. He sets them where they are clearly visible.*]

Jean: Tonight she's wild again. Miss Julie's absolutely wild!

Christine: You took your time getting back!

Jean: I took the Count down to the station, and on my way back as I passed the barn I went in for a dance. And there was Miss Julie leading the dance with the game warden. But then she noticed me. And she ran right into my arms and chose me for the ladies' waltz. And she's been dancing ever since like—like I don't know what. She's absolutely wild!

Christine: That's nothing new. But she's been worse than ever during the last two weeks, ever since her engagement was broken off.

Jean: Yes, I never did hear all there was to that. He was a good man, too, even if he wasn't rich. Well, that's a woman for you. (*He sits down at the end of the table.*) But, tell me, isn't it strange that a young girl like her—all right, young woman—prefers to stay home here with the servants rather than go with her father to visit her relatives?

Christine: I suppose she's ashamed to face them after that fiasco with her young man.

Jean: No doubt. He wouldn't take any nonsense from her. Do you know what happened, Christine? I do. I saw the whole thing, even though I didn't let on.

Christine: Don't tell me you were there?

Jean: Well, I was. They were in the barnyard one evening—and she was training him, as she called it. Do you know what she was doing? She was making him jump over her riding whip—training him like a dog. He jumped over twice, and she whipped him both times. But the third time, he grabbed the whip from her, broke it in a thousand pieces—and walked off.

Christine: So that's what happened. Well, what do you know!

Jean: Yes, that put an end to that affair.—What have you got for me that is really good, Christine?

Christine (*serving him from the frying pan*). Just a little bit of kidney. I cut it especially for you.

Jean (*smelling it*). Wonderful! My special *délice!* (*Feeling the plate.*) Hey, you didn't warm the plate!

Christine: You're more fussy than the Count himself when you set your mind to it. (*She rumples his hair gently.*)

Jean (*irritated*). Cut it out! Don't muss up my hair. You know I don't like that!

Christine: Oh, now don't get mad. Can I help it if I like you?

[JEAN *eats.* CHRISTINE *gets out a bottle of beer.*]

Jean: Beer on Midsummer Eve! No thank you! I've got something much better than that. (*He opens a drawer in the table and takes out a bottle of red wine with a gold seal.*) Do you see that? Gold Seal. Now give me a glass.—No, a wine glass of course. I'm drinking it straight.

Christine (*goes back to the stove and puts on a small saucepan*). Lord help the woman who gets you for a husband. You're an old fussbudget!

Jean: Talk, talk! You'd consider yourself lucky if you got yourself a man as good as me. It hasn't done you any harm to have people think I'm your fiancé. (*He tastes the wine.*) Very good. Excellent. But warmed just a little too little. (*Warming the glass in his hands.*) We bought this in Dijon. Four francs a liter, unbottled—and the tax on top of that. . . . What on earth are you cooking? It smells awful!

Christine: Some damn mess that Miss Julie wants for her dog.

Jean: You should watch your language, Christine. . . . Why do you have to stand in front of the stove on a holiday, cooking for that mutt? Is it sick?

Christine: Oh, she's sick, all right! She sneaked out to the gatekeeper's mongrel and—got herself in a fix. And you know Miss Julie, she can't stand anything like that.

Jean: She's too stuck-up in some ways and not proud enough in others. Just like her mother. The Countess felt right at home in the kitchen or down in the barn with the cows, but when she went driving, *one* horse wasn't enough for her; she had to have a pair. Her sleeves were always dirty, but her buttons had the royal crown on them. As for Miss Julie, she doesn't seem to care how she looks and acts. I mean, she's not really refined, not really. Just now, down at the barn, she grabbed the game warden right from under Anna's eyes and asked him to dance. You wouldn't see anybody in our class doing a thing like that. But that's what happens when the gentry try to act like the common people—they become common! . . . But she *is* beautiful! Statuesque! Ah, those shoulders—those—and so forth, and so forth!

Christine: Oh, don't exaggerate. Clara tells me all about her, and Clara dresses her.

Jean: Clara, pooh! You women are always jealous of each other. *I've* been out riding with her . . . And how she can dance . . . !

Christine: Listen, Jean, you *are* going to dance with me, aren't you, when I am finished here?

Jean: Certainly! Of course I am.

Christine: Promise?

Jean: Promise! Listen if I say I'm going to do a thing, I do it. . . . Christine, I thank you for a delicious meal. (*He shoves the cork back into the bottle.*)

[MISS JULIE *appears in the doorway, talking to someone outside.*]

Miss Julie: I'll be right back. Don't wait for me.

[JEAN *slips the bottle into the table drawer quickly and rises respectfully.* MISS JULIE *comes in and crosses over to* CHRISTINE, *who is at the stove.*]

Miss Julie: Did you get it ready?

[CHRISTINE *signals that* JEAN *is present.*]

Jean (*polite and charming*). Are you ladies sharing secrets?

Miss Julie (*flipping her handkerchief in his face*). Don't be nosey!

Jean: Oh, that smells good! Violets.

Miss Julie (*flirting with him*). Don't be impudent! And don't tell me you're an expert on perfumes, too. I know you're an expert dancer,—No, don't look! Go away!

Jean (*inquisitive, but deferential*). What are you cooking? A witch's brew for Midsummer Eve? Something that reveals what the stars have in store for you, so you can see the face of your future husband?

Miss Julie (*curtly*). You'd have to have good eyes to see that. [*To* CHRISTINE.] Pour it into a small bottle, and seal it tight. . . . Jean, come and dance a schottische with me.

Jean (*hesitating*). I hope you don't think I'm being rude, but I've already promised this dance to Christine.

Miss Julie: She can always find someone else. Isn't that so, Christine? You don't mind if I borrow Jean for a minute, do you?

Christine: It isn't up to me. If Miss Julie is gracious enough to invite you, it isn't right for you to say no, Jean. You go on, and thank her for the honor.

Jean: Frankly, Miss Julie, I don't want to hurt your feelings, but I wonder if it is wise—I mean for you to dance twice in a row with the same partner. Especially since the people around here are so quick to spread gossip.

Miss Julie (*bridling*). What do you mean? What kind of gossip? What are you trying to say?

Jean (*retreating*). If you insist on misunderstanding me, I'll have to speak more plainly. It just doesn't look right for you to prefer one of your servants to the others who are hoping for the same unusual honor.

Miss Julie: Prefer! What an idea! I'm really surprised. I, the mistress of the house, am good enough to come to their dance, and when I feel like dancing, I want to dance with someone who knows how to lead. After all I don't want to look ridiculous.

Jean: As you wish. I am at your orders.

Miss Julie (*gently*). Don't take it as an order. Tonight we're all just happy people at a party. There's no question of rank. Now give me your arm.—Don't worry, Christine. I won't run off with your boy friend.

[JEAN *gives her his arm and leads her out.*]

PANTOMIME SCENE

[*This should be played as if the actress were actually alone. She turns her back on the audience when she feels like it; she does not look out into the auditorium; she does not hurry as if she were afraid the audience would grow impatient.*]

CHRISTINE *alone. In the distance the sound of the violins playing the schottische.* CHRISTINE, *humming in time with the music, cleans up after* JEAN, *washes the dishes, dries them, and puts them away in a cupboard. Then she takes off her apron, takes a little mirror from one of the table drawers, and leans it against the jar of lilacs on the table. She lights a tallow candle, heats a curling iron, and curls the bangs on her forehead. Then she goes to the doorway and stands listening to the music. She comes back to the table and finds the handkerchief that* MISS JULIE *left behind. She smells it, spreads it out, and then, as if lost in thought, stretches it, smooths it out, and folds it in four.*

[JEAN *enters alone.*]

Jean: I told you she was wild! You should have seen the way she was dancing. Everyone was peeking at her from behind the doors and laughing at her. Can you figure her out, Christine?

Christine: You might know it's her monthlies, Jean. She always acts peculiar then. . . . Well, are you going to dance with me?

Jean: You're not mad at me because I broke my promise?

Christine: Of course not. Not for a little thing like that, you know that. And I know my place.

Jean (*grabs her around the waist*). You're a sensible girl, Christine. You're going to make somebody a good wife—

[MISS JULIE, *coming in, sees them together. She is unpleasantly surprised.*]

Miss Julie (*with forced gaiety*). Well, aren't you the gallant beau—running away from your partner!

Jean: On the contrary, Miss Julie. As you can see, I've hurried back to the partner I deserted.

Miss Julie (*changing tack*). You know, you're the best dancer I've met.—But why are you wearing livery on a holiday? Take it off at once.

Jean: I'd have to ask you to leave for a minute. My black coat is hanging right here—(*He moves to the right and points.*)

Miss Julie: You're not embarrassed because I'm here, are you? Just to change your coat? Go in your room and come right back again. Or else you can stay here and I'll turn my back.

Jean: If you'll excuse me, Miss Julie. (*He goes off to the right. His arm can be seen as he changes his coat.*)

Miss Julie (*to* CHRISTINE). Tell me something, Christine. Is Jean your fiancé? He seems so intimate with you.

Christine: Fiancé? I suppose so. At least that's what we say.

Miss Julie: What do you mean?

Christine: Well, Miss Julie, you have had fiancés yourself, and you know—

Miss Julie: But we were properly engaged—!

Christine: I know, but did anything come of it?

[JEAN *comes back, wearing a cutaway coat and derby.*]

Miss Julie: *Très gentil, monsieur Jean! Très gentil!*

Jean: *Vous voulez plaisanter, madame.*

Miss Julie: *Et vous voulez parler français!* Where did you learn to speak French?

Jean: In Switzerland. I was *sommelier* in one of the biggest hotels in Lucerne.

Miss Julie: But you look quite the gentleman in that coat! *Charmant!* (*She sits down at the table.*)

Jean: Flatterer!

Miss Julie (*stiffening*). Who said I was flattering you?

Jean: My natural modesty would not allow me to presume that you were paying sincere compliments to someone like me, and therefore I assumed that you were exaggerating, or, in other words, flattering me.

Miss Julie: Where on earth did you learn to talk like that? Do you go to the theater often?

Jean: And other places. You don't think I stayed in the house for six years when I was a valet in Stockholm, do you?

Miss Julie: But weren't you born in this district?

Jean: My father worked as a farm hand on the district attorney's estate, next door to yours. I used to see you when you were little. But of course you didn't notice me.

Miss Julie: Did you really?

Jean: Yes. I remember one time in particular—. But I can't tell you about that!

Miss Julie: Of course you can. Oh, come on, tell me. Just this once—for me.

Jean: No. No, I really couldn't. Not now. Some other time maybe.

Miss Julie: Some other time? That means never. What's the harm in telling me now?

Jean: There's no harm. I just don't feel like it.—Look at her. (*He nods at* CHRISTINE, *who has fallen asleep in a chair by the stove.*)

Miss Julie: Won't she make somebody a pretty wife! I'll bet she snores, too.

Jean: No, she doesn't. But she talks in her sleep.

Miss Julie (*cynically*). Now how would you know she talks in her sleep?

Jean (*coolly*). I've heard her. . . .

[*Pause. They look at each other.*]

Miss Julie: Why don't you sit down?

Jean: I wouldn't take the liberty in your presence.

Miss Julie: But if I were to order you—?

Jean: I'd obey.

Miss Julie: Well then, sit down.—Wait a minute. Could you get me something to drink first?

Jean: I don't know what there is in the icebox. Only beer, I suppose.

Miss Julie: *Only* beer?! I have simple tastes. I prefer beer to wine.

[JEAN *takes a bottle of beer from the icebox and opens it. He looks in the cupboard for a glass and a saucer, and serves her.*]

Jean: At your service.

Miss Julie: Thank you. Don't you want to drink, too?

Jean: I'm not much of a beer-drinker, but if it's your wish—

Miss Julie: My wish! I should think a gentleman would want to keep his lady company.

Jean: That's a point well taken! (*He opens another bottle and takes a glass.*)

Miss Julie: Now drink a toast to me! (JEAN *hesitates.*) You're not shy, are you? A big, strong man like you? (*Playfully,* JEAN *kneels and raises his glass in mock gallantry.*)

Jean: To my lady's health!

Miss Julie: Bravo! Now if you would kiss my shoe, you will have hit it off perfectly. (JEAN *hesitates, then boldly grasps her foot and touches it lightly with his lips.*) Superb! You should have been an actor.

Jean (*rising*). This has got to stop, Miss Julie! Someone might come and see us.

Miss Julie: What difference would that make?

Jean: People would talk, that's what! If you knew how their tongues were wagging out there just a few minutes ago, you wouldn't—

Miss Julie: What sort of things did they say? Tell me. Sit down and tell me.

Jean: I don't want to hurt your feelings, but they used expressions that—that hinted at certain—you know what I mean. After all, you're not a child. And when they see a woman drinking, alone with a man—and a servant at that—in the middle of the night—well . . .

Miss Julie: Well what? Besides, we're not alone. Christine is here.

Jean: Sleeping!

Miss Julie: I'll wake her up then. (*She goes over to* CHRISTINE.) Christine! Are you asleep? (CHRISTINE *babbles in her sleep.*) Christine!—My, how sound she sleeps!

Christine (*talking in her sleep*). Count's boots are brushed . . . put on the coffee . . . right away, right away, right . . . mm—mm . . . poofff . . .

[MISS JULIE *grabs* CHRISTINE'S *nose.*]

Miss Julie: Wake up, will you!

Jean (*sternly*). Let her alone!

Miss Julie (*sharply*). What!

Jean: She's been standing over the stove all day. She's worn out when evening comes. Anyone asleep is entitled to some respect.

Miss Julie (*changing tack*). That's a very kind thought. It does you credit. Thank you. (*She offers* JEAN *her hand.*) Now come on out and pick some lilacs for me.

[*During the following,* CHRISTINE *wakes up and, drunk with sleep, shuffles off to the right to go to bed. A polka can be heard in the distance.*)

Jean: With you, Miss Julie?

Miss Julie: Yes, with me.

Jean: That's no good. Absolutely not.

Miss Julie: I don't know what you're thinking. Maybe you're letting your imagination run away with you.

Jean: I'm not. The other people are.

Miss Julie: In what way? Imagining that I'm—*verliebt* in a servant?

Jean: I'm not conceited, but it's been known to happen. And to these people nothing's sacred.

Miss Julie: Why, I believe you're an aristocrat!

Jean: Yes, I am.

Miss Julie: I'm climbing down—

Jean: Don't climb down, Miss Julie! Take my advice. No one will ever believe that you climbed down deliberately. They'll say you fell.

Miss Julie: I think more highly of these people than you do. Let's see who's right! Come on! (*She looks him over, challenging him.*)

Jean: You know, you're very strange.

Miss Julie: Perhaps. But then so are you. . . . Besides, everything is strange. Life, people, everything. It's all scum, drifting and drifting on the water until it sinks—drowns. There's a dream I have every now and then. It's coming back to to me now. I'm sitting on top of a pillar that I've climbed up somehow and I don't know how to get back down. When I look down I get dizzy. I have to get down but I don't have the courage to jump. I can't hold on much longer and I want to fall; but I don't fall. I know I won't have any peace until I get down; no rest until I get down, down on the ground. And if I ever get down on the ground, I'd want to go farther down, right down into the earth. . . . Have you ever felt anything like that?

Jean: Never! I used to dream that I'm lying under a tall tree in a dark woods. I want to get up, up to the very top, to look out over the bright landscape with the sun shining on it, to rob the bird's nest up there with the golden eggs in it. And I climb and I climb, but the trunk is so thick, and so smooth, and it's such a long way to that first branch. But I know that if I could just reach that first branch, I'd go right to the top as if on a ladder. I've never reached it yet, but some day I will—even if only in my dreams.

Miss Julie: Here I am talking about dreams with you. Come out with me. Only into the park a way. (*She offers him her arm, and they start to go.*)

Jean: Let's sleep on nine midsummer flowers, Miss Julie, and then our dreams will come true!

[MISS JULIE *and* JEAN *suddenly turn around in the doorway.* JEAN *is holding his hand over one eye.*]

Miss Julie: You've caught something in your eye. Let me see.

Jean: It's nothing. Just a bit of dust. It'll go away.

Miss Julie: The sleeve of my dress must have grazed your eye. Sit down and I'll help you. (*She takes him by the arm and sits him down. She takes his head and leans it back. With the corner of her handkerchief she tries to get out the bit of dust.*) Now sit still, absolutely still. (*She slaps his hand.*) Do as you're told. Why, I believe you're trembling—a big, strong man like you. (*She feels his biceps.*) With such big arms!

Jean (*warningly*). Miss Julie!

Miss Julie: Yes, *Monsieur Jean?*

Jean: *Attention! Je ne suis qu'un homme!*

Miss Julie: Sit still, I tell you! . . . There now! It's out. Kiss my hand and thank me!

Jean (*rising to his feet*). Listen to me, Miss Julie—Christine has gone to bed!—Listen to me, I tell you!

Miss Julie: Kiss my hand first!

Jean: Listen to me!

Miss Julie: Kiss my hand first!

Jean: All right. But you'll have no one to blame but yourself.

Miss Julie: For what?

Jean: For what! Are you twenty-five years old and still a child? Don't you know it's dangerous to play with fire?

Miss Julie: Not for me. I'm insured!

Jean (*boldly*). Oh, no you're not! And even if you are, there's inflammable stuff next door.

Miss Julie: Meaning you?

Jean: Yes. Not just because it's me, but because I'm a young man—

Miss Julie: And irresistibly handsome? What incredible conceit! A Don Juan, maybe! Or a Joseph! Yes, bless my soul, that's it: you're a Joseph!

Jean: You think so?!

Miss Julie: I'm almost afraid so! (JEAN *boldly steps up to her, grabs her around the waist, kisses her. She slaps his face.*) None of that!

Jean: Are you still playing games or are you serious?

Miss Julie: I'm serious.

Jean: Then you must have been serious just a moment ago, too! You take your games too seriously and that's dangerous. Well, I'm tired of your games, and if you'll excuse me, I'll return to my work. (*Takes up the boots and starts to brush them.*) The Count will be wanting his boots on time, and it's long past midnight.

Miss Julie: Put those boots down.

Jean: No! This is my job. It's what I'm here for. But I never undertook to be a playmate for you. That's something I could never be. I consider myself too good for that.

Miss Julie: You are proud.

Jean: In some ways. Not in others.

Miss Julie: Have you ever been in love?

Jean: We don't use that word around here. But I've been interested in a lot of girls, if that's what you mean. . . . I even got sick once because I couldn't have the one I wanted—really sick, like the princes in the Arabian Nights—who couldn't eat or drink for love.

Miss Julie: Who was the girl? (JEAN *does not reply.*) Who was she?

Jean: You can't make me tell you that.

Miss Julie: Even if I ask you as an equal—ask you—as a friend? . . . Who was she?

Jean: You.

Miss Julie (*sitting down*). How—amusing. . . .

Jean: Yes, maybe so. Ridiculous. . . . That's why I didn't want to tell you about it before. Want to hear the whole story? . . . Have you any idea what you and your people look like from down below? Of course not. Like hawks or eagles, that's what: you hardly ever see their backs because they're always soaring so high up. I lived with seven brothers and sisters—and a pig—out on the waste land where there wasn't even a tree growing. But from my window I could see the wall of the Count's garden with the apple trees sticking up over it. That was the Garden of Eden for me, and there were many angry angels with flaming swords standing guard over it. But in spite of them, I and the other boys found a way to the Tree of Life. . . . I'll bet you despise me.

Miss Julie: All boys steal apples.

Jean: That's what you say now. But you still despise me. Never mind. One day I went with my mother into this paradise to weed the onion beds. Next to the vegetable garden stood a Turkish pavilion, shaded by jasmine and hung all over with honeysuckle. I couldn't imagine what it was used for; I only knew I had never seen such a beautiful building. People went in, and came out again. And one day the door was left open. I sneaked in. The walls were covered with portraits of kings and emperors, and the windows had red curtains with tassels on them.—You dc know what kind of place I'm talking about, don't you? . . . I—(*He breaks off a lilac and holds it under* MISS JULIE'S *nose.*) I had never been inside a castle, never seen anything besides the church. But this was more beautiful. And no matter what I tried to think about, my thoughts always came back—to that little pavilion. And little by little there arose in me a desire to experience just for once the whole pleasure of. . . . *Enfin,* I sneaked in, looked about, and marveled. And just then I heard someone coming! There was only one way out—for the upper-class people. But for me there was one more—a lower one. And I had no other choice but to take it. (MISS JULIE, *who has taken the lilac from* JEAN, *lets it fall to the table.*) Then I began to run like mad, plunging through the raspberry bushes, ploughing through the strawberry patches, and came up on the rose terrace. And there I caught sight of a pink dress and a pair of white stockings. You! I crawled under—well, you can imagine what it was like—under thistles that pricked me and wet dirt that stank to high heaven. And all the while I could see you walking among the roses. I said to myself, "If it's true that a thief can enter heaven and be with the angels, isn't it strange that a poor man's child here on God's green earth can't enter the Count's park and play with the Count's daughter."

Miss Julie (*sentimentally*). Do you think all poor children have felt that way?

Jean (*hesitatingly at first, then with mounting conviction*). If all poor ch—? Yes—yes, naturally. Of course!

Miss Julie: It must be terrible to be poor.

Jean (*with deep feeling, his words charged with emotion*). Oh, Miss Julie! You don't know! A dog can lie on the sofa with its mistress; a horse can have its nose stroked by the hand of a countess; but a servant—! (*Changing his tone*) Of course, now and then you meet somebody with guts enough to work his way up in the world, but how often?—Anyway, you know what I did afterwards? I threw myself into the millstream with all my clothes on. Got fished out and spanked. But the following Sunday, when Pa and everybody else in the house went to visit Grandma, I arranged things so I'd be left behind. Then I washed myself all over with soap and warm water, put on my best clothes, and went off to church—just to see you there once more. I saw you, and then I went home determined to die. But I wanted to die beautifully and comfortably, without pain. I remembered that it was fatal to sleep under an elderberry bush. And we had a big one that had just blossomed out. I stripped it of every leaf and blossom it had and made a bed of them in a bin of oats. Have you ever noticed how smooth oats are? As smooth to the touch as human skin. . . . So I pulled the lid of the bin shut and closed my eyes—fell asleep. And when they woke me I was really very sick. But I didn't die, as you can see.—What was I trying to prove? I don't know. There was no hope of winning you. But you were a symbol of the absolute hopelessness of my ever getting out of the circle I was born in.

Miss Julie: You know, you have a real gift for telling stories. Did you go to school?

Jean: A little. But I've read a lot of novels and gone to the theater. And I've also listened to educated people talk. That's how I've learned the most.

Miss Julie: You mean to tell me you stand around listening to what we're saying!

Jean: Certainly! And I've heard an

awful lot, I can tell you—sitting on the coachman's seat or rowing the boat. One time I heard you and a girl friend talking——

Miss Julie: Really? . . . And just what did you hear?

Jean: Well, now, I don't know if I could repeat it. I can tell you I was a little amazed. I couldn't imagine where you had learned such words. Maybe at bottom there isn't such a big difference as you might think, between people and people.

Miss Julie: How vulgar! At least people in my class don't behave like you when we're engaged.

Jean (*looking her in the eye*). Are you sure?—Come on now, it's no use playing the innocent with me.

Miss Julie: He was a beast. The man I offered my love was a beast.

Jean: That's what you all say—afterwards.

Miss Julie: All?

Jean: I'd say so, since I've heard the same expression used several times before in similar circumstances.

Miss Julie: What kind of circumstances?

Jean: That kind we're talking about. I remember the last time I—

Miss Julie (*rising*). That's enough! I don't want to hear any more.

Jean: How strange! Neither did she! . . . Well, now if you'll excuse me, I'll go to bed.

Miss Julie (*softly*). Go to bed on Midsummer Eve?

Jean: That's right. Dancing with that crowd up there really doesn't amuse me.

Miss Julie: Jean, get the key to the boathouse and row me out on the lake. I want to see the sun come up.

Jean: Do you think that's wise?

Miss Julie: You sound as if you were worried about your reputation.

Jean: Why not? I don't particularly care to be made ridiculous, or to be kicked out without a recommendation just when I'm trying to establish myself. Besides, I have a certain obligation to Christine.

Miss Julie: Oh, I see. It's Christine now.

Jean: Yes, but I'm thinking of you, too. Take my advice, Miss Julie, and go up to your room.

Miss Julie: When did you start giving me orders?

Jean: Just this once. For your own sake! Please! It's very late. You're so tired, you're drunk; you don't know what you're doing. Go to bed, Miss Julie.—Besides, if my ears aren't deceiving me, they're coming this way, looking for me. If they find us here together, you're done for!

The Chorus (*is heard coming nearer, singing*).

Two ladies came from out the clover,
Tri-di-ri-di-ralla, tri-di-ri-di-ra.
And one of them was green all over,
Tri-di-ri-di-ralla-la.
They told us they had gold aplenty,
Tri-di-ri-di-ralla, tri-di-ri-di-ra.
But neither of them owned a penny.
Tri-di-ri-di-ralla-la.
This wreath for you I may be plaiting,
Tri-di-ri-di-ralla, tri-di-ri-di-ra.
But it's for another I am waiting,
Tri-di-ri-di-ralla-la!

Miss Julie: I know these people. I love them just as they love me. Let them come. You'll find out.

Jean: Oh, no, Miss Julie, they don't love you! They take the food you give them, but they spit on it as soon as your back is turned. Believe me! Just listen to them. Listen to what they're singing.—No, you'd better not listen.

Miss Julie (*listening*). What are they singing?

Jean: A dirty song—about you and me!

Miss Julie: How disgusting! Oh, what cowardly, sneaking—

Jean: That's what the mob always is—cowards! You can't fight them; you can only run away.

Miss Julie: Run away? Where? There's no way out of here. And we can't go in to Christine.

Jean: What about my room? What do you say? The rules don't count in a situation like this. You can trust me. I'm your friend, remember? Your true, devoted, and respectful friend.

Miss Julie: But suppose—suppose they look for you there?

Jean: I'll bolt the door. If they try to break it down, I'll shoot. Come, Miss Julie! (*On his knees.*) Please, Miss Julie!

Miss Julie (*meaningfully*). You promise me that you—?

Jean: I swear to you!

[MISS JULIE *goes out quickly to the right.* JEAN *follows her impetuously.*]

THE BALLET

[*The country people enter in festive costumes, with flowers in their hats. The fiddler is in the lead. A keg of small beer and a little keg of liquor, decorated with greenery, are set up on the table. Glasses are brought out. They all drink, and start to sing the song. Then they form a circle and sing and dance the round dance, "Two ladies came from out the clover." At the end of the dance they all leave singing.*

[MISS JULIE *comes in alone; looks at the devastated kitchen; clasps her hands together; then takes out a powder puff and powders her face.* JEAN *enters. He is in high spirits.*]

Jean: You see! You heard them, didn't you? You've got to admit it's impossible to stay here.

Miss Julie: No, I don't. But even if I did, what could we do?

Jean: Go away, travel, get away from here!

Miss Julie: Travel? Yes—but where?

Jean: Switzerland, the Italian lakes. You've never been there?

Miss Julie: No. Is it beautiful?

Jean: Eternal summer, oranges, laurel trees, ah . . . !

Miss Julie: But what are we going to do there?

Jean: I'll set up a hotel—a first-class hotel with a first-class clientele.

Miss Julie: Hotel?

Jean: I tell you that's the life! Always new faces, new languages. Not a minute to think about yourself or worry about your nerves. No looking for something to do. The work keeps you busy. Day and night the bells ring, the trains whistle, the busses come and go. And all the while the money comes rolling in. I tell you it's the life!

Miss Julie: Yes, that's the life. But what about me?

Jean: The mistress of the whole place, the star of the establishment! With your looks—and your personality—it can't fail. It's perfect! You'll sit in the office like a queen, setting your slaves in motion by pressing an electric button. The guests will file before your throne and timidly lay their treasures on your table. You can't imagine how people tremble when you shove a bill in their face! I'll salt the bills and you'll sugar them with your prettiest smile. Come on, let's get away from here— (*He takes a timetable from* *his pocket.*)—right away—the next train! We'll be in Malmö at 6:30; Hamburg 8:40 in the morning; Frankfurt to Basle in one day; and to Como by way of the Gotthard tunnel in—let me see—three days! Three days!

Miss Julie: You make it sound so wonderful. But, Jean, you have to give me strength. Tell me you love me. Come and put your arms around me.

Jean (*hesitates*). I want to . . . but I don't dare. Not any more, not in this house. I do love you—without a shadow of a doubt. How can you doubt that, Miss Julie?

Miss Julie (*shyly, very becomingly*). You don't have to be formal with me, Jean. You can call me Julie. There aren't any barriers between us now. Call me Julie.

Jean (*agonized*). I can't! There are still barriers between us, Miss Julie, as long as we stay in this house! There's the past, there's the Count. I've never met anyone I feel so much respect for. I've only got to see his gloves lying on a table and I shrivel up. I only have to hear that bell ring and I shy like a frightened horse. I only have to look at his boots standing there so stiff and proud and I feel my spine bending. (*He kicks the boots.*) Superstitions, prejudices that they've drilled into us since we were children! But they can be forgotten just as easily! Just wait till we get to another country where they have a republic! They'll crawl on their hands and knees when they see my uniform. On their hands and knees, I tell you! But not me! Oh, no. I'm not made for crawling. I've got guts, backbone. And once I grab that first branch, you just watch me climb. I may be a valet now, but next year I'll be owning property; in ten years, I'll be living off my investments. Then I'll go to Rumania, get myself some decorations, and maybe—notice I only say maybe—end up as a count!

Miss Julie: How wonderful, wonderful.

Jean: Listen, in Rumania you can buy titles. You'll be a countess after all. *My* countess.

Miss Julie: But I'm not interested in that. I'm leaving all that behind. Tell me you love me, Jean, or else—or else what difference does it make what I am?

Jean: I'll tell you a thousand times—but later! Not now. And not here. Above all, let's keep our feelings out of this or we'll make a mess of everything. We have to look at this thing calmly and coolly, like sensible people. (*He takes out a cigar, clips the end, and lights it.*) Now you sit there and I'll sit here, and we'll talk as if nothing had happened.

Miss Julie (*in anguish*). My God, what are you? Don't you have any feelings?

Jean: Feelings? Nobody's got more feelings than I have. But I've learned how to control them.

Miss Julie: A few minutes ago you were kissing my shoe—and now—!

Jean (*harshly*). That was a few minutes ago. We've got other things to think about now!

Miss Julie: Don't speak to me like that, Jean!

Jean: I'm just trying to be sensible. We've been stupid once; let's not be stupid again. Your father might be back at any moment, and we've got to decide our future before then.—Now what do you think about my plans? Do you approve or don't you?

Miss Julie: I don't see anything wrong with them. Except one thing. For a big undertaking like that, you'd need a lot of capital. Have you got it?

Jean (*chewing on his cigar*). Have I got it? Of course I have. I've got my knowledge of the business, my vast experience, my familiarity with languages. That's capital that counts for something, let me tell you.

Miss Julie: You can't even buy the railway tickets with it.

Jean: That's true. That's why I need a backer—someone to put up the money.

Miss Julie: Where can you find him on a moment's notice?

Jean: You'll find him—if you want to be my partner.

Miss Julie: I can't. And I don't have a penny to my name. (*Pause.*)

Jean: Then you can forget the whole thing.

Miss Julie: Forget—?

Jean: And things will stay just the way they are.

Miss Julie: Do you think I'm going to live under the same roof with you as your mistress? Do you think I'm going to have people sneering at me behind my back? How do you think I'll ever be able to look my father in the face after this? No, no! Take me away from here, Jean—the shame, the humiliation. . . . What have I done? Oh, my God, my God! What have I done? (*She bursts into tears.*)

Jean: Now don't start singing that tune. It won't work. What have you done that's so awful? You're not the first.

Miss Julie (*crying hysterically*). Now you despise me!—I'm falling, I'm falling!

Jean: Fall down to me, and I'll lift you up again!

Miss Julie: What awful hold did you have over me? What drove me to you? The weak to the strong? The falling to the rising! Or maybe it was love? Love? This? You don't know what love is!

Jean: Want to bet? Did you think I was a virgin?

Miss Julie: You're coarse—vulgar! The things you say, the things you think!

Jean: That's the way I was brought up and that's the way I am! Now don't get hysterical. And don't play the fine lady with me. We're eating off the same platter now. . . . That's better. Come over here and be a good girl and I'll treat you to something special. (*He opens the table drawer and takes out the wine bottle. He pours the wine into two used glasses.*)

Miss Julie: Where did you get that wine?

Jean: From the wine cellar.

Miss Julie: My father's burgundy!

Jean: Should be good enough for his son-in-law.

Miss Julie: I was drinking beer and you—!

Jean: Shows that I have better taste that you.

Miss Julie: Thief!

Jean: You going to squeal on me?

Miss Julie: Oh, God! Partner in crime with a petty house thief! I must have been drunk; I must have been walking in my sleep. Midsummer Night! Night of innocent games—

Jean: Yes, very innocent!

Miss Julie (*pacing up and down*). Is there anyone here on earth as miserable as I am?

Jean: Why be miserable? After such a conquest! Think of poor Christine in there. Don't you think she's got any feelings?

Miss Julie: I thought so a while ago, but I don't now. A servant's a servant—

Jean: And a whore's a whore!

Miss Julie (*falls to her knees and clasps her hands together*). Oh, God in heaven, put an end to my worthless life! Lift me out of this awful filth I'm sinking in! Save me! Save me!

Jean: I feel sorry for you, I have to admit it. When I was lying in the onion beds, looking up at you on the rose terrace, I—I'm telling you the truth now—I had the same dirty thoughts that all boys have.

Miss Julie: And you said you wanted to die for me!

Jean: In the oat bin? That was only a story.

Miss Julie: A lie, you mean.

Jean (*beginning to get sleepy*). Practically. I think I read it in a paper about a chimney sweep who curled up in a wood-bin with some lilacs because they were going to arrest him for non-support of his child.

Miss Julie: Now I see you as you really are.

Jean: What did you expect me to do? It's always the fancy talk that gets the women.

Miss Julie: You dog!

Jean: You bitch!

Miss Julie: Well, now you've seen the eagle's back—

Jean: Wasn't exactly its back—!

Miss Julie: I was going to be your first branch—!

Jean: A rotten branch—

Miss Julie: I was going to be the window dressing for your hotel—!

Jean: And I the hotel—!

Miss Julie: Sitting at the desk, attracting your customers, padding your bills—!

Jean: I could manage that myself—!

Miss Julie: How can a human soul be so dirty and filthy?

Jean: Then why don't you clean it up?

Miss Julie: You lackey! You shoeshine boy! Stand up when I talk you!

Jean: You lackey lover! You bootblack's tramp! Shut your mouth and get out of here! Who do you think you are telling me I'm coarse? I've never seen anybody in my class behave as crudely as you did tonight. Have you ever seen any of the girls around here grab at a man like you did? Do you think any of the girls of my class would throw themselves at a man like that? I've never seen the like of it except in animals and prostitutes!

Miss Julie (*crushed*). That's right! Hit me! Walk all over me! It's all I deserve. I'm rotten. But help me! Help me to get out of this—if there is any way out for me!

Jean (*less harsh*). I'd be doing myself an injustice if I didn't admit that part of the credit for this seduction belongs to me. But do you think a person in my position would have dared to look twice at you if you hadn't asked for it? I'm still amazed—

Miss Julie: And still proud.

Jean Why not? But I've got to confess the victory was a little too easy to give me any real thrill.

Miss Julie: Go on, hit me again!

Jean (*standing up*). No. . . . I'm sorry I said that. I never hit a person who's down, especially a woman. I can't deny that, in one way, it was good to find out that what I saw glittering up above was only fool's gold, to have seen that the eagle's back was as gray as its belly, that the smooth cheek was just powder, and that there could be dirt under the manicured nails, that the handkerchief was soiled even though it smelled of perfume. But, in another way, it hurt me to find that everything I was striving for wasn't very high above me after all, wasn't even real. It hurts me to see you sink far lower than your own cook. Hurts, like seeing the last flowers cut to pieces by the autumn rains and turned to muck.

Miss Julie: You talk as if you already stood high above me.

Jean: Well, don't I? Don't forget I could make you a countess but you can never make me a count.

Miss Julie: But I have a father for a count. You can never have that!

Jean: True. But I might father my own counts—that is, if—

Miss Julie: You're a thief! I'm not!

Jean: There are worse things than being a thief. A lot worse. And besides, when I take a position in a house, I consider myself a member of the family—in a way, like a child in the house. It's no crime for a child to steal a few ripe cherries when they're falling off the trees, is it? (*He begins to feel passionate again*). Miss Julie, you're a beautiful woman, much too good for the likes of me. You got carried away by your emotions and now you want to cover up your mistake by telling yourself that you love me. You don't love me. You might possibly have been attracted by my looks—in which case your kind of love is no better than mine. But I could never be satisfied to be just an animal for you, and I could never make you love me.

Miss Julie: How do you know that for sure?

Jean: You mean there's a chance? I could love you, there's no doubt about that. You're beautiful, you're refined—(*He goes up to her and takes her hand.*) —educated, lovable when you want to be, and once you set a man's heart on fire, I'll bet it burns forever. (*He puts his arm around her waist.*) You're like hot wine with strong spices. One of your kisses is enough to—(*He attempts to lead her out, but she rather reluctantly breaks away from him.*)

Miss Julie: Let me go. You don't get me that way.

Jean: Then how? Not by petting you and not with pretty words, not by planning for the future, not by saving you from humiliation! Then how, tell me how?

Miss Julie: How? How? I don't know how! I don't know at all!—I hate you like I hate rats, but I can't get away from you.

Jean: Then come away *with* me!

Miss Julie (*pulling herself together*). Away? Yes, we'll go away!—But I'm so tired. Pour me a glass of wine, will you? (JEAN *pours the wine.* MISS JULIE *looks at her watch.*) Let's talk first. We still have a little time. (*She empties the glass of wine and holds it out for more.*)

Jean: Don't overdo it. You'll get drunk.

Miss Julie: What difference does it make?

Jean: What difference? It looks cheap. —What did you want to say to me?

Miss Julie: We're going to run away together, right? But we'll talk first—that is, I'll talk. So far you've done all the talking. You've told me your life, now I'll tell you mine. That way we'll know each other through and through before we become traveling companions.

Jean: Wait a minute. Excuse me, but are you sure you won't regret this afterwards, when you've surrendered your secrets to me?

Miss Julie: I thought you were my friend.

Jean: I am—sometimes. But don't count on me.

Miss Julie: You don't mean that. Anyway, everybody knows my secrets.—My mother's parents were very ordinary people, just commoners. She was brought up, according to the theories of her time, to believe in equality, the independence of women, and all that. And she had a strong aversion to marriage. When my father proposed to her, she swore she would never become his wife, but that she might possibly consent to become his mistress. So he told her he didn't want to see the woman he loved enjoy less respect than he did. But she said she didn't care what the world thought—and he, believing that he couldn't live without her, accepted her conditions. That did it. From then on he was cut off from his old circle of friends and left without anything to do in the house, which couldn't have kept him occupied anyway. Then I came into the world—against my mother's wishes, as far as I can make out. My mother decided to bring me up as a nature child. And on top of that I had to learn everything a boy learns, so I could be living proof that women were just as good as men. I had to wear boy's clothes, learn to handle horses—but not to milk the cows. I was made to groom the horses and handle them, and learn farming and go hunting—I even had to learn how to slaughter the animals. It was disgusting. And on the estate all the men were set to doing women's chores, and the women to doing men's work—with the result that the whole place threatened to fall to pieces, and we became the local laughing-stock. Finally my father must have come out of his trance. He rebelled, and everything was changed according to his wishes. Then my mother got sick. I don't know what kind of sickness it was, but she often had convulsions, and she would hide herself in the attic or in the garden, and sometimes she would stay out all night. Then there occurred that big fire you've heard about. The house, the stables, the cowsheds, all burned down—and under very peculiar circumstances that led one to suspect arson. You see, the accident occurred the day after the insurance expired, and the premiums on the new policy, which my father had sent in, were delayed through the messenger's carelessness, and didn't arrive on time. (*She refills her glass and drinks.*)

Jean: You've had enough.

Miss Julie: Who cares!—We were left without a penny to our name. We had to sleep in the carriages. My father didn't know where to turn for money to rebuild the house. Then Mother suggested to him that he might try to borrow money from an old friend of hers, who owned a brick factory not far from here. Father took out a loan, but there wasn't any interest charged, which surprised him. So the place was rebuilt. (*She drinks some more.*) Do you know who set fire to the place?

Jean: Your honorable mother!

Miss Julie: Do you know who the brick manufacturer was?

Jean: Your mother's lover?

Miss Julie: Do you know whose money it was?

Jean: Let me think a minute. . . . No, I give up.

Miss Julie: It was my mother's!

Jean: The Count's, you mean. Or was there a marriage settlement?

Miss Julie: There wasn't a settlement. My mother had a little money of her own which she didn't want under my father's control, so she invested it with her—friend.

Jean: Who grabbed it!

Miss Julie: Right! He appropriated it. Well, my father found out what happened. But he couldn't go to court, couldn't pay his wife's lover, couldn't prove that it's his wife's money. That was how my mother got her revenge because he had taken control of the house. He was on the verge of shooting himself. There was even a rumor that he tried and failed. But he took a new lease on life and he forced my mother to pay for her mistakes. Can you imagine what those five years were like for me? I loved my father, but I took my mother's side because I didn't know the whole story. She had taught me to hate all men—you've heard how she hated men—and I swore to her that I'd never be slave to any man.

Jean: But you got engaged to the attorney.

Miss Julie: Only to make him my slave.

Jean: But he didn't like the idea, did he?

Miss Julie: Oh, he wanted to well enough. I didn't give him the chance. I got bored with him.

Jean: Yes, so I noticed—in the barnyard.

Miss Julie: What did you notice?

Jean: I saw what I saw. *He* broke off the engagement.

Miss Julie: That's a lie! It was I who broke it off. Did he tell you that? He's beneath contempt!

Jean: Come on now, he isn't as bad as that. So you hate men, Miss Julie?

Miss Julie: Yes, I do. . . . Most of the time. But sometimes, when I can't help myself—oh. . . . (*She shudders in disgust.*)

Jean: Then you hate me, too?

Miss Julie: You have no idea how much! I'd like to see you killed like an animal—

Jean: Like when you're caught in the act with an animal: you get two years at hard labor and the animal is killed. Right?

Miss Julie: Right.

Jean: But there's no one to catch us—and *no animal!*—So what are we going to do?

Miss Julie: Go away from here.

Jean: To torture ourselves to death?

Miss Julie: No. To enjoy ourselves for a day or two, or a week, for as long as we can—and then—to die—

Jean: Die? How stupid! I've got a better idea: start a hotel!

Miss Julie (*continuing without hearing* JEAN) —on the shores of Lake Como, where the sun is always shining, where the laurels bloom at Christmas, and the golden oranges glow on the trees.

Jean: Lake Como is a stinking wet hole, and the only oranges I saw there were on the fruit stands. But it's a good tourist spot with a lot of villas and cottages that are rented out to lovers. Now there's a profitable business. You know why? They rent the villa for the whole season, but they leave after three weeks.

Miss Julie (*naïvely*). Why after only three weeks?

Jean: Because they can't stand each other any longer. Why else? But they still have to pay the rent. You see, then you rent it out again to another couple, and so on. There's no shortage of love—even if it doesn't last very long.

Miss Julie: Then you don't want to die with me?

Jean: I don't want to die at all! I enjoy life too much. And moreover, I consider taking your own life a sin against the Providence that gave us life.

Miss Julie: You believe in God? You?

Jean: Yes, certainly I do! I go to church every other Sunday.—Honestly, I've had enough of this talk. I'm going to bed.

Miss Julie: Really? You think you're going to get off that easy? Don't you know that a man owes something to the woman he's dishonored?

Jean (*takes out his purse and throws a silver coin on the table*). There you are. I don't want to owe anybody anything.

Miss Julie (*ignoring the insult*). Do you know what the law says—?

Jean: Aren't you lucky the law says nothing about the women who seduce men!

Miss Julie (*still not hearing him*). What else can we do but go away from here, get married, and get divorced?

Jean: Suppose I refuse to enter into this *mésalliance?*

Miss Julie: *Mésalliance?*

Jean: For me! I've got better ancestors than you. I don't have any female arsonist in my family.

Miss Julie: How can you know?

Jean: You can't prove the opposite because we don't have any family records —except in the police courts. But I've read the whole history of your family in that book on the drawing-room table. Do you know who the founder of your family line was? A miller—who let his wife sleep with the king one night during the Danish war. I don't have any ancestors like that. I don't have any ancestors at all! But I can become an ancestor myself.

Miss Julie: This is what I get for baring my heart and soul to someone too low to understand, for sacrificing the honor of my family—

Jean: Dishonor!—I warned you, remember? Drinking makes one talk, and talking's bad.

Miss Julie: Oh, how sorry I am! . . . If only it had never happened! . . . If only you at least loved me!

Jean: For the last time— What do you want me to do? Cry? Jump over your whip? Kiss you? Lure you to Lake Como for three weeks and then—? What am I supposed to do? What do you want? I've had more than I can take. This is what I get for involving myself with women. . . . Miss Julie, I can see that you're unhappy; I know that you're suffering; but I simply cannot understand you. My people don't behave like this. We don't hate each other. We make love for the fun of it, when we can get any time off from our work. But we don't have time for it all day and all night like you do. If you ask me, you're sick, Miss Julie. Your mother's mind was affected, you know. There are whole counties affected with pietism. That was your mother's trouble—pietism. Everybody's catching it.

Miss Julie: You can be understanding, Jean. You're talking to me like a human being now.

Jean: Well, be human yourself. You spit on me but you don't let me wipe it off —on you.

Miss Julie: Help me, Jean. Help me. Tell me what I should do, that's all— which way to go.

Jean: For Christ's sake, if only I knew myself!

Miss Julie: I've been crazy—I've been out of my mind—but does that mean there's no way out for me?

Jean: Stay here as if nothing had happened. Nobody knows anything.

Miss Julie: Impossible! Everybody who works here knows. Christine knows.

Jean: They don't know a thing. And anyhow they'd never believe it.

Miss Julie (*slowly, significantly*). But . . . it might happen again.

Jean: That's true!

Miss Julie: And there might be consequences.

Jean (*stunned*). Consequences! What on earth have I been thinking of! You're right. There's only one thing to do: get away from here! Immediately! I can't go with you—that would give the whole game away. You'll have to go by yourself. Somewhere—I don't care where!

Miss Julie: By myself? Where?—Oh, no, Jean, I can't. I can't!

Jean: You've got to! Before the Count comes back. You know as well as I do what will happen if you stay here. After one mistake, you figure you might as well go on—the damage is already done. Then you get more and more careless until—finally you're exposed. I tell you, you've got to get out of the country. Afterwards you can write to the Count and tell him everything—leaving me out, of course. He'd never guess it was me. Anyway, I don't think he'd exactly like to find that out.

Miss Julie: I'll go—if you'll come with me!

Jean: Lady, are you out of your mind!? "Miss Julie elopes with her footman." The day after tomorrow it would be in all the papers. The Count would never live it down.

Miss Julie: I can't go away. I can't stay. Help me. I'm so tired, so awfully tired. . . . Tell me what to do. Order me. Start me going. I can't think any more, can't move any more. . . .

Jean: Now do you realize how weak you all are? What gives you the right to go strutting around with your noses in the air as if you owned the world? All right, I'll give you your orders. Go up and get dressed. Get some traveling money. And come back down here.

Miss Julie (*almost in a whisper*). Come up with me!

Jean: To your room? . . . You're going crazy again! (*He hesitates a moment.*) No! No! Go! Right now! (*He takes her hand and leads her out.*)

Miss Julie (*as she is leaving*). Don't be so harsh, Jean.

Jean: Orders always sound harsh. You've never had to take them.

[JEAN, *left alone, heaves a sigh of relief and sits down at the table. He takes out a notebook and a pencil and begins to calculate, counting aloud now and then. The pantomime continues until* CHRISTINE *enters, dressed for church, and carrying* JEAN'S *white tie and shirt front in her hand.*]

Christine: Lord in Heaven, what a mess! What on earth have you been doing?

Jean: It was Miss Julie. She dragged the whole crowd in here. You must have been sleeping awfully sound if you didn't hear anything.

Christine: I slept like a log.

Jean: You already dressed for church?

Christine: Yes, indeed. Don't you remember you promised to go to Communion with me today?

Jean: Oh, yes, of course. I remember. I see you've brought my things. All right. Come on, put it on me. (*He sits down, and* CHRISTINE *starts to put the white tie and shirt front on him. Pause.*)

Jean (*yawning*). What's the lesson for today?

Christine: The beheading of John the Baptist, I suppose.

Jean: My God, that will go on forever.—Hey, you're choking me! . . . Oh, I'm so sleepy, so sleepy.

Christine: What were you doing up all night? You look green in the face.

Jean: I've been sitting here talking with Miss Julie.

Christine: That girl! She doesn't know how to behave herself!

[*Pause.*]

Jean: Tell me something, Christine. . . .

Christine: Well, what?

Jean: Isn't it strange when you think about it? Her, I mean.

Christine: What's so strange?

Jean: Everything!

[*Pause.* CHRISTINE *looks at the half-empty glasses on the table.*]

Christine: Have you been drinking with her?

Jean: Yes!

Christine: Shame on you!—Look me in the eyes! You haven't . . . ?

Jean: Yes!

Christine: Is it possible? Is it really possible?

Jean (*after a moment's consideration*). Yes. It is.

Christine: Oh, how disgusting! I could never have believed anything like this would happen! No. No. This is too much!

Jean: Don't tell me you're jealous of her?

Christine: No, not of her. If it had been Clara—or Sophie—I would have scratched your eyes out! But her—? That's different. I don't know why. . . . But it's still disgusting!

Jean: Then you're not mad at her?

Christine: No. Mad at you. You were mean and cruel to do a thing like that, very mean. The poor girl! . . . But let me tell you, I'm not going to stay in this house a moment longer, not when I can't have any respect for my employers.

Jean: Why do you want to respect them?

Christine: Don't try to be smart. You don't want to work for people who behave immorally, do you? Well, do you? If you ask me, you'd be lowering yourself by doing that.

Jean: Oh, I don't know. I think it's rather comforting to find out that they're not one bit better than we are.

Christine: Well, I don't. If they're not any better, there's no point in us trying to be like them.—And think of the Count. Think of all the sorrows he's been through in his time. No, sir, I won't stay in this house any longer. . . . Imagine! You, of all people! If it had been the attorney fellow; if it had been somebody respectable—

Jean: Now just a minute—!

Christine: Oh, you're all right in your own way. But there's a big difference between one class and another. You can't deny that.—No, this is something I can never get over. She was so proud, and so sarcastic about men, you'd never believe she'd go and throw herself at one. And at someone like you! And *she* was going to have Diana shot, because the poor thing ran after the gatekeeper's mongrel!—Well, I tell you, I've had enough! I'm not going to stay here any longer. On the twenty-fourth of October, I'm leaving.

Jean: Then what'll you do?

Christine: Well, since you brought it up, it's about time that you got yourself a decent place, if we're going to get married.

Jean: Why should I go looking for another place? I could never get a place like this if I'm married.

Christine: Well, of course not! But you could get a job as a porter, or maybe try to get a government job as a caretaker somewhere. The government don't pay much, but they pay regular. And there's a pension for the wife and children.

Jean (*wryly.*) Fine, fine! But I'm not the kind of guy who thinks about dying for his wife and children this early in the game. I hate to say it, but I've got slightly bigger plans than that.

Christine: Plans! Hah! What about your obligations? You'd better start giving them a little thought!

Jean: Don't start nagging me about obligations! I know what I have to do without you telling me. (*He hears a sound upstairs.*) Anyhow, we'll have plenty of chance to talk about this later. You just go and get yourself ready, and we'll be off to church.

Christine: Who is that walking around up there?

Jean: I don't know. Clara, I suppose. Who else?

Christine (*starting to leave*). It can't be the Count, can it? Could he have come back without anybody hearing him?

Jean (*frightened*). The Count? No, it can't be. He would have rung.

Christine (*leaving*). God help us! I've never heard of the like of this.

[*The sun has now risen and strikes the tops of the trees in the park. The light shifts gradually until it is shining very obliquely through the windows.* JEAN *goes to the door and signals.* MISS JULIE *enters, dressed for travel, and carrying a small bird cage, covered with a towel. She sets the cage down on a chair.*]

Miss Julie: I'm ready now.

Jean: Shh! Christine's awake.

Miss Julie (*she is extremely tense and nervous during the following*). Did she suspect anything?

Jean: She doesn't know a thing.—My God, what happened to you?

Miss Julie: What do you mean? Do I look so strange?

Jean: You're white as a ghost, and you've—excuse me—but you've got dirt on your face.

Miss Julie: Let me wash it off. (*She goes over to the wash basin and washes her face and hands.*) There! Do you have a towel? . . . Oh, look, the sun's coming up!

Jean: That breaks the magic spell!

Miss Julie: Yes, we were spellbound last night, weren't we? Midsummer madness . . . Jean, listen to me! Come with me. I've got the money!

Jean (*suspiciously*). Enough?

Miss Julie: Enough for a start. Come with me, Jean. I can't travel alone today. Midsummer Day on a stifling hot train, packed in with crowds of people, all staring at me—stopping at every station when I want to be flying. I can't, Jean, I can't! . . . And everything will remind me of the past. Midsummer Day when I was a child and the church was decorated with leaves—birch leaves and lilacs . . . the table spread for dinner with friends and relatives . . . and after dinner, dancing in the park, with flowers and games. Oh, no matter how far you travel, the memories tag right along in the baggage car . . . and the regrets and the remorse.

Jean: All right, I'll go with you! But it's got to be now—before it's too late! This very instant!

Miss Julie: Hurry and get dressed! (*She picks up the bird cage.*)

Jean: But no baggage! It would give us away.

Miss Julie: Nothing. Only what we can take to our seats.

Jean (*as he gets his hat*). What in the devil have you got there? What is that?

Miss Julie: It's only my canary. I can't leave it behind.

Jean: A canary! My God, do you expect us to carry a bird cage around with us? You're crazy. Put that cage down!

Miss Julie: It's the only thing I'm taking with me from my home—the only living thing who loves me since Diana was unfaithful to me! Don't be cruel, Jean. Let me take it with me.

Jean: I told you to put that cage down!—And don't talk so loud. Christine can hear us.

Miss Julie: No, I won't leave it with a stranger. I won't. I'd rather have you kill it.

Jean: Let me have the little pest and I'll wring its neck.

Miss Julie: Yes, but don't hurt it. Don't—. No, I can't do it!

Jean: Don't worry, I can. Give it here.

[MISS JULIE *takes the bird out of the cage and kisses it.*]

Miss Julie: Oh, my little Serena, must you die and leave your mistress?

Jean: You don't have to make a scene of it. It's a question of your whole life and future. You're wasting time! (JEAN *grabs the canary from her, carries it to the chopping block, and picks up a meat cleaver.* MISS JULIE *turns away.*) You should have learned how to kill chickens instead of shooting revolvers—(*He brings the cleaver down.*)—then a drop of blood wouldn't make you faint.

Miss Julie (*screaming*). Kill me too! Kill me! You can kill an innocent creature without turning a hair—then kill me. Oh, how I hate you! I loathe you! There's blood between us. I curse the moment I first laid eyes on you! I curse the moment I was conceived in my mother's womb.

Jean: What good does your cursing do? Let's get out of here!

Miss Julie (*approaches the chopping block as if drawn to it against her will*). No, I don't want to go yet. I can't.—I have to see.—Shh! I hear a carriage coming! (*She listens but keeps her eyes fastened on the chopping block and cleaver.*) You don't think I can stand the sight of blood, do you? You think I'm so weak, don't you? Oh, how I'd love to see your blood, your brains on that chopping block. I'd love to see the whole of your sex swimming in a sea of blood just like that. The way I feel I could drink out of your skull. I'd like to use your chest as a foot bath and dip my toes in your guts! I could eat your heart roasted whole! —You think I'm weak! You think I loved you because my womb hungered for your semen. You think I want to carry your brood under my heart and feed it with my blood! Bear your child and take your name!—Come to think of it, what is your name anyway? I've never even heard your last name. I'll bet you don't even have one. I'd be Mrs. Doorman or Madame Garbageman. You dog with *my* name on your collar—you lackey with *my* initials on your buttons! Do you think I'm going to share you with my cook and fight over you with my maid?! Ohhh!—You think I'm a coward who's going to run away! No, I'm going to stay—come hell or high water. My father will come home—find his desk broken into—his money gone. He'll ring—on that bell—two rings for the valet. And then he'll send for the sheriff—and I'll tell him everything. Everything! Oh, what a relief it'll be to have it all over . . . if only it will be over. . . . He'll have a stroke and die . . . and there'll be an end to all of us. There'll be peace . . . and quiet . . . forever. . . . The coat of arms will be broken on his coffin; the Count's line will be extinct—while the valet's breed will continue in an orphanage, win triumphs in the gutter, and end in jail!

[CHRISTINE *enters, dressed for church and with a hymn-book in her hand.* MISS JULIE *rushes over to her and throws herself into her arms as if seeking protection.*]

Miss Julie: Help me, Christine! Help me against this man!

Christine (*cold and unmoved*). This is a fine way to behave on a holy day! (*She sees the chopping block.*) Just look at the mess you've made there! How do you explain that? And what's all this shouting and screaming about?

Miss Julie: Christine, you're a woman, you're my friend! I warn you, watch out for this—this monster!

Jean (*ill at ease and a little embarrassed*). If you ladies are going to talk, I think I'll go and shave. (*He slips out to the right.*)

Miss Julie: You've got to understand, Christine! You've got to listen to me!

Christine: No, I don't. I don't understand this kind of shenanigans at all. Where do you think you're going dressed like that? And Jean with his hat on?—Well?—Well?

Miss Julie: Listen to me, Christine! If you'll just listen to me, I'll tell you everything.

Christine: I don't want to know anything.

Miss Julie: You've got to listen to me—!

Christine: What about? About your stupid behavior with Jean? I tell you that doesn't bother me at all, because it's none of my business. But if you have any silly idea about talking him into skipping out with you, I'll soon put a stop to that.

Miss Julie (*extremely tense*). Christine, please don't get upset. Listen to me. I can't stay here, and Jean can't stay here. So you see, we have to go away.

Christine: Hm, hm, hm.

Miss Julie (*suddenly brightening up*). Wait! I've got an idea! Why couldn't all three of us go away together?—out of the country—to Switzerland—and start a hotel. I've got the money, you see. Jean and I would be responsible for the whole affair—and Christine, you could run the kitchen, I thought. Doesn't that sound wonderful! Say yes! Say you'll come, Christine, then everything will be settled. Say you will! Please! (*She throws her arms around* CHRISTINE *and pats her.*)

Christine (*remaining aloof and unmoved*). Hm. Hm.

Miss Julie (*presto tempo*). You've never been traveling, Christine. You have to get out and see the world. You can't imagine how wonderful it is to travel by train—constantly new faces—new countries. We'll go to Hamburg, and stop over to look at the zoo—you'll love that. And we'll go to the theater and the opera. And then when we get to Munich, we'll go to the museums, Christine. They have Rubenses and Raphaels there—those great painters, you know. Of course you've heard about Munich where King Ludwig lived—you know, the king who went mad. And then we can go and see his castles—they're built just like the ones you read about in fairy tales. And from there it's just a short trip to Switzerland—with the Alps. Think of the Alps,

Christine, covered with snow in the middle of summer. And oranges grow there, and laurel trees that are green the whole year round.—(JEAN *can be seen in the wings at the right, sharpening his straight razor on a strap held between his teeth and his left hand. He listens to* MISS JULIE *with a satisfied expression on his face, now and then nodding approvingly.* MISS JULIE *continues tempo prestissimo.*)—And that's where we'll get a hotel. I'll sit at the desk while Jean stands at the door and receives the guests, goes out shopping, writes the letters. What a life that will be! The train whistle blowing, then the bus arriving, then a bell ringing upstairs, then the bell in the restaurant rings—and I'll be making out the bills—and I know just how much to salt them—you can't imagine how timid tourists are when you shove a bill in their face!—And you, Christine, you'll run the whole kitchen—there'll be no standing at the stove for you—of course not. If you're going to talk to the people, you'll have to dress neatly and elegantly. And with your looks—I'm not trying to flatter you, Christine—you'll run off with some man one fine day—a rich Englishman, that's who it'll be, they're so easy to—(*slowing down*)—to catch.—Then we'll all be rich.—We'll build a villa on Lake Como.—Maybe it does rain there sometimes, but—(*more and more lifelessly*)—the sun has to shine sometimes, too—even if it looks cloudy.—And—then . . . Or else we can always travel some more—and come back . . . (*pause*)—here . . . or somewhere else. . . .

Christine: Do you really believe a word of that yourself, Miss Julie?

Miss Julie (*completely beaten*). Do I believe a word of it myself?

Christine: Do you?

Miss Julie (*exhausted*). I don't know. I don't believe anything any more. (*She sinks down on the bench and lays her head between her arms on the table.*) Nothing. Nothing at all.

Christine (*turns to the right and faces* JEAN). So! You were planning to run away, were you?

Jean (*nonplused, lays his razor down on the table*). We weren't exactly going to run away! Don't exaggerate. You heard Miss Julie's plans. Even if she's tired now after being up all night, her plans are perfectly practical.

Christine: Well, just listen to you! Did you really think you could get me to cook for that little—

Jean (*sharply*). You keep a respectful tongue in your mouth when you talk to your mistress! Understand?

Christine: Mistress!

Jean: Yes, mistress!

Christine: Well of all the—! I don't have to listen—

Jean: Yes, you do! You need to listen more and talk less. Miss Julie is your mistress. Don't forget that! And if you're going to despise her for what she did, you ought to despise yourself for the same reason.

Christine: I've always held myself high enough to—

Jean: High enough to make you look down on others!

Christine: —enough to keep from lowering myself beneath my position. No one can say that the Count's cook has ever had anything to do with the stable groom or the swineherd. No one can say that!

Jean: Yes, aren't you lucky you got involved with a decent man!

Christine: What kind of a decent

man is it who sells the oats from the Count's stables?

Jean: Listen to who's talking! You get a commission on the groceries and take bribes from the butcher!

Christine: How can you say a thing like that!

Jean: And you tell me you can't respect your employers any more! You! You!

Christine: Are you going to church or aren't you? I should think you'd need a good sermon after your exploits.

Jean: No, I'm not going to church! You can go alone and confess your own sins.

Christine: Yes, I'll do just that. And I'll come back with enough forgiveness to cover yours, too. Our Redeemer suffered and died on the cross for all our sins, and if we come to Him in faith and with a penitent heart, He will take all our sins upon Himself.

Jean: Grocery sins included?

Miss Julie: Do you really believe that, Christine?

Christine: With all my heart, as sure as I'm standing here. It was the faith I was born into, and I've held on to it since I was a little girl, Miss Julie. Where sin aboundeth, there grace aboundeth also.

Miss Julie: If I had your faith, Christine, if only—

Christine: But you see, that's something you can't have without God's special grace. And it is not granted to everyone to receive it.

Miss Julie: Then who receives it?

Christine: That's the secret of the workings of grace, Miss Julie, and God is no respecter of persons. With Him the last shall be the first—

Miss Julie: In that case, He does have respect for the last, doesn't He?

Christine (*continuing*). —and it is easier for a camel to go through the eye of a needle than for a rich man to enter the kingdom of God. That's how things are, Miss Julie. I'm going to leave now —alone. And on my way out I'm going to tell the stable boy not to let any horses out, in case anyone has any ideas about leaving before the Count comes home. Goodbye. (*She leaves.*)

Jean: She's a devil in skirts!—And all because of a canary!

Miss Julie (*listlessly*). Never mind the canary. . . . Do you see any way out of this, any end to it?

Jean (*after thinking for a moment*). No.

Miss Julie: What would you do if you were in my place?

Jean: In your place? Let me think. . . . An aristocrat, a woman, and—fallen. . . . I don't know.—Or maybe I do.

Miss Julie (*picks up the razor and makes a gesture with it*). Like this?

Jean: Yes. But *I* wouldn't do it, you understand. That's the difference between us.

Miss Julie: Because you're a man and I'm a woman? What difference does that make?

Jean: Just the difference that there is —between a man and a woman.

Miss Julie (*holding the razor in her hand*). I want to! But I can't do it. My father couldn't do it either, that time he should have done it.

Jean: No, he was right not to do it. He had to get his revenge first.

Miss Julie: And now my mother is getting her revenge again through me.

Jean: Haven't you ever loved your father, Miss Julie?

Miss Julie: Yes, enormously. But I must have hated him too. I must have hated him without knowing it. It was he who brought me up to despise my own sex, to be half woman and half man. Who's to blame for what has happened? My father, my mother, myself? Myself? I don't have a self that's my own. I don't have a single thought I didn't get from my father, not an emotion I didn't get from my mother. And that last idea—about all people being equal—I got that from him, my fiancé. That's why I say he's beneath contempt. How can it be my own fault? Put the blame on Jesus, like Christine does? I'm too proud to do that—and too intelligent, thanks to what my father taught me. . . . A rich man can't get into heaven? That's a lie. But at least Christine, who's got money in the savings bank, won't get in. . . . Who's to blame? What difference does it make who's to blame? I'm still the one who has to bear the guilt, suffer the consequences—

Jean: Yes, but—

[*The bell rings sharply twice,* MISS JULIE *jumps up.* JEAN *changes his coat.*]

Jean: The Count's back! What if Christine—? (*He goes to the speaking tube, taps on it, and listens.*)

Miss Julie: Has he looked in his desk yet?

Jean: This is Jean, sir! (*Listens. The audience cannot hear what the* COUNT *says.*) Yes, sir! (*Listens.*) Yes, sir! Yes, as soon as I can. (*Listens.*) Yes, at once, ssir! (*Listens.*) Very good, sir! In half an hour.

Miss Julie (*trembling with anxiety*). What did he say? For God's sake, what did he say?

Jean: He ordered his boots and his coffee in half an hour.

Miss Julie: Half an hour then! . . . Oh, I'm so tired. I can't bring myself to do anything. Can't repent, can't run away, can't stay, can't live . . . can't die. Help me, Jean. Command me, and I'll obey like a dog. Do me this last favor. Save my honor, save his name. You know what I ought to do but can't force myself to do. Let me use your will power. You command me and I'll obey.

Jean: I don't know—I can't either, not now. I don't know why. It's as if this coat made me—. I can't give you orders in this. And now, after the Count has spoken to me, I—I can't really explain it—but—I've got the backbone of a damned lackey! If the Count came down here now and ordered me to cut my throat, I'd do it on the spot.

Miss Julie: Pretend that you're him, and that I'm you. You were such a good actor just a while ago, when you were kneeling before me. You were the aristocrat then. Or else—have you ever been to the theater and seen a hypnotist? (JEAN *nods.*) He says to his subject, "Take this broom!" and he takes it. He says, "Now sweep!" and he sweeps.

Jean: But the person has to be asleep!

Miss Julie (*ecstatic, transposed*). I'm already asleep. The whole room has turned to smoke. You seem like an iron stove, a stove that looks like a man in black with a high hat. Your eyes are glowing like coals in a dying fire. Your face is a white smudge, like ashes. (*The sun is now shining in on the floor and falls on* JEAN.) It's so good and warm— (*She rubs her hands together as if warming them at a fire.*) —and so bright—and so peaceful.

Jean (*takes the razor and puts it in her hand*). There's the broom. Go now, when the sun is up—out into the barn—and— (*He whispers in her ear*).

Miss Julie (*waking up*). Thanks! I'm going to get my rest. But tell me one thing. Tell me that the first can also receive the gift of grace. Tell me that, even if you don't believe it.

Jean: The first? I can't tell you that. —But wait a moment, Miss Julie. I know what I can tell you. You're no longer one of the first. You're one of—the last.

Miss Julie: That's true! I'm one of the last. I am the very last!—Oh!—Now I can't go! Tell me just once more, tell me to go!

Jean: Now I can't either. I can't!

Miss Julie: And the first shall be the last. . . .

Jean: Don't think—don't think! You're taking all my strength away. You're making me a coward. . . . What! I thought I saw the bell move. No. . . . Let me stuff some paper in it.—Afraid of a bell! But it isn't just a bell. There's somebody behind it. A hand that makes it move. And there's something that makes the hand move.—Stop your ears, that's it, stop your ears! But it only rings louder. Rings louder and louder until you answer it. And then it's too late. Then the sheriff comes—and then— (*There are two sharp rings on the bell.* JEAN *gives a start, then straightens himself up.*) It's horrible! But there's no other way for it to end.—Go! (MISS JULIE *walks resolutely out through the door.*)

DISCUSSION QUESTIONS

1. To what extent has Strindberg broken with the "well-made," fully unified, melodramatic conventions of nineteenth-century theatre?
2. How is Strindberg's tragedy naturalistic?
3. To what extent does Strindberg diverge from naturalism—impose values, that is, upon his art?
4. How does Strindberg link his play's tragic qualities to aspects of pity and terror?
5. What are the central conflicts in the play?
6. How is Jean's character a mixture of virtues and vices?
7. How does the character of Jean affect the outcome of the play?
8. How are the boots which Jean brings in with him symbolic?
9. How does the initial dialogue between Jean and Christine introduce factors likely to motivate Miss Julie's behavior later in the play?
10. How are Jean's comments on Miss Julie ironic, both in regard to her character and to his point of view?
11. How does Miss Julie resemble her wayward dog?
12. How does Christine serve as a foil or illuminating contrast to Miss Julie?
13. How does Strindberg divide his partialities between Jean and Julie?
14. How are the forces which propel Jean and Julie toward their fates symbolized in their recurring dreams?
15. How does Jean's story of the Turkish outhouse reveal his basic motivation?
16. How does Jean's behavior towards both Julie and the Count reflect his underlying tensions?
17. How do the attitudes of Jean and Julie towards the sexual act differ?

18. How does the song the peasants sing indirectly parody the three major characters (and even some of the minor or absent characters)?
19. How does the situation in which Jean and Julie find themselves as the peasants enter symbolize the operations of fate?
20. How do Jean's plans reveal his completely materialistic values?
21. What kind of formal, dramatic design has Strindberg imposed on his loose, natural, and compact action?
22. How is Jean's story of his one-time attempted suicide symbolic?
23. What does Julie recognize about Jean after they withdraw to his bedroom?
24. What does Jean recognize about Julie after they return from his bedroom?
25. How is Julie's parentage revealed to be the main source of her problems?
26. How does Miss Julie's inner conflict continue to poison her relationship with Jean?
27. What incongruous inner conflict continues to torture Jean?
28. What traits in Christine's character are reinforced by her second appearance?
29. What is Christine's function in the play, particularly regarding illusions held by Jean and Julie?
30. What thematic, symbolic contrasts emerge from the struggle between Jean and Julie?
31. How does Jean's killing of the bird symbolize his role?
32. To what extent is Julie's suicide a victory for Jean?
33. To what extent is Julie's suicide a victory for her?
34. How does Jean's cringing at the bell add an additional touch of irony?

THE CHERRY ORCHARD

Anton Chekhov

Translated by
BLAZE ODELL BONAZZA and EMIL ROY

Introductory Comment

It is ironic that because of the unfamiliar language in which it was written, *The Cherry Orchard* had no more impact on European drama than it did and that despite its apparent lack of action, its influence has been so pervasive. The play has no chases, no eavesdropping scenes by jealous lovers, no obvious heroes or villains, very little violence, no significant passions, few theatrical speeches and no secrets to be revealed at the last moment in a hidden letter. The play's historical importance is ambiguous, and none of the characters are very deep thinkers. A faithful translation probably loses less than English versions of most literature, and very few, if any, of the speeches are very quotable.

What gives the play its unique position in modern drama is the significance of the orchard itself as a potent symbol of renewal and freshness. Chekhov's insistence on the beauty of the trees, even though characters who rhapsodize about it are usually most sentimental and self-deluded when they do so, is part of the subtle unfolding of the play's complex texture. The loss of the orchard is poignant and avoidable, despite the inevitability with which it slips through everyone's fingers. But the failure, the inability of any of the characters to reach intellectual or even emotional assent on the significance of what they are enacting is integral to the play's form. By applying the term "comedy" to his play, Chekhov did not rule out the despair at man's limited knowledge, the racking pain of isolation, and the apparent loss of a spiritual center which emerge from tragedy, particularly as it approaches its crisis. However, while the larger implications of the play are unmistakably tragic, the moment-by-moment progress of the action is often grotesque and farcical. Fools repeat laughable petty vices, a penetrating and judicious speech is deliberately mocked by a pratfall, sensitive and intense characters deflate once-genuine emotions, and even climactic moments of pathos are subtly undercut by both our and the sufferers' sense that they rather perversely enjoy the lassitude of an apparently hopeless situation. Like Ibsen and Shaw, Chekhov has managed to lift commonplace, routine feelings into the realm of art by placing them in juxtaposition. He joins the acute, the self-pitying, the random and witty in contexts where people seem least aware that their inner feelings are being exposed. We are shown how the comforting religious, social, and family myths have been replaced by conditioning and sentimentality. Unlike the theatres of Sophocles and Shakespeare, that of Chekhov and his contemporaries is stark, myopic, and dead-end. It is impossible for us to imagine Chekhov's commonplace, unimaginative, and frustrated people acting in any other way than they do. What does surprise us is that with such mundane concerns and trite notions of behavior, they are capable of both undergoing and evoking from us such a broad range of contradictory feelings, often simultaneously. Although Chekhov's down-at-the-heel aristocrats, their hangers-on, and their society have responded to their situation with a variety of usually ineffective, but revealing acts, it is not only their failures but their occasional flashes of insight, compassion, and resolution which form a viable image of human nature in as many varied facets as the contemporary world seems to allow.

Cast of Characters

RANEVSKY, LYUBOV ANDREYEVNA, *a landowner*
ANYA, *her daughter, age 17*
VARYA, *her foster daughter, age 22*
GAYEV, LEONID ANDREYEVICH, *Mme. Ranevsky's brother*
LOPAHIN, YERMOLAY ALEXEYEVICH, *a businessman*
TROFIMOV, PYOTR SERGEYEVICH, *a student*
SEMYONOV-PISHCHIK, BORIS BORISOVICH, *a landowner*
CHARLOTTA IVANOVNA, *a governess*
EPIHODOV, SEMYON PANTELEYEVICH, *a clerk on the Ranevsky estate*
DUNYASHA, *a maidservant*
FIRS, *an old manservant, age 87*
YASHA, *a young manservant*
A TRAMP
STATIONMASTER
POST OFFICE CLERK
GUESTS, SERVANTS

The action takes place on the Ranevsky estate around 1900.

ACT I

[*A room which until now has been called the "nursery." One of the doors leads into* ANYA'S *room. It is early morning, the sun is about to rise. It is May, the cherry trees are in blossom, but it is cold in the orchard, with the frost of early morning. The windows of the room are closed. Enter* DUNYASHA *with a candle and* LOPAHIN *with a book in his hand.*]

Lopahin: The train has arrived, thank God! what time is it?

Dunyasha: Almost two. (*Blows out the candle.*) It's light already.

Lopahin: How late is the train then? Two hours at least. (*Yawns and stretches.*) What a fool I've made of myself. I came here on purpose to meet them at the station, and then all at once I miss them by sleeping too long . . . I fell asleep sitting in a chair. What a shame. You could have awakened me.

Dunyasha: I thought you had left. (*Listens.*) I think they're coming now.

Lopahin (*listens*). No, they have to pick up their luggage, and take care of this and that. (*Pause.*) Lyubov Andreyevna has spent five years abroad . . . I don't know what she's like now . . . She's a nice, easy-going, simple sort of person. I remember once when I was a boy of fifteen, my poor dead father—he ran a store here in the village at that time—punched me in the face with his fist, and my nose started bleeding. We had come into the yard together for one reason or another—he was a little tipsy. Lyubov Andreyevna, how well I still remember her, so young and slender—brought me in to the washstand . . . right here in this very room, the nursery. "Don't cry, little peasant," she said, "It will be well in time for your wedding." (*Pause.*) Little peasant . . . my father was a peasant, it's true, but look at me with my white vest and yellow shoes. Like a pig with his snout in a pastry shop . . . only in this case, I'm a rich one, I've got lots of money, but if you think about it and observe closely, you'll see I'm still an ordinary peasant. (*Thumbs through the book.*) Look here, I've been reading this book and got absolutely nothing out of it. I was reading and I fell asleep. (*Pause.*)

Dunyasha: The dogs didn't sleep all night long. They can sense that their masters are coming.

Lopahin: What's the matter with you, Dunyasha?

Dunyasha: My hands are shaking. I'm going to faint.

Lopahin: You're just too delicate, Dunyasha. Here you are, all dressed up like a lady, and with your hair all done up. That just won't do. You should keep your place.

[*Enter* EPIHODOV *with a bouquet; he wears a jacket and highly polished boots which squeak loudly; he drops the bouquet coming in.*]

Epihodov (*picking up the bouquet*). Here, the gardener sent them. He says to put them in the dining room. (*Gives* DUNYASHA *the bouquet.*)

Lopahin: And bring me some kvass.[1]

Dunyasha: Yes, sir. (*Goes out.*)

Epihodov: It's frosty this morning . . . three degrees below zero, yet the cherry trees are all in bloom. I can't say I approve of our climate. (*Sighs.*) I can't. Our climate just can't seem to cooperate right. Look here, Yermolay Alexeyich, may I add that I bought some boots for myself the day before yesterday, and they squeak so much, I assure you, I just can't stand it. What can I grease them with?

Lopahin: Oh, leave me alone. You annoy me.

Epihodov: Every day brings some new mishap or other to me, but I never complain. I'm used to it . . I even smile.

[DUNYASHA *comes in, serving* LOPAHIN *the kvass.*]

Epihodov: I'm leaving. (*Stumbles into a chair which topples over.*) There! (*With an air of triumph.*) There, by the way, you see, if you'll pardon my saying so, is the kind of thing I mean. It's simply remarkable. (*Goes out.*)

Dunyasha: I simply must tell you, Yermolay Alexeyich—Epihodov has proposed to me.

Lopahin: Ah!

Dunyasha: I just don't know what to do about it . . . He's a mild-mannered man, but sometimes when he begins talking, you just can't understand a word. It's nice and tender . . . but you just can't make heads or tails of it. I like him I guess, and he's wild about me. He's an unlucky fellow . . . something happens to him every day. We tease him about it by calling him "a born loser."

Lopahin (*listening*). There! I think they're coming. . . .

Dunyasha: They're coming! What's the matter with me? I feel cold all over.

Lopahin: They really are coming. Let's go and meet them. Will she recognize me? We haven't seen one another in five years.

Dunyasha (*confused*). I just know I'm going to faint . . . Oh, I'm fainting!

[*Two carriages are heard driving up to the house.* LOPAHIN *and* DUNYASHA *go*

[1] A Russian fermented drink made from rye or barley and resembling beer.

out hurriedly. The stage is empty. In the adjoining room a noise starts up. FIRS, *who had gone to meet* LYUBOV, *hurries across the stage, leaning on a stick. He wears old-fashioned livery and a high hat. He mumbles something to himself, but not a word can be understood. The offstage noise gets louder and louder. A voice:* "Look, let's go through here . . ." LYUBOV, ANYA, *and* CHARLOTTA, *with a small dog on a chain, all of them dressed for traveling,* VARYA *wearing an overcoat and kerchief,* GAYEV, SEMYONOV-PISHCHIK, LOPAHIN, DUNYASHA, *with a bundle and an umbrella, servants with pieces of luggage—all walk across the room.*]

Anya: Let's go through here. Mama, do you remember what room this is?

Lyubov (*joyfully, tearfully*). The nursery!

Varya: It's so cold my hands are numb. (*To* LYUBOV.) Your rooms, the white one and the violet one, are the same as they always were, Mama dear.

Lyubov: The nursery, my dear, lovely room! . . . I slept here when I was a little girl . . . (*weeps*). And now I am like a little girl again. . . . (*Kisses her brother and* VARYA, *and then her brother again.*) And Varya is the same as ever, she looks just like a nun. And I recognized Dunyasha . . . (*kisses Dunyasha*).

Gayev: The train was two hours late. What do you think of that? Some efficiency!

Charlotta (*To* PISHCHIK). My dog eats nuts too.

Pishchik (*Astonished*). Can you imagine that!

[*All go out, except* ANYA *and* DUNYASHA.]

Dunyasha: We waited so long for you we got tired. (*Takes* ANYA'S *coat and hat.*)

Anya: I couldn't sleep for four nights on the trip . . . now I'm frozen.

Dunyasha: When you left during Lent there was snow and frost, but now look at it! My darling! (*She laughs and kisses her.*) We waited for you so long, my darling, my joy . . . but I must tell you something right away, I can't hold off a minute longer.

Anya (*wearily*). What is it this time?

Dunyasha: The clerk, Epihodov, proposed to me just after Easter.

Anya: You've got a one-track mind. (*Rearranges her hair.*) I've lost all my hair-pins . . . (*She is very tired, almost to the point of falling over.*)

Dunyasha: I really don't know what to think. He loves me, he loves me so much!

Anya (*looks toward the door of her own room, tenderly*). My own room, my own windows. It's just as if I had never been away. I'm home! Tomorrow morning I'll get up and run straight to the orchard . . . Oh, if only I could get some sleep! I didn't sleep on the entire trip, I was so worried.

Dunyasha: Pyotr Sergeyich got here the day before yesterday.

Anya (*joyfully*). Petya!

Dunyasha: He's sleeping in the bath house, he's settled down in there. He says he's afraid of being in the way. (*Looking at her pocket watch.*) I would have awakened him, but Varvara Mihailovna gave orders not to. "Don't you wake him up," she says to me.

[*Enter* VARYA, *with a bunch of keys at her waist.*]

Varya: Dunyasha, coffee, and hurry . . . Mama dear is asking for coffee.

Dunyasha (*goes out*). It'll be ready in a minute.

Varya: Well, thank goodness, you're back. You're home again! (*Caressing her.*) My darling has come back! My little sweetheart has returned!

Anya: You'll never know what I've been through.

Varya: I can well imagine!

Anya: When I left during Holy Week, it was so cold. And Charlotta insitted on talking the entire trip and kept doing her tricks. Why did you have to burden me with Charlotta?

Varya: You know you couldn't go all by yourself, darling. At seventeen years of age!

Anya: When we got to Paris, it was cold and snowing. You know I speak terrible French. Mama lived on the fifth floor, I went up to her room, and there were all kinds of French people with her —ladies, an old priest with a big book. It was so smoky in there and so drab. All at once I felt so sorry for Mama, so sorry . . . I held her head in my arms and hugged her and couldn't let go of her. Then Mama kept petting me and crying . . .

Varya (*through her tears*). Don't, don't . . .

Anya: She had already sold her villa near Mentone and had nothing left, nothing. And I didn't have a penny left either, scarcely enough to get back home on. But Mama just didn't understand! When we had dinner at the train stations, she would always order the most expensive dishes and tip each of the waiters a whole rouble. Charlotta did exactly the same thing. Yasha would also order something for himself. It was simply terrible. You know Mama has Yasha as her manservant. We brought him back with us.

Varya: Yes, I've seen the despicable fellow.

Anya: Well, how is everything? Have you paid the interest on the mortgage?

Varya: How could we!

Anya: Good heavens, good heavens.

Varya: The estate will be put up for sale in August.

Anya: Good heavens . . .

Lopahin (*Looking in through the doorway and moos*). Moo . . . ooo. (*Goes away.*)

Varya (*tearfully*). Oh, how I'd like to hit him one! (*Shakes her fist.*)

Anya (*embracing* VARYA, *gently*). Has he proposed to you yet, Varya? (VARYA *shakes her head.*) But he loves you, doesn't he? Why don't you come to an understanding? What are you waiting for?

Varya: I don't think anything will come of it between us. He's got so much to do, he has no time to spare for me . . . he never pays any attention to me. God bless him! (*Ironically.*) . . . it hurts me just to see him. Everyone talks about our wedding, they all congratulate me, but there's really nothing to it. It's all a dream . . . (*Changes her tone.*) Your new brooch looks like a bee.

Anya (*sorrowfully*). Mama bought it. (*Goes into her own room, speaks in a cheerful, childlike tone.*) When I was in Paris, I went up in a balloon!

Varya: My darling has come back! My little sweetheart's home again!

[DUNYASHA *returns with the coffee pot and gets the coffee ready.*]

Varya (*standing near the door*). All day long, darling, as I go about on my housekeeping duties I keep dreaming. If we could only marry you to a rich man, then I would be at peace. I would gladly go to a convent, then to Kiev, to Moscow, and then go on traveling from one holy place to another . . . I would go on and on. What bliss!

Anya: The birds are singing in the orchard. What time is it?

Varya: It must be after two. It's time for you to be asleep, darling. (*They go into* ANYA'S *room.*) What bliss!

[YASHA *comes in with a plaid blanket and a small traveling bag.*]

Yasha (*Crosses the stage, speaks in an affected voice*). May I go through here, ma'am?

Dunyasha: I didn't recognize you, Yasha. You changed so much while you were abroad.

Yasha: Hm . . . and who are you?

Dunyasha: When you left here, I was this high . . . (*measures her height from the floor*). I'm Dunyasha, the daughter of Fyodor Kozoyedov. You don't remember me!

Yasha: Hmm . . . what a cute little cucumber! (*Looking around and putting his arms around her; she squeals and drops a saucer. Yasha hurries out.*)

Varya (*in the doorway, in an irritated tone*). What happened here?

Dunyasha (*tearfully*). I broke a saucer.

Varya: That's a good omen.

Anya (*comes out of her room*). We should warn Mama in advance that Petya's here.

Varya: I told them not to wake him up.

Anya (*thoughtfully*). Six years ago father died. A month later brother Grisha drowned in the river. He was such a cute little boy and only seven. Mama couldn't bear it. She went away, she went away without looking back . . . (*shudders*). How well I understand her, if she only knew. (*Pause.*) And Petya Trofimov was Grisha's tutor, he might stir up memories . . .

[FIRS *comes in; he is wearing a jacket and a white vest.*]

Firs (*goes over to the coffee pot, anxiously*). Madame will have her coffee in here. (*Puts on white gloves.*) Is the coffee ready? (*To* DUNYASHA, *sternly.*) You! Where's the cream?

Dunyasha: Oh, good heavens . . . (*Hurries out.*)

Firs (*fiddling with the coffee pot*). Ah, you half-wit . . . (*Mutters to himself.*) They've come back from Paris . . . and the old master used to go to Paris in days gone by . . . in a horse-carriage . . . (*Laughs.*)

Varya: Firs, what are you laughing about?

Firs: What can I do for you, Madame? (*Joyfully.*) My mistress is home again! At last I've seen her. Now I would be willing to die . . . (*Weeps with joy.*)

[LYUBOV, GAYEV, *and* SEMYONOV-PISHCHIK *come in.* PISHCHIK *is wearing a snug-waisted, pleated coat of fine broadcloth and full trousers. As* GAYEV *comes in, he makes motions with his hands and body as if he were playing billiards.*]

Lyubov: How does that go? Let me see if I remember. . . . Yellow ball in the corner pocket! Combination shot in the side pocket!

Gayev: I'll cut it into the corner pocket! Once upon a time, little sister, you and I used to sleep in this very same room, and now I'm fifty-one, strange as it may seem . . .

Lopahin: Yes, time flies.

Gayev: What?

Lopahin: Time flies, I said.

Gayev: It smells of shaving lotion in here.

Anya: I'm going to bed. Good night, Mama. (*Kisses her.*)

Lyubov: My beloved child. (*Kisses her hands.*) Are you happy now that you're home again? I still haven't got used to the idea myself.

Anya: Good-bye, Uncle.

Gayev (*kisses her face and hands*). The Lord be with you. How much you resemble your mother. (*To his sister.*) At her age, Lyuba, you looked exactly like her.

[ANYA *shakes hands with* LOPAHIN *and* PISHCHIK, *leaves, and closes the door after her.*]

Lyubov: She's very tired.

Pishchik: It was a long journey, to be sure.

Varya (*to* LOPAHIN *and* PISHCHIK). Well, gentlemen, what about it? It's after two . . . time to put an end to this.

Lyubov (*laughing*). You're the same as ever, Varya. (*Draws her near and kisses her.*) I'll finish this coffee and then we'll all go. (FIRS *places a cushion under her feet.*) Thank you, dear. I've gotten used to coffee. I drink it day and night. Thank you, my dear old fellow. (*Kisses* FIRS.)

Varya: I'd better look and see if all the luggage has been brought in . . . (*Goes out.*)

Lyubov: Is it really me sitting here? (*Laughs.*) I feel like leaping about and tossing my arms around. (*Covers her face with her hands.*) All of a sudden, I'll find out I'm only dreaming. God only knows I love my country, I love it dearly. I could hardly look out of the train windows I was crying so much. (*Through her tears.*) Still, I must finish my coffee. Thank you, Firs, thank you, my dear old fellow. I'm so happy you're still alive.

Firs: The day before yesterday.

Gayev: He doesn't hear very well.

Lopahin: I have to leave for Kharkov soon, at five in the morning. What a nuisance! I wanted to take a good look at you, to talk to you . . . you look as magnificent as ever.

Pishchik (*breathing heavily*). She's ever more beautiful. Decked out in the latest Parisian fashions. She sweeps you right off your feet.

Lopahin: Your brother, Leonid Andreyevich, is always saying that I'm a vulgar fellow, a money-grubber, but I don't care . . . let him talk. I only want you to believe in me as you used to. I want your trusting, wonderful, soft eyes to look upon me as they used to. Merciful God. My father was a serf of your father's and your grandfather's, but you, you yourself, did so much for me once that I have forgotten all that and love you like my very own, even more than my very own.

Lyubov: I can't sit still. I'm in such a state. (*Jumps up and walks about extremely agitated.*) I simply can't bear this joy! Go ahead and laugh at me, I'm so silly . . . my very own little bookcase. (*Kisses the bookcase.*) My darling little table!

Gayev: Nurse died while you were away.

Lyubov (*sits down and drinks her coffee*). Yes, may she rest in peace. They wrote me about it.

Gayev: Anastasy died too. Petrushka Kossoy has left me and is now in town working for the police captain. (*Takes a box of hard candy from his pocket and sucks on a piece.*)

Pishchik: My daughter, Dashenka, sends her best regards.

Lopahin: I want to tell you something very pleasant . . . it'll cheer you up. (*Glancing at his watch.*) I'll be leaving soon. I don't have much time to talk . . . but I'll tell you in a few words. As you already know, your cherry orchard will be sold to pay off the debt on it. The auction will be held on the twenty-second of August, but don't worry, my dear, rest easy, there's a way out . . . here's my plan. Pay attention. Your estate is only fifteen miles out of town and close to where they ran the railroad. Now, if you divided up the cherry orchard and the property along the river bank and leased it out for summer cottages, you would realize an income of 25,000 roubles a year at the very least.

Gayev: Pardon me, but what twaddle!

Lyubov: I don't completely understand you, Yermolay Alexeyich.

Lopahin: You will get an annual rent from the summer residents of at least ten roubles an acre, and if you start advertising right away, I'll guarantee you anything you want, you won't have a single piece of land left by autumn . . . everything will be taken. In a word, I congratulate you, you're saved. The location is ideal, the river is nice and deep there. But naturally, you'll have to get it cleared and ready . . . let's say, for example, you tear down all the old buildings and this house here, which is no longer worth anything anyway, and cut down the cherry orchard . . .

Lyubov: Cut down the cherry orchard! My dear fellow, forgive me, but you simply don't understand. If there is one thing in this whole province that's interesting . . . in fact, remarkable . . . it's nothing else but this very orchard.

Lopahin: The only remarkable thing about this orchard is that it's so big. It bears a crop of cherries once every two years, and you can't do anything with them. Nobody wants to buy them.

Gayev: Why, this orchard is even mentioned in the encyclopedia.

Lopahin (*glancing at his watch*). If we can't think of anything or come up with something, this cherry orchard and the whole estate are going to be sold at auction. Make up your minds. There's no other way out. I swear to you, none whatsoever.

Firs: In the good old days, forty or fifty years ago, they used to dry the cherries, soak them, pickle them, and make them into preserves, and we used to . . .

Gayev: Keep quiet, Firs.

Firs: And they used to ship out the dried cherries by the cartload, to Moscow and Kharkov. The money there was in them! And the cherries used to be so soft and juicy, and sweet, and fragrant . . . They knew the way to do it in the good old days.

Lyubov: But where is the recipe now?

Firs: They've forgotten. No one remembers.

Pishchik: What's going on in Paris? How are things? Did you eat frogs there?

Lyubov: I ate crocodiles.

Pishchik: Can you imagine that!

Lopahin: Up until now there were only landowners and peasants living in the country, but now there are all these summer residents. All the towns, even the very small ones, are surrounded by summer cottages. And I can tell you, in another twenty years the number of summer residents will increase tremendously. Right now, the summer vacationer merely drinks his tea on the porch, but it could very well be that he'll start doing some farming on his couple of acres, and then your cherry orchard will be a happy, rich, magnificent place . . .

Gayev (*angrily*). What twaddle!

[VARYA *and* YASHA *come in.*]

Varya: Two telegrams came for you, Mama dear. (*Selects a key and, with a jingling noise, opens an old fashioned bookcase.*) Here they are.

Lyubov: They're from Paris. (*Tears the telegrams up, without reading them.*) I'm finished with Paris . . .

Gayev: Lyuba, do you know how old that bookcase is? Last week I pulled out the lower drawer, and I looked, and there was the date branded on it. That bookcase was made exactly one hundred years ago. What do you think of that? Perhaps we should celebrate its anniversary. True, it's just an inanimate object, but all the same, everything considered, a bookcase . . .

Pishchik (*astonished*). A hundred years! Can you imagine that?

Gayev: Yes . . . (*Patting it.*) That's really something. Dear, esteemed bookcase, I salute your existence which, for more than a hundred years, has contributed to the ideals of goodness and justice. Your silent call to productive efforts has never weakened in the course of these one hundred years, (*tearfully*) sustaining, from one generation of our family to the next, our courage and our faith in a brighter future and inculcating in us ideals of righteousness and social awareness. (*Pause.*)

Lopahin: Yes . . .

Lyubov: You're just the same as ever, Lyonya.

Gayev (*a little flustered*). Carom shot off the ball on the right into the corner pocket! Cut shot into the side pocket!

Lopahin (*glancing at his watch*). Well, it's time for me to leave . . .

Yasha (*hands some medicine to* LYUBOV). Perhaps you would like to take your pills now . . .

Pishchik: You should never take any medicines, my dear madame. They don't do a thing. Let me have them here . . . highly esteemed lady. (*Takes the pills, shakes them out on his hand, blows on them, puts them in his mouth, and drinks them down with some kvass.*) There!

Lyubov (*alarmed*). You must be out of your mind!

Pishchik: I've taken all the pills.

Lopahin: What a glutton! (*Everybody laughs.*)

Firs: When they visited us during Easter, they ate half a bucket of pickles . . . (*Mutters.*)

Lyubov: What's he talking about?

Varya: He's been muttering like that for the past three years. We're used to it now.

Yasha: His sunset years. (*Ironically.*)

[CHARLOTTA, *very thin, tightly laced, in a white dress, a lorgnette at her waist, walks across the stage.*]

Lopahin: Pardon me, Charlotta Ivanovna, I haven't had time yet to greet you. (*Tries to kiss her hand.*)

Charlotta (*pulling her hand away*). If I allowed you to kiss my hand, next you'll want to kiss my arm and then my shoulder . . .

Lopahin: I guess I'm just out of luck today. (*Everybody laughs.*) Charlotta, show us a trick!

Charlotta: I don't want to. I want to go to bed. (*Goes out.*)

Lopahin: We'll be meeting again in three weeks. (*Kisses* LYUBOV'S *hand.*) Good-bye until then. It's time for me to go. (*To* GAYEV.) So long. (*Kisses* PISH-

CHIK.) So long. (*Shakes hands with* VARYA, *then with* FIRS *and* YASHA.). I really don't want to go. (*To* LYUBOV.) If you think over this summer cottage business and make up your mind, let me know, I can get you a loan of 50,000 roubles. Give it some serious thought.

Varya (*angrily*). Well, you're finally leaving!

Lopahin: I'm leaving, I'm leaving . . . (*Goes out.*)

Gayev: Vulgar fellow. Oh, pardon me . . . I forgot, Varya is going to marry him. He's Varya's boyfriend.

Varya: Don't talk so much, Uncle dear.

Lyubov: What of it, Varya, I would be very happy. He's a nice man.

Pishchik: Yes, you have to admit, he's a most worthy fellow . . . and my Dashenka . . . she also says that . . . she says a lot of things. (*Snores, but wakes up right away.*) Just the same, worthy lady, would you let me have . . . as a loan, of course, two hundred and forty roubles . . . I've got to pay the interest on my mortgage tomorrow . . .

Varya (*frightened*). We can't, we don't have any money!

Pishchik: Oh, well, I'll find it. (*Laughs.*) I never give up hope. Once before, I thought all was lost, finished, when lo and behold, the railroad came through my property . . . and they paid me for it. You'll see, something else will turn up again, if not today, then tomorrow . . . Dashenka will win 200,000 . . . she's got a lottery ticket.

Lyubov: Now that we've had our coffee, we can go to bed.

Firs (*brushing off* GAYEV'S *clothes, reprovingly*). You've put on the wrong trousers again! What am I going to do with you!

Varya (*gently*). Anya's sleeping. (*Quietly opens the window.*) The sun has come up already, it's not cold at all. Look Mama dear, what beautiful trees. And my goodness, what air! The starlings are singing.

Gayev (*opens another window*). The orchard is all white. You haven't forgotten it, have you Lyuba? Look at that long avenue that runs so straight, as if it were a stretched-out string. How it shines on moonlight nights. Do you remember? You haven't forgotten, have you?

Lyubov (*looking out the window into the orchard*). Oh, my childhood, my innocence! I used to sleep in this nursery and look out from here into the orchard . . . And every morning happiness awakened with me. The orchard was just as it is now, nothing has changed. (*Laughs with delight.*) All white, all white! Oh, my orchard. After the dark and dismal autumn and the cold winter, you are young again, and full of happiness, the heavenly angels have never left you . . . If only I could take this heavy burden off my chest and shoulders! If I could only forget my past!

Gayev: Yes, and the orchard will be sold to pay our debts, strange as it may seem . . .

Lyubov: Look, our poor dead mother is walking in the orchard . . . all dressed in white (*Laughs joyfully.*) There she is.

Gayev: Where?

Varya: God bless you, Mama.

Lyubov: No one is there, it was just an illusion. To the right, at the turn to the arbor, is a little white tree bending over. It looks just like a woman . . .

[TROFIMOV *enters, dressed in a worn student's uniform and wearing glasses.*]

Lyubov: What a wonderful orchard! White masses of blossoms, a blue sky . . .

Trofimov: Lyubov Andreyevna! (*She*

looks him over.) I'll just pay my respects and then I'll leave right away. (*Kisses her hand warmly.*) I was told to wait until morning, but I didn't have enough patience . . .

[*Lyubov looks at him, perplexed.*]

Varya (*tearfully*). This is Petya Trofimov . . .

Trofimov: Petya Trofimov, your Grisha's former tutor . . . Is it possible that I have changed so much?

[LYUBOV *embraces him and weeps quietly.*]

Gayev (*flustered*). Now, now, Lyubov.

Varya (*crying*). But Petya, I told you to have patience until tomorrow.

Lyubov: My Grisha . . . my boy . . . Grisha . . . son . . .

Varya: What can we do, Mama dear, it was God's will.

Trofimov (*gently, tearfully*). There . . . there . . .

Lyubov (*weeping quietly*). My little boy died, drowned . . . why? Why, my friend? (*More quietly.*) Anya's asleep in there, and here I am talking so loud . . . making so much noise . . . But what has happened, Petya? Why have you become so homely? Why have you grown so old?

Trofimov: A peasant woman on the train called me a mangy-looking gentleman.

Lyubov: You were only a boy then, a darling little student, and now your hair isn't thick anymore and you're wearing glasses. Is it possible that you're still a student? (*Goes toward the door.*)

Trofimov: It's very likely I'll be a perpetual student.

Lyubov (*kisses her brother, then* VARYA). Well, go to bed now . . . You've grown older too, Leonid.

Pishchik (*follows her*). Well, I guess I'll be going to bed now. Oh, my gout. I'll stay here with you . . . Lyubov Andreyevna, my dear, if you would give me tomorrow morning . . . 240 roubles . . .

Gayev: It's always the same story with him.

Lyubov: But I don't have any money, my friend.

Pishchik: I'll pay it back, my dear . . . it's a trifling sum.

Lyubov: Oh, well, Leonid will give it to you . . . you give it to him, Leonid.

Gayev: Sure, I'll give it to him (*Ironically.*) Here, hold your pockets open.

Lyubov: What can you do? Give it to him . . . he needs it . . . he'll repay us.

[LYUBOV, TROFIMOV, PISHCHIK, *and* FIRS *go out;* GAYEV, VARYA, *and* YASHA *remain.*]

Gayev: My sister hasn't lost her habit of tossing money around. (*To* YASHA.) Go away, my good fellow, you smell of chickens.

Yasha (*grinning.*) And you, Leonid Andreyevich, are the same as you always were.

Gayev: What? (*To* VARYA.) What did he say?

Varya (*to* YASHA). Your mother's here from the village. She's been sitting in the servant's room since yesterday, waiting to see you . . .

Yasha: God bless her! (*Ironically*).

Varya: You shameless wretch!

Yasha: She's all I need. She could have waited until tomorrow.

[*Goes out.*]

Varya: Mama is the same as always, she hasn't changed a bit. If she had her own way, she'd give away everything she has.

Gayev: Yes . . . (*Pause.*) If a great

many remedies are recommended for a disease, you can rest assured it's incurable. I keep thinking and racking my brains. I have many remedies, a great many, and, as a matter of fact, that really means I have none. It would be fine if we inherited something from someone, or if we married off Anya to a very rich man, or if we went to Yaroslavl to try our luck with our dear aunt, the Countess. Auntie's very, very rich, you know . . .

Varya (*weeping*). If only God would help us!

Gayev: Stop bawling! Auntie's very rich, but she doesn't care very much for us. First of all, sister married a lawyer, not a nobleman . . . (ANYA *appears in the doorway.*) . . . she didn't marry a nobleman and, you must admit, didn't conduct herself very virtuously. She's good, she's kind, she's sweet, I love her very much, but, but no matter how many allowances you make for her, you must admit she's an immoral woman. Why, you can sense it in her slightest movement!

Varya (*whispering*). Anya's standing in the doorway.

Gayev: Who? (*Pause.*) That's odd, something got into my right eye . . . I can't see very well . . . and on Thursday, when I was at the District Court . . .

[*Enter* ANYA.]

Varya: Why aren't you asleep, Anya?

Anya: I couldn't fall asleep.

Gayev: My dear child. (*Kisses* ANYA'S *face and hands.*) My child . . . (*Tearfully.*) You are not my niece, you are my angel . . . you're everything to me. Believe me, believe me . . .

Anya: I believe you, Uncle. Everybody loves you and respects you . . . but, dear Uncle, you must keep quiet . . . just keep quiet. What were you saying just now about my mama, about your own sister? Why did you say that?

Gayev: Yes, yes . . . (*He covers his face with her hands.*) Really, that was terrible! My goodness! Heaven help me! And today, I delivered a speech to the bookcase . . . so idiotic! Not until I got through did I see how idiotic it was.

Varya: That's right, uncle dear, you should keep quiet. Just keep quiet, that's all.

Anya: If you could keep quiet, you would have more peace for yourself too.

Gayev: I'll keep quiet. (*Kisses* ANYA *and* VARYA *on the hands.*) I will. Only, there's this business. Last Thursday I went to the District Court, and well, I got together with some friends, and we got talking about this and that, one thing after another, and it seemed to me that I might be able to arrange a loan on a promissory note so we could pay the interest off at the bank.

Varya: If only God would help us!

Gayev: On Tuesday I'll go and talk about it again. (*To* VARYA.) Stop bawling. (*To* ANYA.) Your mama will talk to Lopahin; and, naturally, he wouldn't refuse her . . . and, as soon as you're rested, you will go to your great-aunt, the Countess, in Yaroslavl. So we'll be working in three directions at the same time—and our business will be all wrapped up. We'll pay off the interest on the mortgage, I'm positive of that . . . (*Puts a piece of candy in his mouth.*) On my honor, I swear by anything you like, the estate won't be sold! (*Excitedly.*) I swear by my own happiness, the estate will not be sold. Here is my hand on it, call me the vilest, meanest of men if I let the estate go at an auction! I swear by my whole being.

Anya (*a quiet mood returns to her and*

she is happy again). How good you are, Uncle! How clever! (*Embraces him.*) Now I am at peace. Now I'm happy!

[FIRS *comes in.*]

Firs (*reproachfully*). Leonid Andreyevich, have you no fear of God? When are you going to bed?

Gayev: Right away, right away. Go away, Firs. I'll undress myself this time. Come, children, nightie-night . . . We'll go over the details tomorrow, but now go to bed. (*Kisses* ANYA *and* VARYA.) I'm a man of the 1880's . . . They don't have much to say for that period nowadays. But all the same, I can honestly say that I have suffered more than a little for my principles in my lifetime. It's not for nothing that the peasants love me. One must know the peasant! One must understand, what . . .

Anya: You're at it again, Uncle!

Varya: Uncle dear, please be quiet.

Firs (*angrily*). Leonid Andreyevich!

Gayev: I'm coming, I'm coming . . . Go to bed. Double cushion shot into the side pocket! There goes a nice clean shot . . . (*Goes out;* FIRS *totters after him.*)

Anya: My mind's at rest now. I don't want to go to Yaroslavl. I don't like Great-Aunt, but now my mind is completely at rest. Thanks to Uncle.

Varya: We must get to bed. While you were gone, something unpleasant occurred. In the old servant's quarters, as you know, there are only a few old servants: Ephimyushka, Polya, Evstigney, and Karp also. They began to let all sorts of tramps spend the night . . . I kept quiet at first. But then, I heard they had been spreading a story that I had given orders to feed them nothing but peas. Out of stinginess, you understand . . . it was all because of Evstigney . . . Fine, I say. If that's the way it is, I say, just you wait. I call Evstigney . . . (*Yawns.*) He comes . . . "What's this all about, Evstigney?" I say . . . "What a fool you are . . ." (*Looks at* ANYA.) Anitchka! . . . (*Pause.*) She fell asleep . . . (*Takes her by the hand.*) Let's go to bed . . . Let's go . . . (*Leads her.*) My little darling has fallen asleep! Let's go . . . (*They go.*)

[*Far off beyond the orchard a shepherd plays his pipe.* TROFIMOV *crosses the stage and, seeing* VARYA *and* ANYA, *stops.*]

Varya: Shh . . . She's asleep . . . she's asleep . . . Let's go, dear.

Anya (*softly, half-asleep*). I'm so tired . . . All those bells . . . Uncle . . . dear . . . Mama and Uncle . . .

Varya: Let's go, my dear, let's go . . . (*They both go into* ANYA'S *room.*)

Trofimov (*with feeling*). My sunshine! My springtime!

ACT II

[*A field. An old, long neglected little chapel, leaning over to one side, near it, a well, large stones, apparently former tombstones, and an old bench. A road to* GAYEV'S *property can be seen. At one side, poplar trees rise up darkly at the edge of the cherry orchard. In the middle distance is a row of telegraph poles, and in the far distance, on the horizon, a large city, which is fully visible only on a clear day, can be indistinctly made out. The sun will soon set.* CHARLOTTA, YASHA *and* DUNYASHA *are sitting on the bench.* EPIHODOV *stands nearby, playing a guitar. They are all absorbed in thought.* CHARLOTTA *is wearing an old cap; she has lowered a gun from her shoulder and is adjusting the buckle on the shoulder strap.*]

Charlotta (*absorbed in thought*). I don't have a regular passport. I don't even know how old I am, and yet it always seems to me that I'm very young. When I was a little girl, my father and mother used to go to different fairs and give performances, very good ones too. And I used to do the flying somersault and other little stunts. And when Papa and Mama died, a German lady took me in and gave me an education. Well and good. When I grew up, I started working as a governess. But where I came from and who I am—I don't know. I don't really know who my parents were, perhaps they weren't even married. (*Takes a cucumber out of her pocket and eats it.*) I don't know a thing. (*Pause.*) I want to talk to someone so badly, but there's no one to talk to . . . I don't have anybody.

Epihodov (*plays on the guitar and sings*). "What is the worrisome world to me, what is friend or foe to me?" How pleasant it is to play the mandolin.

Dunyasha: It's a guitar, not a mandolin. (*She looks at herself in a pocket mirror and powders her face.*)

Epihodov: To a madman in love, it's a mandolin . . . (*Sings.*) "Would that my heart were warmed by the warmth of love returned . . ." (YASHA *sings along with him.*)

Charlotta: How wretchedly these people sing . . . phooey! They sound like jackals.

Dunyasha (*to* YASHA). At least you've been fortunate enough to have traveled abroad.

Yasha: Yes, of course. I can't help but agree with you. (*Yawns, then lights a cigar.*)

Epihodov: To be sure. Everything abroad has long since attained a state of perfection.

Yasha: That goes without saying.

Epihodov: I'm a cultured man. I read all sorts of remarkable books, but I can't determine the precise direction to take—to be honest about it—whether to go on living or to shoot myself. But nevertheless, I always carry a revolver on me. Here it is . . . (*Shows a revolver.*)

Charlotta: I'm all through, I'm leaving now. (*Slings the gun over her shoulder.*) You're a very clever fellow, Epihodov, and a very fearsome one. The women must just love you to distraction. Brrr! . . . (*Going.*) These clever people are all so ridiculous. There's nobody I can talk to . . . I'm always alone, all alone. I don't have anyone . . . And who I am and why I am, no one knows . . .

[*Leaves in a leisurely fashion.*]

Epihodov: To be honest about it, not referring to anything else, I must say this about myself, among other things, fate buffets me without pity, as a storm does a small boat. If we admit for a moment that I might be wrong, why then, for instance, do I wake up this morning and see on my chest a great big spider . . . look, this big . . . (*demonstrating with both hands*). And then when I go to drink some kvass, what do I see there but something extremely loathesome, like a cockroach.

(*Pause.*) Have you read the [English] historian Buckle? (*Pause.*) Avdotya Fyodorovna, I would like to trouble you with a few words.

Dunyasha: Go ahead and talk.

Epihodov: I would like to speak to you privately. (*Sighs.*)

Dunyasha (*in confusion*). Very well . . . but first bring me my cape . . . It's by the cupboard . . . It's a little damp here . . .

Epihodov: Yes, milady . . . I will fetch it, milady . . . Now I know what to do with my revolver . . . (*Takes the guitar and goes off, strumming it.*)

Yasha: A born loser! Between you and me, I must say he's a stupid fellow . . . (*Yawns.*)

Dunyasha: God forbid that he should shoot himself. (*Pause.*) I've become so nervous lately. I'm always upset. I was only a little girl when they took me into the master's house, and now I'm unaccustomed to the simple life. Look, my hands are as white as any lady's. I've become so delicate and genteel, I'm afraid of everything . . . simply terrified. And if you deceive me, Yasha, I don't know what will become of my nerves!

Yasha (*kisses her*). You little cucumber! Of course, a girl should know enough not to lose her head. And what I dislike most of all is a girl not behaving herself right.

Dunyasha: I've fallen madly in love with you. You're so educated. You can talk about anything.

Yasha (*yawns*). Yes, ma'am . . . To my way of thinking, if a girl loves someone, then she's immoral. (*Pause.*) It's pleasant smoking a cigar out in the fresh air. (*Listens.*) Someone's coming this way . . . it's the ladies and gentlemen. (DUNYASHA *embraces him impulsively.*)

Yasha: Go back to the house as if you had gone down to the river to bathe. Take this path, or they'll run into you and think that I had arranged to meet you here. I can't stand their thinking that.

Dunyasha (*coughs quietly*). Your cigar has given me a headache . . .

[*Leaves.*]

[YASHA remains, sitting near the chapel. LYUBOV, GAYEV, *and* LOPAHIN *come in.*]

Lopahin: Sooner or later you've got to make up your mind . . . Time doesn't stand still. The whole question is very easy to settle, you know. Do you agree to rent your land out for summer cottages or not? Answer one word, yes or no. Only one word!

Lyubov: Who smokes those disgusting cigars out here? (*Sits.*)

Gayev: It's nice and convenient for us, having the railroad close by . . . (*Sits down.*) . . . To be able to go into town and have lunch as we did . . . yellow ball in the side pocket! Maybe first I should go into the house and play just one game . . .

Lyubov: You've got plenty of time.

Lopahin: Only one word! (*entreatingly.*) Please give me your answer!

Gayev (*yawning*). What?

Lyubov (*looks into her purse*). Yesterday there was a lot of money in my purse, but today there's scarcely any. My poor Varya tries to save money by feeding all of us milk soup, and in the kitchen she gives them nothing but peas to eat while I manage to spend it foolishly somehow, in one absurd way or another. (*Drops the purse, scattering gold coins all over.*) There they go—pouring out . . . (*Annoyed.*)

Yasha: Allow me . . . I'll pick them up. (*Picks up the money.*)

Lyubov: If you would be so kind, Yasha. And why did I go out to lunch . . . Your trashy old restaurant with its music, those table cloths smelling of soap . . . Why drink so much, Lyonya? Why eat so much? Why talk so much? Today again in the restaurant you were talking so much and so pointlessly. About the 1870's, about the decadents. And to whom? To waiters, about decadents!

Lopahin: Yes.

Gayev (*waving his hand*). I'm incorrigible, that's obvious. (*To* YASHA, *irritably.*) What's the matter with you, always buzzing around in front of me . . .

Yasha (*laughs*). I can't hear your voice without laughing.

Gayev (*to his sister*). Either he or I . . .

Lyubov: Get out of here, Yasha. Be on your way . . .

Yasha (*gives* LYUBOV *her purse*). I'm leaving right now. (*Scarcely able to restrain his laughter.*) This very minute . . . (*Leaves.*)

Lopahin: That rich fellow Deriganov intends to buy your estate. They say he's going to come to the auction himself.

Lyubov: And where did you hear this?

Lopahin: They're saying it in town.

Gayev: Our aunt in Yaroslavl promised to send us some money; but when and how much she will send, nobody knows . . .

Lopahin: How much is she going to send? A hundred thousand? Two hundred?

Lyubov: Well . . . ten or fifteen thousand, and we'd be grateful for that even.

Lopahin: Pardon me, but such heedless, unbusinesslike, odd people as you, I never met before in my life. You are told in plain language that your estate is going to be sold, but it's just as if you didn't understand a word.

Lyubov: But what can we do? Tell us, what can we do?

Lopahin: I've been telling you every day. Every day I keep telling you the same old thing. It's urgent that the cherry orchard and the land be leased for summer cottages. And it must be done now—right away—the auction is right under your nose! Get this straight! Once you've definitely made up your mind to have the cottages, you can have as much money as you want, and you'll be saved.

Lyubov: Cottages and summer residents—pardon me, but this is all so trivial.

Gayev: I'm absolutely in agreement with you.

Lopahin: I'm either going to break down and cry or start shouting, or maybe even pass out. I just can't stand it! You've worn me out! (*To* GAYEV.) You old woman!

Gayev: What?

Lopahin: Old woman. (*Starts to go.*)

Lyubov (*alarmed*). No, don't go! Please stay, my friend. I beg you. Perhaps we can think of something!

Lopahin: What is there to think of?

Lyubov: Don't go, I beg you. At least it's more cheerful when you're here. (*Pause.*) I've been expecting something to happen all the time . . . It's as if the house was ready to fall apart around us.

Gayev: (*Reflecting sadly*). Combination shot in the corner . . . Bank shot in the side pocket. . . .

Lyubov: What great sinners we have been.

Lopahin: How have you sinned . . . ?

Gayev (*puts a piece of candy in his*

mouth). They say that I've spent my fortune on candy! (*laughs.*)

Lyubov: Oh, my sins! . . . I have always thrown money around recklessly, like someone out of his mind, and I married a man who did nothing but go into debt. My husband drowned himself in champagne . . . he drank with a passion. And then, to my misfortune, I fell in love with someone else. I gave myself to him. And just at that time came my first punishment, a real low blow—right here in this river my poor little boy was drowned. And I went abroad . . . went away for good . . . never to return, never to see this river again . . . I closed my eyes and ran, not knowing what I was doing. But he ran after me . . . pitilessly, callously. I bought a villa near Mentone, because he fell sick there, and for three years I knew no rest, day or night. The sick man wore me out, my soul shriveled up. And then this past year, when the villa was sold to pay my debts, I went to Paris, and there he robbed me, deserted me, and took up with another woman. I tried to poison myself . . . How stupid it was, how shameful! . . . And suddenly I was overwhelmed by a deep longing for Russia, my native land, for my little girl . . . (*Wipes her tears away.*) Dear God, Dear God, be merciful, forgive me my sins! Don't punish me any more! (*Takes a telegram out of her pocket.*) I received this from Paris today . . . he begs my forgiveness, pleads with me to return to him . . . (*Tears up the telegram.*) . . . Can that be music somewhere? (*Listens.*)

Gayev: That's our famous Jewish orchestra. You know—four violins, a flute, and a double bass.

Lyubov: Are they still around? We ought to have them over sometime to give a little party.

Lopahin (*listens*). I don't hear anything . . . (*Sings quietly.*) "A German will turn a Russian into a Frenchman for money." (*Laughs.*) What a play I saw at the theater yesterday—really funny.

Lyubov: There was probably nothing funny about it at all. Instead of looking at plays, you should look at yourselves more often. What colorless lives you lead, how much of what you talk about is so useless!

Lopahin: You're right. To be frank about it, the kind of life we lead is stupid . . . (*Pause.*) My father was a peasant, an idiot; he didn't know a thing and never taught me anything. All he did was beat me whenever he got drunk, and always with a stick. Actually, I'm as much of a blockhead and idiot as he was. I was never taught anything. My handwriting is horrible. I write like a pig, so bad I'm even ashamed to have people see it.

Lyubov: You should get married, my friend.

Lopahin: Yes . . . that's true.

Lyubov: To our Varya. She's a good girl.

Lopahin: Yes.

Lyubov: She comes from simple people, works hard all day long, but, most important, she's in love with you. And besides, you've liked her for a long time.

Lopahin: Why not? I'm not opposed to the idea . . . She's a good girl. (*Pause.*)

Gayev: They've offered me a position at the bank. Six thousand a year. Have you heard about it?

Lyubov: How can you even think of it! You stay right where you are!

[FIRS *comes in, carrying an overcoat.*]

Firs: Please, sir, put this on. It's damp here.

Gayev (*puts on the overcoat*). I'm tired of you, friend.

Firs: There's no use arguing. This morning you went off without letting me know. (*Looks him over.*)

Lyubov: How old you've gotten, Firs!

Firs: Can I do something for you, Madame?

Lopahin: She says you've grown old.

Firs: I've lived a long time. They were rounding up a wife for me before your father even came into this world . . . (*Laughs.*) When freedom came, I was already the head footman. I wouldn't agree to being set free, but stayed on with my masters . . . As I remember, they were all very happy, but what they were happy about, they themselves didn't know.

Lopahin: Things were fine in the old days. At least they used to flog.

Firs (*not hearing clearly*). Certainly it was. The peasants were for the masters, and the masters for the peasants, but today everything's fallen apart. You don't know what's going on.

Gayev: Keep quiet, Firs. Tomorrow I have to go into town. They have promised to introduce me to some general who might lend us money on a promissory note.

Lopahin: Nothing will come of that. Don't you realize you won't even be able to pay the interest?

Lyubov: Oh, he's just talking nonsense. There isn't any such general.

[TROFIMOV, ANYA *and* VARYA *come in.*]

Gayev: Here come the young people.

Anya: There's Mama, sitting on the bench.

Lyubov (*tenderly*). Come, come . . . my darlings . . . (*Embraces* ANYA *and* VARYA.) If you only knew how much I love the two of you! Sit down beside me, right here. (*They all sit down.*)

Lopahin: Our perpetual student is always going around with the young ladies.

Trofimov: That's none of your business.

Lopahin: He'll soon be fifty, and he's still a student!

Trofimov: Why don't you lay off those stupid jokes of yours?

Lopahin: What are you so upset about, you odd fellow?

Trofimov: You just never stop teasing, do you?

Lopahin (*laughing*). Let me ask you. What's your opinion of me?

Trofimov: My opinion of you is this, Yermolay Alexeyevich: you're a rich man, you'll soon be a millionaire. In the same way that a carnivorous beast that eats everything that comes along is necessary in the nature of things, so also are you necessary. (*Everybody laughs.*)

Varya: Petya, maybe you'd better talk about the planets.

Lyubov: Let's take up where we left off yesterday.

Trofimov: What were we talking about?

Gayev: About human pride.

Trofimov: We talked a long time yesterday, but we didn't settle anything. As you use the term there is something mystical about human pride. You may be right from the way you look at it, but if we discuss this simply without splitting hairs, then what reason is there for pride? Is there any justification for it considering that man is so poorly put together physiologically, considering that in the overwhelming majority of instances he is crude, stupid, and extremely unhappy? We should stop admiring ourselves. The only thing we should do is work.

Gayev: In spite of all this, you will die.

Trofimov: Who knows? And what

does it mean when you say, "You will die"? Perhaps man is endowed with a hundred senses and maybe only those five known to us perish, while the other ninety-five stay alive.

Lyubov: How clever you are, Petya . . . !

Lopahin (*ironically*). Amazingly clever!

Trofimov: Mankind moves ever forward constantly perfecting its powers. Everything that is now beyond our reach will some day come within our grasp and be easily understood. But the only thing is we must work and help with all our strength those who seek the truth. Among us in Russia so far only a very few of us work. The overwhelming majority of the intellectuals, as far as I know, are not seeking anything. They do nothing and as yet are unfit for work. They call themselves the intelligentsia, yet they address their servants contemptuously, they treat the peasants like animals, they don't bother to get an education, they never read anything serious and do absolutely nothing at all, except merely talk about science, and they scarcely have any acquaintance with art at all. They all pretend to be very serious people and they go about with stern faces. They all talk about nothing but very weighty matters and go about spouting philosophy, but at the same time the overwhelming majority among us, ninety-nine out of a hundred, live like savages. For the flimsiest reason—at the smallest provocation—bang goes a punch in the mouth and insulting language. They eat disgustingly, sleep in filthy, suffocating rooms, with bedbugs, stench, sliminess and moral corruption . . . Obviously, all our elevated conversation does is to divert the attention of ourselves and others from this real evil. Tell me, where are our kindergartens which we have been told about so much and often, where are all the libraries? They only write about them in novels, but in actuality, there aren't any. There is only filth, triviality and oriental torpor. I'm afraid that I don't like this serious philosophizing very much. I'm afraid of these lofty speculations of theirs. We'd be better off just keeping still!

Lopahin: Do you realize that I get up at five in the morning and work from morning until evening? I'm constantly dealing with my own money and money belonging to strangers, and I see what people are like. You only have to start doing something, anything at all, to learn how few honest and decent people there are in this world. Sometimes, when I can't get to sleep, I think: "Oh Lord, Thou hast given us exceedingly great forests, vast plains, and the widest horizons, and living here on earth, we should ourselves verily be giants . . ."

Lyubov: You're asking for giants . . . They're only good in fairy tales; in real life they only frighten us.

[EPIHODOV *goes across the rear of the stage, strumming on the guitar.*]

Lyubov (*musingly*). Here comes Epihodov.

Anya (*musingly*). Here comes Epihodov.

Gayev: The sun has set, ladies and gentlemen.

Trofimov: Yes.

Gayev (*rather softly, as if reciting*). Oh, wonderful Nature, Thou shinest with perpetual radiance, beautiful and indifferent, Thou, whom we call Mother, contain within Thyself both life and death, Thou createst and Thou destroyest . . .

Varya (*entreatingly*). Uncle dear!

Anya: Uncle, you're at it again!

Trofimov: You'd better play a combination shot off the yellow ball into the side pocket.

Gayev: I'll keep quiet, I'll keep quiet.

[*They all sit deep in thought. Silence. The only sound is* FIRS *muttering softly to himself. Suddenly, a far-off sound is heard, as if coming from the sky, the sound of a snapped string dying sorrowfully away.*]

Lyubov: What's that?

Lopahin: I don't know. Somewhere far away in a mine-shaft a bucket must have fallen down. But somewhere very far away.

Gayev: Maybe it was some kind of bird—like a heron.

Trofimov: Or an owl . . .

Lyubov (*shudders*). Well, anyway, it was unpleasant.

Firs: Before the calamity the same thing happened—the owl screeched and the samovar droned away without stopping.

Gayev: Before what calamity?

Firs: Before the freeing of the serfs. (*Pause.*)

Lyubov: My friends, we'd better be going. It's getting dark. (*To* ANYA.) You have tears in your eyes . . . What is it, my little girl? (*Embraces her.*)

Anya: It's nothing, Mama.

Trofimov: Someone's coming.

[A TRAMP *appears, dressed in a white cap and an overcoat; he is slightly drunk.*]

Tramp: Permit me to inquire of you, can I get to the station straight through here?

Gayev: Yes, you can. Take that road.

Tramp: My sincerest thanks to you. (*Coughing.*) The weather is splendid. (*Declaims.*) "Brother of mine, my suffering brother . . . come out to the Volga, whose moans . . . (*To* VARYA.) Mademoiselle, could you please allow a hungry Russian thirty kopecks? (VARYA, *frightened, cries out.*)

Lopahin (*angrily*). Every impropriety has its limits, you know!

Lyubov (*losing her composure*). Here . . . take this . . . (*fumbling in her purse*). I haven't any small change, but never mind, here's a gold piece.

Tramp: My sincerest thanks to you. (*Goes out. Laughter.*)

Varya (*frightened*). I'm going—I'm going . . . Oh, Mama dear, at home the servants have nothing to eat, and you give him a gold piece.

Lyubov: What can you do with foolish me! When we get back home, I'll give you everything that I have. Yermolay Alexeyich, will you let me borrow some more? . . .

Lopahin: Of course.

Lyubov: Let us go, ladies and gentlemen, it's time. We have definitely arranged your engagement. Congratulations.

Varya (*tearfully*). You shouldn't joke about something like that, Mama.

Lopahin: "Akmelia, get thee to a nunnery!"

Gayev: My hands are trembling; it's been a long time since I've played billiards.

Lopahin: Akmelia, oh nymph, remember me in all thy prayers!

Lyubov: Let's go, ladies and gentlemen. It'll soon be time for supper.

Varya: That tramp frightened me so. My heart is still pounding.

Lopahin: I want to remind you, ladies and gentlemen—the cherry orchard will be put up for sale on the twenty-second of August. Think about it! Think! . . .

[*They all go out except* TROFIMOV *and* ANYA.]

Anya (*laughing*). I'm glad that tramp frightened Varya, now we're alone.

Trofimov: Varya's afraid we might suddenly fall in love with one another. She hasn't left us alone all day. Her narrow mind just can't comprehend that we are above love. To shun the petty and illusory, all that keeps us from being free and happy, that is the purpose and meaning of our lives. Forward! We move on irresistibly toward that bright star that burns far off in the distance. Forward! Do not stay behind, friends!

Anya (*clapping her hands together.*): How well you speak! (*Pause.*) It's wonderful here today!

Trofimov: Yes, the weather is marvelous.

Anya: What have you done with me, Petya? Why don't I love the cherry orchard the way I used to. I used to love it so tenderly that I thought there was no better place on earth than our orchard.

Trofimov: All Russia is our orchard. The land is vast and beautiful, there are many marvelous places in it. (*Pause.*) Just think, Anya, your grandfather, your great-grandfather, and all your forefathers were supporters of serfdom, the owners of living souls. Isn't it possible that from every cherry tree in the orchard, from every leaf, from every trunk a human being is looking at you? Is it possible that you do not hear their voices? . . . Oh, this is terrible! Your orchard is a frightening place. When in the evening or at night you walk through the orchard, the old bark on the trees glistens dimly and it seems that the cherry trees see in their dreams what happened a hundred or two hundred years ago and they are in torment from their sorrowful visions. What can you say! We are behind at least two hundred years, as yet we have absolutely nothing, no definite attitude toward the past. We only spout philosophy, complain of boredom, or drink vodka. But it's so obvious: in order to begin life in the present, we must first of all atone for our past, do away with it, and we can atone for it only through suffering, only through extraordinary, unremitting toil. Remember this, Anya.

Anya: The house we live in has not been ours for a long time, and I will leave, I give you my word.

Trofimov: If you have the household keys, hurl them into the well and go away. Be as free as the wind.

Anya (*ecstatically*). How well you put it!

Trofimov: Believe me, Anya, believe me! I'm not yet thirty, I'm young, I'm still a student, but I have already endured so much! When winter comes I am hungry, sick, distressed, poor as a beggar. And where hasn't fate driven me, where haven't I been? And yet all this while, my soul, every minute of the day and night, has been full of unexplainable intimations. I have a premonition of happiness, Anya, I see it already . . .

Anya (*pensively*). The moon is rising.

[*The sound of* EPIHODOV *playing the same sorrowful tune on the guitar. The moon rises. Somewhere near the poplars* VARYA *is looking for* ANYA *and calling*: "Anya, where are you?"]

Trofimov: Yes, the moon is rising. (*Pause.*) There it is—happiness, here it comes approaching ever nearer and nearer. I can already hear its footsteps. And if we don't see it, if we don't recognize it, what does it matter? Others will see it.

Varya's Voice: Anya! Where are you?

Trofimov: That Varya again! (*Angrily.*) It's shocking!

Anya: It doesn't matter. Let's go down to the river. It's beautiful there.

Trofimov: Let's go. (*They go out.*)

Varya's Voice: Anya! Anya!

ACT III

[*The salon, separated from the ballroom by an arch. A chandelier is burning. A Jewish orchestra, the one mentioned in Act II, is heard playing in the anteroom. In the ballroom they are dancing the "Grand Rond." The voice of* SEMYON-PISHCHIK: "Promenade à une paire!" *They come into the salon: the first couple is* PISHCHIK *and* CHARLOTTA; *the second,* TROFIMOV *and* LYUBOV ANDREYEVNA; *the third,* ANYA *and the* POST OFFICE CLERK; *the fourth,* VARYA *and the* STATIONMASTER, etc. VARYA *is weeping quietly as she dances, wiping away her tears at the same time. In the last couple is* DUNYASHA. *They all promenade through the salon.* PISHCHIK *shouts:* "Grand Rond, balancez!" *and* "Les cavaliers à genoux et remerciez vos dames!"]

[FIRS, *attired in a swallow-tailed coat, brings in soda water on a tray.* PISHCHIK *and* TROFIMOV *enter the salon.*]

Pishchik: I've got high blood pressure, you know. I've already had two strokes. Dancing is a strain on me, but, you know what they say, if you run with the pack, whether you bark or not, you've still got to wag your tail. Actually, though, I'm as strong as a horse. My poor dead father, jokester that he was, used to say, in talking about our family, that the ancient line of the Semyonov-Pishchiks could trace its origin back to that very same horse that Caligula appointed to the Senate . . . (*Sits down.*) But the big difficulty is that I don't have any money! A hungry dog has no faith in anything but meat . . . (*Snores but wakes up instantly.*) That's the way it is with me . . . I can't think of anything but money . . .

Trofimov: Come to think about it, you do look something like a horse.

Pishchik: Oh well, anyway a horse is a good animal—at least you can sell him . . .

[*The sound of billiard playing can be heard coming from the adjoining room.* VARYA *comes into view under the arch leading to the ballroom.*]

Trofimov (*teasing*). Madame Lopahin! Madame Lopahin!

Varya (*angrily*). Mangy-looking gentleman.

Trofimov: Yes, I am a mangy-looking gentleman and I'm proud of it!

Varya (*musing bitterly*). Now we've gone and hired musicians! What are we going to use to pay them with?

Trofimov (*to* PISHCHIK). If you used all that energy you've wasted in your lifetime looking for money to pay the interest on your mortgage, on anything else at all, you probably would have stood the world on its head.

Pishchik: Nietzsche . . . the philosopher . . . the greatest, the most famous of men . . . a man of the highest intellect, says in his writings that it is permissible to make counterfeit banknotes.

Trofimov: And have you read Nietzsche?

Pishchik: Well, not exactly . . . Dashenka told me. And I'm in such a pickle now I could even forge a few banknotes myself . . . The day after tomorrow I've got to pay 310 roubles . . . I've already got my hands on 130 . . . (*Feels in his pockets, frantically.*) The money is gone! I've lost the money! (*Tearfully.*) Where can the money be? (*Joyfully.*) Ah, here it is—inside the lining . . . That sure threw me into a sweat!

[LYUBOV and CHARLOTTA *enter.*]

Lyubov (*humming a popular dance tune*). Why isn't Leonid here yet? What could he be doing in town? (*To* DUNYASHA.) Offer the musicians some tea . . .

Trofimov: In all probability the auction hasn't been held yet.

Lyubov: The musicians came at a bad time, and we arranged the ball at a bad time . . . Well, never mind . . . (*Sits down, humming softly.*)

Charlotta (*handing a deck of cards to* PISHCHIK). Here's a deck of cards. Now just think of a card . . . any card.

Pishchik: All right, I have.

Charlotta: Now shuffle the cards. Very good. Give them back to me now, my dear Mr. Pishchik. Ein, zwei, drei! Now . . . lo and behold, it's in your breast pocket.

Pishchik (*taking a card out of his breast pocket*). The eight of spades! Why, you're absolutely right! (*Astonished.*) Can you imagine that!

Charlotta (*holding the deck of cards in the palm of her hand; to* TROFIMOV). Tell me quickly—what is the top card?

Trofimov: What? Well, then, the queen of spades.

Charlotta: That's it! . . . (*To* PISHCHIK.) Well, now? What card is on top?

Pishchik: The ace of hearts.

Charlotta: That's it! . . . (*She claps her hands and the deck of cards disappears.*) And what beautiful weather we are having today! (*A mysterious feminine voice which seems to come from beneath the floor answers her:* "Oh, yes, splendid weather, madame.") You are such a most perfect ideal . . . (*The voice:* "and you, madame, please me very much.")

Stationmaster (*applauding*). A lady ventriloquist, bravo!

Pishchik (*astonished*). Well, can you imagine that! The most charming Charlotta Ivanovna . . . I'm positively in love with you . . .

Charlotta: In love? (*Shrugging her shoulders.*) Is it possible that you can love? Guter Mensch, aber schlechter Musikant.

Trofimov (*slapping* PISHCHIK *on the shoulder*). What a horse you are . . .

Charlotta: Attention, please. One more trick. (*She takes a plaid blanket from a chair.*) See this very nice plaid. Well, I would like to sell it . . . (*She shakes it out.*) Doesn't anyone want to buy it?

Pishchik (*astonished*). Can you imagine that!

Charlotta: Ein, zwei, drei! (*She quickly raises the plaid blanket; behind it stands* ANYA, *who make a curtsy, runs to her mother, embraces her, and then runs back to the ballroom. Everyone is delighted.*)

Lyubov (*applauding*). Bravo, bravo!

Charlotta: Now, once more. Ein,

zwei, drei! (*She lifts the plaid. Behind it stands* VARYA, *who makes a bow.*)

Pishchik (*astonished*). Can you imagine that!

Charlotta: That's it. (*She tosses the plaid at* PISHCHIK, *makes a curtsy, and runs off to the ballroom.*)

Pishchik (*running after her*). You rascal, you . . . what a woman!

[*Goes out.*]

Lyubov: All this time and Leonid is still not here. I just don't understand what he can be doing in town so long. It must be all over by now. Either the estate has been sold or the auction hasn't been held yet. But why does he keep us in suspense so long?

Varya (*trying to comfort her*). Uncle has bought it. I'm sure of it.

Trofimov (*sarcastically*). Of course he has.

Varya: Our great-aunt has sent him a power of attorney to buy it in her name and transfer the loan. She did it for Anya. I'm certain Uncle will buy it, God willing.

Lyubov: Our great-aunt in Yaroslavl sent us 15,000 in order to buy the estate in her name—she has no confidence in us—but that amount of money wouldn't even be enough to pay the interest on the mortgage. (*She covers her face with her hands.*) Today my fate is being decided, my fate . . .

Trofimov (*teasing* VARYA). Madame Lopahin!

Varya (*angrily*). You perpetual student, you. You've already been dropped from the university twice.

Lyubov: Why do you get so angry, Varya? What if he does tease you about Lopahin? If you want to, go ahead and marry Lopahin. He's a nice, interesting fellow. If you don't want to, then don't marry him. No one is forcing you, my dear.

Varya: To be frank about it, mama, I take this matter very seriously. He is a nice man and I like him.

Lyubov: Well, then, marry him. I don't understand what you're waiting for.

Varya: Mama, I just can't propose to him myself. For the past two years everybody has been talking to me about him—everybody else talks, but he himself either just keeps quiet or cracks jokes. Oh, I can understand all right. He's making money, he's tied up with business matters; he just doesn't have time for me. If there were any money, even a little bit, just a hundred roubles, I would drop everything and go away. I would go to a convent.

Trofimov: Such saintliness!

Varya (*to* TROFIMOV). You ought to have more sense than that! (*Tearfully, softly.*) How homely you have become, Petya. How you have aged. (*To* LYUBOV, *no longer weeping.*) But I just can't get along without something to do, Mama. I have to keep busy every minute.

[YASHA *enters.*]

Yasha (*scarcely able to keep from laughing.*) Epihodov just broke a billiard cue. (*Goes out.*)

Varya: But why is Epihodov here in the first place? Who gave him permission to play billiards? I just don't understand these people . . . (*Goes out.*)

Lyubov: Don't tease her so, Petya. You know she has enough troubles without that.

Trofimov: She's just too officious. She interferes in things that are none of her business. All summer long she wouldn't let Anya or me have any peace at all. She was afraid that a romance might develop between us. What business of hers would that be? Besides, I gave her no grounds for believing so. I'm too far removed from such trivialities. We are both above love!

Lyubov: And I, I suppose, must be beneath love. (*Extremely agitated.*) Why isn't Leonid here? All I would like to know is—has the estate been sold or not? This calamity seems so incredible to me that I still don't know what to think. I've lost all control of myself. I could scream this very moment. I could make a complete fool of myself. Save me, Petya. Tell me anything, anything . . .

Trofimov: Isn't it all the same whether the estate is sold today or not? That was all finished long ago. There is no turning back. The path is all grown over. Calm yourself, my dear. You must not deceive yourself. For once in your life, you must look the truth straight in the eye.

Lyubov: What truth? You can see the difference between truth and illusion, but I seem to have lost my sight. I can see nothing. You have the courage to resolve all your problems. But tell me, my dear boy, isn't that because you are so young and that you have not yet begun to suffer because of your problems? You have the courage to look ahead, but isn't that because you don't see and don't anticipate anything frightening, because life is still veiled from your youthful gaze? You are more courageous, honest, and profound than we are, but think carefully and be generous, just a little bit. Have pity on me. Don't forget I was born here, my father and mother lived here, so did my grandfather. I love this house. I just can't imagine life without the cherry orchard. If it really must be sold, then sell me along with the cherry orchard. (*She embraces* TROFIMOV *and kisses him on the forehead.*) Don't forget, my son was drowned here. (*Weeps.*) Have pity on me, my good, kind friend.

Trofimov: You know I sympathize with you with all my heart.

Lyubov: But you should say it differently, so differently . . . (*She takes out her handkerchief. A telegram falls on the floor.*) I have such a weight on my heart today. You could never imagine. It seems so noisy here to me. My heart quakes at every sound, but I can't go off by myself. When I'm all by myself, the silence terrifies me. Don't be too hard on me, Petya. I love you as though you were one of us. I would gladly let Anya marry you—believe me—but, my dear boy, you must apply yourself to your studies, you must get your degree. You don't do a thing. Fate tosses you from one place to another—it's so strange. It's true, isn't it? And you simply must do something about your beard, to make it grow somehow . . . (*She laughs.*) You look so funny.

Trofimov (*picking up the telegram*). I have no desire to be a dandy.

Lyubov: It's a telegram from Paris. I get one every day—yesterday and today. That uncouth barbarian is sick again. Things are going badly for him now . . . He's begging me to forgive him. He pleads with me to return. And really, I ought to go to Paris to be near him. You are wearing such a stern expression, Petya. But what am I to do, dear boy? What I am I to do? He's ill, all alone, and so miserable. And who is there to look after him? Who is there to keep him from making mistakes? Who is there to give him his medicine on time? And why should I hide it or be silent about it? It's obvious that I'm in love with him. I love him, I love him . . . He's a millstone around my neck, I'm going to the bottom with him, but I love that millstone and can't live without him. (*She presses* TROFIMOV'S *hand.*) Don't think too harshly of me, Petya. Don't say anything just now, don't . . .

Trofimov (*tearfully*). In God's name, please forgive my frankness, but that man is robbing you.

Lyubov: No, no, no. You mustn't say such things. (*She covers her ears.*)

Trofimov: But he's a scoundrel and you're the only one that doesn't know it! He's a petty scoundrel, absolutely worthless . . .

Lyubov (*angry, but in control of herself*). You are twenty-six or twenty-seven years old, but you're acting more like a twelve-year old.

Trofimov: That may very well be.

Lyubov: At your age you should be a mature man. You should be able to understand about people in love. And you should be in love yourself . . . you should fall in love! (*Angrily.*) That's true, that's true! It's not purity in you. It's only prudishness. You are a comical, odd little man . . . a freak . . .

Trofimov (*shocked*). What is she saying!

Lyubov: "I am above love!" You are not above love, but as Firs says, simply a little dull-witted. Imagine not having a sweetheart at your age!

Trofimov (*shocked*). This is terrible! What is she saying? (*Walks quickly toward the ballroom, pressing his hands against his head.*) This is terrible . . . I simply can't—I'm leaving . . . (*Goes out, but comes back at once.*) Everything is finished between us! (*Goes out into the anteroom.*)

Lyubov (*calling after him*). Petya, wait! You odd fellow. I was only joking! Petya!

[*From the anteroom comes the sound of someone running quickly on the stairs and suddenly falling down with a crash.* ANYA *and* VARYA *start screaming, but then immediately start laughing.*]

Lyubov: What was that?

[ANYA *comes running in.*]

Anya (*laughing*). Petya fell down the stairs. (*Runs out.*)

Lyubov: What an odd fellow that Petya is! . . .

[*The* STATIONMASTER *stands in the center of the ballroom reciting* "The Sinner"[1] *by Alexei Tolstoy. The others are listening to him, but he has scarcely recited a few lines when the sound of a waltz comes from the anteroom and the recitation breaks off abruptly. Everyone starts dancing.* TROFIMOV, ANYA, VARYA, *and* LYUBOV *come from the anteroom.*]

Lyubov: There, now, Petya . . . You sweet thing . . . I beg your forgiveness . . . Come dance with me . . . (*Dances with* PETYA.)

[ANYA *and* VARYA *dance.* FIRS *enters, leaving his walking stick near the side door.* YASHA *also comes into the salon and watches the dancers.*]

Yasha: What's up, granddad?

Firs: I don't feel so good. At one time we used to have generals, barons, and admirals dancing here, but now we send for the postal clerk and the stationmaster, and even they don't come willingly. I'm growing weaker every day. My old master —the grandfather—used to give all of us

[1] Also known as "Magdalene."

sealing wax for whatever ailed us. I have been taking sealing wax almost every day now for twenty years, or maybe even longer. Maybe that's why I'm still alive.

Yasha: You bother me, granddad. Why don't you just lie down and die?

Firs: Eh, you . . . you half-wit. (*Mutters.*)

[TROFIMOV *and* LYUBOV *dance in the ballroom, then into the salon.*]

Lyubov: *Merci.* I'll sit down for awhile. (*Sits.*) I'm tired.

[ANYA *enters.*]

Anya (*excitedly*). Just now in the kitchen some man said that the cherry orchard was sold today.

Lyubov: Sold to whom?

Anya: He didn't say to whom. He's gone now. (*Dances with* TROFIMOV. *They go off to the ballroom.*)

Yasha: It was some old man gabbing away in there. Some stranger.

Firs: And Leonid Andreyevich still isn't here. He hasn't come back yet. He was wearing his lightweight overcoat and he's apt to catch cold. Eh, these youngsters!

Lyubov: I'm going to die this very minute. Yasha, go and find out who bought it.

Yasha: But the old man left long ago. (*Laughs.*)

Lyubov (*somewhat vexed*). Well, what are you laughing at? What are you so happy about?

Yasha: That Epihodov is such a clown. What a useless character. He's a born loser.

Lyubov: Firs, if the estate is sold, where will you go?

Firs: I'll go wherever you say.

Lyubov: Why do you look like that? Are you ill? You should go to bed, you know.

Firs: Yes . . . (*with a smile*) . . . If I go to bed, without me here who is to serve things, who will manage things? I'm the only one left in the whole house.

Yasha (*to* LYUBOV). Please permit me to ask a favor of you. If you go back to Paris, please take me with you. It's absolutely impossible for me to remain here. (*Looks around him and speaks in a quiet voice.*) You can see for yourself there's nothing to talk about around here. It's an uncivilized country and the people have no morals at all. Besides that, it's boring. The food they serve in the kitchen is a tasteless mess. And then there's Firs wandering around, muttering all kinds of nonsense. Please take me with you!

[PISHCHIK *comes in.*]

Pishchik: Permit me to ask you . . . for a little waltz, beautiful lady . . . (LYUBOV *goes with him.*) Enchanting creature, I really must borrow a hundred and eighty roubles from you . . . really, I must. (*They dance.*) A hundred and eighty roubles . . .

[*They go off into the ballroom.*]

Yasha (*crooning softly*). "Will you understand the turmoil in my heart"?

[*In the ballroom a figure in a gray top hat and checkered trousers waves both hands and jumps about. There are shouts of,* "Bravo, Charlotta Ivanovna!"]

Dunyasha (*stopping to powder her nose*). The young mistress has ordered me to dance . . . There are a lot of men, but only a few ladies. But every time I dance my head starts spinning around and my heart begins to pound. Firs Nikolyevich, the postal clerk, just told me something that absolutely took my breath away.

[*The music grows softer.*]

Firs: What did he say to you?

Dunyasha: "You are just like a flower," he said.

Yasha (*yawning*). What stupidity. (*Goes out.*)

Dunyasha: "Just like a flower" . . . I'm such a delicate creature. I just love pretty speeches!

Firs: You will lose your head over such things.

[EPIHODOV *comes in.*]

Epihodov: Avdotya Fyodorovna, you try to avoid me . . . just as if I were some kind of insect. (*Sighs.*) Ah, well, that's life!

Dunyasha: What do you want?

Epihodov: No doubt about it, you're probably right. But, of course, if one looks at it from a certain point of view, if I may be permitted to express myself freely, forgive me for speaking so candidly, but you have completely upset my peace of mind. I'm perfectly aware what my fate is. Every day some misfortune or other happens to me, but I've been accustomed to it for such a long time now that I look upon my fate with a smile. You gave me your word and, although I . . .

Dunyasha: Please, let's talk about it some other time. Leave me alone right now. I'm lost in a dream. (*Plays with her fan.*)

Epihodov: Some misfortune happens to me everyday. And, if I may express an opinion, I only smile, even laugh at my misfortunes . . .

[VARYA *enters from the ballroom.*]

Varya: Haven't you left yet, Semyon? Really—what a rude fellow you are. (*To* DUNYASHA.) Get along now, Dunyasha. (*To* EPIHODOV.) First you play billiards and break a cue, then you saunter around the salon like one of the guests.

Epihodov: Allow me to inform you that you are not authorized to reprimand me.

Varya: I am not reprimanding you. I'm merely telling you. All you know how to do is to walk about from place to place instead of tending to your own business. We employ you as a clerk around here but heaven knows why.

Epihodov (*offended*). Whether I work or walk around, eat or play billiards is a matter to be judged only by those with more understanding and maturity.

Varya: You dare to speak to me in this way! (*Enraged.*) You dare suggest that I don't understand anything? Get out of here! This very minute!

Epihodov (*abashed*). I beg you to express yourself in a more discreet manner.

Varya (*beside herself with anger*). Get out of here this minute! Out! (*He goes toward the door, she after him.*) You born loser! I don't want to see hide nor hair of you around here again. (*He goes out; from behind the door comes his voice:* "I shall protest your treatment of me!") Ah, you're coming back? (*She picks up the stick left near the door by* FIRS.) Come on then . . . come on . . . come on . . . I'll show you! Ah, are you coming? Coming? Well, then, here's something for you . . . (*She swings the stick just as* LOPAHIN *enters.*)

Lopahin: Thank you very much.

Varya (*angrily and sarcastically*). I beg your pardon.

Lopahin: Don't mention it. Thank you kindly for the pleasant reception.

Varya: Don't bother thanking me.

(*Moves away, then looks back and asks softly.*) I didn't hurt you, did I?

Lopahin: No, it's nothing. But a big bump is starting to come up.

Voices in the Ballroom: Lopahin has arrived! Yermolay Alexeyevich!

Pishchik: Well, here he is . . . big as life. (*Embraces* LOPAHIN.) You smell of cognac, my dear fellow. We've been entertaining ourselves here too.

[LYUBOV *comes in.*]

Lyubov: Is that you, Yermolay Alexeyevich? What kept you so long? Where is Leonid?

Lopahin: Leonid arrived with me. He's coming . . .

Lyubov (*agitated*). Well, what happened? Did they hold the auction? Tell me!

Lopahin (*embarrassed, afraid of showing his joy*). The auction was all over about four o'clock. We were late for our train and had to wait until nine-thirty. (*Sighing deeply.*) Ugh, my head is spinning around . . .

[GAYEV *enters, with his right hand he carries some purchases, with his left he wipes away his tears.*]

Lyubov: Lyonya, what happened? Well, Lyonya? (*Impatiently, tearfully.*) Hurry up, for God's sake!

Gayev (*not answering, only waving his hand; to* FIRS, *weeping*). Here, take this . . . Here are some anchovies, some herrings . . . I haven't eaten anything all day . . . I've been through so much today!

[*The door to the billiard room is open. One can hear the sound of billiard balls and* YASHA'S *voice saying:* "Seven and eighteen!" *The expression on* GAYEV'S *face changes; he is no longer weeping.*]

Gayev: I'm very tired. Lay out my clothes for me, Firs. I want to change. (*Goes to his own room through the ballroom;* FIRS *follows after.*)

Pishchik: What happened at the auction? Tell us about it!

Lyubov: Has the cherry orchard been sold?

Lopahin: It's been sold.

Lyubov: Who bought it?

Lopahin: I bought it. (*Pause.*)

[LYUBOV *is overwhelmed. She would fall if she weren't standing by a chair and table.* VARYA *takes the keys from her belt, throws them on the floor in the middle of the salon, and goes out.*]

Lopahin: I bought it. Wait a minute, ladies and gentlemen. My head is spinning around and I can't speak. (*Laughs.*) When we got to the auction, Deriganov was already there. Leonid had only 15,000 roubles, and all at once Deriganov bid 30,000 roubles over and above the amount of the mortgage. Seeing how things were, I tangled with him and bid 40,000. He upped it to 45,000. I went to 55,000. He kept raising by 5,000 and I, by 10,000 . . . Well, it was finally over. Over and above the mortgage, I bid 90,000 roubles, and it was sold to me. The cherry orchard belongs to me now. It's mine. (*Laughs boisterously.*) By God, the cherry orchard is mine. Tell me that I'm drunk, that I'm out of my mind, that I've imagined all this. (*Dances a jig.*) Don't laugh at me. If only my father and grandfather could rise from their graves and see all that has happened . . . how their flogged, half-illiterate Yermolay, who used to run around barefoot in the winter-time, that very same Yermolay has bought the most beautiful estate in the whole world! I have bought the estate where my grandfather and father were serfs, where they were not even allowed in the kitchen. I must be asleep, this must be a dream, an illusion. This has to be the result of imagination wrapped in ignorance. (*He picks up the keys, smiling affably.*) She threw down the keys, she wants to show that she is no longer mistress here . . . (*Jingles the keys.*) Well, it doesn't matter. (*The orchestra can be heard tuning up.*) Hey, you musicians, play. I want to hear you. Come on, everybody, see how Yermolay Lopahin will put the axe to the cherry orchard, see how the trees will topple to the ground. We will build a lot of summer homes and our grandsons and great-grandsons will see a new life rising here . . . Let's have a little music! (*The music plays.* LYUBOV *slumps into a chair and weeps softly.*)

Lopahin (*reproachfully*). Why, why didn't you listen to me before? My poor dear, it can't be undone now. (*Tearfully.*) Oh, if only all this would be over quickly. If only we could change our crazy, mixed up lives somehow.

Pishchik (*taking him by the arm, speaking in a quiet voice*). She's crying. Let's go into the ballroom and leave her alone . . . Come on . . . (*Takes him by the arm and leads him into the ballroom.*)

Lopahin: What's the matter. Let's strike up the music! Let's have everything just the way I want it! (*Ironically.*) Here comes the new landlord, the owner of the cherry orchard. (*Accidentally pushes a table, nearly knocking over the candelabra.*) I can pay for anything! (*Goes out with* PISHCHIK.)

[*There is no one left in the ballroom or salon except* LYUBOV, *who sits huddled over, crying bitterly. The music is playing softly.* ANYA *and* TROFIMOV *enter hurriedly.* ANYA *goes over to her mother and kneels down in front of her.* TROFIMOV *remains by the ballroom entrance.*]

Anya: Mama! . . . Mama, are you crying? My dear, good, kind mother, my beautiful one, I love you . . . I bless you. The cherry orchard has been sold. It doesn't exist anymore, that's true, true; but don't cry, Mama. Your life still lies ahead of you. You still have your sweet, pure heart . . . Come with me, come away from here, my darling, come! . . . We will plant a new orchard, more splendid than this one. You will see it, you will understand, and a quiet joy will settle into your heart like the sun setting in the evening! And you will smile, Mama. Come, darling, come! . . .

ACT IV

[*The same setting as in Act I. There are no curtains on the windows or pictures on the walls. A few articles of furniture remain, put together in one corner of the room, as if for sale. An atmosphere of emptiness pervades the room. There is a pile of suitcases, bundles for traveling, etc., near the outer door at the rear of the stage. The door on the left is open and the voices of* ANYA *and* VARYA *can be heard coming through it.* LOPAHIN *stands waiting.* YASHA *is hold-*

ing a tray of wine glasses filled with champagne. In the anteroom EPIHODOV *is tying up a box. A hum of voices comes from behind the scene. It is the peasants. They have come to say good-bye. The voice of* GAYEV *is heard saying:* "Thank you, friends, thank you."]

Yasha: The simple folk have come to say good-bye. In my opinion, Yermolay Alexeyich, the people are good souls but they don't know very much.

[*The drone of voices subsides.* LYUBOV *and* GAYEV *enter through the anteroom. She is not crying, but her face is pale, drawn, and tremulous, and she cannot speak.*]

Gayev: You gave your purse away to them, Lyuba. You shouldn't do such things, you shouldn't . . .

Lyubov: I just couldn't help it! I just couldn't help it!

[*Both leave.*]

Lopahin (*calling after them through the doorway*). Please, I humbly beg of you! A little farewell drink. I didn't think of bringing any champagne from town, and I could only find one bottle at the station. Please! (*Pause.*) Well, then, ladies and gentlemen! Don't you want any? (*Moving away from the door.*) I wouldn't have bought any if I had known. All right, then, I won't drink any either. (YASHA *carefully puts the tray down on a chair.*) Come on, Yasha, you have a drink at least.

Yasha: On behalf of those who are leaving, a toast to those who are staying behind! This champagne isn't the real thing, I can tell you that.

Lopahin: Eight roubles a bottle. (*Pause.*) It's cold as the devil in here!

Yasha: They didn't light the stoves today. But what's the difference. We're all leaving anyway. (*Laughs.*)

Lopahin: What are you laughing for?

Yasha: For sheer delight.

Lopahin: It's October, yet it's sunny and quiet just like summer . . . perfect weather for building. (*Looking at his watch, speaks toward the door.*) Keep in mind, ladies and gentlemen, it's only forty-seven minutes until train time. You know you'd better leave for the station in twenty minutes. Better hurry up.

[TROFIMOV, *wearing an overcoat, comes in from outside.*]

Trofimov: If you ask me, it's time to leave now. The horses are ready. The devil only knows where my galoshes are. They must be lost . . . (*Speaking toward the door.*) Anya, my galoshes aren't here. I can't find them!

Lopahin: As for me, I have to leave for Kharkov. I'm taking the same train you are. I'll be spending the whole winter in Kharkov. I've been lounging around here with you and I'm bored stiff with nothing to do. I just can't get along without work. I don't know what to do with my hands. They just hang limply as if they belonged to somebody else.

Trofimov: Well, we'll be leaving soon, and you can start your useful endeavors again.

Lopahin: Here, have a little drink.

Trofimov: No, I don't want any.

Lopahin: Well, what now . . . are you leaving for Moscow?

Trofimov: Yes, I'll see them off in town, and tomorrow I'll be leaving for Moscow.

Lopahin: I see . . . I'll bet the professors aren't giving any of their lectures until you get there!

Trofimov: That's none of your business.

Lopahin: How many years have you been studying at the university?

Trofimov: Can't you think of anything new? That chestnut is old and stale. (*Looks for his galoshes.*) You know, we probably won't see one another again, so let me give you one farewell piece of advice: Don't swing your arms around the way you do! Get rid of that habit—that arm-swinging. And furthermore, this building of summer homes, this business about summer residents eventually becoming separate land-owners . . . it's all arm-waving, you know . . . But in spite of it all, I'm fond of you. You have delicate, sensitive fingers . . . like an artist, and you have a delicate, sensitive soul . . .

Lopahin (*embracing him*). Good-bye, my dear boy. Thanks for everything. If you need it, take some money from me for your trip.

Trofimov: What for? I don't need it.

Lopahin: But you don't have any.

Trofimov: Yes I do. Thank you. I got some for a translation I did. Here it is in my pocket. (*Anxiously.*) But where can those galoshes be!

Varya (*from the adjoining room*). Take your nasty old things! (*Tosses a pair of rubber galoshes out onto the stage.*)

Trofimov: What are you angry about, Varya? Mm . . . but these aren't my galoshes!

Lopahin: Last spring I sowed 2,700 acres of poppies, and now I've made 40,000 roubles clear profit. When those poppies were in full bloom, what a picture that was! Look, as I was saying, I cleared 40,000 on the deal, and I'm offering you a loan because I can afford it. Why turn your nose up at it? I'm a peasant . . . I speak frankly.

Trofimov: Your father was a peasant, mine was a druggist . . . which proves absolutely nothing. (LOPAHIN *takes out his billfold.*) Put it away, put it away . . . Even if you gave me 200,000 roubles, I wouldn't accept it. I'm a free man. And everything that all of you value so highly and dearly—rich man and poor man alike—hasn't the slightest power over me. It's just like so much fluff floating on air. I can get along without you. I can pass you by. I am strong and proud. Humanity is moving onward to the highest truth, to the highest happiness possible on earth, and I am in the front ranks.

Lopahin: Do you think you'll ever get there?

Trofimov: I'll get there. (*Pause.*) I'll get there, or I'll show others the way to get there.

[*Off in the distance the sound of an axe striking against a tree.*]

Lopahin: Well, good-bye, my boy. It's time to go. We turn our noses up at one another, meanwhile life is passing us by. Whenever I work for a long time without letting up, my spirits are lighter, and I seem to know why I exist. But how many people are there in Russia, my friend, who exist without knowing why. Well, no matter. That's not what keeps things going. They say that Leonid Andreyevich has taken a position in the bank at six thousand a year . . . The only thing is, of course, he won't stay there. He's too lazy . . .

Anya (*in the doorway*). Mama begs you not to cut down the orchard until she's gone.

Trofimov: Really, don't you have any tact at all . . . (*Goes out through the anteroom.*)

Lopahin: Right away, right away . . .

Those men, really . . . (*Goes out after* TROFIMOV.)

Anya: Did they send Firs to the hospital?

Yasha: I told them to this morning. They must have taken him.

Anya (*to* EPIHODOV, *who is passing through the ballroom*). Semyon Panteleyich, find out if they took Firs to the hospital, please.

Yasha (*resentfully*). I told Yegor this morning. Why keep asking?

Epihodov: In my considered opinion, old worn-out Firs is not worth mending. He should join his forefathers. As for me, I can only envy him. (*Puts a suitcase on a cardboard box, crushing it.*) Well, there you are . . . naturally. I expected as much. (*Goes out.*)

Yasha: What a born loser . . . !

Varya (*from the other side of the door*). Did they take Firs to the hospital?

Anya: They did.

Varya: Then why didn't they take the note to the doctor?

Anya: We'll have to send it along after them . . . (*Goes out.*)

Varya (*from the adjoining room*). Where is Yasha. Tell him his mother came to say good-bye to him.

Yasha (*waving his hand*). Ah, all she does is make me lose my patience.

[*All this time* DUNYASHA *has been busying herself around the luggage. Now that* YASHA *is alone, she goes over to him.*]

Dunyasha: You could look at me just one little time, Yasha. After all, you are going away . . . you are leaving me . . . (*Weeps and throws her arms around his neck.*)

Yasha: What are you crying about? (*Drinks champagne.*) In six days I'll be back in Paris. Tomorrow we'll get aboard the express train and away we'll go, and that will be the last you'll see of us. I can hardly believe it myself. *Vive la France!* . . . This place is not for me. I just can't stand it. There's nothing I can do about it. I can't put up with this backwardness . . . It's too much for me. (*Drinks champagne.*) What are you crying about? Behave yourself properly and there won't be anything to cry about.

Dunyasha (*powders her nose and looks into a pocket mirror*). Send me a letter from Paris. I loved you, Yasha, how I loved you! I'm such a delicate creature, Yasha!

Yasha: They're coming. (*Busies himself with the suitcases, humming softly.*)

[LYUBOV, GAYEV, ANYA, *and* CHARLOTTA *enter.*]

Gayev: We should be leaving. We don't have much time left. (*Looks at* YASHA.) Who smells of herring?

Lyubov: In about ten minutes we should be in the carriages. (*Glancing around the room.*) Farewell, dear house, dear old grandfather. Winter will soon pass and spring will come again, but you will no longer be here. They will tear you down to the ground. How much these old walls have seen! (*Kisses her daughter warmly.*) My treasure, you look positively radiant. Your eyes sparkle like two diamonds. Are you happy? Really happy?

Anya: Really happy. A new life is beginning for us, Mama!

Gayev (*cheerfully*). Well, at least everything is all right now. Until the cherry orchard was sold, we were all upset and worried, but then when the matter was finally settled, we all calmed down and even cheered up a bit. I'm a bank employee now . . . a financier . . . the yellow ball in the side pocket . . . Anyway, Lyuba, you're looking better now. There's no denying that.

Lyubov: Yes, my nerves are better, that's true. (*They hand her her hat and coat.*) I sleep well. Take my things out, Yasha. It's time. (*To* ANYA.) My little girl, we'll be seeing one another again soon. I'm leaving for Paris. I'll live there on the money your great aunt in Yaroslavl sent to buy the estate with . . . Long live great aunt; but the money won't last very long.

Anya: But you'll be coming back very soon, Mama . . . won't you? I'll prepare for my exams at the high school and I'll pass them. Then I'll work to help you. We'll read all kinds of books together, Mama, won't we? (*Kisses her mother's hands.*) We'll read together in the autumn evenings. We'll read lots of books, and a new and marvelous world will open up before us . . . (*In a trance.*) Mama, come back . . .

Lyubov: I'll come, my precious. (Embraces ANYA.)

[LOPAHIN *and* CHARLOTTA *enter. She is softly humming a tune.*]

Gayev: Charlotta must be happy. She's singing!

Charlotta (*picks up a bundle resembling a baby in swaddling clothes*). Bye, bye, baby . . . (*The sound of a baby's crying is heard.*) Hush, my darling, my dear little boy. ("Wah! Wah!") I feel so sorry for you! (*Throws the bundle down.*) Would you find a new position for me. I can't get along this way.

Lopahin: We'll find one for you. Charlotta Ivanovna. Don't worry about it.

Gayev: Everyone is deserting us. Varya is going away . . . All of a sudden we're no longer needed.

Charlotta: There's no place for me to live in town. I have to leave . . . (*Hums.*) Oh, well, what does it matter?

[PISHCHIK *enters.*]

Lopahin: Well, here comes one of nature's marvels! . . .

Pishchik (*out of breath*). Oh, let me catch my breath . . . I'm worn out . . . My honored friends . . . let me have some water.

Gayev: Looking for money again, no doubt. Excuse me . . . please, but I'm getting out of harm's way. (*Goes out.*)

Pishchik: It's been quite awhile since I was here last, most charming lady. (*To* LOPAHIN.) So you're here . . . glad to see you . . . a man of the greatest intellect . . . Here, take this . . . take it . . . (*Hands money to* LOPAHIN.) Four hundred roubles . . . I still owe you eight hundred and forty . . .

Lopahin (*shrugging his shoulders, puzzled*). This must be a dream . . . But where did you get it?

Pishchik: Wait . . . I'm hot . . . A most extraordinary occurrence. Some Englishmen came to my place and found some kind of white clay on it . . . (*To* LYUBOV.) And four hundred for you . . . most beautiful . . . most wonderful creature . . . (*Gives her money.*) The rest will come later. (*Drinks some water.*) Just now on the train a young fellow was telling me that some great philosopher recommends jumping off roofs. "Jump," he says, "and you solve all your problems." (*Astonished.*) Can you imagine that! More water, please!

Lopahin: But what about those Englishmen?

Pishchik: I leased them the land with

the clay on it for twenty-four years . . . And now, excuse me . . . I can't stay . . . I must be running along . . . I'm going to Znoykov's . . . To Kardamonov's . . . I owe money to everybody . . . (*Drinks.*) I want to wish the best to all of you . . . I'll stop by on Thursday.

Lyubov: We're going into town any minute now, and tomorrow I'm going abroad.

Pishchik: What? (*In alarm.*) Why into town? Ah, so that's why I see the furniture like this . . . the suitcases . . . Well, never mind . . . (*Tearfully.*) Never mind . . . People of the greatest intellect, these Englishmen . . . Never mind. The best of luck! God will help you . . . Never mind . . . Everything in this world comes to an end . . . (*Kisses* LYUBOV'S *hand.*) If news should ever reach your ears that my end has come, remember this . . . this old horse and say: "There was once on earth such-and-such a fellow . . . Semyonov-Pishchik . . . God rest his soul . . ." Remarkable weather . . . Yes . . . (*Goes out very much upset, but comes back immediately and speaks from the doorway.*) Dashenka sends her greetings.

Lyubov: Now we can leave. I'm leaving with two worries on my mind. The first thing is that Firs is sick. (*Looking at her watch.*) We still have about five minutes.

Anya: Mama, they already sent Firs to the hospital. Yasha sent him this morning.

Lyubov: My other worry is Varya. She's used to getting up early and working and now, without anything to do, she's like a fish out of water. She's grown thin and pale and just cries continually, poor little thing . . . (*Pause.*) But you know all this very well, Yermolay Alexeyevich. I had hoped she would marry you. After all, everything seemed to indicate you would marry her. (*Whispers to* ANYA, *who beckons to* CHARLOTTA, *and both leave.*) She loves you. You like her. I don't know why it is, but you seem to avoid one another. I just don't understand it!

Lopahin: I must admit I don't understand it myself. It's all very strange somehow . . . If there is still time, I'm ready even now . . . Let's take care of it right now and get it over and done with. But without you here, I don't think I could ever propose to her.

Lyubov: Wonderful! Actually, it will only take a minute. I'll call her right away . . .

Lopahin: And appropriately enough, here's the champagne. (*Looking at the glasses.*) Empty. Somebody has already drunk it all. (YASHA *coughs.*) That's what they call guzzling it down . . .

Lyubov (*excitedly*). Wonderful! We'll leave . . . Yasha, *allez!* I'll call her . . . (*In the doorway.*) Varya, leave what you're doing and come here. Come. (*Goes out with* YASHA.)

Lopahin (*looking at his watch*). Yes . . . (*Pause.*)

[*Behind the door there is subdued laughter and whispering; finally* VARYA *comes in.*]

Varya (*looking over the luggage for a long time*). That's strange. I just can't seem to find it . . .

Lopahin: What are you looking for?

Varya: I packed it myself but I just don't remember where. (*Pause.*)

Lopahin: Where will you go now, Varvara Mihailovna?

Varya: I? To the Ragulins . . . I've arranged with them to look after their house . . . sort of a housekeeper. That's what they call it, isn't it?

Lopahin: They live in Yashnevo, don't they? That's about fifty miles from here. (*Pause.*) Well, it looks like life is finished in this house.

Varya (*examining the luggage*). Where can that be . . . Maybe I put it in the trunk . . . Yes, life is finished in this house . . . there won't be any more . . .

Lopahin: And I'm leaving for Kharkov right away . . . on the next train, in fact. I've got a lot to do. I'm leaving Epihodov around here . . . I hired him.

Varya: You have!

Lopahin: By this time last year snow was already falling, if you recall. But now it's quiet, and the sun is shining. The only thing is, it's cold . . . three degrees below zero.

Varya: I hadn't noticed. (*Pause.*) And besides, our thermometer is broken . . . (*Pause.*)

A Voice through the Doorway from Outside: Yermolay Alexeyich! . . .

Lopahin (*as if he had been waiting for this for a long time*). Coming! (*Goes out hurriedly.*)

[VARYA *sits on the floor, puts her head on a bundle, and sobs quietly. The door opens and* LYUBOV *enters cautiously.*]

Lyubov: Well? (*Pause.*) We must be on our way.

Varya (*no longer crying, wipes her eyes*). Yes, it's time, Mama. I'll have time to get to the Ragulins today if we don't miss the train.

Lyubov (*at the door*). Anya, get your things on!

[ANYA *comes in, then* GAYEV, *and* CHARLOTTA IVANOVNA. GAYEV *is wearing a warm overcoat with a hood. Servants and hired coachmen come in.* EPIHODOV *busies himself with the luggage.*]

Lyubov: Now we can be on our way.

Anya (*joyfully*). On our way!

Gayev: My friends, my dear, sweet friends! As I leave this house forever, can I keep silent, can I refrain from expressing at our parting those feelings which are now welling up inside me . . .

Anya (*imploringly*). Uncle!

Varya: Dear Uncle, don't!

Gayev (*dispiritedly*). Combination shot off the yellow ball into the side pocket . . . Yes, I'll keep quiet.

[TROFIMOV *enters, then* LOPAHIN.]

Trofimov: Well, ladies and gentlemen, it's time to leave!

Lopahin: Epihodov, my coat!

Lyubov: I'm going to sit down for a minute. It's as if I had never seen what the walls and ceiling in this house were like before, and now I look at them longingly, with such tender feelings.

Gayev: I remember when I was only six years old, on Trinity Sunday. I was sitting in this window, watching as my father was leaving for church . . .

Lyubov: Have they taken all the luggage out?

Lopahin: It looks that way. Everything's gone. (*To* EPIHODOV *as he puts his coat on.*) Epihodov, see that everything is attended to.

Epihodov (*in a hoarse voice*). Don't worry, Yermolay Alexeyich!

Lopahin: What's wrong with your voice?

Epihodov: I just had a drink of water. It must have been something I swallowed.

Yasha (*contemptuously*). What stupidity . . .

Lyubov: We're leaving . . . There won't be a soul left here.

Lopahin: Until next spring.

Varya (*pulls an umbrella out of a bundle as if to hit someone.* LOPAHIN *pretends* *to be frightened*). Come now, come now . . . I had no intention of . . .

Trofimov: Ladies and gentlemen, let's get into the carriages . . . It's time now! The train will be coming soon!

Varya: Petya, there are your galoshes . . . beside the suitcase. (*Tearfully.*) How dirty they are, how old . . .

Trofimov (*putting the galoshes on*). Let's go, ladies and gentlemen! . . .

Gayev (*greatly distressed, fearful of breaking into tears*). The train . . . the station . . . Bank shot into the side pocket, combination shot off the white ball into the corner pocket . . .

Lopahin: Is everybody here? Anyone in there? (*Locking the side door on the left.*) There are some things stored away in there. It should be kept locked. Let's go! . . .

Anya: Good-bye, house! Good-bye, old life!

Trofimov: Welcome, new life! . . . (*Goes out with* ANYA.)

[VARYA *glances around the room, and, without hurrying, goes out.* YASHA *and* CHARLOTTA, *with her dog, go out.*]

Lopahin: Well, then, until spring. On your way, ladies and gentlemen . . . until we meet again! . . . (*Goes out.*)

[LYUBOV *and* GAYEV *are left alone. As if they had been waiting for this, they throw their arms around one another and sob quietly, in a restrained manner, as if fearful of being overheard.*]

Gayev (*despairingly*). Sister, sister . . .

Lyubov: Oh, my dear, sweet, beautiful orchard! . . . My life, my youth, my happiness, good-bye, good-bye! . . .

Anya's Voice (*gaily, invitingly*). Mama! . . .

Trofimov's Voice (*gaily, excitedly*). Hey! . . .

Lyubov: For the last time, let me look at the walls, the windows . . . My poor dead mother used to love to walk about in this room . . .

Gayev: Sister, sister! . . .

Lyubov: We're coming. (*They go out.*)

[*The stage is deserted. There is the sound of keys locking all the doors, then of carriages driving off. It becomes quiet. In the silence can be heard the sound of an axe striking against a tree, a solitary, melancholy sound. Footsteps are heard.* FIRS *appears in the doorway on the right. He is dressed as usual in a jacket, white vest, and slippers. He is obviously sick.*]

Firs (*goes to the door, grasps the handle*). It's locked. They left. (*Sits down on the sofa.*) They forgot all about me . . . no matter . . . I'll sit here awhile . . . I'll bet Leonid Andreyich didn't put his fur coat on but went off with only his cloth one on . . . (*Sighs anxiously.*) I didn't look after him . . . Ah, these youngsters! (*He mutters something unintelligible.*) Life has gone by just as if I had never lived. (*Lies down.*) I'm going to lie down for awhile . . . You don't have any strength left. There's nothing left, nothing . . . Ah, you worn-out old thing! (*Lies motionless.*)

[*A far-off sound is heard as if from the sky, the sound of a snapped string, mournfully dying away. The silence returns and only the sound of an axe striking against a tree is heard, somewhere far off in the orchard.*]

DISCUSSION QUESTIONS

Act I

1. What elements in the time and setting symbolize the hope of rebirth, renewal, and rejuvenation?
2. What aspects of the first scene suggest frustration, inner conflict, and loss, partly in contrast to the setting?
3. What social occasion provides the center of Act I?
4. Throughout the play most of the characters are easily recognized by their mannerisms, tricks of speech, or gestures (e.g., Pishchik's repeated astonishment at trifles, repeated dozing, his attempts at borrowing money from anyone, faith in unexpected luck). What traits are associated with the following characters: Gayev, Lyubov, Trofimov, Lopahin, Firs, Charlotta, Epihodov, Varya?
5. How do developments in Act I foreshadow or prepare for later action in the play?
6. What mysterious or supernatural events occur, helping to emphasize the tone of unreality, of illusion, and tension?
7. Although Chekhov has called his play a "comedy," he has instilled in Act I an underlying tone of pathos. That is, many of the characters are or have been the weak, helpless victims of external forces. How do the following characters appear "pathetic": Lopahin, Lyubov, the entire party of Lyubov, Firs, Gayev?
8. Lyubov apparently sees her mother walking through the orchard, an illusion that is paralleled in Act II when Trofimov imagines that from "every cherry tree in the orchard, from every leaf, from every trunk a human being is looking at you." What inner need in Lyubov helps explain her hallucination, especially in the light of her eagerness to return home? And how does Trofimov's sense of the orchard's femininity relate to his nationalism, his insight into Lyubov's guilt, and even the future revolution?
9. Although one of the play's major themes is the inability of the characters to establish deep or lasting intimacy with each other, Chekhov has implied a number of love attachments in Act I. What are they and how are they complicated?
10. Throughout the first Act, Chekhov subtly introduces symbolic gestures or stage props (e.g., Epihodov's squeaking shoes, signifying his lack of poise, refinement, and competence). What is the significance of the following articles or incidents: the stick on which Firs leans and with which Varya later strikes Lopahin, the nursery, Dunyasha's broken saucer, Gayev's imaginary billiard-playing, Lopahin's overuse of shaving lotion, Gayev's century-old bookcase, the sound of a shepherd's pipe, Trofimov's comparison of Anya to sunshine and springtime?

Act II

1. Francis Fergusson has noted that although *The Cherry Orchard* has no formal plot, that "nothing happens," the action that all the characters share is the attempt

to save the cherry orchard. What values are seen in the orchard, in the first two Acts, by the following: Lopahin, Firs, Gayev, Lyubov, Trofimov?

2. How does the setting of Act II reflect a significant motif of the play, the contrast between past and future?
3. How are the death motifs of the setting extended to characterization in the first scene of Act II?
4. How does the tone of sentimentality, leisurely relaxation, and illusion of the first scene shift to an atmosphere of irritation, frustration, and fear that follows Lyubov's entrance?
5. What problems are again (as in Act I) brought to the reader's attention?
6. How do Firs' costume and reminiscences combine with the setting to form a particular attitude toward the past?
7. Lyubov's exposition of her immoral and painful past involves enough material for a full-length melodramatic novel. What ironies are involved in her criticism of Lopahin's dull life, her advice that he marry Varya, and the guilt that she and Lopahin share toward the past—especially since she has known what was right has not been done?
8. Lyubov's past is presented through exposition instead of being represented directly. How does Chekhov thus establish an ironic parallel between cheap art and Lyubov's mind, and contrast dead social traditions and the vitality of the orchard?
9. How does Lyubov's exposition establish her intelligence, sensitivity, and despair, while preparing for her repetition of the same kind of mistakes?
10. How do Lopahin's confessions of ignorance, stupidity, and boredom resemble Lyubov's admissions of immorality and impulsiveness?
11. What is the contrast in tone between Firs' vision of a stable social hierarchy and the scene beginning with the entrance of Anya, Varya, and Trofimov?
12. What attitudes toward progress, the past, and human tragedy are conveyed by Trofimov's speech beginning "there is something mystical about human pride," apparently another in a series of confessions?
13. How is the tone affected by Gayev's false, rhetorical apostrophe to nature (an archaic device usually found at the beginning of epics) and the reaction it draws from the other characters?
14. Chekhov often uses music as a signal and inducement when he wishes us to shift our perspectives from the characters in the foreground to their wider setting. What specific-to-general movement occurs with the following: Epihodov's guitar-strumming, the Jewish band, the distant sound of a string snapping?
15. From what motives does Lyubov give money to the tramp?
16. How do Lopahin's misquotes from *Hamlet* (III, i) reveal his relationships to both Lyubov and Varya?
17. How has Anya's young love for Trofimov's intellectual enthusiasm affected her mood and outlook?
18. How are Trofimov's abstract aspirations, involving both the estate and Anya, as defective as the values of the others?

Act III

1. The social occasion at the center of Act III is the hysterical party that Lyubov Ranevsky gives in the drawing room of the Ranevsky house. How is the party related to the preceding action?
2. How do chance comments by Pishchik, Varya, and Lyubov—mostly about material security—build suspense and prepare for the *reversal* of the action that will occur with Lopahin's entrance and announcement?
3. How are Trofimov's and Lyubov's attitudes toward love ironically contrasted?
4. How are Trofimov and Lyubov alike in their power (or lack of it) to struggle?
5. The quarrel between Trofimov and Lyubov is ironic since the party should be celebrating joy and reconciliation. What charges are leveled against Trofimov by Lyubov?
6. How is it ironic that the station-master chooses to recite A. Tolstoy's "The Sinner," and that this veiled warning of disaster is almost immediately interrupted?
7. In what ways do old and new clash in Act III?
8. Why has Lopahin bought the orchard for himself when his desire to save it for Lyubov in Acts I and II was apparently sincere?
9. Although the apparent final loss of the cherry orchard involves shock, horror, and pathos, the tone of Act III is influenced by a series of ludicrous incidents. What are these incidents and their significance, as they involve the following characters: Charlotta, Epihodov, Lyubov and Trofimov, Varya and Lopahin, Lopahin?
10. To what extent are Lopahin's and Anya's views of the future alike, now that the cherry orchard is irrevocably lost?
11. How many hints that the orchard will be sold precede the actual entrance of Lopahin in Act III?

Act IV

1. What social occasion forms the center of Act IV, and how does the setting reflect it?
2. In certain respects, *The Cherry Orchard* approaches Aristotle's definition of comedy: "an imitation of characters of a lower type who are not bad in themselves but whose faults possess something ludicrous in them." What ludicrous mannerisms and gestures reappear in association with the various characters, and what is their significance: Yasha, Lopahin, Pishchik, Trofimov, Gayev, Anya?
3. How does Act IV reveal or parody a sense of what James Joyce has called an *epiphany,* "a sudden spiritual manifestation"? Do the characters recognize their responsibility for the sale of the cherry orchard with any irony?
4. How much time elapses in the course of the play? Is this time lapse symbolic in terms of change, characterization, and free will?
5. Do changes in time of day from Act to Act also relate to the play's unity, its social concerns, and the characters' abilities to plan their lives?
6. How are Gayev's and Lyubov's reactions to disaster characteristically inadequate?

7. How does Pishchik's sudden stroke of good fortune present an ironic parallel to Lyubov's plight and suggest a moral about the value of struggling?
8. What are the implications of the simultaneous axe strokes and breaking string at the end?
9. Although tragedy ends unhappily, it also requires a dominant figure or protagonist who has the ability and will to oppose his fate. He must not be the helpless victim of events, but must put up a good fight against those forces that will ultimately destroy him. In this way he defines both his own character and the nature of the world. To what extent is Lopahin a tragic figure?
10. What inner conflict complicates Lopahin's character?
11. Some critics believe that one theme of the play arises from the symbolism of the orchard: the destruction of beauty by those who are utterly blind to it. Is there any evidence that this is not the *main* theme of the play, that Chekhov is not primarily attacking Lopahin, the man most responsible for the destruction of the orchard?
12. To what extent is Lyubov Ranevsky a tragic figure?
13. Does an inner conflict also afflict Gayev, the only other character remotely capable of saving the orchard?
14. Northrop Frye has suggested that the main theme of the play is the disintegration of a society without anything to take its place. What will predictably happen to the lives of Trofimov, Gayev, Lyubov, and Lopahin after the play ends?
15. In comparison with contemporary melodrama, what possibilities for overt action (love affairs, conflict, violence) has Chekhov suggested but left undeveloped?

HEARTBREAK HOUSE

George Bernard Shaw

Introductory Comment

Heartbreak House is both more traditional in its forms and more topical in its content than nearly any other play in this collection. Ellie Dunn as the Ingenue, Hector Hushabye as the Romantic Lead, and Boss Mangan as the ominous Heavy, to name only a few examples, derive from countless "well-made" melodramas of the nineteenth century. The play also reveals Shaw's long-time interests in social reform through enlightenment, his sophisticated, aphoristic wit, and his penchant for centering his action around a vital, deeply intelligent and charismatic young woman. Yet the very detail and vividness of his mock-ship interior, the wealth of specifics in the personal lives of his characters, and the crackling flashes of insight which occur in the action all suggest unmistakably that pre-war (any war), cultured, complacent Europe appears here in microcosm.

Although Shaw is funnier than Chekhov and Ibsen, with a gift for sparkling dialogue neither of them aspired to, his purposes in this play represent an unusual departure for him. As Robert Brustein has remarked, instead of a consoling myth of social reform, revolving around characters with a high sense of purpose, he is providing in *Heartbreak House* a Chekhovian myth of fatalism, revolving around characters with no sense of direction at all. Ellie may be too brittle, too close to caricature to gain the kind of imaginative assent we provide for Chekhov's Madame Ranevsky or Shakespeare's Cordelia. But the range and intensity of significance which are attached to Shaw's incredibly representative group both lift us toward symbolism and discourage the identification with a single hero or protagonist which Chekhov had likewise avoided. Moreover, the development of character, the unfolding of action proceed at a very leisurely pace—unusual for Shaw, but one of Chekhov's trademarks. Shotover resembles a Shavian spokesman at first glance, although his age and world-weariness, his terrible loss of grip on life are distinctly uncharacteristic of his creator.

As reality fades, dissolves, and re-shapes itself before our eyes, we may be surprised to note that Shaw uses only a single set as clear and precise a a photograph. Yet the super-human intelligence of these characters, Shaw's apocalyptic vision, and the sardonic insights which continuously interact with emotional trauma and startling action lift Heartbreak House above the plane of the commonplace to the level of the universal. The play lacks the deft parody of romanticized history which appears in *The*

Devil's Disciple, the bittersweet catharsis of *Saint Joan,* and the clash of sharply-paired wills of *Pygmalion.* But by adopting the more open forms of Tolstoy and Chekhov, and combining them with a far more dominant moralism and sharper self-awareness than nearly any of his contemporaries instill in character, Shaw has created a masterpiece of vision and penetration.

Cast of Characters

CAPTAIN SHOTOVER
HESIONE HUSHABYE
HECTOR HUSHABYE
ARIADNE UTTERWORD
RANDALL UTTERWORD
ELLIE DUNN
MAZZINI DUNN
BOSS MANGAN
NURSE GUINNESS
THE BURGLAR
THE WOMANSERVANT

ACT I

[The hilly country in the middle of the north edge of Sussex, looking very pleasant on a fine evening at the end of September, is seen through the windows of a room which has been built so as to resemble the after part of an old-fashioned high-pooped ship with a stern gallery; for the windows are ship built with heavy timbering, and run right across the room as continuously as the stability of the wall allows. A row of lockers under the windows provides an unupholstered window-seat interrupted by twin glass doors, respectively halfway between the stern post and the sides. Another door strains the illusion a little by being apparently in the ship's port side, and yet leading, not to the open sea, but to the entrance hall of the house. Between this door and the stern gallery are bookshelves. There are electric light switches beside the door leading to the hall and the glass doors in the stern gallery. Against the starboard wall is a carpenter's bench. The vise has a board in its jaws; and the floor is littered with shavings, overflowing from a waste-paper basket. A couple of planes and a centrebit are on the bench. In the same wall, between the bench and the windows, is a narrow doorway with a half door, above which a glimpse of the room beyond shews that it is a shelved pantry with bottles and kitchen crockery.

On the starboard side, but close to the middle, is a plain oak drawing-table with drawing-board, T-square, straightedges, set squares, mathematical instruments, saucers of water color, a tumbler of discolored water, Indian ink, pencils, and brushes on it. The drawing-board is set so that the draughtsman's chair has the window on its left hand. On the floor at the end of the table, on his right, is a ship's fire bucket. On the port side of the room, near the bookshelves, is a sofa with its back to the windows. It is a sturdy mahogany article, oddly upholstered in sailcloth, including the bolster, with a couple of blankets hanging over the back. Between the sofa and the drawing-table is a big wicker chair, with broad arms and a low sloping back, with its back to the light. A small but stout table of teak, with a round top and gate legs, stands against the port wall between the door and the bookcase. It is the only article in the room that suggests (not at all convincingly) a woman's hand in the furnishing. The uncarpeted floor of narrow boards is caulked and holystoned like a deck.

The garden to which the glass doors lead dips to the south before the landscape rises again to the hills. Emerging from the hollow is the cupola of an observatory. Between the observatory and the house is a flagstaff on a little esplanade, with a hammock on the east side and a long garden seat on the west.

A young lady, gloved and hatted, with a dust coat on, is sitting in the windowseat with her body twisted to enable her to look out at the view. One hand props her chin: the other hangs down with a volume of the Temple Shakespear in it, and her finger stuck in the page she has been reading.

A clock strikes six.

The young lady turns and looks at her watch. She rises with an air of one who waits and is almost at the end of her patience. She is a pretty girl, slender, fair, and intelligent looking, nicely but not expensively dressed, evidently not a smart idler.

With a sigh of weary resignation she comes to the draughtsman's chair; sits down; and begins to read Shakespear. Presently the book sinks to her lap; her eyes close; and she dozes into a slumber.

An elderly womanservant comes in from the hall with three unopened bottles of rum on a tray. She passes through and disappears in the pantry without noticing the young lady. She places the bottles on the shelf and fills her tray with empty bottles. As she returns with these, the young lady lets her book drop, awakening herself, and startling the womanservant so that she all but lets the tray fall.]

The Womanservant: God bless us! (*The young lady picks up the book and places it on the table.*) Sorry to wake you, miss, I'm sure; but you are a stranger to me. What might you be waiting here for now?

The Young Lady: Waiting for somebody to shew some signs of knowing that I have been invited here.

The Womanservant: Oh, youre invited, are you? And has nobody come? Dear! dear!

The Young Lady: A wild-looking old gentleman came and looked in at the window; and I heard him calling out "Nurse: there is a young and attractive female waiting in the poop. Go and see what she wants." Are you the nurse?

The Womanservant: Yes, miss: I'm Nurse Guinness. That was old Captain Shotover, Mrs. Hushabye's father. I heard him roaring; but I thought it was for something else. I suppose it was Mrs. Hushabye that invited you, ducky?

The Young Lady: I understood her to do so. But really I think I'd better go.

Nurse Guinness: Oh, dont think of such a thing, miss. If Mrs. Hushabye has forgotten all about it, it will be a pleasant surprise for her to see you, wont it?

The Young Lady: It has been a very unpleasant surprise to me to find that nobody expects me.

Nurse Guinness: Youll get used to it, miss: this house is full of surprises for them that dont know our ways.

Captain Shotover (*looking in from the hall suddenly: an ancient but still hardy man with an immense white beard, in a reefer jacket with a whistle hanging from his neck*). Nurse: there is a hold-all and a handbag on the front steps for everybody to fall over. Also a tennis racquet. Who the devil left them there?

The Young Lady: They are mine, I'm afraid.

The Captain (*advancing to the drawing-table*). Nurse: who is this misguided and unfortunate young lady?

Nurse Guinness: She says Miss Hessy invited her, sir.

The Captain: And had she no friend, no parents, to warn her against my daughter's invitations? This is a pretty sort of house, by heavens! A young and attractive lady is invited here. Her luggage is left on the steps for hours; and she herself is deposited in the poop and abandoned, tired and starving. This is our hospitality. These are our manners. No room ready. no hot water. No welcoming hostess. Our visitor is to sleep in the toolshed, and to wash in the duckpond.

Nurse Guinness: Now it's all right, Captain: I'll get the lady some tea; and her room shall be ready before she has finished it. (*To the young lady.*) Take off your hat, ducky; and make yourself at home. (*She goes to the door leading to the hall.*)

The Captain (*as she passes him*). Ducky! Do you suppose, woman, that because this young lady has been insulted and neglected, you have the right to address her as you address my wretched children, whom you have brought up in ignorance of the commonest decencies of social intercourse?

Nurse Guinness: Never mind him, doty. (*Quite unconcerned, she goes out into the hall on her way to the kitchen*).

The Captain: Madam: will you favor me with your name? (*He sits down in the big wicker chair.*)

The Young Lady: My name is Ellie Dunn.

The Captain: Dunn! I had a boatswain whose name was Dunn. He was originally a pirate in China. He set up as a ship's chandler with stores which I have every reason to believe he stole from me. No doubt he became rich. Are you his daughter?

Ellie (*indignant*). No: certainly not. I am proud to be able to say that though my father has not been a successful man, nobody has ever had one word to say against him. I think my father is the best man I have ever known.

The Captain: He must be greatly changed. Has he attained the seventh degree of concentration?

Ellie: I don't understand.

The Captain: But how could he, with a daughter? I, madam, have two daughters. One of them is Hesione Hushabye, who invited you here. I keep this house: she upsets it. I desire to attain the seventh degree of concentration: she invites visitors and leaves me to entertain them. (NURSE GUINNESS *returns with the tea tray, which she places on the teak table.*) I have a second daughter who is, thank God, in a remote part of the Empire with her numskull of a husband. As a child she thought the figure-head of my ship, the Dauntless, the most beautiful thing on earth. He resembled it. He had the same expression: wooden yet enterprising. She married him, and will never set foot in this house again.

Nurse Guinness (*carrying the table, with the tea things on it, to* ELLIE'S *side*). Indeed you never were more mistaken. She is in England this very moment. You have been told three times this week that she is coming home for a year for her health. And very glad you should be to see your own daughter again after all these years.

The Captain: I am not glad. The natural term of the affection of the human animal for its offspring is six years. My daughter Ariadne was born when I was forty-six. I am now eighty-eight. If she comes, I am not at home. If she wants anything, let her take it. If she asks for me, let her be informed that I am extremely old, and have totally forgotten her.

Nurse Guinness: Thats no talk to offer to a young lady. Here, ducky, have some tea; and dont listen to him. (*She pours out a cup of tea.*)

The Captain (*rising wrathfully*). Now before high heaven they have given this innocent child Indian tea: the stuff they tan their own leather insides with. (*He seizes the cup and the tea pot and empties both into the leathern bucket.*)

Ellie (*almost in tears*). Oh, please! I am so tired. I should have been glad of anything.

Nurse Guinness: Oh, what a thing to do! The poor lamb is ready to drop.

The Captain: You shall have some of my tea. Do not touch that fly-blown cake: nobody eats it here except the dogs. (*He disappears into the pantry.*)

Nurse Guinness: Theres a man for you! They say he sold himself to the devil in Zanzibar before he was a captain; and the older he grows the more I believe them.

A Woman's Voice (in the hall). Is anyone at home? Hesione! Nurse! Papa! Do come, somebody; and take in my luggage.

[*Thumping heard, as of an umbrella, on the wainscot.*]

Nurse Guinness: My gracious! It's Miss Addy, Lady Utterword, Mrs. Hushabye's sister: the one I told the Captain about. (*Calling.*) Coming, Miss, coming.

[*She carries the table back to its place by the door, and is hurrying out when she is intercepted by* LADY UTTERWORD, *who bursts in much flustered.* LADY UTTERWORD, *a blonde, is very handsome, very well dressed, and so precipitate in speech and action that the first impression (erroneous) is one of comic silliness.*]

Lady Utterword: Oh, is that you, Nurse? How are you? You dont look a day older. Is nobody at home? Where is Hesione? Doesnt she expect me? Where are the servants? Whose luggage is that on the steps? Where's papa? Is everybody asleep? (*Seeing* ELLIE.) Oh! I beg your pardon. I suppose you are one of my nieces. (*Approaching her with outstretched arms.*) Come and kiss your aunt, darling.

Ellie: I'm only a visitor. It is my luggage on the steps.

Nurse Guinness: I'll go get you some fresh tea, ducky. (*She takes up the tray.*)

Ellie: But the old gentleman said he would make some himself.

Nurse Guinness: Bless you! he's forgotten what he went for already. His mind wanders from one thing to another.

Lady Utterword: Papa, I suppose?

Nurse Guinness: Yes, Miss.

Lady Utterword (*vehemently*). Dont be silly, Nurse. Dont call me Miss.

Nurse Guinness (*placidly*). No, lovey. (*She goes out with the tea-tray.*)

Lady Utterword (*sitting down with a flounce on the sofa*). I know what you must feel. Oh, this house, this house! I come back to it after twenty-three years; and it is just the same: the luggage lying on the steps, the servants spoilt and impossible, nobody at home to receive anybody, no regular meals, nobody ever hungry because they are always gnawing bread and butter or munching apples, and, what is worse, the same disorder in ideas, in talk, in feeling. When I was a child I was used to it: I had never known anything better, though I was unhappy, and longed all the time—oh, how I longed!—to be respectable, to be a lady, to live as others did, not to have to think of everything for myself. I married at nineteen to escape from it. My husband is Sir Hastings Utterword, who has been governor of all the crown colonies in succession. I have always been the mistress of Government House. I have been so happy: I had forgotten that people could live like this. I wanted to see my father, my sister, my nephews and nieces (one ought to, you know), and I was looking forward to it. And now the state of the house! the way I'm received! the casual impudence of that woman Guinness, our old nurse! really Hesione might at least have been here: s o m e[1] preparation might have been made for me. You must excuse my going on in this way; but I am really very much hurt and annoyed and disillusioned: and if I had realized it was to be like this, I wouldnt have come. I have a great mind to go away without another word. (*She is on the point of weeping.*)

Ellie (*also very miserable*). Nobody has been here to receive me either. I thought I ought to go away too. But how can I, Lady Utterword? My luggage is on the steps; and the station fly has gone.

[THE CAPTAIN *emerges from the pantry with a tray of Chinese lacquer and a very fine tea-set on it. He rests it provisionally on the end of the table; snatches away the drawing-board, which he stands on the floor against the table legs; and puts the tray in the space thus cleared.* ELLIE *pours out a cup greedily.*]

The Captain: Your tea, young lady. What! another lady! I must fetch another cup. (*He makes for the pantry.*)

[1] For emphasis, Shaw uses letter spacing.

Lady Utterword (*rising from the sofa, suffused with emotion*). Papa! Dont you know me? I'm your daughter.

The Captain: Nonsense! my daughter's upstairs asleep. (*He vanishes through the half door.*)

[LADY UTTERWORD *retires to the window to conceal her tears.*]

Ellie (*going to her with the cup*). Dont be so distressed. Have this cup of tea. He is very old and very strange: he has been just like that to me. I know how dreadful it must be: my own father is all the world to me. Oh, I'm sure he didn't mean it.

[THE CAPTAIN *returns with another cup.*]

The Captain: Now we are complete. (*He places it on the tray.*)

Lady Utterword (*hysterically*). Papa: you can't have forgotten me. I am Ariadne. I'm little Paddy Patkins. Wont you kiss me? (*She goes to him and throws her arms round his neck.*)

The Captain (*woodenly enduring her embrace*). How can you be Ariadne? You are a middle-aged woman: well-preserved, madam, but no longer young.

Lady Utterword: But think of all the years and years I have been away, papa. I have had to grow old, like other people.

The Captain (*disengaging himself*). You should grow out of kissing strange men: they may be striving to attain the seventh degree of concentration.

Lady Utterword: But I'm your daughter. You havnt seen me for years.

The Captain: So much the worse! When our relatives are at home, we have to think of all their good points or it would be impossible to endure them. But when they are away, we console ourselves for their absence by dwelling on their vices. That is how I have come to think my absent daughter Ariadne a perfect fiend; so do not try to ingratiate yourself here by impersonating her. (*He walks firmly away to the other side of the room.*)

Lady Utterword: Ingratiating myself indeed! (*With dignity.*) Very well, papa. (*She sits down at the drawing-table and pours out tea for herself.*)

The Captain: I am neglecting my social duties. You remember Dunn? Billy Dunn?

Lady Utterword: Do you mean that villainous sailor who robbed you?

The Captain (*introducing* ELLIE.) His daughter. (*He sits down on the sofa.*)

Ellie (*protesting.*) No—

[NURSE GUINNESS *returns with fresh tea.*]

The Captain: Take that hogwash away. Do you hear?

Nurse: Youve actually remembered about the tea!

(*To* ELLIE.) O, miss, he didnt forget you after all! You have made an impression.

The Captain (*gloomily*). Youth! beauty! novelty! They are badly wanted in this house. I am excessively old. Hesione is only moderately young. Her children are not youthful.

Lady Utterword: How can children be expected to be youthful in this house? Almost before we could speak we were filled with notions that might have been all very well for pagan philosophers of fifty, but were certainly quite unfit for respectable people of any age.

Nurse: You were always for respectability, Miss Addy.

Lady Utterword: Nurse: will you please remember that I am Lady Utterword, and not Miss Addy, nor lovey, nor darling, nor doty? Do you hear?

Nurse: Yes, ducky: all right. I'll tell them all they must call you my lady. (*She takes her tray out with undisturbed placidity.*)

Lady Utterword: What comfort? what sense is there in having servants with no manners?

Ellie (*rising and coming to the table to put down her empty cup*). Lady Utterword: do you think Mrs. Hushabye really expects me?

Lady Utterword: Oh, dont ask me. You can see for yourself that Ive just arrived; her only sister, after twenty-three years absence! and it seems that *I* am not expected.

The Captain: What does it matter whether the young lady is expected or not? She is welcome. There are beds: there is food. I'll find a room for her myself. (*He makes for the door.*)

Ellie (*following him to stop him*). Oh please—(*He goes out.*) Lady Utterword: I dont know what to do. Your father persists in believing that my father is some sailor who robbed him.

Lady Utterword: You had better pretend not to notice it. My father is a very clever man; but he always forgot things; and now that he is old, of course he is worse. And I must warn you that it is sometimes very hard to feel quite sure that he really forgets.

[MRS. HUSHABYE *bursts into the room tempestuously, and embraces* ELLIE. *She is a couple of years older than* LADY UTTERWORD, *and even better looking. She has magnificent black hair, eyes like the fish pools of Heshbon, and a nobly modelled neck, short at the back and low between her shoulders in front. Unlike her sister she is uncorseted and dressed anyhow in a rich robe of black pile that shews off her white skin and statuesque contour.*]

Mrs. Hushabye: Ellie, my darling, my

pettikins (*kissing her*). How long have you been here? Ive been at home all the time: I was putting flowers and things in your room; and when I just sat down for a moment to try how comfortable the armchair was I went off to sleep. Papa woke me and told me you were here. Fancy your finding no one, and being neglected and abandoned. (*Kissing her again.*) My poor love! (*She deposits* ELLIE *on the sofa. Meanwhile* ADRIADNE *has left the table and come over to claim her share of attention.*) Oh, youve brought someone with you. Introduce me.

Lady Utterword: Hesione: is it possible that you dont know me?

Mrs. Hushabye (*conventionally*). Of course I remember your face quite well. Where have we met?

Lady Utterword: Didnt papa tell you I was here? Oh! this is really too much. (*She throws herself sulkily into the big chair.*)

Mrs. Hushabye: Papa!

Lady Utterword: Yes: Papa. O u r papa, you unfeeling wretch. (*Rising angrily.*) I'll go straight to a hotel.

Mrs. Hushabye (*seizing her by the shoulders*). My goodness gracious goodness, you dont mean to say that youre Addy!

Lady Utterword: I certainly am Addy; and I dont think I can be so changed that you would not have recognized me if you had any real affection for me. And papa didnt think me even worth mentioning!

Mrs. Hushabye: What a lark! Sit down. (*She pushes her back into the chair instead of kissing her, and posts herself behind it.*) You do look a swell. Youre much handsomer than you used to be. Youve made the acquaintance of Ellie, of course. She is going to marry a perfect hog of a millionaire for the sake of her father, who is as poor as a church mouse; and you must help me to stop her.

Ellie: Oh p l e a s e, Hesione.

Mrs. Hushabye: My pettikins, the man's coming here today with your father to begin persecuting you; and everybody will see the state of the case in ten minutes; so whats the use of making a secret of it?

Ellie: He is not a hog, Hesione. You dont know how wonderfully good he was to my father, and how deeply grateful I am to him.

Mrs. Hushabye (*to* LADY UTTERWORD). Her father is a very remarkable man, Addy. His name is Mazzini Dunn. Mazzini was a celebrity of some kind who knew Ellie's grandparents. They were both poets, like the Brownings; and when her father came into the world Mazzini said "Another soldier born for freedom!" So they christened him Mazzini; and he has been fighting for freedom in his quiet way ever since. Thats why he is so poor.

Ellie: I am proud of his poverty.

Mrs. Hushabye: Of course you are, pettikins. Why not leave him in it, and marry someone you love?

Lady Utterword (*rising suddenly and explosively*). Hesione: are you going to kiss me or are you not?

Mrs. Hushabye: What do you want to be kissed for?

Lady Utterword: I dont want to be kissed; but I do want you to behave properly and decently. We are sisters. We have been separated for twenty-three years. You o u g h t to kiss me.

Mrs. Hushabye: Tomorrow morning, dear, before you make up. I hate the smell of powder.

Lady Utterword: Oh, you unfeeling —(*She is interrupted by the return of the captain.*)

The Captain (*to* ELLIE). Your room

is ready. (ELLIE *rises.*) The sheets were damp; but I have changed them.

[*He makes for the garden door on the port side.*]

Lady Utterword: Oh! What about my sheets?

The Captain (*halting at the door*). Take my advice: air them; or take them off and sleep in blankets. You shall sleep in Ariadne's old room.

Lady Utterword: Indeed I shall do nothing of the sort. That little hole! I am entitled to the best spare room.

The Captain (*continuing unmoved*). She married a numskull. She told me she would marry anyone to get away from home.

Lady Utterword: You are pretending not to know me on purpose. I will leave the house.

[MAZZINI DUNN *enters from the hall. He is a little elderly man with bulging credulous eyes and earnest manners. He is dresed in a blue serge jacket suit with an unbuttoned mackintosh over it, and carries a soft black hat of clerical cut.*]

Ellie: At last! Captain Shotover: here is my father.

The Captain: This! Nonsense! not a bit like him. (*He goes away through the garden, shutting the door sharply behind him.*)

Lady Utterword: I will not be ignored and pretended to be somebody else. I will have it out with papa now, this instant. (*To* MAZZINI.) Excuse me. (*She follows the* CAPTAIN *out, making a hasty bow to* MAZZINI, *who returns it.*)

Mrs. Hushabye (*hospitably, shaking hands*). How good of you to come, Mr. Dunn! You dont mind papa, do you? He is as mad as a hatter, you know, but quite harmless, and extremely clever. You will have some delightful talks with him.

Mazzini: I hope so. (*To* ELLIE.) So here you are, Ellie, dear. (*He draws her arm affectionately through his.*) I must thank you, Mrs. Hushabye, for your kindness to my daughter. I'm afraid she would have had no holiday if you had not invited her.

Mrs. Hushabye: Not at all. Very nice of her to come and attract young people to the house for us.

Mazzini (*smiling*). I'm afraid Ellie is not interested in young men, Mrs. Hushabye. Her taste is on the graver, solider side.

Mrs. Hushabye (*with a sudden rather hard brightness in her manner*). Wont you take off your overcoat, Mr. Dunn? You will find a cupboard for coats and hats and things in the corner of the hall.

Mazzini (*hastily releasing* ELLIE). Yes—thank you—I had better—(*He goes out.*)

Mrs. Hushabye (*emphatically*). The old brute!

Ellie: Who?

Mrs. Hushabye: Who! Him. He. It. (*Pointing after* MAZZINI.) "Graver, solider tastes," indeed!

Ellie (*aghast*). You dont mean that you were speaking like that of my father!

Mrs. Hushabye: I was. You know I was.

Ellie (*with dignity*). I will leave your house at once. (*She turns to the door.*)

Mrs. Hushabye: If you attempt it, I'll tell your father why.

Ellie (*turning again*). Oh! How can you treat a visitor like this, Mrs. Hushabye?

Mrs. Hushabye: I thought you were going to call me Hesione.

Ellie: Certainly not now?

Mrs. Hushabye: Very well: I'll tell your father.

Ellie (*distressed*). Oh!

Mrs. Hushabye: If you turn a hair—if you take his part against me and against your own heart for a moment, I'll give that born soldier of freedom a piece of my mind that will stand him on his selfish old head for a week.

Ellie: Hesione! My father selfish! How little you know—

[*She is interrupted by* MAZZINI, *who returns, excited and perspiring.*]

Mazzini: Ellie: Mangan has come: I thought youd like to know. Excuse me, Mrs. Hushabye: the strange old gentleman—

Mrs. Hushabye: Papa. Quite so.

Mazzini: Oh, I beg your pardon: of course: I was a little confused by his manner. He is making Mangan help him with something in the garden; and he wants me to—

[*A powerful whistle is heard.*]

The Captain's Voice: Bosun ahoy! (*The whistle is repeated.*)

Mazzini (*flustered*). Oh dear! I believe he is whistling for me. (*He hurries out.*)

Mrs. Hushabye: Now m y father is a wonderful man if you like.

Ellie: Hesione: listen to me. You dont understand. My father and Mr. Mangan were boys together. Mr. Ma—

Mrs. Hushabye: I dont care what they were: we must sit down if you are going to begin as far back as that. (*She snatches at* ELLIE'S *waist, and makes her sit down on the sofa beside her.*) Now, pettikins: tell me all about Mr. Mangan. They call him Boss Mangan, dont they? He is a Napoleon of industry and disgustingly rich, isnt he? Why isnt your father rich?

Ellie: My poor father should never have been in business. His parents were poets; and they gave him the noblest ideas; but they could not afford to give him a profession.

Mrs. Hushabye: Fancy your grandparents, with their eyes in fine frenzy rolling! And so your poor father had to go into business. Hasnt he succeeded in it?

Ellie: He always used to say he could succeed if he only had some capital. He fought his way along, to keep a roof over our heads and bring us up well; but it was always a struggle: always the same difficulty of not having capital enough. I dont know how to describe it to you.

Mrs. Hushabye: Poor Ellie! I know. Pulling the devil by the tail.

Ellie (*hurt*). Oh no, Not like that. It was at least dignified.

Mrs. Hushabye: That made it all the harder, didnt it? *I* shouldn't have pulled the devil by the tail with dignity. I should have pulled hard—(*between her teeth*) h a r d. Well? Go on.

Ellie: At last it seemed that all our troubles were at an end. Mr. Mangan did an extraordinary noble thing out of pure friendship for my father and respect for his character. He asked him how much capital he wanted, and gave it to him. I dont mean that he lent it to him, or that he invested it in his business. He just simply made him a present of it. Wasn't that splendid of him?

Mrs. Hushabye: On condition that you married him?

Ellie: Oh no, no, no. This was when I was a child. He had never even seen me: he never came to our house. It was absolutely disinterested. Pure generosity.

Mrs. Hushabye: Oh! I beg the gentleman's pardon. Well, what became of the money?

Ellie: We all got new clothes and moved into another house. And I went to another school for two years.

Mrs. Hushabye: Only two years?

Ellie: That was all; for at the end of two years my father was utterly ruined.

Mrs. Hushabye: How?

Ellie: I dont know. I never could understand. But it was dreadful. When we were poor my father had never been in debt. But when he launched out into business on a large scale, he had to incur liabilities. When the business went into liquidation he owed more money than Mr. Mangan had given him.

Mrs. Hushabye: Bit off more than he could chew, I suppose.

Ellie: I think you are a little unfeeling about it.

Mrs. Hushabye: My pettikins: you mustnt mind my way of talking. I was quite as sensitive and particular as you once; but I have picked up so much slang from the children that I am really hardly presentable. I suppose your father had no head for business, and made a mess of it.

Ellie: Oh, that just shews how entirely you are mistaken about him. The business turned out a great success. It now pays forty-four percent after deducting the excess profits tax.

Mrs. Hushabye: Then why arnt you rolling in money?

Ellie: I dont know. It seems very unfair to me. You see, my father was made bankrupt. It nearly broke his heart, because he had persuaded several of his friends to put money into the business. He was sure it would succeed; and events proved that he was quite right. But they all lost their money. It was dreadful. I dont know what we should have done but for Mr. Mangan.

Mrs. Hushabye: What! Did the Boss come to the rescue again, after all his money being thrown away?

Ellie: He did indeed, and never uttered a reproach to my father. He bought what was left of the business—the buildings and the machinery and things—from the official trustee for enough money to enable my father to pay six and eightpence in the pound and get his discharge. Everyone pitied papa so much, and saw so plainly that he was an honorable man, that they let him off at six and eightpence instead of ten shillings. Then Mr. Mangan started a company to take up the business, and made my father a manager in it to save us from starvation; for I wasnt earning anything then.

Mrs. Hushabye: Quite a romance. And when did the Boss develop the tender passion?

Ellie: Oh, that was years after, quite lately. He took the chair one night at a sort of people's concert. I was singing there. As an amateur, you know: half a guinea for expenses and three songs with three encores. He was so pleased with my singing that he asked might he walk home with me. I never saw anyone so taken aback as he was when I took him home and introduced him to my father: his own manager. It was then that my father told me how nobly he had behaved. Of course it was considered a great chance for me, as he is so rich. And—and—we drifted into a sort of understanding—I suppose I should call it an engagement—(*She is distressed and cannot go on.*)

Mrs. Hushabye (*rising and marching about*). You may have drifted into it; but you will bounce out of it, my pettikins, if I am to have anything to do with it.

Ellie (*hopelessly*). No: it's no use. I

am bound in honor and gratitude. I will go through with it.

Mrs. Hushabye (*behind the sofa, scolding down at her*). You know, of course, that it's not honorable or grateful to marry a man you dont love. Do you love this Mangan man?

Ellie: Yes. At least—

Mrs. Hushabye: I dont want to know about "the least": I want to know the worst. Girls of your age fall in love with all sorts of impossible people, especially old people.

Ellie: I like Mr. Mangan very much; and I shall always be—

Mrs. Hushabye (*impatiently completing the sentence and prancing away intolerantly to starboard*). —grateful to him for his kindness to dear father. I know. Anybody else?

Ellie: What do you mean?

Mrs. Hushabye: Anybody else? Are you in love with anybody else?

Ellie: Of course not.

Mrs. Hushabye: Humph! (*The book on the drawing-table catches her eye. She picks it up, and evidently finds the title very unexpected. She looks at* ELLIE, *and asks, quaintly.*) Quite sure youre not in love with an actor?

Ellie: No, no. Why? What put such a thing into your head?

Mrs. Hushabye: This is yours, isn't it? Why else should you be reading Othello?

Ellie: My father taught me to love Shakespear.

Mrs. Hushabye (*flinging the book down on the table*). Really! your father does seem to be about the limit.

Ellie (*naïvely*). Do you never read Shakespear, Hesione? That seems to me so extraordinary. I like Othello.

Mrs. Hushabye: Do you indeed? He was jealous, wasn't he?

Ellie: Oh, not that. I think all the part about jealousy is horrible. But dont you think it must have been a wonderful experience for Desdemona, brought up so quietly at home, to meet a man who had been out in the world doing all sorts of brave things and having terrible adventures, and yet finding something in her that made him love to sit and talk with her and tell her about them?

Mrs. Hushabye: That your idea of romance, is it?

Ellie: Not romance, exactly. It might really happen.

[ELLIE'S *eyes shew that she is not arguing, but in a daydream.* MRS. HUSHABYE, *watching her inquisitively, goes deliberately back to the sofa and resumes her seat beside her.*]

Mrs. Hushabye: Ellie darling: have you noticed that some of those stories that Othello told Desdemona couldnt have happened?

Ellie: Oh no. Shakespear thought they could have happened.

Mrs. Hushabye: Hm! Desdemona thought they could have happened. But they didnt.

Ellie: Why do you look so enigmatic about it? You are such a sphinx: I never know what you mean.

Mrs. Hushabye: Desdemona would have found him out if she had lived, you know. I wonder was that why he strangled her!

Ellie: Othello was not telling lies.

Mrs. Hushabye: How do you know?

Ellie: Shakespear would have said if he was. Hesione: there are men who have done wonderful things: men like Othello, only, of course, white, and very handsome, and—

Mrs. Hushabye: Ah! Now we're coming to it. Tell me all about him. I knew there must be somebody, or youd never have been so miserable about Mangan: youd have thought it quite a lark to marry him.

Ellie (*blushing vividly*). Hesione: you are dreadful. But I dont want to make a secret of it, though of course I dont tell everybody. Besides, I dont know him.

Mrs. Hushabye: Dont know him! What does that mean?

Ellie: Well, of course I know him to speak to.

Mrs. Hushabye: But you want to know him ever so much more intimately, eh?

Ellie: No no: I know him quite—almost intimately.

Mrs. Hushabye: You dont know him; and you know him almost intimately. How lucid!

Ellie: I mean that he does not call on us. I—I got into conversation with him by chance at a concert.

Mrs. Hushabye: You seem to have rather a gay time at your concerts, Ellie.

Ellie: Not at all: we talk to everyone in the green-room waiting for our turns. I thought he was one of the artists: he looked so splendid. But he was only one of the committee. I happened to tell him that I was copying a picture at the National Gallery. I make a little money that way. I cant paint much; but as it's always the same picture I can do it pretty quickly and get two or three pounds for it. It happened that he came to the National Gallery one day.

Mrs. Hushabye: One student's day. Paid sixpence to stumble about through a crowd of easels, when he might have come in next day for nothing and found the floor clear! Quite by accident?

Ellie (*triumphantly*). No. On purpose. He liked talking to me. He knows lots of the most splendid people. Fashionable women who are all in love with him. But he ran away from them to see me at the National Gallery and persuade me to come with him for a drive round Richmond Park in a taxi.

Mrs. Hushabye: My pettikins, you have been going it. It's wonderful what you good girls can do without anyone saying a word.

Ellie: I am not in society, Hesione. If I didnt make acquaintances in that way I shouldnt have any at all.

Mrs. Hushabye: Well, no harm if you know how to take care of yourself. May I ask his name?

Ellie (*slowly and musically*). Marcus Darnley.

Mrs. Hushabye (*echoing the music*). Marcus Darnley! What a splendid name!

Ellie: Oh, I'm so glad you think so. I think so too; but I was afraid it was only a silly fancy of my own.

Mrs. Hushabye: Hm! Is he one of the Aberdeen Darnleys?

Ellie: Nobody knows. Just fancy! He was found in an antique chest—

Mrs. Hushabye: A what?

Ellie: An antique chest, one summer morning in a rose garden, after a night of the most terrible thunderstorm.

Mrs. Hushabye: What on earth was he doing in the chest? Did he get into it because he was afraid of the lightning?

Ellie: Oh no, no: he was a baby. The name Marcus Darnley was embroidered on his babyclothes. And five hundred pounds in gold.

Mrs. Hushabye (*looking hard at her*). Ellie!

Ellie: The garden of the Viscount—

Mrs. Hushabye: —de Rougemont?

Ellie (*innocently*). No: de Larochejaquelin. A French family. A vicomte. His life has been one long romance. A tiger—

Mrs. Hushabye: Slain by his own hand?

Ellie: Oh no: nothing vulgar like that. He saved the life of the tiger from a hunting party: one of King Edward's hunting parties in India. The King was furious: that was why he never had his military services properly recognized. But he doesnt care. He is a Socialist and despises rank, and has been in three revolutions fighting on the barricades.

Mrs. Hushabye: How can you sit there telling me such lies? You, Ellie, of all people! And I thought you were a perfectly simple, straightforward, good girl.

Ellie (*rising, dignified but very angry*). Do you mean to say you dont believe me?

Mrs. Hushabye: Of course I dont believe you. Youre inventing every word of it. Do you take me for a fool?

[ELLIE *stares at her. Her candor is so obvious that* MRS. HUSHABYE *is puzzled.*]

Ellie: Goodbye, Hesione. I'm very sorry. I see now that it sounds very improbable as I tell it. But I cant stay if you think that way about me.

Mrs. Hushabye (*catching her dress*). You shant go. I couldnt be so mistaken: I know too well what liars are like. Somebody has really told you all this.

Ellie (*flushing*). Hesione: dont say that you dont believe h i m. I couldnt bear that.

Mrs. Hushabye (*soothing her*). Of course I believe him, dearest. But you should have broken it to me by degrees. (*Drawing her back to her seat.*) Now tell me all about him. Are you in love with him?

Ellie: Oh no. I'm not so foolish. I dont fall in love with people. I'm not so silly as you think.

Mrs. Hushabye: I see. Only something to think about—to give some interest and pleasure to life.

Ellie: Just so. Thats all, really.

Mrs. Hushabye: It makes the hours go fast, doesnt it? No tedious waiting to go to sleep at nights and wondering whether you will have a bad night. How delightful it makes waking up in the morning! How much better than the happiest dream! All life transfigured! No more wishing one had an interesting book to read, because life is so much happier than any book! No desire but to be alone and not to have to talk to anyone: to be alone and just think about it.

Ellie (*embracing her*). Hesione: you are a witch. How do you know? Oh, you are the most sympathetic woman in the world.

Mrs. Hushabye (*caressing her*). Pettikins, my pettikins: how I envy you! and how I pity you!

Ellie: Pity me! Oh, why?

[*A very handsome man of fifty, with mousquetaire moustaches, wearing a rather dandified curly brimmed hat, and carrying an elaborate walking-stick, comes into the room from the hall, and stops short at sight of the women on the sofa.*]

Ellie (*seeing him and rising in glad surprise*). Oh! Hesione: this is Mr. Marcus Darnley.

Mrs. Hushabye (*rising*). What a lark! He is my husband.

Ellie: But how—(*she stops suddenly; then turns pale and sways*).

Mrs. Hushabye (*catching her and sitting down with her on the sofa*). Steady, my pettikins.

The Man (*with a mixture of confusion and effrontery, depositing his hat and stick on the teak table*). My real name,

Miss Dunn, is Hector Hushabye. I leave you to judge whether that is a name any sensitive man would care to confess to. I never use it when I can possibly help it. I have been away for nearly a month; and I had no idea you knew my wife, or that you were coming here. I am none the less delighted to find you in our little house.

Ellie (*in great distress*). I dont know what to do. Please, may I speak to papa? Do leave me. I cant bear it.

Mrs. Hushabye: Be off, Hector.

Hector: I—

Mrs. Hushabye: Quick, quick. Get out.

Hector: If you think it better—(*He goes out, taking his hat with him but leaving the stick on the table.*)

Mrs. Hushabye (*laying* ELLIE *down at the end of the sofa*). Now, pettikins, he is gone. Theres nobody but me. You can let yourself go. Dont try to control yourself. Have a good cry.

Ellie (*raising her head*). Damn!

Mrs. Hushabye: Splendid! Oh, what a relief! I thought you were going to be brokenhearted. Never mind me. Damn him again.

Ellie: I am not damning him: I am damning myself for being such a fool. (*Rising.*) How could I let myself be taken in so? (*She begins prowling to and fro, her bloom gone, looking curiously older and harder.*)

Mrs. Hushabye (*cheerfully*). Why not, pettikins? Very few young women can resist Hector. I couldnt when I was your age. He is really rather splendid, you know.

Ellie (*turning on her*). Splendid! Yes: splendid looking of course. But how can you love a liar?

Mrs. Hushabye: I dont know. But you can, fortunately. Otherwise there wouldnt be much love in the world.

Ellie: But to lie like that! To be a boaster! a coward!

Mrs. Hushabye (*rising in alarm*). Pettikins: none of that, if you please. If you hint the slightest doubt of Hector's courage, he will go straight off and do the most horribly dangerous things to convince himself that he isnt a coward. He has a dreadful trick of getting out of one third-floor window and coming in at another, just to test his nerve. He has a whole drawerful of Albert Medals for saving people's lives.

Ellie: He never told me that.

Mrs. Hushabye: He never boasts of anything he really did: he cant bear it; and it makes him shy if anyone else does. All his stories are made-up stories.

Ellie (*coming to her*). Do you mean that he is really brave, and really has adventures, and yet tells lies about things that he never did and that never happened?

Mrs. Hushabye: Yes, pettikins, I do. People dont have their virtues and vices in sets: they have them anyhow: all mixed.

Ellie (*staring at her thoughtfully*). Theres something odd about this house, Hesione, and even about you. I dont know why I'm talking to you so calmly. I have a horrible fear that my heart is broken, but that heartbreak is not like what I thought it must be.

Mrs. Hushabye (*fondling her*). It's only life educating you, pettikins. How do you feel about Boss Mangan now?

Ellie (*disengaging herself with an expression of distaste*). Oh, how can you remind me of him, Hesione?

Mrs. Hushabye: Sorry, dear. I think I hear Hector coming back. You dont mind now, do you, dear?

Ellie: Not in the least. I'm quite cured.

[MAZZINI DUNN *and* HECTOR *come in from the hall.*]

Hector (*as he opens the door and allows* MAZZINI *to pass in*). One second more, and she would have been a dead woman!

Mazzini: Dear! dear! What an escape! Ellie, my love: Mr. Hushabye has just been telling me the most extraordinary—

Ellie: Yes: Ive heard it. (*She crosses to the other side of the room.*)

Hector (*following her*). Not this one: I'll tell it to you after dinner. I think youll like it. The truth is, I made it up for you, and was looking forward to the pleasure of telling it to you. But in a moment of impatience at being turned out of the room, I threw it away on your father.

Ellie (*turning at bay with her back to the carpenter's bench, scornfully self-possessed*). It was not thrown away. He believes it. I should not have believed it.

Mazzini (*benevolently*). Ellie is very naughty, Mr. Hushabye. Of course she does not really think that. (*He goes to the bookshelves, and inspects the titles of the volumes.*)

[BOSS MANGAN *comes in from the hall, followed by* THE CAPTAIN. MANGAN, *carefully frock-coated as for church or for a directors' meeting, is about fifty-five, with a careworn, mistrustful expression, standing a little on an entirely imaginary dignity, with a dull complexion, straight, lustreless hair, and features so entirely commonplace that it is impossible to describe them.*]

Captain Shotover (*to* MRS. HUSHABYE, *introducing the newcomer*). Says his name is Mangan. Not ablebodied.

Mrs. Hushabye (*graciously*). How do you do, Mr. Mangan?

Mangan (*shaking hands*). Very pleased.

Captain Shotover: Dunn's lost his muscle, but recovered his nerve. Men seldom do after three attacks of delirium tremens. (*He goes into the pantry.*)

Mrs. Hushabye: I congratulate you, Mr. Dunn.

Mazzini (*dazed*). I am a lifelong teetotaler.

Mrs. Hushabye: You will find it far less trouble to let papa have his own way than try to explain.

Mazzini: But three attacks of delirium tremens, really!

Mrs. Hushabye (*to* MANGAN). Do you know my husband, Mr. Mangan? (*She indicates* HECTOR.)

Mangan (*going to* HECTOR, *who meets him with outstretched hand*). Very pleased. (*Turning to* ELLIE.) I hope, Miss Ellie, you have not found the journey down too fatiguing. (*They shake hands.*)

Mrs. Hushabye: Hector: shew Mr. Dunn his room.

Hector: Certainly. Come along, Mr. Dunn. (*He takes* MAZZINI *out.*)

Ellie: You havnt shewn me my room yet, Hesione.

Mrs. Hushabye: How stupid of me! Come along. Make yourself quite at home, Mr. Mangan. Papa will entertain you. (*She calls to the* CAPTAIN *in the pantry.*) Papa: come and explain the house to Mr. Mangan.

[*She goes out with* ELLIE. *The Captain comes from the pantry.*]

Captain Shotover: Youre going to marry Dunn's daughter. Dont. Youre too old.

Mangan (*staggered*). Well! Thats fairly blunt, Captain.

Captain Shotover: It's true.

Mangan: She doesnt think so.

Captain Shotover: She does.

Mangan: Older men than I have—

Captain Shotover (*finishing the sentence for him*). —made fools of themselves. That, also, is true.

Mangan (*asserting himself*). I dont see that this is any business of yours.

Captain Shotover: It is everybody's business. The stars in their courses are shaken when such things happen.

Mangan: I'm going to marry her all the same.

Captain Shotover: How do you know?

Mangan (*playing the strong man*). I intend to. I mean to. See? I never made up my mind to do a thing yet that I didnt bring it off. Thats the sort of man I am; and there will be a better understanding between us when you make up your mind to that, Captain.

Captain Shotover: You frequent picture palaces.

Mangan: Perhaps I do. Who told you?

Captain Shotover: Talk like a man, not like a movy. You mean that you make a hundred thousand a year.

Mangan: I dont boast. But when I meet a man that makes a hundred thousand a year, I take off my hat to that man, and stretch out my hand to him and call him brother.

Captain Shotover: Then you also make a hundred thousand a year, hey?

Mangan: No. I cant say that. Fifty thousand, perhaps.

Captain Shotover: His half brother only. (*He turns away from* MANGAN *with his usual abruptness, and collects the empty tea-cups on the Chinese tray.*)

Mangan (*irritated*). See here, Captain Shotover. I dont quite understand my position here. I came here on your daughter's invitation. Am I in her house or in yours?

Captain Shotover: You are beneath the dome of heaven, in the house of God. What is true within these walls is true outside them. Go out on the seas; climb the mountains; wander through the valleys. She is still too young.

Mangan (*weakening*). But I'm very little over fifty.

Captain Shotover: You are still less under sixty. Boss Mangan: you will not marry the pirate's child. (*He carries the tray away into the pantry.*)

Mangan (*following him to the half door*). What pirate's child? What are you talking about?

Captain Shotover (*in the pantry*). Ellie Dunn. You will not marry her.

Mangan: Who will stop me?

Captain Shotover (*emerging*). My daughter. (*He makes for the door leading to the hall.*)

Mangan (*following him*). Mrs. Hushabye! Do you mean to say she brought me down here to break it off?

Captain Shotover (*stopping and turning on him*). I know nothing more than I have seen in her eye. She w i l l break it off. Take my advice: marry a West Indian negress: they make excellent wives. I was married to one myself for two years.

Mangan: Well, I a m damned!

Captain Shotover: I thought so. I was, too, for many years. The negress redeemed me.

Mangan (*feebly*). This is queer. I ought to walk out of this house.

Captain Shotover: Why?

Mangan: Well, many men would be offended by your style of talking.

Captain Shotover: Nonsense! It's the other sort of talking that makes quarrels. Nobody ever quarrels with me.

[*A gentleman, whose firstrate tailoring and frictionless manners proclaim the wellbread West Ender, comes in from the hall. He has an engaging air of being young and unmarried, but on close inspection is found to be at least over forty.*]

The Gentleman: Excuse my intruding in this fashion; but there is no knocker on the door; and the bell does not seem to ring.

Captain Shotover: Why should there be a knocker? Why should the bell ring? The door is open.

The Gentleman: Precisely. So I ventured to come in.

Captain Shotover: Quite right. I will see about a room for you. (*He makes for the door.*)

The Gentleman (*stopping him*). But I'm afraid you dont know who I am.

Captain Shotover: Do you suppose that at my age I make distinctions between one fellowcreature and another? (*He goes out. Mangan and the newcomer stare at one another.*)

Mangan: Strange character, Captain Shotover, sir.

The Gentleman: Very.

Captain Shotover (*shouting outside*). Hesione: another person has arrived and wants a room. Man about town, well dressed, fifty.

The Gentleman: Fancy Hesione's feelings! May I ask are you a member of the family?

Mangan: No.

The Gentleman: I am. At least a connexion.

[MRS. HUSHABYE *comes back.*]

Mrs. Hushabye: How do you do? How good of you to come!

The Gentleman: I am very glad indeed to make your acquaintance, Hesione. (*Instead of taking her hand he kisses her. At the same moment the* CAPTAIN *appears in the doorway.*) You will excuse my kissing your daughter, Captain, when I tell you that—

Captain Shotover: Stuff! Everyone kisses my daughter. Kiss her as much as you like. (*He makes for the pantry.*)

The Gentleman: Thank you. One moment, Captain. (THE CAPTAIN *halts and turns. The gentleman goes to him affably.*) Do you happen to remember— but probably you dont as it occurred many years ago—that your younger daughter married a numskull?

Captain Shotover: Yes. She said she'd marry anybody to get away from this house. I should not have recognized you: your head is no longer like a walnut. Your aspect is softened. You have been boiled in bread and milk for years and years, like other married men. Poor devil! (*He disappears into the pantry.*)

Mrs. Hushabye (*going past* MANGAN *to the gentleman and scrutinizing him*). I dont believe you are Hastings Utterword.

The Gentleman: I am not.

Mrs. Hushabye: Then what business had you to kiss me?

The Gentleman: I thought I would like to. The fact is, I am Randall Utterword, the unworthy younger brother of Hastings. I was abroad diplomatizing when he was married.

Lady Utterword (*dashing in*). Hesione: where is the key of the wardrobe in my room? My diamonds are in my dressing-bag: I must lock it up— (*Recognizing the stranger with a shock.*) Randall: how dare you? (*She marches at him past* MRS.

HUSHABYE, *who retreats and joins* MANGAN *near the sofa.*)

Randall: How dare I what? I am not doing anything.

Lady Utterword: Who told you I was here?

Randall: Hastings. You had just left when I called on you at Claridge's; so I followed you down here. You are looking extremely well.

Lady Utterword: Dont presume to tell me so.

Mrs. Hushabye: What is wrong with Mr. Randall, Addy?

Lady Utterword (*recollecting herself*). Oh, nothing. But he has no right to come bothering you and papa without being invited. (*She goes to the window-seat and sits down, turning away from them ill-humoredly and looking into the garden, where* HECTOR *and* ELLIE *are now seen strolling together.*)

Mrs. Hushabye: I think you have not met Mr. Mangan, Addy.

Lady Utterword (*turning her head and nodding coldly to* MANGAN). I beg your pardon. Randall: you have flustered me so: I made a perfect fool of myself.

Mrs. Hushabye: Lady Utterword. My sister. My y o u n g e r sister.

Mangan (*bowing*). Pleased to meet you, Lady Utterword.

Lady Utterword (*with marked interest*). Who is that gentleman walking in the garden with Miss Dunn?

Mrs. Hushabye: I dont know. She quarrelled mortally with my husband only ten minutes ago; and I didnt know anyone else had come. It must be a visitor. (*She goes to the window to look.*) Oh, it i s Hector. Theyve made it up.

Lady Utterword: Your husband! That handsome man?

Mrs. Hushabye: Well, why shouldnt my husband be a handsome man?

Randall (*joining them at the window*). One's husband never is, Ariadne. (*He sits by* LADY UTTERWORD, *on her right.*)

Mrs. Hushabye: One's sister's husband always is, Mr. Randall.

Lady Utterword: Dont be vulgar, Randall. And you, Hesione, are just as bad.

[ELLIE *and* HECTOR *come in from the garden by the starboard door.* RANDALL *rises.* ELLIE *retires into the corner near the pantry.* HECTOR *comes forward; and* LADY UTTERWORD *rises looking her very best.*]

Mrs. Hushabye: Hector: this is Addy.

Hector (*apparently surprised*). Not this lady.

Lady Utterword (*smiling*). Why not?

Hector (*looking at her with a piercing glance of deep but respectful admiration, his moustache bristling*). I thought— (*pulling himself together*) I beg your pardon, Lady Utterword. I am extremely glad to welcome you at last under our roof. (*He offers his hand with grave courtesy.*)

Mrs. Hushabye: She wants to be kissed, Hector.

Lady Utterword: Hesione! (*But she still smiles.*)

Mrs. Hushabye: Call her Addy; and kiss her like a good brother-in-law; and have done with it. (*She leaves them to themselves.*)

Hector: Behave yourself, Hesione. Lady Utterword is entitled not only to hospitality but to civilization.

Lady Utterword (*gratefully*). Thank you, Hector. (*They shake hands cordially.*)

[MAZZINI DUNN *is seen crossing the garden from starboard to port.*]

Captain Shotover (*coming from the pantry and addressing* ELLIE). Your father has washed himself.

Ellie (*quite self-possessed*). He often does, Captain Shotover.

Captain Shotover: A strange conversion! I saw him through the pantry window.

[MAZZINI DUNN *enters through the port window door, newly washed and brushed, and stops, smiling benevolently, between* MANGAN *and* MRS. HUSHABYE.]

Mrs. Hushabye (*introducing*). Mr. Mazzini Dunn, Lady Ut—oh, I forgot: youve met. (*Indicating* ELLIE.) Miss Dunn.

Mazzini (*walking across the room to take* ELLIE'S *hand, and beaming at his own naughty irony*). I have met Miss Dunn also. She is my daughter. (*He draws her arm through his caressingly.*)

Mrs. Hushabye: Of course: how stupid! Mr. Utterword, my sister's-er—

Randall (*shaking hands agreeably*). Her brother-in-law, Mr. Dunn. How do you do?

Mrs. Hushabye: This is my husband.

Hector: We have met, dear. Dont introduce us any more. (*He moves away to the big chair, and adds*): Wont you sit down, Lady Utterword? (*She does so very graciously.*)

Mrs. Hushabye: Sorry. I hate it: it's like making people shew their tickets.

Mazzini (*sententiously*). How little it tells us, after all! The great question is, not who we are, but what we are.

Captain Shotover: Ha! What are you?

Mazzini (*taken aback*). What am I?

Captain Shotover: A thief, a pirate, and a murderer.

Mazzini: I assure you you are mistaken.

Captain Shotover: An adventurous life; but what does it end in? Respectability. A lady-like daughter. The language and appearance of a city missionary. Let it be a warning to all of you. (*He goes out through the garden.*)

Dunn: I hope nobody here believes that I am a thief, a pirate, or a murderer. Mrs. Hushabye: will you excuse me a moment? I must really go and explain. (*He follows* THE CAPTAIN.)

Mrs. Hushabye (*as he goes*). It's no use. Youd really better— (*But* DUNN *has vanished.*) We had better all go out and look for some tea. We never have regular tea; but you can always get some when you want: the servants keep it stewing all day. The kitchen veranda is the best place to ask. May I shew you? (*She goes to the starboard door.*)

Randall (*going with her*). Thank you, I dont think I'll take any tea this afternoon. But if you will shew me the garden—?

Mrs. Hushabye: Theres nothing to see in the garden except papa's observatory, and a gravel pit with a cave where he keeps dynamite and things of that sort. However, it's pleasanter out of doors; so come along.

Randall: Dynamite! Isnt that rather risky?

Mrs. Hushabye: Well, we dont sit in the gravel pit when theres a thunderstorm.

Lady Utterword: Thats something new. What is the dynamite for?

Hector: To blow up the human race if it goes too far. He is trying to discover a psychic ray that will explode all the explosives at the will of a Mahatma.

Ellie: The Captain's tea is delicious, Mr. Utterword.

Mrs. Hushabye (*stopping in the doorway*). Do you mean to say that youve had some of my father's tea? that you got round him before you were ten minutes in the house?

Ellie: I did.

Mrs. Hushabye: You little devil! (*She goes out with* RANDALL.)

Mangan: Wont you come, Miss Ellie?

Ellie: I'm too tired. I'll take a book up to my room and rest a little. (*She goes to the bookshelf.*)

Mangan: Right. You cant do better. But I'm disappointed. (*He follows* RANDALL *and* MRS. HUSHABYE.)

[ELLIE, HECTOR, *and* LADY UTTERWORD *are left.* HECTOR *is close to* LADY UTTERWORD. *They look at* ELLIE, *waiting for her to go.*]

Ellie (*looking at the title of a book*). Do you like stories of adventure, Lady Utterword?

Lady Utterword (*patronizingly*). Of course, dear.

Ellie: Then I'll leave you to Mr. Hushabye. (*She goes out through the hall.*)

Hector: That girl is mad about tales of adventure. The lies I have to tell her!

Lady Utterword (*not interested in* ELLIE). When you saw me what did you mean by saying that you thought, and then stopping short? What did you think?

Hector (*folding his arms and looking down at her magnetically*). May I tell you?

Lady Utterword: Of course.

Hector: It will not sound very civil. I was on the point of saying "I thought you were a plain woman."

Lady Utterword: Oh for shame, Hector! What right had you to notice whether I am plain or not?

Hector: Listen to me, Ariadne. Until today I have seen only photographs of you; and no photograph can give the strange fascination of the daughters of that supernatural old man. There is some damnable quality in them that destroys men's moral sense, and carries them beyond honor and dishonor. You know that, dont you?

Lady Utterword: Perhaps I do, Hector. But let me warn you once for all that I am a rigidly conventional woman. You may think because I'm a Shotover that I'm a Bohemian, because we are all so horribly Bohemian. But I'm not. I hate and loathe Bohemianism. No child brought up in a strict Puritan household every suffered from Puritanism as I suffered from our Bohemianism.

Hector: Our children are like that. They spend their holidays in the houses of their respectable schoolfellows.

Lady Utterword: I shall invite them for Christmas.

Hector: Their absence leaves us both without our natural chaperons.

Lady Utterword: Children are certainly very inconvenient sometimes. But intelligent people can always manage, unless they are Bohemians.

Hector: You are no Bohemian; but you are no Puritan either: your attraction is alive and powerful. What sort of woman do you count yourself?

Lady Utterword: I am a woman of the world, Hector; and I can assure you that if you will only take the trouble always to do the perfectly correct thing, and to say the perfectly correct thing, you can do just what you like. An ill-conducted, careless woman gets simply no chance. An ill-conducted, careless man is never allowed within arms length of any woman worth knowing.

Hector: I see. You are neither a Bohemian woman nor a Puritan woman. You are a dangerous woman.

Lady Utterword: On the contrary, I am a safe woman.

Hector: You are a most accursedly attractive woman. Mind: I am not making love to you. I do not like being attracted. But you had better know how I feel if you are going to stay here.

Lady Utterword: You are an exceedingly clever ladykiller, Hector. And terribly handsome. I am quite a good player, myself, at that game. It is quite understood that we are only playing?

Hector: Quite. I am deliberately playing the fool, out of sheer worthlessness.

Lady Utterword (*rising brightly*). Well, you are my brother-in-law. Hesione asked you to kiss me. (*He seizes her in his arms, and kisses her strenuously.*) Oh! that was a little more than play, brother-in-law. (*She pushes him suddenly away.*) You shall not do that again.

Hector: In effect, you got your claws deeper into me than I intended.

Mrs. Hushabye (*coming in from the garden*). Dont let me distrub you: I only want a cap to put on daddiest. The sun is setting; and he'll catch cold. (*She makes for the door leading to the hall.*)

Lady Utterword: Your husband is quite charming, darling. He has actually condescended to kiss me at last. I shall go into the garden: it's cooler now. (*She goes out by the port door.*)

Mrs. Hushabye: Take care, dear child. I dont believe any man can kiss Addy without falling in love with her. (*She goes into the hall.*)

Hector (*striking himself on the chest*). Fool! Goat!

[MRS. HUSHABYE *comes back with* THE CAPTAIN'S *cap.*]

Hector: Your sister is an extremely enterprising old girl. Wheres Miss Dunn!

Mrs. Hushabye: Mangan says she has gone up to her room for a nap. Addy wont let you talk to Ellie: she has marked you for her own.

Hector: She has the diabolical family fascination. I began making love to her automatically. What am I to do? I cant fall in love; and I cant hurt a woman's feelings by telling her so when she falls in love with me. And as women are always falling in love with my moustache I get landed in all sorts of tedious and terrifying flirtations in which I'm not a bit in earnest.

Mrs. Hushabye: Oh, neither is Addy. She has never been in love in her life, though she has always been trying to fall in head over ears. She is worse than you, because you had one real go at least, with me.

Hector: That was a confounded madness. I cant believe that such an amazing experience is common. It has left its mark on me. I believe that is why I have never been able to repeat it.

Mrs. Hushabye (*laughing and caressing his arm*). We were frightfully in love with one another, Hector. It was such an enchanting dream that I have never been able to grudge it to you or anyone else since. I have invited all sorts of pretty women to the house on the chance of giving you another turn. But it has never come off.

Hector: I dont know that I want it to come off. It was damned dangerous. You fascinated me; but I loved you; so it was heaven. This sister of yours fascinates me; but I hate her; so it is hell. I shall kill her if she persists.

Mrs. Hushabye: Nothing will kill Addy: she is as strong as a horse. (*Releasing him.*) Now *I* am going off to fascinate somebody.

Hector: The Foreign Office toff? Randall?

Mrs. Hushabye: Goodness gracious, no! Why should I fascinate him?

Hector: I presume you dont mean the bloated capitalist, Mangan?

Mrs. Hushabye: Hm! I think he had better be fascinated by me than by Ellie. (*She is going into the garden when* THE CAPTAIN *comes in from it with some sticks in his hand.*) What have you got there, daddiest?

Captain Shotover: Dynamite.

Mrs. Hushabye: Youve been to the gravel pit. Dont drop it about the house: theres a dear. (*She goes into the garden, where the evening light is now very red.*)

Hector: Listen, O sage. How long dare you concentrate on a feeling without risking having it fixed in your consciousness all the rest of your life?

Captain Shotover: Ninety minutes. An hour and a half. (*He goes into the pantry.*)

[HECTOR, *left alone, contracts his brows, and falls into a daydream. He does not move for some time. Then he folds his arms. Then, throwing his hands behind him, and gripping one with the other, he strides tragically once to and fro. Suddenly he snatches his walking-stick from the teak table, and draws it; for it is a sword-stick. He fights a desperate duel with an imaginary antagonist, and after many vicissitudes runs him through the body up to the hilt. He sheathes his sword and throws it on the sofa, falling into another reverie as he does so. He looks straight into the eyes of an imaginary woman; seizes her by the arms; and says in a deep and thrilling tone* "Do you love me!" THE CAPTAIN *comes out of the pantry at this moment; and* HECTOR, *caught with his arms stretched out and his fists clenched, has to account for his attitude by going through a series of gymnastic exercises.*]

Captain Shotover: That sort of strength is no good. You will never be as strong as a gorilla.

Hector: What is the dynamite for?

Captain Shotover: To kill fellows like Mangan.

Hector: No use. They will always be able to buy more dynamite than you.

Captain Shotover: I will make a dynamite that he cannot explode.

Hector: And that you can, eh?

Captain Shotover: Yes: when I have attained the seventh degree of concentration.

Hector: Whats the use of that? You never do attain it.

Captain Shotover: What then is to be done? Are we to be kept for ever in the mud by these hogs to whom the universe is nothing but a machine for greasing their bristles and filling their snouts?

Hector: Are Mangan's bristles worse than Randall's lovelocks?

Captain Shotover: We must win powers of life and death over them both. I refuse to die until I have invented the means.

Hector: Who are we that we should judge them?

Captain Shotover: What are they that they should judge us? Yet they do, unhesitatingly. There is enmity between our seed and their seed. They know it and act on it, strangling our souls. They believe in themselves. When we believe in ourselves, we shall kill them.

Hector: It is the same seed. You forget that your pirate has a very nice daughter. Mangan's son may be a Plato: Randall's a Shelley. What was my father?

Captain Shotover: The damndest scoundrel I ever met. (*He replaces the drawing-board; sits down at the table; and begins to mix a wash of color.*)

Hector: Precisely. Well, dare you kill his innocent grandchildren?

Captain Shotover: They are mine also.

Hector: Just so. We are members one of another. (*He throws himself carelessly on the sofa.*) I tell you I have often thought of this killing of human vermin. Many men have thought of it. Decent men are like Daniel in the lion's den: their survival is a miracle; and they do not always survive. We live among the Mangans and Randalls and Billie Dunns as they, poor devils, live among the disease germs and the doctors and the lawyers and the parsons and the restaurant chefs and the tradesmen and the servants and all the rest of the parasites and blackmailers. What are our terrors to theirs? Give me the power to kill them; and I'll spare them in sheer—

Captain Shotover (*cutting in sharply*). Fellow feeling?

Hector: No. I should kill myself if I believed that. I must believe that my spark, small as it is, is divine, and that the red light over their door is hell fire. I should spare them in simple magnanimous pity.

Captain Shotover: You cant spare them until you have the power to kill them. At present they have the power to kill you. There are millions of blacks over the water for them to train and let loose on us. Theyre going to do it. Theyre doing it already.

Hector: They are too stupid to use their power.

Captain Shotover (*throwing down his brush and coming to the end of the sofa*). Do not deceive yourself: they do use it. We kill the better half of ourselves every day to propitiate them. The knowledge that these people are there to render all our aspirations barren prevents us having the aspirations. And when we are tempted to seek their destruction they bring forth demons to delude us, disguised as pretty daughters, and singers and poets and the like, for whose sake we spare them.

Hector (*sitting up and leaning towards him*). May not Hesione be such a demon, brought forth by you lest I should slay you?

Captain Shotover: That is possible. She has used you up, and left you nothing but dreams, as some women do.

Hector: Vampire women, demon women.

Captain Shotover: Men think the world well lost for them, and lose it accordingly. Who are the men that do things? The husbands of the shrew and of the drunkard, the men with the thorn in the flesh. (*Walking distractedly away towards the pantry.*) I must think these things out. (*Turning suddenly.*) But I go on with the dynamite none the less. I will discover a ray mightier than any X-ray: a mind ray that will explode the ammunition in the belt of my adversary before he can point his gun at me. And I must hurry. I am old: I have no time to waste in talk. (*He is about to go into the pantry, and* HECTOR *is making for the hall, when* HESIONE *comes back.*)

Mrs. Hushabye: Daddiest: you and

Hector must come and help me to entertain all these people. What on earth were you shouting about?

Hector (*stopping in the act of turning the door handle*). He is madder than usual.

Mrs. Hushabye: We all are.

Hector: I must change. (*He resumes his door opening.*)

Mrs. Hushabye: Stop, stop. Come back, both of you. Come back. (*They return, reluctantly.*) Money is running short.

Hector: Money! Where are my April dividends?

Mrs. Hushabye: Where is the snow that fell last year?

Captain Shotover: Where is all the money you had for that patent lifeboat I invented?

Mrs. Hushabye: Five hundred pounds; and I have made it last since Easter!

Captain Shotover: Since Easter! Barely four months! Monstrous extravagance! I could live for seven years on £500.

Mrs. Hushabye: Not keeping open house as we do here, daddiest.

Captain Shotover: Only £500 for that lifeboat! I got twelve thousand for the invention before that.

Mrs. Hushabye: Yes, dear; but that was for the ship with the magnetic keel that sucked up submarines. Living at the rate we do, you cannot afford life-saving inventions. Cant you think of something that will murder half Europe at one bang?

Captain Shotover: No. I am ageing fast. My mind does not dwell on slaughter as it did when I was a boy. Why doesnt your husband invent something? He does nothing but tell lies to women.

Hector: Well, that is a form of invention, is it not? However, you are right: I ought to support my wife.

Mrs. Hushabye: Indeed you shall do nothing of the sort: I should never see you from breakfast to dinner. I want my husband.

Hector (*bitterly*). I might as well be your lapdog.

Mrs. Hushabye: Do you want to be my breadwinner, like the other poor husbands?

Hector: No, by thunder! What a damned creature a husband is anyhow!

Mrs. Hushabye (*to* THE CAPTAIN). What about that harpoon cannon?

Captain Shotover: No use. It kills whales, not men.

Mrs. Hushabye: Why not? You fire the harpoon out of a cannon. It sticks in the enemy's general; you wind him in; and there you are.

Hector: You are your father's daughter, Hesione.

Captain Shotover: There is something in it. Not to wind in generals: they are not dangerous. But one could fire a grapnel and wind in a machine gun or even a tank. I will think it out.

Mrs. Hushabye (*squeezing* THE CAPTAIN'S *arm affectionately*). Saved! You a r e a darling, daddiest. Now we must go back to these dreadful people and entertain them.

Captain Shotover: They have had no dinner. Dont forget that.

Hector: Neither have I. And it is dark: it must be all hours.

Mrs. Hushabye: Oh, Guinness will produce some sort of dinner for them. The servants always take jolly good care that there is food in the house.

Captain Shotover (*raising a strange wail in the darkness*). What a house! What a daughter!

Mrs. Hushabye (*raving*). What a father!

Hector (*following suit*). What a husband!

Captain Shotover: Is there no thunder in heaven?

Hector: Is there no beauty, no bravery, on earth?

Mrs. Hushabye: What do men want? They have their food, their firesides, their clothes mended, and our love at the end of the day. Why are they not satisfied? Why do they envy us the pain with which we bring them into the world, and make strange dangers and torments for themselves to be even with us?

Captain Shotover (*weirdly chanting*).

I builded a house for my daughters, and opened the doors thereof,
That men might come for their choosing, and their betters spring from their love;
But one of them married a numskull;

Hector (*taking up the rhythm*).

The other a liar wed;

Mrs. Hushabye (*completing the stanza*).

And now must she lie beside him, even as she made her bed.

Lady Utterword (*calling from the garden*). Hesione! Hesione! Where are you?

Hector: The cat is on the tiles.

Mrs. Hushabye: Coming, darling, coming. (*She goes quickly into the garden.*)

[THE CAPTAIN *goes back to his place at the table.*]

Hector (*going into the hall*). Shall I turn up the lights for you?

Captain Shotover: No. Give me deeper darkness. Money is not made in the light.

ACT II

[*The same room, with the lights turned up and the curtains drawn.* ELLIE *comes in, followed by* MANGAN. *Both are dressed for dinner. She strolls to the drawing-table. He comes between the table and the wicker chair.*]

Mangan: What a dinner! I dont call it a dinner: I call it a meal.

Ellie: I am accustomed to meals, Mr. Mangan, and very lucky to get them. Besides, the captain cooked some macaroni for me.

Mangan (*shuddering liverishly*). Too rich: I cant eat such things. I suppose it's because I have to work so much with my brain. Thats the worst of being a man of business: you are always thinking, thinking, thinking. By the way, now that we are alone, may I take the opportunity to come to a little understanding with you?

Ellie (*settling into the draughtsman's seat*). Certainly. I should like to.

Mangan (*taken aback*). Should you? That surprises me; for I thought I noticed this afternoon that you avoided me all you could. Not for the first time either.

Ellie: I was very tired and upset. I wasnt used to the way of this extraordinary house. Please forgive me.

Mangan: Oh, thats all right: I dont mind. But Captain Shotover has been talking to me about you. You and me, you know.

Ellie (*interested*). The Captain! What did he say?

Mangan: Well, he noticed the difference between our ages.

Ellie: He notices everything.

Mangan: You dont mind, then?

Ellie: Of course I know quite well that our engagement—

Mangan: Oh! you call it an engagement.

Ellie: Well, isnt it?

Mangan: Oh, yes, yes: no doubt it is if you hold to it. This is the first time youve used the word; and I didnt quite know where we stood: that all. (*He sits down in the wicker chair; and resigns himself to allow her to lead the conversation.*) You were saying—?

Ellie: Was I? I forget. Tell me. Do you like this part of the country? I heard you ask Mr. Hushabye at dinner whether there are any nice houses to let down here.

Mangan: I like the place. The air suits me. I shouldnt be surprised if I settled down here.

Ellie: Nothing would please me better. The air suits me too. And I want to be near Hesione.

Mangan (*with growing uneasiness*). The air may suit us; but the question is, should we suit one another? Have you thought about that?

Ellie: Mr. Mangan: we must be sensible, mustnt we? It's no use pretending that we are Romeo and Juliet. But we can get on very well together if we choose to make the best of it. Your kindness of heart will make it easy for me.

Mangan (*leaning forward, with the beginning of something like deliberate unpleasantness in his voice*). Kindness of heart, eh? I ruined your father, didnt I?

Ellie: Oh, not intentionally.

Mangan: Yes I did. Ruined him on purpose.

Ellie: On purpose!

Mangan: Not out of ill-nature, you know. And youll admit that I kept a job for him when I had finished with him. But business is business; and I ruined him as a matter of business.

Ellie: I dont understand how that can be. Are you trying to make me feel that I need not be grateful to you, so that I may choose freely?

Mangan (*rising aggressively*). No. I mean what I say.

Ellie: But how could it possibly do you any good to ruin my father? The money he lost was yours.

Mangan (*with a sour laugh*). Was mine! It is mine, Miss Ellie, and all the money the other fellows lost too. (*He shoves his hands into his pockets and shews his teeth.*) I just smoked them out like a hive of bees. What do you say to that? A bit of a shock, eh?

Ellie: It would have been, this morning. Now! you cant think how little it matters. But it's quite interesting. Only, you must explain it to me. I dont understand it. (*Propping her elbows on the drawing-board and her chin on her hands, she composes herself to listen with a combination of conscious curiosity with unconscious contempt which provokes him to more and more unpleasantness, and an attempt at patronage of her ignorance.*)

Mangan: Of course you dont understand: what do you know about business? You just listen and learn. Your father's business was a new business; and I dont start new businesses: I let other fellows start them. They put all their money and their friends' money into starting them.

They wear out their souls and bodies trying to make a success of them. Theyre what you call enthusiasts. But the first dead lift of the thing is too much for them; and they havent enough financial experience. In a year or so they have either to let the whole show go bust, or sell out to a new lot of fellows for a few deferred ordinary shares: that is, if theyre lucky enough to get anything at all. As likely as not the very same thing happens to the new lot. They put in more money and a couple of years more work; and then perhaps t h e y have to sell out to a third lot. If it's really a big thing the third lot will have to sell out too, and leave t h e i r work and t h e i r money behind them. And thats where the real business man comes in: where I come in. But I'm cleverer than some: I dont mind dropping a little money to start the process. I took your father's measure. I saw that he had a sound idea, and that he would work himself silly for it if he got the chance. I saw that he was a child in business, and was dead certain to outrun his expenses and be in too great a hurry to wait for his market. I knew that the surest way to ruin a man who doesnt know how to handle money is to give him some. I explained my idea to some friends in the city, and they found the money; for I take no risks in ideas, even when theyre my own. Your father and the friends that ventured their money with him were no more to me than a heap of squeezed lemons. Youve been wasting your gratitude: my kind heart is all rot. I'm sick of it. When I see your father beaming at me with his moist, grateful eyes, regularly wallowing in gratitude, I sometimes feel I must tell him the truth or burst. What stops me is that I know he wouldnt believe me. He'd think it was my modesty, as you did just now. He'd think anything rather than the truth, which is that he's a blamed fool, and I am a man that knows how to take care of himself. (*He throws himself back into the big chair with large self-approval.*) Now what do you think of me, Miss Ellie?

Ellie (*dropping her hands*). How strange! that my mother, who knew nothing at all about business, should have been quite right about you! She always said—not before papa, of course, but to us children—that you were just that sort of man.

Mangan (*sitting up, much hurt*). Oh! did she? And yet she'd have let you marry me.

Ellie: Well, you see, Mr. Mangan, my mother married a very good man—for whatever you may think of my father as a man of business, he is the soul of goodness—and she is not at all keen on my doing the same.

Mangan: Anyhow, you dont want to marry me now, do you?

Ellie (*very calmly*). Oh, I think so. Why not?

Mangan (*rising aghast*). Why not!

Ellie: I dont see why we shouldnt get on very well together.

Mangan: Well, but look here, you know— (*He stops, quite at a loss.*)

Ellie (*patiently*). Well?

Mangan: Well, I thought you were rather particular about people's characters.

Ellie: If we women were particular about men's characters, we should never get married at all, Mr. Mangan.

Mangan: A child like you talking of "we women"! What next! Youre not in earnest?

Ellie: Yes I am. Arnt you?

Mangan: You mean to hold me to it?

Ellie: Do you wish to back out of it?

Mangan: Oh no. Not exactly back out of it.

Ellie: Well?

[*He has nothing to say. With a long whispered whistle, he drops into the wicker chair and stares before him like a beggared gambler. But a cunning look soon comes into his face. He leans over towards her on his right elbow, and speaks in a low steady voice.*]

Mangan: Suppose I told you I was in love with another woman!

Ellie (*echoing him*). Suppose I told you I was in love with another man!

Mangan (*bouncing angrily out of his chair*). I'm not joking.

Ellie: Who told you *I* was?

Mangan: I tell you I'm serious. Youre too young to be serious; but youll have to believe me. I want to be near your friend Mrs. Hushabye. I'm in love with her. Now the murder's out.

Ellie: I want to near your friend Mr. Hushabye. I'm in love with him. (*She rises and adds with a frank air.*) Now we are in one another's confidence, we shall be real friends. Thank you for telling me.

Mangan (*almost beside himself*). Do you think I'll be made a convenience of like this?

Ellie: Come, Mr. Mangan! you made a business convenience of my father. Well, a woman's business is marriage. Why shouldnt I make a domestic convenience of you?

Mangan: Because I dont choose, see? Because I'm not a silly gull like your father. Thats why.

Ellie (*with serene contempt*). You are not good enough to clean my father's boots, Mr. Mangan; and I am paying you a great compliment in condescending to make a convenience of you, as you call it. Of course you are free to throw over our engagement if you like; but, if you do, youll never enter Hesione's house again: I will take care of that.

Mangan (*gasping*). You little devil, youve done me. (*On the point of collapsing into the big chair again he recovers himself.*) Wait a bit, though: youre not so cute as you think. You cant beat Boss Mangan as easy as that. Suppose I go straight to Mrs. Hushabye and tell her that youre in love with her husband.

Ellie: She knows it.

Mangan: You told her!!!

Ellie: She told me.

Mangan (*clutching at his bursting temples*). Oh, this is a crazy house. Or else I'm going clean off my chump. Is she making a swap with you—she to have your husband and you to have hers?

Ellie: Well, you dont want us both, do you?

Mangan (*throwing himself into the chair distractedly*). My brain wont stand it. My head's going to split. Help! Help me to hold it. Quick: hold it: squeeze it. Save me. (ELLIE *comes behind his chair; clasps his head hard for a moment; then begins to draw her hands from his forehead back to his ears.*) Thank you. (*Drowsily.*) Thats very refreshing. (*Waking a little.*) Dont you hypnotize me, though. Ive seen men made fools of by hypnotism.

Ellie (*steadily*). Be quiet. Ive seen men made fools of without hypnotism.

Mangan (*humbly*). You dont dislike touching me, I hope. You never touched me before, I noticed.

Ellie: Not since you fell in love naturally with a grown-up nice woman, who will never expect you to make love to her. And I will never expect him to make love to me.

Mangan: He may, though.

Ellie (*making her passes rhythmically*). Hush. Go to sleep. Do you hear? You are to go to sleep, go to sleep, go to sleep; be quiet, deeply deeply quiet; sleep, sleep, sleep, sleep, sleep.

[*He falls asleep.* ELLIE *steals away; turns the light out; and goes into the garden.*]

[NURSE GUINNESS *opens the door and is seen in the light which comes in from the hall.*]

Guinness (*speaking to someone outside*). Mr. Mangan's not here, ducky: theres no one here. It's all dark.

Mrs. Hushabye (*without*). Try the garden. Mr. Dunn and I will be in my boudoir. Shew him the way.

Guinness: Yes, ducky. (*She makes for the garden door in the dark; stumbles over the sleeping* MANGAN*; and screams.*) Ahoo! Oh Lord, sir! I beg your pardon, I'm sure: I didnt see you in the dark. Who is it? (*She goes back to the door and turns on the light.*) Oh, Mr. Mangan, sir, I hope I havnt hurt you plumping into your lap like that. (*Coming to him.*) I was looking for you, sir. Mrs. Hushabye says will you please— (*Noticing that he remains quite insensible.*) Oh, my good Lord, I hope I havnt killed him. Sir! Mr. Mangan! Sir! (*She shakes him; and he is rolling inertly off the chair on the floor when she holds him up and props him against the cushion.*) Miss Hessy! Miss Hessy! Quick, doty darling. Miss Hessy! (MRS. HUSHABYE *comes in from the hall, followed by* MAZZINI DUNN.) Oh, Miss Hessy, Ive been and killed him.

[MAZZINI *runs round the back of the chair to* MANGAN'S *right hand, and sees that the nurse's words are apparently only too true.*]

Mazzini: What tempted you to commit such a crime, woman?

Mrs. Hushabye (*trying not to laugh*). Do you mean you did it on purpose?

Guinness: Now is it likely I'd kill any man on purpose? I fell over him in the dark; and I'm a pretty tidy weight. He never spoke nor moved until I shook him; and then he would have dropped dead on the floor. Isnt it tiresome?

Mrs Hushabye (*going past the nurse to* MANGAN'S *side, and inspecting him less credulously than* MAZZINI). Nonsense! he is not dead: he is only asleep. I can see him breathing.

Guinness: But why wont he wake?

Mazzini (*speaking very politely into* MANGAN'S *ear*). Mangan! My dear Mangan! (*He blows into* MANGAN'S *ear.*)

Mrs. Hushabye: Thats no good. (*She shakes him vigorously.*) Mr. Mangan: wake up. Do you hear? (*He begins to roll over.*) Oh! Nurse, nurse: he's falling: help me.

[NURSE GUINNESS *rushes to the rescue. With* MAZZINI'S *assistance,* MANGAN *is propped safely up again.*]

Guinness (*behind the chair; bending over to test the case with her nose*). Would he be drunk, do you think, pet?

Mrs. Hushabye: Had he any of papa's rum?

Mazzini: It cant be that: he is most abstemious. I am afraid he drank too much formerly, and has to drink too little now. You know, Mrs. Hushabye, I really think he has been hypnotized.

Guinness: Hip no what, sir?

Mazzini: One evening at home, after we had seen a hypnotizing performance, the children began playing at it; and Ellie stroked my head. I assure you I went off dead asleep; and they had to send for a professional to wake me up after I had slept eighteen hours. They had to carry me upstairs; and as the poor children were not very strong, they let me slip; and I rolled right down the whole flight and never woke up. (MRS. HUSHABYE *sputters.*) Oh, you may laugh, Mrs. Hushabye; but I might have been killed.

Mrs. Hushabye: I couldnt have helped laughing even if you had been, Mr. Dunn. So Ellie has hypnotized him. What fun!

Mazzini: Oh no, no, no. It was such a terrible lesson to her: nothing would induce her to try such a thing again.

Mrs. Hushabye: Then who did it? *I* didnt.

Mazzini: I thought perhaps the Captain might have done it unintentionally. He is so fearfully magnetic: I feel vibrations whenever he comes close to me.

Guinness: The Captain will get him out of it any how, sir: I'll back him for that. I'll go fetch him. (*She makes for the pantry.*)

Mrs. Hushabye: Wait a bit. (*To* MAZZINI.) You say he is all right for eighteen hours?

Mazzini: Well, *I* was asleep for eighteen hours.

Mrs. Hushabye: Were you any the worse for it?

Mazzini: I dont quite remember. They had poured brandy down my throat, you see; and—

Mrs. Hushabye: Quite. Anyhow, you survived. Nurse, darling: go and ask Miss Dunn to come to us here. Say I want to speak to her particularly. You will find her with Mr. Hushabye probably.

Guinness: I think not, ducky: Miss Addy is with him. But I'll find her and send her to you. (*She goes out into the garden.*)

Mrs. Hushabye (*calling* MAZZINI'S *attention to the figure on the chair*). Now, Mr. Dunn, look. Just look. Look hard. Do you still intend to sacrifice your daughter to that thing?

Mazzini (*troubled*). You have completely upset me, Mrs. Hushabye, by all you have said to me. That anyone could imagine that I—*I,* a consecrated soldier of freedom, if I may say so—could sacrifice Ellie to anybody or anyone, or that I should ever have dreamed of forcing her inclinations in any way, is a most painful blow to my—well, I suppose you would say to my good opinion of myself.

Mrs. Hushabye (*rather stolidly*). Sorry.

Mazzini (*looking forlornly at the body).* What is your objection to poor Mangan, Mrs. Hushabye? He looks all right to me. But then I am so accustomed to him.

Mrs Hushabye: Have you no heart? Have you no sense? Look at the brute! Think of poor weak innocent Ellie in the clutches of this slavedriver, who spends his life making thousands of rough violent workmen bend to his will and sweat for him: a man accustomed to have great masses of iron beaten into shape for him by steam-hammers! to fight with women and girls over a halfpenny an hour ruthlessly! a captain of industry, I think you call him, dont you? Are you going to fling your delicate, sweet, helpless child into such a beast's claws just because he will keep her in an expensive house and make her wear diamonds to shew how rich he is?

Mazzini (*staring at her in wide-eyed amazement*). Bless you, dear Mrs. Hushabye, what romantic ideas of business you have! Poor dear Mangan isnt a bit like that.

Mrs. Hushabye (*scornfully*). Poor dear Mangan indeed!

Mazzini: But he doesnt know anything about machinery. He never goes near the men: he couldnt manage them: he is afraid of them. I never can get him to take the least interest in the works: he hardly knows more about them than you do. People are cruelly unjust to Mangan: they think he is all rugged strength just because his manners are bad.

Mrs. Hushabye: Do you mean to tell me he isnt strong enough to crush poor little Ellie?

Mazzini: Of course it's very hard to say how any marriage will turn out; but speaking for myself, I should say that he wont have a dog's chance against Ellie. You know, Ellie has remarkable strength of character. I think it is because I taught her to like Shakespear when she was very young.

Mrs. Hushabye (*contemptuously*). Shakespear! The next think you will tell me is that you could have made a great deal more money than Mangan. (*She retires to the sofa, and sits down at the port end of it in the worst of humors.*)

Mazzini (*following her and taking the other end*). No: I'm no good at making money. I dont care enough for it, somehow. I'm not ambitious! that must be it. Mangan is wonderful about money: he thinks of nothing else. He is so dreadfully afraid of being poor. I am always thinking of other things: even at the works I think of the things we are doing and not of what they cost. And the worst of it is, poor Mangan doesnt know what to do with his money when he gets it. He is such a baby that he doesnt know even what to eat and drink: he had ruined his liver eating and drinking the wrong things; and now he can hardly eat at all. Ellie will diet him splendidly. You will be surprised when you come to know him better: he is really the most helpless of mortals. You get quite a protective feeling towards him.

Mrs. Hushabye: Then who manages his business, pray?

Mazzini: I do. And of course other people like me.

Mrs. Hushabye: Footling people, you mean.

Mazzini: I suppose youd think us so.

Mrs. Hushabye: And pray why dont you do without him if youre all so much cleverer?

Mazzini: Oh, we couldnt: we should ruin the business in a year. I've tried; and I know. We should spend too much on everything. We should improve the quality of the goods and make them too dear. We should be sentimental about the hard cases among the workpeople. But Mangan keeps us in order. He is down on us about every extra half-penny. We could never do without him. You see, he will sit up all night thinking of how to save sixpence. Wont Ellie make him jump, though, when she takes his house in hand!

Mrs. Hushabye: Then the creature is a fraud even as a captain of industry!

Mazzini: I am afraid all the captains of industry are what y o u call frauds, Mrs. Hushabye. Of course there are some manufacturers who really do understand their own works; but they dont make as high a rate of profit as Mangan does. I assure you Mangan is quite a good fellow in his way. He means well.

Mrs. Hushabye: He doesnt look well. He is not in his first youth, is he?

Mazzini: After all, no husband is in his first youth for very long. Mrs. Hushabye. And men cant afford to marry in their first youth nowadays.

Mrs. Hushabye: Now if *I* said that, it would sound witty. Why cant y o u say it wittily? What on earth is the matter with you? Why dont you inspire everybody with confidence? with respect?

Mazzini (*humbly*). I think that what is the matter with me is that I am poor. You dont know what that means at home. Mind: I dont say they have ever complained. Theyve all been wonderful: theyve been proud of my poverty. Theyve even joked about it quite often. But my wife has had a very poor time of it. She has been quite resigned—

Mrs. Hushabye (*shuddering involuntarily*)!!

Mazzini: There! You see, Mrs. Hushabye. I dont want Ellie to live on resignation.

Mrs. Hushabye: Do you want her to have to resign herself to living with a man she doesnt love?

Mazzini (*wistfully*). Are you sure that would be worse than living with a man she did love, if he was a footling person?

Mrs. Hushabye (*relaxing her contemptuous attitude, quite interested in* MAZZINI *now*). You know, I really think you must love Ellie very much; for you become quite clever when you talk about her.

Mazzini: I didnt know I was so very stupid on other subjects.

Mrs. Hushabye: You are, sometimes.

Mazzini (*turning his head away; for his eyes are wet*). I have learnt a good deal about myself from you, Mrs. Hushabye; and I'm afraid I shall not be the happier for your plain speaking. But if you thought I needed it to make me think of Ellie's happiness you were very much mistaken.

Mrs. Hushabye (*leaning towards him kindly*). Have I been a beast?

Mazzini (*pulling himself together*). It doesnt matter about me, Mrs. Hushabye. I think you like Ellie; and that is enough for me.

Mrs. Hushabye: I'm beginning to like you a little. I perfectly loathed you at first. I though you the most odious, self-satisfied, boresome elderly prig I ever met.

Mazzini (*resigned, and now quite cheerful*). I daresay I am all that. I never have been a favorite with gorgeous women like you. They always frighten me.

Mrs. Hushabye (*pleased*). Am I a gorgeous woman, Mazzini? I shall fall in love with you presently.

Mazzini (*with placid gallantry*). No you wont, Hesione. But you would be quite safe. Would you believe it that quite a lot of women have flirted with me because I am quite safe? But they get tired of me for the same reason.

Mrs. Hushabye (*mischievously*). Take care. You may not be so safe as you think.

Mazzini: Oh yes, quite safe. You see, I have been in love really: the sort of love that only happens once. (*Softly.*) Thats why Ellie is such a lovely girl.

Mrs. Hushabye: Well, really, you a r e coming out. Are you quite sure you wont let me tempt you into a second grand passion?

Mazzini: Quite. It wouldnt be natural. The fact is, you dont strike on my box, Mrs. Hushabye; and I certainly dont strike on yours.

Mrs. Hushabye: I see. Your marriage was a safety match.

Mazzini: What a very witty application of the expression I used! I should never have thought of it.

[ELLIE *comes in from the garden, looking anything but happy.*]

Mrs. Hushabye (*rising*). Oh! here is Ellie at last. (*She goes behind the sofa.*)

Ellie (*on the threshold of the starboard door*). Guinness said you wanted me: you and papa.

Mrs. Hushabye: You have kept us

waiting so long that it almost came to—well, never mind. Your father is a very wonderful man (*she ruffles his hair affectionately*): the only one I ever met who could resist me when I made myself really agreeable. (*She comes to the big chair, on* MANGAN'S *left.*) Come here. I have something to shew you. (ELLIE *strolls listlessly to the other side of the chair.*) Look.

Ellie (*contemplating* MANGAN *without interest*). I know. He is only asleep. We had a talk after dinner; and he fell asleep in the middle of it.

Mrs. Hushabye: You did it, Ellie. You put him asleep.

Mazzini (*rising quickly and coming to the back of the chair*). Oh, I hope not. Did you, Ellie?

Ellie (*wearily*). He asked me to.

Mazzini: But it's dangerous. You know what happened to me.

Ellie (*utterly indifferent*). Oh, I daresay I can wake him. If not, somebody else can.

Mrs. Hushabye: It doesnt matter, anyhow, because I have at last persuaded your father that you dont want to marry him.

Ellie (*suddenly coming out of her listlessness, much vexed*). But why did you do that, Hesione? I do want to marry him. I fully intend to marry him.

Mazzini: Are you quite sure, Ellie? Mrs. Hushabye has made me feel that I may have been thoughtless and selfish about it.

Ellie (*very clearly and steadily*). Papa. When Mrs. Hushabye takes it on herself to explain to you what I think or dont think, shut your ears tight; and shut your eyes too. Hesione knows nothing about me: she hasnt the least notion of the sort of person I am, and never will. I promise you I wont do anything I dont want to do and mean to do for my own sake.

Mazzini: You are quite, quite sure?

Ellie: Quite, quite sure. Now you must go away and leave me to talk to Mrs. Hushabye.

Mazzini: But I should like to hear. Shall I be in the way?

Ellie (*inexorable*). I had rather talk to her alone.

Mazzini (*affectionately*). Oh, well, I know what a nuisance parents are, dear. I will be good and go. (*He goes to the garden door.*) By the way, do you remember the address of that professional who woke me up? Dont you think I had better telegraph to him?

Mrs. Hushabye (*moving towards the sofa*). It's too late to telegraph tonight.

Mazzini: I suppose so. I do hope he'll wake up in the course of the night. (*He goes out into the garden.*)

Ellie (*turning vigorously on Hesione the moment her father is out of the room*). Hesione: what the devil do you mean by making mischief with my father about Mangan?

Mrs. Hushabye (*promptly losing her temper*). Dont you dare speak to me like that, you little minx. Remember that you are in my house.

Ellie: Stuff! Why dont you mind your own business? What is it to you whether I choose to marry Mangan or not?

Mrs. Hushabye: Do you suppose you can bully me, you miserable little matrimonial adventurer?

Ellie: Every woman who hasnt any money is a matrimonial adventurer. It's easy for you to talk: you have never know what it is to want money; and you can pick up men as if they were daisies. I am poor and respectable—

Mrs. Hushabye (*interrupting*). Ho! respectable! How did you pick up Mangan? How did you pick up my husband?

You have the audacity to tell me that I am a—a—a—

Ellie: A siren. So you are. You were born to lead men by the nose: if you werent, Marcus would have waited for me, perhaps.

Mrs. Hushabye (*suddenly melting and half laughing*). Oh, my poor Ellie, my pettikins, my unhappy darling! I am so sorry about Hector. But what can I do? It's not my fault: I'd give him to you if I could.

Ellie: I dont blame you for that.

Mrs. Hushabye: What a brute I was to quarrel with you and call you names! Do kiss me and say youre not angry with me.

Ellie (*fiercely*). Oh, dont slop and gush and be sentimental. Dont you see that unless I can be hard—as hard as nails—I shall go mad? I dont care a damn about your calling me names: do you think a woman in my situation can feel a few hard words?

Mrs. Hushabye: Poor little woman! Poor little situation!

Ellie: I suppose you think youre being sympathetic. You are just foolish and stupid and selfish. You see me getting a smasher right in the face that kills a whole part of my life: the best part that can never come again; and you think you can help me over it by a little coaxing and kissing. When I want all the strength I can get to lean on: something iron, something stony, I dont care how cruel it is, you go all mushy and want to slobber over me. I'm not angry; I'm not unfriendly; but for God's sake do pull yourself together; and dont think that because youre on velvet and always have been, women who are in hell can take it as easily as you.

Mrs. Hushabye (*shrugging her shoulders*). Very well. (*She sits down on the sofa in her old place.*) But I warn you that when I am neither coaxing and kissing nor laughing, I am just wondering how much longer I can stand living in this cruel, damnable world. You object to the siren: well, I drop the siren. You want to rest your wounded bosom against a grindstone. Well (*folding her arms*), here is the grindstone.

Ellie (*sitting down beside her, appeased*). Thats better: you really have the trick of falling in with everyone's mood; but you dont understand, because you are not the sort of woman for whom there is only one man and only one chance.

Mrs. Hushabye: I certainly dont understand how your marrying that object (*indicating* MANGAN) will console you for not being able to marry Hector.

Ellie: Perhaps you dont understand why I was quite a nice girl this morning, and am now neither a girl nor particularly nice.

Mrs. Hushabye: Oh yes, I do. It's because you have made up your mind to do something despicable and wicked.

Ellie: I dont think so, Hesione. I must make the best of my ruined house.

Mrs. Hushabye: Pooh! youll get over it. Your house isnt ruined.

Ellie: Of course I shall get over it. You dont suppose I'm going to sit down and die of a broken heart, I hope, or be an old maid living on a pittance from the Sick and Indigent Room-keepers' Association. But my heart i s broken, all the same. What I mean by that is that I know that what has happened to me with Marcus will not happen to me ever again. In the world for me there is Marcus and a lot of other men of whom one is just the same as another. Well, if I cant have love, thats no reason why I should have poverty.

If Mangan has nothing else, he has money.

Mrs. Hushabye: And are there no y o u n g men with money?

Ellie: Not within my reach. Besides, a young man would have the right to expect love from me, and would perhaps leave me when he found I could not give it to him. Rich young men can get rid of their wives, you know, pretty cheaply. But this object, as you call him, can expect nothing more from me than I am prepared to give him.

Mrs. Hushabye: He will be your owner, remember. If he buys you, he will make the bargain pay him and not you. Ask your father.

Ellie (*rising and strolling to the chair to contemplate their subject*). You need not trouble on that score, Hesione. I have more to give Boss Mangan than he has to give me: it is I who am buying him, and at a pretty good price too, I think. Women are better at that sort of bargain than men. I have taken the Boss's measure; and ten Boss Mangans shall not prevent me doing far more as I please as his wife than I have ever been able to do as a poor girl. (*Stooping to the recumbent figure.*) Shall they, Boss? I think not. (*She passes on to the drawing-table, and leans against the end of it, facing the windows.*) I shall not have to spend most of my time wondering how long my gloves will last, anyhow.

Mrs. Hushabye (*rising superbly*). Ellie: you are a wicked sordid little beast. And to think that I actually condescended to fascinate that creature there to save you from him! Well, let me tell you this: if you make this disgusting match, you will never see Hector again if I can help it.

Ellie (*unmoved*). I nailed Mangan by telling him that if he did not marry me he should never see you again. (*She lifts herself on her wrists and seats herself on the end of the table.*)

Mrs. Hushabye (*recoiling*). Oh!

Ellie: So you see I am not unprepared for your playing that trump against me. Well, you just try it: thats all. I should have made a man of Marcus, not a household pet.

Mrs. Hushabye (*flaming*). You dare!

Ellie (*looking almost dangerous*). Set him thinking about me if y o u dare.

Mrs. Hushabye: Well, of all the impudent little fiends I ever met! Hector says there is a certain point at which the only answer you can give to a man who breaks all the rules is to knock him down. What would you say if I were to box your ears?

Ellie (*calmly*). I should pull your hair.

Mrs. Hushabye (*mischievously*). That wouldnt hurt me. Perhaps it comes off at night.

Ellie (*so taken aback that she drops off the table and runs to her*). Oh, you dont mean to say, Hesione, that your beautiful black hair is false?

Mrs. Hushabye (*patting it*). Dont tell Hector. He believes in it.

Ellie (*groaning*). Oh! Even the hair that ensnared him false! Everything false!

Mrs. Hushabye: Pull it and try. Other women can snare men in their hair; but I can swing a baby on mine. Aha! you cant do that, Goldylocks.

Ellie (*heartbroken*). No. You have stolen m y babies.

Mrs. Hushabye: Pettikins: dont make me cry. You know, what you said about my making a household pet of him is a little true. Perhaps he ought to have waited for you. Would any other woman on earth forgive you?

Ellie: Oh, what right had you to take him all for yourself! (*Pulling herself together.*) There! You couldnt help it: neither of us could help it. He couldnt help it. No: dont say anything more: I cant bear it. Let us wake the object. (*She begins stroking* MANGAN'S *head, reversing the movement with which she put him to sleep.*) Wake up, do you hear? You are to wake up at once. Wake up, wake up, wake—

Mangan (*bouncing out of the chair in a fury and turning on them*). Wake up! So you think Ive been asleep, do you? (*He kicks the chair violently back out of his way, and gets between them.*) You throw me into a trance so that I cant move hand or foot—I might have been buried alive! it's a mercy I wasnt—and then you think I was only asleep. If youd let me drop the two times you rolled me about, my nose would have been flattened for life against the floor. But Ive found you all out, anyhow. I know the sort of people I'm among now. Ive heard every word youve said, you and your precious father, and (*to* MRS. HUSHABYE) you too. So I'm an object, am I? I'm a thing, am I? I'm a fool that hasnt sense enough to feed myself properly, am I? I'm afraid of the men that would starve if it werent for the wages I give them, am I? I'm nothing but a disgusting old skinflint to be made a convenience of by designing women and fool managers of my works, am I? I'm—

Mrs. Hushabye (*with the most elegant aplomb*). Sh-sh-sh-sh-sh! Mr. Mangan: you are bound in honor to obliterate from your mind all you heard while you were pretending to be asleep. It was not meant for you to hear.

Mangan: Pretending to be asleep! Do you think if I was only pretending that I'd have sprawled there helpless, and listened to such unfairness, such lies, such injustice and plotting and backbiting and slandering of me, if I could have up and told you what I thought of you! I wonder I didnt burst.

Mrs. Hushabye (*sweetly*). You dreamt it all, Mr. Mangan. We were only saying how beautifully peaceful you looked in your sleep. That was all, wasnt it, Ellie? Believe me, Mr. Mangan, all those unpleasant things came into your mind in the last half second before you woke. Ellie rubbed your hair the wrong way; and the disagreeable sensation suggested a disagreeable dream.

Mangan (*doggedly*). I believe in dreams.

Mrs. Hushabye: So do I. But they go by contraries, dont they?

Mangan (*depths of emotion suddenly welling up in him*). I shant forget, to my dying day, that when you gave me the glad eye that time in the garden, you were making a fool of me. That was a dirty low mean thing to do. You had no right to let me come near you if I disgusted you. It isnt my fault if I'm old and havnt a moustache like a bronze candlestick as your husband has. There are things no decent woman would do to a man—like a man hitting a woman in the breast.

[HESIONE, *utterly shamed, sits down on the sofa and covers her face with her hands.* MANGAN *sits down also on his chair and begins to cry like a child.* ELLIE *stares at them.* MRS. HUSHABYE, *at the distressing sound he makes, takes down her hands and looks at him. She rises and runs to him.*]

Mrs. Hushabye: Dont cry: I cant bear it. Have I broken your heart? I didnt know you had one. How could I?

Mangan: I'm a man aint I?

Mrs. Hushabye (*half coaxing, half rallying, altogether tenderly*). Oh no:

not what I call a man. Only a Boss: just that and nothing else. What business has a Boss with a heart?

Mangan: Then youre not a bit sorry for what you did, nor ashamed?

Mrs. Hushabye: I was ashamed for the first time in my life when you said that about hitting a woman in the breast, and I found out what I'd done. My very bones blushed red. Youve had your revenge, Boss. Arnt you satisfied?

Mangan: Serve you right! Do you hear? Serve you right! Youre just cruel. Cruel.

Mrs. Hushabye: Yes. cruelty would be delicious if one could only find some sort of cruelty that didnt really hurt. By the way (*sitting down beside him on the arm of the chair*), whats your name? It's not really Boss, is it?

Mangan (*shortly*). If you want to know, my name's Alfred.

Mrs. Hushabye (*springing up*). Alfred! Ellie: he was christened after Tennyson!!!

Mangan (*rising*). I was christened after my uncle, and never had a penny from him, damn him! What of it?

Mrs. Hushabye: It comes to me suddenly that you are a real person: that you had a mother, like anyone else. (*Putting her hands on his shoulders and surveying him.*) Little Alf!

Mangan: Well, you have a nerve.

Mrs. Hushabye: And you have a heart, Alfy, a whimpering little heart, but a real one. (*Releasing him suddenly.*) Now run and make it up with Ellie. She has had time to think what to say to you, which is more than I had. (*She goes out quickly into the garden by the port door.*)

Mangan: That woman has a pair of hands that go right through you.

Ellie: Still in love with her, in spite of all we said about you?

Mangan: Are all women like you two? Do they never think of anything about a man except what they can get out of him? You werent even thinking about me. You were only thinking whether your gloves would last.

Ellie: I shall not have to think about that when we are married.

Mangan: And you think I am going to marry you after what I heard there!

Ellie: You heard nothing from me that I did not tell you before.

Mangan: Perhaps you think I can't do without you.

Ellie: I think you would feel lonely without us all now, after coming to know us so well.

Mangan (*with something like a yell of despair*). Am I never to have the last word?

Captain Shotover (*appearing at the starboard garden door*). There is a soul in torment here. What is the matter?

Mangan: This girl doesnt want to spend her life wondering how long her gloves will last.

Captain Shotover (*passing through*). Dont wear any. I never do. (*He goes into the pantry.*)

Lady Utterword (*appearing at the port garden door, in a handsome dinner dress*). Is anything the matter?

Ellie: This gentleman wants to know is he never to have the last word?

Lady Utterword (*coming forward to the sofa*). I should let him have it, my dear. The important thing is not to have the last word, but to have your own way.

Mangan: She wants both.

Lady Utterword: She wont get them, Mr. Mangan. Providence always has the last word.

Mangan (*desperately*). Now you are going to come religion over me. In this house a man's mind might as well be a football. I'm going. (*He makes for the hall, but is stopped by a hail from* THE CAPTAIN, *who has just emerged from his pantry.*)

Captain Shotover: Whither away, Boss Mangan?

Mangan: To hell out of this house: let that be enough for you and all here.

Captain Shotover: You were welcome to come: you are free to go. The wide earth, the high seas, the spacious skies are waiting for you outside.

Lady Utterword: But your things, Mr. Mangan. Your bags, your comb and brushes, your pyjamas—

Hector: (*who has just appeared in the port doorway in a handsome Arab costume*). Why should the escaping slave take his chains with him?

Mangan: That's right, Hushabye. Keep the pyjamas, my lady; and much good may they do you.

Hector (*advancing to* LADY UTTERWORD'S *left hand*). Let us all go out into the night and leave everything behind us.

Mangan: You stay where you are, the lot of you. I want no company, especially female company.

Ellie: Let him go. He is unhappy here. He is angry with us.

Captain Shotover: Go, Boss Mangan; and when you have found the land where there is happiness and where there are no women, send me its latitude and longitude; and I will join you there.

Lady Utterword: You will certainly not be comfortable without your luggage, Mr. Mangan.

Ellie (*impatient*). Go, go: why dont you go? It is a heavenly night: you can sleep on the heath. Take my waterproof to lie on: it is hanging up in the hall.

Hector: Breakfast at nine, unless you prefer to breakfast with the Captain at six.

Ellie: Good night, Alfred.

Hector: Alfred! (*He runs back to the door and calls into the garden.*) Randall: Mangan's Christian name is Alfred.

Randall (*appearing in the starboard doorway in evening dress*). Then Hesione wins her bet.

[MRS. HUSHABYE *appears in the port doorway. She throws her left arm round* HECTOR'S *neck; draws him with her to the back of the sofa; and throws her right arm round* LADY UTTERWORD'S *neck.*]

Mrs. Hushabye: They wouldnt believe me. Alf.

[*They contemplate him.*]

Mangan: Is there any more of you coming in to look at me, as if I was the latest thing in a menagerie?

Mrs. Hushabye: You a r e the latest thing in this menagerie.

[*Before* MANGAN *can retort, a fall of furniture is heard from upstairs; then a pistol shot, and a yell of pain. The staring group breaks up in consternation.*]

Mazzini's Voice (*from above*). Help! A burglar! Help!

Hector (*His eyes blazing*). A burglar!!!

Mrs. Hushabye: No, Hector: youll be shot. (*But it is too late: he has dashed out past* MANGAN, *who hastily moves towards the bookshelves out of his way.*)

Captain Shotover (*blowing his whistle*). All hands aloft! (*He strides out after* HECTOR.)

Lady Utterword: My diamonds. (*She follows* THE CAPTAIN.)

Randall (*rushing after her*). No, Ariadne. Let me.

Ellie: Oh, is papa shot? (*She runs out.*)

Mrs. Hushabye: Are you frightened, Alf?

Mangan: No. It aint my house, thank God.

Mrs. Hushabye: If they catch a burglar, shall we have to go into court as witnesses, and be asked all sorts of questions about our private lives?

Mangan: You wont be believed if you tell the truth.

[MAZZINI, *terribly upset, with a duelling pistol in his hand, comes from the hall, and makes his way to the drawing-table.*]

Mazzini: Oh, my dear Mrs. Hushabye, I might have killed him. (*He throws the pistol on the table and staggers round to the chair.*) I hope you wont believe I really intended to.

[HECTOR *comes in, marching an old and villainous looking man before him by the collar. He plants him in the middle of the room and releases him.*]

[ELLIE *follows, and immediately runs across to the back of her father's chair and pats his shoulders.*]

Randall (*entering with a poker*). Keep your eye on this door, Mangan. I'll look after the other. (*He goes to the starboard door and stands on guard there.*)

[LADY UTTERWORD *comes in after* RANDALL, *and goes between* MRS. HUSHABYE *and* MANGAN.]

[NURSE GUINNESS *brings up the rear, and waits near the door, on* MANGAN'S *left.*]

Mrs. Hushabye: What has happened?

Mazzini: Your housekeeper told me there was somebody upstairs, and gave me a pistol that Mr. Hushabye had been practising with. I thought it would frighten him; but it went off at a touch.

The Burglar: Yes, and took the skin off my ear. Precious near took the top off my head. Why dont you have a proper revolver instead of a thing like that, that goes off if you as much as blow on it?

Hector: One of my duelling pistols. Sorry.

Mazzini: He put his hands up and said it was a fair cop.

The Burglar: So it was. Send for the police.

Hector: No, by thunder! It was not a fair cop. We were four to one.

Mrs. Hushabye: What will they do to him?

The Burglar: Ten years. Beginning with solitary. Ten years off my life. I shant serve it all: I'm too old. It will see me out.

Lady Utterword: You should have thought of that, before you stole my diamonds.

The Burglar: Well, you've got them back, lady: havnt you? Can you give me back the years of my life you are going to take from me?

Mrs. Hushabye: Oh, we cant bury a man alive for ten years for a few diamonds.

The Burglar: Ten little shining diamonds! Ten long black years!

Lady Utterword: Think of what it is for us to be dragged through the horrors of a criminal court, and have all our family affairs in the papers! If you were a native, and Hastings could order you a good beating and send you away, I shouldn't mind; but here in England there is no real protection for any respectable person.

The Burglar: I'm too old to be giv a hiding, lady. Send for the police and have done with it. It's only just and right you should.

Randall (*who has relaxed his vigilance on seeing the burglar so pacifically disposed, and comes forward swinging the poker between his fingers like a well-folded umbrella*). It is neither just nor right that we should be put to a lot of inconvenience to gratify your moral enthusiasm, my friend. You had better get out, while you have the chance.

The Burglar (*inexorably*). No. I must work my sin off my conscience. This has come as a sort of call to me. Let me spend the rest of my life repenting in a cell. I shall have my reward above.

Mangan (*exasperated*). The very burglars cant behave naturally in this house.

Hector: My good sir: you must work out your salvation at somebody else's expense. Nobody here is going to charge you.

The Burglar: Oh, you wont charge me, wont you?

Hector: No. I'm sorry to be inhospitable; but will you kindly leave the house?

The Burglar: Right. I'll go to the police station and give myself up. (*He turns resolutely to the door; but* HECTOR *stops him.*)

HECTOR.	Oh no. You mustn't do that.
RANDALL.	No, no. Clear out, man, cant you; and dont be a fool.
LADY HUSHABYE.	Don't be silly. Cant you repent at home?

Lady Utterword: You will have to do as you are told.

The Burglar: It's compounding a felony, you know.

Mrs. Hushabye: This is utterly ridiculous. Are we to be forced to prosecute this man when we dont want to?

The Burglar: Am I to be robbed of my salvation to save you the trouble of spending a day at the sessions? Is that justice? Is it right? Is it fair to me?

Mazzini (*rising and leaning across the table persuasively as if it were a pulpit desk or a shop counter*). Come, come! let me shew you how you can turn your very crimes to account. Why not set up as a locksmith? You must know more about locks than most honest men?

The Burglar: That's true, sir, but I couldnt set up as a locksmith under twenty pounds.

Randall: Well, you can easily steal twenty pounds. You will find it in the nearest bank.

The Burglar (*horrified*). Oh what a thing for a gentleman to put into the head of a poor criminal scrambling out of the bottomless pit as it were! Oh, shame on you, sir! Oh, God forgive you! (*He throws himself into the big chair and covers his face as if in prayer.*)

Lady Utterword: Really, Randall!

Hector: It seems to me that we shall have to take up a collection for this inopportunely contrite sinner.

Lady Utterword: But twenty pounds is ridiculous.

The Burglar (*looking up quickly*). I shall have to buy a lot of tools, lady.

Lady Utterword: Nonsense: you have your burgling kit.

The Burglar: Whats a jimmy and a centre-bit and an acetylene welding plant and a bunch of skeleton keys? I shall want a forge, and a smithy, and a shop, and fittings. I cant hardly do it for twenty.

Hector: My worthy friend, we havnt got twenty pounds.

The Burglar (*now master of the situation*). You can raise it among you, cant you?

Mrs. Hushabye: Give him a sovereign, Hector, and get rid of him.

Hector (*giving him a pound*). There! Off with you.

The Burglar (*rising and taking the money very ungratefully*). I wont promise nothing. You have more on you than a quid: all the lot of you, I mean.

Lady Utterword (*vigorously*). Oh, let us prosecute him and have done with it. I have a conscience too, I hope; and I do not feel at all sure that we have any right to let him go, especially if he is going to be greedy and impertinent.

The Burglar (*quickly*). All right, lady, all right. Ive no wish to be anything but agreeable. Good evening, ladies and gentlemen; and thank you kindly.

[*He is hurrying out when he is confronted in the doorway by* CAPTAIN SHOTOVER.]

Captain Shotover (*fixing* THE BURGLAR *with a piercing regard*). What's this? Are there two of you?

The Burglar (*falling on his knees before* THE CAPTAIN *in abject terror*). Oh my good Lord, what have I done? Dont tell me its y o u r house Ive broken into, Captain Shotover.

[THE CAPTAIN *seizes him by the collar; drags him to his feet; and leads him to the middle of the group,* HECTOR *falling back beside his wife to make way for them.*]

Captain Shotover (*turning him towards* ELLIE). Is that your daughter? (*He releases him.*)

The Burglar: Well, how do I know, Captain? You know the sort of life you and me has led. Any young lady of that age might be my daughter anywhere in the wide world, as you might say.

Captain Shotover (*to* MAZZINI). You are not Billy Dunn. This is Billy Dunn. Why have you imposed on me?

The Burglar (*indignantly to* MAZZINI). Have you been giving yourself out to be me? You, that nigh blew my head off! Shooting y o u r s e l f, in a manner of speaking!

Mazzini: My dear Captain Shotover, ever since I came into this house I have done hardly anything else but assure you that I am not Mr. William Dunn, but Mazzini Dunn, a very different person.

The Burglar: He dont belong to my branch, Captain. Theres two sets in the family: the thinking Dunns and the drinking Dunns, each going their own ways. I'm a drinking Dunn: he's a thinking Dunn. But that didnt give him any right to shoot me.

Captain Shotover: So youve turned burglar, have you?

The Burglar: No, Captain: I wouldn't disgrace our old sea calling by such a thing. I am no burglar.

Lady Utterword: What were you doing with my diamonds?

Guinness: What did you break into the house for if youre no burglar?

Randall: Mistook the house for your own and came in by the wrong window, eh?

The Burglar: Well, it's no use telling you a lie: I can take in most captains, but not Captain Shotover, because he sold himself to the devil in Zanzibar, and can divine water, spot gold, explode a cartridge in your pocket with a glance of his eye, and see the truth hidden in the heart of man. But I'm no burglar.

Captain Shotover: Are you an honest man?

The Burglar: I dont set up to be better than my fellow-creatures, and never did, as you well know, Captain. But what I do is innocent and pious. I enquire about for houses where the right sort of people live. I work it on them same as I worked it here. I break into the house; put a few spoons or diamonds in my pocket; make a noise; get caught; and take up a collection. And you wouldnt believe how hard it is to get caught when youre actually trying to. I have knocked over all the chairs in a room without a soul paying any attention to me. In the end I have had to walk out and leave the job.

Randall: When that happens, do you put back the spoons and diamonds?

The Burglar: Well, I dont fly in the face of Providence, if thats what you want to know.

Captain Shotover: Guinness: you remember this man?

Guinness: I should think I do, seeing I was married to him, the blackguard!

HESIONE
LADY UTTERWORD. } (*exclaiming together*). { Married to him! Guinness!!

The Burglar: It wasnt legal. Ive been married to no end of women. No use coming that over me.

Captain Shotover: Take him to the forecastle. (*He flings him to the door with a strength beyond his years.*)

Guinness: I suppose you mean the kitchen. They wont have him there. Do you expect servants to keep company with thieves and all sorts?

Captain Shotover: Land-thieves and water-thieves are the same flesh and blood. I'll have no boatswain on my quarter-deck. Off with you both.

The Burglar: Yes, Captain. (*He goes out humbly.*)

Mazzini: Will it be safe to have him in the house like that?

Guinness: Why didn't you shoot him, sir? If I'd known who he was, I'd have shot him myself. (*She goes out.*)

Mrs. Hushabye: Do sit down, everybody. (*She sits down on the sofa.*)

[*They all move except* ELLIE. MAZZINI *resumes his seat.* RANDALL *sits down in the window seat near the starboard door, again making a pendulum of his poker, and studying it as Galileo might have done.* HECTOR *sits on his left, in the middle.* MANGAN, *forgotten, sits in the port corner.* LADY UTTERWORD *takes the big chair.* CAPTAIN SHOTOVER *goes into the pantry in deep abstraction. They all look after him; and* LADY UTTERWOOD *coughs consciously.*]

Mrs. Hushabye: So Billy Dunn was poor nurse's little romance. I knew there had been somebody.

Randall: They will fight their battles over again and enjoy themselves immensely.

Lady Utterword (*irritably*). You are not married; and you know nothing about it, Randall. Hold your tongue.

Randall: Tyrant!

Mrs. Hushabye: Well, we have had a very exciting evening. Everything will be an anticlimax after it. We'd better all go to bed.

Randall: Another burglar may turn up.

Mazzini: Oh, impossible! I hope not.

Randall: Why not? There is more than one burglar in England.

Mrs. Hushabye: What do you say, Alf?

Mangan (*huffily*). Oh, I dont matter.

I'm forgotten. The burglar has put my nose out of joint. Shove me into a corner and have done with me.

Mrs. Hushabye (*jumping up mischievously, and going to him*). Would you like a walk on the heath, Alfred? With me?

Ellie: Go, Mr. Mangan. It will do you good. Hesione will soothe you.

Mrs. Hushabye (*slipping her arm under his and pulling him upright*). Come, Alfred. There is a moon: it's like the night in Tristan and Isolde. (*She caresses his arm and draws him to the port garden door.*)

Mangan (*writhing but yielding*). How you can have the face—the heart— (*He breaks down and is heard sobbing as she takes him out.*)

Lady Utterword: What an extraordinary way to behave! What is the matter with the man?

Ellie (*in a strangely calm voice, staring into an imaginary distance*). His heart is breaking: that is all. (THE CAPTAIN *appears at the pantry door, listening.*) It is a curious sensation: the sort of pain that goes mercifully beyond our powers of feeling. When your heart is broken, your boats are burned: nothing matters any more. It is the end of happiness and the beginning of peace.

Lady Utterword (*suddenly rising in a rage, to the astonishment of the rest*). How dare you?

Hector: Good heavens! What's the matter?

Randall (*in a warning whisper*). Tch—tch—tch! Steady.

Ellie (*surprised and haughty*). I was not addressing you particularly, Lady Utterwood. And I am not accustomed to be asked how dare I.

Lady Utterword: Of course not. Anyone can see how badly you have been brought up.

Mazzini Oh, I hope not, Lady Utterwood. Really!

Lady Utterword: I know very well what you meant. The impudence!

Ellie: What on earth do you mean?

Captain Shotover (*advancing to the table*). She means that her heart will not break. She has been longing all her life for someone to break it. At last she has become afraid she has none to break.

Lady Utterword (*flinging herself on her knees and throwing her arms round him*). Papa: dont say you think Ive no heart.

Captain Shotover (*raising her with grim tenderness*). If you had no heart how could you want to have it broken, child?

Hector (*rising with a bound*). Lady Utterword: you are not to be trusted. You have made a scene. (*He runs out into the garden through the starboard door.*)

Lady Utterword: Oh! Hector, Hector! (*She runs out after him.*)

Randall: Only nerves, I assure you. (*He rises and follows her, waving the poker in his agitation.*) Ariadne! Ariadne! For God's sake be careful. You will— (*He is gone.*)

Mazzini (*rising*). How distressing! Can I do anything, I wonder?

Captain Shotover (*promptly taking his chair and setting to work at the drawing-board*). No. Go to bed. Goodnight.

Mazzini (*bewildered*). Oh! Perhaps you are right.

Ellie: Goodnight, dearest. (*She kisses him.*)

Mazzini: Goodnight, love. (*He makes for the door, but turns aside to the bookshelves.*) I'll just take a book. (*He takes *one.*) Goodnight. (*He goes out, leaving* ELLIE *alone with* THE CAPTAIN.)

[THE CAPTAIN *is intent on his drawing.* ELLIE, *standing sentry over his chair, contemplates him for a moment.*]

Ellie: Does nothing ever disturb you, Captain Shotover?

Captain Shotover: Ive stood on the bridge for eighteen hours in a typhoon. Life here is stormier; but I can stand it.

Ellie: Do you think I ought to marry Mr. Mangan?

Captain Shotover (*never looking up*). One rock is as good as another to be wrecked on.

Ellie: I am not in love with him.

Captain Shotover: Who said you were?

Ellie: You are not surprised?

Captain Shotover: Surprised! at my age!

Ellie: It seems to me quite fair. He wants me for one thing: I want him for another.

Captain Shotover: Money?

Ellie: Yes.

Captain Shotover: Well, one turns the cheek: the other kisses it. One provides the cash: the other spends it.

Ellie: Who will have the best of the bargain, I wonder?

Captain Shotover: You. These fellows live in an office all day. You will have to put up with him from dinner to breakfast; but you will both be asleep most of that time. All day you will be quit of him; and you will be shopping with his money. If that is too much for you, marry a seafaring man: you will be bothered with him only three weeks in the year, perhaps.

Ellie: That would be best of all, I suppose.

Captain Shotover: It's a dangerous thing to be married right up to the hilt, like my daughter's husband. The man is at home all day, like a damned soul in hell.

Ellie: I never thought of that before.

Captain Shotover: If youre marrying for business, you cant be too businesslike.

Ellie: Why do women always want other women's husbands?

Captain Shotover: Why do horse-thieves prefer a horse that is broken-in to one that is wild?

Ellie (*with a short laugh*). I suppose so. What a vile world it is!

Captain Shotover: It doesnt concern me. I'm nearly out of it.

Ellie: And I'm only just beginning.

Captain Shotover: Yes; so look ahead.

Ellie: Well, I think I am being very prudent.

Captain Shotover: I didnt say prudent. I said look ahead.

Ellie: Whats the difference?

Captain Shotover: It's prudent to gain the whole world and lose your own soul. But dont forget that your soul sticks to you if you stick to it; but the world has a way of slipping through your fingers.

Ellie (*wearily, leaving him and beginning to wander restlessly about the room*). I'm sorry, Captain Shotover; but it's no use talking like that to me. Old-fashioned people are no use to me. Old-fashioned people think you can have a soul without money. They think the less money you have, the more soul you have. Young people nowadays know better. A soul is a very expensive thing to keep: much more so than a motor car.

Captain Shotover: Is it? How much does your soul eat?

Ellie: Oh, a lot. It eats music and pictures and books and mountains and lakes and beautiful things to wear and nice people to be with. In this country you cant have them without lots of money: that is why our souls are so horribly starved.

Captain Shotover: Mangan's soul lives on pigs' food.

Ellie: Yes: money is thrown away on him. I suppose his soul was starved when he was young. But it will not be thrown away on me. It is just because I want to save my soul that I am marrying for money. All the women who are not fools do.

Captain Shotover: There are other ways of getting money. Why dont you steal it?

Ellie: Because I dont want to go to prison.

Captain Shotover: Is that the only reason? Are you quite sure honesty has nothing to do with it?

Ellie: Oh, you are very old-fashioned, Captain. Does any modern girl believe that legal and illegal ways of getting money are the honest and dishonest ways? Mangan robbed my father and my father's friends. I should rob all the money back from Mangan if the police would let me. As they wont, I must get it back by marrying him.

Captain Shotover: I can't argue: I'm too old: my mind is made up and finished. All I can tell you is that, old-fashioned or new-fashioned, if you sell yourself, you deal your soul a blow that all the books and pictures and concerts and scenery in the world wont heal. (*He gets up suddenly and makes for the pantry.*)

Ellie (*running after him and seizing him by the sleeve.*) Then why did you sell yourself to the devil in Zanzibar?

Captain Shotover (*stopping, startled*). What?

Ellie: You shall not run away before you answer. I have found out that trick of yours. If you sold yourself, why shouldnt I?

Captain Shotover: I had to deal with men so degraded that they wouldnt obey me unless I swore at them and kicked them and beat them with my fists. Foolish people took young thieves off the streets; flung them into a training ship where they were taught to fear the cane instead of fearing God; and thought theyd made men and sailors of them by private subscription. I tricked these thieves into believing I'd sold myself to the devil. It saved my soul from the kicking and swearing that was damning me by inches.

Ellie (*releasing him*). I shall pretend to sell myself to Boss Mangan to save my soul from the poverty that is damning me by inches.

Captain Shotover: Riches will damn you ten times deeper. Riches wont save even your body.

Ellie: Old-fashioned again. We know now that the soul is the body, and the body the soul. They tell us they are different because they want to persuade us that we can keep our souls if we let them make slaves of our bodies. I am afraid you are no use to me, Captain.

Captain Shotover: What did you expect? A Savior, eh? Are you old-fashioned enough to believe in that?

Ellie: No. But I thought you were very wise, and might help me. Now I have found you out. You pretend to be busy, and think of fine things to say, and run in and out to surprise people by saying them, and get away before they can answer you.

Captain Shotover: It confuses me to be answered. It discourages me. I cannot bear men and women. I have to run away. I must run away now. (*He tries to*).

Ellie (*again seizing his arm*). You shall not run away from me. I can hypnotize you. You are the only person in the house I can say what I like to. I know you are fond of me. Sit down. (*She draws him to the sofa*).

Captain Shotover (*yielding*). Take care: I am in my dotage. Old men are dangerous: it doesnt matter to them what is going to happen to the world.

[*They sit side by side on the sofa. She leans affectionately against him with her head on his shoulder and her eyes half closed.*]

Ellie (*dreamily*). I should have thought nothing else mattered to old men. They cant be very interested in what is going to happen to themselves.

Captain Shotover: A man's interest in the world is only the overflow from his interest in himself. When you are a child your vessel is not yet full; so you care for nothing but your own affairs. When you grow up, your vessel overflows; and you are a politician, a philosopher, or an explorer and adventurer. In old age the vessel dries up: there is no overflow: you are a child again. I can give you the memories of my ancient wisdom: mere scraps and leavings; but I no longer really care for anything but my own little wants and hobbies. I sit here working out my old ideas as a means of destroying my fellow-creatures. I see my daughters and their men living foolish lives of romance and sentiment and snobbery. I see you, the younger generation, turning from their romance and sentiment and snobbery to money and comfort and hard common sense. I was ten times happier on the bridge in the typhoon, or frozen into Arctic ice for months in darkness, than you or they have ever been. You are looking for a rich husband. At your age I looked for hardship, danger, horror, and death, that I might feel the life in me more intensely. I did not let the fear of death govern my life; and my reward was, I had my life. You are going to let the fear of poverty govern your life; and your reward will be that you will eat, but you will not live.

Ellie (*sitting up impatiently*). But what can I do? I am not a sea captain: I cant stand on bridges in typhoons, or go slaughtering seals and whales in Greenland's icy mountains. They wont let women be captains. Do you want me to be a stewardess?

Captain Shotover: There are worse lives. The stewardesses could come ashore if they liked; but they sail and sail and sail.

Ellie: What could they do ashore but marry for money? I dont want to be a stewardess: I am too bad a sailor. Think of something else for me.

Captain Shotover: I cant think so long and continuously. I am too old. I must go in and out. (*He tries to rise.*)

Ellie (*pulling him back*). You shall not. You are happy here, arnt you?

Captain Shotover: I tell you it's dangerous to keep me. I cant keep awake and alert.

Ellie: What do you run away for? To sleep?

Captain Shotover: No. To get a glass of rum.

Ellie (*frightfully disillusioned*). Is that it? How disgusting! Do you like being drunk?

Captain Shotover: No: I dread being drunk more than anything in the world. To be drunk means to have dreams; to go soft; to be easily pleased and deceived; fall into the clutches of women. Drink does that for you when you are young. But when you are old: very very old, like me, the dreams come by themselves. You dont know how terrible that is: you are young: you sleep at night only, and sleep soundly. But later on you will sleep in the afternoon. Later still you will sleep even in the morning; and you will awake tired, tired of life. You will never be free from dozing and dreams: the dreams will steal upon your work every ten minutes unless you can awaken yourself with rum. I drink now to keep sober; but the dreams are conquering: rum is not what it was: I have had ten glasses since you came; and it might be so much water. Go get me another: Guinness knows where it is. You had better see for yourself the horror of an old man drinking.

Ellie: You shall not drink. Dream. I like you to dream. You must never be in the real world when we talk together.

Captain Shotover: I am too weary to resist or too weak. I am in my second childhood. I do not see you as you really are. I cant remember what I really am. I feel nothing but the accursed happiness I have dreaded all my life long: the happiness that comes as life goes, the happiness of yielding and dreaming instead of resisting and doing, the sweetness of the fruit that is going rotten.

Ellie: You dread it almost as much as I used to dread losing my dreams and having to fight and do things. But that is all over for me: m y dreams are dashed to pieces. I should like to marry a very old, very rich man. I should like to marry you. I had much rather marry you than marry Mangan. Are you very rich?

Captain Shotover: No. Living from hand to mouth. And I have a wife somewhere in Jamaica: a black one. My first wife. Unless she's dead.

Ellie: What a pity! I feel so happy with you. (*She takes his hand, almost unconsciously, and pats it.*) I thought I should never feel happy again.

Captain Shotover: Why?

Ellie: Dont you know?

Captain Shotover: No.

Ellie: Heartbreak. I fell in love with Hector, and didnt know he was married.

Captain Shotover: Heartbreak? Are you one of those who are so sufficient to themselves that they are only happy when they are stripped of everything, even of hope?

Ellie (*gripping the hand*). It seems so; for I feel now as if there was nothing I could not do, because I want nothing.

Captain Shotover: Thats the only real strength. Thats genius. Thats better than rum.

Ellie (*throwing away his hand*). Rum! Why did you spoil it?

[HECTOR *and* RANDALL *come in from the garden through the starboard door.*]

Hector: I beg your pardon. We did not know there was anyone here.

Ellie (*rising*). That means that you want to tell Mr. Randall the story about the tiger. Come, Captain: I want to talk to my father; and you had better come with me.

Captain Shotover (*rising*). Nonsense! the man is in bed.

Ellie: Aha! Ive caught you. My real father has gone to bed; but the father you gave me is in the kitchen. You knew quite well all along. Come. (*She draws him out into the garden with her through the port door.*)

Hector: That's an extraordinary girl. She has the Ancient Mariner on a string like a Pekinese dog.

Randall: Now that they have gone, shall we have a friendly chat?

Hector: You are in what is supposed to be my house. I am at your disposal.

[HECTOR *sits down in the draughtsman's chair, turning it to face* RANDALL, *who remains standing, leaning at his ease against the carpenter's bench.*]

Randall: I take it that we may be quite frank. I mean about Lady Utterword.

Hector: You may. I have nothing to be frank about. I never met her until this afternoon.

Randall (*straightening up*). What! But you are her sister's husband.

Hector: Well, if you come to that, you are her husband's brother.

Randall: But you seem to be on intimate terms with her.

Hector: So do you.

Randall: Yes; but I am on intimate terms with her. I have known her for years.

Hector: It took her years to get to the same point with you that she got to with me in five minutes, it seems.

Randall (*vexed*). Really, Ariadne is the limit. (*He moves away huffishly towards the windows.*)

Hector (*cooly*). She is, as I remarked to Hesione, a very enterprising woman.

Randall (*returning, much troubled*). You see, Hushabye, you are what women consider a good-looking man.

Hector: I cultivated that appearance in the days of my vanity; and Hesione insists on my keeping it up. She makes me wear these ridiculous things (*indicating his Arab costume*) because she thinks me absurd in evening dress.

Randall: Still, you do keep it up, old chap. Now, I assure you I have not an atom of jealousy in my disposition—

Hector: The question would seem to be rather whether your brother has any touch of that sort.

Randall: What! Hastings! Oh, dont trouble about Hastings. He has the gift of being able to work sixteen hours a day at the dullest detail, and actually likes it. That gets him to the top wherever he goes. As long as Ariadne takes care that he is fed regularly, he is only too thankful to anyone who will keep her in good humor for him.

Hector: And as she has all the Shotover fascination, there is plenty of competition for the job, eh?

Randall (*angrily*). She encourages them. Her conduct is perfectly scandalous. I assure you, my dear fellow, I havnt an atom of jealousy in my composition; but she makes herself the talk of every place she goes to by her thoughtlessness. It's nothing more: she doesnt really care for the men she keeps hanging about her; but how is the world to know that? It's not fair to Hastings. It's not fair to me.

Hector: Her theory is that her conduct is so correct—

Randall: Correct! She does nothing but make scenes from morning till night. You be careful, old chap. She will get you into trouble: that is, she would if she really cared for you.

Hector: Doesn't she?

Randall: Not a scrap. She may want your scalp to add to her collection; but her true affection has been engaged years ago. You had really better be careful.

Hector: Do you suffer much from this jealousy?

Randall: Jealousy! I jealous! My dear fellow, havnt I told you that there is not an atom of—

Hector: Yes. And Lady Utterwood told me she never made scenes. Well, dont waste your jealousy on my moustache.

Never waste jealousy on a real man: it is the imaginary hero that supplants us all in the long run. Besides, jealousy does not belong to your easy man-of-the-world pose, which you carry so well in other respects.

Randall: Really, Hushabye, I think a man may be allowed to be a gentleman without being accused of posing.

Hector: It is a pose like any other. In this house we know all the poses: our game is to find out the man under the pose. The man under your pose is apparently Ellie's favorite, Othello.

Randall: Some of your games in this house are damned annoying, let me tell you.

Hector: Yes: I have been their victim for many years. I used to writhe under them at first; but I became accustomed to them. At last I learned to play them.

Randall: If its all the same to you, I had rather you didnt play them on me. You evidently dont quite understand my character, or my notions of good form.

Hector: Is it your notion of good form to give away Lady Utterword?

Randall (*a childishly plaintive note breaking into his huff*). I have not said a word against Lady Utterword. This is just the conspiracy over again.

Hector: What conspiracy?

Randall: You know very well, sir. A conspiracy to make me out to be pettish and jealous and childish and everything I am not. Everyone knows I am just the opposite.

Hector (*rising*). Something in the air of the house has upset you. It often does have that effect. (*He goes to the garden door and calls* LADY UTTERWORD *with commanding emphasis.*) Ariadne!

Lady Utterword (*at some distance*). Yes.

Randall: What are you calling her for? I want to speak—

Lady Utterword (*arriving breathless*). Yes. You really are a terribly commanding person. Whats the matter?

Hector: I do not know how to manage your friend Randall. No doubt you do.

Lady Utterword: Randall: have you been making yourself ridiculous, as usual? I can see it in your face. Really, you are the most pettish creature.

Randall: You know quite well, Ariadne, that I have not an ounce of pettishness in my disposition. I have made myself perfectly pleasant here. I have remained absolutely cool and imperturbable in the face of a burglar. Imperturbability is almost too strong a point of mine. But (*putting his foot down with a stamp, and walking angrily up and down the room*) I i n s i s t on being treated with a certain consideration. I will not allow Hushabye to take liberties with me. I will not stand your encouraging people as you do.

Hector: The man has a rooted delusion that he is your husband.

Lady Utterword: I know. He is jealous. As if he had any right to be! He compromises me everywhere. He makes scenes all over the place. Randall: I will not allow it. I simply will not allow it. You had no right to discuss me with Hector. I will not be discussed by men.

Hector: Be reasonable, Ariadne. Your fatal gift of beauty forces men to discuss you.

Lady Utterword: Oh indeed! what about y o u r fatal gift of beauty?

Hector: How can I help it?

Lady Utterword: You could cut off your moustache: I cant cut off my nose. I get my whole life messed up with people falling in love with me. And then Randall says I run after men.

Randall: I—

Lady Utterword: Yes you do: you said it just now. Why cant you think of something else than women? Napoleon was quite right when he said that women are the occupation of the idle man. Well, if ever there was an idle man on earth, his name is Randall Utterword.

Randall: Ariad—

Lady Utterword (*overwhelming him with a torrent of words*). Oh yes you are: it's no use denying it. What have you ever done? What good are you? You are as much trouble in the house as a child of three. You couldnt live without your valet.

Randall: This is—

Lady Utterword: Laziness! You are laziness incarnate. You are selfishness itself. You are the most uninteresting man on earth. You cant even gossip about anything but yourself and your grievances and your ailments and the people who have offended you. (*Turning to* HECTOR.) Do you know what they call him, Hector?

Hector } (*speaking together*). { Please dont tell me.
Randall } { I'll not stand it—

Lady Utterword: Randall the Rotter: that is his name in good society.

Randall (*shouting*). I'll not bear it, I tell you. Will you listen to me, you infernal—(*He chokes.*)

Lady Utterword: Well: go on. What were you going to call me? An infernal what? Which unpleasant animal is it to be this time?

Randall (*foaming*). There is no animal in the world so hateful as a woman can be. You are a maddening devil. Hushabye: you will not believe me when I tell you that I have loved this demon all my life; but God knows I have paid for it. (*He sits down in the draughtsman's chair, weeping.*)

Lady Utterword (*standing over him with triumphant contempt*). Cry-baby!

Hector (*gravely, coming to him*). My friend: the Shotover sisters have two strange powers over men. They can make them love; and they can make them cry. Thank your stars that you are not married to one of them.

Lady Utterword (*haughtily*). And pray, Hector—

Hector (*suddenly catching her round the shoulders; swinging her right round him and away from* RANDALL; *and gripping her throat with the other hand*). Ariadne: if you attempt to start on me, I'll choke you: do you hear? The cat-and-mouse game with the other sex is a good game; but I can play your head off at it. (*He throws her, not at all gently, into the big chair, and proceeds, less fiercely but firmly.*) It is true that Napoleon said that woman is the occupation of the idle man. But he added that she is the relaxation of the warrior. Well, *I* am the warrior. So take care.

Lady Utterword (*not in the least put out, and rather pleased by his violence*). My dear Hector: I have only done what you asked me to do.

Hector: How do you make that out, pray?

Lady Utterword: You called me in to manage Randall, didnt you? You said you couldnt manage him yourself.

Hector: Well, what if I did? I did not ask you to drive the man mad.

Lady Utterword: He isnt mad. Thats the way to manage him. If you were a mother, youd understand.

Hector: Mother! What are you up to now?

Lady Utterword: It's quite simple. When the children got nerves and were naughty, I smacked them just enough to give them a good cry and a healthy nervous shock. They went to sleep and were quite good afterwards. Well, I cant smack Randall: he is too big; so when he gets nerves and is naughty, I just rag him till he cries. He will be all right now. Look: he is half asleep already (*which is quite true*).

Randall (*waking up indignantly*). I'm not. You are most cruel, Ariadne. (*Sentimentally.*) But I suppose I must forgive you, as usual. (*He checks himself in the act of yawning.*)

Lady Utterword (*to* HECTOR). Is the explanation satisfactory, dread warrior?

Hector: Some day I shall kill you, if you go too far. I thought you were a fool.

Lady Utterword (*laughing*). Everybody does, at first. But I am not such a fool as I look. (*She rises complacently.*) Now, Randall: go to bed. You will be a good boy in the morning.

Randall (*only very faintly rebellious*). I'll go to bed when I like. It isnt ten yet.

Lady Utterword: It is long past ten. See that he goes to bed at once, Hector. (*She goes into the garden.*)

Hector: Is there any slavery on earth viler than this slavery of men to women?

Randall (*rising resolutely*). I'll not speak to her tomorrow. I'll not speak to her for another week. I'll give her such a lesson. I'll go straight to bed without bidding her goodnight. (*He makes for the door leading to the hall.*)

Hector: You are under a spell, man. Old Shotover sold himself to the devil in Zanzibar. The devil gave him a black witch for a wife; and these two demon daughters are their mystical progeny. I am tied to Hesione's apron-string; but I'm her husband; and if I did go stark staring mad about her, at least we became man and wife. But why should you let yourself be dragged about and beaten by Ariadne as a toy donkey is dragged about and beaten by a child? What do you get by it? Are you her lover?

Randall: You must not misunderstand me. In a higher sense—in a Platonic sense—

Hector: Psha! Platonic sense! She makes you her servant; and when pay-day comes round, she bilks you: that is what you mean.

Randall (*feebly*). Well, if I dont mind, I dont see what business it is of yours. Besides, I tell you I am going to punish her. You shall see: *I* know how to deal with women. I'm really very sleepy. Say goodnight to Mrs. Hushabye for me, will you, like a good chap. Goodnight. (*He hurries out.*)

Hector: Poor wretch! Oh women! women! women! (*He lifts his fists in invocation to heaven.*) Fall. Fall and crush. (*He goes out into the garden.*)

ACT III

[*In the garden,* HECTOR, *as he comes out through the glass door of the poop, finds* LADY UTTERWORD *lying voluptuously in the hammock on the east side of the flagstaff, in the circle of light cast by the electric arc, which is like a moon in its opal globe. Beneath the head of the hammock, a campstool. On the other side of the flagstaff, on the long garden seat,* CAPTAIN SHOTOVER *is asleep, with* ELLIE *beside hin, leaning affectionately against him on his right hand. On his left is a deck chair. Behind them in the gloom,* HESIONE *is strolling about with* MANGAN. *It is a fine still night, moonless.*]

Lady Utterword: What a lovely night! It seems made for us.

Hector: The night takes no interest in us. What are we to the night? (*He sits down moodily in the deck chair.*)

Ellie (*dreamily, nestling against* THE CAPTAIN). Its beauty soaks into my nerves. In the night there is peace for the old and hope for the young.

Hector: Is that remark your own?

Ellie: No. Only the last thing the Captain said before he went to sleep.

Captain Shotover: I'm not asleep.

Hector: Randall is. Also Mr. Mazzini Dunn. Mangan too, probably.

Mangan: No.

Hector: Oh, you are there. I thought Hesione would have sent you to bed by this time.

Mrs. Hushabye (*coming to the back of the garden seat, into the light, with* MANGAN). I think I shall. He keeps telling me he has a presentiment that he is going to die. I never met a man so greedy for sympathy.

Mangan (*plaintively*). But I have a presentiment. I really have. And you wouldnt listen.

Mrs. Hushabye: I was listening for something else. There was a sort of splendid drumming in the sky. Did none of you hear it? It came from a distance and then died away.

Mangan: I tell you it was a train.

Mrs. Hushabye: And *I* tell you, Alf, there is no train at this hour. The last is nine fortyfive.

Mangan: But a goods train.

Mrs. Hushabye: Not on our little line. They tack a truck on to the passenger train. What can it have been, Hector?

Hector: Heaven's threatening growl of disgust at us useless futile creatures. (*Fiercely.*) I tell you, one of two things must happen. Either out of that darkness some new creation will come to supplant us as we have supplanted the animals, or the heavens will fall in thunder and destroy us.

Lady Utterword (*in a cool instructive manner, wallowing comfortably in her hammock*). We have not supplanted the animals, Hector. Why do you ask heaven to destroy this house, which could be made quite comfortable if Hesione had any notion of how to live? Dont you know what is wrong with it?

Hector: We are wrong with it. There is no sense in us. We are useless, dangerous, and ought to be abolished.

Lady Utterword: Nonsense! Hastings told me the very first day he came here, nearly twentyfour years ago, what is wrong with the house.

Captain Shotover: What! The numskull said there was something wrong with my house!

Lady Utterword: I said Hastings said it; and he is not in the least a numskull.

Captain Shotover: Whats wrong with my house?

Lady Utterword: Just what is wrong with a ship, papa. Wasnt it clever of Hastings to see that?

Captain Shotover: The man's a fool. Theres nothing wrong with a ship.

Lady Utterword: Yes there is.

Mrs. Hushabye: But what is it? Dont be aggravating, Addy.

Lady Utterword: Guess.

Hector: Demons. Daughters of the witch of Zanzibar. Demons.

Lady Utterword: Not a bit. I assure you, all this house needs to make it a sensible, healthy, pleasant house, with good appetites and sound sleep in it, is horses.

Mrs. Hushabye: Horses! What rubbish!

Lady Utterword: Yes: horses. Why have we never been able to let this house? Because there are no proper stables. Go anywhere in England where there are natural, wholesome, contented, and really nice English people; and what do you always find? That the stables are the real centre of the household; and that if any visitor wants to play the piano the whole room has to be upset before it can be opened, there are so many things piled on it. I never lived until I learned to ride; and I shall never ride really well because I didnt begin as a child. There are only two classes in good society in England: the equestrian classes and the neurotic classes. It isnt mere convention: everybody can see that the people who hunt are the right people and the people who dont are the wrong ones.

Captain Shotover: There is some truth in this. My ship made a man of me; and a ship is the horse of the sea.

Lady Utterword: Exactly how Hastings explained your being a gentleman.

Captain Shotover: Not bad for a numskull. Bring the man here with you next time: I must talk to him.

Lady Utterword: Why is Randall such an obvious rotter? He is well bred; he has been at a public school and a university; he has been in the Foreign Office; he knows the best people and has lived all his life among them. Why is he so unsatisfactory, so contemptible? Why cant he get a valet to stay with him longer than a few months? Just because he is too lazy and pleasure-loving to hunt and shoot. He strums the piano, and sketches, and runs after married women, and reads literary books and poems. He actually plays the flute: but I never let him bring it into my house. If he would only—(*She is interrupted by the melancholy strains of a flute coming from an open window above. She raises herself indignantly in the hammock.*) Randall: you have not gone to bed. Have you been listening? (*The flute replies pertly*):

How vulgar! Go to bed instantly, Randall: how dare you? (*The window is slammed down. She subsides.*) How can anyone care for such a creature!

Mrs. Hushabye: Addy: do you think Ellie ought to marry poor Alfred merely for his money?

Mangan (*much alarmed*). Whats that? Mrs. Hushabye: are my affairs to be discussed like this before everybody?

Lady Utterword: I dont think Randall is listening now.

Mangan: Everybody is listening. It isnt right.

Mrs. Hushabye: But in the dark, what does it matter? Ellie doesnt mind. Do you, Ellie?

Ellie: Not in the least. What is your opinion, Lady Utterword? You have so much good sense.

Mangan: But it isnt right. It—(MRS. HUSHABYE *puts her hand on his mouth.*) Oh, very well.

Lady Utterword: How much money have you, Mr. Mangan?

Mangan: Really—No: I cant stand this.

Lady Utterword: Nonsense, Mr. Mangan! It all turns on your income, doesnt it?

Mangan: Well, if you come to that, how much money has she?

Ellie: None.

Lady Utterword: You are answered, Mr. Mangan. And now, as you have made Miss Dunn throw her cards on the table, you cannot refuse to shew your own.

Mrs. Hushabye: Come, Alf! out with it! How much?

Mangan (*baited out of all prudence*). Well, if you want to know, I have no money and never had any.

Mrs. Hushabye: Alfred: you mustnt tell naughty stories.

Mangan: I'm not telling you stories. I'm telling you the raw truth.

Lady Utterword: Then what do you live on, Mr. Mangan?

Mangan: Travelling expenses. And a trifle of commission.

Captain Shotover: What more have any of us but travelling expenses for our life's journey?

Mrs. Hushabye: But you have factories and capital and things?

Mangan: People think I have. People think I'm an industrial Napoleon. Thats why Miss Ellie wants to marry me. But I tell you I have nothing.

Ellie: Do you mean that the factories are like Marcus's tigers? That they dont exist?

Mangan: They exist all right enough. But theyre not mine. They belong to syndicates and shareholders and all sorts of lazy good-for-nothing capitalists. I get money from such people to start the factories. I find people like Miss Dunn's father to work them, and keep a tight hand so as to make them pay. Of course I make them keep me going pretty well; but it's a dog's life; and I dont own anything.

Mrs. Hushabye: Alfred, Alfred: you are making a poor mouth of it to get out of marrying Ellie.

Mangan: I'm telling the truth about my money for the first time in my life; and it's the first time my word has ever been doubted.

Lady Utterword: How sad! Why dont you go in for politics, Mr. Mangan?

Mangan: Go in for politics! Where have you been living? I a m in politics.

Lady Utterword: I'm sure I beg your pardon. I never heard of you.

Mangan: Let me tell you, Lady Utterword, that the Prime Minister of this country asked me to join the Government without even going through the nonsense of an election, as the dictator of a great public department.

Lady Utterword: As a Conservative or a Liberal?

Mangan: No such nonsense. As a practical business man. (*They all burst out laughing.*) What are you all laughing at?

Mrs. Hushabye: Oh, Alfred, Alfred!

Ellie: You! who have to get my father to do everything for you!

Mrs. Hushabye: You! who are afraid of your own workmen!

Hector: You! with whom three women have been playing cat and mouse all the evening!

Lady Utterword: You must have given an immense sum to the party funds, Mr. Mangan.

Mangan: Not a penny out of my own pocket. The syndicate found the money: they knew how useful I should be to them in the Government.

Lady Utterword: This is most interesting and unexpected, Mr. Mangan. And what have your administrative achievements been, so far?

Mangan: Achievements? Well, I dont know what you call achievements; but Ive jolly well put a stop to the games of the other fellows in the other departments. Every man of them thought he was going to save the country all by himself, and do me out of the credit and out of my chance of a title. I took good care that if they wouldnt let me do it they shouldnt do it themselves either. I may not know anything about my own machinery; but I know how to stick a ramrod into the other fellow's. And now they all look the biggest fools going.

Hector: And in heaven's name, what do you look like?

Mangan: I look like the fellow that was too clever for all the others, dont I? If that isnt a triumph of practical business, what is?

Hector: Is this England, or is it a madhouse?

Lady Utterword: Do you expect to save the country, Mr. Mangan?

Mangan: Well, who else will? Will your Mr. Randall save it?

Lady Utterword: Randall the rotter! Certainly not.

Mangan: Will your brother-in-law save it with his moustache and his fine talk?

Hector: Yes, if they will let me.

Mangan (*sneering*). Ah! Will they let you?

Hector: No. They prefer you.

Mangan: Very well then, as youre in a world where I'm appreciated and youre not, youd best be civil to me, hadnt you? Who else is there but me?

Lady Utterword: There is Hastings. Get rid of your ridiculous sham democracy; and give Hastings the necessary powers, and a good supply of bamboo to bring the British native to his senses: he will save the country with the greatest ease.

Captain Shotover: It had better be lost. Any fool can govern with a stick in his hand. *I* could govern that way. It is not God's way. The man is a numskull.

Lady Utterword: The man is worth all of you rolled into one. What do you say, Miss Dunn?

Ellie: I think my father would do very well if people did not put upon him and cheat him and despise him because he is so good.

Mangan (*contemptuously*). I think I see Mazzini Dunn getting into parliament or pushing his way into the Government. Weve not come to that yet, thank God! What do you say, Mrs. Hushabye?

Mrs. Hushabye: Oh, *I* say it matters very little which of you governs the country so long as we govern you.

Hector: We? Who is we, pray?

Mrs. Hushabye: The devil's granddaughters, dear. The lovely women.

Hector (*raising his hands as before*). Fall, I say; and deliver us from the lures of Satan!

Ellie: There seems to be nothing real in the world except my father and Shakespear. Marcus's tigers are false; Mr. Mangan's millions are false; there is nothing really strong and true about Hesione but her beautiful black hair; and Lady Utterword's is too pretty to be real. The one thing that was left to me was the Captain's seventh degree of concentration; and that turns out to be—

Captain Shotover: Rum.

Lady Utterword (*placidly*). A good

deal of my hair is quite genuine. The Duchess of Dithering offered me fifty guineas for this (*touching her forehead*) under the impression that it was a transformation; but it is all natural except the color.

Mangan (*wildly*). Look here: I'm going to take off all my clothes. (*He begins tearing off his coat.*)

Lady Utterword	(*in consternation*).	Mr. Mangan!
Captain Shotover		Whats that?
Hector		Ha! ha! Do. Do.
Ellie		Please dont.

Mrs. Hushabye (*catching his arm and stopping him*). Alfred: for shame! Are you mad?

Mangan: Shame! What shame is there in this house? Let's all strip stark naked. We may as well do the thing thoroughly when we're about it. Weve stripped ourselves morally naked: well, let us strip ourselves physically naked as well, and see how we like it. I tell you I cant bear this. I was brought up to be respectable. I dont mind the women dyeing their hair and the men drinking: it's human nature. But it's not human nature to tell everybody about it. Every time one of you opens your mouth I go like this (*he cowers as if to avoid a missile*) afraid of what will come next. How are we to have any self-respect if we dont keep it up that we're better than we really are?

Lady Utterword: I quite sympathize with you, Mr. Mangan. I have been through it all; and I know by experience that men and women are delicate plants and must be cultivated under glass. Our family habit of throwing stones in all directions and letting the air in is not only unbearably rude, but positively dangerous. Still, there is no use catching physical colds as well as moral ones; so please keep your clothes on.

Mangan: I'll do as I like: not what you tell me. Am I a child or a grown man? I wont stand this mothering tyranny. I'll go back to the city, where I'm respected and made much of.

Mrs. Hushabye: Goodbye, Alf. Think of us sometimes in the city. Think of Ellie's youth!

Ellie: Think of Hesione's eyes and hair!

Captain Shotover: Think of this garden in which you are not a dog barking to keep the truth out!

Hector: Think of Lady Utterword's beauty! her good sense! her style!

Lady Utterword: Flatterer. Think, Mr. Mangan, whether you can really do any better for yourself elsewhere: that is the essential point, isnt it?

Mangan (*surrendering*). All right: all right. I'm done. Have it your own way. Only let me alone. I dont know whether I'm on my head or my heels when you all start on me like this. I'll stay. I'll marry her. I'll do anything for a quiet life. Are you satisfied now?

Ellie: No. I never really intended to make you marry me, Mr. Mangan. Never in the depths of my soul. I only wanted to feel my strength: to know that you could not escape if I chose to take you.

Mangan (*indignantly*). What! Do you mean to say you are going to throw me over after my acting so handsome?

Lady Utterword: I should not be too hasty, Miss Dunn. You can throw Mr. Mangan over at any time up to the last moment. Very few men in his position go bankrupt. You can live very comfortably on his reputation for immense wealth.

Ellie: I cannot commit bigamy, Lady Utterword.

Mrs. Hushabye } (*exclaiming all together*). Bigamy! Whatever on earth are you talking about, Ellie?
Lady Utterword } Bigamy! What do you mean, Miss Dunn?
Mangan } Bigamy! Do you mean to say youre married already?
Hector } Bigamy! This is some enigma.

Ellie: Only half an hour ago I became Captain Shotover's white wife.

Mrs. Hushabye: Ellie! What nonsense! Where?

Ellie: In heaven, where all true marriages are made.

Lady Utterword: Really, Miss Dunn! Really, papa!

Mangan: He told me *I* was too old! And him a mummy!

Hector (*quoting Shelley*).

"Their altar the grassy earth outspread,
And their priest the muttering wind."

Ellie: Yes: I, Ellie Dunn, give my broken heart and my strong sound soul to its natural captain, my spiritual husband and second father.

[*She draws* THE CAPTAIN'S *arm through hers, and pats his hand.* THE CAPTAIN *remains fast asleep.*]

Mrs. Hushabye: Oh, thats very clever of you, pettikins. V e r y clever. Alfred: you could never have lived up to Ellie. You must be content with a little share of me.

Mangan (*sniffing and wiping his eyes*). It isnt kind—(*His emotion chokes him.*)

Lady Utterword: You are well out of it, Mr. Mangan. Miss Dunn is the most conceited young woman I have met since I came back to England.

Mrs. Hushabye: Oh, Ellie isnt conceited. Are you, pettikins?

Ellie: I know my strength now, Hesione.

Mangan: Brazen, I call you. Brazen.

Mrs. Hushabye: Tut tut, Alfred: dont be rude. Dont you feel how lovely this marriage night is, made in heaven? Arnt you happy, you and Hector? Open your eyes: Addy and Ellie look beautiful enough to please the most fastidious man: we live and love and have not a care in the world. We women have managed all that for you. Why in the name of common sense do you go on as if you were two miserable wretches?

Captain Shotover: I tell you happiness is no good. You can be happy when you are only half alive. I am happier now I am half dead than ever I was in my prime. But there is no blessing on my happiness.

Ellie (*her face lighting up*). Life with a blessing! that is what I want. Now I know the real reason why I couldnt marry Mr. Mangan: there would be no blessing on our marriage. There is a blessing on my broken heart. There is a blessing on your beauty, Hesione. There is a blessing on your father's spirit. Even on the lies of Marcus there is a blessing; but on Mr. Mangan's money there is none.

Mangan: I dont understand a word of that.

Ellie: Neither do I. But I know it means something.

Mangan: Dont say there was any

difficulty about the blessing. I was ready to get a bishop to marry us.

Mrs. Hushabye: Isnt he a fool, pettikins?

Hector (*fiercely*). Do not scorn the man. We are all fools.

[MAZZINI, *in pyjamas and a richly colored silk dressing-gown, comes from the house, on* LADY UTTERWORD'S *side.*]

Mrs. Hushabye: Oh! here comes the only man who ever resisted me. Whats the matter, Mr. Dunn? Is the house on fire?

Mazzini: Oh no: nothing's the matter: but really it's impossible to go to sleep with such an interesting conversation going on under one's window, and on such a beautiful night too. I just had to come down and join you all. What has it all been about?

Mrs. Hushabye: Oh, wonderful things, soldier of freedom.

Hector: For example, Mangan, as a practical business man, has tried to undress himself and has failed ignominiously; whilst you, as an idealist, have succeeded brilliantly.

Mazzini: I hope you dont mind my being like this, Mrs. Hushabye. (*He sits down on the campstool.*)

Mrs. Hushabye: On the contrary, I could wish you always like that.

Lady Utterword: Your daughter's match is off, Mr. Dunn. It seems that Mr. Mangan, whom we all supposed to be a man of property, owns absolutely nothing.

Mazzini: Well of course I knew that, Lady Utterword. But if people believe in him and are always giving him money, whereas they dont believe in me and never give me any, how can I ask poor Ellie to depend on what I can do for her?

Mangan: Dont you run away with this idea that I have nothing. I—

Hector: Oh, dont explain. We understand. You have a couple of thousand pounds in exchequer bills, 50,000 shares worth ten-pence a dozen, and half a dozen tabloids of cynanide of potassium to poison yourself with when you are found out. Thats the reality of your millions.

Mazzini: Oh no, no, no. He is quite honest: the businesses are genuine and perfectly legal.

Hector (*disgusted*). Yah! Not even a great swindler!

Mangan: So you think. But Ive been too many for some honest men, for all that.

Lady Utterword: There is no pleasing you, Mr. Mangan. You are determined to be neither rich nor poor, honest nor dishonest.

Mangan: There you go again. Ever since I came into this silly house I have been made to look like a fool, though I'm as good a man in this house as in the city.

Ellie (*musically*). Yes: this silly house, this strangely happy house, this agonizing house, this house without foundations. I shall call it Heartbreak House.

Mrs. Hushabye: Stop, Ellie; or I shall howl like an animal.

Mangan (*breaks into a low snivelling*)!!!

Mrs. Hushabye: There! you have set Alfred off.

Ellie: I like him best when he is howling.

Captain Shotover: Silence! (MANGAN *subsides into silence.*) I say, let the heart break in silence.

Hector: Do you accept that name for your house?

Captain Shotover: It is not my house: it is only my kennel.

Hector: We have been too long here. We do not live in this house: we haunt it.

Lady Utterword (*heart torn*). It is dreadful to think how you have been here all these years while I have gone round the world. I escaped young; but it has drawn me back. It wants to break my heart too. But it shant. I have left you and it behind. It was silly of me to come back. I felt sentimental about papa and Hesione and the old place. I felt them calling to me.

Mazzini: But what a very natural and kindly and charming human feeling, Lady Utterword!

Lady Utterword: So I thought, Mr. Dunn. But I know now that it was only the last of my influenza. I found that I was not remembered and not wanted.

Captain Shotover: You left because you did not want us. Was there no heartbreak in that for your father? You tore yourself up by the roots; and the ground healed up and brought forth fresh plants and forgot you. What right had you to come back and probe old wounds?

Mrs. Hushabye: You were a complete stranger to me at first, Addy; but now I feel as if you had never been away.

Lady Utterword: Thank you, Hesione; but the influenza is quite cured. The place may be Heartbreak House to you, Miss Dunn, and to this gentleman from the city who seems to have so little self-control; but to me it is only a very ill-regulated and rather untidy villa without any stables.

Hector: Inhabited by—?

Ellie: A crazy old sea captain and a young singer who adores him.

Mrs. Hushabye: A sluttish female, trying to stave off a double chin and an elderly spread, vainly wooing a born soldier of freedom.

Mazzini: Oh, really, Mrs. Hushabye—

Mangan: A member of His Majesty's Government that everybody sets down as a nincompoop: dont forget him, Lady Utterword.

Lady Utterword: And a very fascinating gentleman whose chief occupation is to be married to my sister.

Hector: All heartbroken imbeciles.

Mazzini: Oh no. Surely, if I may say so, rather a favorable specimen of what is best in our English culture. You are very charming people, most advanced, unprejudiced, frank, humane, unconventional, democratic, free-thinking, and everything that is delightful to thoughtful people.

Mrs. Hushabye: You do us proud, Mazzini.

Mazzini: I am not flattering, really. Where else could I feel perfectly at ease in my pyjamas? I sometimes dream that I am in very distinguished society, and suddenly I have nothing on but my pyjamas! Sometimes I havnt even pyjamas. And I always feel overwhelmed with confusion. But here, I dont mind in the least: it seems quite natural.

Lady Utterword: An infallible sign that you are not now in really distinguished society, Mr. Dunn. If you were in my house, you w o u l d feel embarrassed.

Mazzini: I shall take particular care to keep out of your house, Lady Utterword.

Lady Utterword: You will be quite wrong, Mr. Dunn. I should make you very comfortable; and you would not have the trouble and anxiety of wondering whether you should wear your purple and gold or your green and crimson dressing-gown at dinner. You complicate life instead of simplifying it by doing these ridiculous things.

Ellie: Y o u r house is not Heartbreak House: is it, Lady Utterword?

Hector: Yet she breaks hearts, easy as her house is. That poor devil upstairs with his flute howls when she twists his heart, just as Mangan howls when my wife twists his.

Lady Utterword: That is because Randall has nothing to do but have his heart broken. It is a change from having his head shampooed. Catch anyone breaking Hastings' heart!

Captain Shotover: The numskull wins, after all.

Lady Utterword: I shall go back to my numskull with the greatest satisfaction when I am tired of you all, clever as you are.

Mangan (*huffily*). I never set up to be clever.

Lady Utterword: I forgot you, Mr. Mangan.

Mangan: Well, I dont see that quite, either.

Lady Utterword: You may not be clever, Mr. Mangan; but you are successful.

Mangan: But I dont want to be regarded merely as a successful man. I have an imagination like anyone else. I have a presentiment—

Mrs. Hushabye: Oh, you are impossible, Alfred. Here I am devoting myself to you; and you think of nothing but your ridiculous presentiment. You bore me. Come and talk poetry to me under the stars. (*She drags him away into the darkness.*)

Mangan (*tearfully, as he disappears*). Yes: it's all very well to make fun of me; but if you only knew—

Hector (*impatiently*). How is all this going to end?

Mazzini: It wont end, Mr. Hushabye. Life doesnt end: it goes on.

Ellie: Oh, it cant go on for ever. I'm always expecting something. I dont know what it is; but life must come to a point sometime.

Lady Utterword: The point for a young woman of your age is a baby.

Hector: Yes, but, damn it, I have the same feeling; and *I* cant have a baby.

Lady Utterword: By deputy, Hector.

Hector: But I have children. All that is over and done with for me: and yet I too feel that this cant last. We sit here talking, and leave everything to Mangan and to chance and to the devil. Think of the powers of destruction that Mangan and his mutual admiration gang wield! It's madness: it's like giving a torpedo to a badly brought up child to play at earthquakes with.

Mazzini: I know. I used often to think about that when I was young.

Hector: Think! Whats the good of thinking about it? Why didnt you do something?

Mazzini: But I did. I joined societies and made speeches and wrote pamphlets. That was all I could do. But, you know, though the people in the societies thought they knew more than Mangan, most of them wouldnt have joined if they had known as much. You see they had never had any money to handle or any men to manage. Every year I expected a revolution, or some frightful smash-up: it seemed impossible that we could blunder and muddle on any longer. But nothing happened, except, of course, the usual poverty and crime and drink that we are used to. Nothing ever does happen. It's amazing how well we get along, all things considered.

Lady Utterword: Perhaps somebody cleverer than you and Mr. Mangan was at work all the time.

Mazzini: Perhaps so. Though I was brought up not to believe in anything, I often feel that there is a great deal to be said for the theory of an overruling Providence, after all.

Lady Utterword: Providence! I meant Hastings.

Mazzini: Oh, I beg your pardon, Lady Utterword.

Captain Shotover: Every drunken skipper trusts to Providence. But one of the ways of Providence with drunken skippers is to run them on the rocks.

Mazzini: Very true, no doubt, at sea. But in politics, I assure you, they only run into jellyfish. Nothing happens.

Captain Shotover: At sea nothing happens to the sea. Nothing happens to the sky. The sun comes up from the east and goes down to the west. The moon grows from a sickle to an arc lamp, and comes later and later until she is lost in the light as other things are lost in the darkness. After the typhoon, the flying-fish glitter in the sunshine like birds. It's amazing how t h e y get along, all things considered. Nothing happens, except something not worth mentioning.

Ellie: What is that, O Captain, my captain?

Captain Shotover (*savagely*). Nothing but the smash of the drunken skipper's ship on the rocks, the splintering of her rotten timbers, the tearing of her rusty plates, the drowning of the crew like rats in a trap.

Ellie: Moral: dont take rum.

Captain Shotover (*vehemently*). That is a lie, child. Let a man drink ten barrels of rum a day, he is not a drunken skipper until he is a drifting skipper. Whilst he can lay his course and stand on his bridge and steer it, he is no drunkard. It is the man who lies drinking in his bunk and trusts to Providence that I call the drunken skipper, though he drank nothing but the waters of the River Jordan.

Ellie: Splendid! And you havnt had a drop for an hour. You see you dont need it: your own spirit is not dead.

Captain Shotover: Echoes: nothing but echoes. The last shot was fired years ago.

Hector: And this ship that we are all in? This soul's prison we call England?

Captain Shotover: The captain is in his bunk, drinking bottled ditch-water; and the crew is gambling in the forecastle. She will strike and sink and split. Do you think the laws of God will be suspended in favor of England because you were born in it?

Hector: Well, I dont mean to be drowned like a rat in a trap. I still have the will to live. What am I to do?

Captain Shotover: Do? Nothing simpler. Learn your business as an Englishman.

Hector: And what may my business as an Englishman be, pray?

Captain Shotover: Navigation. Learn it and live; or leave it and be damned.

Ellie: Quiet, quiet: youll tire yourself.

Mazzini: I thought all that once, Captain; but I assure you nothing will happen.

[*A dull distant explosion is heard.*]

Hector (*starting up*). What was that?

Captain Shotover: Something happening. (*He blows his whistle.*) Breakers ahead!

[*The light goes out.*]

Hector (*furiously*). Who put that light out? Who dared put that light out?

Nurse Guinness (*running in from the house to the middle of the esplanade*). I did, sir. The police have telephoned to say we'll be summoned if we dont put that light out: it can be seen for miles.

Hector: It shall be seen for a hundred miles. (*He dashes into the house.*)

Nurse Guinness: The rectory is nothing but a heap of bricks, they say. Unless we can give the rector a bed he has nowhere to lay his head this night.

Captain Shotover: The Church is on the rocks, breaking up. I told him it would unless it headed for God's open sea.

Nurse Guinness: And you are all to go down to the cellars.

Captain Shotover: Go there yourself, you and all the crew. Batten down the hatches.

Nurse Guinness: And hide beside the coward I married! I'll go on the roof first. (*The lamp lights up again.*) There! Mr. Hushabye's turned it on again.

The Burglar (*hurrying in and appealing to* NURSE GUINNESS). Here: wheres the way to that gravel pit? The boot-boy says theres a cave in the gravel pit. Them cellars is no use. Wheres the gravel pit, Captain?

Nurse Guinness: Go straight on past the flagstaff until you fall into it and break your dirty neck. (*She pushes him contemptuously towards the flagstaff, and herself goes to the foot of the hammock and waits there, as it were by* ARIADNE'S *cradle*).

[*Another and louder explosion is heard. The burglar stops and stands trembling.*]

Ellie (*rising*). That was nearer.

Captain Shotover: The next one will get us. (*He rises.*) Stand by, all hands, for judgment.

The Burglar: Oh my Lordy God! (*He rushes away frantically past the flagstaff into the gloom.*)

Mrs. Hushabye (*emerging panting from the darkness*). Who was that running away? (*She comes to* ELLIE.) Did you hear the explosions? And the sound in the sky: it's splendid: it's like an orchestra: it's like Beethoven.

Ellie: By thunder, Hesione: it is Beethoven.

[*She and* HESIONE *throw themselves into one another's arms in wild excitement. The light increases.*]

Mazzini (*anxiously*). The light is getting brighter.

Nurse Guinness (*looking up at the house*). It's Mr. Hushabye turning on all the lights in the house and tearing down the curtains.

Randall (*rushing in in his pyjamas, distractedly waving a flute*). Ariadne: my soul, my precious, go down to the cellars: I beg and implore you, go down to the cellars!

Lady Utterword (*quite composed in her hammock*). The governor's wife in the cellars with the servants! Really, Randall!

Randall: But what shall I do if you are killed?

Lady Utterword: You will probably be killed, too, Randall. Now play your flute to shew that you are not afraid; and be good. Play us *Keep the home fires burning.*

Nurse Guinness (*grimly*). Theyll keep the home fires burning for us: them up there.

Randall (*having tried to play*). My lips are trembling. I cant get a sound.

Mazzini: I hope poor Mangan is safe.

Mrs. Hushabye: He is hiding in the cave in the gravel pit.

Captain Shotover: My dynamite

drew him there. It is the hand of God.

Hector (*returning from the house and striding across to his former place*). There is not half light enough. We should be blazing to the skies.

Ellie (*tense with excitement*). Set fire to the house, Marcus.

Mrs. Hushabye: My house! No.

Hector: I thought of that; but it would not be ready in time.

Captain Shotover: The judgment has come. Courage will not save you; but it will shew that your souls are still alive.

Mrs. Hushabye: Sh-sh! Listen: do you hear it now? It's magnificent.

[*They all turn away from the house and look up, listening.*]

Hector (*gravely*). Miss Dunn: you can do no good here. We of this house are only moths flying into the candle. You had better go down to the cellar.

Ellie (*scornfully*). I d o n t think.

Mazzini: Ellie, dear, there is no disgrace in going to the cellar. An officer would order his soldiers to take cover. Mr. Hushabye is behaving like an amateur. Mangan and the burglar are acting very sensibly; and it is they who will survive.

Ellie: Let them. I shall behave like an amateur. But why should you run any risk?

Mazzini: Think of the risk those poor fellows up there are running!

Nurse Guinness: Think of t h e m, indeed, the murdering blackguards! What next?

[*A terrific explosion shakes the earth. they reel back into their seats, or clutch the nearest support. They hear the falling of the shattered glass from the windows.*]

Mazzini: Is anyone hurt?

Hector: Where did it fall?

Nurse Guinness (*in hideous triumph*). Right in the gravel pit: I seen it. Serve un right! I seen it. (*She runs away towards the gravel pit, laughing harshly.*)

Hector: One husband gone.

Captain Shotover: Thirty pounds of good dynamite wasted.

Mazzini: Oh, poor Mangan!

Hector: Are you immortal that you need pity him? Our turn next.

[*They wait in silence and intense expectation.* HESIONE *and* ELLIE *hold each other's hand tight.*]

[*A distant explosion is heard.*]

Mrs. Hushabye (*relaxing her grip*). Oh! they have passed us.

Lady Utterword: The danger is over, Randall. Go to bed.

Captain Shotover: Turn in, all hands. The ship is safe. (*He sits down and goes asleep*).

Ellie (*disappointedly*). Safe!

Hector (*disgustedly*). Yes, safe. And how damnably dull the world has become again suddenly! (*He sits down.*)

Mazzini (*sitting down*). I was quite wrong, after all. It is we who have survived; and Mangan and the burglar—

Hector: —the two burglars—

Lady Utterword: —the two practical men of business—

Mazzini: —both gone. And the poor clergyman will have to get a new house.

Mrs. Hushabye: But what a glorious experience! I hope theyll come again tomorrow night.

Ellie (*radiant at the prospect*). Oh, I hope so.

[RANDALL *at last succeeds in keeping the home fires burning on his flute.*]

DISCUSSION QUESTIONS

Act I

1. Shaw has said that "Heartbreak House is cultured, leisured Europe before the war." How are the various aspects of the setting representative or symbolic of meaning beyond their literal significance?
2. Shaw has also said that *Heartbreak House,* which he called "a fantasia in the Russian manner on English themes," was influenced by a production of Chekhov's *The Cherry Orchard.* What themes, patterns, and devices does Shaw's play have in common with Chekhov's play?
3. To what extent does Shaw make ironic use of the form of the melodramatic conflict between completely good and completely evil characters over an item of no spiritual value, as well as other conventions of the romantic theatre?
4. In constructing his play, Shaw has observed the so-called three unities (of time—usually less than 24 hours—place, and action), has made all his characters but Ellie at least middle-aged, and has put together a recognizable microcosm (or miniature world) of early twentieth-century England. How has he, at the same time, managed entrances and exits, the kind of speeches, and the concerns of the characters to convey an atmosphere of nightmare, confusion, and boding chaos?
5. What exposition is presented in Act I?
6. How do comments and actions in Act I prepare for action to come in this Act and later?
7. How do the names of the following characters give some clue to their traits (see a good outline or history of classical mythology): Captain Shotover, Hesione and Hector Hushabye, Ariadne Utterword, Boss Mangan, Mazzini Dunn, Ellie Dunn?
8. What does Ellie Dunn learn from her recognition of "Marcus Darnley" as Hector Hushabye, the husband of her friend Hesione?
9. How does Ellie's disillusionment both resemble and differ from past recognitions by all the other characters?
10. In Shakespeare's *Othello,* which Ellie and Hesione discuss, a Moorish general wins over the daughter of a Venetian senator through tales of his prowess in battle. Influenced by the malign insinuations of Iago, he becomes insanely jealous, strangles Desdemona his wife, and then commits suicide. What parallels to this play occur in *Heartbreak House?*
11. Mrs. Hushabye's comment to Ellie that without lies "there wouldn't be much love in the world" suggests that melodramatic illusion is somehow more acceptable than reality. Explain how Shaw might relate the unreal stage conventions of melodrama to the conflict between illusion and reality in "real" life.

12. What is ironic about Mrs. Hushabye's complaint that since household money is running low, Captain Shotover must invent more devices of mass destruction?

Act II

1. In the "well-made play," which *Heartbreak House* only superficially resembles, a series of secrets are revealed. What secrets or recognitions emerge in Act II?
2. What comments and actions in Act II prepare for action to come in the act and later?
3. In *The Simpleton of the Unexpected Isles,* Shaw says that four characters represent Love, Pride, Heroism, and Empire, and his biographer, Archibald Henderson, has found these same abstractions personified in *Heartbreak House.* How do all the characters in the play "stand for" these ideas and others?
4. Hesione Hushabye tells Ellie Dunn that "people don't have virtues and vices in sets: they have them all mixed." How are the following characters made up of contrasting, ironic traits: Captain Shotover, Ellie Dunn, Hesione Hushabye, Lady Ariadne Utterword, Mazzini Dunn, Boss Mangan, Randall Utterword?
5. In her conversation with Mangan, Ellie refers to the values of "we women," and is later compared to the Captain's daughters by Mangan. How does she resemble Hesione and Ariadne?
6. How is Hesione disillusioned, just as Ellie has been, about Mangan?
7. How is Hesione's recognition of Mazzini's traits, as well as Dunn's characterization, furthered by her new insight into Mangan's character?
8. What is ironic about Mangan's violent reaction to what he has heard during his trance?
9. Although Shaw says (in *Crude Criminology*) that the presence of the blackmailing burglar is "a comic dramatization of a process going on every day," the role has been criticized as padding. What arguments could be presented for and against the use of this character by Shaw?
10. As in Act I, Ellie gains a further significant recognition of truth. What is it, and what are its effects?
11. In Marlowe's *Doctor Faustus,* a highly intelligent man sells his soul to the devil for a specified length of time. In return, he is given extraordinary power over people and things. How is Captain Shotover characterized as a Faustian hero and with what ironic significance?
12. How have Captain Shotover's seagoing experiences increased his wisdom, leading toward his spiritual salvation?
13. How does Captain Shotover's explanation of his Faustian reputation serve as an attack on England's history of colonial exploitation?
14. How did the relationships between Captain Shotover and the burglar Billy Dunn, on the one hand, both differ from and resemble that between Boss Mangan and Mazzini Dunn, on the other?
15. How do Shotover's admissions to Ellie establish him as a fit critic of society?

16. How is Lady Utterword's characterization furthered by her attack on Ellie, followed by both Captain Shotover's and Hector's rejection of her?

Act III

1. How does Lady Utterword's distinction between the equestrian and the neurotic classes group and characterize the people of the play?
2. How is the denouement (or unraveling) foreshadowed in Act III?
3. How is Boss Mangan characterized, personally and symbolically, by his admission that he owns nothing?
4. How does Mangan's attempt to tear off his clothes reveal his inner stresses, his delusions, his false respectability?
5. How is Hastings Utterword—a character who never appears in the play—characterized in relation to Shotover and Mangan?
6. What contrasting, complementary qualities are united symbolically in the marriage of Ellie Dunn to Captain Shotover?
7. What final recognition has Ellie achieved?
8. What weakness, symbolic of an entire class, does Lady Utterword reveal in her attack on Ellie's "conceit"?
9. What ironic contrast does Hector draw between Mazzini and Mangan?
10. By the end of the play, Ellie Dunn has been three times disillusioned—once in each act, by Hector, by Mangan, by Shotover. How is her state of mind circular, arriving back to the beginning again?
11. What is the psychological and social significance of the welcome that the characters present to impending destruction?

DESIRE UNDER THE ELMS

Eugene O'Neill

Introductory Comment

In *Desire Under the Elms* O'Nell has taken the elements of sensational, tabloid journalism—a story of adultery and infanticide—and turned them into the substance of serious drama. The bold headlinues of a newspaper article, reporting the incidents the play is based on, might have read, FAITHLESS WIFE KILLS NEWBORN BABY FOR LOVER—Infant Fathered by Stepson-Lover. The accompanying news story would have been just as lurid but more detailed and been the occasion for conventionally shocked disbelief and automatic moral condemnation. In using such material for serious drama, however, O'Neill is actually following a long-established tradition in the history of the theater rather than starting anything new. The same sort of headlines could be framed for almost any one of the world's great tragedies and still be as sensational as the one suggested for this play. Consider, for example, the eye-catching headline possibilities offered by the incest, suicide, and self-mutilation in *Oedipus Rex,* the treacherous assassination, cruel murders, and insanity brought about by guilt in *Macbeth,* or the appearance of a ghost of a murdered king, the deadly sexual intrigue, and the wholesale slaughter in *Hamlet.*

Success in converting the raw material of illicit sex with incestuous overtones and a fatal outcome into significant drama depends primarily on the playwright's vision and his ability to create sympathetic characters credibly motivated and bringing about their own destruction in their conflict with one another and with the circumstances of their lives. O'Neill has to see in the lives of old Cabot, Abbie, and Eben something which fires his imagination as a dramatist and which he can transmit to us through dialogue, action, and setting. Where we might see only the sordid story of a young woman marrying an old man for security and then falling disastrously in love with her husband's son and bearing him a child she kills with her own hand, O'Neill's vision discloses something much more significant. At the end of the play he has us feeling that Abbie and Eben have somehow gained something as important as what they have lost.

In reading this play one should be alert to how O'Neill attempts to create tragedy through the use of speech and action which develop sympathetic characters in Abbie and Eben. One should also carefully note how he uses language and setting with ironic and symbolic ambiguities and how he judiciously selects and arranges his events to make us aware of the conflicts and their inevitable outcome. Whether he succeeds in doing this as well as Sophocles or Shakespeare is debatable and depends also on the criteria one chooses to apply. The material O'Neill has chosen for his tragedy is not the limiting factor. Even if O'Neill is judged to have fallen short of high tragedy in this play, it is still worthwhile and interesting to draw parallels and see how a modern American dramatist grapples with essentially the same problems in fundamentally the same way and in substantially the same form as an ancient Greek or a Renaissance English tragic playwright.

Cast of Characters

EPHRAIM CABOT	ABBIE PUTNAM
SIMEON, PETER, EBEN } *his sons*	YOUNG GIRL, *two* FARMERS, *the* FIDDLER, *a* SHERIFF, *and other folk from the neighboring farms*

[The action of the entire play takes place in, and immediately outside of, the Cabot farmhouse in New England, in the year 1850. The south end of the house faces front to a stone wall with a wooden gate at center opening on a country road. The house is in good condition but in need of paint. Its walls are a sickly grayish, the green of the shutters faded. Two enormous elms are on each side of the house. They bend their trailing branches down over the roof. They appear to protect and at the same time subdue. There is a sinister maternity in their aspect, a crushing, jealous absorption. They have developed from their intimate contact with the life of man in the house an appalling humaneness. They brood oppressively over the house. They are like exhausted women resting their sagging breasts and hands and hair on its roof, and when it rains their tears trickle down monotonously and rot on the shingles.

There is a path running from the gate around the right corner of the house to the front door. A narrow porch is on this side. The end wall facing us has two windows in its upper story, two larger ones on the floor below. The two upper are those of the father's bedroom and that of the brothers. On the left, ground floor, is the kitchen—on the right, the parlor, the shades of which are always drawn down.]

PART I

SCENE I

[Exterior of the farmhouse. It is sunset of a day at the beginning of summer in the year 1850. There is no wind and everything is still. The sky above the roof is suffused with deep colors, the green of the elms glows, but the house is in shadow, seeming pale and washed out by contrast.

A door opens and EBEN CABOT *comes to the end of the porch and stands looking down the road to the right. He has a large bell in his hand and this he swings mechanically, awakening a deafening clangor. Then he puts his hands on his hips and stares up at the sky. He sighs with a puzzled awe and blurts out with halting appreciation.]*

Eben: God! Purty! (*His eyes fall*

and he stares about him frowningly. He is twenty-five, tall and sinewy. His face is well-formed, good-looking, but its expression is resentful and defensive. His defiant, dark eyes remind one of a wild animal's in captivity. Each day is a cage in which he finds himself trapped but inwardly unsubdued. There is a fierce repressed vitality about him. He has black hair, mustache, a thin curly trace of beard. He is dressed in rough farm clothes.

He spits on the ground with intense disgust, turns and goes back into the house.

SIMEON *and* PETER *come in from their work in the fields. They are tall men, much older than their half-brother* [SIMEON *is thirty-nine and* PETER *thirty-seven*], *built on a squarer, simpler model, fleshier in body, more bovine and homelier in face, shrewder and more practical. Their shoulders stoop a bit from years of farm work. They clump heavily along in their clumsy thick-soled boots caked with earth. Their clothes, their faces, hands, bare arms, and throats are earth-stained. They smell of earth. They stand together for a moment in front of the house and, as if with one impulse, stare dumbly up at the sky, leaning on their hoes. Their faces have a compressed, unresigned expression. As they look upward, this softens.*)

Simeon (*grudgingly*). Purty.

Peter: Ay-eh.

Simeon (*suddenly*). Eighteen year ago.

Peter: What?

Simeon: Jenn. My woman. She died.

Peter: I'd fergot.

Simeon: I rec'lect—now an' agin. Makes it lonesome. She'd hair long's a hoss' tail—an' yaller like gold!

Peter: Waal—she's gone. (*This with indifferent finality—then after a pause.*) They's gold in the West, Sim.

Simeon (*still under the influence of sunset—vaguely*). In the sky?

Peter: Waal—in a manner o' speakn'—thar's the promise. (*Growing excited.*) Gold in the sky—in the West—Golden Gate—Californi-a!—Goldest West!—fields o' gold!

Simeon (*excited in his turn*). Fortunes layin' just atop o' the ground waitin' t' be picked! Solomon's mines, they say! (*For a moment they continue looking up at the sky—then their eyes drop.*)

Peter (*with sardonic bitterness*). Here—it's stones atop o' the ground—stones atop o' stones—makin' stone walls—year atop o' year—him 'n' yew 'n' me 'n' then Eben—makin' stone walls fur him to fence us in!

Simeon: We've wuked. Give our strength. Give our years. Plowed 'em under in the ground—(*he stamps rebelliously*)—rottin'—makin' soil for his crops! (*A pause.*) Waal—the farm pays good for hereabouts.

Peter: If we plowed in Californi-a, they'd be lumps o' gold in the furrow!

Simeon: Californi-a's t'other side o' earth, a'most. We got t' calc'late—

Peter (*after a pause*). 'Twould be hard fur me, too, to give up what we've 'arned here by our sweat. (*A pause,* EBEN *sticks his head out of the dining-room window, listening.*)

Simeon: Ay-eh. (*A pause.*) Mebbe—he'll die soon.

Peter (*doubtfully*). Mebbe.

Simeon: Mebbe—fur all we knows—he's dead now.

Peter: Ye'd need proof.

Simeon: He's been gone two months—with no word.

Peter: Left us in the fields an evenin' like this. Hitched up an' druv off into the West. That's plum onnateral. He hain't never been off this farm 'ceptin' t' the village in thirty year or more, not since he married Eben's maw. (*A pause. Shrewdly.*) I calc'late we might get him declared crazy by the court.

Simeon: He skinned 'em too slick. He got the best o' all on 'em. They'd never b'lieve him crazy. (*A pause.*) We got t' wait—till he's under ground.

Eben (*with a sardonic chuckle*). Honor thy father! (*They turn, startled, and stare at him. He grins, then scowls.*) I pray he's died. (*They stare at him. He continues matter-of-factly.*) Supper's ready.

Simeon *and* **Peter** (*together*). Ay-eh.

Eben (*gazing up at the sky.*) Sun's downin' purty.

Simeon *and* **Peter** (*together*). Ay-eh. They's gold in the West.

Eben: Ay-eh. (*Pointing.*) Yonder atop o' the hill pasture, ye mean?

Simeon *and* **Peter** (*together*). In Californi-a!

Eben: Hunh? (*Stares at them indifferently for a second, then drawls.*) Waal—supper's gittin' cold. (*He turns back into kitchen.*)

Simeon (*startled—smacks his lips*). I air hungry!

Peter (*sniffing*). I smells bacon!

Simeon (*with hungry appreciation*). Bacon's good!

Peter (*in same tone*). Bacon's bacon! (*They turn, shouldering each other, their bodies bumping and rubbing together as they hurry clumsily to their food, like two friendly oxen toward their evening meal. They disappear around the right corner of house and can be heard entering the door.*)

SCENE II

[*The color fades from the sky. Twilight begins. The interior of the kitchen is now visible. A pine table is at center, a cook-stove in the right rear corner, four rough wooden chairs, a tallow candle on the table. In the middle of the rear wall is fastened a big advertising poster with a ship in full sail and the word "California" in big letters. Kitchen utensils hang from nails. Everything is neat and in order but the atmosphere is of a men's camp kitchen rather than that of a home.*

Places for three are laid. EBEN *takes boiled potatoes and bacon from the stove and puts them on the table, also a loaf of bread and a crock of water.* SIMEON *and* PETER *shoulder in, slump down in their chairs without a word.* EBEN *joins them. The three eat in silence for a moment, the two elder as naturally unrestrained as beasts of the field,* EBEN *picking at his food without appetite, glancing at them with a tolerant dislike.*]

Simeon (*suddenly turns to* EBEN). Looky here! Ye'd oughtn't t' said that, Eben.

Peter: 'Twa'n't righteous.

Eben: What?

Simeon: Ye prayed he'd died.

Eben: Waal—don't yew pray it? (*A pause.*)

Peter: He's our Paw.

Eben (*violently*). Not mine!

Simeon (*dryly*). Ye'd not let no one else say that about yer Maw! Ha! (*He gives one abrupt sardonic guffaw.* PETER *grins.*)

Eben (*very pale*). I meant—I hain't his'n—I hain't like him—he hain't me!

Peter (*dryly*). Wait till ye've growed his age!

Eben (*intensely*). I'm Maw—every drop o' blood! (*A pause. They stare at him with indifferent curiosity.*)

Peter (*reminiscently*). She was good t' Sim 'n' me. A good Stepmaw's scurse.

Simeon: She was good t' everyone.

Eben (*greatly moved, gets to his feet and makes an awkward bow to each of them—stammering*). I be thankful t'ye. I'm her—her heir. (*He sits down in confusion.*)

Peter (*after a pause—judicially*). She was good even t' him.

Eben (*fiercely*). An' fur thanks he killed her!

Simeon (*after a pause*). No one never kills nobody. It's allus somethin'. That's the murderer.

Eben: Didn't he slave Maw t' death?

Peter: He slaved himself t' death. He's slaved Sim 'n' me 'n' yew t' death —on'y none o' us hain't died—yit.

Simeon: It's somethin'—drivin' him —t' drive us!

Eben (*vengefully*). Waal—I hold him t' jedgment! (*Then scornfully.*) Somethin'! What's somethin'?

Simeon: Dunno.

Eben (*sardonically*). What's drivin' yew to Californi-a, mebbe. (*They look at him in surprise.*) Oh, I've heerd ye! (*Then, after a pause.*) But ye'll never go t' the gold fields!

Peter (*assertively*). Mebbe!

Eben: Whar'll ye git the money?

Peter: We kin walk. It's an a'mighty ways—Californi-a—but if yew was t' put all the steps we've walked on this farm end t' end we'd be in the moon!

Eben: The Injuns'll skulp ye on the plains.

Simeon (*with grim humor*). We'll mebbe make 'em pay a hair fur a hair!

Eben (*decisively*). But t'ain't that. Ye won't never go because ye'll wait here fur yer share o' the farm, thinkin' allus he'll die soon.

Simeon (*after a pause*). We've a right.

Peter: Two-thirds belongs t' us.

Eben (*jumping to his feet*). Ye've no right! She wa'n't yewr Maw! It was her farm! Didn't he steal it from her? Shes' dead. It's my farm.

Simeon (*sardonically*). Tell that t' Paw—when he comes! I'll bet ye a dollar he'll laugh—fur once in his life. Ha! (*He laughs himself in one single mirthless bark.*)

Peter (*amused in turn, echoes his brother*). Ha!

Simeon (*after a pause*). What've ye got held agin us, Eben? Year after year it's skulked in yer eye—somethin'.

Peter: Ay-eh.

Eben: Ay-eh. They's somethin'. (*Suddenly exploding.*) Why didn't ye never stand between him 'n' my Maw when he was slavin' her to her grave—t' pay her back fur the kindness she done t' yew? (*There is a long pause. They stare at him in surprise.*)

Simeon: Waal—the stock'd got t' be watered.

Peter: 'R they was woodin' t' do.

Simeon: 'R plowin'.

Peter: 'R hayin'.

Simeon: 'R spreadin' manure.

Peter: 'R weedin'.

Simeon: 'R prunin'.

Peter: 'R milkin'.

Eben (*breaking in harshly.*) An' makin' walls—stone atop o' stone—makin' walls till yer heart's a stone ye heft up out o' the way o' growth onto a stone wall t' wall in yer heart!

Simeon (*matter-of-factly*). We never had no time t' meddle.

Peter (*to* EBEN). Yew was fifteen afore yer Maw died—an' big fur yer age. Why didn't ye never do nothin'?

Eben (*harshly*). They was chores t' do, wa'n't they? (*A pause—then slowly.*) It was on'y arter she died I come to think o' it. Me cookin'—doin' her work—that made me know her, suffer her sufferin'—she'd come back t' help—come back t' bile potatoes—come back t' fry bacon—come back t' bake biscuits—come back all cramped up t' shake the fire, an' carry ashes, her eyes weepin' an' bloody with smoke an' cinders same's they used t' be. She still comes back—stands by the stove thar in the evenin'—she can't find it nateral sleepin' an' restin' in peace. She can't git used t' bein' free—even in her grave.

Simeon: She never complained none.

Eben: She'd got too tired. She'd got too used t' bein' too tired. That was what he done. (*With vengeful passion.*) An' sooner'r later, I'll meddle. I'll say the thin's I didn't say then t' him! I'll yell 'em at the top o' my lungs. I'll see t' it my Maw gits some rest an 'sleep in her grave! (*He sits down again, relapsing into a brooding silence. They look at him with a queer indifferent curiosity.*)

Peter (*after a pause*). Whar in tarnation d'ye s'pose he went, Sim?

Simeon: Dunno. He druv off in the buggy, all spick an' span, with the mare all breshed an' shiny, druv off clackin' his tongue an' wavin' his whip. I remember it right well. I was finishin' plowin', it was spring an' May an' sunset, an' gold in the West, an' he druv off into it. I yells "Whar ye goin', Paw?" an' he hauls up by the stone wall a jiffy. His old snake's eyes was glitterin' in the sun like he'd been drinkin' a jugful an' he says with a mule's grin: "Don't ye run away till I come back!"

Peter: Wonder if he knowed we was wantin' fur Californi-a?

Simeon: Mebbe. I didn't say nothin' and he says, lookin' kinder queer an' sick: "I been hearin' the hens cluckin' an' the roosters crowin' all the durn day. I been listenin' t' the cows lowin' an' everythin' else kickin' up till I can't stand it no more. It's spring an' I'm feelin' damned," he says. "Damned like an old bare hickory tree fit on'y fur burnin'," he says. An' then I calc-late I must've looked a mite hopeful, fur he adds real spry and vicious: "But don't git no fool idee I'm dead. I've sworn t' live a hundred an' I'll do it, if on'y t' spite yer sinful greed! An' now I'm ridin' out t' learn God's message t' me in the spring, like the prophets done. An' yew git back t' yer plowin'," he says. An' he druv off singin' a hymn. I thought he was drunk—'r I'd stopped him goin'.

Eben (*scornfully*). No, ye wouldn't! Ye're scared o' him. He's stronger—inside—than both o' ye put together!

Peter (*sardonically*). An' yew—be yew Samson?

Eben: I'm gittin' stronger. I kin feel it growin' in me—growin' an' growin'—till it'll bust out—! (*He gets up and puts on his coat and a hat. They watch him, gradually breaking into grins.* EBEN *avoids their eyes sheepishly.*) I'm goin' out fur a spell—up the road.

Peter: T' the village?

Simeon: T' see Minnie?

Eben (*defiantly*). Ay-eh!

Peter (*jeeringly*). The Scarlet Woman!

Simeon: Lust—that's what's growin' in ye!

Eben: Waal—she's purty!

Peter: She's been purty fur twenty year!

Simeon: A new coat o' paint'll make a heifer out of forty.

Eben: She hain't forty!

Peter: If she hain't, she's teeterin' on the edge.

Eben (*desperately*). What d'yew know—

Peter: All they is . . . Sim knew her—an' then me arter—

Simeon: An' Paw kin tell yew somethin' too! He was fust!

Eben: D'ye mean t 'say he . . . ?

Simeon (*with a grin*). Ay-eh! We air his heirs in everythin'!

Eben (*intensely*). That's more to it! That grows on it! It'll bust soon! (*Then violently.*) I'll go smash my fist in her face! (*He pulls open the door in rear violently.*)

Simeon (*with a wink at* PETER—*drawlingly*). Mebbe—but the night's wa'm—purty—by the time ye git thar mebbe ye'll kiss her instead!

Peter: Sart'n he will! (*They both roar with coarse laughter.* EBEN *rushes out and slams the door—then the outside front door—comes around the corner of the house and stands still by the gate, staring up at the sky.*)

Simeon (*looking after him*). Like his Paw.

Peter: Dead spit an' image!

Simeon: Dog'll eat dog!

Peter: Ay-eh. (*Pause. With yearning.*) Mebbe a year from now we'll be in Californi-a.

Simeon: Ay-eh. (*A pause. Both yawn.*) Let's git t'bed. (*He blows out the candle. They go out door in rear.* EBEN *stretches his arms up to the sky—rebelliously.*)

Eben: Waal—thar's a star, an' somewhar's they's him, an' there's me, an' thar's Min up the road—in the same night. What if I does kiss her? She's like t'night, she's soft 'n' wa'm, her eyes kin wink like a star, her mouth's wa'm, her arms're wa'm, she smells like a wa'm plowed field, she's purty . . . Ay-eh! By God A'mighty she's purty, an' I don't give a damn how many sins she's sinned afore mine or who's she's sinned 'em with, my sin's as purty as any one on 'em!

[*He strides off down the road to the left.*]

SCENE III

[*It is the pitch darkness just before dawn.* EBEN *comes in from the left and goes around to the porch, feeling his way, chuckling bitterly and cursing half-aloud to himself.*]

Eben: The cussed old miser! (*He can be heard going in the front door. There is a pause as he goes upstairs, then a loud knock on the bedroom door of the brothers.*) Wake up!

Simeon (*startedly*). Who's thar?

Eben (*pushing open the door and coming in, a lighted candle in his hand. The bedroom of the brothers is revealed. Its ceiling is the sloping roof. They can stand upright only close to the center dividing wall of the upstairs.* SIMEON *and* PETER *are in a double bed, front.* EBEN'S *cot is to the rear.* EBEN *has a mixture of silly grin and vicious scowl on his face*). I be!

Peter (*angrily*). What in hell's-fire . . . ?

Eben: I got news fur ye! Ha! (*He gives one abrupt sardonic guffaw.*)

Simeon (*angrily*). Couldn't ye hold it 'til we'd got our sleep?

Eben: It's nigh sunup. (*Then explosively.*) He's gone an' married agen!

Simeon *and* **Peter** (*explosively*). Paw?

Eben: Got himself hitched to a female 'bout thirty-five—an' purty, they says . . .

Simeon (*aghast*). It's a durn lie!

Peter: Who says?

Simeon: They been stringin' ye!

Eben: Think I'm a dunce, do ye? The hull village says. The preacher from New Dover, he brung the news—told it t'our preacher—New Dover, that's whar the old loon got himself hitched—that's whar the woman lived—

Peter (*no longer doubting—stunned*). Waal . . . !

Simeon (*the same*). *Waal . . . !*

Eben (*sitting down on a bed—with vicious hatred*). Ain't he a devil out o' hell? It's jest t' spite us—the damned old mule!

Peter (*after a pause*). Everythin'll go t' her now.

Simeon: Ay-eh. (*A pause—dully.*) Waal—if it's done—

Peter: It's done us. (*Pause—then persuasively.*) They's gold in the fields o' Californi-a, Sim. No good a-stayin' here now.

Simeon: Jest what I was a-thinkin'. (*Then with decision.*) S'well fust's last! Let's light out and git this mornin'.

Peter: Suits me.

Eben: Ye must like walkin'.

Simeon (*sardonically*). If ye'd grow wings on us we'd fly thar!

Eben: Ye'd like ridin' better—on a boat, wouldn't ye? (*Fumbles in his pocket and takes out a crumpled sheet of foolscap.*) Waal, if ye sign this ye kin ride on a boat. I've had it writ out an' ready in case ye'd ever go. It says fur three hundred dollars t' each ye agree yewr shares o' the farm is sold t' me. (*They look suspiciously at the paper. A pause.*)

Simeon (*wonderingly*). But if he's hitched agen—

Peter: An' whar'd yew git that sum o' money, anyways?

Eben (*cunningly*). I know whar it's hid. I been waitin'—Maw told me. She knew whar it lay fur years, but she was waitin' . . . It's her'n—the money he hoarded from her farm an' hid from Maw. It's my money by rights now.

Peter: Whar's it hid?

Eben (*cunningly*). Whar yew won't never find it without me. Maw spied on him—'r she'd never knowed. (*A pause. They look at him suspiciously, and he at them.*) Waal, is it fa'r trade?

Simeon: Dunno.

Peter: Dunno.

Simeon (*looking at window*). Sky's grayin'.

Peter: Ye better start the fire, Eben.

Simeon: An' fix some vittles.

Eben: Ay-eh. (*Then with a forced jocular heartiness.*) I'll git ye a good one. If ye're startin' t' hoof it t' Californi-a ye'll need somethin' that'll stick t' yer ribs. (*He turns to the door, adding meaningly.*) But ye kin ride on a boat if ye'll swap. (*He stops at the door and pauses. They stare at him.*)

Simeon (*suspiciously.*) Whar was ye all night?

Eben (*defiantly*). Up t' Min's. (*Then slowly.*) Walkin' thar, fust I felt 's if I'd kiss her; then I got a-thinkin' o' what ye'd said o' him an' her an' I says, I'll bust her nose fur that! Then I got t' the village an' heerd the news an' I got madder'n hell an' run all the way t' Min's not knowin' what I'd do— (*He* *pauses—then sheepishly but more defiantly.*) Waal—when I seen her, I didn't hit her—nor I didn't kiss her nuther—I begun t' beller like a calf an' cuss at the same time, I was so durn mad—an' she got scared—an' I jest grabbed holt an' tuk her! (*Proudly.*) Yes, sirree! I tuk her. She may've been his'n—an' your'n, too—but she's mine now!

Simeon (*dryly*). In love, air yew?

Eben (*with lofty scorn*). Love! I don't take no stock in sech slop!

Peter (*winking at* SIMEON). Mebbe Eben's aimin' t' marry, too.

Simeon: Min'd make a true faithful he'pmeet! (*They snicker.*)

Eben: What do I care fur her—'ceptin' she's round an' wa'm? The p'int is she was his'n—an' now she belongs t' me! (*He goes to the door—then turns—rebelliously.*) An' Min hain't sech a bad un. They's worse'n Min in the world, I'll bet ye! Wait'll we see this cow the Old Man's hitched t'! She'll beat Min, I got a notion! (*He starts to go out.*)

Simeon (*suddenly*). Mebbe ye'll try t' make her your'n, too?

Peter: Ha! (*He gives a sardonic laugh of relish at this idea.*)

Eben (*spitting with disgust*). Her—here—sleepin' with him—stealin' my Maw's farm! I'd as soon pet a skunk 'r kiss a snake! (*He goes out. The two stare after him suspiciously. A pause. They listen to his steps receding.*)

Peter: He's startin' the fire.

Simeon: I'd like t' ride t' Californi-a—but—

Peter: Min might o' put some scheme in his head.

Simeon: Mebbe it's all a lie 'bout Paw marryin'. We'd best wait an' see the bride.

Peter: An' don't sign nothin' till we does!

Simeon: Nor till we've tested it's good money! (*Then with a grin.*) But if Paw's hitched we'd be sellin' Eben somethin' we'd never git nohow!

Peter: We'll wait an' see. (*Then with sudden vindictive anger.*) An' till he comes, let's yew 'n' me not wuk a lick, let Eben tend to thin's if he's a mind t', let's us jest sleep an' eat an' drink likker, an' let the hull damned farm go t' blazes!

Simeon (*excitedly*). By God, we've 'arned a rest! We'll play rich fur a change. I hain't a-goin' to stir outa bed till breakfast's ready.

Peter: An' on the table!

Simeon (*after a pause—thoughtfully*). What d' ye calc'late she'll be like—our new Maw? Like Eben thinks?

Peter: More'n likely.

Simeon (*vindictively*). Waal—I hope she's a she-devil that'll make him wish he was dead an' livin' in the pit o' hell fur comfort!

Peter (*fervently*). Amen!

Simeon (*imitating his father's voice*). "I'm ridin' out t' learn God's message t' me in the spring like the prophets done," he says. I'll bet right then an' thar he knew plumb well he was goin' whorin', the stinkin' old hypocrite!

SCENE IV

[*Same as Scene II—shows the interior of the kitchen with a lighted candle on table. It is gray dawn outside.* SIMEON *and* PETER *are just finishing their breakfast.* EBEN *sits before his plate of untouched food, brooding frowningly.*]

Peter (*glancing at him rather irritably*). Lookin' glum don't help none.

Simeon (*sarcastically*). Sorrowin' over his lust o' the flesh!

Peter (*with a grin*). Was she yer fust?

Eben (*angrily*). None o' yer business. (*A pause.*) I was thinkin' o' him. I got a notion he's gettin' near—I kin feel him comin' on like yew kin feel malaria chill afore it takes ye.

Peter: It's too early yet.

Simeon: Dunno. He'd like t' catch us nappin'—jest t' have somethin' t' hoss us 'round over.

Peter (*mechanically gets to his feet.* SIMEON *does the same*). Waal—let's git t' wuk. (*They both plod mechanically toward the door before they realize. Then they stop short.*)

Simeon (*grinning*). Ye're a cussed fool, Pete—and I be wuss! Let him see we hain't wukin'! We don't give a durn!

Peter (*as they go back to the table*). Not a damned durn! It'll serve t' show him we're done with him. (*They sit down again.* EBEN *stares from one to the other with surprise.*)

Simeon (*grins at him*). We're aimin' t' start bein' lilies o' the field.

Peter: Nary a toil 'r spin 'r lick o' wuk do we put in!

Simeon: Ye're sole owner—till he comes—that's what ye wanted. Waal, ye got t' be sole hand, too.

Peter: The cows air bellerin'. Ye better hustle at the milkin'.

Eben (*with excited joy*). Ye mean ye'll sign the paper?

Simeon (*dryly*). Mebbe.

Peter: Mebbe.

Simeon: We're considerin'. (*Peremptorily.*) Ye better git t' wuk.

Eben (*with queer excitement*). It's Maw's farm agen! It's my farm! Them's my cows! I'll milk my durn fingers off fur cows o' mine! (*He goes out door in rear, they stare after him indifferently.*)

Simeon: Like his Paw.

Peter: Dead spit 'n' image!

Simeon: Waal—let dog eat dog! (EBEN *comes out of front door and around the corner of the house. The sky is beginning to grow flushed with sunrise.* EBEN *stops by the gate and stares around him with glowing, possessive eyes. He takes in the whole farm with his embracing glance of desire.*)

Eben: It's purty! It's damned purty! It's mine! (*He suddenly throws his head back boldly and glares with hard, defiant eye at the sky.*) Mine, d'ye hear? Mine! (*He turns and walks quickly off left, rear, toward the barn. The two brothers light their pipes.*)

Simeon (*putting his muddy boots up on the table, tilting back his chair, and puffing defiantly*). Waal—this air solid comfort—fur once.

Peter: Ay-eh. (*He follows suit. A pause. Unconsciously they both sigh.*)

Simeon (*suddenly*). He never was much o' a hand at milkin', Eben wa'n't.

Peter (*with a snort*). His hands air like hoofs! (*A pause.*)

Simeon: Reach down the jug thar! Let's take a swaller. I'm feelin' kind o' low.

Peter: Good idee! (*He does so—gets two glasses—they pour out drinks of whisky.*) Here's t' the gold in Californi-a!

Simeon: An' luck t' find it! (*They drink—puff resolutely—sigh—take their feet down from the table.*)

Peter: Likker don't 'pear t' sot right.

Simeon: We hain't used t' it this early. (*A pause. They become very restless.*)

Peter: Gittin' close in this kitchen.

Simeon (*with immense relief*). Let's git a breath o' air. (*They arise briskly and go out rear—appear around house and stop by the gate. They stare up at the sky with a numbed appreciation.*)

Peter: Purty!

Simeon: Ay-eh. Gold's t' the East now.

Peter: Sun's startin' with us fur the Golden West.

Simeon (*staring around the farm, his compressed face tightened, unable to conceal his emotion*). Waal—it's our last mornin'—mebbe.

Peter (*the same*). Ay-eh.

Simeon (*stamps his foot on the earth and addresses it desperately*). Waal—ye've thirty year o' me buried in ye—spread out over ye—blood an' bone an' sweat—rotted away—fertilizin' ye—richin' yer soul—prime manure, by God, that's what I been t' ye!

Peter: Ay-eh! An' me!

Simeon: An' yew, Peter. (*He sighs—then spits.*) Waal—no use'n cryin' over spilt milk.

Peter: They's gold in the West—an' freedom, mebbe. We been slaves t' stone walls here.

Simeon (*defiantly*). We hain't nobody's slaves from this out—nor no thin's slaves nuther. (*A pause—restlessly.*) Speakin' o' milk, wonder how Eben's managin'?

Peter: I s'pose he's managin'.

Simeon: Mebbe we'd ought t' help—this once.

Peter: Mebbe. The cows knows us.

Simeon: An' likes us. They don't know him much.

Peter: An' the hosses, an' pigs, an' chickens. They don't know him much.

Simeon: They knows us like brothers—an' likes us! (*Proudly.*) Hain't we raised 'em t' be fust-rate, number one prize stock?

Peter: We hain't—not no more.

Simeon (*dully*). I was fergittin'. (*Then resignedly.*) Waal, let's go help Eben a spell an' git waked up.

Peter: Suits me. (*They are starting off down left, rear, for the barn when* EBEN *appears from there hurrying toward them, his face excited.*)

Eben (*breathlessly*). Waal—har they be! The old mule an' the bride! I seen 'em from the barn down below at the turnin'.

Peter: How could ye tell that far?

Eben: Hain't I as far-sight as he's near-sight? Don't I know the mare 'n' buggy, an' two people settin' in it? Who else . . . ? An' I tell ye I kin feel 'em a-comin', too! (*He squirms as if he had the itch.*)

Peter (*beginning to be angry*). Waal—let him do his own unhitchin'!

Simeon (*angry in his turn*). Let's hustle in an' git our bundles an' be a-goin' as he's a-comin'. I don't want never t' step inside the door agen arter he's back. (*They both start back around the corner of the house.* EBEN *follows them.*)

Eben (*anxiously*). Will ye sign it afore ye go?

Peter: Let's see the color o' the old skinflint's money an' we'll sign. (*They disappear left. The two brothers clump upstairs to get their bundles.* EBEN *appears in the kitchen, runs to the window, peers out, comes back and pulls up a strip of flooring in under stove, takes out a canvas bag and puts it on table, then sets the floorboard back in place. The two brothers appear a moment after. They carry old carpet bags.*)

Eben (*puts his hand on bag guardingly*). Have ye signed?

Simeon (*shows paper in his hand.*) Ay-eh. (*Greedily.*) Be that the money?

Eben (*opens bag and pours out pile of twenty-dollar gold pieces*). Twenty-dollar pieces—thirty on 'em. Count 'em. (PETER *does so, arranging them in stacks of five, biting one or two to test them.*)

Peter: Six hundred. (*He puts them in bag and puts it inside his shirt carefully.*)

Simeon (*handing paper to* EBEN). Har ye be.

Eben (*after a glance, folds it carefully and hides it under his shirt—gratefully*). Thank yew.

Peter: Thank yew fur the ride.

Simeon: We'll send ye a lump o' gold fur Christmas. (*A pause.* EBEN *stares at them and they at him.*)

Peter (*awkwardly*). Waal — we're a-goin'.

Simeon: Comin' out t' the yard?

Eben: No. I'm waitin' in here a spell. (*Another silence. The brothers edge awkwardly to the door in rear—then turn and stand.*)

Simeon: Waal—good-by.

Peter: Good-by.

Eben: Good-by. (*They go out. He sits down at the table, faces the stove and pulls out the paper. He looks from it to the stove. His face, lighted up by the shaft of sunlight from the window, has an expression of trance. His lips move. The two brothers come out to the gate.*)

Peter (*looking off toward barn*). Thar he be—unhitchin'.

Simeon (*with a chuckle*). I'll bet ye he's riled!

Peter: An' thar she be.

Simeon: Let's wait 'n' see what our new Maw looks like.

Peter (*with a grin*). An' give him our partin' cuss!

Simeon (*grinning*). I feel like raisin' fun. I feel light in my head an' feet.

Peter: Me, too. I feel like laffin' till I'd split up the middle.

Simeon: Reckon it's the likker?

Peter: No. My feet feel itchin' t' walk an' walk—an' jump high over thin's —an' . . . .

Simeon: Dance? (*A pause.*)

Peter (*puzzled*). It's plumb onnateral.

Simeon (*a light coming over his face*). I calc'late it's 'cause school's out. It's holiday. Fur once we're free!

Peter (*dazedly*). Free?

Simeon: The halter's broke—the harness is busted—the fence bars is down—the stone walls air crumblin' an' tumblin'! We'll be kickin' up an' tearin' away down the road!

Peter (*drawing a deep breath—oratorically*). Anybody that wants this stinkin' old rock-pile of a farm kin hev it. 'Tain't our'n, no sirree!

Simeon (*takes the gate off its hinges and puts it under his arm*). We harby 'bolishes shet gates an' open gates, an' all gates, by thunder!

Peter: We'll take it with us fur luck an' let 'er sail free down some river.

Simeon (*as a sound of voices comes from left, rear*). Har they comes! (*The two brothers congeal into two stiff, grim-visaged statues.* EPHRAIM CABOT *and* ABBIE PUTNAM *come in.* CABOT *is seventy-five, tall and gaunt, with great, wiry, concentrated power, but stoop-shouldered from toil. His face is as hard as if it were hewn out of a boulder, yet there is a weakness in it, a petty pride in its own narrow strength. His eyes are small, close together, and extremely near-sighted, blinking continually in the effort to focus on objects, their stare having a straining, ingrowing quality. He is dressed in his dismal black Sunday suit.* ABBIE *is thirty-five, buxom, full of vitality. Her round face is pretty but marred by its rather gross sensuality. There is strength and obstinacy in her jaw, a hard determination in her eyes, and about her whole personality the same unsettled, untamed,* *desperate quality which is so apparent in* EBEN.)

Cabot (*as they enter—a queer strangled emotion in his dry cracking voice*). Har we be t' hum, Abbie.

Abbie (*with lust for the word*). Hum! (*Her eyes gloating on the house without seeming to see the two stiff figures at the gate.*) It's purty—purty! I can't b'lieve it's r'ally mine.

Cabot (*sharply*). Yewr'n? Mine! (*He stares at her penetratingly. She stares back. He adds relentingly.*) Our'n—mebbe! It was lonesome too long. I was growin' old in the spring. A hum's got t' hev a woman.

Abbie (*her voice taking possession*). A woman's got t' hev a hum!

Cabot (*nodding uncertainly*). Ay-eh. (*Then irritably.*) Whar be they? Ain't thar nobody about—'r wukin'—r' nothin'?

Abbie (*sees the brothers. She returns their stare of cold appraising contempt with interest—slowly*). Thar's two men loafin' at the gate an' starin' at me like a couple o' strayed hogs.

Cabot (*straining his eyes*). I kin see 'em—but I can't make out. . . .

Simeon: It's Simeon.

Peter: It's Peter.

Cabot (*exploding*). Why hain't ye wukin'?

Simeon (*dryly*). We're waitin' t' welcome ye hum—yew an' the bride!

Cabot (*confusedly*). Huh? Waal—this be yer new Maw, boys. (*She stares at them and they at her.*)

Simeon (*turns away and spits contemptuously*). I see her!

Peter (*spits also*). An' I see her!

Abbie (*with the conqueror's conscious superiority*). I'll go in an' look at *my* house. (*She goes slowly around to porch.*)

Simeon (*with a snort*). *Her* house!

Peter (*calls after her*). Ye'll find Eben inside. Ye better not tell him it's *yewr* house.

Abbie (*mouthing the name*). Eben. (*Then quietly.*) I'll tell Eben.

Cabot (*with a contemptuous sneer*). Ye needn't heed Eben. Eben's a dumb fool—like his Maw—soft an' simple!

Simeon (*with his sardonic burst of laughter*). Ha! Eben's a chip o' yew—spit 'n' image—hard 'n' bitter's a hickory tree! Dog'll eat dog. He'll eat ye yet, old man!

Cabot (*commandingly*). Ye git t' wuk!

Simeon (*as* ABBIE *disappears in house—winks at* PETER *and says tauntingly*). So that thar's our new Maw, be it? Whar in hell did ye dig her up? (*He and* PETER *laugh.*)

Peter: Ha! Ye'd better turn her in the pen with the other sows. (*They laugh uproariously, slapping their thighs.*)

Cabot (*so amazed at their effrontery that he stutters in confusion*). Simeon! Peter! What's come over ye? Air ye drunk?

Simeon: We're free, old man—free o' yew an' the hull damned farm! (*They grow more and more hilarious and excited.*)

Peter: An' we're startin' out fur the gold fields o' Californi-a!

Simeon: Ye kin take this place an' burn it!

Peter: An' bury it—fur all we cares!

Simeon: We're free, old man! (*He cuts a caper.*)

Peter: Free! (*He gives a kick in the air.*)

Simeon (*in a frenzy*). Whoop!

Peter: Whoop! (*They do an absurd Indian war dance about the old man who is petrified between rage and the fear that they are insane.*)

Simeon: We're free as Injuns! Lucky we don't sculp ye!

Peter: An' burn yer barn an' kill the stock!

Simeon: An' rape yer new woman! Whoop! (*He and* PETER *stop their dance, holding their sides, rocking with wild laughter.*)

Cabot (*edging away*). Lust fur gold —fur the sinful, easy gold o' Californi-a! It's made ye mad!

Simeon (*tauntingly*). Wouldn't ye like us to send ye back some sinful gold, ye old sinner?

Peter: They's gold besides what's in Californi-a! (*He retreats back beyond the vision of the old man and takes the bag of money and flaunts it in the air above his head, laughing.*)

Simeon: And sinfuller, too!

Peter: We'll be voyagin' on the sea! Whoop! (*He leaps up and down.*)

Simeon: Livin' free! Whoop! (*He leaps in turn.*)

Cabot (*suddenly roaring with rage*). My cuss on ye!

Simeon: Take our'n in trade fur it! Whoop!

Cabot: I'll hev ye both chained up in the asylum!

Peter: Ye old skinflint! Good-by!

Simeon: Ye old blood sucker! Good-by!

Cabot: Go afore I . . . !

Peter: Whoop! (*He picks a stone from the road.* SIMEON *does the same.*)

Simeon: Maw'll be in the parlor.

Peter: Ay-eh! One! Two!

Cabot (*frightened*). What air ye . . . ?

Peter: Three! (*They both throw, the stones hitting the parlor window with a crash of glass, tearing the shade.*)

Simeon: Whoop!

Peter: Whoop!

Cabot (*in a fury now, rushing toward them*). If I kin lay hands on ye—I'll break yer bones fur ye! (*But they beat a capering retreat before him,* SIMEON *with the gate still under his arm.* CABOT *comes back, panting with impotent rage. Their voices as they go off take up the song of the gold-seekers to the old tune of "Oh, Susannah!"*)

"I jumped aboard the Liza ship,
And traveled on the sea,
And every time I thought of home
I wished it wasn't me!
Oh! Californi-a,
That's the land fur me!
I'm off to Californi-a!
With my wash bowl on my knee."

[*In the meantime, the window of the upper bedroom on right is raised and* ABBIE *sticks her head out. She looks down at* CABOT*—with a sigh of relief.*]

Abbie: Waal—that's the last o' them two, hain't it? (*He doesn't answer. Then in possessive tones.*) This here's a nice bedroom, Ephraim. It's a r'al nice bed. Is it my room, Ephraim?

Cabot (*grimly—without looking up*). Our'n! (*She cannot control a grimace of aversion and pulls back her head slowly and shuts the window. A sudden horrible thought seems to enter* CABOT'S *head.*) They been up to somethin'! Mebbe—mebbe they've pizened the stock—'r somethin'! (*He almost runs off down toward the barn. A moment later the kitchen door is slowly pushed open and* ABBIE *enters. For a moment she stands looking at* EBEN. *He does not notice her at first. Her eyes take him in penetratingly with a calculating appraisal of his strength as against hers. But under this her desire is dimly awakened by his youth and good looks. Suddenly he becomes conscious of her presence and looks up.*

Their eyes meet. He leaps to his feet, glowering at her speechlessly.)

Abbie (*in her most seductive tones which she uses all through this scene*). Be you—Eben? I'm Abbie—(*She laughs.*) I mean, I'm yer new Maw.

Eben (*viciously*). No, damn ye!

Abbie (*as if she hadn't heard—with a queer smile*). Yer Paw's spoke a lot o' yew. . . .

Eben: Ha!

Abbie: Ye mustn't mind him. He's an old man. (*A long pause. They stare at each other.*) I don't want t' pretend playin' Maw t' ye, Eben. (*Admiringly.*) Ye're too big an' too strong fur that. I want t' be frens with ye. Mebbe with me fur a fren ye'd find ye'd like livin' here better. I kin make it easy fur ye with him, mebbe. (*With a scornful sense of power.*) I calc'late I kin git him t' do most anythin' fur me.

Eben (*with bitter scorn*). Ha! (*They stare again,* EBEN *obscurely moved, physically attracted to her—in forced stilted tones.*) Yew kin go t' the devil!

Abbie (*calmly*). If cussin' me does ye good, cuss all ye've a mind t'. I'm all prepared t' have ye agin me—at fust. I don't blame ye nuther. I'd feel the same at any stranger comin' t' take my Maw's place. (*He shudders. She is watching him carefully.*) Yew must've cared a lot fur yewr Maw, didn't ye? My Maw died afore I'd growed. I don't remember her none. (*A pause.*) But yew won't hate me long, Eben. I'm not the wust in the world—an' yew an' me've got a lot in common. I kin tell that by lookin' at ye. Waal—I've had a hard life, too—oceans o' trouble an' nuthin' but wuk fur reward. I was a orphan early an' had t' wuk fur others in other folks' hums. Then I married an' he turned out a drunken spreer an' so he had to wuk fur others an' me too agen in other folks' hums, an' the baby died, an' my husband got sick an' died too, an' I was glad sayin' now I'm free fur once, on'y I diskivered right away all I was free fur was t' wuk agen in other folks' hums, doin' other folks' wuk till I'd most give up hope o' ever doin' my own wuk in my own hum, an' then your Paw come. . . . (CABOT *appears returning from the barn. He comes to the gate and looks down the road the brothers have gone. A faint strain of their retreating voices is heard: "Oh, Californi-a! That's the place for me." He stands glowering, his fist clenched, his face grim with rage.*)

Eben (*fighting against his growing attraction and sympathy—harshly*). An' bought yew—like a harlot! (*She is stung and flushes angrily. She has been sincerely moved by the recital of her troubles. He adds furiously:*) An' the price he's payin' ye—this farm—was my Maw's, damn ye!—an' mine now!

Abbie (*with a cool laugh of confidence*). Yewr'n? We'll see 'bout that! (*Then strongly.*) Waal—what if I did need a hum? What else'd I marry an old man like him fur?

Eben (*maliciously*): I'll tell him ye said that!

Abbie (*smiling*). I'll say ye're lyin' a-purpose—an' he'll drive ye off the place!

Eben: Ye devil!

Abbie (*defying him*) This be my farm—this be my hum—this be my kitchen—!

Eben (*furiously, as if he were going to attack her*). Shut up, damn ye!

Abbie (*walks up to him—a queer coarse expression of desire in her face and body—slowly*). An' upstairs—that be my bedroom—an' my bed! (*He stares into her eyes, terribly confused and torn. She adds softly:*) I hain't bad nor mean —'ceptin' fur an enemy—but I got t' fight fur what's due me out o' life, if I ever 'spect t' git it. (*Then putting her hand on his arm—seductively.*) Let's yew 'n' me be frens, Eben.

Eben (*stupidly—as if hypnotized*). Ay-eh. (*Then furiously flinging off her arm.*) No, ye durned old witch! I hate ye! (*He rushes out the door.*)

Abbie (*looks after him smiling satisfiedly—then half to herself, mouthing the word*). Eben's nice. (*She looks at the table, proudly.*) I'll wash up *my* dishes now. (EBEN *appears outside, slamming the door behind him. He comes around corner, stops on seeing his father, and stands staring at him with hate.*)

Cabot (*raising his arms to heaven in the fury he can no longer control*). Lord God o' Hosts, smite the undutiful sons with Thy wust cuss!

Eben (*breaking in violently*). Yew 'n' yewr God! Allus cussin' folks—allus naggin' 'em!

Cabot (*oblivious to him—summoningly*). God o' the old! God o' the lonesome!

Eben (*mockingly*). Naggin' His sheep t' sin! T' hell with yewr God! (CABOT *turns. He and* EBEN *glower at each other.*)

Cabot (*harshly*). So it's yew. I might've knowed it. (*Shaking his finger threateningly at him.*) Blasphemin' fool! (*Then quickly.*) Why hain't ye t' wuk?

Eben: Why hain't yew? They've went. I can't wuk it all alone.

Cabot (*contemptuously*). Nor noways! I'm wuht ten o' ye yit, old's I be! Ye'll never be more'n half a man! (*Then, matter-of-factly.*) Waal—let's git t' the barn. (*They go. A last faint note of the "Californi-a" song is heard from the distance.* ABBIE *is washing her dishes.*)

PART II

SCENE I

[*The exterior of the farmhouse, as in Part I—a hot Sunday afternoon two months later.* ABBIE, *dressed in her best, is discovered sitting in a rocker at the end of the porch. She rocks listlessly, enervated by the heat, staring in front of her with bored, half-closed eyes.*

EBEN *sticks his head out of his bedroom window. He looks around furtively and tries to see—or hear—if anyone is on the porch, but although he has been carefeul to make no noise,* ABBIE *has sensed his movement. She stops rocking, her face grows animated and eager, she waits attentively.* EBEN *seems to feel her presence, he scowls back his thoughts of her and spits with exaggerated disdain—then withdraws back into the room.* ABBIE *waits, holding her breath as she listens with passionate eagerness for every sound within the house.*

EBEN *comes out. Their eyes meet. His falter, he is confused, he turns away and slams the door resentfully. At this gesture,* ABBIE *laughs tantalizingly, amused but at the same time piqued and irritated. He scowls, strides off the porch to the path and starts to walk past her to the road with a grand swagger of ignoring her existence. He is dressed in his store suit, spruced up, his face shines from soap and water.* ABBIE *leans forward on her chair, her eyes hard and angry now, and, as he passes her, gives a sneering, taunting chuckle.*]

Eben (*stung—turns on her furiously*). What air yew cacklin' 'bout?

Abbie (*triumphant*). Yew!

Eben: What about me?

Abbie: Ye look all slicked up like a prize bull.

Eben (*with a sneer*). Waal—ye hain't so durned purty yerself, be ye? (*They stare into each other's eyes, his held by hers in spite of himself, hers glowingly possessive. Their physical attraction becomes a palpable force quivering in the hot air.*)

Abbie (*softly*). Ye don't mean that, Eben. Ye may think ye mean it, mebbe, but ye don't. Ye can't. It's agin nature, Eben. Ye been fightin' yer nature ever since the day I come—tryin' t' tell yerself I hain't purty t'ye. (*She laughs a low humid laugh without taking her eyes from his. A pause—her body squirms desirously—she murmurs languorously.*) Hain't the sun strong an' hot? Ye kin feel it burnin' into the earth—Nature—makin' thin's grow—bigger 'n' bigger—burnin' inside ye—makin' ye want t' grow—into somethin' else—till ye're jined with it—an' it's yourn—but it owns ye, too—an' makes ye grow bigger—like a tree—like them elums—(*She laughs again softly, holding his eyes. He takes a step toward her, compelled against his will.*) Nature'll beat ye, Eben. Ye might's well own up t' it fust 's last.

Eben (*trying to break from her spell—confusedly*). If Paw'd hear ye goin' on. . . . (*Resentfully.*) But ye've made such a damned idjit out o' the old devil . . . ! (ABBIE *laughs.*)

Abbie: Waal—hain't it easier fur yew with him changed softer?

Eben (*defiantly*). No. I'm fightin' him—fightin' yew—fightin' fur Maw's rights t' her hum! (*This breaks her spell for him. He glowers at her.*) An' I'm onto ye. Ye hain't foolin' me a mite. Ye're aimin' t' swaller up everythin' an' make it your'n. Waal, you'll find I'm a heap sight bigger hunk nor yew kin chew! (*He turns from her with a sneer.*)

Abbie (*trying to regain her ascendancy—seductively*). Eben!

Eben: Leave me be! (*He starts to walk away.*)

Abbie (*more commandingly*). Eben!

Eben (*stops—resentfully*). What d'ye want?

Abbie (*trying to conceal a growing excitement*). Whar air ye goin'?

Eben (*with malacious nonchalance*). Oh—up the road a spell.

Abbie: T' the village?

Eben (*airily*). Mebbe.

Abbie (*excitedly*). T' see that Min, I s'pose?

Eben: Mebbe.

Abbie (*weakly*). What d'ye want t' waste time on her fur?

Eben (*revenging himself now—grinning at her*). Ye can't beat Nature, didn't ye say? (*He laughs and again starts to walk away.*)

Abbie (*bursting out*). An ugly old hake!

Eben (*with a tantalizing sneer*). She's purtier'n yew be!

Abbie: That every wuthless drunk in the country has. . . .

Eben (*tauntingly*). Mebbe—but she's better'n yew. She owns up fa'r 'n' squar' t' her doin's.

Abbie (*furiously*). Don't ye dare compare. . . .

Eben: She don't go sneakin' an' stealin'—what's mine.

Abbie (*savagely seizing on his weak point*). Your'n? Yew mean—my farm?

Eben: I mean the farm yew sold yerself fur like any other old whore—my farm!

Abbie (*stung—fiercely*). Ye'll never live t' see the day when even a stinkin' weed on it'll belong t' ye! (*Then in a scream.*) Git out o' my sight! Go on t' yer slut—disgracin' yer Paw 'n' me! I'll git yer Paw t' horsewhip ye off the place if I want t'! Ye're only livin' here 'cause I tolerate ye! Git along! I hate the sight o' ye! (*She stops, panting and glaring at him.*)

Eben (*returning her glance in kind*). An' I hate the sight o' yew! (*He turns and strides off up the road. She follows his retreating figure with concentrated hate. Old* CABOT *appears coming up from the barn. The hard, grim expression of his face has changed. He seems in some queer way softened, mellowed. His eyes have taken on a strange, incongruous dreamy quality. Yet there is no hint of physical weakness about him—rather he looks more robust and younger.* ABBIE *sees him and turns away quickly with unconcealed aversion. He comes slowly up to her.*)

Cabot (*mildly*): War yew an' Eben quarrelin' agen?

Abbie (*slowly*). No.

Cabot: Ye was talkin' a'mighty loud. (*He sits down on the edge of porch.*)

Abbie (*snappishly*). If ye heered us they hain't no need askin' questions.

Cabot: I didn't hear what ye said.

Abbie (*relieved*). Waal—it wa'n't nothin' t' speak on.

Cabot (*after a pause*). Eben's queer.

Abbie (*bitterly*). He's the dead spit 'n' image o' yew!

Cabot (*queerly interested*). D'ye think so, Abbie? (*After a pause, ruminatingly.*) Me 'n' Eben's allus fit 'n' fit. I never could b'ar him noways. He's so thunderin' soft—like his Maw.

Abbie (*scornfully*). Ay-eh! 'Bout as soft as yew be!

Cabot (*as if he hadn't heard*). Mebbe I been too hard on him.

Abbie (*jeeringly*). Waal—ye're gettin' soft now—soft as slop! That's what Eben was sayin'.

Cabot (*his face instantly grim and ominous*). Eben was sayin'? Waal, he'd best not do nothin' t' try me 'r he'll soon diskiver. . . . (*A pause. She keeps her face turned away. His gradually softens. He stares up at the sky.*) Purty, hain't it?

Abbie (*crossly*). I don't feel nothin' purty.

Cabot: The sky. Feels like a wa'm field up thar.

Abbie (*sarcastically*). Air yew aimin' t' buy up over the farm too? (*She snickers contemptuously.*)

Cabot (*strangely*). I'd like t' own my place up thar. (*A pause.*) I'm gittin' old, Abbie, I'm gittin' ripe on the bough. (*A pause. She stares at him mystified. He goes on.*) It's allus lonesome cold in the house—even when it's bilin' hot outside. Hain't yew noticed?

Abbie: No.

Cabot: It's wa'm down t' the barn—

nice smellin' an' warm—with the cows. (*A pause.*) Cows is queer.

Abbie: Like yew?

Cabot: Like Eben. (*A pause.*) I'm gittin' t' feel resigned t' Eben—jest as I got t' feel 'bout his Maw. I'm gittin' t' learn to b'ar his softness—jest like her'n. I calc'late I c'd a'most take t' him—if he wa'n't sech a dumb fool! (*A pause.*) I s'pose it's old age a-creepin' in my bones.

Abbie (*indifferently*). Waal — ye hain't dead yet.

Cabot (*roused*). No, I hain't, yew bet—not by a hell of a sight—I'm sound 'n' tough as hickory! (*Then moodily.*) But arter three score and ten the Lord warns ye t' prepare. (*A pause.*) That's why Eben's come in my head. Now that his cussed sinful brothers is gone their path t' hell, they's no one left but Eben.

Abbie (*resentfully*). They's me, hain't they? (*Agitatedly.*) What's all this sudden likin' ye tuk to Eben? Why don't ye say nothin' 'bout me? Hain't I yer lawful wife?

Cabot (*simply*). Ay-eh. Ye be. (*A pause—he stares at her desirously—his eyes grow avid—then with a sudden movement he seizes her hands and squeezes them, declaiming in a queer camp meeting preacher's tempo:*) Yew air my Rose o' Sharon! Behold, yew air fair; yer eyes air doves; yer lips air like scarlet; yer two breasts air like two fawns; yer navel be like a round goblet; yer belly be like a heap o' wheat. . . . (*He covers her hand with kisses. She does not seem to notice. She stares before her with hard angry eyes.*)

Abbie (*jerking her hands away—harshly*). So ye're plannin' t' leave the farm t' Eben, air ye?

Cabot (*dazedly*). Leave. . . ? (*Then with resentful obstinacy.*) I hain't a-givin' it t' no one!

Abbie (*remorselessly*). Ye can't take it with ye.

Cabot (*thinks a moment—then reluctantly*). No, I calc'late not. (*After a pause—with a strange passion.*) But if I could, I would, by the Etarnal! 'R if I could, in my dyin' hour, I'd set it afire an' watch it burn—this house an' every ear o' corn an' every tree down t' the last blade o' hay! I'd sit an' know it was all a-dying with me an' no one else'd ever own what was mine, what I'd made out o' nothin' with my own sweat 'n' blood! (*A pause—then he adds with a queer affection.*) 'Ceptin' the cows. Them I'd turn free.

Abbie (*harshly*). An' me?

Cabot (*with a queer smile*). Ye'd be turned free, too.

Abbie (*furiously*). So that's the thanks I git fur marryin' ye—t' have ye change kind to Eben who hates ye, an' talk o' turnin' me out in the road.

Cabot (*hastily*). Abbie! Ye know I wa'n't. . . .

Abbie (*vengefully*). Just let me tell ye a thing or two 'bout Eben. Whar's he gone? T' see that harlot, Min! I tried fur t' stop him. Disgracin' yew an' me—on the Sabbath, too!

Cabot (*rather guiltily*). He's a sinner—nateral-born. It's lust eatin' his heart.

Abbie (*enraged beyond endurance—wildly vindictive*). An' his lust fur me! Kin ye find excuses fur that?

Cabot (*stares at her—after a dead pause*). Lust—fur yew?

Abbie (*defiantly*). He was tryin' t' make love t' me—when ye heerd us quarrelin'.

Cabot (*stares at her—then a terrible expression of rage comes over his face—he springs to his feet shaking all over*). By the A'mighty God—I'll end him!

Abbie (*frightened now for* EBEN). No! Don't ye!

Cabot (*violently*). I'll git the shotgun an' blow his soft brains t' the top o' them elums!

Abbie (*throwing her arms around him.*) No, Ephraim!

Cabot (*pushing her away violently*). I will, by God!

Abbie (*in a quieting tone*). Listen, Ephraim. 'Twa'n't nothin' bad—on'y a boy's foolin'—'twa'n't meant serious—jest jokin' an' teasin'. . . .

Cabot: Then why did ye say—lust?

Abbie: It must hev sounded wusser'n I meant. An' I was mad at thinkin'—ye'd leave him the farm.

Cabot (*quieter but still grim and cruel.*) Waal then, I'll horsewhip him off the place if that much'll content ye.

Abbie (*reaching out and taking his hand*). No. Don't think o' me! Ye mustn't drive him off. 'Taint sensible. Who'll yew get to help ye on the farm? They's no one hereabouts.

Cabot (*considers this—then nodding his appreciation*). Ye got a head on ye. (*Then irritably:*) Waal, let him stay. (*He sits down on the edge of the porch. She sits beside him. He murmurs contemptuously:*) I oughtn't git riled so—at that 'ere fool calf. (*A pause.*) But har's the p'int. What son o' mine'll keep on here t' the farm—when the Lord does call me? Simeon an' Peter air gone t' hell—an' Eben's follerin' 'em.

Abbie: They's me.

Cabot: Ye're on'y a woman.

Abbie: I'm yewr wife.

Cabot: That hain't me. A son is me—my blood—mine. Mine ought t' git mine. An' then it's still mine—even though I be six foot under. D'ye see?

Abbie (*giving him a look of hatred*). Ay-eh. I see. (*She becomes very thoughtful, her face growing shrewd, her eyes studying* CABOT *craftily.*)

Cabot: I'm gittin' old—ripe on the bough. (*Then with a sudden forced reassurance.*) Not but what I hain't a hard nut t' crack even yet—an' fur many a year t' come! By the Etarnal, I kin break most o' the young fellars' backs at any kind o' work any day o' the year!

Abbie (*suddenly*). Mebbe the Lord'll give *us* a son.

Cabot (*turns and stares at her eagerly*). Ye mean—a son—t' me 'n' yew?

Abbie (*with a cajoling smile*). Ye're a strong man yet, hain't ye? 'Tain't noways impossible, be it? We know that. Why d'ye stare so? Hain't ye never thought o' that afore? I been thinkin' o' it all along. Ay-eh—an' I been prayin' it'd happen, too.

Cabot (*his face growing full of joyous pride and a sort of religious ecstasy*). Ye been prayin', Abbie?—fur a son?—t' us?

Abbie: Ay-eh. (*With a grim resolution.*) I want a son now.

Cabot (*excitedly clutching both of her hands in his*). It'd be a blessin' o' God, Abbie—the blessin' o' God A'mighty on me—in my old age—in my lonesomeness! They hain't nothin' I wouldn't do fur ye then, Abbie. Ye'd hev on'y t' ask it—anythin' ye'd a mind t'!

Abbie (*interrupting*). Would ye will the farm t' me then—t' me an' it . . .?

Cabot (*vehemently*). I'd do anythin' ye axed, I tell ye! I swar it! May I be ever-lastin' damned t' hell if I wouldn't! (*He sinks to his knees pulling her down with him. He trembles all over with the fervor of his hopes.*) Pray t' the Lord agen, Abbie. It's the Sabbath! I'll jine ye! Two prayers air better nor one. "An' God hearkened unto Rachel"! An' God hearkened unto Abbie! Pray, Abbie! Pray fur him to hearken! (*He bows his head, mumbling. She pretends to do likewise but gives him a side glance of scorn and triumph.*)

SCENE II

[*About eight in the evening. The interior of the two bedrooms on the top floor is shown*—EBEN *is sitting on the side of his bed in the room on the left. On account of the heat he has taken off everything but his undershirt and pants. His feet are bare. He faces front, brooding moodily, his chin propped on his hands, a desperate expression on his face. In the other room* CABOT *and* ABBIE *are sitting side by side on the edge of their bed, an old four-poster with feather mattress. He is in his night shirt, she in her nightdress. He is still in the queer, excited mood into which the notion of a son has thrown him. Both rooms are lighted dimly and flickeringly by tallow candles.*]

Cabot: The farm needs a son.

Abbie: I need a son.

Cabot: Ay-eh. Sometimes ye air the farm an' sometimes the farm be yew. That's why I clove t' ye in my lonesomeness. (*A pause. He pounds his knee with his fist.*) Me an' the farm has got t' beget a son!

Abbie: Ye'd best go t' sleep. Ye're gittin' thin's all mixed.

Cabot (*with an impatient gesture*). No, I hain't. My mind's clear's a well. Ye don't know me, that's it. (*He stares hopelessly at the floor.*)

Abbie (*indifferently*). Mebbe. (*In the next room* EBEN *gets up and paces up and down distractedly.* ABBIE *hears him. Her eyes fasten on the intervening wall with concentrated attention.* EBEN *stops and stares. Their hot glances seem to meet through the wall. Unconsciously he stretches out his arms for her and she half rises. Then aware, he mutters a curse at himself and flings himself face downward on the bed, his clenched fists above his head, his face buried in the pillow.* ABBIE *relaxes with a faint sigh but her eyes remain fixed on the wall; she listens with all her attention for some movement from* EBEN.)

Cabot (*suddenly raises his head and looks at her—scornfully*). Will ye ever know me—'r will any man 'r woman? (*Shaking his head.*) No. I calc'late 't wa'n't t' be. (*He turns away.* ABBIE *looks at the wall. Then, evidently unable to keep silent about his thoughts, without looking at his wife, he puts out his hand and clutches her knee. She starts violently, looks at him, sees he is not watching her, concentrates again on the wall and pays no attention to what he says.*) Listen, Abbie. When I come here fifty odd year ago—I was jest twenty an' the strongest an' hardest ye ever seen—ten times as strong an' fifty times as hard as Eben. Waal—this place was nothin' but fields o' stones. Folks laughed when I tuk it. They couldn't know what I knowed. When ye kin make corn sprout out o' stones, God's livin' in yew! They wa'n't strong enuf fur that! They reckoned God was easy. They laughed. They don't laugh no more. Some died hereabouts. Some went West an' died. They're all under ground—fur follerin' arter an easy God. God hain't easy. (*He shakes his head slowly.*) An' I growed hard. Folks kept allus sayin' he's a hard man like 'twas sinful t' be hard, so's at last I said back at 'em: Waal then, by thunder, ye'll git me hard an' see how ye like it! (*Then suddenly.*) But I give in t' weakness once. 'Twas arter I'd been here two year. I got weak—despairful—they was so many stones. They was a party leavin', givin' up, goin' West. I jined 'em. We tracked on 'n' on. We come t' broad medders, plains, whar the soil was black an' rich as gold. Nary a stone. Easy. Ye'd on'y to plow an' sow an' then set an' smoke yer pipe an' watch thin's grow. I could o' been a rich man—but somethin' in me fit me an' fit me—the voice o' God sayin': "This hain't wuth nothin' t' Me. Get ye back t' hum!" I got afeerd o' that voice an' I lit out back t' hum here, leavin' my claim an' crops t' whoever'd a mind t' take 'em. Ay-eh. I actoolly give up what was rightful mine! God's hard, not easy! God's in the stones! Build my church on a rock—out o' stones an' I'll be in them! That's what He meant t' Peter! (*He sighs heavily—a pause.*) Stones. I picked 'em up an' piled 'em into walls. Ye kin read the years o' my life in them walls, every day a hefted stone, climbin' over the hills up and down, fencin' in the fields that was mine, whar I'd made thin's grow out o' nothin—like the will o' God, like the servant o' His hand. It wa'n't easy. It was hard an' He made me hard fur it. (*He pauses.*) All the time I kept gittin' lonesomer. I tuk a wife. She bore Simeon an' Peter. She was a good woman. She wuked hard. We was married twenty year. She never knowed me. She helped but she never knowed what she was helpin'. I was allus lonesome. She died. After that it wa'n't so lonesome fur a spell. (*A pause.*) I lost count o' the years. I had no time t' fool away countin' 'em. Sim an' Peter helped. The farm growed. It was all mine! When I thought o' that I didn't feel lonesome. (*A pause.*) But ye can't hitch yer mind t' one thin' day an' night. I tuk another wife—Eben's Maw. Her folks was contestin' me at law over my deeds t' the farm—my farm! That's why Eben keeps a-talkin' his fool talk o' this bein' his Maw's farm. She bore Eben. She was purty—but soft. She tried t' be hard. She couldn't. She never knowed me nor nothin'. It was lonesomer 'n hell with her. After a matter o' sixteen odd years, she died. (*A pause.*) I lived with the boys. They hated me 'cause I was hard. I hated them 'cause they was soft. They coveted the farm without knowin' what it meant. It made me bitter 'n wormwood. It aged me—them coveting what I'd made fur mine. Then this spring the call come—the voice o' God cryin' in my wilderness, in my lonesomeness—t' go out an' seek an' find! (*Turning to her with strange passion.*) I sought ye an' I found ye! Yew air my Rose o' Sharon! Yer eyes air like. . . . (*She has turned a blank face, resentful eyes to his. He stares at her for a moment—then harshly.*) Air ye any the wiser fur all I've told ye?

Abbie (*confusedly*). Mebbe.

Cabot (*pushing her away from him—angrily*). Ye don't know nothin'—nor never will. If ye don't hev a son t' redeem ye . . . (*This in a tone of cold threat.*)

Abbie (*resentfully*). I've prayed, hain't I?

Cabot (*bitterly*). Pray agen—fur understandin'!

Abbie (*a veiled threat in her tone*). Ye'll have a son out o' me, I promise ye.

Cabot: How kin ye promise?

Abbie: I got second-sight mebbe. I kin foretell. (*She gives a queer smile.*)

Cabot: I believe ye have. Ye give me the chills sometimes. (*He shivers.*) It's cold in this house. It's oneasy. They's thin's pokin' about in the dark—in the corners. (*He pulls on his trousers, tucking in his night shirt, and pulls on his boots.*)

Abbie (*surprised*). Whar air ye goin'?

Cabot (*queerly*). Down whar it's restful—whar it's warm—down t' the barn. (*Bitterly.*) I kin talk t' the cows. They know. They know the farm an' me. They'll give me peace. (*He turns to go out the door.*)

Abbie (*a bit frightenedly*). Air ye ailin' to-night, Ephraim?

Cabot: Growin'. Growin' ripe on the bough. (*He turns and goes, his boots clumping down the stairs.* EBEN *sits up with a start, listening.* ABBIE *is conscious of his movement and stares at the wall.* CABOT *comes out of the house around the corner and stands by the gate, blinking at the sky. He stretches up his hands in a tortured gesture*) God A'mighty, call from the dark! (*He listens as if expecting an answer. Then his arms drop, he shakes his head and plods off toward the barn.* EBEN *and* ABBIE *stare at each other through the wall.* EBEN *sighs heavily and* ABBIE *echoes it. Both become terribly nervous, uneasy. Finally* ABBIE *gets up and listens, her ear to the wall. He acts as if he saw every move she was making, he becomes resolutely still. She seems driven into a decision—goes out the door in rear determinedly. His eyes follow her. Then as the door of his room is opened softly, he turns away, waits in an attitude of strained fixity.* ABBIE *stands for a second staring at him, her eyes burning with desire. Then with a litle cry she runs over and throws her arms about his neck, she pulls his head back and covers his mouth with kisses. At first, he submits dumbly; then he puts his arms about her neck and returns her kisses, but finally, suddenly aware of his hatred, he hurls her away from him, springing to his feet. They stand speechless and breathless, panting like two animals.*)

Abbie (*at last—painfully*). Ye shouldn't, Eben—ye shouldn't—I'd make ye happy!

Eben (*harshly*). I don't want t' be happy—from yew!

Abbie (*helplessly*). Ye do, Eben! Ye do! Why d'ye lie?

Eben (*viciously*). I don't take t'ye, I tell ye! I hate the sight o' ye!

Abbie (*with an uncertain troubled laugh*). Waal, I kissed ye anyways—an' ye kissed back—yer lips was burnin'—ye can't lie 'bout that! (*Intensely.*) If ye don't care, why did ye kiss me back—why was yer lips burnin'?

Eben (*wiping his mouth*). It was like pizen on 'em (*Then tauntingly.*) When I kissed ye back, mebbe I thought 'twas someone else.

Abbie (*wildly*). Min?

Eben: Mebbe.

Abbie (*torturedly*). Did ye go t' see her? Did ye r'ally go? I thought ye mightn't. Is that why ye throwed me off jest now?

Eben (*sneeringly*). What if it be?

Abbie (*raging*). Then ye're a dog, Eben Cabot!

Eben (*threateningly*). Ye can't talk that way t' me!

Abbie (*with a shrill laugh*). Can't I? Did ye think I was in love with ye—a weak thin' like yew? Not much—I on'y wanted ye fur a purpose o' my own—an' I'll hev ye fur it yet 'cause I'm stronger'n yew be!

Eben (*resentfully*). I knowed well it was on'y part o' yer plan t' swaller everythin'!

Abbie (*tauntingly*). Mebbe!

Eben (*furious*). Git out o' my room!

Abbie: This air my room an' ye're on'y hired help!

Eben (*threateningly*). Git out afore I murder ye!

Abbie (*quite confident now*). I hain't a mite afeerd. Ye want me, don't ye? Yes, ye do! An' yer Paw's son'll never kill what he wants! Look at yer eyes! They's lust fur me in 'em, burnin' 'em up! Look at yer lips now! They're tremblin' an' longin' t' kiss me, an' yer teeth t' bite. (*He is watching her now with a horrible fascination. She laughs a crazy triumphant laugh.*) I'm a-goin' t' make all o' this hum my hum! They's one room hain't mine yet, but it's a-goin' t' be tonight. I'm a-goin' down now an' light up! (*She makes him a mocking bow.*) Won't ye come courtin' me in the best parlor, Mister Cabot?

Eben (*staring at her—horribly confused—dully*). Don't ye dare! It hain't been opened since Maw died an' was laid out thar! Don't ye . . . ! (*But her eyes are fixed on his so burningly that his will seems to wither before hers. He stands swaying toward her helplessly.*)

Abbie (*holding his eyes and putting all her will into her words as she backs out the door*). I'll expect ye afore long, Eben.

Eben (*stares after her for a while, walking toward the door. A light appears in the parlor window. He murmurs*). In the parlor? (*This seems to arouse connotations for he comes back and puts on his white shirt, collar, half ties the tie mechanically, puts on coat, takes his hat, stands barefooted looking about him in bewilderment, mutters wonderingly:*) Maw! Whar air yew? (*Then goes slowly toward the door in rear.*)

SCENE III

[*A few minutes later. The interior of the parlor is shown. A grim, repressed room like a tomb in which the family has been interred alive.* ABBIE *sits on the edge of the horsehair sofa. She has lighted all the candles and the room is revealed in all its preserved ugliness. A change has come over the woman. She looks awed and frightened now, ready to run away.*

The door is opened and EBEN *appears. His face wears an expression of obsessed confusion. He stands staring at her, his arms hanging disjointedly from his shoulders, his feet bare, his hat in his hand.*]

Abbie (*after a pause—with a nervous, formal politeness*). Won't ye set?

Eben (*dully*). Ay-eh. (*Mechanically he places his hat carefully on the floor near the door and sits stiffly beside her on the edge of the sofa. A pause. They both remain rigid, looking straight ahead with eyes full of fear.*)

Abbie: When I fust came in—in the dark—they seemed somethin' here.

Eben (*simply*). Maw.

Abbie: I kin still feel—somethin'. . . . .

Eben: It's Maw.

Abbie: At fust I was feered o' it. I wanted t' yell an' run. Now—since yew come—seems like it's growin' soft an' kind t' me. (*Addressing the air—queerly.*) Thank yew.

Eben: Maw allus loved me.

Abbie: Maybe it knows I love yew too. Mebbe that makes it kind t' me.

Eben (*dully*). I dunno. I should think she'd hate ye.

Abbie (*with certainty*). No. I kin feel it don't—not no more.

Eben: Hate ye fur stealin' her place here in her hum—settin' in her parlor whar she was laid— (*He suddenly stops, staring stupidly before him.*)

Abbie: What is it, Eben?

Eben (*in a whisper*). Seems like Maw didn't want me t' remind ye.

Abbie (*excitedly*). I knowed, Eben! It's kind t' me! It don't b'ar me no grudges fur what I never knowed an' couldn't help!

Eben: Maw b'ars him a grudge.

Abbie: Waal, so does all o' us.

Eben: Ay-eh. (*With passion.*) I does, by God!

Abbie (*taking one of his hands in hers and patting it*). Thar! Don't git riled thinkin' o' him. Think o' yer Maw who's kind t' us. Tell me about yer Maw, Eben.

Eben: They hain't nothin' much. She was kind. She was good.

Abbie (*putting one arm over his shoulder. He does not seem to notice—passionately*). I'll be kind an' good t' ye!

Eben: Sometimes she used t' sing fur me.

Abbie: I'll sing fur ye!

Eben: This was her hum. This was her farm.

Abbie: This is my hum! This is my farm!

Eben: He married her t' steal 'em. She was soft an' easy. He couldn't 'preciate her.

Abbie: He can't 'preciate me!

Eben: He murdered her with his hardness.

Abbie He's murderin' me!

Eben: She died. (*A pause.*) Sometimes she used to sing fur me. (*He bursts into a fit of sobbing.*)

Abbie (*both her arms around him—with wild passion*). I'll sing fur ye! I'll die fur ye! (*In spite of her overwhelming desire for him, there is a sincere maternal love in her manner and voice—a horribly frank mixture of lust and mother love.*) Don't cry, Eben! I'll take yer Maw's place! I'll be everythin' she was t' ye! Let me kiss ye, Eben! (*She pulls his head around. He makes a bewildered pretense of resistance. She is tender.*) Don't be afeered! I'll kiss ye pure, Eben—same 's if I was a Maw t' ye—an' ye kin kiss me back 's if yew was my son—my boy—sayin' good-night t' me! Kiss me, Eben. (*They kiss in restrained fashion. Then suddenly wild passion overcomes her. She kisses him lustfully again and again and he flings his arms about her and returns her kisses. Suddenly, as in the bedroom, he frees himself from her violently and springs to his feet. He is trembling all over, in a strange state of terror.* ABBIE *strains her arms toward him with fierce pleading.*) Don't ye leave me, Eben! Can't ye see it hain't enuf—lovin' ye like a Maw—can't ye see it's got t' be that an' more—much more—a hundred times more—fur me t' be happy—fur yew t' be happy?

Eben (*to the presence he feels in the room*). Maw! Maw! What d'ye want? What air ye tellin' me?

Abbie: She's tellin' ye t' love me. She knows I love ye an' I'll be good t' ye. Can't ye feel it? Don't ye know? She's tellin' ye t' love me, Eben!

Eben: Ay-eh. I feel—mebbe she—but—I can't figger out—why—when ye've stole her place—here in her hum—in the parlor whar she was—

Abbie (*fiercely*). She knows I love ye!

Eben (*his face suddenly lighting up with a fierce triumphant grin*). I see it! I sees why. It's her vengeance on him—so's she kin rest quiet in her grave!

Abbie (*wildly*). Vengeance o' God on the hull o' us! What d'we give a durn? I love ye, Eben! God knows I love ye! (*She stretches out her arms for him.*)

Eben (*throws himself on his knees beside the sofa and grabs her in his arms*

—releasing all his pent-up passion). An' I love yew, Abbie!—now I kin say it! I been dyin' for want o' ye—every hour since ye come! I love ye! (*Their lips meet in a fierce, bruising kiss.*)

SCENE IV

[*Exterior of the farmhouse. It is just dawn. The front door at right is opened and* EBEN *comes out and walks around to the gate. He is dressed in his working clothes. He seems changed. His face wears a bold and confident expression, he is grinning to himself with evident satisfaction. As he gets near the gate, the window of the parlor is heard opening and the shutters are flung back and* ABBIE *sticks her head out. Her hair tumbles over her shoulders in disarray, her face is flushed, she looks at* EBEN *with tender, languorous eyes and calls softly.*]

Abbie: Eben (*As he turns—playfully.*) Jest one more kiss afore ye go. I'm goin' to miss ye fearful all day.

Eben: An' me yew, ye kin bet! (*He goes to her. They kiss several times. He draws away, laughingly.*) Thar. That's enuf, hain't it? Ye won't hev none left fur next time.

Abbie: I got a million o' 'em left fur yew! (*Then a bit anxiously.*) D'ye r'ally love me Eben?

Eben (*emphatically*). I like ye better'n any gal I ever knowed! That's gospel!

Abbie: Likin' hain't lovin'.

Eben: Waal then—I love ye. Now air yew satisfied?

Abbie: Ay-eh, I be. (*She smiles at him adoringly.*)

Eben: I better git t' the barn. The old critter's liable t' suspicion an' come sneakin' up.

Abbie (*with a confident laugh*). Let him! I kin allus pull the wool over his eyes. I'm goin' t' leave the shutters open and let in the sun 'n' air. This room's been dead long enuf. Now it's goin' t' be my room!

Eben (*frowning*). Ay-eh.

Abbie (*hastily*). I meant—our room.

Eben: Ay-eh.

Abbie: We made it our'n last night, didn't we? We give it life—our lovin' did. (*A pause.*)

Eben (*with a strange look*). Maw's gone back t' her grave. She kin sleep now.

Abbie: May she rest in peace! (*Then tenderly rebuking.*) Ye oughtn't t' talk o' sad thin's—this mornin'.

Eben: It jest come up in my mind o' itself.

Abbie: Don't let it. (*He doesn't answer. She yawns.*) Waal, I'm a-goin' t' steal a wink o' sleep. I'll tell the Old Man I hain't feelin' pert. Let him git his own vittles.

Eben: I see him comin' from the barn. Ye better look smart an' git upstairs.

Abbie: Ay-eh. Don't fergit me. (*She throws him a kiss. He grins—then squares his shoulders and awaits his father confidently.* CABOT *walks slowly up from the left, staring up at the sky with a vague face.*)

Eben (*jovially*). Mornin', Paw. Stargazin' in daylight?

Cabot: Purty, hain't it?

Eben (*looking around him possessively*). It's a durned purty farm.

Cabot: I mean the sky.

Eben (*grinning*). How d'ye know? Them eyes o' your'n can't see that fur.

(*This tickles his humor and he slaps his thigh and laughs.*) Ho-ho! That's a good un!

Cabot (*grimly sarcastic*). Ye're feelin' right chipper, hain't ye? Whar'd ye steal the likker?

Eben (*good-naturedly*). 'Tain't likker. Jest life. (*Suddenly holding out his hand—soberly.*) Yew 'n' me is quits. Let's shake hands.

Cabot (*suspiciously*). What's come over ye?

Eben: Then don't. Mebbe it's jest as well. (*A moment's pause.*) What's come over me? (*Queerly.*) Didn't ye feel her passin'—goin' back t' her grave?

Cabot (*dully*). Who?

Eben: Maw. She kin rest now an' sleep content. She's quits with ye.

Cabot (*confusedly*). I rested. I slept good—down with the cows. They know how t' sleep. They're teachin' me.

Eben (*suddenly jovial again*). Good fur the cows! Waal—ye better git t' work.

Cabot (*grimly amused*). Air yew bossn' me, ye calf?

Eben (*beginning to laugh*). Ay-eh! I'm bossin' yew! Ha-ha-ha! see how ye like it! Ha-ha-ha! I'm the prize rooster o' this roost. Ha-ha-ha! (*He goes off toward the barn laughing.*)

Cabot (*looks after him with scornful pity*). Soft-headed. Like his Maw. Dead spit 'n' image. No hope in him! (*He spits with contemptuous disgust.*) A born fool! (*Then matter-of-factly.*) Waal—I'm gittin' peckish. (*He goes toward door.*)

PART III

SCENE I

[*A night in late spring the following year. The kitchen and the two bedrooms upstairs are shown. The two bedrooms are dimly lighted by a tallow candle in each.* EBEN *is sitting on the side of the bed in his room, his chin propped on his fists, his face a study of the struggle he is making to understand his conflicting emotions. The noisy laughter and music from below where a kitchen dance is in progress annoy and distract him. He scowls at the floor.*

In the next room a cradle stands beside the double bed.

In the kitchen all is festivity. The stove has been taken down to give more room to the dancers. The chairs, with a wooden benches added, have been pushed back against the wall. On these are seated, squeezed in tight against one another, farmers and their wives and their young folks of both sexes from the neighboring farms. They are all chattering and laughing loudly. They evidently have some secret joke in common. There is no end of winking, of nudging, of meaning nods of the head toward CABOT *who, in a state of extreme hilarious excitement increased by the amount he has drunk, is standing near the rear door where there is a small keg of whisky and serving drinks to all the men. In the left corner, front, dividing the attention with her husband,* ABBIE *is sitting in a rocking chair, a shawl wrapped about her shoulders. She is very pale, her face is thin and drawn, her eyes are fixed anxiously on the open door in rear as if waiting for someone.*

The musician in tuning up his fiddle, seated in the far right corner. He is a lanky young fellow with a long, weak face. His pale eyes blink incessantly and he grins about him slyly with a greedy malice.]

Abbie (*suddenly turning to a young girl on her right*). Whar's Eben?

Young Girl (*eyeing her scornfully*). I dunno, Mrs. Cabot. I hain't seen Eben in ages. (*Meaningly.*) Seems like he's spent most o' his time t' hum since yew come.

Abbie (*vaguely*). I tuk his Maw's place.

Young Girl: Ay-eh. So I heerd. (*She turns away to retail this bit of gossip to her mother sitting next to her.* ABBIE *turns to her left to a big stoutish middle-aged man whose flushed face and staring eyes show the amount of "likker" he has consumed.*)

Abbie: Ye hain't seen Eben, hev ye?

Man: No, I hain't. (*Then he adds with a wink.*) If yew hain't, who would?

Abbie: He's the best dancer in the county. He'd ought t' come an' dance.

Man (*with a wink*). Mebbe he's doin' the dutiful an' walkin' the kid t' sleep. It's a boy, hain't it?

Abbie (*nodding vaguely*). Ay-eh—born two weeks back—purty's a picter.

Man: They all is—t' their Maws. (*Then in a whisper, with a nudge and a leer.*) Listen, Abbie—if ye ever git tired o' Eben, remember me! Don't fergit now! (*He looks at her uncomprehending face for a second—then grunts disgustedly.*) Waal—guess I'll likker agin. (*He goes over and joins* CABOT *who is arguing noisily with an old farmer over cows. They all drink.*)

Abbie (*this time appealing to nobody in particular*). Wonder what Eben's a-doin'? (*Her remark is repeated down the line with many a guffaw and titter until it reaches the fiddler. He fastens his blinking eyes on* ABBIE.)

Fiddler (*raising his voice*). Bet I kin tell ye, Abbie, what Eben's doin'! He's down t' the church offerin' up prayers o' thanksgivin'. (*They all titter expectantly.*)

Man: What fur? (*Another titter.*)

Fiddler: 'Cause unto him a—(*he hesitates just long enough*)—brother is born! (*A roar of laughter. They all look from* ABBIE *to* CABOT. *She is oblivious, staring at the door.* CABOT, *although he hasn't heard the words, is irritated by the laughter and steps forward, glaring about him. There is an immediate silence.*)

Cabot: What're ye all bleatin' about—like a flock o' goats? Why don't ye dance, damn ye? I axed ye here t' dance—t' eat, drink an' be marry—an' thar ye set cacklin' like a lot o' wet hens with the pip! Ye've swilled my likker an' guzzled my vittles like hogs, hain't ye? Then dance fur me, can't ye? That's fa'r an' squar', hain't it? (*A grumble of resentment goes around but they are all evidently in too much awe of him to express it openly.*)

Fiddler (*slyly*). We're waitin' fur Eben. (*A suppressed laugh.*)

Cabot (*with a fierce exultation*). T'hell with Eben! Eben's done fur now! I got a new son! (*His mood switching with drunken suddenness.*) But ye needn't t' laugh at Eben, none o' ye! He's my blood, if he be a dumb fool. He's better nor any o' yew! He kin do a day's work a'most up t' what I kin—an' that'd put any o' yew pore critters t' shame!

Fiddler: An' he kin do a good night's work, too! (*A roar of laughter.*)

Cabot: Laugh, ye damn fools! Ye're right jist the same, Fiddler. He kin work day an' night too, like I kin, if need be!

Old Farmer (*from behind the keg where he is weaving drunkenly back and forth—with great simplicity*). They hain't many t' touch ye, Ephraim—a son at seventy-six. That's a hard man fur ye! I be on'y sixty-eight an' I couldn't do it. (*A roar of laughter in which* CABOT *joins uproariously.*)

Cabot (*slapping him on the back*). I'm sorry fur ye, Hi. I'd never suspicion sech weakness from a boy like yew!

Old Farmer: An' I never reckoned yew had it in ye nuther, Ephraim. (*There is another laugh.*)

Cabot (*suddenly grim*). I got a lot in me—a hell of a lot—folks don't know on. (*Turning to the* FIDDLER.) Fiddle 'er up, durn ye! Give 'em somethin' t' dance t'! What air ye, an ornament? Hain't this a celebration? Then grease yer elbow an' go it!

Fiddler (*seizes a drink which the* OLD FARMER *holds out to him and downs it*). Here goes! (*He starts to fiddle "Lady of the Lake." Four young fellows and four girls form in two lines and dance a square dance. The* FIDDLER *shouts directions for the different movements, keeping his words in the rhythm of the music and interspersing them with jocular personal remarks to the dancers themselves. The people seated along the walls stamp their feet and clap their hands in unison.* CABOT *is especially active in this respect. Only* ABBIE *remains apathetic, staring at the door as if she were alone in a silent room.*)

Fiddler: Swing your partner t' the right! That's it, Jim! Give her a b'ar hug! Her Maw hain't lookin'. (*Laughter.*) Change partners! That suits ye, don't it, Essie, now ye got Reub afore ye? Look at her redden up, will ye! Waal, life is short an' so's love, as the feller says. (*Laughter.*)

Cabot (*excitedly, stamping his foot*). Go it, boys! Go it, gals!

Fiddler (*with a wink at the others*). Ye're the spryest seventy-six ever I sees, Ephraim! Now if ye'd on'y good eyesight . . . ! (*Suppressed laughter. He gives* CABOT *no chance to retort but roars.*) Promenade! Ye're walkin' like a bride down the aisle, Sarah! Waal, while they's life they's allus hope. I've heerd tell. Swing your partner to the left! Gosh A'mighty, look at Johnny Cook highsteppin'! They hain't goin' t' be much strength left fur howin' in the corn lot t'morrow. (*Laughter.*)

Cabot: Go it! Go it! (*Then suddenly, unable to restrain himself any longer, he prances into the midst of the dancers, scattering them, waving his arms about wildly.*) Ye're all hoofs! Git out o' my road! Give me room! I'll show ye dancin'. Ye're all too soft! (*He pushes them roughly away. They crowd back toward the walls, muttering, looking at him resentfully.*)

Fiddler (*jeeringly*). Go it, Ephraim! Go it! (*He starts "Pop Goes the Weasel," increasing the tempo with every verse until at the end he is fiddling crazily as fast as he can go.*)

Cabot (*starts to dance, which he does very well and with tremendous vigor. Then he begins to improvise, cuts incredibly grotesque capers, leaping up and cracking his heels together, prancing around in a circle with body bent in an Indian war dance, then suddenly straightening up and kicking as high as he can with both legs. He is like a monkey on a *string. And all the while he intersperses his antics with shouts and derisive comments*): Whoop! Here's dancin' fur ye! Whoop! See that! Seventy-six, if I'm a day! Hard as iron yet! Beatin' the young 'uns like I allus done! Look at me! I'd invite ye t' dance on my hundredth birthday on'y ye'll all be dead by then. Ye're a sickly generation! Yer hearts air pink, not red! Yer veins is full o' mud an' water! I be the on'y man in the county! Whoop! See that! I'm a Injun! I've killed Injuns in the West afore ye was born—an' skulped 'em too! They's a arrer wound on my backside I c'd show ye! The hull tribe chased me. I outrun 'em all—with the arrer stuck in me! An' I tuk vengeance on 'em. Ten eyes fur an eye that was my motter! Whoop! Look at me! I kin kick the ceilin' off the room! Whoop!

Fiddler (*stops playing—exhaustedly*). God A'mighy, I got enuf. Ye got the devil's strength in ye.

Cabot (*delightedly*). Did I beat yew, too? Wa'al, ye played smart. Hev a swig. (*He pours whisky for himself and* FIDDLER. *They drink. The others watch* CABOT *silently with cold, hostile eyes. There is a dead pause. The* FIDDLER *rests.* CABOT *leans against the keg, panting, glaring around him confusedly. In the room above,* EBEN *gets to his feet and tiptoes out the door in rear, appearing a moment later in the other bedroom. He moves silently, even frightenedly, toward the cradle and stands there looking down at the baby. His face is as vague as his reactions are confused, but there is a trace of tenderness, of interested discovery. At the same moment that he reaches the cradle,* ABBIE *seems to sense something. She gets up weakly and goes to* CABOT.)

Abbie: I'm goin' up t' the baby.

Cabot (*with real solicitude*). Air ye able fur the stairs? D'ye want me t' help ye, Abbie?

Abbie: No. I'm able. I'll be down agen soon.

Cabot: Don't ye git wore out. He needs ye, remember—our son does! (*He grins affectionately, patting her on the back. She shrinks from his touch.*)

Abbie (*dully*). Don't—tech me. I'm goin'—up. (*She goes.* CABOT *looks after her. A whisper goes around the room.* CABOT *turns. It ceases. He wipes his forehead streaming with sweat. He is breathing pantingly.*)

Cabot: I'm a-goin' out t' git fresh air. I'm feelin' a mite dizzy. Fiddle up thar! Dance, all o' ye! Here's likker fur them as wants it. Enjoy yerselves. I'll be back. (*He goes, closing the door behind him.*)

Fiddler (*sarcastically*). Don't hurry none on our account! (*A suppressed laugh. He imitates* ABBIE.) What's Eben? (*More laughter.*)

A Woman (*loudly*). What's happened in this house is plain as the nose on yer face! (ABBIE *appears in the doorway upstairs and stands looking in surprise and adoration at* EBEN *who does not see her.*)

A Man: Ssshh! He's li'ble t' be listenin' at the door. That'd be like him. (*Their voices die to an intensive whispering. Their faces are concentrated on this gossip. A noise as of dead leaves in the wind comes from the room.* CABOT *has come out from the porch and stands by the gate, leaning on it, staring at the sky blinkingly.* ABBIE *comes across the room silently.* EBEN *does not notice her until quite near.*)

Eben (*starting*). Abbie!

Abbie: Ssshh! (*She throws her arms around him. They kiss—then bend over* *the cradle together.*) Ain't he purty?—dead spit 'n' image o' yew!

Eben (*pleased*). Air he? I can't tell none.

Abbie: E-zactly like!

Eben (*frowningly*). I don't like this. I don't like lettin' on what's mine's his'n. I been doin' that all my life. I'm gittin' t' the end o' b'arin' it!

Abbie (*putting her finger on his lips*). We're doin' the best we kin. We got t' wait. Somethin's bound t' happen. (*She puts her arms around him.*) I got t' go back.

Eben: I'm goin' out. I can't b'ar it with the fiddle playin' an' the laughin'.

Abbie: Don't git feelin' low. I love ye, Eben. Kiss me. (*He kisses her. They remain in each other's arms.*)

Cabot (*at the gate, confusedly*). Even the music can't drive it out—somethin'. Ye kin feel it droppin' off the elums, climbin' up the roof, sneakin' down the chimney, pokin' in the corners! They's no peace in houses, they's no rest livin' with folks. Somethin's always livin' with ye. (*With a deep sigh.*) I'll go t' the barn an' rest a spell. (*He goes wearily toward the barn.*)

Fiddler (*tuning up*). Let's celebrate the old skunk gittin' fooled! We kin have some fun now he's went. (*He starts to fiddle "Turkey in the Straw." There is real merriment now. The young folks get up to dance.*)

SCENE II

[*A half hour later—exterior—*EBEN *is standing by the gate looking up at the sky, an expression of dumb pain bewildered by itself on his face.* CABOT *appears, returning from the barn, walking wearily his eyes on the ground. He sees* EBEN *and his whole mood immediately changes. He becomes excited, a cruel, triumphant grin comes to his lips, he strides up and slaps* EBEN *on the back. From within comes the whining of the fiddle and the noise of stamping feet and laughing voices.*]

Cabot: So har ye be!

Eben (*startled, stares at him with hatred for a moment—then dully*). Ay-eh.

Cabot (*surveying him jeeringly*). Why hain't ye been in t' dance? They was all axin' fur ye.

Eben: Let 'em ax!

Cabot: They's a hull passal o' purty gals.

Eben: T' hell with 'em!

Cabot: Ye'd ought t' be marryin' one o' 'em soon.

Eben: I hain't marryin' no one.

Cabot: Ye might 'arn a share o' a farm that way.

Eben (*with a sneer*). Like yew did, ye mean? I hain't that kind.

Cabot (*stung*). Ye lie! 'Twas yer Maw's folks aimed t' steal my farm from me.

Eben: Other folks don't say so. (*After a pause—defiantly.*) An' I got a farm, anyways!

Cabot (*derisively*). Whar?

Eben (*stamps a foot on the ground*). Har!

Cabot (*throws his head back and laughs coarsely*). Ho-ho! Ye hev, hev ye? Waal, that's a good un!

Eben (*controlling himself—grimly*). Ye'll see!

Cabot (*stares at him suspiciously, trying to make him out—a pause—then with scornful confidence*). Ay-eh. I'll see.

So'll ye. It's ye that's blind—blind as a mole underground. (EBEN *suddenly laughs, one short sardonic bark: "Ha." A pause,* CABOT *peers at him with renewed suspicion.*) What air ye hawin' 'bout? (EBEN *turns away without answering.* CABOT *grows angry.*) God A'migthty, yew air a dumb dunce! They's nothin' in that thick skull o' your'n but noise—like a empty keg it be! (EBEN *doesn't seem to hear*—CABOT'S *rage grows.*) Yewr farm! God A'mighty! If ye wa'n't a born donkey ye'd know ye'll never own stick nor stone on it, specially now arter him bein' born. It's his'n, I tell ye—his'n arter I die—but I'll live a hundred jest t' fool ye all—an' he'll be growed then—yewr age a'most! (EBEN *laughs again his sardonic "Ha." This drives* CABOT *into a fury.*) Ha? Ye think ye kin git 'round that someways, do ye? Waal, it'll be her'n, too —Abbie's—ye won't git 'round her—she knows yer tricks—she'll be too much fur ye—she wants the farm her'n—she was afeerd o' ye—she told me ye was sneakin' 'round tryin' t' make love t' her t' git her on yer side . . . ye . . . ye mad fool, ye! (*He raises his clenched fists threateningly.*)

Eben (*is confronting him choking with rage*). Ye lie, ye old skunk! Abbie said no sech thing!

Cabot (*suddenly triumphant when he sees how shaken* EBEN *is*). She did. An' I says, I'll blow his brains t' the top o' them elums—an' she says no, that hain't sense, who'll ye git t' help ye on the farm in his place—an' then she says yew'n me ought t' have a son—I know we kin, she says—an' I says, if we do, ye kin have anythin' I've got ye've a mind t'. An' she says, I wants Eben cut off so's this farm'll be mine when ye die! (*With terrible gloating.*) An' that's what's happened, hain't it? An' the farm's her'n! An' the dust o' the road—that's you'rn! Ha! Now who's hawin'?

Eben (*has been listening, petrified with grief and rage—suddenly laughs wildly and brokenly*). Ha-ha-ha! So that's her sneakin' game—all along!—like I suspicioned at fust—t' swaller it all—an' me, too . . . ! (*Madly.*) I'll murder her! (*He springs toward the porch but* CABOT *is quicker and gets in between.*)

Cabot: No, ye don't!

Eben: Git out o' my road! (*He tries to throw* CABOT *aside. They grapple in what becomes immediately a murderous struggle. The old man's concentrated strength is too much for* EBEN. CABOT *gets one hand on his throat and presses him back across the stone wall. At the same moment,* ABBIE *comes out on the porch. With a stifled cry she runs toward them.*)

Abbie: Eben! Ephraim! (*She tugs at the hand on* EBEN'S *throat.*) Let go, Ephraim! Ye're chokin' him!

Cabot (*removes his hand and flings* EBEN *sideways full length on the grass, gasping and choking. With a cry,* ABBIE *kneels beside him, trying to take his head on her lap, but he pushes her away.* CABOT *stands looking down with fierce triumph*). Ye needn't fret, Abbie, I wa'n't aimin' t' kill him. He hain't wuth hangin' fur—not by a hell of a sight! (*More and more triumphantly.*) Seventy-six an' him not thirty yit—an' look whar he be fur thinkin' his Paw was easy! No, by God, I hain't easy! An' him upstairs, I'll raise him t' be like me! (*He turns to leave them.*) I'm goin' in an' dance!—sing an' celebrate! (*He walks to the porch—then turns with a great grin.*) I don't calc-late it's left in him, but if he gits pesky, Abbie, ye jest sing out. I'll come a-runnin' an' by the Etarnal, I'll put him across my knee an' birch him! Ha-ha-ha! (*He goes into the house laughing. A moment later his loud "whoop" is heard.*)

Abbie (*tenderly*). Eben. Air ye hurt? (*She tries to kiss him but he pushes her violently away and struggles to a sitting position.*)

Eben (*gaspingly*). T'hell—with ye!

Abbie (*not believing her ears*). It's me, Eben—Abbie—don't ye know me?

Eben (*glowering at her with hatred*). Ay-eh—I know ye—now! (*He suddenly breaks down, sobbing weakly.*)

Abbie (*fearfully*). Eben—what's happened t' ye—why did ye look at me 's if ye hated me?

Eben (*violently, between sobs and gasps*). I do hate ye! Ye're a whore—a damn trickin' whore!

Abbie (*shrinking back horrified*). Eben! Ye don't know what ye're sayin'!

Eben (*scrambling to his feet and following her—accusingly*). Ye're nothin' but a stinkin' passel o' lies! Ye've been lyin' t' me every word ye spoke, day an' night, since we fust—done it. Ye've kept sayin' ye loved me. . . .

Abbie (*frantically*). I do love ye! (*She takes his hands but he flings hers away.*)

Eben (*unheeding*). Ye've made a fool o' me—a sick, dumb fool—a-purpose! Ye've been on'y playin' yer sneakin', stealin' game all along—gittin' me t' lie with ye so's ye'd hev a son he'd think was his'n, an' makin' him promise he'd give ye the farm and let me eat dust, if ye did git him a son! (*Staring at her with anguished, bewildered eyes.*) They must be a devil livin' in ye! 'Tain't human t' be as bad as that be!

Abbie (*stunned—dully*). He told yew . . . ?

Eben: Hain't it true? It hain't no good in yew lyin'.

Abbie (*pleadingly*). Eben, listen—ye must listen—it was long ago—afore we done nothin'—yew was scornin' me—goin' t' see Min—when I was lovin' ye—an' I said it t' him t' git vengeance on ye!

Eben (*unheedingly. With tortured passion*). I wish ye was dead! I wish I was dead along with ye afore this come! (*Ragingly.*) But I'll git my vengeance too! I'll pray Maw t' come back t' help me—t' put her cuss on yew an' him!

Abbie (*brokenly*). Don't ye, Eben! Don't ye! (*She throws herself on her knees before him, weeping.*) I didn't mean t' do bad t'ye! Fergive me, won't ye?

Eben (*not seeming to hear her—fiercely*). I'll git squar' with the old skunk—an' yew! I'll tell him the truth 'bout the son he's so proud o'! Then I'll leave ye here t' pizen each other—with Maw comin' out o' her grave at nights—an' I'll go t' the gold fields o' Californi-a whar Sim an' Peter be!

Abbie (*terrified*). Ye won't—leave me? Ye can't!

Eben (*with fierce determination*). I'm a-goin' I tell ye! I'll git rich thar an' come back an' fight him fur the farm he stole—an' I'll kick ye both out in the road—t' beg an' sleep in the woods—an' yer son along with ye—t' starve an' die! (*He is hysterical at the end.*)

Abbie (*with a shudder—humbly*). He's yewr son, too, Eben.

Eben (*torturedly*). I wish he never was born! I wish he'd die this minit! I wish I'd never sot eyes on him! it's him—yew havin' him—a-purpose t' steal—that's changed everythin'!

Abbie (*gently*). Did ye believe I loved ye—afore he come?

Eben: Ay-eh—like a dumb ox!

Abbie: An' ye don't believe no more?

Eben: B'lieve a lyin' thief! Ha!

Abbie (*shudders—then humbly*). And did ye r'ally love me afore?

Eben (*brokenly*). Ay-eh—an' ye was trickin' me!

Abbie: An' ye don't love me now!

Eben (*violently*). I hate ye, I tell ye!

Abbie: An' ye're truly goin' West—goin' t' leave me—all account o' him being born?

Eben: I'm a-goin' in the mornin'—or may God strike me t' hell!

Abbie (*after a pause—with a dreadful cold intensity—slowly*). If that's what his comin's done t' me—killin' yewr love—takin' yew away—my on'y joy—the on'y joy I've ever knowed—like heaven t' me—purtier'n heaven—then I hate him, too, even if I be his Maw!

Eben (*bitterly*). Lies! Ye love him! He'll steal the farm fur ye! (*Brokenly.*) But 'tain't the farm so much—not no more—it's yew foolin' me—gittin' me t' love ye—lyin' yew loved me—jest t' git a son t' steal!

Abbie (*distractedly*). He won't steal! I'd kill him fust! I do love ye! I'll prove t' ye . . . !

Eben (*harshly*). 'Tain't no use lyin' no more. I'm deaf t' ye! (*He turns away.*) I hain't seein' ye agen. Good-by!

Abbie (*pale with anguish*). Hain't ye even goin' t' kiss me—not once—arter all we loved?

Eben (*in a hard voice*). I hain't wantin' t' kiss ye never agen! I'm wantin' t' forgit I ever sot eyes on ye!

Abbie: Eben!—ye mustn't—wait a spell—I want t' tell ye. . . .

Eben: I'm a-goin' in t' git drunk. I'm a-goin' t' dance.

Abbie (*clinging to his arm—with passionate earnestness*). If I could make it—'s if he'd never come up between us—if I could prove t' ye I wa'n't schemin' t' steal from ye—so's everythin' could be jest the same with us, lovin' each other jest the same, kissin' an' happy the same's we've been happy afore he come—if I could do it—ye'd love me agen, wouldn't ye? Ye'd kiss me agen? Ye wouldn't never leave me, would ye?

Eben (*moved*). I calc'late not. (*Then shaking her hand off his arm—with a bitter smile.*) But ye hain't God, be ye?

Abbie (*exultantly*). Remember ye've promised! (*Then with strange intensity.*) Mebbe I kin take back one thin' God does!

Eben (*peering at her*). Ye're gittin' cracked, hain't ye? (*Then going towards door.*) I'm a-goin' t' dance.

Abbie (*calls after him intensely*). I'll prove t' ye! I'll prove I love ye better'n. . . . (*He goes in the door, not seeming to hear. She remains standing where she is, looking after him—then she finishes desperately:*) Better'n everythin' else in the world!

SCENE III

[Just before dawn in the morning—shows the kitchen and CABOT'S *bedroom. In the kitchen, by the light of a tallow candle on the table,* EBEN *is sitting, his chin propped on his hands, his drawn face blank and expressionless. His carpetbag is on the floor beside him. In the bedroom, dimly lighted by a small whale-oil lamp,* CABOT *lies*

asleep. ABBIE *is bending over the cradle, listening, her face full of terror yet with an undercurrent of desperate triumph. Suddenly, she breaks down and sobs, appears about to throw herself on her knees beside the cradle; but the old man turns restlessly, groaning in his sleep, and she controls herself, and shrinking away from the cradle with a gesture of horror, backs swiftly toward the door in rear and goes out. A moment later she comes into the kitchen and, running to* EBEN, *flings her arms about his neck and kisses him wildly. He hardens himself, he remains unmoved and cold, he keeps his eyes straight ahead*].

Abbie (*hysterically*). I done it. Eben! I told ye I'd do it! I've proved I love ye—better'n everythin'—so's ye can't never doubt me no more!

Eben (*dully*). Whatever ye done, it hain't no good now.

Abbie (*wildly*). Don't ye say that! Kiss me, Eben, won't ye? I need ye t' kiss me arter what I done! I need ye t' say ye love me!

Eben (*kisses her without emotion—dully*). That's fur good-by. I'm a-goin' soon.

Abbie: No! No! Ye won't go—not now!

Eben (*going on with his own thoughts*). I been a-thinkin'—an' I hain't goin' t' tell Paw nothin'. I'll leave Maw t' take vengeance on ye. If I told him, the old skunk'd jest be stinkin' mean enuf to take it out on that baby. (*His voice showing emotion in spite of him.*) An' I don't want nothin' bad t' happen t' him. He hain't t' blame fur yew. (*He adds with a certain queer pride*:) An' he looks like me! An' by God, he's mine! An' some day I'll be a-comin' back an' . . . !

Abbie (*too absorbed in her own thoughts to listen to him—pleadingly*). They's no cause fur ye t' go now—they's no sense—it's all the same's it was—they's nothin' come b'tween us now—arter what I done!

Eben (*something in her voice arouses him. He stares at her a bit frightenedly*). Ye look mad, Abbie. What did ye do?

Abbie: I—I killed him, Eben.

Eben (*amazed*). Ye killed him?

Abbie (*dully*). Ay-eh.

Eben (*recovering from his astonishment—savagely*). An' serves him right! But we got t' do somethin' quick t' make it look s'if the old skunk'd killed himself when he was drunk. We kin prove by 'em all how drunk he got.

Abbie (*wildly*). No! No! Not him! (*Laughing distractedly.*) But that's what I ought t' done, hain't it? I oughter killed him instead! Why didn't ye tell me?

Eben (*appalled*). Instead? What d'ye mean?

Abbie: Not him.

Eben (*his face grown ghastly*). Not—not that baby!

Abbie (*dully*). Ay-eh!

Eben (*falls to his knees as if he'd been struck—his voice trembling with horror*). Oh, God A'mighty! A'mighty God! Maw, whar was ye, why didn't ye stop her?

Abbie (*simply*). She went back t' her grave that night we fust done it, remember? I hain't felt her about since. (*A pause.* EBEN *hides his head in his hands, trembling all over as if he had the ague. She goes on dully*:) I left the pillar over his little face. Then he killed himself. He stopped breathin'. (*She begins to weep softly.*)

Eben (*rage beginning to mingle with grief*). He looked like me. He was mine, damn ye!

Abbie (*slowly and broken*). I didn't want t' do it. I hated myself fur doin' it. I loved him. He was so purty—dead spit 'n' image o' yew. But I loved yew more—an' yew was goin' away—far off whar I'd never see ye agen, never kiss ye, never feel ye pressed again me agen—an' ye said ye hated me fur havin' him—ye said ye hated him an' wished he was dead —ye said if it hadn't been fur him comin' it'd be the same's afore between us.

Eben (*unable to endure this, springs to his feet in a fury, threatening her, his twitching fingers seeming to reach out for her throat*). Ye lie! I never said—I never dreamed ye'd—I'd cut off my head afore I'd hurt his finger!

Abbie (*piteously, sinking on her knees*). Eben, don't ye look at me like that—hatin' me—not after what I done fur ye—fur us—so's we could be happy agen—

Eben (*furiously now*). Shut up, or I'll kill ye! I see yer game now—the same old sneakin' trick—ye're aimin' t' blame me fur the murder ye done!

Abbie (*moaning—putting her hands over her ears*). Don't ye, Eben! Don't ye! (*She grasps his legs.*)

Eben (*his mood suddenly changing to horror, shrinks away from her*). Don't ye tech me! Ye're pizen! How could ye —t' murder a poor little critter—Ye must've swapped yer soul t' hell! (*Sudden raging.*) Ha! I kin see why ye done it! Not the lies ye jest told—but 'cause ye wanted t' steal agen—steal the last thin' ye'd left me—my part o' him—no, the hull o' him—ye saw he looked like me—ye knowed he was all mine—an' ye couldn't b'ar it—I know ye! Ye killed him fur bein' mine! (*All this has driven him almost insane. He makes a rush past her for the door—then turns—shaking both fists at her, violently.*) But I'll take vengeance now! I'll git the Sheriff! I'll tell him everythin'! Then I'll sing "I'm off to Californi-a!" an' go—gold—Golden Gate—gold sun—fields o' gold in the West! (*This last he half shouts, half croons incoherently, suddenly breaking off passionately.*) I'm a-goin' fur the Sheriff t' come an' git ye! I want ye tuk away, locked up from me! I can't stand t' luk at ye! Murderer an' thief 'r not, ye still tempt me! I'll give ye up t' the Sheriff! (*He turns and runs out, around the corner of house, panting and sobbing, and breaks into a swerving sprint down the road.*)

Abbie (*struggling to her feet, runs to the door, calling after him*). I love ye, Eben! I love ye! (*She stops at the door weakly, swaying, about to fall.*) I don't care what ye do—if ye'll on'y love me agen—(*She falls limply to the floor in a faint.*)

SCENE IV

[*About an hour later. Same as Scene III. Shows the kitchen and* CABOT'S *bedroom. It is after dawn. The sky is brilliant with the sunrise. In the kitchen,* ABBIE *sits at the table, her body limp and exhausted, her head bowed down over her arms, her face hidden. Upstairs,* CABOT *is still asleep but awakens with a start. He looks toward the window and gives a snort of surprise and irritation—throws back the covers and begins hurriedly pulling on his clothes. Without looking be-*

hind him, he begins talking to ABBIE *whom he supposes beside him.*]

Cabot: Thunder 'n' lightnin', Abbie! I hain't slept this late in fifty years! Looks 's if the sun was full riz a'most. Must've been the dancin' an' likker. Must be gittin' old. I hope Eben's t'wuk. Ye might've tuk the trouble t' rouse me, Abbie. (*He turns—sees no one there—surprised.*) Waal—whar air she? Gittin' vittles, I calc'late. (*He tiptoes to the cradle and peers down—proudly.*) Mornin', sonny. Purty's a picter! Sleepin' sound. He don't beller all night like most o' 'em. (*He goes quietly out the door in rear—a few moments later enters kitchen—sees* ABBIE*—with satisfaction.*) So thar ye be. Ye got any vittles cooked?

Abbie (*without moving*). No.

Cabot (*coming to her, almost sympathetically*). Ye feelin' sick?

Abbie: No.

Cabot (*pats her on shoulder. She shudders*). Ye'd best lie down a spell. (*Half jocularly.*) Yer son'll be needin' ye soon. He'd ought t' wake up with a gnashin' appetite, the sound way he's sleepin'.

Abbie (*shudders—then in a dead voice*). He ain't never goin' to wake up.

Cabot (*jokingly*). Takes after me this mornin'. I ain't slept so late in . . .

Abbie: He's dead.

Cabot (*stares at her—bewilderedly*). What . . .

Abbie: I killed him.

Cabot (*stepping back from her—aghast*). Air ye drunk—'r crazy—'r . . . !

Abbie (*suddenly lifts her head and turns on him—wildly*). I killed him, I tell ye! I smothered him. Go up an' see if ye don't b'lieve me! (CABOT *stares at her a second, then bolts out the rear door, can be heard bounding up the stairs, and rushes into the bedroom and over to the cradle.* ABBIE *has sunk back lifelessly into her former position.* CABOT *puts his hand on the body in the crib. An expression of fear and horror comes over his face.*)

Cabot (*shrinking away—tremblingly*). God A'mighty! God A'mighty. (*He stumbles out the door—in a short while returns to the kitchen—comes to* ABBIE, *the stunned expression still on his face—hoarsely.*) Why did ye do it? Why? (*As she doesn't answer, he grabs her violently by the shoulder and shakes her.*) I ax ye why ye done it! Ye'd better tell me 'r . . . !

Abbie (*gives him a furious push which sends him staggering back and springs to her feet—with wild rage and hatred*). Don't ye dare tech me! What right hev ye t' question me 'bout him? He wa'n't yewr son! Think I'd have a son by yew? I'd die fust! I hate the sight o' ye an' allus did! It's yew I should've murdered, if I'd had good sense! I hate ye! I love Eben. I did from the fust. An' he was Eben's son—mine an' Eben's—not your'n'!

Cabot (*stands looking at her dazedly—a pause—finding his words with an effort—dully*). That was it—what I felt—pokin' round the corners—while ye lied—holdin' yerself from me—sayin' ye'd a'ready conceived—(*He lapses into crushed silence—then with a strange emotion.*) He's dead, sart'n. I felt his heart. Pore little critter! (*He blinks back one tear, wiping his sleeve across his nose.*)

Abbie (*hysterically*). Don't ye! Don't ye! (*She sobs unrestrainedly.*)

Cabot (*with a concentrated effort that stiffens his body into a rigid line and hardens his face into a stony mask—through his teeth to himself*). I got t' be—like a stone—a rock o' jedgement! (*A pause. He gets complete control over himself—harshly.*) If he was Eben's, I be glad he air gone! An' mebbe I suspicioned it all along. I felt they was somethin' onnateral—somewhars—the house got so lonesome—an' cold—drivin' me down t' the barn—t' the beasts o' the field. . . . Ay-eh. I must've suspicioned—somethin'. Ye didn't fool me—not altogether, leastways—I'm too old a bird—growin' ripe on the bough. . . . (*He becomes aware he is wandering, straightens again, looks at* ABBIE *with a cruel grin.*) So ye'd liked t' hev murdered me 'stead o' him, would ye? Waal, I'll live to a hundred! I'll live t' see ye hung! I'll deliver ye up t' the jedgment o' God an' the law! I'll git the Sheriff now. (*Starts for the door.*)

Abbie (*dully*). Ye needn't. Eben's gone fur him.

Cabot (*amazed*). Eben—gone fur the Sheriff?

Abbie: Ay-eh.

Cabot: T' inform agen ye?

Abbie: Ay-eh.

Cabot (*considers this—a pause—then in a hard voice*). Waal, I'm thankful fur him savin' me the trouble. I'll git t' wuk. (*He goes to the door—then turns—in a voice full of strange emotion.*) He'd ought t' been my son, Abbie. Ye'd ought t' loved me. I'm a man. If ye'd loved me, I'd never told no Sheriff on ye no matter what ye did, if they was t' brile me alive!

Abbie (*defensively*). They's more to it nor yew know, makes him tell.

Cabot (*dryly*). Fur yewr sake, I hope they be. (*He goes out—comes around to the gate—stares up at the sky. His control relaxes. For a moment he is old and weary. He murmurs despairingly:*) God A'mighty, I be lonesomer'n ever! (*He hears running footsteps from the left, immediately is himself again.* EBEN *runs in, panting exhaustedly, wild-eyed and mad looking. He lurches through the gate.* CABOT *grabs him by the shoulder.* EBEN *stares at him dumbly.*) Did ye tell the Sheriff?

Eben (*nodding stupidly*). Ay-eh.

Cabot (*gives him a push away that sends him sprawling—laughing with withering contempt*). Good fur ye! A prime chip o' yer Maw ye be! (*He goes toward the barn, laughing harshly.* EBEN *scrambles to his feet. Suddenly* CABOT *turns—grimly threatening.*) Git off this farm when the Sheriff takes her—or, by God, he'll have t' come back an' git me fur murder, too! (*He stalks off.* EBEN *does not appear to have heard him. He runs to the door and comes into the kitchen.* ABBIE *looks up with a cry of anguished joy.* EBEN *stumbles over and throws himself on his knees beside her—sobbing brokenly.*)

Eben: Fergive me!

Abbie (*happily*). Eben! (*She kisses him and pulls his head over against her breast.*)

Eben: I love ye! Fergive me!

Abbie (*ecstatically*). I'd fergive ye all the sins in hell fur sayin' that! (*She kisses his head, pressing it to her with a fierce passion of possession.*)

Eben (*brokenly*). But I told the Sheriff. He's comin' fur ye!

Abbie: I kin b'ar what happens t' me—now!

Eben: I woke him up. I told him. He says, wait 'til I git dressed. I was waiting. I got to thinkin' o' yew. I got to thinkin' how I'd loved ye. It hurt like somethin' was bustin' in my chest an' head. I got t' cryin'. I knowed sudden I loved ye yet, an' allus would love ye!

Abbie (*caressing his hair—tenderly*). My boy, hain't ye?

Eben: I begun t' run back. I cut across the fields an' through the woods. I thought ye might have time t' run away —with me—an' . . .

Abbie (*shaking her head*). I got t' take my punishment—t' pay fur my sin.

Eben: Then I want t' share it with ye.

Abbie: Ye didn't do nothin'.

Eben: I put it in yer head. I wisht he was dead! I as much as urged ye t' do it!

Abbie: No. It was me alone!

Eben: I'm as guilty as yew be! He was the child o' our sin.

Abbie (*lifting her head as if defying God*). I don't repent that sin! I hain't askin' God t' fergive that!

Eben: Nor me—but it led up t' the other—an' the murder ye did, ye did 'count o' me—an' it's my murder, too, I'll tell the Sheriff—an' if ye deny it, I'll say we planned it t'gether—an' they'll all b'lieve me, fur they suspicion everythin' we've done, an' it'll seem likely an' true to 'em. An' it is true—way down. I did help ye—somehow.

Abbie (*laying her head on his—sobbing*). No! I don't want yew t' suffer!

Eben: I got t' pay fur my part o' the sin! An' I'd suffer wuss leavin' ye, goin' West, thinkin' o' ye day an' night, bein' out when yew was in—(*lowering his voice*)—'r bein' alive when yew was dead. (*A pause.*) I want t' share with ye, Abbie —prison 'r death 'r hell 'r anythin'! (*He looks into her eyes and forces a trembling smile.*) If I'm sharin' with ye, I won't feel lonesome, leastways.

Abbie (*weakly*). Eben! I won't let ye! I can't let ye!

Eben (*kissing her—tenderly*). Ye can't he'p yerself. I got ye beat fur once!

Abbie (*forcing a smile—adoringly*). I hain't beat—s'long's I got ye!

Eben (*hears the sound of feet outside*). Ssshh! Listen! They've come t' take us!

Abbie: No, it's him. Don't give him no chance to fight ye, Eben. Don't say nothin'—no matter what he says. An' I won't neither. (*It is* CABOT. *He comes up from the barn in a great state of excitement and strides into the house and then into the kitchen.* EBEN *is kneeling beside* ABBIE, *his arm around her, hers around him. They stare straight ahead.*)

Cabot (*stares at them, his face hard. A long pause—vindictively*). Ye make a slick pair o' murderin' turtle doves! Ye'd ought t' be both hung on the same limb an' left thar t' swing in the breeze an' rot—a warnin' t' old fools like me t' b'ar their lonesomeness alone—an' fur young fools like ye t' hobble their lust. (*A pause. The excitement returns to his face, his eyes snap, he looks a bit crazy.*) I couldn't work today. I couldn't take no interest. T' hell with the farm! I'm leavin' it. I've turned the cows an' other stock loose! I've druv 'em into the woods whar they kin be free! By freein' 'em, I'm freein' myself! I'm quittin' here today! I'll set fire t' house an' barn an' watch 'em burn, an' I'll leave yer Maw t' haunt the ashes, an' I'll will the fields back t' God, so that nothin' human kin never touch 'em! I'll be a-goin' to Californi-a —t' jine Simeon an' Peter—true sons o' mine if they be dumb fools—an' the Cabots'll find Solomon's Mines t'gether! (*He suddenly cuts a mad caper.*) Whoop! What was the song they sung? "Oh, Californi-a! That's the land fur me." (*He sings this—then gets on his knees by the floorboard under which the money was hid.*) An' I'll sail thar on one o' the finest clippers I kin find! I've got the money! Pity ye didn't know whar this was hidden so's ye could steal . . . (*He has pulled up the board. He stares—feels —stares again. A pause of dead silence. He slowly turns, slumping into a sitting position on the floor, his eyes like those of a dead fish, his face the sickly green of an attack of nausea. He swallows painfully several times—forces a weak smile at last.*) So—ye did steal it!

Eben (*emotionlessly*). I swapped it t' Sim an' Peter fur their share o' the farm —t' pay their passage t' Californi-a.

Cabot (*with one sardonic*) *Ha!* (*He begins to recover. Gets slowly to his feet —strangely*). I calc'late God give it to 'em—not yew! God's hard, not easy! Mebbe they's easy gold in the West but it hain't God's gold. It hain't fur me. I kin hear His voice warnin' me agen t' be hard an' stay on my farm. I kin see his hand usin' Eben t' steal t' keep me from weakness. I kin feel I be in the palm o' His hand, His fingers guidin' me. (*A pause—then he mutters sadly:*) It's a-goin' t' be lonesomer now than ever it war afore —an' I'm gittin' old, Lord—ripe on the bough. . . . (*Then stiffening.*) Waal— what d'ye want? God's lonesome, hain't He? God's hard an' lonesome! (*A pause. The* SHERIFF *with two men comes up the road from the left. They move cautiously to the door. The* SHERIFF *knocks on it with the butt of his pistol.*)

Sheriff: Open in the name o' the law! (*They start.*)

Cabot: They've come fur ye. (*He goes to the rear door.*) Come in, Jim! (*The three men enter.* CABOT *meets them in doorway.*) Jest a minit, Jim. I got 'em safe here. (*The* SHERIFF *nods. He and his companions remain in the doorway.*)

Eben (*suddenly calls*). I lied this mornin', Jim. I helped her to do it. Ye kin take me, too.

Abbie (*brokenly*). No!

Cabot: Take 'em both. (*He comes forward—stares at* EBEN *with a trace of grudging admiration.*) Purty good—fur yew! Waal, I got t' round up the stock. Good-by.

Eben: Good-by.

Abbie: Good-by. (CABOT *turns and strides past the men—comes out and around the corner of the house, his shoulders squared, his face stony, and stalks grimly toward the barn. In the meantime the* SHERIFF *and men have come into the room.*)

Sheriff (*embarrassedly*). Waal—we'd best start.

Abbie: Wait. (*Turns to* EBEN.) I love ye, Eben.

Eben: I love ye, Abbie. (*They kiss. The three men grin and shuffle embarrassedly.* EBEN *takes* ABBIE'S *hand. They go out the door in the rear, the men following, and come from the house, walking hand in hand to the gate.* EBEN *stops there and points to the sunrise sky.*) Sun's a-risin'. Purty, hain't it?

Abbie: Ay-eh. (*They both stand for a moment looking up raptly in attitudes strangely aloof and devout.*)

Sheriff (*looking around at the farm enviously—to his companion*). It's a jim-dandy farm, no denyin'. Wished I owned it!

DISCUSSION QUESTIONS

Part I

1. How does O'Neill use stage setting and description to help establish the mood of the scene?
2. What do the manner of ringing the bell, the comment on the sunset, and the spitting establish about the character of Eben?
3. What purpose does it serve to have Simeon and Peter older than Eben and only his half-brothers?
4. What expository information concerning character and events is provided by the conversation between Simeon and Peter and between them and Eben?
5. How does their conversation serve to initiate the characterization of their father?
6. How does the *double entendre* over the remark concerning Eben's parentage illustrate the difference in character between him and his brothers?
7. What conflicts are set up between Eben and his brothers?
8. What is the effect of the monosyllabic interchange between Simeon and Peter concerning Eben's mother, and what excuse do they give to extenuate their failure to lighten her burden?
9. What conflicts exist between Eben and his father?
10. What does O'Neill do in this scene to create suspense that will carry interest over to later scenes? What clues does he give?
11. What purpose does the mention of the town prostitute serve?
12. What do Simeon's predictions and Eben's concluding soliloquy in this scene establish about Eben's future behavior?
13. What purpose does it serve to have Eben learn the news of Cabot's new wife before Simeon and Peter do?
14. How does the manner in which Eben spent the night relate to his father's marriage?
15. What is the symbolic significance of the room that the three brothers occupy?
16. How do Eben's possession of the money and the bargain he seeks to strike with his brothers further his characterization?
17. How does the news of a new wife serve as a motivating force in the plot? On Simeon and Peter? On Eben?
18. What purpose does Simeon's inquiry, "Whar was ye all night?" serve in furthering the characterization of Eben?
19. What preparation is provided by the conversation between Eben and Simeon in which Eben boasts of having been with Min?
20. What is the unhinged gate symbolic of for Simeon and Peter?
21. What is Ephraim Cabot's nearsightedness symbolic of?
22. What is ironic about Cabot's appraisal of Eben's character?

23. What characterization of Abbie is achieved in this scene as exhibited in her conversations with the other characters?
24. What events do Cabot's final remarks prepare for?
25. What is the purpose, tonally and in terms of action, of having the "Californi-a" song heard off in the distance?

Part II

1. What is the symbolic significance of the heat mentioned in the description of the setting for Part II?
2. What is the imagery suggestive of in such words and phrases "cacklin'," "prize bull," and those in Abbie's speech on nature?
3. What is the irony in Abbie's protest against being compared with Min?
4. What is ironic about Cabot's overhearing the quarrel between Abbie and Eben and his attitude toward it?
5. What is ironic about Cabot's biblical allusions in this scene?
6. What is ironic about Abbie's complaint to Cabot that Eben will disgrace them by going to see Min and that she tried to stop him?
7. What further characterization of Abbie is accomplished here?
8. How does O'Neill use stage setting as an active element in this scene? (Scene ii.)
9. How is his hardness of temperament Ephraim Cabot's greatest strength and greatest weakness at the same time?
10. What is the dramatic irony inherent in Abbie's promise of a son to Cabot?
11. Why does Abbie emerge victorious in her clash with Eben in this scene? (Scene ii.)
12. Of what is the closed parlor a symbol, and how does Abbie use it as part of her conquest of Eben?
13. What is ironic about the parlor courting-scene between Abbie and Eben?
14. What is ironic about Abbie's identifying herself with Eben's mother?
15. Besides their mutual passion, what serves as the motivating force to permit Eben to surrender to his desire for Abbie?
16. In Scene iv what is symbolic about the opening of the parlor windows and the appearance of Abbie and Eben?
17. What exchange of roles between the two lovers has occurred since the last scene?
18. What is the irony Eben intends in his jest about his father's star-gazing?
19. Why does Eben now feel that his mother's spirit can go back to her grave and rest content?
20. What is the ambiguous significance of Eben's remark, "I'm bossin' hew! Ha-ha-ha."

Part III

1. What is the expository purpose of the remarks made by the young girl and the stout man in their conversation with Abbie?

2. What is the function of the fiddler in relation to the illicit love affair of Abbie and Eben, and how does it relate to the general attitude toward Cabot?
3. What is ironic in Cabot's retort about Eben to the fiddler, "He kin work day and night like I kin, if need be"?
4. What do Cabot's dance and victory over the fiddler do to characterize him and symbolize the conflict between him and society?
5. How does Cabot's soliloquy at the end of Scene i prepare for subsequent action?
6. In the quarrel between Eben and Cabot, why is Eben at first self-controlled and confident?
7. How does this behavior on the part of Eben act as a motivating force on Cabot?
8. What is ironic about Eben's situation as he now conceives it to be?
9. How is the physical struggle between Cabot and Eben symbolic of their entire relationship?
10. What is the difference between the circumstances connected with Cabot's dancing after the fight and those connected with his dancing earlier in the evening?
11. What is ironic about the accusation Eben hurls at Abbie?
12. What preparation is provided by Abbie's questioning of Eben concerning his love for her and the obstacle between them?
13. What is the mood at the end of this scene and how is it achieved?
14. Why is Abbie still a sympathetic figure even after she has killed the baby?
15. What is the dramatic irony in Abbie's killing the baby?
16. What redeeming feature does Cabot exhibit in this scene?
17. How does Abbie achieve tragic stature in this closing scene?

OUR TOWN

Thornton Wilder

A Play in Three Acts

Introductory Comment

Many of the plays in this collection are centered around some "dramatic" or violent action involving physical conflict and death by suicide or murder. In *Antigone* we have civil strife brought about through the violation of a stern edict by a rebellious member of the state's ruling family; in *Lear* we have actual civil war growing out of bitter family rivalry and inordinate ambition and lust for power; in *An Enemy of the People* the conflict takes a less violent form but we still have emotional antagonisms and community upheaval resulting from a verbal attack on the town's main source of income. Like *The Cherry Orchard* and *The Glass Menagerie, Our Town* belongs to that class of play in which essentially "undramatic" events form the center of the action. Wilder, like Chekhov and Williams, is drawing his dramatic power from the commonplace, as Emerson put it, "from the pot on the hearth."

As a result of this approach, events in *Our Town* are all low-keyed and rather routine: babies are born, wives make sacrifices for their husbands, brothers and sisters tease one another at breakfast, children go to school, form attachments, grow up, get married and have their own children, people die, but life goes on in the even tenor of its ways. It is almost as though Wilder were telling us directly that life itself is dramatic in a very real sense—that everything we do and feel is unique and important because of our individuality and human mortality.

This play, then, may be considered a kind of homily in dramatic form. Through the lives of the Webbs and the Gibbs and the other citizens of "our town" Wilder is trying to get us to see our own lives more clearly—for we too are citizens of the

OUR TOWN, *A Play in Three Acts, by Thornton Wilder.*

same community—and to lead them with a greater awareness of what it means to be alive, to love, to know hope and grief, and to come to grips with our mortality and accept it as part of the human condition.

Our Town might well be considered a modern equivalent of the medieval morality play *Everyman,* in which the central figure, standing for all mankind, as his name implies, prepares himself to meet the summons of Death. In hasty, last-minute preparations for which he pleads he needs more time, he discovers, within the framework of medieval religious belief, what the really important things in life are. The only things he can take with him into the after-life, he finds, are the good deeds he has performed in this life; all else deserts him—his friends, his strength, his beauty, his intelligence, his senses. In Wilder's play we the audience are invited to witness the events on the stage and participate emotionally in them, asking ourselves as we do what the important things in life really are as we live each moment of our existence only once on our way to inevitable death. With such a dramatic purpose shaping the play, we can easily understand why the common-place and the routine are treated as though they were of the highest dramatic importance.

Cast of Characters

STAGE MANAGER
DR. GIBBS
JOE CROWELL
HOWIE NEWSOME
MRS. GIBBS
MRS. WEBB
GEORGE GIBBS
REBECCA GIBBS
WALLY WEBB
EMILY WEBB
PROFESSOR WILLARD
MR. WEBB
WOMAN IN THE BALCONY
MAN IN THE AUDITORIUM
LADY IN THE BOX
SIMON STIMSON
MRS. SOAMES
CONSTABLE WARREN
SI CROWELL
THREE BASEBALL PLAYERS
SAM CRAIG
JOE STODDARD

The entire play takes place in Grover's Corners, New Hampshire.

ACT I

[*No curtain.*

No scenery.

The audience, arriving, sees an empty stage in half-light.

Presently the STAGE MANAGER, *hat on and pipe in mouth, enters and begins placing a table and three chairs downstage left, and a table and three chairs downstage right. He also places a low bench at the corner of what will be the Webb house, left.*

"Left" and "right" are from the point of view of the actor facing the audience.

"Up" is toward the back wall.

As the house lights go down he has finished setting the stage and leaning against the right proscenium pillar watches the late arrivals in the audience.

When the auditorium is in complete darkness he speaks:]

Stage Manager: "This play is called 'Our Town.' It was written by Thornton Wilder; produced and directed by A. . . . (or: produced by A. . . . ; directed by B. . . .). In it you will see Miss C. . . . ; Miss D. . . . ; Miss E. . . . ; and Mr. F. . . . ; Mr. G. . . . ; Mr. H. . . . ; and many others. The name of the town is Grover's Corners, New Hampshire—just across the Massachusetts line: latitude 42 degrees 40 minutes; longitude 70 degrees 37 minutes. The First Act shows a day in our town. The day is May 7, 1901. The time is just before dawn." A rooster crows.

"The sky is beginning to show some

streaks of light over in the East there, behind our mount'in.

"The morning star always gets wonderful bright the minute before it has to go, —doesn't it?" He stares at it for a moment, then goes upstage.

"Well, I'd better show you how our town lies. Up here—" (That is: parallel with the back wall.) "is Main Street. Way back there is the railway station; tracks go that way. Polish Town's across the tracks, and some Canuck families."

Toward the left. "Over there is the Congregational Church; across the street's the Presbyterian.

"Methodist and Unitarian are over there.

"Baptist is down in the holla' by the river.

"Catholic Church is over beyond the tracks.

"Here's the Town Hall and Post Office combined; jail's in the basement.

"Bryan once made a speech from these very steps here.

"Along here's a row of stores. Hitching posts and horse blocks in front of them. First automobile's going to come along in about five years—belonged to Banker Cartwright, our richest citizen . . . lives in the big white house up on the hill.

"Here's the grocery store and here's Mr. Morgan's drugstore.

Most everybody in town manages to look into those two stores once a day.

"Public School's over yonder. High School's still farther over.

Quarter of nine mornings, noontimes, and three o'clock afternoons, the hull town can hear the yelling and screaming from those schoolyards."

He approaches the table and chairs downstage right.

"This is our doctor's house,—Doc Gibbs'. This is the back door." Two arched trellises, covered with vines and flowers, are pushed out, one by each proscenium pillar. "There's some scenery for those who think they have to have scenery.

"This is Mrs. Gibbs' garden. Corn . . . peas . . . beans . . . hollyhocks . . . heliotrope . . . and a lot of burdock." Crosses the stage.

"In those days our newspaper come out twice a week—the Grover's Corners *Sentinel*—and this is Editor Webb's house.

"And this is Mrs. Webb's garden.

"Just like Mrs. Gibbs', only it's got a lot of sunflowers, too."

He looks upward, center stage.

"Right here . . . 's a big butternut tree."

He returns to his place by the right proscenium pillar and looks at the audience for a minute.

"Nice town, y'know what I mean?

—"Nobody very remarkable ever come out of it, s'far as we know.

"The earliest tombstones in the cemetery up there on the mountain say 1670-1680—they're Grovers and Cartwrights and Gibbses and Herseys—same names as are around here now.

"Well, as I said: it's about dawn.

"The only lights on in town are in a cottage over by the tracks where a Polish mother's just had twins. And in the Joe Crowell house, where Joe Junior's getting up so as to deliver the paper. And in the depot, where Shorty Hawkins is gettin' ready to flag the 5:45 for Boston." A train whistle is heard. The STAGE MANAGER takes out his watch and nods.

"Naturally, out in the country—all around—there've been lights on for some time, what with milkin's and so on. But town people sleep late."

"So—another day's begun.

"There's Doc Gibbs comin' down Main Street now, comin' back from that baby case. And here's his wife comin' downstairs to get breakfast." MRS. GIBBS, a plump, pleasant woman in the middle thirties, comes "downstairs" right. She pulls up an imaginary window shade in her kitchen and starts to make a fire in her stove.

"Doc Gibbs died in 1930. The new hospital's named after him.

"Mrs. Gibbs died first—long time ago, in fact. She went out to visit her daughter, Rebecca, who married an insurance man in Canton, Ohio, and died there—pneumonia—but her body was brought back here. She's up in the cemetery there now—in with a whole mess of Gibbses and Herseys—she was Julia Hersey 'fore she married Doc Gibbs in the Congregational Church over there.

"In our town we like to know the facts about everybody.

"There's Mrs. Webb, coming downstairs to get her breakfast, too.

"—That's Doc Gibbs. Got that call at half past one this morning. And there comes Joe Crowell, Jr., delivering Mr. Webb's *Sentinel*."

Dr. Gibbs has been coming along Main Street from the left. At the point where he would turn to approach his house, he stops, sets down his—imaginary—black bag, takes off his hat, and rubs his face with fatigue, using an enormous handkerchief.

Mrs. Webb, a thin, serious, crisp woman, has entered her kitchen, left, tying on an apron. She goes through the motions of putting wood into a stove, lighting it, and preparing breakfast.

Suddenly, JOE CROWELL, JR., eleven, starts down Main Street from the right, hurling imaginary newspapers into doorways.

Joe Crowell, Jr.: "Morning, Doc Gibbs."

Dr. Gibbs: "Morning, Joe."

Joe Crowell, Jr.: "Somebody been sick, Doc?"

Dr. Gibbs: "No. Just some twins born over in Polish Town."

Joe Crowell, Jr.: "Do you want your paper now?"

Dr. Gibbs: "Yes, I'll take it.—Anything serious goin' on in the world since Wednesday?"

Joe Crowell, Jr.: "Yessir. My schoolteacher, Miss Foster, 's getting married to a fella over in Concord."

Dr. Gibbs: "I declare.—How do you boys feel about that?"

Joe Crowell, Jr.: "Well, of course, it's none of my business—but I think if a person starts out to be a teacher, she ought to stay one."

Dr. Gibbs: "How's your knee, Joe?"

Joe Crowell, Jr.: "Fine, Doc, I never think about it at all. Only like you said, it always tells me when it's going to rain."

Dr. Gibbs: "What's it telling you today? Goin' to rain?

Joe Crowell, Jr.: "No, sir."

Dr. Gibbs: "Sure?"

Joe Crowell, Jr.: "Yessir."

Dr. Gibbs: "Knee ever make a mistake?"

Joe Crowell, Jr.: "No, sir." Joe goes off. DR. GIBBS stands reading his paper.

Stage Manager: "Want to tell you something about that boy Joe Crowell there. Joe was awful bright—graduated from high school here, head of his class. So he got a scholarship to Massachusetts Tech. Graduated head of his class there, too. It was all wrote up in the Boston paper at the time. Goin' to be a great engineer, Joe was. But the war broke out and he died in France.—All that education for nothing."

Howie Newsome, off left: "Giddap, Bessie! What's the matter with you today?"

Stage Manager: "Here comes Howie Newsome, deliverin' the milk." HOWIE NEWSOME, about thirty, in overalls, comes along Main Street from the left, walking beside an invisible horse and wagon and carrying an imaginary rack with milk bottles. The sound of clinking milk bottles is heard. He leaves some bottles at Mrs. Webb's trellis, then, crossing the stage to Mrs. Gibbs', he stops center to talk to Dr. Gibbs.

Howie Newsome: "Morning, Doc."

Dr. Gibbs: "Morning, Howie."

Howie Newsome: "Somebody sick?"

Dr. Gibbs: "Pair of twins over to Mrs. Goruslawski's."

Howie Newsome: "Twins, eh? This town's gettin' bigger every year."

Dr. Gibbs: "Goin' to rain, Howie?"

Howie Newsome: "No, no. Fine day—that'll burn through. Come on, Bessie."

Dr. Gibbs: "Hello Bessie." He strokes the horse, which has remained up center. "How old is she, Howie?"

Howie Newsome: "Going on seventeen. Bessie's all mixed up about the route ever since the Lockharts stopped takin' their quart of milk every day. She wants to leave 'em a quart just the same—keeps scolding me the hull trip." He reaches Mrs. Gibbs' back door. She is waiting for him.

Mrs. Gibbs: "Good morning, Howie."

Howie Newsome: "Morning, Mrs. Gibbs. Doc's just comin' down the street."

Mrs. Gibbs: "Is he? Seems like you're late today."

Howie Newsome: "Yes, Somep'n went wrong with the separator. Don't know what 'twas." He passes Dr. Gibbs up center. "Doc!"

Dr. Gibbs: "Howie!"

Mrs. Gibbs, calling upstairs: "Children! Children! Time to get up."

Howie Newsome: "Come on, Bessie!" He goes off right.

Mrs. Gibbs: "George! Rebecca!" DR. GIBBS arrives at his back door and passes through the trellis into his house.

Mrs. Gibbs: "Everything all right, Frank?"

Dr. Gibbs: "Yes. I declare—easy as kittens."

Mrs. Gibbs: "Bacon'll be ready in a minute. Set down and drink your coffee. You can catch a couple hours' sleep this morning, can't you?"

Dr. Gibbs: "Hm! . . . Mrs. Wentworth's coming at eleven. Guess I know what it's about, too. Her stummick ain't what it ought to be."

Mrs. Gibbs: "All told, you won't get more'n three hours' sleep. Frank Gibbs, I don't know what's goin' to become of you. I do wish I could get you to go away someplace and take a rest. I think it would do you good."

Mrs. Webb: "Emileeee! Time to get up! Wally! Seven o'clock!"

Mrs. Gibbs: "I declare, you got to speak to George. Seems like something's come over him lately. He's no help to me at all. I can't even get him to cut me some wood."

Dr. Gibbs, washing and drying his hands at the sink. MRS. GIBBS is busy at the stove: "Is he sassy to you?"

Mrs. Gibbs: "No. He just whines! All he thinks about is that baseball—George! Rebecca! You'll be late for school."

Dr. Gibbs: "M-m-m . . ."

Mrs. Gibbs: "George!"

Dr. Gibbs: "George, look sharp!"

George's Voice: "Yes, Pa!"

Dr. Gibbs, as he goes off the stage: "Don't you hear your mother calling you? I guess I'll go upstairs and get forty winks."

Mrs. Webb: "Walleee! Emileee! You'll be late for school! Walleee! You wash yourself good or I'll come up and do it myself."

Rebecca Gibbs' Voice: "Ma! What dress shall I wear?"

Mrs. Gibbs: "Don't make a noise. Your father's been out all night and needs his sleep. I washed and ironed the blue gingham for you special."

Rebecca: "Ma, I hate that dress."

Mrs. Gibbs: "Oh, hush-up-with-you."

Rebecca: "Every day I go to school dressed like a sick turkey."

Mrs. Gibbs: "Now, Rebecca, you always look *very* nice."

Rebecca: "Mama, George's throwing soap at me."

Mrs. Gibbs: "I'll come and slap the both of you,—that's what I'll do." A factory whistle sounds. The CHILDREN dash in and take their places at the tables. Right, GEORGE, about sixteen, and REBECCA, eleven. Left, EMILY and WALLY, same ages. They carry strapped schoolbooks.

Stage Manager: "We've got a factory in our town too—hear it? Makes blankets. Cartwrights own it and it brung 'em a fortune."

Mrs. Webb: "Children! Now I won't have it. Breakfast is just as good as any other meal and I won't have you gobbling like wolves. It'll stunt your growth,—that's a fact. Put away your book, Wally."

Wally: "Aw, Ma! By ten o'clock I got to know all about Canada."

Mrs. Webb: "You know the rule's well as I do—no books at table. As for me, I'd rather have my children healthy than bright."

Emily: "I'm both, Mama: you know I am. I'm the brightest girl in school for my age. I have a wonderful memory."

Mrs. Webb: "Eat your breakfast."

Wally: "I'm bright, too, when I'm looking at my stamp collection."

Mrs. Gibbs: "I'll speak to your father about it when he's rested. Seems to me twenty-five cents a week's enough for a boy your age. I declare I don't know how you spend it all."

George: "Aw, Ma,—I gotta lotta things to buy."

Mrs. Gibbs: "Strawberry phosphates—that's what you spend it on."

George: "I don't see how Rebecca comes to have so much money. She has more'n a dollar."

Rebecca, spoon in mouth, dreamily: "I've been saving it up gradual."

Mrs. Gibbs: "Well, dear, I think it's a good thing to spend some every now and then."

Rebecca: "Mama, do you know what I love most in the world—do you?—Money."

Mrs. Gibbs: "Eat your breakfast."

The Children: "Mama, there's first bell.—I gotta hurry.—I don't want any more.—I gotta hurry." The CHILDREN rise, seize their books and dash out through the trellises. They meet, down center, and chattering, walk to Main Street, then turn left. The STAGE MANAGER goes off, unobtrusively, right.

Mrs. Webb: "Walk fast, but you don't have to run. Wally, pull up your pants at the knee. Stand up straight, Emily."

Mrs. Gibbs: "Tell Miss Foster I send her my best congratulations—can you remember that?"

Rebecca: "Yes, Ma."

Mrs. Gibbs: "You look real nice, Rebecca. Pick up your feet."

All: "Good-by." MRS. GIBBS fills her apron with food for the chickens and comes down to the footlights.

Mrs. Gibbs: "Here, chick, chick, chick.

"No, go away, you. Go away.

"Here, chick, chick, chick.

"What's the matter with *you*? Fight, fight, fight,—that's all you do. Hm . . . *you* don't belong to me. Where'd you come from?" She shakes her apron.

"Oh, don't be so scared. Nobody's going to hurt you." MRS. WEBB is sitting on the bench by her trellis, stringing beans.

"Good Morning, Myrtle. How's your cold?"

Mrs. Webb: "Well, I still get that tickling feeling in my throat. I told Charles I didn't know as I'd go to choir practice tonight. Wouldn't be any use."

Mrs. Webb: "Have you tried singing over your voice?"

Mrs. Webb: "Yes, but somehow I can't do that and stay on the key. While I'm resting myself I thought I'd string some of these beans."

Mrs. Gibbs, rolling up her sleeves as she crosses the stage for a chat: "Let me help you. Beans have been good this year."

Mrs. Webb: "I've decided to put up forty quarts if it kills me. The children say they hate 'em, but I notice they're able to get 'em down all winter." Pause. Brief sound of chickens cackling.

Mrs. Gibbs: "Now, Myrtle. I've got to tell you something, because if I don't tell somebody I'll burst."

Mrs. Webb: "Why, Julia Gibbs!"

Mrs. Gibbs: "Here, give me some more of those beans. Myrtle, did one of those secondhand-furniture men from Boston come to see you last Friday?"

Mrs. Webb: "No-o."

Mrs. Gibbs: "Well, he called on me. First I thought he was a patient wantin' to see Dr. Gibbs. 'N he wormed his way into my parlor, and, Myrtle Webb, he offered me three hundred and fifty dollars for Grandmother Wentworth's highboy, as I'm sitting here!"

Mrs. Webb: "Why, Julia Gibbs!"

Mrs. Gibbs: "He did! That old thing! Why, it was so big I didn't know where to put it and I almost give it to Cousin Hester Wilcox."

Mrs. Webb: "Well, you're going to take it, aren't you?"

Mrs. Gibbs: "I don't know."

Mrs. Webb: "You don't know—three hundred and fifty dollars! What's come over you?"

Mrs. Gibbs: "Well, if I could get the Doctor to take the money and go away someplace on a real trip, I'd sell it like that.—Y'know, Myrtle, it's been the dream of my life to see Paris, France.—Oh, I don't know. It sounds crazy, I suppose, but for years I've been promising myself that if we ever had the chance—"

Mrs. Webb: "How does the Doctor feel about it?"

Mrs. Gibbs: Well, I did beat about the bush a little and said that if I got a legacy—that's the way I put it—I'd make him take me somewhere."

Mrs. Webb: "M-m-m . . . What did he say?"

Mrs. Gibbs: "You know how he is. I haven't heard a serious word out of him since I've known him. No, he said, it might make him discontented with Grover's Corners to go traipsin' about Europe; better let well enough alone, he says. Every two years he makes a trip to the battlefields of the Civil War and that's enough treat for anybody, he says."

Mrs. Webb: "Well, Mr. Webb just

admires the way Dr. Gibbs knows everything about the Civil War. Mr. Webb's a good mind to give up Napoleon and move over to the Civil War, only Dr. Gibbs being one of the greatest experts in the country just makes him despair."

Mrs. Gibbs: "It's a fact! Dr. Gibbs is never so happy as when he's at Antietam or Gettysburg. The times I've walked over those hills, Myrtle, stopping at every bush and pacing it all out, like we were going to buy it."

Mrs. Webb: "Well, if that secondhand man's really serious about buyin' it, Julia, you sell it. And then you'll get to see Paris, all right. Just keep droppin' hints from time to time—that's how I got to see the Atlantic Ocean, y'know."

Mrs. Gibbs: "Oh, I'm sorry I mentioned it. Only it seems to me that once in your life before you die you ought to see a country where they don't talk in English and don't even want to." The STAGE MANAGER enters briskly from the right. He tips his hat to the ladies, who nod their heads.

Stage Manager: "Thank you, ladies. Thank you very much."

MRS. GIBBS and MRS. WEBB gather up their things, return into their homes and disappear.

"Now, we're going to skip a few hours.

"But first we want a little more information about the town, kind of a scientific account, you might say.

"So I've asked Professor Willard of our State University to sketch in a few details of our past history here.

"Is Professor Willard here?" PROFESSOR WILLARD, a rural savant, pince-nez on a wide satin ribbon, enters from the right with some notes in his hand.

"May I introduce Professor Willard of our State University. A few brief notes, thank you, Professor,—unfortunately our time is limited."

Professor Willard: "Grover's Corners . . . let me see . . . Grover's Corners lies on the old Pleistocene granite of the Appalachian range. I may say it's some of the oldest land in the world. We're very proud of that. A shelf of Devonian basalt crosses it with vestiges of Mesozoic shale, and some sandstone outcroppings; but that's all more recent: two hundred, three hundred million years old.

"Some highly interesting fossils have been found . . . I may say: unique fossils . . . two miles out of town, in Silas Peckham's cow pasture. They can be seen at the museum in our University at any time—that is, at any reasonable time. Shall I read some of Professor Gruber's notes on the meteorological situation—mean precipitation, et cetera?"

Stage Manager: "Afraid we won't have time for that, Professor. We might have a few words on the history of man here."

Professor Willard: "Yes . . . anthropological data: Early Amerindian stock. Cotahatchee tribes . . . no evidence before the tenth century of this era . . . hm . . . now entirely disappeared . . . possible traces in three families. Migration toward the end of the seventeenth century of English brachiocephalic blue-eyed stock . . . for the most part. Since then some Slav and Mediterranean—"

Stage Manager: "And the population, Professor Willard?"

Professor Willard: "Within the town limits: 2,640."

Stage Manager: "Just a moment, Professor." He whispers into the professor's ear.

Professor Willard: "Oh, yes, indeed? —The population, *at the moment,* is 2,642. The Postal District brings in 507 more, making a total of 3,149.—Mortality and birth rates: constant.—By MacPherson's gauge: 6.032."

Stage Manager: "Thank you very much, Professor. We're all very much obliged to you, I'm sure."

Professor Willard: "Not at all, sir; not at all."

Stage Manager: "This way, Professor, and thank you again." Exit PROFESSOR WILLARD. "Now the political and social report: Editor Webb.—Oh, Mr. Webb?" MRS. WEBB appears at her back door.

Mrs. Webb: "He'll be here in a minute. . . . He just cut his hand while he was eatin' an apple."

Stage Manager: "Thank you, Mrs. Webb.

Mrs. Webb: "Charles! Everybody's waitin'." Exit MRS. WEBB.

Stage Manager: "Mr. Webb is Publisher and Editor of the Grover's Corners *Sentinel.* That's our local paper, y'know." MR. WEBB enters from his house, pulling on his coat. His finger is bound in a handkerchief.

Mr. Webb: "Well . . . I don't have to tell you that we're run here by a Board of Selectmen.—All males vote at the age of twenty-one. Women vote indirect. We're lower middle class: sprinkling of professional men . . . ten per cent illiterate laborers. Politically, we're eighty-six per cent Republicans; six per cent Democrats; four per cent Socialists; rest, indifferent.

"Religiously, we're eighty-five per cent Protestants; twelve per cent Catholics; rest, indifferent."

Stage Manager: "Have you any comments, Mr. Webb?"

Mr. Webb: "Very ordinary town, if you ask me. Little better behaved than most. Probably a lot duller.

"But our young people here seem to like it well enough. Ninety per cent of 'em graduating from high school settle down right here to live—even when they've been away to college."

Stage Manager: "Now, is there anyone in the audience who would like to ask Editor Webb anything about the town?"

Woman in the Balcony: "Is there much drinking in Grover's Corners?"

Mr. Webb: "Well, ma'am, I wouldn't know what you'd call *much.* Satiddy nights the farmhands meet down in Ellery Greenough's stable and holler some. We've got one or two town drunks, but they're always having remorses every time an evangelist comes to town. No, ma'am, I'd say likker ain't a regular thing in the home here, except in the medicine chest. Right good for snake bite, y'know—always was."

Belligerent Man at Back of Auditorium: "Is there no one in town aware of—"

Stage Manager: "Come forward, will you, where we can all hear you—What were you saying?"

Belligerent Man: "Is there no one in town aware of social injustice and industrial inequality?"

Mr. Webb: "Oh, yes, everybody is—somethin' terrible. Seems like they spend most of their time talking about who's rich and who's poor."

Belligerent Man: "Then why don't they do something about it?" He withdraws without waiting for an answer.

Mr. Webb: "Well, I dunno. . . . I guesss we're all hunting like everybody else for a way the diligent and sensible can rise to the top and the lazy and quarrelsome can sink to the bottom. But it ain't easy to find. Meanwhile, we do all we can to help those that can't help themselves and those that can we leave alone. —Are there any other questions?"

Lady in a Box: "Oh, Mr. Webb? Mr. Webb, is there any culture or love of beauty in Grover's Corners?"

Mr. Webb: "Well, ma'am, there ain't much—not in the sense you mean. Come to think of it, there's some girls that play the piano at High School Commencement; but they ain't happy about it. No, ma'am, there isn't much culture; but maybe this is the place to tell you that we've got a lot of pleasures of a kind here: we like the sun comin' up over the mountain in the morning, and we all notice a good deal about the birds. We pay a lot of attention to them. And we watch the change of the seasons; yes, everybody knows about them. But those other things—you're right, ma'am,—there ain't much.—*Robinson Crusoe* and the Bible; and Handel's 'Largo,' we all know that; and Whistler's 'Mother'—those are just about as far as we go."

Lady in a Box: "So I thought. Thank you, Mr. Webb."

Stage Manager: "Thank you, Mr. Webb." MR. WEBB retires. "Now, we'll go back to the town. It's early afternoon. All 2,642 have had their dinners and all the dishes have been washed." MR. WEBB, having removed his coat, returns and starts pushing a lawn mower to and fro beside his house. "There's an early-afternoon calm in our town: a buzzin' and a hummin' from the school buildings; only a few buggies on Main Street—the horses dozing at the hitching posts; you all remember what it's like. Doc Gibbs is in his office, tapping people and making them say 'ah.' Mr. Webb's cuttin' his lawn over there; one man in ten thinks it's a privilege to push his own lawn mover.

"No, sir. It's later than I thought. There are the children coming home from school already." Shrill girls' voices are heard, off left. EMILY comes along Main Street, carrying some books. There are some signs that she is imagining herself to be a lady of startling elegance.

Emily: "I *can't,* Lois. I've got to go home and help my mother. I *promised.*"

Mr. Webb: "Emily, walk simply. Who do you think you are today?"

Emily: "Papa, you're terrible. One minute you tell me to stand up straight and the next minute you call me names. I just don't listen to you." She gives him an abrupt kiss.

Mr. Webb: "Golly, I never got a kiss from such a great lady before." He goes out of sight. EMILY leans over and picks some flowers by the gate of her house. GEORGE GIBBS comes careening down Main Street. He is throwing a ball up to dizzying heights, and waiting to catch it again. This sometimes requires his taking six steps backward. He bumps into an OLD LADY invisible to us.

George: "Excuse me, Mrs. Forrest."

Stage Manager, as Mrs. Forrest: "Go out and play in the fields, young man. You got no business playing baseball on Main Street."

George: "Awfully sorry, Mrs. Forrest. —Hello, Emily."

Emily: "H'lo."

George: "You made a fine speech in class."

Emily: "Well . . . I was really ready to make a speech about the Monroe Doctrine, but at the last minute Miss Corcoran made me talk about the Louisiana Purchase instead. I worked an awful long time on both of them."

George: "Gee, it's funny, Emily. From my window up there I can just see your head nights when you're doing your homework over in your room."

Emily: "Why, can you?"

George: "You certainly do stick to it, Emily. I don't see how you can sit still that long. I guess you like school."

Emily: "Well, I always feel it's something you have to go through."

George: "Yeah."

Emily: "I don't mind it really. It passes the time."

George: "Yeah.—Emily, what do you think? We might work out a kinda telegraph from your window to mine; and once in a while you could give me a kinda hint or two about one of those algebra problems. I don't mean the answers, Emily, of course not . . . just some little hint . . ."

Emily: "Oh, I think hints are allowed.—So—ah—if you get stuck, George, you whistle to me; and I'll give you some hints."

George: "Emily, you're just naturally bright, I guess."

Emily: "I figure that it's just the way a person's born."

George: "Yeah. But, you see, I want to be a farmer, and my Uncle Luke says whenever I'm ready I can come over and work on his farm and if I'm good I can just gradually have it."

Emily: "You mean the house and everything?" Enter MRS. WEBB with a large bowl and sits on the bench by her trellis.

George: "Yeah. Well, thanks . . . I better be getting out to the baseball field. Thanks for the talk, Emily.—Good afternoon, Mrs. Webb."

Mrs. Webb: "Good afternoon, George."

George: "So long, Emily."

Emily: "So long, George."

Mrs. Webb: "Emily, come and help me string these beans for the winter. George Gibbs let himself have a real conversation, didn't he? Why, he's growing up. How old would George be?"

Emily: "I don't know."

Mrs. Webb: "Let's see. He must be almost sixteen."

Emily: "Mama, I made a speech in class today and I was very good."

Mrs. Webb: "You must recite it to your father at supper. What was it about?"

Emily: "The Louisiana Purchase. It was like silk off a spool. I'm going to make speeches all my life.—Mama, are these big enough?"

Mrs. Webb: "Try and get them a little bigger if you can."

Emily: "Mama, will you answer me a question, serious?"

Mrs. Webb: "Seriously, dear—not serious."

Emily: "Seriously, will you?"

Mrs. Webb: "Of course, I will."

Emily: "Mama, am I good looking?"

Mrs. Webb: "Yes, of course you are. All my children have got good features; I'd be ashamed if they hadn't."

Emily: "Oh, Mama, that's not what I mean. What I mean is: am I *pretty?*"

Mrs. Webb: "I've already told you, yes. Now that's enough of that. You have a nice young pretty face. I never heard of such foolishness."

Emily: "Oh, Mama, you never tell us the truth about anything."

Mrs. Webb: "I *am* telling you the truth."

Emily: "Mama, were *you* pretty?"

Mrs. Webb: "Yes, I was, if I do say it. I was the prettiest girl in town next to Mamie Cartwright."

Emily: "But, Mama, you've got to say *some*thing about me. Am I pretty enough . . . to get anybody . . . to get people interested in me?"

Mrs. Webb: "Emily, you make me tired. Now stop it. You're pretty enough for all normal purposes.—Come along now and bring that bowl with you."

Emily: "Oh, Mama, you're no help at all."

Stage Manager: "Thank you. Thank you! That'll do. We'll have to interrupt again here. Thank you, Mrs. Webb; thank you, Emily." MRS. WEBB and EMILY withdraw. "There are some more things we want to explore about this town." He comes to the center of the stage. During the following speech the lights gradually dim to darkness, leaving only a spot on him. "I think this is a good time to tell you that the Cartwright interests have just begun building a new bank in Grover's Corners—had to go to Vermont for the marble, sorry to say. And they've asked a friend of mine what they should put in the cornerstone for people to dig up . . . a thousand years from now. . . . Of course, they've put in a copy of the *New York Times* and a copy of Mr. Webb's *Sentinel*. . . . We're kind of interested in this because some scientific fellas have found a way of painting all that reading matter with a glue—a silicate glue—that'll make it keep a thousand—two thousand years.

"We're putting in a Bible . . . and the Constitution of the United States—and a copy of William Shakespeare's plays. What do you say, folks? What do you think?

"Y'know—Babylon once had two million people in it, and all we know about 'em is the names of the kings and some copies of wheat contracts . . . and contracts for the sale of slaves. Yet every night all those families sat down to supper, and the father came home from his work, and the smoke went up the chimney,—same as here. And even in Greece and Rome, all we know about the *real* life of the people is what we can piece together out of the joking poems and the comedies they wrote for the theatre back then.

"So I'm going to have a copy of this play put in the cornerstone and the people a thousand years from now'll know a few simple facts about us—more than the Treaty of Versailles and the Lindbergh flight.

"See what I mean?

"So—people a thousand years from now—this is the way we were in the provinces north of New York at the beginning of the twentieth century.—This is the way we were: in our growing up and in our marrying and in our living and in our dying." A choir partially concealed in the orchestra pit has begun singing "Blessed Be the Tie That Binds." SIMON STIMSON stands directing them. Two ladders have been pushed onto the stage; they serve as indication of the second story in the Gibbs and Webb houses. GEORGE and EMILY mount them, and apply themselves to their schoolwork. DR. GIBBS has entered and is seated in his kitchen reading.

"Well!—good deal of time's gone by. It's evening.

"You can hear choir practice going on in the Congregational Church.

"The children are at home doing their schoolwork.

"The day's running down like a tired clock."

Simon Stimson: "Now look here, everybody. Music come into the world to give pleasure.—Softer! Softer! Get it out of your heads that music's only good when it's loud. You leave loudness to the Methodists. You couldn't beat 'em, even if you wanted to. Now again. Tenors!"

George: "Hssst! Emily!"

Emily: "Hello."

George: "Hello!"

Emily: "I can't work at all. The moonlight's so *terrible*."

George: "Emily, did you get the third problem?"

Emily: "Which?"

George: "The *third*?"

Emily: "Why, yes, George—that's the easiest of them all."

George: "I don't see it. Emily, can you give me a hint?"

Emily: "I'll tell you one thing: the answer's in yards."

George: "! ! ! In yards? How do you mean?"

Emily: "In *square* yards."

George: "Oh . . . in square yards."

Emily: "Yes, George, don't you see?"

George: "Yeah."

Emily: "In square yards of *wallpaper*."

George: "Wallpaper,—oh, I see. Thanks a lot, Emily."

Emily: "You're welcome. My, isn't the moonlight *terrible*? And choir practice going on.—I think if you hold your breath you can hear the train all the way to Contoocook. Hear it?"

George: "M-m-m—What do you know!"

Emily: "Well, I guess I better go back and try to work."

George: "Good night, Emily. And thanks."

Emily: "Good night, George."

Simon Stimson: "Before I forget it: how many of you will be able to come in Tuesday afternoon and sing at Fred Hersey's wedding?—show your hands. That'll be fine; that'll be right nice. We'll do the same music we did for Jane Trowbridge's last month.

"—Now we'll do: 'Art Thou Weary; Art Thou Languid?' It's a question, ladies and gentlemen, make it talk. Ready."

Dr. Gibbs: "Oh, George, can you come down a minute?"

George: "Yes, Pa." He descends the ladder.

Dr. Gibbs: "Make yourself comfortable, George; I'll only keep you a minute. George, how old are you?"

George: "I? I'm sixteen, almost seventeen."

Dr. Gibbs: "What do you want to do after school's over?"

George: "Why, you know, Pa. I want to be a farmer on Uncle Luke's farm."

Dr. Gibbs: "You'll be willing, will you, to get up early and milk and feed the stock . . . and you'll be able to hoe and hay all day?"

George: "Sure, I will. What are you . . . what do you mean, Pa?"

Dr. Gibbs: "Well, George, while I was in my office today I heard a funny sound . . . and what do you think it was? It was your mother chopping wood. There you see your mother—getting up early; cooking meals all day long; washing and ironing;—and still she has to go out in the back yard and chop wood. I suppose she just got tired of asking you. She just gave up and decided it was easier to do it herself. And you eat her meals, and put on the clothes she keeps nice for you, and you run off and play baseball,—like she's some hired girl we keep around the house but that we don't like very much. Well, I knew all I had to do was call your attention to it. Here's a handkerchief, son. George, I've decided to raise your spending money twenty-five cents a week. Not, of course, for chopping wood for your mother, because that's a present you give her, but because you're getting older—and I imagine there are lots of things you must find to do with it."

George: "Thanks, Pa."

Dr. Gibbs: "Let's see—tomorrow's your payday. You can count on it—Hmm. Probably Rebecca'll feel she ought to have some more too. Wonder what could have happened to your mother. Choir practice never was as late as this before."

George: "It's only half past eight, Pa."

Dr. Gibbs: "I don't know why she's in that old choir. She hasn't any more voice than an old crow. . . . Traipsin' around the streets at this hour of the night . . . just about time you retired, don't you think?"

George: "Yes, Pa." GEORGE mounts to his place on the ladder. Laughter and good nights can be heard on stage left and presently MRS. GIBBS, MRS. SOAMES and MRS. WEBB come down Main Street. When they arrive at the corner of the stage they stop.

Mrs. Soames: "Good night, Martha. Good night, Mr. Foster."

Mrs. Webb: "I'll tell Mr. Webb; I *know* he'll want to put it in the paper."

Mrs. Gibbs: "My, it's late!"

Mrs. Soames: "Good night, Irma."

Mrs. Gibbs: "Real nice choir practice, wa'n't it? Myrtle Webb! Look at that moon, will you? Tsk-tsk-tsk. Potato weather, for sure." They are silent a moment, gazing up at the moon.

Mrs. Soames: "Naturally, I didn't want to say a word about it in front of those others, but now we're alone—really, it's the worst scandal that ever was in this town!"

Mrs. Gibbs: "What?"

Mrs. Soames: "Simon Stimson!"

Mrs. Gibbs: "Now, Louella!"

Mrs. Soames: "But, Julia! To have the organist of a church *drink* and *drunk* year after year. You know he was drunk tonight."

Mrs. Gibbs: "Now, Louella! We all know about Mr. Stimson, and we all know about the troubles he's been through, and Dr. Ferguson knows too, and if Dr. Ferguson keeps him on there in his job the only thing the rest of us can do is just not to notice it."

Mrs. Soames: *"Not to notice it!* But it's getting worse."

Mrs. Webb: "No, it isn't, Louella. It's getting better. I've been in that choir twice as long as you have. It doesn't happen anywhere near so often. . . . My, I hate to go to bed on a night like this.—I better hurry. Those children'll be sitting up till all hours. Good night, Louella." They all exchange good nights. She hurries downstage, enters her house and disappears.

Mrs. Gibbs: "Can you get home safe, Louella?"

Mrs. Soames: "It's as bright as day. I can see Mr. Soames scowling at the window now. You'd think we'd been to a dance the way the menfolk carry on." More good nights. MRS. GIBBS arrives at her home and passes through the trellis into the kitchen.

Mrs. Gibbs: "Well, we had a real good time."

Dr. Gibbs: "You're late enough."

Mrs. Gibbs: "Why, Frank, it ain't any later 'n usual."

Dr. Gibbs: "And you stopping at the corner to gossip with a lot of hens."

Mrs. Gibbs: "Now, Frank, don't be grouchy. Come out and smell the heliotrope in the moonlight." They stroll out arm in arm along the footlights. "Isn't that wonderful? What did you do all the time I was away?"

Dr. Gibbs: "Oh, I read—as usual. What were the girls gossiping about tonight?"

Mrs. Gibbs: "Well, believe me, Frank—there is something to gossip about."

Dr. Gibbs: "Hmm! Simon Stimson far gone, was he?"

Mrs. Gibbs: "Worst I've ever seen him. How'll that end, Frank? Dr. Ferguson can't forgive him forever."

Dr. Gibbs: "I guess I know more

about Simon Stimson's affairs than anybody in this town. Some people ain't made for smalltown life. I don't know how that'll end; but there's nothing we can do but just leave it alone. Come, get in."

Mrs. Gibbs: "No, not yet . . . Frank, I'm worried about you."

Dr. Gibbs: "What are you worried about?"

Mrs. Gibbs: "I think it's my duty to make plans for you to get a real rest and change. And if I get that legacy, well, I'm going to insist on it."

Dr. Gibbs: "Now, Julia, there's no sense in going over that again."

Mrs. Gibbs: "Frank, you're just *unreasonable*!"

Dr. Gibbs, starting into the house: "Come on, Julia, it's getting late. First thing you know you'll catch cold. I gave George a piece of my mind tonight. I reckon you'll have your wood chopped for a while anyway. No, no, start getting upstairs."

Mrs. Gibbs: "Oh, dear. There's always so many things to pick up, seems like. You know, Frank, Mrs. Fairchild always locks her front door every night. All those people up that part of town do."

Dr. Gibbs, blowing out the lamp: "They're all getting citified, that's the trouble with them. They haven't got nothing fit to burgle and everybody knows it." They disappear. REBECCA climbs up the ladder beside GEORGE.

George: "Get out, Rebecca. There's only room for one at this window. You're always spoiling everything."

Rebecca: "Well, let me look just a minute."

George: "Use your own window."

Rebecca: "I did, but there's no moon there. . . . George, do you know what I think, do you? I think maybe the moon's getting nearer and nearer and there'll be a big 'splosion."

George: "Rebecca, you don't know anything. If the moon were getting nearer, the guys that sit up all night with telescopes would see it first and they'd tell about it, and it'd be in all the newspapers."

Rebecca: "George, is the moon shining on South America, Canada and half the whole world?"

George: "Well—prob'ly is." The STAGE MANAGER strolls on. Pause. The sound of crickets is heard.

Stage Manager: "Nine thirty. Most of the lights are out. No, there's Constable Warren trying a few doors on Main Street. And here comes Editor Webb, after putting his newspaper to bed." MR. WARREN, an elderly policeman, comes along Main Street from the right, MR. WEBB from the left.

Mr. Webb: "Good evening, Bill."

Constable Warren: "Evenin', Mr. Webb."

Mr. Webb: "Quite a moon!"

Constable Warren: "Yepp."

Mr. Webb: "All quiet tonight?"

Constable Warren: "Simon Stimson is rollin' around a little. Just saw his wife movin' out to hunt for him so I looked the other way—there he is now." SIMON STIMSON comes down Main Street from the left, only a trace of unsteadiness in his walk.

Mr. Webb: "Good evening, Simon . . . Town seems to have settled down for the night pretty well. . . ." SIMON STIMSON comes up to him and pauses a moment and stares at him, swaying slightly. "Good evening . . . Yes, most of the town's settled down for the night,

Simon. . . . I guess we better do the same. Can I walk along a ways with you?" SIMON STIMSON continues on his way without a word and disappears at the right. "Good night."

Constable Warren: "I don't know how that's goin' to end, Mr. Webb."

Mr. Webb: "Well, he's seen a peck of trouble, one thing after another. . . . Oh, Bill . . . if you see my boy smoking cigarettes, just give him a word, will you? He thinks a lot of you, Bill."

Constable Warren: "I don't think he smokes no cigarettes, Mr. Webb. Leastways, not more'n two or three a year."

Mr. Webb: "Hm . . . I hope not.—Well, good night, Bill."

Constable Warren: "Good night, Mr. Webb." Exit.

Mr. Webb: "Who's that up there? Is that you, Myrtle?"

Emily: "No, it's me, Papa."

Mr. Webb: "Why aren't you in bed?"

Emily: "I don't know. I just can't sleep yet, Papa. The moonlight's so *wonderful.* And the smell of Mrs. Gibbs' heliotrope. Can you smell it?"

Mr. Webb: "Hm . . . Yes. Haven't any troubles on your mind, have you, Emily?"

Emily: *"Troubles,* Papa? *No."*

Mr. Webb: "Well, enjoy yourself, but don't let your mother catch you. Good night, Emily."

Emily: "Good night, Papa." MR. WEBB crosses into the house, whistling 'Blessed Be the Tie That Binds' and disappears.

Rebecca: "I never told you about that letter Jane Crofut got from her minister when she was sick. He wrote Jane a letter and on the envelope the address was like this: It said: Jane Crofut; The Crofut Farm; Grover's Corners; Sutton County; New Hampshire; United States of America."

George: "What's funny about that?"

Rebecca: "But listen, it's not finished: the United States of America; Continent of North America; Western Hemisphere; the Earth; the Solar System; the Universe; the Mind of God—that's what it said on the envelope."

George: "What do you know!"

Rebecca: "And the postman brought it just the same."

George: "What do you know!"

Stage Manager: "That's the end of the First Act, friends. You can go and smoke now, those that smoke."

ACT II

[*The tables and chairs of the two kitchens are still on the stage.*

The ladders and the small bench have been withdrawn.

The STAGE MANAGER *has been at his accustomed place watching the audience return to its seats.*]

Stage Manager: "Three years have gone by.

"Yes, the sun's come up over a thousand times.

"Summers and winters have cracked the mountains a little bit more and the rains have brought down some of the dirt.

"Some babies that weren't even born before have begun talking regular sentences already; and a number of people who thought they were right young and spry have noticed that they can't bound up a flight of stairs like they used to, without their heart fluttering a little.

"All that can happen in a thousand days.

"Nature's been pushing and contriving in other ways, too; a number of young people fell in love and got married.

"Yes, the mountain got bit away a few fractions of an inch; millions of gallons of water went by the mill; and here and there a new home was set up under a roof.

"Almost everybody in the world gets married,—you know what I mean? In our town there aren't hardly any exceptions. Most everybody in the world climbs into their graves married.

"The First Act was called the Daily Life. This act is called Love and Marriage. There's another act coming after this: I reckon you can guess what that's about.

"So:

"It's three years later. It's 1904.

"It's July 7th, just after High School Commencement.

"That's the time most of our young people jump up and get married.

"Soon as they've passed their last examinations in solid geometry and Cicero's Orations, looks like they suddenly feel themselves fit to be married.

"It's early morning. Only this time it's been raining. It's been pouring and thundering.

"Mrs. Gibbs' garden, and Mrs. Webb's here: drenched.

"All those bean poles and pea vines: drenched.

"All yesterday over there on Main Street, the rain looked like curtains being blown along.

"Hm . . . it may begin again any minute.

"There! You can hear the 5:45 for Boston." MRS. GIBBS and MRS. WEBB enter their kitchen and start the day as in the First Act. "And there's Mrs. Gibbs and Mrs. Webb come down to make breakfast, just as though it were an ordinary day. I don't have to point out to the women in my audience that those ladies they see before them, both of those ladies cooked three meals a day—one of 'em for twenty years, the other for forty —and no summer vacation. They brought up two children apiece, washed, cleaned the house,—and *never a nervous breakdown.*

"It's like what one of those Middle West poets said: You've got to love life to have life, and you've got to have life to love life. . . .

"It's what they call a vicious circle."

Howie Newsome, off stage left: "Giddap, Bessie!"

Stage Manager: "Here comes Howie Newsome delivering the milk. And there's Si Crowell delivering the papers like his brother before him." SI CROWELL has entered hurling imaginary newspapers into doorways; HOWIE NEWSOME has come along Main Street with Bessie.

Si Crowell: "Morning, Howie."

Howie Newsome: "Morning, Si.—Anything in the papers I ought to know?"

Si Crowell: "Nothing much, except we're losing about the best baseball pitcher Grover's Corners ever had—George Gibbs."

Howie Newsome: "Reckon he is."

Si Crowell: "He could hit and run bases, too."

Howie Newsome: "Yep. Mighty fine ball player.—Whoa! Bessie! I guess I can stop and talk if I've a mind to!"

Si Crowell: "I don't see how he could give up a thing like that just to get marrried. Would you, Howie?"

Howie Newsome: "Can't tell, Si. Never had no talent that way." CONSTABLE WARREN enters. They exchange good mornings. "You're up early, Bill."

Constable Warren: "Seein' if there's anything I can do to prevent a flood. River's been risin' all night."

Howie Newsome: "Si Crowell's all worked up here about George Gibbs' retiring from baseball."

Constable Warren: "Yes, sir; that's the way it goes. Back in '84 we had a player, Si—even George Gibbs couldn't touch him. Name of Hank Todd. Went down to Maine and became a parson. Wonderful ball player.—Howie, how does the weather look to you?"

Howie Newsome: "Oh, 'tain't bad. Think maybe it'll clear up for good." CONSTABLE WARREN and SI CROWELL continue on their way. HOWIE NEWSOME brings the milk first to MRS. GIBBS' house. She meets him by the trellis.

Mrs. Gibbs: "Good morning, Howie. Do you think it's going to rain again?"

Howie Newsome: "Morning, Mrs. Gibbs. It rained so heavy, I think maybe it'll clear up."

Mrs. Gibbs: "Certainly hope it will."

Howie Newsome: "How much did you want today?"

Mrs. Gibbs: "I'm going to have a houseful of relations, Howie. Looks to me like I'll need three-a-milk and two-a-cream."

Howie Newsome: "My wife says to tell you we both hope they'll be very happy, Mrs. Gibbs. Know they *will*."

Mrs. Gibbs: "Thanks a lot, Howie. Tell your wife I hope she gits there to the wedding."

Howie Newsome: "Yes, she'll be there; she'll be there if she kin." HOWIE NEWSOME *crosses to* MRS. WEBB'S house. "Morning, Mrs. Webb."

Mrs. Webb: "Oh, good morning, Mr. Newsome. I told you four quarts of milk, but I hope you can spare me another."

Howie Newsome: "Yes'm . . . and the two of cream."

Mrs. Webb: "Will it start raining again, Mr. Newsome?"

Howie Newsome: "Well. Just sayin' to Mrs. Gibbs as how it may lighten up. Mrs. Newsome told me to tell you as how we hope they'll both be very happy, Mrs. Webb. Know they *will*."

Mrs. Webb: "Thank you, and thank Mrs. Newsome and we're counting on seeing you at the wedding."

Howie Newsome: "Yes, Mrs. Webb. We hope to git there. Couldn't miss that. Come on, Bessie." Exit HOWIE NEWSOME. DR. GIBBS descends in shirt sleeves, and sits down at his breakfast table.

Dr. Gibbs: "Well, Ma, the day has come. You're losin' one of your chicks."

Mrs. Gibbs: "Frank Gibbs, don't you say another word. I feel like crying every minute. Sit down and drink your coffee."

Dr. Gibbs: "The groom's up shaving himself—only there ain't an awful lot to shave. Whistling and singing, like he's glad to leave us.—Every now and then he says 'I do' to the mirror, but it don't sound convincing to me."

Mrs. Gibbs: "I declare, Frank, I don't know how he'll get along. I've arranged his clothes and seen to it he's put warm things on,—Frank! they're too *young.* Emily won't think of such things. He'll catch his death of cold within a week."

Dr. Gibbs: "I was remembering my wedding morning, Julia."

Mrs. Gibbs: "Now don't start that, Frank Gibbs."

Dr. Gibbs: "I was the scaredest young fella in the State of New Hampshire. I thought I'd make a mistake for sure. And when I saw you comin' down that aisle I thought you were the prettiest girl I'd ever seen, but the only trouble was that I'd never seen you before. There I was in the Congregational Church marryin' a total stranger."

Mrs. Gibbs: "And how do you think I felt!—Frank, weddings are perfectly awful things. Farces,—that's what they are!" She puts a plate before him. "Here, I've made something for you."

Dr. Gibbs: "Why, Julia Hersey—French toast!"

Mrs. Gibbs: " 'Tain't hard to make and I had to do *some*thing." Pause. DR. GIBBS' pours on the syrup.

Dr. Gibbs: "How'd you sleep last night, Julia?"

Mrs. Gibbs: "Well, I heard a lot of the hours struck off."

Dr. Gibbs: "Ye-e-s! I get a shock every time I think of George setting out to be a family man—that great gangling thing!—I tell you Julia, there's nothing so terrifying in the world as a *son.* The relation of father and son is the darndest, awkwardest—"

Mrs. Gibbs: "Well, mother and daughter's no picnic, let me tell you."

Dr. Gibbs: "They'll have a lot of troubles, I suppose, but that's none of our business. Everybody has a right to their own troubles."

Mrs. Gibbs, at the table, drinking her coffee, meditatively: "Yes . . . people are meant to go through life two by two. 'Tain't natural to be lonesome." Pause. *Dr.* GIBBS starts laughing.

Dr. Gibbs: "Julia, do you know one of the things I was scared of when I married you?"

Mrs. Gibbs: "Oh, go along with you!"

Dr. Gibbs: "I was afraid we wouldn't have material for conversation more'n'd last us a few weeks." Both laugh. "I was afraid we'd run out and eat our meals in silence, that's a fact.—Well, you and I been conversing for twenty years now without any noticeable barren spells."

Mrs. Gibbs: "Well,—good weather, bad weather—'tain't very choice, but I always find something to say." She goes to the foot of the stairs. "Did you hear Rebecca stirring around upstairs?"

Dr. Gibbs: "No. Only day of the year Rebecca hasn't been managing everybody's business up there. She's hiding in her room.—I got the impression she's crying."

Mrs. Gibbs: "Lord's sakes!—This has got to Stop.—Rebecca! Rebecca! Come and get your breakfast." GEORGE comes rattling down the stairs, very brisk.

George: "Good morning, everybody. Only five more hours to live." Makes the gesture of cutting his throat, and a loud "k-k-k," and starts through the trellis.

Mrs. Gibbs: "George Gibbs, where are you going?"

George: "Just stepping across the grass to see my girl."

Mrs. Gibbs: "Now, George! You put on your overshoes. It's raining torrents. You don't go out of this house without you're prepared for it."

George: "Aw, Ma. It's just a *step!"*

Mrs. Gibbs: "George! You'll catch your death of cold and cough all through the service."

Dr. Gibbs: "George, do as your mother tells you!" DR. GIBBS goes upstairs. GEORGE returns reluctantly to the kitchen and pantomimes putting on overshoes.

Mrs. Gibbs: "From tomorrow on you can kill yourself in all weathers, but while you're in my house you'll live wisely, thank you.—Maybe Mrs. Webb isn't used to callers at seven in the morning.—Here, take a cup of coffee first."

George: "Be back in a minute." He crosses the stage, leaping over the puddles. "Good morning, Mother Webb."

Mrs. Webb: "Goodness! You frightened me!—Now, George, you can come in a minute out of the wet, but you know I can't ask you in."

George: "Why not—?"

Mrs. Webb: "George, you know's well as I do: the groom can't see his bride on his wedding day, not until he sees her in church."

George: "Aw!—that's just a superstition.—Good morning, Mr. Webb." Enter MR. WEBB.

Mr. Webb: "Good morning, George."

George: "Mr. Webb, you don't believe in that superstition, do you?"

Mr. Webb: "There's a lot of common sense in some superstitions, George." He sits at the table, facing right.

Mrs. Webb: "Millions have folla'd it, George, and you don't want to be the first to fly in the face of custom."

George: "How is Emily?"

Mrs. Webb: "She hasn't waked up yet. I haven't heard a sound out of her."

George: "Emily's *asleep!!!*"

Mrs. Webb: "No wonder! We were up 'til all hours, sewing and packing. Now I'll tell you what I'll do; you set down here a minute with Mr. Webb and drink this cup of coffee; and I'll go upstairs and see she doesn't come down and surprise you. There's some bacon, too; but don't be long about it." Exit MRS. WEBB. Embarrassed silence. MR. WEBB dunks doughnuts in his coffee. More silence.

Mr. Webb, suddenly and loudly: "Well, George, how are you?"

George, startled, choking over his coffee: "Oh, fine, I'm fine." Pause. "Mr. Webb, what sense could there be in a superstition like that?"

Mr. Webb: "Well, you see,—on her wedding morning a girl's head's apt to be full of . . . clothes and one thing and another. Don't you think that's probably it?"

George: "Ye-e-s. I never thought of that."

Mr. Webb: "A girl's apt to be a mite nervous on her wedding day." Pause.

George: "I wish a fellow could get married without all that marching up and down."

Mr. Webb: "Every man that's ever lived has felt that way about it, George; but is hasn't been any use. It's the womenfolk who've built up weddings, my boy. For a while now the women have it all their own. A man looks pretty small at a wedding, George. All those good women standing shoulder to shoulder making sure that the knot's tied in a mighty public way."

George: "But . . . you *believe* in it, don't you, Mr. Webb?"

Mr. Webb, with alacrity. "Oh, yes; *oh, yes.* Don't you misunderstand me, my boy. Marriage is a wonderful thing,—wonderful thing. And don't you forget that, George."

George: "No, sir.—Mr. Webb, how old were you when you got married?"

Mr. Webb: "Well, you see: I'd been

to college and I'd taken a little time to get settled. But Mrs. Webb—she wasn't much older than what Emily is. Oh, age hasn't much to do with it, George,—not compared with . . . uh . . . other things."

George: "What were you going to say, Mr. Webb?"

Mr. Webb: "Oh, I don't know.—Was I going to say something?" Pause. "George, I was thinking the other night of some advice my father gave me when I got married. Charles, he said, Charles, start out early showing who's boss, he said. Best thing to do is to give an order, even if it don't make sense; just so she'll learn to obey. And he said: If anything about your wife irritates you—her conversation, or anything—just get up and leave the house. That'll make it clear to her, he said. And, oh, yes! he said never, *never* let your wife know how much money you have, never."

George: "Well, Mr. Webb . . . I don't think I could . . ."

Mr. Webb: "So I took the opposite of my father's advice and I've been happy ever since. And let that be a lesson to you, George, never to ask advice on personal matters.—George, are you going to raise chickens on your farm?"

George: "What?"

Mr. Webb: "Are you going to raise chickens on your farm?"

George: "Uncle Luke's never been much interested, but I thought—"

Mr. Webb: "A book came into my office the other day, George, on the Philo System of raising chickens. I want you to read it. I'm thinking of beginning in a small way in the back yard, and I'm going to put an incubator in the cellar—" Enter MRS. WEBB.

Mrs. Webb: "Charles, are you talking about that old incubator again? I thought you two'd be talking about other things worth while."

Mr. Webb, bitingly: "Well, Myrtle, if you want to give the boy some good advice, I'll go upstairs and leave you alone with him."

Mrs. Webb, pulling GEORGE up: "George, Emily's got to come downstairs and eat her breakfast. She sends you her love but she doesn't want to lay eyes on you. Good-by."

George: "Good-by." GEORGE crosses the stage to his own home, bewildered and crestfallen. He slowly dodges a puddle and disappears into his house.

Mr. Webb: "Myrtle, I guess you don't know about that older superstition."

Mrs. Webb: "What do you mean, Charles?"

Mr. Webb: "Since the cave men: no bridegroom should see his father-in-law on the day of the wedding, or near it. Now remember that." Both leave the stage.

Stage Manager: Thank you very much, Mr. and Mrs. Webb.—Now I have to interrupt again here. You see, we want to know how all this began—this wedding, this plan to spend a lifetime together. I'm awfully interested in how big things like that begin.

"You know how it is: you're twenty-one or twenty-two and you make some decisions; then whisssh! you're seventy: you've been a lawyer for fifty years, and that white-haired lady at your side has eaten over fifty thousand meals with you.

"How do such things begin?

"George and Emily are going to show you now the conversation they had when they first knew that . . . that . . . as the saying goes . . . they were meant for one another. "But before they do it I want you to try and remember what it was like to have been very young.

"And particularly the days when you were first in love; when you were like a person sleepwalking, and you didn't quite see the street you were in, and didn't quite hear everything that was said to you.

"You're just a little bit crazy. Will you remember that, please?

"Now they'll be coming out of high school at three o'clock. George has just been elected President of the Junior Class, and as it's June, that means he'll be President of the Senior Class all next year. And Emily's just been elected Secretary and Treasurer. I don't have to tell you how important that is." He places a board across the backs of two chairs, which he takes from those at the Gibb's family table. He brings two high stools from the wings and places them behind the board. Persons sitting on the stools will be facing the audience. This is the counter of Mr. Morgan's drugstore. The sounds of young people's voices are heard off left. "Yepp, —there they are coming down Main Street now." EMILY, carrying an armful of—imaginary—schoolbooks, comes along Main Street from the left.

Emily: "I can't, Louise. I've got to go home. Good-by. Oh, Ernestine! Ernestine! Can you come over tonight and do Latin? Isn't that Cicero the worst thing—! Tell your mother you *have* to. G'by, G'by, Helen. G'by, Fred." GEORGE, also carrying books, catches up with her.

George: "Can I carry your books home for you, Emily?"

Emily, cooly: "Why . . . uh . . . Thank you. It isn't far." She gives them to him.

George: "Excuse me a minute, Emily. —Say, Bob, if I'm a little late, start practice anyway. And give Herb some long high ones."

Emily: "Good-by, Lizzy.

George: "Good-by, Lizzie. —I'm awfully glad you were elected, too, Emily."

Emily: "Thank you." They have been standing on Main Street, almost against the back wall. They take the first steps toward the audience when GEORGE stops and says:

George: "Emily, why are you mad at me?"

Emily: "I'm not mad at you."

George: "You've been treating me so funny lately."

Emily: "Well, since you ask me, I might as well say it right out, George,—" She catches sight of a teacher passing. "Good-by, Miss Corcoran."

George: "Good-by, Miss Corcoran.— Wha—what is it?"

Emily, not scoldingly; finding it difficult to say: "I don't like the whole change that's come over you in the last year. I'm sorry if that hurts your feelings, but I've got to—tell the truth and shame the devil."

George: "A *change?*—Wha—what do you mean?"

Emily: "Well, up to a year ago I used to like you a lot. And I used to watch you as you did everything . . . because we'd been friends so long . . . and then you began spending all your time at *baseball* . . . and you never stopped to speak to anybody any more. Not even to your own family you didn't . . . and, George, it's a fact, you've got awful conceited and stuck-up, and all the girls say so. They may not say so to your face, but that's what they say about you behind your back, and it hurts me to hear them say it, but I've got to agree with them a little. I'm sorry if it hurts your feelings . . . but I can't be sorry I said it."

George: "I . . . I'm glad you said it, Emily. I never thought that such a thing was happening to me. I guess it's hard for a fella not to have faults creep into his character." They take a step or two in silence, then stand still in misery.

Emily: "I always expect a man to be perfect and I think he should be."

George: "Oh . . . I don't think it's possible to be perfect, Emily."

Emily: "Well my *father* is, and as far as I can see *your* father is. There's no reason on earth why you shouldn't be, too."

George: "Well, I feel it's the other way round. That men aren't naturally good; but girls are."

Emily: "Well, you might as well know right now that I'm not perfect. It's not as easy for a girl to be perfect as a man, because we girls are more—more—nervous.—Now I'm sorry I said all that about you. I don't know what made me say it."

George: "Emily,—"

Emily: "Now I can see it's not the truth at all. And suddenly I feel that it isn't important, anyway."

George: "Emily . . . would you like an ice-cream soda, or something, before you go home?"

Emily: "Well, thank you. . . . I would." They advance toward the audience and make an abrupt right turn, opening the door of Morgan's drugstore. Under strong emotion, EMILY keeps her face down. GEORGE speaks to some passers-by.

George: "Hello, Stew,—how are you?—Good afternoon, Mrs. Slocum." The STAGE MANAGER, wearing spectacles and assuming the role of MR. MORGAN, enters abruptly from the right and stands between the audience and the counter of his soda fountain.

Stage Manager: "Hello, George. Hello, Emily.—What'll you have?—Why, Emily Webb,—what have you been crying about?"

George, he gropes for an explanation: "She . . . she just got an awful scare, Mr. Morgan. She almost got run over by that hardware-store wagon. Everybody says that Tom Huckins drives like a crazy man."

Stage Manager, drawing a drink of water: "Well, now! You take a drink of water, Emily. You look all shook up. I tell you, you've got to look both ways before you cross Main Street these days. Gets worse every year.—What'll you have?"

Emily: "I'll have a strawberry phosphate, thank you, Mr. Morgan."

George: "No, no, Emily. Have an ice-cream soda with me. Two strawberry ice-cream sodas, Mr. Morgan."

Stage Manager, working the faucets: "Two strawberry ice-cream sodas, yes sir. Yes, sir. There are a hundred and twenty-five horses in Grover's Corners this minute I'm talking to you. State Inspector was in here yesterday. And now they're bringing in these automobiles, the best thing to do is to just stay home. Why, I can remember when a dog could go to sleep all day in the middle of Main Street and nothing come along to disturb him." He sets the imaginary glasses before them: "There they are. Enjoy 'em." He sees a customer, right. "Yes, Mrs. Ellis. What can I do for you?" He goes out right.

Emily: "They're so expensive."

George: "No, no,—don't you think of that. We're celebrating our election. And then do you know what else I'm celebrating?"

Emily: "No-no."

George: "I'm celebrating because I've got a friend who tells me all the things that ought to be told me."

Emily: "George, *please* don't think of that. I don't know why I said it. It's not true. You're—"

George: "No, Emily, you stick to it.

I'm glad you spoke to me like you did. But you'll *see*: I'm going to change so quick —you bet I'm going to change. And, Emily, I want to ask you a favor."

Emily: "What?"

George: "Emily, if I go away to State Agriculture College next year, will you write me a letter once in a while?"

Emily: "I certainly will. I certainly will, George . . ." Pause. They start sipping the sodas through the straws. "It certainly seems like being away three years you'd get out of touch with things. Maybe letters from Grover's Corners wouldn't be so interesting after a while. Grover's Corners isn't a very important place when you think of all—New Hampshire; but I think it's a very nice town."

George: "The day wouldn't come when I wouldn't want to know everything that's happening here. I know *that's* true, Emily."

Emily: "Well, I'll try to make my letters interesting." Pause.

George: "Y'know. Emily, whenever I meet a farmer I ask him if he thinks it's important to go to Agriculture School to be a good farmer."

Emily: "Why, George—"

George: "Yeah, and some of them say that it's even a waste of time. You can get all those things, anyway, out of the pamphlets the government sends out. And Uncle Luke's getting old,—he's about ready for me to start taking over his farm tomorrow, if I could.

Emily: "My!"

George: "And, like you say, being gone all that time . . . in other places and meeting other people . . . Gosh, if anything like that can happen I don't want to go away. I guess new people aren't any better than old ones. I'll bet they almost never are. Emily . . . I feel that you're as good a friend as I've got. I don't need to go and meet the people in other towns."

Emily: "But, George, maybe it's very important for you to go and learn all that about—cattle judging and soils and those things. . . . Of course, I don't know."

George, after a pause, very seriously: "Emily, I'm going to make up my mind right now. I won't go. I'll tell Pa about it tonight."

Emily: "Why, George, I don't see why you have to decide right now. It's a whole year away."

George: "Emily, I'm glad you spoke to me about that . . . that fault in my character. What you said was right; but there was *one* thing wrong in it, and that was when you said that for a year I wasn't noticing people, and . . . you, for instance. Why, you say you were watching me when I did everything . . . I was doing the same about you all the time. Why, sure,—I always thought about you as one of the chief people I thought about. I always made sure where you were sitting on the bleachers, and who you were with, and for three days now I've been trying to walk home with you; but something's always got in the way. Yesterday I was standing over against the wall waiting for you, and you walked home with Miss Corcoran."

Emily: "George! . . . Life's awful funny! How could I have known that? Why, I thought—"

George: "Listen, Emily, I'm going to tell you why I'm not going to Agriculture School. I think that once you've found a person that you're very fond of . . . I mean a person who's fond of you, too, and likes you enough to be interested in your character . . . Well, I think that's just as important as college is, and even more so. That's what I think."

Emily: "I think it's awfully important, too."

George: "Emily."

Emily: "Y-yes, George."

George: "Emily, if I *do* improve and make a big change . . . would you be . . . I mean: *could* you be . . ."

Emily: "I . . . I am now; I always have been."

George, pause: "So I guess this is an important talk we've been having."

Emily: Yes . . . yes."

George, takes a deep breath and straightens his back: "Wait just a minute and I'll walk you home." With mounting alarm he digs into his pockets for the money. The STAGE MANAGER enters, right. GEORGE, deeply embarrassed, but direct, says to him: "Mr. Morgan, I'll have to go home and get the money to pay you for this. It'll only take me a minute."

Stage Manager, pretending to be affronted: "What's that? George Gibbs, do you mean to tell me—!"

George: "Yes but I had reasons, Mr. Morgan.—Look, here's my gold watch to keep until I come back with the money."

Stage Manager: "That's all right. Keep your watch, I'll trust you."

George: "I'll be back in five minutes."

Stage Manager: "I'll trust you ten years, George,—not a day over.—Got all over your shock, Emily?"

Emily: "Yes, thank you, Mr. Morgan. It was nothing."

George, taking up the books from the counter: "I'm ready." They walk in grave silence across the stage and pass through the trellis at the WEBBS' back door and disappear. The STAGE MANAGER watches them go out, then turns to the audience, removing his spectacles.

Stage Manager: "Well,—" He claps his hand as a signal. "Now we're ready to get on with the wedding." He stands waiting while the set is prepared for the next scene. STAGEHANDS remove the chairs, tables and trellises from the GIBBS and WEBB houses. They arrange the pews for the church in the center of the stage. The congregation will sit facing the back wall. The aisle of the church starts at the center of the back wall and comes toward the audience. A small platform is placed against the back wall on which the STAGE MANAGER will stand later, playing the minister. The image of a stained-glass window is cast from a lantern slide upon the back wall. When all is ready the STAGE MANAGER strolls to the center of the stage, down front, and, musingly, addresses the audience. "There are a lot of things to be said about a wedding; there are a lot of thoughts that go on during a wedding.

"We can't get them all into one wedding, naturally, and especially not into a wedding at Grover's Corners, where they're awfully plain and short.

"In this wedding I play the minister. That gives me the right to say a few things more about it.

"For a while now, the play gets pretty serious.

"Y'see, some churches say that marriage is a sacrament. I don't quite know what that means, but I can guess. Like Mrs. Gibbs said a few minutes ago: People were made to live two-by-two.

"This is a good wedding, but people are so put together that even at a good wedding there's a lot of confusion way down deep in people's minds and we thought that that ought to be in our play, too.

"The real hero of this scene isn't on the stage at all, and you know who that is. It's like what one of those European fellas said: every child born into the world is nature's attempt to make a perfect human being. Well, we've seen nature pushing and contriving for some time now. We all know that nature's interested in quantity; but I think she's interested in quality, too—that's why I'm in the ministry.

"And don't forget all the other witnesses at this wedding,—the ancestors. Millions of them. Most of them set out to live two-by-two, also. Millions of them.

"Well, that's all my sermon. 'Twan't very long, anyway." The organ starts playing Handel's 'Largo.' The congregation streams into the church and sits in silence. Church bells are heard. MRS. GIBBS sits in the front row, the first seat on the aisle, the right section; next to her are REBECCA and DR. GIBBS. Across the aisle are MRS. WEBB, WALLY and MR. WEBB. A small choir takes its place, facing the audience under the stained-glass window. MRS. WEBB, on the way to her place, turns back and speaks to the audience.

Mrs. Webb: "I don't know why on earth I should be crying. I suppose there's nothing to cry about. It came over me at breakfast this morning; there was Emily eating her breakfast as she's done for seventeen years and now she's going off to eat it in someone else's house, I suppose that's it.

"And Emily! She suddenly said: I can't eat another mouthful, and she put her head down on the table and *she* cried." She starts toward her seat in the church, but turns back and adds: "Oh, I've got to say it: you know, there's something downright cruel about sending our girls out into marriage this way. I hope some of her girl friends have told her a thing or two. It's cruel, I know, but I couldn't bring myself to say anything. I went into it blind as a bat myself." In half-amused exasperation. "The whole world's wrong, that's what's the matter.

"There they come." She hurries to her place in the pew. GEORGE starts to come down the right aisle of the theatre, through the audience. Suddenly THREE MEMBERS of his baseball team appear by the right proscenium pillar and start whistling and cat-calling to him. They are dressed for the ball field.

The Basball Players: "Eh, George, George! Hast—yaow! Look at him, fellas—he looks scared to death. Yaow! George, don't look so innocent, you old geezer. We know what you're thinking. Don't disgrace the team, big boy. Whoo-oo-oo."

Stage Manager: "All right! All right! That'll do. That's enough of that." Smiling, he pushes them off the stage. They lean back to shout a few more catcalls. "There used to be an awful lot of that kind of thing at weddings in the old days,—Rome, and later. We're more civilized now,—so they say." The choir starts singing 'Love Divine, All Love Excelling—.' GEORGE has reached the stage. He stares at the congregation a moment, then takes a few steps of withdrawal, toward the right proscenium pillar. His mother, from the front row, seems to have felt his confusion. She leaves her seat and comes down the aisle quickly to him.

Mrs. Gibbs: "George! George! What's the matter?"

George: "Ma, I don't want to grow old. Why's everybody pushing me so?"

Mrs. Gibbs: "Why, George . . . you wanted it."

George: "No, Ma, listen to me—"

Mrs. Gibbs: "No, no, George,—you're a man now."

George: "Listen, Ma,—for the last

time I ask you . . . All I want to do is to be a fella—"

Mrs. Gibbs: "George! If anyone should hear you! Now stop. Why, I'm ashamed of you!"

George, he comes to himself and looks over the scene: "What? Where's Emily?"

Mrs. Gibbs, relieved: "George! You gave me such a turn."

George: "Cheer up, Ma, I'm getting married."

Mrs. Gibbs: "Let me catch my breath a minute."

George, comforting her: Now, Ma, you save Thursday nights. Emily and I are coming over to dinner every Thursday night . . . you'll see. Ma, what are you crying for? Come on; we've got to get ready for this." MRS. GIBBS, mastering her emotion, fixes his tie and whispers to him. In the meantime, EMILY, in white and wearing her wedding veil, has come through the audience and mounted onto the stage. She too draws back, frightened, when she sees the congregation in the church. The choir begins: 'Blessed Be the Tie That Binds.'

Emily: "I never felt so alone in my whole life. And George over there, looking so . . . ! I *hate* him. I wish I were dead. Papa! Papa!"

Mr. Webb, leaves his seat in the pews and comes toward her anxiously: "Emily! Emily! Now don't get upset. . . ."

Emily: "But, Papa,—I don't want to get married. . . ."

Mr. Webb: "Sh—sh—Emily. Everything's all right."

Emily: "Why can't I stay for a while just as I am? Let's go away,—"

Mr. Webb: "No, no, Emily. Now stop and think a minute."

Emily: "Don't you remember that you used to say,—all the time you used to say—all the time: that I was *your* girl! There must be lots of places we can go to. I'll work for you. I could keep house."

Mr. Webb: "Sh . . . you musn't think of such things. You're just nervous, Emily," He turns and calls: "George! George! Will you come here a minute?" He leads her toward George. "Why you're marrying the best young fellow in the world. George is a fine fellow."

Emily: "But Papa,—" MRS. GIBBS returns unobtrusively to her seat. MR. WEBB has one arm around his daughter. He places his hand on GEORGE's shoulder.

Mr. Webb: "I'm giving away my daughter, George. Do you think you can take care of her?"

George: "Mr. Webb, I want to . . . I want to try. Emily, I'm going to do my best. I love you, Emily. I need you."

Emily: "Well, if you love me, help me. All I want is someone to love me."

George: "I will, Emily. Emily, I'll try."

Emily: "And I mean for *ever*. Do you hear? For ever and ever." They fall into each other's arms. The March from *Lohengrin* is heard. The STAGE MANAGER, as CLERGYMAN, stands on the box, up center.

Mr. Webb: "Come, they're waiting for us. Now you know it'll be all right. Come, quick." GEORGE slips away and takes his place beside the STAGE MANAGER-CLERGYMAN. EMILY proceeds up the aisle on her father's arm.

Stage Manager: "Do you, George, take this woman, Emily, to be your wedded wife, to have . . ." MRS. SOAMES has been sitting in the last row of the congregation. She now turns to her neighbors and speaks in a shrill voice. Her chatter drown out the rest of the clergyman's words.

Mrs. Soames: "Perfectly lovely wedding! Loveliest wedding I ever saw. Oh, I do love a good wedding, don't you? Doesn't she make a lovely bride?"

George: "I do."

Stage Manager: "Do you, Emily, take this man, George, to be your wedded husband,—" Again his further words are covered by those of MRS. SOAMES.

Mrs. Soames: "Don't know *when* I've seen such a lovely wedding. But I always cry. Don't know why it is, but I always cry. I just like to see young people happy, don't you? Oh, I think it's lovely." The ring. The kiss. The stage is suddenly arrested into silent tableaux. The STAGE MANAGER, his eyes on the distance, as though to himself:

Stage Manager: "I've married over two hundred couples in my day.

"Do I believe in it?

"I don't know.

"M. . . . marries N. . . . millions of them.

"The cottage, the go-cart, the Sunday-afternoon drives in the Ford, the first rheumatism, the grandchildren, the second rheumatism, the deathbed, the reading of the will,—" He now looks at the audience for the first time, with a warm smile that removes any sense of cynicism from the next line. "Once in a thousand times it's interesting.

"—Well, let's have Mendelssohn's 'Wedding March'!" The organ picks up the March. The BRIDE and GROOM come down the aisle, radiant, but trying to be very dignified.

Mrs. Soames: "Aren't they a lovely couple? Oh, I've never been to such a nice wedding. I'm sure they'll be happy. I always say: *happiness,* that's the great thing! The important thing is to be happy." The BRIDE and GROOM reach the steps leading into the audience. A bright light is thrown upon them. They descend into the auditorium and run up the aisle joyously.

Stage Manager: "That's all the Second Act, folks. Ten minutes' intermission."

ACT III

[*During the intermission the audience has seen the* STAGEHANDS *arranging the stage. On the right-hand side, a little right of the center, ten or twelve ordinary chairs have been placed in three openly spaced rows facing the audience.*

These are graves in the cemetery.

Toward the end of the intermission the ACTORS *enter and take their places. The front row contains: toward the center of the stage, an empty chair; then* MRS. GIBBS; SIMON STIMSON.

The third row has WALLY WEBB.

The dead do not turn their heads or their eyes to right or left, but they sit in a quiet without stiffness. When they speak their tone is matter-of-fact, without sentimentality and, above all, without lugubriousness.

The STAGE MANAGER *takes his accustomed place and waits for the house lights to go down.*]

Stage Manager: "This time nine years have gone by, friends—summer, 1913.

"Gradual changes in Grover's Corners. Horses are getting rarer.

"Farmers coming into town in Fords.

"Everybody locks their house doors now at night. Ain't been any burglars in town yet, but everybody's heard about 'em.

"You'd be surprised, though—on the whole, things don't change much around here.

"This is certainly an important part of Grover's Corners. It's on a hilltop—a windy hilltop—lots of sky, lots of clouds, —often lots of sun and moon and stars.

"You come up here, on a fine afternoon and you can see range on range of hills—awful blue they are—up there by Lake Sunapee and Lake Winnipesaukee . . . and way up, if you've got a glass, you can see the White Mountains and Mt. Washington—where North Conway and Conway is. And, of course, our favorite mountain, Mt. Monadnock, 's right here —and all these towns that lie around it: Jaffrey, 'n East Jaffrey, 'n Peterborough, 'n Dublin; and" Then pointing down in the audience. "there, quite a ways down, is Grover's Corners."

"Yes, beatuiful spot up here. Mountain laurel and li-lacks. I often wonder why people like to be buried in Woodlawn and Brooklyn when they might pass the same time up here in New Hampshire. Over there—" Pointing to stage left. "are the old stones,—1670, 1680. Strong-minded people that come a long way to be independent. Summer people walk around there laughing at the funny words on the tombstones . . . it don't do any harm. And genealogists come up from Boston—get paid by city people for looking up their ancestors. They want to make sure they're Daughters of the American Revolution and of the *Mayflower*. . . . Well, I guess that don't do any harm, either. Wherever you come near the human race, there's layers and layers of nonsense. . . .

"Over there are some Civil War veterans. Iron flags on their graves . . . New Hampshire boys . . . had a notion that the Union ought to be kept together, though they'd never seen more than fifty miles of it themselves. All they knew was the name, friends—the United States of America. The United States of America. And they went and died about it.

"This here is the new part of the cemetery. Here's your friend Mrs. Gibbs. 'N let me see—Here's Mr. Stimson, organist at the Congregational Church. And Mrs. Soames who enjoyed the wedding so—you remember? Oh, and a lot of others. And Editor Webb's boy, Wallace, whose appendix burst while he was on a Boy Scout trip to Crawford Notch. Yes, an awful lot of sorrow has sort of quieted down up here.

"People just wild with grief have brought their relatives up to this hill. We all know how it is . . . and then time . . . and sunny days . . . and rainy days . . . 'n snow . . . We're all glad they're in a beautiful place and we're coming up here ourselves when our fit's over.

"Now there are some things we all know, but we don't take'm out and look at'm very often. We all know that *something* is eternal. And it ain't houses, and it ain't names, and it ain't earth, and it ain't even the stars . . . everybody knows in their bones that *something* is eternal, and that something has to do with human beings. All the greatest people ever lived have been telling us that for five thousand years and yet you'd be surprised how people are always losing hold of it. There's something way down deep that's eternal about every human being." Pause.

"You know as well as I do that the dead don't stay interested in us living people for very long. Gradually, gradually, they lose hold of the earth . . . and the ambitions they had . . . and the pleasures they had . . . and the things they suffered . . . and the people they loved.

"They get weaned away from earth— that's the way I put it,—weaned away.

"And they stay here while the earth part of 'em burns away, burns out; and all that time they slowly get indifferent to what's goin' on in Grover's Corners.

"They're waitin'. They're waitin' for something that they feel is comin'. Something important, and great. Aren't they waitin' for the eternal part in them to come out clear?

"Some of the things they're going to say maybe'll hurt your feelings—but that's the way it is: mother'n daughter . . . husband'n wife . . . enemy'n enemy . . . money'n miser . . . all those terribly important things kind of grow pale around here. And what's left when memory's gone, and your identity, Mrs. Smith?" He looks at the audience a minute, then turns to the stage.

"Well! There are some *living* people. There's Joe Stoddard, our undertaker, supervising a new-made grave. And here comes a Grover's Corners boy, that left town to go out West." JOE STODDARD has hovered about in the background. SAM CRAIG enters left, wiping his forehead from the exertion. He carries an umbrella and strolls front.

Sam Craig: "Good afternoon, Joe Stoddard."

Joe Stoddard: "Good afternoon, good afternoon. Let me see now: do I know you?"

Sam Craig: "I'm Sam Craig."

Joe Stoddard: "Gracious sakes' alive! Of all people! I should'a knowed you'd be back for the funeral. You've been away a long time, Sam."

Sam Craig: "Yes, I've been away over twelve years. I'm in business out in Buffalo now, Joe. But I was in the East when I got news of my cousin's death, so I thought I'd combine things a little and come and see the old home. You look well."

Joe Stoddard: "Yes, yes, can't complain. Very sad, our journey today, Samuel."

Sam Craig: "Yes."

Joe Stoddard: "Yes, yes. I always say I hate to supervise when a young person is taken. They'll be here in a few minutes now. I had to come here early today— my son's supervisin' at the home."

Sam Crag, reading stones: "Old Farmer McCarty, I used to do chores for him— after school. He had the lumbago."

Joe Stoddard: "Yes, we brought Farmer McCarthy here a number of years ago now."

Sam Craig staring at MRS. GIBB's knees: "Why, this is my Aunt Julia . . . I'd forgotten that she'd . . . of course, of course."

Joe Stoddard: "Yes, Doc Gibbs lost his wife two-three years ago . . . about this time. And today's another pretty bad blow for him, too."

Mrs. Gibbs, to Simon Stimson: in an even voice: "That's my sister Carrie's boy, Sam . . . Sam Craig."

Simon Stimson: "I'm always uncomfortable when *they're* around."

Mrs. Gibbs: "Simon."

Sam Craig: "Do they choose their own verses much, Joe?"

Joe Stoddard: "No . . . not usual. Mostly the bereaved pick a verse."

Sam Craig: "Doesn't sound like Aunt Julia. There aren't many of those Hersey sisters left now. Let me see: where are . . . I wanted to look at my father's and mother's . . ."

Joe Stoddard: "Over there with the Craigs . . . Avenue F."

Sam Craig, reading SIMON STIMSON'S epitaph: "He was organist at church, wasn't he?—Hm, drank a lot, we used to say."

Joe Stoddard: "Nobody was supposed to know about it. He'd seen a peck of trouble." Behind his hand. "Took his own life, y' know?"

Sam Craig: "Oh, did he?"

Joe Stoddard: "Hung himself in the attic. They tried to hush it up, but of course it got around. He chose his own epy-taph. You can see it there. It ain't a verse exactly."

Sam Craig: "Why, it's just some notes of music—what is it?"

Joe Stoddard: "Oh, I wouldn't know. It was wrote up in the Boston papers at the time."

Sam Craig: "Joe, what did she die of?"

Joe Stoddard: "Who?"

Sam Craig: "My cousin."

Joe Stoddard: "Oh, didn't you know? Had some trouble bringing a baby into the world. 'Twas her second, though. There's a little boy 'bout four years old."

Sam Craig, opening his umbrella: "The grave's going to be over there?"

Joe Stoddard: "Yes, there ain't much more room over here among the Gibbses, so they're opening up a whole new Gibbs section over by Avenue B. You'll excuse me now. I see they're comin'." From left to center, at the back of the stage, comes a procession. FOUR MEN carry a casket, invisible to us. All the rest are under umbrellas. One can vaguely see: DR. GIBBS, GEORGE, the WEBBS, etc. They gather about a grave in the back center of the stage, a little to the left of center.

Mrs. Soames: "Who is it, Julia?"

Mrs. Gibbs, without raising her eyes: "My daughter-in-law, Emily Webb."

Mrs. Soames, a little surprised, but no emotion: "Well, I declare! The road up here must have been awful muddy. What did she die of, Julia?"

Mrs. Gibbs: "In childbirth."

Mrs. Soames: "Childbirth." Almost with a laugh. "I'd forgotten all about that. My, wasn't life awful—" With a sigh, "and wonderful."

Simon Stimson, with a sideways glance: "Wonderful, was it?"

Mrs. Gibbs: "Simon! Now, remember!"

Mrs. Soames: "I remember Emily's wedding. Wasn't it a lovely wedding! And I remember her reading the class poem at Graduation Exercises. Emily was one of the brightest girls ever graduated from High School. I've heard Principal Wilkins say so time after time. I called on them at their new farm, just before I died. Perfectly beautiful farm."

A Woman among the dead: "It's on the same road we lived on."

A Man among the dead: "Yepp, right smart farm." They subside. The group by the grave starts singing 'Blessed Be the Tie That Binds.'

A Woman among the dead: "I always liked that hymn. I was hopin' they'd sing a hymn." Pause. Suddenly EMILY appears from among the umbrellas. She is wearing a white dress. Her hair is down her back and tied by a white ribbon like a little girl. She comes slowly, gazing wonderingly at the dead, a little dazed. She stops halfway and smiles faintly. After looking at the mourners for a moment, she walks slowly to the vacant chair beside MRS. GIBBS and sits down.

Emily, to them all, quietly, smiling: "Hello."

Mrs. Soames: "Hello, Emily."

A Man among the dead: "Hello, M's. Gibbs."

Emily, warmly: "Hello, Mother Gibbs."

Mrs. Gibbs: "Emily."

Emily: "Hello." With surprise. "It's raining."

Her eyes drift back to the funeral company.

Mrs. Gibbs: "Yes . . . They'll be gone soon, dear. Just rest yourself."

Emily: "It seems thousands and thousands of years since I . . . Papa remembered that that was my favorite hymn.

"Oh, I wish I'd been here a long time. I don't like being new here.—How do you do, Mr. Stimson?"

Simon Stimson: "How do you do, Emily." EMILY continues to look about her with a wondering smile; as though to shut out from her mind the thought of the funeral company she starts speaking to MRS. GIBBS with a touch of nervousness.

Emily: "Mother Gibbs, George and I have made that farm into just the best place you ever saw. We thought of you all the time. We wanted to show you the new barn and a great long ce-ment drinking fountain for the stock. We bought that out of the money you left us."

Mrs. Gibbs: "I did?"

Emily: "Don't you remember, Mother Gibbs—the legacy you left us? Why, it was over three hundred and fifty dollars."

Mrs. Gibbs: "Yes, yes, Emily."

Emily: "Well, there's a patent device on the drinking fountain so that it never overflows, Mother Gibbs, and it never sinks below a certain mark they have there. It's fine." Her voice trails off and her eyes return to the funeral group. "It won't be the same to George without me, but it's a lovely farm." Suddenly she looks directly at MRS. GIBBS. "Live people don't understand, do they?"

Mrs. Gibbs: "No, dear—not very much."

Emily: "They're sort of shut up in little boxes, aren't they? I feel as though I knew them last a thousand years ago . . . My boy is spending the day at Mrs. Carter's." She sees MR. CARTER among the dead. "Oh, Mr. Carter, my little boy is spending the day at your house."

Mr. Carter: "Is he?"

Emily: "Yes, he loves it there.—Mother Gibbs, we have a Ford, too. Never gives any trouble. I don't drive, though. Mother Gibbs, when does this feeling go away?—Of being . . . one of *them?* How long does it . . . ?

Mrs. Gibbs: "Sh! dear. Just wait and be patient.

Emily, with a sigh: "I know.—Look, they're finished. They're going."

Mrs. Gibbs: "Sh—." The umbrellas leave the stage. DR. GIBBS has come over to his wife's grave and stands before it a moment. EMILY looks up at his face. MRS. GIBBS does not raise her eyes.

Emily: "Look! Father Gibbs is bringing some of my flowers to you. He looks just like George, doesn't he? Oh, Mother Gibbs, I never realized before how troubled and how . . . how in the dark live persons are. Look at him. I loved him so. From morning till night, that's all they are —troubled." DR. GIBBS goes off.

The Dead: "Little cooler than it was.—Yes, that rain's cooled it off a little. Those northeast winds always do the same thing, don't they? If it isn't a rain, it's a three-day blow.—" A patient calm falls on the stage. The STAGE MANAGER appears at his proscenium pillar, smoking. EMILY sits up abruptly with an idea.

Emily: "But, Mother Gibbs, one can go back; one can go back there again . . . into the living. I feel it. I know it. Why just then for a moment I was thinking about . . . about the farm . . . and for a minute I *was* there, and my baby was on my lap as plain as day."

Mrs. Gibbs: "Yes, of course you can."

Emily: "I can go back there and live all those days over again . . . why not?"

Mrs. Gibbs: "All I can say is, Emily, don't."

Emily, she appeals urgently to the STAGE MANAGER: "But it's true isn't it? I can go and live . . . back there . . . again."

Stage Manager: "Yes, some have tried—but they soon come back here."

Mrs. Gibbs: "Don't do it, Emily."

Mrs. Soames: "Emily, don't. It's not what you think it'd be."

Emily: "But I won't live over a sad day. I'll choose a happy one—I'll choose the day I first knew that I loved George. Why should that be painful?" They are silent. Her question turns to the STAGE MANAGER.

Stage Manager: "You not only live it; but you watch yourself living it."

Emily: "Yes?"

Stage Manager: "And as you watch it, you see the thing that they—down there—never know. You see the future. You know what's going to happen afterwards."

Emily: "But is that—painful? Why?"

Mrs. Gibbs: "That's not the only reason why you shouldn't do it, Emily. When you've been here longer you'll see that our life here is to forget all that, and think only of what's ahead, and be ready for what's ahead. When you've been here longer you'll understand.

Emily, softly: "But Mother Gibbs, how can I *ever* forget that life? It's all I know. It's all I had."

Mrs. Soames: "Oh, Emily. It isn't wise. Really, it isn't."

Emily: "But it's a thing, I must know for myself. I'll choose a happy day, anyway."

Mrs. Gibbs: "No!—At least, choose an unimportant day. Choose the least important day in your life. It will be important enough."

Emily, to herself: "Then it can't be since I was married; or since the baby was born." To the STAGE MANAGER, eagerly. "I can choose a birthday at least, can't I?—I choose my twelfth birthday."

Stage Manager: "All right. February 11th, 1899. A Tuesday.—Do you want any special time of day?"

Emily: "Oh, I want the whole day."

Stage Manager: "We'll begin at dawn. You remember it had been snowing for several days; but it had stopped the night before, and they had begun clearing the roads. The sun's coming up."

Emily, with a cry; rising: "There's Main Street . . . why, that's Mr. Morgan's drugstore before he changed it! . . . And there's the livery stable." The stage at no time in this act has been very dark; but now the left half of the stage gradually becomes very bright—the brightness of a crisp winter morning. EMILY walks toward Main Street.

Stage Manager: "Yes, it's 1899. This is fourteen years ago."

Emily: "Oh, that's the town I knew as a little girl. And, *look,* there's the old white fence that used to be around our house. Oh, I'd forgotten that! Oh, I love it so! Are they inside?"

Stage Manager: "Yes, your mother'll be coming downstairs in a minute to make breakfast."

Emily, softly: "Will she?"

Stage Manager: "And you remember: your father had been away for several days; he came back on the early-morning train."

Emily: "No . . . ?"

Stage Manager: "He'd been back to his college to make a speech—in western New York, at Clinton."

Emily: "Look! There's Howie Newsome. There's our policeman. But he's *dead;* he *died.*" The voices of HOWIE NEWSOME, CONSTABLE WARREN and JOE CROWELL, JR., are heard at the left of the stage. EMILY listens in delight.

Howie Newsome: "Whoa, Bessie!—Bessie! 'Morning, Bill."

Constable Warren: "Morning, Howie."

Howie Newsome: "You're up early."

Constable Warren: "Been rescuin' a party; darn near froze to death, down by Polish Town thar. Got drunk and lay out in the snowdrifts. Thought he was in bed when I shook'm."

Emily: "Why, there's Joe Crowell. . . ."

Joe Crowell: "Good morning, Mr. Warren. 'Morning, Howie." MRS. WEBB has appeared in her kitchen, but EMILY does not see her until she calls.

Mrs. Webb: "Chil-*dren!* Wally! Emily! . . . Time to get up."

Emily: "Mama, I'm here! Oh! how young Mama looks! I didn't know Mama was ever that young."

Mrs. Webb: "You can come and dress by the kitchen fire, if you like; but hurry." HOWIE NEWSOME has entered along Main Street and brings the milk to MRS. WEBB'S door. "Good morning, Mr. Newsome. Whhhh—it's cold."

Howie Newsome: "Ten below by my barn, Mrs. Webb."

Mrs. Webb: "Think of it! Keep yourself wrapped up." She takes her bottles in, shuddering.

Emily, with an effort: "Mama, I can't find my blue hair ribbon anywhere."

Mrs. Webb: "Just open your eyes, dear, that's all. I laid it out for you special—on the dresser, there. If it were a snake it would bite you."

Emily: "Yes, yes . . ." She puts her hand on her heart. MR. WEBB comes along Main Street, where he meets CONSTABLE WARREN. Their movements and voices are increasingly lively in the sharp air.

Mr. Webb: "Good morning, Bill."

Constable Warren: "Good morning, Mr. Webb. You're up early."

Mr. Webb: "Yes, just been back to my old college in New York State. Been any trouble here?"

Constable Warren: "Well, I was called up this mornin' to rescue a Polish fella—darn near froze to death he was."

Mr. Webb: "We must get it in the paper."

Constable Warren: " 'Twan't much."

Emily, whispers: "Papa." MR. WEBB shakes the snow off his feet and enters his house. CONSTABLE WARREN goes off, right.

Mr. Webb: "Good morning, Mother."

Mrs. Webb: "How did it go, Charles?"

Mr. Webb: "Oh, fine, I guess. I told'm a few things.—Everything all right here?"

Mrs. Webb: "Yes—can't think of anything that's happened, special. Been right cold. Howie Newsome says it's ten below over to his barn."

Mr. Webb: "Yes, well, it's colder

than that at Hamilton College. Student's ears are falling off. It ain't Christian.—Paper have any mistakes in it?"

Mrs. Webb: "None that I noticed. Coffee's ready when you want it." He starts upstairs. "Charles! Don't forget; it's Emily's birthday. Did you remember to get her something?"

Mr. Webb, patting his pocket: "Yes, I've got something here." Calling up the stairs. "Where's my girl? Where's my birthday girl?" He goes off left.

Mrs. Webb: "Don't interrupt her now, Charles. You can see her at breakfast. She's slow enough as it is. Hurry up, children! It's seven o'clock. Now, I don't want to call you again."

Emily, softly, more in wonder than in grief: "I can't bear it. They're so young and beautiful. Why did they ever have to get old? Mama, I'm here. I'm grown up. I love you all, everything.—I can't look at everything hard enough." She looks questioningly at the STAGE MANAGER, saying or suggesting: "Can I go in?" He nods briefly. She crosses to the inner door to the kitchen, left of her mother, and as though entering the room, says, suggesting the voice of a girl of twelve: "Good morning, Mama."

Mrs. Webb, crossing to embrace and kiss her; in her characteristic matter-of-fact manner: "Well, now, dear, a very happy birthday to my girl and many happy returns. There are some surprises waiting for you on the kitchen table."

Emily: "Oh, Mama, you *shouldn't* have." She throws an anguished glance at the STAGE MANAGER. "I can't—I can't."

Mrs. Webb, facing the audience, over her stove: "But birthday or no birthday, I want you to eat your breakfast good and slow. I want you to grow up and be a good strong girl. That in the blue paper is from your Aunt Carrie; and I reckon you can guess who brought the post-card album. I found it on the doorstep when I brought in the milk—George Gibbs . . . must have come over in the cold pretty early . . . right nice of him."

Emily, to herself: "Oh, George! I'd forgotten that. . . ."

Mrs. Webb: "Chew that bacon good and slow. It'll help keep you warm on a cold day."

Emily, with mounting urgency: "Oh, Mama, just look at me one minute as though you really saw me. Mama, fourteen years have gone by. I'm dead. You're a grandmother, Mama. I married George Gibbs, Mama. Wally's dead, too. Mama, his appendix burst on a camping trip to North Conway. We felt just terrible about it—don't you remember? But, just for a moment now we're all together. Mama, just for a moment we're happy. *Let's look at one another."*

Mrs. Webb: "That in the yellow paper is something I found in the attic among your grandmother's things. You're old enough to wear it now, and I thought you'd like it."

Emily: "And this is from you. Why, Mama, it's just lovely and it's just what I wanted. It's beautiful!" She flings her arms around her mother's neck. HER MOTHER goes on with her cooking, but is pleased.

Mrs. Webb: "Well, I hoped you'd like it. Hunted all over. Your Aunt Norah couldn't find one in Concord, so I had to send all the way to Boston." Laughing.

"Wally has something for you, too. He made it at manual-training class and he's very proud of it. Be sure you make a big fuss about it.—Your father has a surprise for you, too; dont' know what it is myself. Sh—here he comes."

Mr. Webb, off stage: "Where's my girl? Where's my birthday girl?"

Emily, in a loud voice to the STAGE MANAGER: "I can't. I can't go on. It goes so fast. We don't have time to look at one another." She breaks down sobbing. The lights dim on the left half of the stage. MRS. WEBB disappears.

"I didn't realize. So all that was going on and we never noticed. Take me back—up the hill—to my grave. But first: Wait! One more look.

"Good-by, Good-by, world. Good-by, Grover's Corners . . . Mama and Papa. Good-by to clocks ticking . . . and Mama's sunflowers. And food and coffee. And new-ironed dresses and hot baths . . . and sleeping and waking up. Oh, earth, you're too wonderful for anybody to realize you." She looks toward the STAGE MANAGER and asks abruptly, through her tears:

"Do any human beings ever realize life while they live it?—every, every minute?"

Stage Manager: "No." Pause. "The saints and poets, maybe—they do some."

Emily: "I'm ready to go back." She returns to her chair beside MRS. GIBBS. Pause.

Mrs. Gibbs: "Were you happy?"

Emily: "No . . . I should have listened to you. That's all human beings are! Just blind people."

Mrs. Gibbs: "Look, it's clearing up. The stars are coming out."

Emily: "Oh, Mr. Stimson, I should have listened to them."

Simon Stimson, with mounting violence; bitingly: "Yes, now you know. Now you know! That's what it was to be alive. To move about in a cloud of ignorance; to go up and down trampling on the feelings of those . . . of those about you. To spend and waste time as though you had a million years. To be always at the mercy of one self-centered passion, or another. Now you know—that's the happy existence you wanted to go back to. Ignorance and blindness."

Mrs. Gibbs, spiritedly: "Simon Stimson, that ain't the whole truth and you know it. Emily, look at that star. I forget its name."

A Man among the Dead: "My boy Joel was a sailor,—knew 'em all. He'd set on the porch evenings and tell 'em all by name. Yes, sir, wonderful!"

Another Man among the Dead: "A star's mighty good company."

A Woman among the Dead: "Yes, Yes, 'tis."

Simon Stimson: "Here's one of *them* coming."

The Dead: "That's funny. 'Tain't no time for one of them to be here.—Goodness sakes."

Emily: "Mother Gibbs, it's George."

Mrs. Gibbs: "Sh, dear. Just rest yourself."

Emily: "It's George." GEORGE enters from the left, and slowly comes toward them.

A Man from among the Dead: "And my boy, Joel, who knew the stars—he used to say it took millions of years for that speck of light to git to the earth. Don't seem like a body could believe it, but that's what he used to say—millions of years." GEORGE sinks to his knees then falls full length at Emily's feet.

A Woman among the Dead: "Goodness! That ain't no way to behave!"

Mrs. Soames: "He ought to be home."

Emily: "Mother Gibbs?"

Mrs. Gibbs: "Yes, Emily?"

Emily: "They don't understand, do they?"

Mrs. Gibbs: "No, dear. They don't understand." The STAGE MANAGER appears at the right, one hand on a dark curtain which he slowly draws across the scene. In the distance a clock is heard striking the hour very faintly.

Stage Manager: "Most everybody's asleep in Grover's Corners. There are a few lights on: Shorty Hawkins, down at the depot, has just watched the Albany train go by. And at the livery stable somebody's setting up late and talking.—Yes, it's clearing up. There are the stars—doing their old, old crisscross journeys in the sky. Scholars haven't settled the matter yet, but they seem to think there are no living beings up there. Just chalk . . . or fire. Only this one is straining away, straining away all the time to make something of itself. The strain's so bad that every sixteen hours everybody lies down and gets a rest." He winds his watch. "Hm. . . . Eleven o'clock in Grover's Corners.—You get a good rest, too. Good night."

DISCUSSION QUESTIONS

Act I

1. What purpose does the absence of a curtain and scenery serve?
2. What purpose is served by having the Stage Manager seen arranging the furniture?
3. What dramatic function does the Stage Manager perform? Also, what doesn't he do?
4. What *persona* does the Stage Manager assume?
5. What is the significance of the various details the Stage Manager refers to in his description of the layout of the town? How do they help to create mood and atmosphere?
6. What is the significance of the time in which the play is set for mood and atmosphere?
7. How is time treated generally in the play? What does this suggest thematically?
8. What is the significance of the Stage Manager's remark, "There's some scenery for those who think they have to have scenery"?
9. What is the thematic significance of the gardens belonging to Mrs. Gibbs and Mrs. Webb?
10. What is the significance of the mention of the cemetery on the mountain and the names on the tombstones?
11. What characterization of Dr. Gibbs is provided by the mention of his presence on Main Street in the early hours of the morning?
12. What is the significance, literally and symbolically, of the new hospital being named after Dr. Gibbs?
13. Why does the newsboy hurl imaginary newspapers instead of real ones?
14. What is the irony and significance of the interchange between Dr. Gibbs and Joe Jr. concerning, "Anything serious goin' on in the world since Wednesday"?

15. What is the basis of the humor in Joe's remark on school teachers and marriage?
16. What does the conversation about Howie's horse contribute to the atmosphere of the play?
17. What is ironic about Mrs. Gibb's solicitude about Dr. Gibbs getting more rest and sleep? What is the thematic significance of the conversation?
18. What is the significance of George's response to his mother's calling him and to his father's calling him to get up for school?
19. What do the mention of Rebecca's dress and the throwing of soap do for the atmosphere of the scene?
20. What conflict is set up between George and Rebecca as to money matters, how does it characterize them, and what is the significance of this characterization thematically?
21. What does the shelling of the beans do to characterize Mrs. Gibbs and Mrs. Webb and how does it function thematically?
22. What does Mrs. Gibb's "secret" do to characterize her?
23. What purpose does it serve to have the Stage Manager break up the conversation between the two women?
24. What is the purpose of the interview with Professor Willard?
25. What is the significance of the information about life in the town provided by Mr. Webb?
26. What do the remarks on drinking establish?
27. What is the significance of the incident involving the question asked by the belligerent man at the back of the auditorium concerning social injustice and industrial inequality?
28. What characterization and preparation is provided in the after-school encounter between George and Emily?
29. What is the significance of the conversation between Emily and her mother concerning Emily's "prettiness" as far as characterization and theme are concerned?
30. What is the thematic significance of the Stage Manager's remarks about the cornerstone of the new bank in Grover's Corners?
31. What does the scene between George and his father do toward furthering the atmosphere and theme of the play?
32. What does the conversation between Mrs. Gibbs and Mrs. Soames do to characterize Mrs. Gibbs and add to the theme of the play?
33. What is the significance of the conversation over locking one's front door?
34. What does the encounter between Mr. Webb and Constable Warren establish in the way of atmosphere?
35. What transition does the address on the envelope to Jane Crofut prepare for?

Act II

1. What preparation for Act II do the Stage Manager's opening remarks provide?
2. What preparation for Act III do the Stage Manager's opening remarks provide?
3. What do the images of stair-climbing, erosion, and the flow of water accomplish?

4. What is the implication of the Stage Manager's remark about Mrs. Gibbs and Mrs. Webb, ". . . and never had a nervous breakdown"?
5. What is the significance of the discussion of the news between Howie Newsome and Si Crowell?
6. What is the purpose of the conversation between Howie and Mrs. Gibbs and Mrs. Webb?
7. What is the purpose of the breakfast conversation between Dr. Gibbs and Mrs. Gibbs?
8. What is the significance of Mr. Webb's ironic advice to George?
9. What traits of Emily and George are brought out in the flashback scene that augur well for a happy marriage?
10. What is the significance of the baseball players at the wedding?
11. How is the wisdom of the parents demonstrated?
12. Why does the wedding scene end in a silent tableau?

Act III

1. What is the significance of the stage directions concerning the empty chair in the front row?
2. What is the significance of the date, horses getting rarer, everyone locking his door at night, etc.?
3. What does the use of Indian place names—"Lake Sunapee" and "Lake Winipausakee"—accomplish thematically?
4. What is the irony of the remark, "I often wonder why people like to be buried in Woodlawn and Brooklyn when they might pass the same time up here in New Hampshire"?
5. What is the ironic significance of the Stage Manager's remarks on genealogy?
6. What is the thematic significance of the death of young Wallace?
7. What is the Stage Manager's attitude toward death?
8. What is the significance of the Stage Manager's metaphor, "They get weaned away from earth"?
9. What is the irony of Joe Stoddard's presence?
10. What is comic about Joe Stoddard's mention of his son?
11. What function does Sam Craig serve in the scene?
12. What is the irony in Mrs. Stimson's remark to Mrs. Gibbs?
13. What is the significance of the rain and the umbrellas?
14. What is the irony in the manner of Emily's death?
15. What is the significance of Mrs. Gibb's failure to remember the money she had left to George and Emily?
16. In this scene particularly, how does the playwright use the concept of time that prevails throughout the play?
17. What is the price that Emily must pay for reversing the direction of time?
18. How do Mr. Stimson's remarks bear on the theme of the play?

19. What is the thematic significance behind Mrs. Gibbs' admonition to Emily to choose an unimportant day?
20. What is significant about Emily's reaction to her mother's youthful appearance?
21. What events are stressed as being "important" on this "unimportant" day and what do they establish?
22. What is the significance thematically of the stage direction, "Crossing to embrace and kiss her; in her characteristic matter-of-fact manner"?
23. What is the thematic significance of Emily's remark, "Let's look at one another"?
24. What is the thematic significance of the Stage Manager's remark about "saints and poets"?
25. What is the conflict between Mr. Stimson and Mrs. Gibbs and how is it resolved?
26. What is the thematic significance of the remark, ". . . it took millions of years for the speck o' light to git to earth"?
27. What is significant about Emily's shifting from the pronoun "we" to "they" in her remarks?
28. What is the significance of the absence of the long-dead from the company of the dead?

THE GLASS MENAGERIE

✦ *Tennessee Williams*

Introductory Comment

The Glass Menagerie is Williams' first successful play and possibly his best. Despite his use of an actor who doubles as narrator, the unconventional lantern slides, and the tricky playing with lights which mean so much to Williams, the play is likely to impress us more through its often sentimental, evocative moods and its crisp, idiomatic speech. The presence in the play of an often silly and coquettish mother with absurd and childish illusions of refinement, a fragile daughter whose crippled leg manifests deep inner disturbances, and a rebellious poet of a son is hardly unusual. Considering Williams' penchant for the bizarre, what is most surprising about the play is the relative normality of all the characters: sexual aberrations, violent crime and emotional psychoses are almost totally absent. Yet Williams has fleshed out a set of patterns he uses again in more grotesque settings: in Amanda, we have the frightened fugitive from a distasteful reality, moving through a haze of self-deceptions and rosy illusions; in her children, we also have the helpless siblings who try to love and protect her; and finally, a stranger, Jim O'Connor, enters from "normality," seems to promise escape and safety, but finally withdraws, unaware of the family's deeper problems.

Beyond the confused and self-deceiving struggles of his trapped characters, we dimly vision glacial social and emotional forces in conflict. The sophistication and refinement of the South which Amanda remembers has existed mainly in sentimental fiction like *Gone With the Wind.* But the burning, decaying urban centers which crush the aspirations of Amanda and her kind provide no viable alternatives. The land which nurtured her impossible dreams went down to defeat through inefficiency, perverse individualism, and an often eccentric emphasis on an artificial chivalric code. But their replacement by warehouses and factories, high-rise apartment buildings and lushly-colored movies shown in rococo palaces hardly expands man's outlets for creative self-expression. Yet the social protest in Williams is muted. He is more interested in people than in the political and economic issues which have preoccupied writers like Ibsen, Shaw, and Miller. The comic inventiveness which proliferates through all the speeches heightens the pathetic and often bitter disappointments in the play. At the same time, the closeness of his types—ageing belle, gee-whiz stock boy, poetic adolescent—to caricature only enhances their theatricality and, paradoxically, their typicality. In garrulousness and reticence, tenderness and anger, malicious fun and self-pitying withdrawal, the authentic tones of American experience in the depressed thirties emerge from their encounters. In spite of the occasional hazy sentimentality which Williams is sometimes prone to, his delicious aphorisms, funny anecdotes, and compelling symbols crystallize into palpable, fresh patterns of experience. And the condensed, picture-frame vision of reality which Williams has portrayed manages to expand the apparently humdrum into images of universal significance. With only four characters, scant properties, a single setting, and deft lighting, Williams has presented the simple, lifelike difficulties of an alienated, transplanted family pathetically trying to escape a soul-crushing ugliness.

✣ *Production Notes*

Being a "memory play," *The Glass Menagerie* can be presented with unusual freedom of convention. Because of its considerably delicate or tenuous material, atmospheric touches and subtleties of direction play a particularly important part. Expressionism and all other unconventional techniques in drama have only one valid aim, and that is a closer approach to truth. When a play employs unconventional techniques, it is not, or certainly shouldn't be, trying to escape its responsibility of dealing with reality, or interpreting experience, but is actually or should be attempting to find a closer approach, a more penetrating and vivid expression of things as they are. The straight realistic play with its genuine frigidaire and authentic ice-cubes, its characters that speak exactly as its audience speaks, corresponds to the academic landscape and has the same virtue of a photographic likeness. Everyone should know nowadays the unimportance of the photographic in art: that truth, life, or reality is an organic thing which the poetic imagination can represent or suggest, in essence, only through transformation, through changing into other forms than those which were merely present in appearance.

These remarks are not meant as comments only on this particular play. They have to do with a conception of a new, plastic theatre which must take the place of the exhausted theatre of realistic conventions if the theatre is to resume vitality as a part of our culture.

The Screen Device

There is *only one important difference between the original and acting version of the play* and that is the *omission* in the latter of the device which I tentatively included in my *original* script. This device was the use of a screen on which were projected magic-lantern slides bearing images or titles. I do not regret the omission of this device from the present Broadway production. The extraordinary power of Miss Taylor's performance made it suitable to have the utmost simplicity in the physical production. But I think it may be interesting to some readers to see how this device was conceived. So I am putting it into the published manuscript. These images and legends, projected from behind, were cast on a section of wall between the front-room and dining-room areas, which should be indistinguishable from the rest when not in use.

The purpose of this will probably be apparent. It is to give accent to certain values in each scene. Each scene contains a particular point (or several) which is structurally the most important. In an episodic play, such as this, the basic structure or narrative line may be obscured from the audience; the effect may seem fragmentary rather than architectural. This may not be the fault of the play so much as a lack of attention in the audience. The legend or image upon the screen will strengthen the effect of what is merely allusion in the writing and allow the primary point to be made more simply and lightly than if the entire responsibility were on the spoken lines. Aside from this structural value, I think the screen will have a definite emotional appeal, less definable but just as important. An imaginative producer or director may invent many other uses for this device than those indicated in the present script. In fact the possibilities of the device seem much larger to me than the instance of this play can possibly utilize.

The Music

Another extra-literary accent in this play is provided by the use of music. A single recurring tune, "The Glass Menagerie," is used to give emotional emphasis to suitable passages. This tune is like circus music, not when you are on the grounds or in the immediate vicinity of the parade, but when you are at some distance and very likely thinking of something else. It seems under those circumstances to continue almost interminably and it weaves in and out of your preoccupied consciousness; then it is the lightest, most delicate music in the world and perhaps the saddest. It expresses the surface vivacity of life with the underlying strain of immutable and inexpressible sorrow. When you look at a piece of delicately spun glass you think of two things: how beautiful it is and how easily it can be broken. Both of those ideas should be woven into the recurring tune, which dips in and out of the play as if it were carried on a wind that changes. It serves as a thread of connection and allusion between the narrator with his separate point in time and space and the subject of his story. Between each episode it returns as reference to the emotion, nostalgia, which is the first condition of the play. It is primarily Laura's music and therefore comes out most clearly when the play focuses upon her and the lovely fragility of glass which is her image.

The Lighting

The lighting in the play is not realistic. In keeping with the atmosphere of memory, the stage is dim. Shafts of light are focused on selected areas or actors, sometimes in contradistinction to what is the apparent center. For instance, in the quarrel scene between Tom and Amanda, in which Laura has no active part, the clearest pool of light is on her figure. This is also true of the supper scene, when her silent figure on the sofa should remain the visual center. The light upon Laura should be distinct from the others, having a peculiar pristine clarity such as light used in early religious portraits of female saints or madonnas. A certain correspondence to light in religious paintings, such as El Greco's, where the figures are radiant in atmosphere that is relatively dusky, could be effectively used throughout the play. (It will also permit a more effective use of the screen.) A free, imaginative use of light can be of enormous value in giving a mobile, plastic quality to plays of a more or less static nature.

T. W.

Cast of Characters

AMANDA WINGFIELD, *the mother.*
LAURA WINGFIELD, *the daughter.*
TOM WINGFIELD, *her son.*
JIM O'CONNOR, *the gentleman caller.*

Scene: An alley in St. Louis.
Part I. *Preparation for a Gentleman Caller.*
Part II. *The Gentleman calls.*
Time: *Now and the Past.*

SCENE I

[*The Wingfield apartment is in the rear of the building, one of those vast hive-like conglomerations of cellular living-units that flower as warty growths in overcrowded urban centers of lower middle-class population and are symptomatic of the impulse of this largest and fundamentally enslaved section of American society to avoid fluidity and differentiation and to exist and function as one interfused mass of automatism.*

The apartment faces an alley and is entered by a fire-escape, a structure whose name is a touch of accidental poetic truth, for all of these huge buildings are always burning with the slow and implacable fires of human desperation. The fire-escape is included in the set—that is, the landing of it and steps descending from it.

The scene is memory and is therefore non-realistic. Memory takes a lot of poetic license. It omits some details; others are exaggerated, according to the emotional value of the articles it touches, for memory is seated predominantly in the heart. The interior is therefore rather dim and poetic.

At the rise of the curtain, the audience is faced with the dark, grim rear wall of the Wingfield tenement. This building, which runs parallel to the footlights, is flanked on both sides by dark, narrow alleys which run into murky canyons of tangled clotheslines, garbage cans and the sinister lattice-work of neighboring fire-escapes. It is up and down these side alleys that exterior entrances and exits are made, during the play. At the end of TOM'S *opening commentary, the dark tenement wall slowly reveals (by means of a transparency) the interior of the ground floor Wingfield apartment.*

Downstage is the living room, which also serves as a sleeping room for LAURA, *the sofa unfolding to make her bed. Upstage, center, and divided by a wide arch or second proscenium with transparent faded portieres (or second curtain), is the dining room. In an old-fashioned what-not in the living room are seen scores of transparent glass animals. A blown-up photograph of the father hangs on the wall of the living room, facing the audience, to the left of the archway. It is the face of a very handsome young man in a doughboy's First World War cap. He is gallantly smiling, ineluctably smiling, as if to say, "I will be smiling forever."*

The audience hears and sees the opening scene in the dining room through both the transparent fourth wall of the building and the transparent gauze portieres of the dining room arch. It is during this revealing scene that the fourth wall slowly ascends, out of sight. This transparent exterior wall is not brought down again until the very end of the play, during TOM'S *final speech.*

The narrator is an undisguised convention of the play. He takes whatever license with dramatic convention as is convenient to his purposes.

TOM *enters dressed as a merchant sailor from alley, stage left, and strolls across the front of the stage to the fire-escape. There he stops and lights a cigarette. He addresses the audience.*]

Tom: Yes, I have tricks in my pocket, I have things up my sleeve. But I am the opposite of a stage magician. He gives you illusion that has the appearance of truth. I give you truth in the pleasant disguise of illusion. To begin with, I turn back time. I reverse it to that quaint period, the thirties, when the huge middle class of America was matriculating in a school for the blind. Their eyes had failed them, or they had failed their eyes, and so they were having their fingers pressed forcibly down on the fiery Braille alphabet of a dissolving economy. In Spain there was revolution. Here there was only shouting and confusion. In Spain there was Guernica. Here there were disturbances of labor, sometimes pretty violent, in otherwise peaceful cities such as Chicago, Cleveland, Saint Louis . . . This is the social background of the play.

[*Music.*]

The play is memory. Being a memory play, it is dimly lighted, it is sentimental, it is not realistic. In memory everything seems to happen to music. That explains the fiddle in the wings. I am the narrator of the play, and also a character in it. The other characters are my mother, Amanda, my sister, Laura, and a gentleman caller who appears in the final scenes. He is the most realistic character in the play, being an emissary from a world of reality that we were somehow set apart from. But since I have a poet's weakness for symbols, I am using this character also as a symbol; he is the long delayed but always expected something that we live for. There is a fifth character in the play who doesn't appear except in this larger-than-life photograph over the mantel. This is our father who left us a long time ago. He was a telephone man who fell in love with long distances; he gave up his job with the telephone company and skipped the light fantastic out of town . . . The last we heard of him was a picture post-card from Mazatlan, on the Pacific coast of Mexico, containing a message of two words—"Hello—Goodbye!" and no address. I think the rest of the play will explain itself. . . .

[AMANDA'S *voice becomes audible through the portieres.*]

[*Legend on screen: "Où sont les neiges."*]

[*He divides the portieres and enters the upstage area.*]

[AMANDA *and* LAURA *are seated at a drop-leaf table. Eating is indicated by gestures without food or utensils.*

AMANDA *faces the audience.* TOM *and* LAURA *are seated in profile.*]

[*The interior has lit up softly and through the scrim we see* AMANDA *and* LAURA *seated at the table in the upstage area.*]

Amanda (*calling*). Tom?

Tom: Yes, Mother.

Amanda: We can't say grace until you come to the table!

Tom: Coming, Mother. (*He bows slightly and withdraws, reappearing a few moments later in his place at the table.*)

Amanda (*to her son*). Honey, don't *push* with your *fingers.* If you have to push with something, the thing to push with is a crust of bread. And chew—chew! Animals have sections in their stomachs which enable them to digest food without mastication, but human beings are supposed to chew their food before they swallow it down. Eat food leisurely, son, and really enjoy it. A well-cooked meal has lots of delicate flavors that have to be held in the mouth for appreciation. So chew your food and give your salivary glands a chance to function!

[TOM *deliberately lays his imaginary fork down and pushes his chair back from the table.*]

Tom: I haven't enjoyed one bite of this dinner because of your constant directions on how to eat it. It's you that make me rush through meals with your hawk-like attention to every bite I take. Sickening—spoils my appetite—all this discussion of animals' secretion—salivary glands—mastication!

Amanda (*lightly*). Temperament like a Metropolitan star! (*He rises and crosses downstage.*) You're not excused from the table.

Tom: I'm getting a cigarette.

Amanda: You smoke too much.

[LAURA *rises.*]

Laura: I'll bring in the blanc mange.

[*He remains standing with his cigarette by the portieres during the following.*]

Amanda (*rising*). No, sister, no, sister—you be the lady this time and I'll be the darky.

Laura: I'm already up.

Amanda: Resume your seat, little sister—I want you to stay fresh and pretty—for gentlemen callers!

Laura: I'm not expecting any gentlemen callers.

Amanda (*crossing out to kitchenette. Airily*). Sometimes they come when they are least expected! Why, I remember one Sunday afternoon in Blue Mountain—(*Enters kitchenette.*)

Tom: I know what's coming!

Laura: Yes. But let her tell it.

Tom: Again?

Laura: She loves to tell it.

[AMANDA *returns with bowl of dessert.*]

Amanda: One Sunday afternoon in Blue Mountain—your mother received—*seventeen!*—gentlemen callers! Why, sometimes there weren't chairs enough to accommodate them all. We had to send the nigger over to bring in folding chairs from the parish house.

Tom (*remaining at portieres*). How did you entertain those gentlemen callers?

Amanda: I understood the art of conversation!

Tom: I bet you could talk.

Amanda: Girls in those days *knew* how to talk, I can tell you.

Tom: Yes?

[*Image:* AMANDA *as a girl on a porch, greeting callers.*]

Amanda: They knew how to entertain their gentlemen callers. It wasn't enough for a girl to be possessed of a pretty face and a graceful figure—although I wasn't slighted in either respect. She also needed to have a nimble wit and a tongue to meet all occasions.

Tom: What did you talk about?

Amanda: Things of importance going on in the world! Never anything coarse or common or vulgar. (*She addresses* TOM *as though he were seated in the vacant chair at the table though he remains by portieres. He plays this scene as though he held the book.*) My callers were gentlemen—all! Among my callers were some of the most prominent young planters of the Mississippi Delta—planters and sons of planters!

[TOM *motions for music and a spot of light on* AMANDA.]

[*Her eyes lift, her face glows, her voice becomes rich and elegiac.*]

[*Screen legend: "Où sont les neiges."*]

There was young Champ Laughlin who later became vice-president of the Delta Planters Bank. Hadley Stevenson who was drowned in Moon Lake and left his widow one hundred and fifty thousand in Government bonds. There were the Cutrere brothers, Wesley and Bates. Bates was one of my bright particular beaux! He got in a quarrel with that wild Wainwright boy. They shot it out on the floor of Moon Lake Casino. Bates was shot through the stomach. Died in the ambulance on his way to Memphis. His widow was also well-provided for, came into eight or ten thousand acres, that's all. She married him on the rebound—never loved her—carried my picture on him the night he died! And there was that boy that every girl in the Delta had set her cap for! That beautiful, brilliant young Fitzhugh boy from Greene County!

Tom: What did he leave his widow?

Amanda: He never married! Gracious, you talk as though all of my old admirers had turned up their toes to the daisies!

Tom: Isn't this the first you've mentioned that still survives?

Amanda: That Fitzhugh boy went North and made a fortune—came to be known as the Wolf of Wall Street! He had the Midas touch, whatever he touched turned to gold! And I could have been Mrs. Duncan J. Fitzhugh, mind you! But—I picked your *father!*

Laura (*rising*). Mother, let me clear the table.

Amanda: No, dear, you go in front and study your typewriter chart. Or practice your shorthand a little. Stay fresh and pretty!—It's almost time for our gentlemen callers to start arriving. (*She flounces girlishly toward the kitchenette.*) How many do you suppose we're going to entertain this afternoon?

[TOM *throws down the paper and jumps up with a groan.*]

Laura (*alone in the dining room*). I don't believe we're going to receive any, Mother.

Amanda (*reappearing, airily*). What? No one—not one? You must be joking! (LAURA *nervously echoes her laugh. She slips in a fugitive manner through the half-open portieres and draws them gently behind her. A shaft of very clear light is thrown on her face against the faded tapestry of the curtains. Music: "The Glass Menagerie" under faintly. Lightly:*) Not one gentleman caller? It can't be true! There must be a flood, there must have been a tornado!

Laura: It isn't a flood, it's not a tornado, Mother. I'm just not popular like you were in Blue Mountain. . . . (TOM *utters another groan.* LAURA *glances at him with a faint, apologetic smile. Her voice catching a little.*) Mother's afraid I'm going to be an old maid.

[*The scene dims out with "Glass Menagerie" music.*]

SCENE II

[*"Laura, Haven't You Ever Liked Some Boy?"*

On the dark stage the screen is lighted with the image of blue roses.

Gradually LAURA'S *figure becomes apparent and the screen goes out.*

The music subsides.

LAURA *is seated in the delicate ivory chair at the small claw-foot table.*

She wears a dress of soft violet material for a kimono—her hair tied back from her forehead with a ribbon.

She is washing and polishing her collection of glass.

AMANDA *appears on the fire-escape. At the sound of her ascent,* LAURA *catches her breath, thrusts the bowl of ornaments away and seats herself stiffly before the diagram of the typewriter keyboard as though it held her spellbound. Something has happened to* AMANDA. *It is written in her face as she climbs to the landing: a look that is grim and hopeless and a little absurd.*

She has on one of those cheap or imitation velvety-looking cloth coats with imitation fur collar. Her hat is five or six years old, one of those dreadful cloche hats that were worn in the late twenties and she is clasping an enormous black patent-leather pocketbook with nickel clasps and initials. This is her full-dress outfit, the one she usually wears to the D.A.R.

Before entering she looks through the door.

She purses her lips, opens her eyes wide, rolls them upward and shakes her head.

Then she slowly lets herself in the door. Seeing her mother's expression LAURA *touches her lips with a nervous gesture.*]

Laura: Hello, Mother, I was—(*She makes a nervous gesture toward the chart on the wall.* AMANDA *leans against the shut door and stares at* LAURA *with a martyred look.*)

Amanda: Deception? Deception? (*She slowly removes her hat and gloves, continuing the sweet suffering stare. She lets the hat and gloves fall on the floor—a bit of acting.*)

Laura (*shakily*). How was the D.A.R. meeting? (AMANDA *slowly opens her purse and removes a dainty white handkerchief which she shakes out delicately and delicately touches to her lips and nostrils.*) Didn't you go to the D.A.R. meeting, Mother?

Amanda (*faintly, almost inaudibly*).

—No.—No. (*Then more forcibly:*) I did not have the strength—to go to the D.A.R. In fact, I did not have the courage! I wanted to find a hole in the ground and hide myself in it forever! (*She crosses slowly to the wall and removes the diagram of the typewriter keyboard. She holds it in front of her for a second, staring at it sweetly and sorrowfully—then bites her lips and tears it in two pieces.*)

Laura (*faintly*). Why did you do that, Mother? (AMANDA *repeats the same procedure with the chart of the Gregg Alphabet.*) Why are you—

Amanda: Why? Why? How old are you, Laura?

Laura: Mother, you know my age.

Amanda: I thought that you were an adult; it seems that I was mistaken. (*She crosses slowly to the sofa and sinks down and stares at* LAURA.)

Laura: Please don't stare at me, Mother.

[AMANDA *closes her eyes and lowers her head. Count ten.*]

Amanda: What are we going to do, what is going to become of us, what is the future?

[*Count ten.*]

Laura: Has something happened, Mother? (AMANDA *draws a long breath and takes out the handkerchief again. Dabbing process.*) Mother, has—something happened?

Amanda: I'll be all right in a minute. I'm just bewildered—(*Count five*)—by life. . . .

Laura: Mother, I wish that you would tell me what's happened!

Amanda: As you know, I was supposed to be inducted into my office at the D.A.R. this afternoon. (*Image: A swarm of typewriters.*) But I stopped off at Rubicam's Business College to speak to your teachers about your having a cold and ask them what progress they thought you were making down there.

Laura: Oh. . . .

Amanda: I went to the typing instructor and introduced myself as your mother. She didn't know who you were. Wingfield, she said. We don't have any such student enrolled at the school! I assured her she did, that you had been going to classes since early in January. "I wonder," she said, "if you could be talking about that terribly shy little girl who dropped out of school after only a few days' attendance?" "No," I said, "Laura, my daughter has been going to school every day for the past six weeks!" "Excuse me," she said. She took the attendance book out and there was your name, unmistakably printed, and all the dates you were absent until they decided that you had dropped out of school. I still said, "No, there must have been some mistake! There must have been some mix-up in the records!" And she said, "No—I remember her perfectly now. Her hands shook so that she couldn't hit the right keys! The first time we gave a speed-test, she broke down completely—was sick at the stomach and almost had to be carried into the wash-room! After that morning she never showed up any more. We phoned the house but never got any answer"—while I was working at Famous and Barr, I suppose, demonstrating those—Oh! I felt so weak I could barely keep on my feet! I had to sit down while they got me a glass of water! Fifty dollars' tuition, all of our plans—my hopes and ambitions for you—just gone up the spout, just gone up the spout like that. (LAURA *draws a long breath and gets awkwardly to her feet. She crosses to the victrola and winds it up.*) What are you doing?

Laura: Oh! (*She releases the handle and returns to her seat.*)

Amanda: Laura, where have you been going when you've gone out pretending that you were going to business college?

Laura: I've just been going out walking.

Amanda: That's not true.

Laura: It is. I just went walking.

Amanda: Walking? Walking? In winter? Deliberately courting pneumonia in that light coat? Where did you walk to, Laura?

Laura: All sorts of places—mostly in the park.

Amanda: Even after you'd started catching that cold?

Laura: It was the lesser of two evils, Mother. (*Image: winter scene in park.*) I couldn't go back up. I—threw up—on the floor!

Amanda: From half past seven till after five every day you mean to tell me you walked around in the park, because you wanted to make me think that you were still going to Rubicam's Business College?

Laura: It wasn't as bad as it sounds. I went inside places to get warmed up.

Amanda: Inside where?

Laura: I went in the art museum and the bird-houses at the Zoo. I visited the penguins every day! Sometimes I did without lunch and went to the movies. Lately I've been spending most of my afternoons in the Jewel-box, that big glass house where they raise the tropical flowers.

Amanda: You did all this to deceive me, just for deception? (LAURA *looks down.*) Why?

Laura: Mother, when you're disappointed, you get that awful suffering look on your face, like the picture of Jesus' mother in the museum!

Amanda: Hush!

Laura: I couldn't face it.

[*Pause. A whisper of strings.*]

[*Legend: "The Crust of Humility."*]

Amanda (*hopelessly fingering the huge pocketbook*). So what are we going to do the rest of our lives? Stay home and watch the parades go by? Amuse ourselves with the glass menagerie, darling? Eternally play those worn-out phonograph records your father left as a painful reminder of him? We won't have a business career—we've given that up because it gave us nervous indigestion! (*Laughs wearily.*) What is there left but dependency all our lives? I know so well what becomes of unmarried women who aren't prepared to occupy a position. I've seen such pitiful cases in the South—barely tolerated spinsters living upon the grudging patronage of sister's husband or brother's wife!—stuck away in some little mouse-trap of a room—encouraged by one in-law to visit another—little birdlike women without any nest—eating the crust of humility all their life! Is that the future that we've mapped out for ourselves? I swear it's the only alternative I can think of! It isn't a very pleasant alternative, is it? Of course—some girls *do marry.* (LAURA *twists her hands nervously.*) Haven't you ever liked some boy?

Laura: Yes. I liked one once. (*Rises.*) I came across his picture a while ago.

Amanda (*with some interest*). He gave you his picture?

Laura: No, it's in the year-book.

Amanda (*disappointed*). Oh—a high-school boy.

[*Screen image:* JIM *as high-school hero bearing a silver cup.*]

Laura: Yes. His name was Jim. (LAURA *lifts the heavy annual from the claw-foot table.*) Here he is in *The Pirates of Penzance.*

Amanda (*absently*). The what?

Laura: The operetta the senior class put on. He had a wonderful voice and we sat across the aisle from each other Mondays, Wednesdays and Fridays in the Aud. Here he is with the silver cup for debating! See his grin?

Amanda (*absently*). He must have had a jolly disposition.

Laura: He used to call me—Blue Roses.

[*Image: Blue roses.*]

Amanda: Why did he call you such a name as that?

Laura: When I had that attack of pleurosis—he asked me what was the matter when I came back. I said pleurosis—he thought that I said Blue Roses! So that's what he always called me after that. Whenever he saw me, he'd holler, "Hello, Blue Roses!" I didn't care for the girl that he went out with. Emily Meisenbach. Emily was the best-dressed girl at Soldan. She never struck me, though, as being sincere . . . It says in the Personal Section—they're engaged. That's—six years ago! They must be married by now.

Amanda: Girls that aren't cut out for business careers usually wind up married to some nice man. (*Gets up with a spark of revival.*) Sister, that's what you'll do!

[LAURA *utters a startled, doubtful laugh. she reaches quickly for a piece of glass.*]

Laura: But, Mother—

Amanda: Yes? (*Crossing to photograph.*)

Laura (*in a tone of frightened apology*). I'm—crippled!

[*Image: screen.*]

Amanda: Nonsense! Laura, I've told you never, never to use that word. Why, you're not crippled, you just have a little defect—hardly noticeable, even! When people have some slight disadvantage like that, they cultivate other things to make up for it—develop charm—and vivacity—and—*charm!* That's all you have to do! (*She turns again to the photograph.*) One thing your father had *plenty of*—was *charm!*

[TOM *motions to the fiddle in the wings.*]

[*The scene fades out with music.*]

SCENE III

[*Legend on screen: "After the fiasco—"*]

[TOM *speaks from the fire-escape landing.*]

Tom: After the fiasco at Rubicam's Business College, the idea of getting a gentleman caller for Laura began to play a more important part in Mother's calculations. It became an obsession. Like some archetype of the universal unconscious, the image of the gentleman caller haunted our small apartment. . . . (*Image: Young man at door with flowers.*) An evening at home rarely passed without some allusion to this image, this spectre, this hope. . . . Even when he wasn't mentioned, his presence hung in Mother's preoccupied look and in my sister's frightened, apologetic manner—hung like a sentence passed upon the Wingfields! Mother was a woman of action as well as words. She began to take logical steps in the planned direction. Late that winter and in the early spring—realizing that extra money would be needed to properly feather the nest and plume the bird—she conducted a vigorous campaign on the telephone, roping in subscribers to one of those magazines for matrons called *The Homemaker's Companion,* the type of journal that features the serialized sublimations of ladies of letters who think in terms of delicate cup-like breasts, slim, tapering waists, rich, creamy thighs, eyes like woodsmoke in autumn, fingers that soothe and caress like strains of music, bodies as powerful as Etruscan sculpture.

[*Screen images: Glamor magazine cover.*]

[AMANDA *enters with phone on long extension cord. She is spotted in the dim stage.*]

Amanda: Ida Scott? This is Amanda Wingfield! We *missed* you at the D.A.R. last Monday! I said to myself: She's probably suffering with that sinus condition! How is that sinus condition? Horrors! Heaven have mercy!—You're a Christian martyr, yes, that's what you are, a Christian martyr! Well, I just now happened to notice that your subscription to the *Companion's* about to expire! Yes, it expires with the next issue, honey!—just when that wonderful new serial by Bessie Mae Hopper is getting off to such an exciting start. Oh, honey, it's something that you can't miss! You remember how *Gone With the Wind* took everybody by storm? You simply couldn't go out if you hadn't read it. All everybody *talked* was Scarlett O'Hara. Well, this is a book that critics already compare to *Gone With the Wind.* It's the *Gone With the Wind* of the post-World War generation!—What?—Burning?—Oh, honey, don't let them burn, go take a look in the oven and I'll hold the wire! Heavens—I think she's hung up!

[*Dim out.*]

[*Legend on screen: "You think I'm in love with Continental Shoemakers?"*]

[*Before the stage is lighted, the violent voices of* TOM *and* AMANDA *are heard.*]

[*They are quarreling behind the portieres. In front of them stands* LAURA *with clenched hands and panicky expression.*]

[*A clear pool of light on her figure throughout this scene.*]

Tom: What in Christ's name am I—

Amanda: (*shrilly*). Don't you use that—

Tom: Supposed to do!

Amanda: Expression! Not in my—

Tom: Ohhh!

Amanda: Presence! Have you gone out of your senses?

Tom: I have that's true, *driven* out!

Amanda: What is the matter with you, you—big—big—*idiot!*

Tom: Look—I've got *no thing,* no single thing—

Amanda: Lower your voice!

Tom: In my life here that I can call my *own!* Everything is—

Amanda: Stop that shouting!

Tom: Yesterday you confiscated my books! You had the nerve to—

Amanda: I took that horrible novel back to the library—yes! That hideous book by that insane Mr. Lawrence. (TOM *laughs wildly.*) I cannot control the output of diseased minds or people who cater to them—(TOM *laughs still more wildly.*) BUT I WON'T ALLOW SUCH FILTH BROUGHT INTO MY HOUSE! No, no, no, no, no!

Tom: House, house! Who pays the rent on it, who makes a slave of himself to—

Amanda: (*fairly screeching*). Don't you DARE to—

Tom: No, no, *I* mustn't say things! *I've* got to just—

Amanda: Let me tell you—

Tom: I don't want to hear any more! (*He tears the portieres open. The upstage area is lit with a turgid smoky red glow.*)

[AMANDA'S *hair is in metal curlers and she wears a very old bathrobe, much too large for her slight figure, a relic of the faithless Mr. Wingfield.*]

[*An upright typewriter and a wild disarray of manuscripts is on the drop-leaf table. The quarrel was probably precipitated by* AMANDA'S *interruption of his creative labor. A chair lying overthrown on the floor.*]

[*Their gesticulating shadows are cast on the ceiling by the fiery glow.*]

Amanda: You *will* hear more, you—

Tom: No, I won't hear more, I'm going out!

Amanda: You come right back in—

Tom: Out, out, out! Because I'm—

Amanda: Come back here, Tom Wingfield! I'm not through talking to you!

Tom: Oh, go—

Laura (*desperately*). —Tom!

Amanda: You're going to listen, and no more insolence from you! I'm at the end of my patience! (*He comes back toward her.*)

Tom: What do you think I'm at? Aren't I supposed to have any patience to reach the end of, Mother? I know, I know. It seems unimportant to you, what I'm *doing*—what I *want* to do—having a little *difference* between them! You don't think that—

Amanda: I think you've been doing things that you're ashamed of. That's why you act like this. I don't believe that you go every night to the movies. Nobody goes to the movies night after night. Nobody in their right minds goes to the movies as often as you pretend to. People don't go to the movies at nearly midnight, and movies don't let out at two A.M. Come in stumbling. Muttering to yourself like a maniac! You get three hours' sleep and then go to work. Oh, I can picture the way you're doing down there. Moping, doping, because you're in no condition.

Tom (*wildly*). No, I'm in no condition!

Amanda: What right have you got to jeopardize your job? Jeopardize the security of us all? How do you think we'd manage if you were—

Tom: Listen! You think I'm crazy *about* the *warehouse?* (*He bends fiercely toward her slight figure.*) You think I'm in love with the Continental Shoemakers? You think I want to spend fifty-five *years* down there in that—*celotex interior!* with —*fluorescent*—*tubes!* Look! I'd rather somebody picked up a crowbar and battered out my brains—than go back mornings! I *go!* Every time you come in yelling that God damn *"Rise and Shine!" "Rise and Shine!"* I say to myself, "How *lucky dead* people are!" But I get up. I *go!* For sixty-five dollars a month I give up all that I dream of doing and being *ever!* And you say self—*self's* all I ever think of. Why, listen, if self is what I thought of, Mother, I'd be where he is —GONE! (*Pointing to father's picture.*) As far as the system of transportation reaches! (*He starts past her. She grabs his arm.*) Don't grab at me, Mother!

Amanda: Where are you going?

Tom: I'm going to the *movies!*

Amanda: I don't believe that lie!

Tom (*crouching toward her, overtowering her tiny figure. She backs away, gasping*). I'm going to opium dens! Yes, opium dens, dens of vice and criminals' hang-outs, Mother. I've joined the Hogan gang, I'm a hired assassin, I carry a tommy-gun in a violin case! I run a string of cat-houses in the Valley! They call me Killer, Killer Wingfield, I'm leading a double-life, a simple honest warehouse worker by day, by night, a dynamic *czar* of the *underworld, Mother.* I go to gambling casinos, I spin away fortunes on the roulette table! I wear a patch over one eye and a false mustache, sometimes I put on green whiskers. On those occasions they call me—*El Diablo!* Oh, I could tell you things to make you sleepless! My enemies plan to dynamite this place. They're going to blow us all sky-high some night! I'll be glad, very happy, and so will you! You'll go up, up on a broomstick, over Blue Mountain with seventeen gentlemen callers! You ugly—babbling old—*witch. . . .* (*He goes through a series of violent, clumsy movements, seizing his overcoat, lunging to the door, pulling it fiercely open. The women watch him, aghast. His arm catches in the sleeve of the coat as he struggles to pull it on. For a moment he is pinioned by the bulky garment. With an outraged groan he tears the coat off again, splitting the shoulder of it, and hurls it across the room. It strikes against the shelf of* LAURA'S *glass collection, there is a tinkle of shattering glass.* LAURA *cries out as if wounded.*)

[*Music legend: "The Glass Menagerie."*

Laura (*shrilly*). *My glass!*—menagerie. . . .

(*She covers her face and turns away.*)

[*But* AMANDA *is still stunned and stupefied by the "ugly witch" so that she barely notices this occurrence. Now she recovers her speech.*]

Amanda (*in an awful voice.*) I won't speak to you—until you apologize! (*She crosses through the portiers and draws them together behind her.* TOM *is left with* LAURA. LAURA *clings weakly to the mantel with her face averted.* TOM *stares at her stupidly for a moment. Then he crosses to shelf. Drops awkwardly on his knees to collect the fallen glass, glancing at* LAURA *as if he would speak but couldn't.*)

[*"The Glass Menagerie" steals in as the scene dims out.*]

SCENE IV

[*The interior is dark. Faint light in the alley.*

A deep-voice bell in a church is tolling the hour of five as the scene commences.

TOM *appears at the top of the alley. After each solemn boom of the bell in the tower, he shakes a little noise-maker or rattle as if to express the tiny spasm of man in contrast to the sustained power and dignity of the Almighty. This and the unsteadiness of his advance make it evident that he has been drinking.*

As he climbs the few steps to the fire-escape landing light steals up inside. LAURA *appears in night-dress, observing* TOM'S *empty bed in the front room.*

TOM *fishes in his pockets for the door-key, removing a motley assortment of articles in the search, including a perfect shower of movie-ticket stubs and an empty bottle. At last he finds the key, but just as he is about to insert it, it slips from his fingers. He strikes a match and crouches below the door.*]

Tom (*bitterly*). One crack—and it falls through!

[LAURA *opens the door.*]

Laura: Tom! Tom, what are you doing?

Tom: Looking for a door-key.

Laura: Where have you been all this time?

Tom: I have been to the movies.

Laura: All this time at the movies?

Tom: There was a very long program. There was a Garbo picture and a Mickey Mouse and a travelogue and a newsreel and a preview of coming attractions. And there was an organ solo and a collection for the milk-fund—simultaneously—which ended up in a terrible fight between a fat lady and an usher!

Laura (*innocently*). Did you have to stay through everything?

Tom: Of course! And, oh, I forgot! There was a big stage show! The headliner on this stage show was Malvolio the Magician. He performed wonderful tricks, many of them, such as pouring water back and forth between pitchers. First it turned to wine and then it turned to beer and then it turned to whiskey. I know it was whiskey it finally turned into because he needed somebody to come up out of the audience to help him, and I came up—both shows! It was Kentucky Straight Bourbon. A very generous fellow, he gave souvenirs. (*He pulls from his back pocket a shimmering rainbow-colored scarf.*) He gave me this. This is his magic scarf. You can have it, Laura. You wave it over a canary cage and you get a bowl of gold-fish. You wave it over the gold-fish bowl and they fly away canaries. . . . But the wonderfullest trick of all was the coffin trick. We nailed him into a coffin and he got out of the coffin without removing one nail. (*He has come inside.*) There is a trick that would come in handy for me—get me out of this 2 by 4 situation! (*Flops onto bed and starts removing shoes.*)

Laura: Tom—Shhh!

Tom: What're you shushing me for?

Laura: You'll wake up Mother.

Tom: Goody, goody! Pay 'er back for all those "Rise an' Shines." (*Lies down, groaning.*) You know it don't take much intelligence to get yourself into a nailed-up coffin, Laura. But who in hell ever got himself out of one without removing one nail?

[*As if in answer, the father's grinning photograph lights up.*]

[*Scene dims out.*]

[*Immediately following: The church bell is heard striking six. At the sixth stroke the alarm clock goes off in* AMANDA'S *room, and after a few moments we hear her calling: "Rise and Shine! Rise and Shine! Laura, go tell your brother to rise and shine!"*]

Tom (*Sitting up slowly*). I'll rise—but I won't shine.

[*The light increases.*]

Amanda: Laura, tell your brother his coffee is ready.

[LAURA *slips into front room.*]

Laura: Tom it's nearly seven. Don't make Mother nervous. (*He stares at her stupidly. Beseechingly.*) Tom, speak to Mother this morning. Make up with her, apologize, speak to her!

Tom: She won't to me. It's her that started not speaking.

Laura: If you just say you're sorry she'll start speaking.

Tom: Her not speaking—is that such a tragedy?

Laura: Please—please!

Amanda (*calling from kitchenette*). Laura, are you going to do what I asked you to do, or do I have to get dressed and go out myself?

Laura: Going, going—soon as I get on my coat! (*She pulls on a shapeless felt hat with nervous, jerky movement, pleadingly glancing at* TOM. *Rushes awkwardly for coat. The coat is one of* AMANDA'S, *inaccurately made-over, the sleeves too short for* LAURA.) Butter and what else?

Amanda (*entering upstage*). Just butter. Tell them to charge it.

Laura: Mother, they make such faces when I do that.

Amanda: Sticks and stones can break our bones, but the expression on Mr. Garfinkel's face won't harm us! Tell your brother his coffee is getting cold.

Laura (*at door*). Do what I asked you, will you, will you, Tom?

[*He looks sullenly away.*]

Amanda: Laura, go now or just don't go at all!

Laura (*rushing out*). Going—going! (*A second later she cries out.* TOM *springs up and crosses to door.* AMANDA *rushes anxiously in.* TOM *opens the door.*)

Tom: Laura?

Laura: I'm all right. I slipped, but I'm all right.

Amanda (*peering anxiously after her*). If anyone breaks a leg on those fire-escape steps, the landlord ought to be sued for every cent he possesses! (*She shuts door. Remembers she isn't speaking and returns to other room.*)

[*As* TOM *enters listlessly for his coffee, she turns her back to him and stands rigidly facing the window on the gloomy gray vault of the areaway. Its light on her face with its aged but childish features is cruelly sharp, satirical as a Daumier print.*]

[*Music under: "Ave Maria."*]

[TOM *glances sheepishly but sullenly at her averted figure and slumps at the table. The coffee is scalding hot; he sips it and gasps and spits it back in the cup. At his gasp,* AMANDA *catches her breath and half turns. Then catches herself and turns back to window.*]

[TOM *blows on his coffee, glancing sidewise at his mother. She clears her throat.* TOM *clears his. He starts to rise. Sinks back down again, scratches his head, clears his throat again.* AMANDA *coughs.* TOM *raises his cup in both hands to blow on it, his eyes staring over the rim of it at his mother for several moments. Then he slowly sets the cup down and awkwardly and hesitantly rises from the chair.*]

Tom (*hoarsely*). Mother. I—I apologize, Mother. (AMANDA *draws a quick, shuddering breath. Her face works grotesquely. She breaks into childlike tears.*) I'm sorry for what I said, for everything that I said, I didn't mean it.

Amanda (*sobbingly*). My devotion has made me a witch and so I make myself hateful to my children!

Tom: *No,* you *don't.*

Amanda: I worry so much, don't sleep, it makes me nervous!

Tom (*gently*). I understand that.

Amanda: I've had to put up a solitary battle all these years. But you're my right-hand bower! Don't fall down, don't fail!

Tom (*gently*). I try, Mother.

Amanda (*with great enthusiasm*). Try and you will SUCCEED! (*The notion makes her breathless.*) Why, you—you're just *full* of natural endowments! Both of my children—they're *unusual* children! Don't you think I know it? I'm so—*proud!* Happy and—feel I've—so much to be thankful for but—Promise me one thing, son!

Tom: What, Mother?

Amanda: Promise, son, you'll—never be a drunkard!

Tom (*turns to her grinning*). I will never be a drunkard, Mother.

Amanda: That's what frightened me so, that you'd be drinking! Eat a bowl of Purina!

Tom: Just coffee, Mother.

Amanda: Shredded wheat biscuit?

Tom: No. No, Mother, just coffee.

Amanda: You can't put in a day's work on an empty stomach. You've got ten minutes—don't gulp! Drinking too-hot liquids makes cancer of the stomach. . . . Put cream in.

Tom: No, thank you.

Amanda: To cool it.

Tom: No! No, thank you, I want it black.

Amanda: I know, but it's not good for you. We have to do all that we can to build ourselves up. In these trying times we live in, all that we have to cling to is—each other. . . . That's why it's so important to—Tom, I— I sent out your sister so I could discuss something with you. If you hadn't spoken I would have spoken to you. (*Sits down.*)

Tom (*gently*). What is it, Mother, that you want to discuss?

Amanda: *Laura!*

[TOM *puts his cup down slowly.*]

[*Legend on screen: "Laura."*]

[*Music: "The Glass Menagerie."*]

Tom: —Oh.—Laura . . .

Amanda (*touching his sleeve*). You know how Laura is. So quiet but—still water runs deep! She notices things and I think she—broods about them. (TOM *looks up*). A few days ago I came in and she was crying.

Tom: What about?

Amanda: You.

Tom: Me?

Amanda: She has an idea that you're not happy here.

Tom: What gave her that idea?

Amanda: What gives her any idea? However, you do act strangely. I—I'm not criticizing, understand *that!* I know your ambitions do not lie in the warehouse, that like everybody in the whole wide world—you've had to—make sacrifices, but—Tom—Tom—life's not easy, it calls for—Spartan endurance! There's so many things in my heart that I cannot describe to you! I've never told you but I—*loved* your father. . . .

Tom (*gently*). I know that, Mother.

Amanda: And you—when I see you taking after his ways! Staying out late—and—well, you *had* been drinking the night you were in that—terrifying condition! Laura says that you hate the apartment and that you go out nights to get away from it! Is that true, Tom?

Tom: No. You say there's so much in your heart that you can't describe to me. That's true of me, too. There's so much in my heart that I can't describe to *you!* So let's respect each other's—

Amanda: But, why—*why,* Tom—are you always so *restless*? Where do you *go* to, nights?

Tom: I—go to the movies.

Amanda: Why do you go to the movies so much, Tom?

Tom: I go to the movies because—I like adventure. Adventure is something I don't have much of at work, so I go to the movies.

Amanda: But, Tom, you go to the movies *entirely* too *much!*

Tom: I like a lot of adventure.

[AMANDA *looks baffled, then hurt. As the familiar inquisition resumes he becomes hard and impatient again.* AMANDA *slips back into her querulous attitude toward him.*]

[*Image on screen: Sailing vessel with Jolly Roger.*]

Amanda: Most young men find adventure in their careers.

Tom: Then most young men are not employed in a warehouse.

Amanda: The world is full of young men employed in warehouses and offices and factories.

Tom: Do all of them find adventure in their careers?

Amanda: They do or they do without it! Not everybody has a craze for adventure.

Tom: Man is by instinct a lover, a hunter, a fighter, and none of those instincts are given much play at the warehouse!

Amanda: Man is by instinct! Don't quote instinct to me! Instinct is something that people have got away from! It belongs to animals! Christian adults don't want it!

Tom: What do Christian adults want, then, Mother?

Amanda: Superior things! Things of the mind and the spirit! Only animals have to satisfy instincts! Surely your aims are somewhat higher than theirs! Than monkeys—pigs—

Tom: I reckon they're not.

Amanda: You're joking. However, that isn't what I wanted to discuss.

Tom (*rising*). I haven't much time.

Amanda (*pushing his shoulders*). Sit down.

Tom: You want me to punch in red at the warehouse, Mother?

Amanda: You have five minutes. I want to talk about Laura.

[*Legend: "Plans and Provisions."*]

Tom: All right! What about Laura?

Amanda: We have to be making plans and provisions for her. She's older than you, two years, and nothing has happened. She just drifts along doing nothing. It frightens me terribly how she just drifts along.

Tom: I guess she's the type that people call home girls.

Amanda: There's no such type, and if there is, it's a pity! That is unless the home is hers, with a husband!

Tom: What?

Amanda: Oh, I can see the handwriting on the wall as plain as I see the nose in front of my face! It's terrifying! More and more you remind me of your father! He was out all hours without explanation —Then *left! Good-bye!* And me with the bag to hold. I saw that letter you got from the Merchant Marine. I know what you're dreaming of. I'm not standing here blindfolded. Very well then. Then *do* it! But not till there's somebody to take your place.

Tom: What do you mean?

Amanda: I mean that as soon as Laura has got somebody to take care of her, married, a home of her own, independent—why, then you'll be free to go wherever you please, on land, on sea, whichever way the wind blows you! But until that time you've got to look out for your sister. I don't say me because I'm old and don't matter! I say for your sister because she's young and dependent. I put her in business college—a dismal failure! Frightened her so it made her sick to her stomach. I took her over to the Young People's League at the church. Another fiasco. She spoke to nobody, nobody spoke to her. Now all she does is fool with those pieces of glass and play those worn-out records. What kind of a life is that for a girl to lead?

Tom: What can I do about it?

Amanda: Overcome selfishness! Self, self, self is all that you ever think of! (TOM *springs up and crosses to get his coat. It is ugly and bulky. He pulls on a cap with earmuffs.*) Where is your muffler? Put your wool muffler on! (*He snatches it angrily from the closet and tosses it around his neck and pulls both ends tight.*) Tom! I haven't said what I had in mind to ask you.

Tom: I'm too late to—

Amanda (*catching his arm—very importunately. Then shyly*). Down at the warehouse, aren't there some—nice young men?

Tom: No!

Amanda: There *must* be—*some . . .*

Tom: Mother—

[*Gesture.*]

Amanda: Find out one that's clean-living—doesn't drink and—ask him out for sister!

Tom: What?

Amanda: For *sister!* To *meet!* Get *acquainted!*

Tom (*stamping to door*). Oh, my *go-osh!*

Amanda: Will you? (*He opens door. Imploringly.*) Will you? (*He starts down.*) Will you? *Will* you, dear?

Tom (*calling back*). YES!

[AMANDA *closes the door hesitantly and with a troubled but faintly hopeful expression.*]

[*Screen image: Glamour magazine cover.*]

[*Spot* AMANDA *at phone.*]

Amanda: Ella Cartwright? This is Amanda Wingfield! How are you, honey? How is that kidney condition? (*Count five*). *Horrors!* (*Count five.*) You're a Christian martyr, yes, honey, that's what you are, a Christian martyr! Well, I just happened to notice in my little red book that your subscription to the *Companion* has just run out! I knew that you wouldn't want to miss out on the wonderful serial starting in this new issue. It's by Bessie Mae Hopper, the first thing she's written since *Honeymoon for Three.* Wasn't that a strange and interesting story? Well, this one is even lovelier, I believe. It has a sophisticated, society background. It's all about the horsey set on Long Island!

[*Fade out.*]

SCENE V

[*Legend on screen: "Annunciation." Fade with music.*]

[*It is early dusk of a spring evening. Supper has just been finished in the Wingfield apartment.* AMANDA *and* LAURA *in light colored dresses are removing dishes from the table, in the upstage area, which is shadowy, their movements formalized almost as a dance or ritual, their moving forms as pale and silent as moths.*

TOM, *in white shirt and trousers rises from the table and crosses toward the fire-escape.*]

Amanda (*as he passes her*). Son, will you do me a favor?

Tom: What?

Amanda: Comb your hair! You look so pretty when your hair is combed! (TOM *slouches on sofa with evening paper. Enormous caption "Franco Triumphs."*) There is only one respect in which I would like you to emulate your father.

Tom: What respect is that?

Amanda: The care he always took of his appearance. He never allowed himself to look untidy. (*He throws down the paper and crosses to fire-escape.*) Where are you going?

Tom: I'm going out to smoke.

Amanda: You smoke too much. A pack a day at fifteen cents a pack. How much would that amount to in a month? Thirty times fifteen is how much, Tom? Figure it out and you will be astounded at what you could save. Enough to give you a night-school course in accounting at Washington U! Just think what a wonderful thing that would be for you, son!

[TOM *is unmoved by the thought.*]

Tom: I'd rather smoke. (*He steps out on landing, letting the screen door slam.*)

Amanda (*sharply*). I know! That's the tragedy of it. . . . (*Alone, she turns to look at her husband's picture.*)

[*Dance music: "All the World Is Waiting for the Sunrise!"*]

Tom (*to the audience*). Across the alley from us was the Paradise Dance Hall. On evenings in spring the windows and doors were open and the music came outdoors. Sometimes the lights were turned out except for a large glass sphere that hung from the ceiling. It would turn slowly about and filter the dusk with delicate rainbow colors. Then the orchestra played a waltz or a tango, something that had a slow and sensuous rhythm. Couples would come outside, to the relative privacy of the alley. You could see them kissing behind ash-pits and telephone poles. This was the compensation for lives that passed like mine, without any change or adventure. Adventure and change were imminent in this year. They were waiting around the corner for all these kids. Suspended in the mist over Berchtesgaden, caught in the folds of Chamberlain's umbrella—In Spain there was Guernica! But here there was only hot swing music and liquor, dance halls, bars, and movies, and sex that hung in the gloom like a chandelier and flooded the world with brief, deceptive rainbows. . . . All the world was waiting for bombardments!

[AMANDA *turns from the picture and comes outside.*]

Amanda (*Sighing*). A fire-escape landing's a poor excuse for a porch. (*She spreads a newspaper on a step and sits down, gracefully and demurely as if she were settling into a swing on a Mississippi veranda.*) What are you looking at?

Tom: The moon.

Amanda: Is there a moon this evening?

Tom: It's rising over Garfinkel's Delicatessen.

Amanda: So it is! A little silver slipper of a moon. Have you made a wish on it yet?

Tom: Um-hum.

Amanda: What did you wish for?

Tom: That's a secret.

Amanda: A secret, huh? Well, I won't tell mine either. I will be just as mysterious as you.

Tom: I bet I can guess what yours is.

Amanda: Is my head so transparent?

Tom: You're not a sphinx.

Amanda: No, I don't have secrets. I'll tell you what I wished for on the moon. Success and happiness for my precious children! I wish for that whenever there's a moon, and when there isn't a moon, I wish for it, too.

Tom: I thought perhaps you wished for a gentleman caller.

Amanda: Why do you say that?

Tom: Don't you remember asking me to fetch one?

Amanda: I remember suggesting that it would be nice for your sister if you brought home some nice young man from the warehouse. I think that I've made that suggestion more than once.

Tom: Yes, you have made it repeatedly.

Amanda: Well?

Tom: We are going to have one.

Amanda: *What?*

Tom: A gentleman caller!

[*The annunciation is celebrated with music.*]

[AMANDA *rises.*]

[*Image on screen: Caller with bouquet.*]

Amanda: You mean you have asked some nice young man to come over?

Tom: Yep. I've asked him to dinner.

Amanda: You really did?

Tom: I did!

Amanda: You did, and did he—*accept?*

Tom: He did!

Amanda: Well, well—well, well! That's—lovely!

Tom: I thought that you would be pleased.

Amanda: It's definite, then?

Tom: Very definite.

Amanda: Soon?

Tom: Very soon.

Amanda: For heaven's sake, stop putting on and tell me some things, will you?

Tom: What things do you want me to tell you?

Amanda: *Naturally* I would like to know when he's *coming!*

Tom: He's coming tomorrow.

Amanda: Tomorrow?

Tom: Yep. Tomorrow.

Amanda: But, Tom!

Tom: Yes, Mother?

Amanda: Tomorrow gives me no time!

Tom: Time for what?

Amanda: Preparations! Why didn't you phone me at once, as soon as you asked him, the minute that he accepted? Then, don't you see, I could have been getting ready!

Tom: You don't have to make any fuss.

Amanda: Oh, Tom, Tom, Tom, of course I have to make a fuss! I want things nice, not sloppy! Not thrown together. I'll certainly have to do some fast thinking, won't I?

Tom: I don't see why you have to think at all.

Amanda: You just don't know. We can't have a gentleman caller in a pig-sty! All my wedding silver has to be polished, the monogrammed table linen ought to be laundered! The windows have to be washed and fresh curtains put up. And how about clothes? We have to *wear* something, don't we?

Tom: Mother, this boy is no one to make a fuss over!

Amanda: Do you realize he's the first young man we've introduced to your sister? It's terrible, dreadful, disgraceful that poor little sister has never received a single gentleman caller! Tom, come inside! (*She opens the screen door.*)

Tom: What for?

Amanda: I want to ask you some things.

Tom: If you're going to make such a fuss, I'll call it off, I'll tell him not to come!

Amanda: You certainly won't do anything of the kind. Nothing offends people worse than broken engagements. It simply means I'll have to work like a Turk! We won't be brilliant, but we will pass inspection. Come on inside. (TOM *follows, groaning.*) Sit down.

Tom: Any particular place you would like me to sit?

Amanda: Thank heavens I've got that new sofa! I'm also making payments on a floor lamp I'll have sent out! And put the chintz covers on, they'll brighten things up! Of course I'd hoped to have these walls repapered. . . . What is the young man's name?

Tom: His name is O'Connor.

Amanda: That, of course, means fish —tomorrow is Friday! I'll have that salmon loaf—with Durkee's dressing! What does he do? He works at the warehouse?

Tom: Of course! How else would I—

Amanda: Tom, he—doesn't drink?

Tom: Why do you ask me that?

Amanda: Your father *did!*

Tom: Don't get started on that!

Amanda: He *does* drink, then?

Tom: Not that I know of!

Amanda: Make sure, be certain! The last thing I want for my daughter's a boy who drinks!

Tom: Aren't you being a little bit premature? Mr. O'Connor has not yet appeared on the scene!

Amanda: But will tomorrow. To meet your sister, and what do I know about his character? Nothing! Old maids are better off than wives of drunkards!

Tom: Oh, my God!

Amanda: Be still!

Tom (*leaning forward to whisper*). Lots of fellows meet girls whom they don't marry!

Amanda: Oh, talk sensibly, Tom—and don't be sarcastic! (*She has gotten a hairbrush.*)

Tom: What are you doing?

Amanda: I'm brushing that cow-lick down! What is this young man's position at the warehouse?

Tom (*submitting grimly to the brush and the interrogation*). This young man's position is that of a shipping clerk, Mother.

Amanda: Sounds to me like a fairly responsible job, the sort of a job *you* would be in if you just had more *get-up*. What is his salary? Have you any idea?

Tom: I would judge it to be approximately eighty-five dollars a month.

Amanda: Well—not princely, but—

Tom: Twenty more than I make.

Amanda: Yes, how well I know! But for a family man, eighty-five dollars a month is not much more than you can just get by on. . . .

Tom: Yes, but Mr. O'Connor is not a family man.

Amanda: He might be, mightn't he? Some time in the future?

Tom: I see. Plans and provisions.

Amanda: You are the only young man that I know of who ignores the fact that the future becomes the present, the present the past, and the past turns into everlasting regret if you don't plan for it!

Tom: I will think that over and see what I can make of it.

Amanda: Don't be supercilious with your mother! Tell me some more about this—what do you call him?

Tom: James D. O'Connor. The D. is for Delaney.

Amanda: Irish on *both* sides! *Gracious!* And doesn't drink?

Tom: Shall I call him up and ask him right this minute?

Amanda: The only way to find out about those things is to make discreet inquiries at the proper moment. When I was a girl in Blue Mountain and it was suspected that a young man drank, the girl whose attentions he had been receiving, if any girl *was,* would sometimes speak to the minister of his church, or rather her father would if her father was living, and sort of feel him out on the young man's character. That is the way such things are discreetly handled to keep a young woman from making a tragic mistake!

Tom: Then how did you happen to make a tragic mistake?

Amanda: That innocent look of your father's had everyone fooled! He *smiled*—the world was *enchanted!* No girl can do worse than put herself at the mercy of a handsome appearance! I hope that Mr. O'Connor is not too good-looking.

Tom: No, he's not too good-looking. He's covered with freckles and hasn't too much of a nose.

Amanda: He's not right-down homely, though?

Tom: Not right-down homely. Just medium homely, I'd say.

Amanda: Character's what to look for in a man.

Tom: That's what I've always said, Mother.

Amanda: You've never said anything of the kind and I suspect you would never give it a thought.

Tom: Don't be so suspicious of me.

Amanda: At least I hope he's the type that's up and coming.

Tom: I think he really goes in for self-improvement.

Amanda: What reason have you to think so?

Tom: He goes to night school.

Amanda (*beaming*). Splendid! What does he do, I mean study?

Tom: Radio engineering and public speaking!

Amanda: Then he has visions of being advanced in the world! Any young man who studies public speaking is aiming to have an executive job some day! And radio engineering? A thing for the future! Both of these facts are very illuminating. Those are the sort of things that a mother should know concerning any young man who comes to call on her daughter. Seriously or—not.

Tom: One little warning. He doesn't know about Laura. I didn't let on that we had dark ulterior motives. I just said, why don't you come and have dinner with us? He said okay and that was the whole conversation.

Amanda: I bet it was! You're eloquent as an oyster. However, he'll know about Laura when he gets here. When he sees how lovely and sweet and pretty she is, he'll thank his lucky stars he was asked to dinner.

Tom: Mother, you mustn't expect too much of Laura.

Amanda: What do you mean?

Tom: Laura seems all those things to you and me because she's ours and we love her. We don't even notice she's crippled any more.

Amanda: Don't say crippled! You know that I never allow that word to be used!

Tom: But face facts, Mother. She is and—that's not all—

Amanda: What do you mean "not all"?

Tom: Laura is very different from other girls.

Amanda: I think the difference is all to her advantage.

Tom: Not quite all—in the eyes of others—strangers—she's terribly shy and lives in a world of her own and those things make her seem a little peculiar to people outside the house.

Amanda: Don't say peculiar.

Tom: Face the facts. She is.

[*The dance-hall music changes to a tango that has a minor and somewhat ominous tone.*]

Amanda: In what way is she peculiar—may I ask?

Tom (*gently*). She lives in a world of her own—a world of—little glass ornaments, Mother. . . . (*Gets up.* AMANDA *remains holding brush, looking at him, troubled.*) She plays old phonograph records and—that's about all—(*He glances at himself in the mirror and crosses to door.*)

Amanda (*sharply*). Where are you going?

Tom: I'm going to the movies. (*Out screen door.*)

Amanda: Not to the movies, every night to the movies! (*Follows quickly to screen door.*) I don't believe you always go to the movies! (*He is gone.* AMANDA *looks worriedly after him for a moment. Then vitality and optimism return and she turns from the door. Crossing to por-*

tieres.) Laura! Laura! (LAURA *answers from kitchenette.*)

Laura: Yes, Mother.

Amanda: Let those dishes go and come in front! (LAURA *appears with dish towel. Gaily.*) Laura, come here and make a wish on the moon!

Laura (*entering*). Moon—moon?

Amanda: A little silver slipper of a moon. Look over your left shoulder, Laura, and make a wish! (LAURA looks *faintly puzzled as if called out of sleep.* AMANDA *seizes her shoulders and turns her at an angle by the door.*) No! Now, darling, *wish!*

Laura: What shall I wish for, Mother?

Amanda (*her voice trembling and her eyes suddenly filling with tears*). Happiness! Good Fortune!

[*The violin rises and the stage dims out.*]

SCENE VI

[*Image: High school hero.*]

Tom: And so the following evening I brought Jim home to dinner. I had known Jim slightly in high school. In high school Jim was a hero. He had tremendous Irish good nature and vitality with the scrubbed and polished look of white chinaware. He seemed to move in a continual spotlight. He was a star in basketball, captain of the debating club, president of the senior class and the glee club and he sang the male lead in the annual light operas. He was always running or bounding, never just walking. He seemed always at the point of defeating the law of gravity. He was shooting with such velocity through his adolescence that you would logically expect him to arrive at nothing short of the White House by the time he was thirty. But Jim apparently ran into more interference after his graduation from Soldan. His speed had definitely slowed. Six years after he left high school he was holding a job that wasn't much better than mine.

[*Image: Clerk.*]

He was the only one at the warehouse with whom I was on friendly terms. I was valuable to him as someone who could remember his former glory, who had seen him win basketball games and the silver cup in debating. He knew of my secret practice of retiring to a cabinet of the washroom to work on poems when business was slack in the warehouse. He called me Shakespeare. And while the other boys in the warehouse regarded me with suspicious hostility, Jim took a humorous attitude toward me. Gradually his attitude affected the others, their hostility wore off and they also began to smile at me as people smile at an oddly fashioned dog who trots across their path at some distance.

I knew that Jim and Laura had known each other at Soldan, and I had heard Laura speak admiringly of his voice. I didn't know if Jim remembered her or not. In high school Laura had been as unobtrusive as Jim had been astonishing. If he did remember Laura, it was not as my sister, for when I asked him to dinner, he grinned and said, "You know,

Shakespeare, I never thought of you as having folks!"

He was about to discover that I did. . . .

[*Light up stage.*]

[*Legend on screen: "The accent of a coming foot."*]

[*Friday evening. It is about five o'clock of a late spring evening which comes "scattering poems in the sky."*]

[*A delicate lemony light is in the Wingfield apartment.*]

[AMANDA *has worked like a Turk in preparation for the gentleman caller. The results are astonishing. The new floor lamp with its rose-silk shade is in place, a colored paper lantern conceals the broken light fixture in the ceiling, new billowing white curtains are at the windows, chintz covers are on chairs and sofa, a pair of new sofa pillows make their initial appearance.*]

[*Open boxes and tissue paper are scattered on the floor.*]

[LAURA *stands in the middle with lifted arms while* AMANDA *crouches before her, adjusting the hem of the new dress, devout and ritualistic. The dress is colored and designed by memory. The arrangement of* LAURA'S *hair is changed; it is softer and more becoming. A fragile, unearthly prettiness has come out in* LAURA: *she is like a piece of translucent glass touched by light, given a momentary radiance, not actual, not lasting.*]

Amanda (*impatiently*). Why are you trembling?

Laura: Mother, you've made me so nervous!

Amanda: How have I made you nervous?

Laura: By all this fuss! You make it seem so important!

Amanda: I don't understand you, Laura. You couldn't be satisfied with just sitting home, and yet whenever I try to arrange something for you, you seem to resist it. (*She gets up.*) Now take a look at yourself. No, wait! Wait just a moment —I have an idea!

Laura: What is it now?

[AMANDA *produces two powder puffs which she wraps in handkerchiefs and stuffs in* LAURA'S *bosom.*]

Laura: Mother, what are you doing?

Amanda: They call them "Gay Deceivers"!

Laura: I won't wear them!

Amanda: You will!

Laura: Why should I?

Amanda: Because, to be painfully honest, your chest is flat.

Laura: You make it seem like we were setting a trap.

Amanda: All pretty girls are a trap, a pretty trap, and men expect them to be. (*Legend: "A pretty trap."*) Now look at yourself, young lady. This is the prettiest you will ever be! I've got to fix myself now! You're going to be surprised by your mother's appearance! (*She crosses through portieres, humming gaily.*)

[LAURA *moves slowly to the long mirror and stares solemnly at herself.*]

[*A wind blows the white curtains inward in a slow, graceful motion and with a faint, sorrowful sighing.*]

Amanda (*off stage*). It isn't dark enough yet. (*She turns slowly before the mirror with a troubled look.*)

[*Legend on screen: 'This is my sister: celebrate her with strings!" Music.*]

Amanda (*laughing, off*). I'm going to show you something. I'm going to make a spectacular appearance!

Laura: What is it, Mother?

Amanda: Possess your soul in patience —you will see! Something I've resurrected from that old trunk! Styles haven't changed so terribly much after all. . . . (*She parts the portieres.*) Now just look at your mother! (*She wears a girlish frock of yellowed voile with a blue silk sash. She carries a bunch of jonquils—the legend of her youth is nearly revived. Feverishly*) This is the dress in which I led the cotillion. Won the cake-walk twice at Sunset Hill, wore one spring to the Governor's ball in Jackson! See how I sashayed around the ballroom, Laura? (*She raises her skirt and does a mincing step around the room.*) I wore it on Sundays for my gentlemen callers! I had it on the day I met your father—I had malaria fever all that spring. The change of climate from East Tennessee to the Delta—weakened resistance—I had a little temperature all the time—not enough to be serious—just enough to make me restless and giddy! Invitations poured in—parties all over the Delta!—"Stay in bed," said Mother, "you have fever!"—but I just wouldn't.—I took quinine but kept on going, going!—Evenings, dances! Afternoons, long, long rides! Picnics—lovely!—So lovely, that country in May. —All lacy with dogwood, literally flooded with jonquils!—That was the spring I had the craze for jonquils. Jonquils became an absolute obsession. Mother said, "Honey, there's no more room for jonquils." And still I kept on bringing in more jonquils. Whenever, wherever I saw them, I'd say, "Stop! Stop! I see jonquils!" I made the young men help me gather the jonquils! It was a joke, Amanda and her jonquils! Finally there were no more vases to hold them, every available space was filled with jonquils. No vases to hold them? All right, I'll hold them myself! And then I—(*She stops in front of the picture. Music.*) met your father! Malaria fever and jonquils and then—this —boy. . . . (*She switches on the rose-colored lamp.*) I hope they get here before it starts to rain. (*She crosses upstage and places the jonquils in bowl on table.*) I gave your brother a little extra change so he and Mr. O'Connor could take the service car home.

Laura (*with altered look*). What did you say his name was?

Amanda: O'Connor.

Laura: What is his first name?

Amnada: I don't remember. Oh, yes, I do. It was—Jim!

[LAURA *sways slightly and catches hold of a chair.*]

[*Legend on screen: "Not Jim!"*]

Laura (*faintly*). Not—Jim!

Amanda: Yes, that was it, it was Jim! I've never known a Jim that wasn't nice! [*Music: Ominous.*]

Laura: Are you sure his name is Jim O'Connor?

Amanda: Yes. Why?

Laura: Is he the one that Tom used to know in high school?

Amanda: He didn't say so. I think he just got to know him at the warehouse.

Laura: There was a Jim O'Connor we both knew in high school—(*Then, with effort.*) If that is the one that Tom is bringing to dinner—you'll have to excuse me, I won't come to the table.

Amanda: What sort of nonsense is this?

Laura: You asked me once if I'd ever

liked a boy. Don't you remember I showed you this boy's picture?

Amanda: You mean the boy you showed me in the year book?

Laura: Yes, that boy.

Amanda: Laura, Laura, were you in love with that boy?

Laura: I don't know, Mother. All I know is I couldn't sit at the table if it was him!

Amanda: It won't be him! It isn't the least bit likely. But whether it is or not, you will come to the table. You will not be excused.

Laura: I'll have to be, Mother.

Amanda: I don't intend to humor your silliness, Laura. I've had too much from you and your brother, both! So just sit down and compose yourself till they come. Tom has forgotten his key so you'll have to let them in, when they arrive.

Laura (*panicky*). Oh, Mother—*you* answer the door!

Amanda (*lightly*). I'll be in the kitchen—busy!

Laura: Oh, Mother, please answer the door, don't make me do it!

Amanda (*crossing into kitchenette*). I've got to fix the dressing for the salmon. Fuss, fuss—silliness!—over a gentleman caller!

[*Door swings shut.* LAURA *is left alone.*]

[*Legend: "Terror!"*]

[*She utters a low moan and turns off the lamp—sits stiffly on the edge of the sofa, knotting her fingers together.*]

[*Legend on screen: "The opening of a door!"*]

[TOM *and* JIM *appear on the fire-escape steps and climb to landing. Hearing their approach,* LAURA *rises with a panicky gesture. She retreats to the portieres.*]

[*The doorbell.* LAURA *catches her breath and touches her throat. Low drums.*]

Amanda (*calling*). Laura, sweetheart! The door!

[LAURA *stares at it without moving.*]

Jim: I think we just beat the rain.

Tom: Uh-huh. (*He rings again, nervously*). JIM *whistles and fishes for a cigarette.*)

Amanda (*very, very gaily*). Laura, that is your brother and Mr. O'Connor! Will you let them in, darling?

[LAURA *crosses toward kitchenette door.*]

Laura (*breathlessly*). Mother—you go to the door!

[AMANDA *steps out of kitchenette and stares furiously at* LAURA. *She points imperiously at the door.*]

Laura: Please, please!

Amanda (*in a fierce whisper*). What is the matter with you, you silly thing?

Laura: (*desperately*). Please, you answer it, *please!*

Amanda: I told you I wasn't going to humor you, Laura. Why have you chosen this moment to lose your mind?

Laura: Please, please, please, you go!

Amanda: You'll have to go to the door because I can't!

Laura (*despairingly*). I can't either!

Amanda: *Why?*

Laura: I'm *sick!*

Amanda: I'm sick, too—of your nonsense! Why can't you and your brother be normal people? Fantastic whims and behavior! (TOM *gives a long ring.*) Preposterous goings on! Can you give me one reason—(*Calls out lyrically:*) COMING!

JUST ONE SECOND!—why you should be afraid to open a door? Now you answer it, Laura!

Laura: Oh, oh, oh . . . (*She returns through the portieres. Darts to the victrola and winds it frantically and turns it on.*)

Amanda: Laura Wingfield, you march right to that door!

Laura: Yes—yes, Mother!

[*A faraway, scratchy rendition of "Dardanella" softens the air and gives her strength to move through it. She slips to the door and draws it cautiously open.*]

[TOM *enters with the caller,* JIM O'CONNOR.]

Tom: Laura, this is Jim. Jim, this is my sister, Laura.

Jim (*stepping inside*). I didn't know that Shakespeare had a sister!

Laura (*retreating stiff and trembling from the door*). How—how do you do?

Jim (*heartily extending his hand*). Okay!

[LAURA *touches it hesitantly with hers.*]

Jim: Your hand's *cold,* Laura!

Laura: Yes, well—I've been playing the victrola. . . .

Jim: Must have been playing classical music on it! You ought to play a little hot swing music to warm you up!

Laura: Excuse me—I haven't finished playing the victrola. . . .

[*She turns awkwardly and hurries into the front room. She pauses a second by the victrola. Then catches her breath and darts through the portieres like a frightened deer.*]

Jim (*grinning*). What was the matter?

Tom: Oh—with Laura? Laura is—terribly shy.

Jim: Shy, huh? It's unusual to meet a shy girl nowadays. I don't believe you ever mentioned you had a sister.

Tom: Well, now you know. I have one. Here is the *Post Dispatch.* You want a piece of it?

Jim: Uh-huh.

Tom: What piece? The comics?

Jim: Sports! (*Glances at it.*) Ole Dizzy Dean is on his bad behavior.

Tom (*disinterest*). Yeah? (*Lights cigarette and crosses back to fire-escape door.*)

Jim: Where are *you* going?

Tom: I'm going out on the terrace.

Jim (*goes after him*). You know, Shakespeare—I'm going to sell you a bill of goods!

Tom: What goods?

Jim: A course I'm taking.

Tom: Huh?

Jim: In public speaking! You and me, we're not the warehouse type.

Tom: Thanks—that's good news. But what has public speaking got to do with it?

Jim: It fits you for—executive positions!

Tom: Awww.

Jim: I tell you it's done a helluva lot for me.

[*Image: Executive at desk.*]

Tom: In what respect?

Jim: In every! Ask yourself what is the difference between you an' me and men in the office down front? Brains?—No!—Ability?—No! Then what? Just one little thing—

Tom: What is that one little thing?

Jim: Primarily it amounts to—social

poise! Being able to square up to people and hold your own on any social level!

Amanda (*off stage*). Tom?

Tom: Yes, Mother?

Amanda: Is that you and Mr. O'Connor?

Tom: Yes, Mother.

Amanda: Well, you just make yourselves comfortable in there.

Tom: Yes, Mother.

Amanda: Ask Mr. O'Connor if he would like to wash his hands.

Jim: Aw, no—no—thank you—I took care of that at the warehouse. Tom—

Tom: Yes?

Jim: Mr. Mendoza was speaking to me about you.

Tom: Favorably?

Jim: What do you think?

Tom: Well—

Jim: You're going to be out of a job if you don't wake up.

Tom: I am waking up—

Jim: You show no signs.

Tom: The signs are interior.

[*Image on screen: The sailing vessel with Jolly Roger again.*]

Tom: I'm planning to change. (*He leans over the rail speaking with quiet exhilaration. The incandescent marquees and signs of the first-run movie houses light his face from across the alley. He looks like a voyager.*) I'm right at the point of committing myself to a future that doesn't include the warehouse and Mr. Mendoza or even a night-school course in public speaking.

Jim: What are you gassing about?

Tom: I'm tired of the movies.

Jim: Movies!

Tom: Yes, movies! Look at them—(*A wave toward the marvels of Grand Avenue.*) All of those glamorous people—having adventures—hogging it all, gobbling the whole thing up! You know what happens? People go to the *movies* instead of *moving!* Hollywood characters are supposed to have all the adventures for everybody in America, while everybody in America sits in a dark room and watches them have them! Yes, until there's a war. That's when adventure becomes available to the masses! *Everyone's* dish, not only Gable's! Then the people in the dark room come out of the dark room to have some adventures themselves—Goody, goody!—It's our turn now, to go to the South Sea Island—to make a safari—to be exotic, far-off!—But I'm not patient. I don't want to wait till then. I'm tired of the *movies* and I am *about* to *move!*

Jim (*incredulously*). Move?

Tom: Yes.

Jim: When?

Tom: Soon!

Jim: Where? Where?

[*Theme three music seems to answer the question, while* TOM *thinks it over. He searches among his pockets.*]

Tom: I'm starting to boil inside. I know I seem dreamy, but inside—well, I'm boiling! Whenever I pick up a shoe, I shudder a little thinking how short life is and what I am doing!—Whatever that means, I know it doesn't mean shoes—except as something to wear on a traveler's feet! (*Finds paper.*) Look—

Jim: What?

Tom: I'm a member.

Jim (*reading*). The Union of Merchant Seamen.

Tom: I paid my dues this month, instead of the light bill.

Jim: You will regret it when they turn the lights off.

Tom: I won't be here.

Jim: How about your mother?

Tom: I'm like my father. The bastard son of a bastard! See how he grins? And he's been absent going on sixteen years!

Jim: You're just talking, you drip. How does your mother feel about it?

Tom: Shhh!—Here comes Mother! Mother is not acquainted with my plans!

Amanda (*enters portieres*). Where are you all?

Tom: On the terrace, Mother.

[*They start inside. She advances to them.* TOM *is distinctly shocked at her appearance. Even* JIM *blinks a little. He is making his first contact with girlish Southern vivacity and in spite of the night-school course in public speaking is somewhat thrown off the beam by the unexpected outlay of social charm.*]

[*Certain responses are attempted by* JIM *but are swept aside by* AMANDA'S *gay laughter and chatter.* TOM *is embarrassed but after the first shock* JIM *reacts very warmly. Grins and chuckles, is altogether won over.*]

[*Image:* AMANDA *as a girl.*]

Amanda (*coyly smiling, shaking her girlish ringlets*). Well, well, well, so this is Mr. O'Connor. Introductions entirely unnecessary. I've heard so much about you from my boy. I finally said to him, Tom—good gracious!—why don't you bring this paragon to supper? I'd like to meet this nice young man at the warehouse!—Instead of just hearing him sing your praises so much! I don't know why my son is so stand-offish—that's not Southern behavior! Let's sit down and—I think we could stand a little more air in here! Tom, leave the door open. I felt a nice fresh breeze a moment ago. Where has it gone to? Mmm, so warm already! And not quite summer, even. We're going to burn up when summer really gets started. However, we're having—we're having a very light supper. I think light things are better fo' this time of year. The same as light clothes are. Light clothes an' light food are what warm weather calls fo'. You know our blood gets so thick during th' winter—it takes a while fo' us to *adjust* ou'selves!—when the season changes . . . It's come so quick this year. I wasn't prepared. All of a sudden—heavens! Already summer!—I ran to the trunk an' pulled out this light dress—Terribly old. Historical almost! But feels so good—so good an' co-ol, y'know. . . .

Tom: Mother—

Amanda: Yes, honey?

Tom: How about—supper?

Amanda: Honey, you go ask Sister if supper is ready! You know that Sister is in full charge of supper! Tell her you hungry boys are waiting for it. (*To* JIM.) Have you met Laura?

Jim: She—

Amanda: Let you in? Oh, good, you've met already! It's rare for a girl as sweet an' pretty as Laura to be domestic! But Laura is, thank heavens, not only pretty but also very domestic. I'm not at all. I never was a bit. I never could make a thing but angel-food cake. Well, in the South we had so many servants. Gone, gone, gone. All vestige of gracious living! Gone completely! I wasn't prepared for what the future brought me. All of my gentlemen callers were sons of planters and so of course I assumed that I would be married to one and raise my family on a large piece of land with plenty of servants. But man proposes—and woman accepts the proposal!—To vary that old, old saying a little bit—I married no planter! I married a man who worked for the telephone company!—That gallantly smiling gentleman over there! (*Points to* *the picture.*) A telephone man who—fell in love with long-distance!—Now he travels and I don't even know where!—But what am I going on for about my—tribulations? Tell me yours—I hope you don't have any! Tom?

Tom (*returning*). Yes, Mother?

Amanda: Is supper nearly ready?

Tom: It looks to me like supper is on the table.

Amanda: Let me look—(*She rises prettily and looks through portieres.*) Oh, lovely!—But where is Sister?

Tom: Laura is not feeling well and she says that she thinks she'd better not come to the table.

Amanda: What?—Nonsense!—Laura? Oh, Laura!

Laura (*off stage, faintly*). Yes, Mother.

Amanda: You really must come to the table. We won't be seated until you come to the table! Come in, Mr. O'Connor. You sit over there, and I'll—Laura? Laura Wingfield! You're keeping us waiting, honey! We can't say grace until you come to the table!

[*The back door is pushed weakly open and* LAURA *comes in. She is obviously quite faint, her lips trembling, her eyes wide and staring. She moves unsteadily toward the table.*]

[*Legend: "Terror!"*]

[*Outside a summer storm is coming abruptly. The white curtains billow inward at the windows and there is a sorrowful murmur and deep blue dusk.*]

[LAURA *suddenly stumbles—she catches at a chair with a faint moan.*]

Tom: Laura!

Amanda: Laura! (*There is a clap of thunder.*) (*Legend: "Ah!"*) (*Despairingly*). Why, Laura, you *are* sick, darling! Tom, help your sister into the living room, dear! Sit in the living room, Laura—rest on the sofa. Well! (*To the gentleman caller.*) Standing over the hot stove made her ill!—I told her that it was just too warm this evening, but—(TOM *comes back in.* LAURA *is on the sofa.*) Is Laura all right now?

Tom: Yes.

Amanda: What *is* that? Rain? A nice cool rain has come up! (*She gives the gentleman caller a frightened look.*) I think we may—have grace—now . . . (TOM *looks at her stupidly.*) Tom, honey—you say grace!

Tom: Oh . . . "For these and all thy mercies—" (*They bow their heads,* AMANDA *stealing a nervous glance at* JIM. *In the living room* LAURA, *stretched on the sofa, clenches her hand to her lips, to hold back a shuddering sob.*) God's Holy Name be praised—

[*The scene dims out.*]

SCENE VII

[A Souvenir.]

[*Half an hour later. Dinner is just being finished in the upstage area which is concealed by the drawn portieres.*

As the curtain rises LAURA *is still huddled upon the sofa, her feet drawn under her, her head resting on a pale blue pillow, her eyes wide and mysteriously watchful. The new floor lamp with its shade of rose-colored silk gives a soft, becoming light to her face, bringing out the fragile, unearthly prettiness which usually escapes attention. There is a steady murmur of rain, but it is slackening and stops soon after the scene begins; the air outside becomes pale and luminous as the moon breaks out.*

A moment after the curtain rises, the lights in both rooms flicker and go out.]

Jim: Hey, there, Mr. Light Bulb!

[AMANDA *laughs nervously.*]

[*Legend: "Suspension of a public service."*]

Amanda: Where was Moses when the lights went out? Ha-ha. Do you know the answer to that one, Mr. O'Connor?

Jim: No, Ma'am, what's the answer?

Amanda: In the dark! (JIM *laughs appreciably.*) Everybody sit still. I'll light the candles. Isn't it lucky we have them on the table? Where's a match? Which of you gentlemen can provide a match?

Jim: Here.

Amanda: Thank you, sir.

Jim: Not at all, Ma'am!

Amanda: I guess the fuse has burnt out. Mr. O'Connor, can you tell a burnt-out fuse? I know I can't and Tom is a total loss when it comes to mechanics. (*Sound: Getting up: Voices recede a little to kitchenette.*) Oh, be careful you don't bump into something. We don't want our gentleman caller to break his neck. Now wouldn't that be a fine howdy-do?

Jim: Ha-ha! Where is the fuse-box?

Amanda: Right here next to the stove. Can you see anything?

Jim: Just a minute.

Amanda: Isn't electricity a mysterious thing? Wasn't it Benjamin Franklin who tied a key to a kite? We live in such a mysterious universe, don't we? Some people say that science clears up all the mysteries for us. In my opinion it only creates more! Have you found it yet?

Jim: No, Ma'am. All these fuses look okay to me.

Amanda: Tom!

Tom: Yes, Mother?

Amanda: That light bill I gave you several days ago. The one I told you we got the notices about?

Tom: Oh.—Yeah.

[*Legend: "Ha!"*]

Amanda: You didn't neglect to pay it by any chance?

Tom: Why, I—

Amanda: Didn't! I might have known it!

Jim: Shakespeare probably wrote a poem on that light bill, Mrs. Wingfield.

Amanda: I might have known better than to trust him with it! There's such a high price for negligence in this world!

Jim: Maybe the poem will win a ten-dollar prize.

Amanda: We'll just have to spend the remainder of the evening in the nineteenth century, before Mr. Edison made the Mazda lamp!

Jim: Candlelight is my favorite kind of light.

Amanda: That shows you're romantic! But that's no excuse for Tom. Well, we got through dinner. Very considerate of them to let us get through dinner before they plunged us into everlasting darkness, wasn't it, Mr. O'Connor?

Jim: Ha-ha!

Amanda: Tom, as a penalty for your carelessness you can help me with the dishes.

Jim: Let me give you a hand.

Amanda: Indeed you will not!

Jim: I ought to be good for something.

Amanda: Good for something? (*Her tone is rhapsodic.*) *You?* Why, Mr. O'Connor, nobody, *nobody's* given me this much entertainment in years—as you have!

Jim: Aw, now, Mrs. Wingfield!

Amanda: I'm not exaggerating, not one bit! But Sister is all by her lonesome. You go keep her company in the parlor! I'll give you this lovely old candelabrum that used to be on the altar at the church of the Heavenly Rest. It was melted a little out of shape when the church burnt down. Lightning struck it one spring. Gypsy Jones was holding a revival at the time and he intimated that the church was destroyed because the Episcopalians gave card parties.

Jim: Ha-ha.

Amanda: And how about you coaxing Sister to drink a little wine? I think it would be good for her! Can you carry both at once?

Jim: Sure. I'm Superman!

Amanda: Now, Thomas, get into this apron!

[*The door of kitchenette swings closed on* AMANDA'S *gay laughter; the flickering light approaches the portieres.*]

[LAURA *sits up nervously as he enters. Her speech at first is low and breathless from the almost intolerable strain of being alone with a stranger.*]

[*Legend: "I don't suppose you remember me at all!"*]

[*In her first speeches in this scene, before* JIM'S *warmth overcomes her paralyzing shyness,* LAURA'S *voice is thin and breathless as though she has just run up a steep flight of stairs.*]

[JIM'S *attitude is gently humorous. In playing this scene it should be stressed that while the incident is apparently unimportant, it is to* LAURA *the climax of her secret life.*]

Jim: Hello, there, Laura.

Laura: (*faintly*). Hello. (*She clears her throat.*)

Jim: How are you feeling now? Better?

Laura: Yes. Yes, thank you.

Jim: This is for you. A little dandelion wine. (*He extends it toward her with extravagant gallantry.*)

Laura: Thank you.

Jim: Drink it—but don't get drunk! (*He laughs heartily.* LAURA *takes the glass uncertainly; laughs shyly.*) Where shall I set the candles?

Laura: Oh—oh, anywhere . . .

Jim: How about here on the floor? Any objections?

Laura: No.

Jim: I'll spread a newspaper under to catch the drippings. I like to sit on the floor. Mind if I do?

Laura: Oh, no.

Jim: Give me a pillow?

Laura: What?

Jim: A pillow!

Laura: Oh . . . (*Hands him one quickly.*)

Jim: How about you? Don't you like to sit on the floor?

Laura: Oh—yes.

Jim: Why don't you, then?

Laura: I—will.

Jim: Take a pillow! (LAURA *does. Sits on the other side of the candelabrum.* JIM *crosses his legs and smiles engagingly at her.*) I can't hardly see you sitting way over there.

Laura: I can—see you.

Jim: I know, but that's not fair, I'm in the limelight. (LAURA *moves her pillow closer.*) Good! Now I can see you! Comfortable?

Laura: Yes.

Jim: So am I. Comfortable as a cow. Will you have some gum?

Laura: No, thank you.

Jim: I think that I will indulge, with your permission. (*Musingly unwraps it and holds it up.*) Think of the fortune made by the guy that invented the first piece of chewing gum. Amazing, huh? The Wrigley Building is one of the sights of Chicago.—I saw it summer before last when I went up to the Century of Progress. Did you take in the Century of Progress?

Laura: No, I didn't.

Jim: Well, it was quite a wonderful exposition. What impressed me most was the Hall of Science. Gives you an idea of what the future will be in America, even more wonderful than the present time is! (*Pause. Smiling at her.*) Your brother tells me you're shy. Is that right, Laura?

Laura: I—don't know.

Jim: I judge you to be an old-fashioned type of girl. Well, I think that's a pretty good type to be. Hope you don't think I'm being too personal—do you?

Laura (*hastily, out of embarrasment*). I believe I *will* take a piece of gum, if you—don't mind. (*Clearing her throat.*) Mr. O'Connor, have you—kept up with your singing?

Jim: Singing? Me?

Laura: Yes. I remember what a beautiful voice you had.

Jim: When did you hear me sing?

[*Voice off stage in the pause.*]

VOICE (*off stage*):

O blow ye winds, heigh-ho,
A-roving I will go!
I'm off to my love
With a boxing glove—
Ten thousand miles away!

Jim: You say you've heard me sing?

Laura: Oh, yes! Yes, very often . . . I—don't suppose you remember me—at all?

Jim (*smiling doubtfully*). You know I have an idea I've seen you before. I had that idea soon as you opened the door. It seemed almost like I was about to remember your name. But the name that I started to call you—wasn't a name! And so I stopped myself before I said it.

Laura: Wasn't it—Blue Roses?

Jim (*springs up. Grinning*). Blue Roses! My gosh, yes—Blue Roses! That's what I had on my tongue when you opened the door! Isn't it funny what tricks your memory plays? I didn't connect you with high school somehow or other. But that's where it was; it was high school. I didn't even know you were Shakespeare's sister! Gosh, I'm sorry.

Laura: I didn't expect you to. You—barely knew me!

Jim: But we did have a speaking acquaintance, huh?

Laura: Yes, we—spoke to each other.

Jim: When did you recognize me?

Laura: Oh, right away!

Jim: Soon as I came in the door?

Laura: When I heard your name I thought it was probably you. I knew that Tom used to know you a little in high school. So when you came in the door—Well, then I was—sure.

Jim: Why didn't you *say* something, then?

Laura (*breathlessly*). I didn't know what to say, I was—too surprised!

Jim: For goodness' sakes! You know, this sure is funny!

Laura: Yes! Yes, isn't it, though . . .

Jim: Didn't we have a class in something together?

Laura: Yes, we did.

Jim: What class was that?

Laura: It was—singing—Chorus!

Jim: Aw!

Laura: I sat across the aisle from you in the Aud.

Jim: Aw.

Laura: Mondays, Wednesdays and Fridays.

Jim: Now I remember—you always came in late.

Laura: Yes, it was so hard for me, getting upstairs. I had that brace on my leg—it clumped so loud!

Jim: I never heard any clumping.

Laura (*wincing at the recollection*). To me it sounded like—thunder!

Jim: Well, well, well, I never even noticed.

Laura: And everybody was seated before I came in. I had to walk in front of all those people. My seat was in the back row. I had to go clumping all the way up the aisle with everyone watching!

Jim: You shouldn't have been self-conscious.

Laura: I know, but I was. It was always such a relief when the singing started.

Jim: Aw, yes, I've placed you now! I used to call you Blue Roses. How was it that I got started calling you that?

Laura: I was out of school a little while with pleurosis. When I came back you asked me what was the matter. I said I had pleurosis—you thought I said Blue Roses. That's what you always called me after that!

Jim: I hope you didn't mind.

Laura: Oh, no—I liked it. You see, I wasn't acquainted with many—people. . . .

Jim: As I remember you sort of stuck by yourself.

Laura: I—I—never have had much luck at—making friends.

Jim: I don't see why you wouldn't.

Laura: Well, I—started out badly.

Jim: You mean being—

Laura: Yes, it sort of—stood between me—

Jim: You shouldn't have let it!

Laura: I know, but it did, and—

Jim: You were shy with people!

Laura: I tried not to be but never could—

Jim: Overcome it?

Laura: No, I—I never could!

Jim: I guess being shy is something you have to work out of kind of gradually.

Laura (*sorrowfully*). Yes—I guess it—

Jim: Takes time!

Laura: Yes—

Jim: People are not so dreadful when you know them. That's what you have to remember! And everybody has problems, not just you, but practically everybody has got some problems. You think of yourself as having the only problems, as being the only one who is disappointed. But just look around you and you will see lots of people as disappointed as you are. For instance, I hoped when I was going to high school that I would be further along at this time, six years later, than I am now—You remember that wonderful write-up I had in *The Torch?*

Laura: Yes! (*She rises and crosses to table.*)

Jim: It said I was bound to succeed in anything I went into! (LAURA *returns with the annual.*) Holy Jeez! *The Torch!* (*He accepts it reverently. They smile* *across it with mutual wonder.* LAURA *crouches beside him and they begin to turn through it.* LAURA'S *shyness is dissolving in his warmth.*)

Laura: Here you are in *Pirates of Penzance!*

Jim (*wistfully*). I sang the baritone lead in that operetta.

Laura (*rapidly*). So—*beautifully!*

Jim (*protesting*). Aw—

Laura: Yes, yes—beautifully—beautifully!

Jim: You heard me?

Laura: All three times!

Jim: No!

Laura: Yes!

Jim: All three performances?

Laura (*looking down*). Yes.

Jim: Why?

Laura: I—wanted to ask you to—autograph my program.

Jim: Why didn't you ask me to?

Laura: You were always surrounded by your own friends so much that I never had a chance to.

Jim: You should have just—

Laura: Well, I—thought you might think I was—

Jim: Thought I might think you was—what?

Laura: Oh—

Jim (*with reflective relish*). I was beleaguered by females in those days.

Laura: You were terribly popular!

Jim: Yeah—

Laura: You had such a—friendly way—

Jim: I was spoiled in high school.

Laura: Everybody—liked you!

Jim: Including you?

Laura: I—Yes, I—I did, too—(*She gently closes the book in her lap.*)

Jim: Well, well, well!—Give me that program, Laura. (*She hands it to him. He signs it with a flourish.*) There you are—better late than never!

Laura: Oh, I—what a—surprise!

Jim: My signature isn't worth very much right now. But some day—maybe—it will increase in value! Being disappointed is one thing and being discouraged is something else. I am disappointed but I am not discouraged. I'm twenty-three years old. How old are you?

Laura: I'll be twenty-four in June.

Jim: That's not old age!

Laura: No, but—

Jim: You finished high school?

Laura (*with difficulty*). I didn't go back.

Jim: You mean you dropped out?

Laura: I made bad grades in my final examinations. (*She rises and replaces the book and the program. Her voice strained.*) How is—Emily Meisenbach getting along?

Jim: Oh, that kraut-head!

Laura: Why do you call her that?

Jim: That's what she was.

Laura: You're not still—going with her?

Jim: I never see her.

Laura: It said in the Personal Section that you were—engaged!

Jim: I know, but I wasn't impressed by that—propaganda!

Laura: It wasn't—the truth?

Jim: Only in Emily's optimistic opinion!

Laura: Oh—

[*Legend: "What have you done since high school?"*]

[JIM *lights a cigarette and leans indolently back on his elbows smiling at* LAURA *with a warmth and charm which lights her inwardly with altar candles. She remains by the table and turns in her hands a piece of glass to cover her tumult.*]

Jim (*after several reflective puffs on a cigarette*). What have you done since high school? (*She seems not to hear him.*) Huh? (LAURA *looks up.*) I said what have you done since high school, Laura?

Laura: Nothing much.

Jim: You must have been doing something these six long years.

Laura: Yes.

Jim: Well, then, such as what?

Laura: I took a business course at business college—

Jim: How did that work out?

Laura: Well, not very very—well—I had to drop out, it gave me—indigestion—

[JIM *laughs gently.*]

Jim: What are you doing now?

Laura: I don't do anything—much. Oh, please don't think I sit around doing nothing! My glass collection takes up a good deal of time. Glass is something you have to take good care of.

Jim: What did you say—about glass?

Laura: Collection I said—I have one —(*She clears her throat and turns away again, acutely shy.*)

Jim (*abruptly*). You know what I judge to be the trouble with you? Inferiority complex! Know what that is? That's what they call it when someone low-rates himself! I understand it because I had it, too. Although my case was not so aggravated as yours seems to be. I had it until I took up public speaking, developed my voice, and learned that I had an aptitude for science. Before that time I never thought of myself as being outstanding in any way whatsoever! Now I've never made a regular study of it, but I have a friend who says I can analyze people better than doctors that make a profession of it. I don't claim that to be necessarily true, but I can sure guess a person's psychology, Laura! (*Takes out his gum.*) Excuse me, Laura. I always take it out when the flavor is gone. I'll use this scrap of paper to wrap it in. I know how it is to get it stuck on a shoe. Yep—that's what I judge to be your principal trouble. A lack of confidence in yourself as a person. You don't have the proper amount of faith in yourself. I'm basing that fact on a number of your remarks and also on certain observations I've made. For instance that clumping you thought was so awful in high school? You say that you even dreaded to walk into class. You see what you did? You dropped out of school, you gave up an education because of a clump, which as far as I know was practically nonexistent! A little physical defect is what you have. Hardly noticeable even! Magnified thousands of times by imagination! You know what my strong advice to you is? Think of yourself as *superior* in some way!

Laura: In what way would I think?

Jim: Why, man alive, Laura! Just look about you a little. What do you see? A world full of common people! All of 'em born and all of 'em going to die! Which of them has one-tenth of your good points! Or mine! Or anyone else's, as far as that goes—Gosh! Everybody excels in some one thing. Some in many! (*Unconsciously glances at himself in the mirror.*) All you've got to do is discover in *what!* Take me, for instance. (*He adjusts his tie at the mirror.*) My interest happens to lie in electro-dynamics. I'm taking a course in radio engineering at night school, Laura, on top of a fairly responsible job at the warehouse. I'm taking that course and studying public speaking.

Laura: Ohhhh.

Jim: Because I believe in the future of television! (*Turning back to her.*) I wish to be ready to go up right along with it. Therefore I'm planning to get in on the ground floor. In fact I've already made the right connections and all that remains is for the industry itself to get under way! Full steam—(*His eyes are starry.*) *Knowledge*—Zzzzzp! *Money!*—Zzzzzzp!—*Power!* That's the cycle democracy is built on! (*His attitude is convincingly dynamic.* LAURA *stares at him, even her shyness eclipsed in her absolute wonder. He suddenly grins.*) I guess you think I think a lot of myself!

Laura: No—o-o-o, I—

Jim: Now how about you? Isn't there something you take more interest in than anything else?

Laura: Well, I do—as I said—have my—glass collection—

[*A peal of girlish laughter from the kitchen.*]

Jim: I'm not right sure I know what you're talking about. What kind of glass is it?

Laura: Little articles of it, they're ornaments mostly! Most of them are little animals made out of glass, the tiniest little animals in the world. Mother calls them a glass menagerie! Here's an example of one, if you'd like to see it! This one is one of the oldest. It's nearly thirteen. (*Music: "The Glass Menagerie."*) (*He stretches out his hand.*) Oh, be careful—if you breathe, it breaks!

Jim: I'd better not take it. I'm pretty clumsy with things.

Laura: Go on, I trust you with him! (*Places it in his palm.*) There now—you're holding him gently! Hold him over the light, he loves the light! You see how the light shines through him?

Jim: It sure does shine!

Laura: I shouldn't be partial, but he is my favorite one.

Jim: What kind of a thing is this one supposed to be?

Laura: Haven't you noticed the single horn on his forehead?

Jim: A unicorn, huh?

Laura: Mmm-hmmm!

Jim: Unicorns, aren't they extinct in the modern world?

Laura: I know!

Jim: Poor little fellow, he must feel sort of lonesome.

Laura (*smiling*). Well, if he does he doesn't complain about it. He stays on a shelf with some horses that don't have horns and all of them seem to get along nicely together.

Jim: How do you know?

Laura (*lightly*). I haven't heard any arguments among them!

Jim (*grinning*). No arguments, huh? Well, that's a pretty good sign. Where shall I set him?

Laura: Put him on the table. They all like a change of scenery once in a while!

Jim (*stretching*). Well, well, well, well—Look how big my shadow is when I stretch!

Laura: Oh, oh, yes—it stretches across the ceiling!

Jim (*crossing to door*). I think it's stopped raining. (*Opens fire-escape door.*) Where does the music come from?

Laura: From the Paradise Dance Hall across the alley.

Jim: How about cutting the rug a little, Miss Wingfield?

Laura: Oh, I—

Jim: Or is your program filled up? Let me have a look at it. (*Grasps imaginary card.*) Why, every dance is taken! I'll just have to scratch some out. (*Waltz music: "La Golondrina"*) Ahhh, a waltz! (*He executes some sweeping turns by himself then holds his arms toward* LAURA.)

Laura (*breathlessly*). I—can't dance!

Jim: There you go, that inferiority stuff!

Laura: I've never danced in my life!

Jim: Come on, try!

Laura: Oh, but I'd step on you!

Jim: I'm not made out of glass.

Laura: How—how—how do we start?

Jim: Just leave it to me. You hold your arms out a little.

Laura: Like this?

Jim: A little bit higher. Right. Now don't tighten up, that's the main thing about it—relax.

Laura (*laughing breathlessly*). It's hard not to.

Jim: Okay.

Laura: I'm afraid you can't budge me.

Jim: What do you bet I can't? (*He swings her into motion.*)

Laura: Goodness, yes, you can!

Jim: Let yourself go, now, Laura, just let yourself go.

Laura: I'm—

Jim: Come on!

Laura: Trying!

Jim: Not so stiff—Easy does it!

Laura: I know but I'm—

Jim: Loosen th' backbone! There now, that's a lot better.

Laura: Am I?

Jim: Lots, lots better! (*He moves her about the room in a clumsy waltz.*)

Laura: Oh, my!

Jim: Ha-ha!

Laura: Oh, my goodness!

Jim: Ha-ha-ha! (*They suddenly bump into the table.* JIM *stops.*) What did we hit on?

Laura: Table.

Jim: Did something fall off it? I think—

Laura: Yes.

Jim: I hope that it wasn't the little glass horse with the horn!

Laura: Yes.

Jim: Aw, aw, aw. Is it broken?

Laura: Now it is just like all the other horses.

Jim: It's lost its—

Laura: Horn! It doesn't matter. Maybe it's a blessing in disguise.

Jim: You'll never forgive me. I bet that that was your favorite piece of glass.

Laura: I don't have favorites much. It's no tragedy, Freckles. Glass breaks so easily. No matter how careful you are. The traffic jars the shelves and things fall off them.

Jim: Still I'm awfully sorry that I was the cause.

Laura (*smiling*). I'll just imagine he had an operation. The horn was removed to make him feel less—freakish! (*They both laugh.*) Now he will feel more at home with the other horses, the ones that don't have horns . . .

Jim: Ha-ha, that's very funny! (*Suddenly serious.*) I'm glad to see that you have a sense of humor. You know—you're—well—very different! Surprisingly different from anyone else I know! (*His voice becomes soft and hesitant with a genuine feeling.*) Do you mind me telling you that? (LAURA *is abashed beyond speech.*) I mean it in a nice way . . . (LAURA *nods shyly, looking away.*) You make me feel sort of—I don't know how to put it! I'm usually pretty good at expressing things, but—This is something that I don't know how to say! (LAURA *touches her throat and clears it—turns the broken unicorn in her hands.*) (*Even softer.*) Has anyone ever told you that you were pretty? (*Pause: Music.*) (LAURA *looks up slowly, with wonder, and shakes her head.*) Well, you are! In a very different way from anyone else. And all the nicer because of the difference, too. (*His voice becomes low and husky.* LAURA *turns away, nearly faint with the novelty of her emotions.*) I wish that you were my sister. I'd teach you to have some confidence in yourself. The different people are not like other people, but being different is nothing to be ashamed of. Because other people are not such wonderful people. They're one hundred times one thousand. You're one times one! They walk all over the earth. You just stay here. They're common as—weeds, but—you—well, you're—*Blue Roses!*

[*Image on screen: Blue roses.*]

[*Music changes.*]

Laura: But blue is wrong for—roses . . .

Jim: It's right for you—You're—pretty!

Laura: In what respect am I pretty?

Jim: In all respects—believe me! Your eyes—your hair—are pretty! Your hands are pretty! (*He catches hold of her hand.*) You think I'm making this up because I'm invited to dinner and have to be nice. Oh, I could do that! I could put on an act for you, Laura, and say lots of things without being very sincere. But this time I am. I'm talking to you sincerely. I happened to notice you had this inferiority complex that keeps you from feeling comfortable with people. Somebody needs to build your confidence up and make you proud instead of shy and turning away and—blushing—Somebody ought to—Ought to—*kiss* you, Laura! (*His hand slips slowly up her arm to her shoulder.*) (*Music swells tumultuously.*) (*He suddenly turns her about and kisses her on the lips.*) (*When he releases her* LAURA *sinks on the sofa with a bright, dazed look.*) (JIM *backs away and fishes in his pocket for a cigarette.*) (*Legend on screen: "Souvenir."*) Stumble-john! (*He lights the cigarette, avoiding her look.*) (*There is a peal of girlish laughter from* AMANDA *in the kitchen.*) (LAURA *slowly raises and opens her hand. It still contains the little broken glass animal. She looks at it with a tender, bewildered expression.*) Stumble-john! I shouldn't have done that—That was way off the beam. You don't smoke, do you? (*She looks up, smiling, not hearing the question.*) (*He sits besides her a little gingerly. She looks at him speechlessly—waiting.*) (*He coughs decorously and moves a little farther aside as he considers the situation and senses her feelings, dimly, with perturbation.*) (*Gently.*) Would you—care for a—mint? (*She doesn't seem to hear him but her look grows brighter even.*) Peppermint—Life Saver? My pocket's a regular drug store—wherever I go . . . (*He pops a mint in his mouth. Then gulps and decides to make a clean breast of it. He speaks slowly and gingerly.*) Laura, you know, if I had a sister like you, I'd do the same thing as Tom. I'd bring out fellows and—introduce her to them. The right type of boys of a type to—appreciate her. Only—well—he made a mistake about me. Maybe I've got no call to be saying this. That may not have been the idea in having me over. But what if it was? There's nothing wrong about that. The only trouble is that in my case—I'm not in a situation to—do the right thing. I can't take down your number and say I'll phone. I can't call up next week and—ask for a date. I thought I had better explain the situation in case you misunderstood it and—hurt your feelings. . . . (*Pause.*) (*Slowly, very slowly,* LAURA'S *look changes, her eyes returning slowly from his to the ornament in her palm.*)

[AMANDA *utters another gay laugh in the kitchen.*]

Laura (*faintly*). You—won't—call again?

Jim: No, Laura, I can't. (*He rises from the sofa.*) As I was just explaining, I've—got strings on me, Laura, I've—been going steady! I go out all the time with a girl named Betty. She's a home-girl like you, and Catholic, and Irish, and in a great many ways we—get along fine. I met her last summer on a moonlight boat trip up the river to Alton, on the *Majestic.* Well—right away from the start it was—love! (*Legend: Love!*) (LAURA *sways slightly forward and grips the arm of the sofa. He fails to notice, now enrapt in his own comfortable being.*) Being in love has made a new man of me! (*Leaning stiffly forward, clutching the arm of the sofa,* LAURA *struggles visibly with her storm. But* JIM *is oblivious, she is a long way off.*) The power of love is really pretty tremendous! Love is something that—changes the whole world, Laura! (*The storm abates a little and* LAURA *leans back. He notices her again.*) It happened that Betty's aunt took sick, she got a wire and had to go to Centralia. So Tom—when he asked me to dinner—I naturally just accepted the invitation, not knowing that you—that he—that I—(*He stops awkwardly.*) Huh—I'm a stumble-john! (*He flops back on the sofa.*) (*The holy candles in the altar of* LAURA'S *face have been snuffed out. There is a look of almost infinite desolation.*) (JIM *glances at her uneasily.*) I wish that you would—say something. (*She bites her lip which was trembling and then bravely smiles. She opens her hand again on the broken glass ornament. Then she gently takes his hand and raises it level with her own. She carefully places the unicorn in the palm of his hand, then pushes his fingers closed upon it.*) What are you—doing that for? You want me to have him?—Laura? (*She nods.*) What for?

Laura: A—souvenir . . .

[*She rises unsteadily and crouches beside the victrola to wind it up.*]

[*Legend on screen: "Things have a way of turning out so badly!"*]

[*Or image: "Gentleman caller waving goodbye!—Gaily."*]

[*At this moment* AMANDA *rushes brightly back in the front room. She bears a pitcher of fruit punch in an old-fashioned cut-glass pitcher and a plate of macaroons. The plate has a gold border and poppies painted on it.*]

Amanda: Well, well, well! Isn't the air delightful after the shower? I've made you children a little liquid refreshment. (*Turns gaily to the gentleman caller.*) Jim, do you know that song about lemonade?

"Lemonade, lemonade
Made in the shade and stirred with a spade—
Good enough for my old maid!"

Jim (*uneasily*). Ha-ha! No—I never heard it.

Amanda: Why, Laura! You look so serious!

Jim: We were having a serious conversation.

Amanda: Good! Now you're better acquainted!

Jim (*uncertainly*). Ha-ha! Yes.

Amanda: You modern young people are much more serious-minded than my generation. I was so gay as a girl!

Jim: You haven't changed, Mrs. Wingfield.

Amanda: Tonight I'm rejuvenated! The gaiety of the occasion, Mr. O'Connor! (*She tosses her head with a peal of laughter. Spills lemonade.*) Oooo! I'm baptizing myself!

Jim: Here—let me—

Amanda (*setting the pitcher down*). There now. I discovered we had some maraschino cherries. I dumped them in, juice and all!

Jim: You shouldn't have gone to that trouble, Mrs. Wingfield.

Amanda: Trouble, trouble? Why it was loads of fun! Didn't you hear me cutting up in the kitchen? I bet your ears were burning! I told Tom how outdone with him I was for keeping you to himself so long a time! He should have brought you over much, much sooner! Well, now that you've found your way, I want you to be a very frequent caller! Not just occasional but all the time. Oh, we're going to have a lot of gay times together! I see them coming! Mmm, just breathe that air! So fresh, and the moon's so pretty! I'll skip back out—I know where my place is when young folks are having a—serious conversation!

Jim: Oh, don't go out, Mrs. Wingfield. The fact of the matter is I've got to be going.

Amanda: Going, now? You're joking! Why, it's only the shank of the evening, Mr. O'Connor!

Jim: Well, you know how it is.

Amanda: You mean you're a young workingman and have to keep workingmen's hours. We'll let you off early tonight. But only on the condition that next time you stay later. What's the best night for you? Isn't Saturday night the best night for you workingmen?

Jim: I have a couple of time-clocks to punch, Mrs. Wingfield. One at morning, another one at night!

Amanda: My, but you *are* ambitious! You work at night, too?

Jim: No, Ma'am, not work but—Betty! (*He crosses deliberately to pick up his hat. The band at the Paradise Dance Hall goes into a tender waltz.*)

Amanda: Betty? Betty? Who's—Betty? (*There is an ominous cracking sound in the sky.*)

Jim: Oh, just a girl. The girl I go steady with! (*He smiles charmingly. The sky falls.*)

[*Legend: "The sky falls."*]

Amanda (*a long-drawn exhalation*). Ohhhh . . . Is it a serious romance, Mr. O'Connor?

Jim: We're going to be married the second Sunday in June.

Amanda: Ohhhh—how nice! Tom didn't mention that you were engaged to be married.

Jim: The cat's not out of the bag at the warehouse yet. You know how they are. They call you Romeo and stuff like that. (*He stops at the oval mirror to put on his hat. He carefully shapes the brim and the crown to give a discreetly dashing effect.*) It's been a wonderful evening, Mrs. Wingfield. I guess this is what they mean by Southern hospitality.

Amanda: It really wasn't anything at all.

Jim: I hope it don't seem like I'm rushing off. But I promised Betty I'd pick her up at the Wabash depot, an' by the time I get my jalopy down there her train'll be in. Some women are pretty upset if you keep 'em waiting.

Amanda: Yes, I know—The tyranny of women! (*Extends her hand.*) Good-bye, Mr. O'Connor. I wish you luck—and happiness—and success! All three of them, and so does Laura!—Don't you, Laura?

Laura: Yes!

Jim (*taking her hand*). Good-bye, Laura. I'm certainly going to treasure that souvenir. And don't you forget the good advice I gave you. (*Raises his voice to a cheery shout.*) So long, Shakespeare! Thanks again, ladies—Good night!

[*He grins and ducks jauntily out.*]

[*Still bravely grimacing,* AMANDA *closes the door on the gentleman caller. Then she turns back to the room with a puzzled expression. She and* LAURA *don't dare to face each other.* LAURA *crouches beside the victrola to wind it.*]

Amanda (*faintly*). Things have a way of turning out so badly. I don't believe that I would play the victrola. Well, well—well—Our gentleman caller was engaged to be married! Tom!

Tom (*from back*). Yes, Mother?

Amanda: Come in here a minute. I want to tell you something awfully funny.

Tom (*enters with macaroon and a glass of the lemonade*). Has the gentleman caller gotten away already?

Amanda: The gentleman caller has made an early departure. What a wonderful joke you played on us!

Tom: How do you mean?

Amanda: You didn't mention that he was engaged to be married.

Tom: Jim? Engaged?

Amanda: That's what he just informed us.

Tom: I'll be jiggered! I didn't know about that.

Amanda: That seems very peculiar.

Tom: What's peculiar about it?

Amanda: Didn't you call him your best friend down at the warehouse?

Tom: He is, but how did I know?

Amanda: It seems extremely peculiar that you wouldn't know your best friend was going to be married!

Tom: The warehouse is where I work, not where I know things about people!

Amanda: You don't know things anywhere! You live in a dream; you manufacture illusions! (*He crosses to door.*) Where are you going?

Tom: I'm going to the movies.

Amanda: That's right, now that you've had us make such fools of ourselves. The effort, the preparations, all the expense! The new floor lamp, the rug, the clothes for Laura! All for what? To entertain some other girl's fiancé! Go to the movies, go! Don't think about us, a mother deserted, an unmarried sister who's crippled and has no job! Don't let anything interfere with your selfish pleasure! Just go, go, go—to the movies!

Tom: All right, I will! The more you shout about my selfishness to me the quicker I'll go, and I won't go to the movies!

Amanda: Go, then! Then go to the moon—you selfish dreamer!

[TOM *smashes his glass on the floor. He plunges out on the fire-escape, slamming the door.* LAURA *screams—cut by door.*]

[*Dance-hall music up.* TOM *goes to the rail and grips it desperately, lifting his face in the chill white moonlight penetrating the narrow abyss of the alley.*]

[*Legend on screen: "And so good-bye . . ."*]

[TOM'S *closing speech is timed with the interior pantomime. The interior scene is played as though viewed through soundproof glass.* AMANDA *appears to be making a comforting speech to* LAURA *who is huddled upon the sofa. Now that we cannot hear the mother's speech, her silliness is gone and she has dignity and tragic beauty.* LAURA'S *dark hair hides her face until at the end of the speech she lifts it to smile at her mother.* AMANDA'S *gestures are slow and graceful, almost dance-like, as she comforts the daughter. At the end of her speech she glances a moment at the father's picture—then withdraws through the portieres. At close of* TOM'S *speech,* LAURA *blows out the candles, ending the play.*]

Tom: I didn't go to the moon, I went much further—for time is the longest distance between two places—Not long after that I was fired for writing a poem on the lid of a shoe-box. I left Saint Louis. I descended the steps of this fire-escape for a last time and followed, from then on, in my father's footsteps, attempting to find in motion what was lost in space—I traveled around a great deal. The cities swept about me like dead leaves, leaves that were brightly colored but torn away from the branches. I would have stopped, but I was pursued by something. It always came upon me unawares, taking me altogether by surprise. Perhaps it was a familiar bit of music. Perhaps it was only a piece of transparent glass—Perhaps I am walking along a street at night, in some strange city, before I have found companions. I pass the lighted window of a shop where perfume is sold. The window is filled with pieces of colored glass, tiny transparent bottles in delicate colors, like bits of a shattered rainbow. Then all at once my sister touches my shoulder. I turn around and look into her eyes . . . Oh, Laura, Laura, I tried to leave you behind me, but I am more faithful than I intended to be! I reach for a cigarette, I cross the street, I run into the movies or a bar, I buy a drink, I speak to the nearest stranger—anything that can blow your candles out! [LAURA *bends over the candles.*]—for nowadays the world is lit by lightning! Blow out your candles, Laura—and so good-bye. . . .

[*She blows the candles out.*]

[*The scene dissolves.*]

DISCUSSION QUESTIONS

Scenes I and II

1. What elements in the setting involve an implicit social consciousness?
2. How is the alley symbolic for each of the characters?
3. How is the fire escape symbolic, especially for Tom?
4. What does Williams gain by presenting Tom both as stage manager and as a character in the play?

5. How is Amanda characterized by her quarrel with Tom and her stories of past courtships?
6. How does Amanda heighten the anxieties that already torment her children?
7. How are the glass menagerie, yearbook, and phonograph symbolic?
8. Does Amanda's role-playing at the beginning of Scene II add complexity to her character?
9. How does Laura ironically reflect her mother's traits?
10. What does the photograph of Amanda's deserted husband symbolize?

Scenes III and IV

1. What masculine traits appear in Amanda's character?
2. How are both Amanda's magazine selling and censorship of Tom's reading ironic?
3. To what extent is Amanda insensitive toward her son's situation?
4. What traits of Tom's character emerge from his angry attack on his mother?
5. What situation is Laura placed in by the quarrels between Amanda and Tom?
6. How does Tom's hurling his coat against Laura's glass collection support the theme?
7. How does the reconciliation between Tom and Amanda ironically involve more, similar conflicts?
8. What do the illnesses of Amanda's "customers" and the stories of the *Companion* have in common?
9. How does the clash over values between Amanda and Tom ironically reveal traits they have in common?

Scenes V and VI

1. How does the Paradise Dance Hall both differ from and resemble the Wingfield apartment?
2. How does the disagreement between Tom and Amanda over the significance of the gentleman caller's visit prepare for disillusionment?
3. How does Tom expose the weaknesses in Amanda's value system?
4. How does the friendship between Tom and Jim O'Connor involve mutual dependency?
5. What contrast in the personalities of Jim and Tom emerges?
6. What contrast in the personalities of Laura and Tom emerges?
7. What elements in Amanda's exaggerated anecdote have parallels in Scene VI?
8. Do Jim's acts and gestures recall Laura's and Tom's previous characterizations of him?
9. How does Tom's continuing exposition foreshadow a crisis?

Scene VII

1. How is the darkness in the apartment both dramatically and symbolically effective?
2. How do Amanda's actions in the last scene sharply accent long-smouldering anxieties?

3. Scene VII is wholly occupied with the climactic "game of passion" between Jim and Laura, although Williams stresses the disproportion between the apparent casualness of the encounter and its heavy emotional impact on Laura. How are Jim's actions in this scene natural extensions of his character as previously described?
4. The play reaches its reversal when the little glass unicorn falls to the ground and loses the horn that made it unique. Does the incident, in view of Jim's ambitions, involve symbolic parallels in both Jim's and Laura's situations?
5. How does Amanda's recognition of the collapse of her plans highlight both her virtues and vices?
6. What significance is suggested by Laura's blowing out the candles while Tom says goodbye?
7. What is the meaning of the play?
8. To what extent is Tom a tragic figure?
9. Is Amanda tragic in any way?

MOTHER COURAGE AND HER CHILDREN

Bertolt Brecht

An English version by
ERIC BENTLEY

Introductory Comment

As an active proponent of Marxism, Brecht operates from a different premise than most traditional dramatists. Marxian dialectic affirms that human nature is a product of circumstances and that there is no fixed human identity, that human traits do not exist in the absolute but are created or destroyed by the economic forces in society. In *Mother Courage* Brecht is dealing with the destructive effect of war on human life, attitudes, and values. In it we see war breeding cynicism, callousness, greed, and cruelty and destroying innocence, hope, sensitivity, and compassion. Yet, in spite of his Marxian bias, Brecht seems ultimately to be demonstrating through his characters and their actions that there is a solid substratum of human worth, of concern for others, and of courage and tenacity regardless of the folly and evil inherent in the economic structure of a particular society.

In the mute and victimized Kattrin he creates a conscience of humanity that can only communicate through deeds not words. Her actions convey her yearning for life and her love of beauty, her unselfish devotion to her family, and her infinite compassion and deep love for all mankind. Life is of no value to her unless she can manifest her love and good will to others.

According to Marxian ethics Mother Courage's profit-making concerns and petty bourgeois values should make her unattractive; yet Brecht's characterization of her succeeds in making her apparently objectionable traits seem to be defensive weapons against a hostile fate, and her toughness comes through as a kind of psychic stamina and stubborn fortitude that springs from a fundamental strength in human nature that makes survival possible in the face of intolerable conditions. Rather than impressing us as a cynical, disillusioned misanthrope motivated chiefly by greed and crass practicality, she wins our sympathy and admiration by rising to the heights of tragic endurance and acceptance of fate. Thus, because of her tremendous vitality and resilience, she becomes a compelling and ultimately attractive figure even though Brecht's ideological bent would have her made otherwise.

Ironically, in achieving this paradoxical effect, Brecht uses a stage technique that is also unmaterialistic and unrealistic. Instead of the earth-bound staging of Ibsen and his followers, he uses settings and actions suggestive of myth and fantasy, not of reality. Even though the physical and temporal setting of the play is that of seventeenth-century Europe during a period of extended religious wars, the real setting is that of the world of free imagination untrammeled by time and space. Brecht is clearly not interested in history for its own sake but only as a vehicle for his ideas. Stage objects and scenery are not intended to represent literal reality as an end in itself. Instead they are designed primarily to be symbolic and universal. The canteen wagon, the cash box, Yvette's red boots and hat, the drum Kattrin beats on are all symbolically related to the theme of the play—the degradation and ruin produced by war and (unwittingly for Brecht) the triumph of the human spirit over it. Even the music and songs are used symbolically to create contrasting moods and underscore the meaning of the play.

From this play one might conclude that Brecht is a propagandist in drama who is betrayed by his integrity as an artist. He tries to write a play expounding a Marxian materialistic concept of history and human destiny but comes very close to writing great mythic tragedy instead. He eschews psychological characterization and yet ironically achieves memorable dramatic figures in Mother Courage and Kattrin. One might say that he is a dramatist in spite of himself and that, because of his considerable talent and artistic vision as a dramatist, he succeeds at a task he did not consciously select for himself.

Cast of Characters

RECRUITING OFFICER
SERGEANT
MOTHER COURAGE
EILIF
SWISS CHEESE
KATTRIN
COOK
COMMANDER
CHAPLAIN
ORDNANCE OFFICER
YVETTE POTTIER
ONE EYE
COLONEL
SCRIVENER
OLDER SOLDIER
YOUNGER SOLDIER
FIRST SOLDIER
OLD PEASANT
SECOND SOLDIER
PEASANT WOMEN
SOLDIER, *singing*
OLD WOMAN
VOICES, *two*
YOUNG MAN
VOICE, *girl singing*
LIEUTENANT
YOUNG PEASANT
(ONE SUPER)
(TWO EXTRAS)

The time: 1624-1636
The place: Sweden, Poland, Germany

SCENE I

[*Spring, 1624. In Dalarna, the Swedish Commander Oxenstierna is recruiting for the campaign in Poland. The canteen woman Anna Fierling, commonly known as* MOTHER COURAGE, *loses a son.*]

[*Highway outside a town. A* SERGEANT *and a* RECRUITING OFFICER *stand shivering.*]

Recruiting Officer: How the hell can you line up a company in a place like this? You know what I keep thinking about, Sergeant? Suicide. I'm supposed to knock four platoons together by the twelfth—four platoons the Chief's asking for! And they're so friendly around here, I'm scared to go to sleep at night. Suppose I do get my hands on some character and squint at him so I don't notice he's pigeon-chested and has varicose veins. I get him drunk and relaxed, he signs on the dotted line. I pay for the drinks, he steps outside for a minute. I have a hunch I should follow him to the door, and am I right? Away he's gone like a louse from a scratch. You can't take a man's word any more, Sergeant. There's no loyalty left in the world, no trust, no faith, no sense of honour. I'm losing my confidence in mankind, Sergeant.

Sergeant: What they could do with around here is a good war. What else can you expect with peace running wild all over the place? You know what the trouble with peace is? No organization. And when do you get organization? In a war. Peace is one big waste of equipment. Anything goes, no one gives a damn. See the way they eat? Cheese on pumpernickel, bacon on the cheese? Disgusting! How many horses have they got in this town? How many young men? Nobody knows! They haven't bothered to count 'em! That's peace for you! I've been in places where they haven't had a war for seventy years and you know what? The people haven't even been given names! They don't know who they are! It takes a war to fix that. In a war, everyone registers, everyone's name's on a list. Their shoes are stacked, their corn's in the bag, you count it all up—cattle, men, *et cetera* —and you take it away! That's the story: no organization, no war!

Recruiting Officer: It's God's truth, you know.

Sergeant: Of course, a war's like any good deal: hard to get going. But when it does get moving, it's a winner, and they're all scared of peace, like a dice player who daren't stop—'cause when peace comes they have to pay up. Of course, *until* it gets going, they're just as scared of war, it's such a novelty!

Recruiting Officer: Hey, look, here's a canteen wagon. Two women and a couple of young lads. Stop the old lady, Sergeant. And if there's nothing doing this time, you won't catch me freezing my arse in the April wind a minute longer.

[*A harmonica is heard. A canteen wagon rolls on, drawn by two young fellows.* MOTHER COURAGE *is sitting on it with her dumb daughter,* KATTRIN.]

Mother Courage: A good day to you, Sergeant!

Sergeant (*barring the way*). Good day to *you!* Who d'you think you are?

Mother Courage: Tradespeople. (*She sings.*)

Here's Mother Courage and her wagon!
  Hey, Captain, let them come and buy!
Beer by the keg! Wine by the flagon!
  Let your men drink before they die!
Sabres and swords are hard to swallow:
  First you must give them beer to drink.
Then they can face what is to follow—
  But let 'em swim before they sink!
    Christians, awake! The winter's gone!
    The snows depart, the dead sleep on.
    And though you may not long survive,
    Get out of bed and look alive!

Your men will march till they are dead, sir.
  But cannot fight unless they eat.
The blood they spill for you is red, sir,
  What fires that blood is my red meat.
For meat and soup and jam and jelly
  In this old cart of mine are found:
So fill the hole up in your belly
  Before you fill one underground.
    Christians, awake! The winter's gone!
    The snows depart, the dead sleep on.
    And though you may not long survive,
    Get out of bed and look alive!

(*She prepares to go.*)

Sergeant: Halt! Where are you from, riffraff?

Eilif: Second Finnish Regiment!

Sergeant: Where are your papers?

Mother Courage: Papers?

Swiss Cheese: But this is Mother Courage!

Sergeant: Never heard of her. Where'd she get a name like that?

Mother Courage: They call me Mother Courage 'cause I was afraid I'd be ruined. So I drove through the bombardment of

Riga like a madwoman, with fifty loaves of bread in my cart. They were going moldly, I couldn't please myself.

Sergeant: No funny business! Where are your papers?

[MOTHER COURAGE *rummages among papers in a tin box and clambers down from her wagon.*]

Mother Courage: Here, Sergeant! Here's a Bible—I got it in Altötting to wrap my cucumbers in. Here's a map of Moravia—God knows if I'll ever get there—the birds can have it. And here's a document saying my horse hasn't got foot and mouth disease—pity he died on us, he cost fifteen gilders, thank God I didn't pay it. Is that enough paper?

Sergeant: Are you making a pass at me? Well, you've got another guess coming. You need a license and you know it.

Mother Courage: Show a little respect for a lady and don't go telling these half-grown children of mine I'm making a pass at you. What would I want with you? My license in the Second Protestant Regiment is an honest face. If *you* wouldn't know how to read it, that's not my fault, I want no rubber stamp on it anyhow.

Recruiting Officer: Sergeant, we have a case of insubordination on our hands. Do you know what we need in the army? Discipline!

Mother Courage: I was going to say sausages.

Sergeant: Name?

Mother Courage: Anna Fierling.

Sergeant: So you're all Fierlings.

Mother Courage: I was talking about me.

Sergeant: And I was talking about your children.

Mother Courage: Must they all have the same name? (*Pointing to the elder son*) This fellow, for instance, I call him Eilif Noyocki—he got the name from his father who told me he was called Koyocki. Or was it Moyocki? Anyhow, the lad remembers him to this day. Only the man he remembers is someone else, a Frenchman with a pointed beard. But he certainly has his father's brains—that man could whip the breeches off a farmer's backside before he could turn around. So we all have our own names.

Sergeant: You're all called something different?

Mother Courage: Are you trying to make out you don't understand?

Sergeant: (*pointing at the younger son*). He's a Chinese, I suppose.

Mother Courage: Wrong again. A Swiss.

Sergeant: After the Frenchman?

Mother Courage: Frenchman? What Frenchman? Don't confuse the issue, Sergeant, or we'll be here all day. He's a Swiss, but he happens to be called Feyos, a name that has nothing to do with his father, who was called something else—a military engineer, if you please, and a drunkard.

[SWISS CHEESE *nods, beaming; even* KATTRIN *smiles.*]

Sergeant: Then how is it his name's Feyos?

Mother Courage: Oh, Sergeant, you have no imagination. *Of course* he's called Feyos: When he came, I was with a Hungarian. He didn't mind. He had a floating kidney, though he never touched a drop. He was a very *honest* man. The boy takes after him.

Sergeant: But that wasn't his father!

Mother Courage: I said: he took after him. I call him Swiss Cheese. Why? Because he's good at pulling wagons.

(*Pointing to her daughter.*) And that is Kattrin Haupt, she's half German.

Sergeant: A nice family, I must say!

Mother Courage: And we've seen the whole wide world together—this wagon-load and me.

Sergeant: We'll need all that in writing. (*He writes.*) You're from Bamberg in Bavaria. What are you doing here?

Mother Courage: I can't wait till the war is good enough to come to Bamberg.

Recruiting Officer: And you two oxen pull the cart. Jacob Ox and Esau Ox! D'you ever get out of harness?

Eilif: Mother! May I smack him in the kisser?

Mother Courage: You stay where you are. And now, gentlemen, what about a brace of pistols? Or a belt? Sergeant? Yours is worn clean through.

Sergeant: It's something else *I'm* looking for. These lads of yours are straight as birch trees, strong limbs, massive chests . . . What are such fine specimens doing out of the army?

Mother Courage (*quickly*). A soldier's life is not for sons of mine.

Recruiting Officer: Why not? It means money. It means fame. Peddling shoes is woman's work. (*To* EILIF.) Step this way and let's see if that's muscle or chicken fat.

Mother Courage: It's chicken fat. Give him a good hard look, and he'll fall right over.

Recruiting Officer: Yes, and kill a calf in the falling! (*He tries to hustle* EILIF *away.*)

Mother Courage: Let him alone! He's not for you!

Recruiting Officer: He called my face a kisser. That is an insult. The two of us will go and settle the affair on the field of honor.

Eilif: Don't worry, Mother, I can handle him.

Mother Courage: Stay here. You're never happy till you're in a fight. He has a knife in his boot and he knows how to use it.

Recruiting Officer: I'll draw it out of him like a milk tooth. Come on, young fellow-me-lad!

Mother Courage: Officer, I'll report you to the Colonel, and he'll throw you in jail. His lieutenant is courting my daughter.

Sergeant (*to* OFFICER). Go easy. (*To* MOTHER COURAGE) What have you got against the service, wasn't his own father a soldier? Didn't you say he died a soldier's death?

Mother Courage: This one's just a baby. You'll lead him like a lamb to the slaughter. I know you. You'll get five gilders for him.

Recruiting Officer (*to* EILIF). First thing you know, you'll have a lovely cap and high boots, how about it?

Eilif: Not from you.

Mother Courage: "Let's you and me go fishing," said the angler to the worm. (*To* SWISS CHEESE) Run and tell everybody they're trying to steal your brother! (*She draws a knife.*) Yes, just you try, and I'll cut you down like dogs! We sell cloth, we sell ham, we are peaceful people!

Sergeant: You're peaceful all right: your knife proves that. Why, you should be ashamed of yourself. Give me that knife, you hag! You admit you live off the war, what else *could* you live off? Now tell me, how can we have a war without soldiers?

Mother Courage: Do they have to be mine?

Sergeant: So that's the trouble. The war should swallow the peach-stone and spit out the peach, hm? Your brood should get fat off the war, but the poor war must ask nothing in return, it can look after itself, can it? Call yourself Mother Courage and then get scared of the war, your breadwinner? Your sons aren't scared, I know that much.

Eilif: Takes more than a war to scare me.

Sergeant: Correct! Take me. The soldier's life hasn't done *me* any harm, has it? I enlisted at seventeen.

Mother Courage: You haven't reached seventy.

Sergeant: I will, though.

Mother Courage: Above ground?

Sergeant: Are you trying to rile me, telling me I'll die?

Mother Courage: Suppose it's the truth? Suppose I see it's your fate? Suppose I *know* you're just a corpse on furlough?

Swiss Cheese: She can look into the future. Everyone says so.

Recruiting Officer: Then by all means look into the sergeant's future. It might amuse him.

Sergeant: I don't believe in that stuff.

Mother Courage: Helmet!

[SERGEANT *gives her his helmet.*]

Sergeant: It means less than a shit in the grass. Anything for a laugh. (MOTHER COURAGE *takes a sheet of parchment and tears it in two.*)

Mother Courage: Eilif, Swiss Cheese, Kattrin! So shall we all be torn in two if we let ourselves get too deep into this war! (*To the* SERGEANT) I'll give you the bargain rate, and do it free. Watch! Death is black, so I draw a black cross.

Swiss Cheese: And the other she leaves blank, see?

Mother Courage: I fold them, put them in the helmet, and mix 'em up, the way all of us are mixed from our mother's womb on. Now draw!

[*The* SERGEANT *hesitates.*]

Recruiting Officer (*to* EILIF). I don't take just anybody. I'm choosy. And you've got guts, I like that.

Sergeant: It's silly. Means as much as blowing your nose.

Swiss Cheese: The black cross! Oh, his number's up!

Recruiting Officer: Don't let them get under your skin. There aren't enough bullets to go round.

Sergeant (*hoarsely*). You cheated me!

Mother Courage: You cheated yourself the day you enlisted. And now we must drive on. There isn't a war every day in the week, we must get to work.

Sergeant: Hell, you're not getting away with this! We're taking that bastard of yours with *us!*

Eilif: I'd like that, Mother.

Mother Courage: Quiet—you Finnish devil, you!

Eilif: And Swiss Cheese wants to be a soldier, too.

Mother Courage: That's news to me. I see I'll have to draw lots for all three of you. (*She goes to the back to draw the crosses on bits of paper.*)

Recruiting Officer (*to* EILIF). People've been saying the Swedish soldier is religious. That kind of loose talk has hurt us a lot. One verse of a hymn every Sunday—and then only if you have a voice . . .

[MOTHER COURAGE *returns with the slips and puts them in the* SERGEANT'S *helmet.*]

Mother Courage: So they'd desert their old mother, would they, the rascals? They take to war like a cat to cream. But

I'll consult these slips, and they'll see the world's no promised land, with a "Join up, son, you're officer material!" Sergeant, I'm afraid for them, very afraid they won't get through this war. They have terrible qualities, all three. (*She holds the helmet out to* EILIF.) There. Draw your lot. (EILIF *fishes in the helmet, unfolds a slip. She snatches it from him.*) There you have it: a cross. Unhappy mother that I am, rich only in a mother's sorrow! He dies. In the springtime of his life, he must go. If he's a soldier, he must bite the dust, that's clear. He's too brave, like his father. And if he doesn't use his head, he'll go the way of all flesh, the slip proves it. (*Hectoring him*) Will you use your head?

Eilif: Why not?

Mother Courage: It's using your head to stay with your mother. And when they make fun of you and call you a chicken, just laugh.

Recruiting Officer: If you're going to wet your pants, I'll try your brother.

Mother Courage: I told you to laugh. Laugh! Now it's your turn, Swiss Cheese. You should be a better bet, you're honest. (*He fishes in the helmet.*) Oh, dear, why are you giving that slip such a funny look? You've drawn a blank for sure. It can't be there's a cross on it. It can't be I'm going to lose *you*. (*She takes the slip.*) A cross? Him too! Could it be 'cause he's so simple-minded? Oh, Swiss Cheese, you'll be a goner too, if you aren't honest, honest, honest the whole time, the way I always brought you up to be, the way you always bring me all the change when you buy me a loaf. It's the only way you can save yourself. Look, Sergeant, if it isn't a black cross!

Sergeant: It's a cross! I don't understand how *I* got one. I always stay well in the rear. (*To the* OFFICER) But it can't be a trick: it gets *her* children too.

Swiss Cheese: It gets me too. But I don't accept it!

Mother Courage (*to* KATTRIN). And now all I have left for certain is you, you're a cross in yourself, you have a good heart. (*She holds the helmet up high toward the wagon but takes the slip out herself.*) Oh, I could give up in despair! There must be some mistake, I didn't mix them right. Don't be too kind, Kattrin, just don't, there's a cross in your path too. Always be very quiet, it can't be hard since you're dumb. Well, so now you know, all of you: be careful, you'll need to be. Now let's climb on the wagon and move on. (*She returns the helmet to the* SERGEANT *and climbs on the wagon.*)

Recruiting Officer (*to the* SERGEANT). Do something!

Sergeant: I don't feel very well.

Recruiting Officer: Maybe you caught a chill when you handed over your helmet in all this wind. Get her involved in a business transaction! (*Aloud*) That belt, Sergeant, you could at least take a look at it. These good people live by trade, don't they? Hey, all of you, the Sergeant wants to buy the belt!

Mother Courage: Half a gilder. A belt like that is worth two gilders. (*She clambers down again from the wagon.*)

Sergeant: It isn't new. But there's too much wind here. I'll go and look at it behind the wagon. (*He does so.*)

Mother Courage: I don't find it windy.

Sergeant: Maybe it's worth half a gilder at that. There's silver on it.

Mother Courage (*following him behind the wagon*). A solid six ounces worth!

Recruiting Officer (*to* EILIF). And we can have a drink, just us men. I'll advance you some money to cover it. Let's go. (EILIF *stands undecided.*)

Mother Courage: Half a gilder, then.

Sergeant: I don't understand it. I always stay in the rear. There's no safer spot for a sergeant to be. You can send the others on ahead in quest of fame. My appetite is ruined. I can tell you right now: I won't be able to get anything down.

Mother Courage: You shouldn't take on so, just because you can't eat. Just stay in the rear. Here, take a slug of brandy, man. (*She gives him brandy.*)

Recruiting Officer (*who has taken* EILIF *by the arm and is making off toward the back*). Ten gilders in advance and you're a soldier of the king and a stout fellow and the women will be mad about you. And you can give me a smack in the kisser for insulting you. (*Both leave. Dumb* KATTRIN *jumps down from the wagon and lets out harsh cries.*)

Mother Courage: Coming Kattrin, coming! The sergeant's just paying up. (*She bites the half gilder.*) I'm suspicious of all money, I've been badly burned, Sergeant. But this money's good. And now we'll be going. Where's Eilif?

Swiss Cheese: Gone with the recruiting officer.

Mother Courage (*stands quite still, then*). Oh, you simpleton! (*To* KATTRIN) You *can't* speak, I know. You are innocent.

Sergeant: That's life, Mother Courage. Take a slug yourself, Mother. Being a soldier isn't the worst that could happen. You want to live off the war and keep you and yours out of it, do you?

Mother Courage: You must help your brother now, Kattrin.

[BROTHER *and* SISTER *get into harness together and pull the wagon.* MOTHER COURAGE *walks at their side. The wagon get under way.*]

Sergeant (*looking after them*).
When a war gives you all you earn
One day it may claim something in return!

SCENE II

[*In the years 1625 and 1626* MOTHER COURAGE *journeys through Poland in the baggage train of the Swedish army. She meets her son again before Wallhof castle. Of the successful sale of a capon and great days for the brave son.*]

[*Tent of the Swedish Commander. Kitchen next to it. Thunder of cannon. The* COOK *is quarreling with* MOTHER COURAGE, *who is trying to sell him a capon.*]

Cook: Sixty hellers for that paltry piece of poultry?

Mother Courage: Paltry poultry? Why, he's the fattest fowl you ever saw! I see no reason why I shouldn't get sixty hellers for him—this Commander can eat till the cows come home—and woe betide you when there's nothing in your pantry . . .

Cook: They're ten hellers a dozen on every street corner.

Mother Courage: A capon like this on every street corner! With a siege going on and people all skin and bones? Maybe you can get a field rat! I said maybe. Because we're all out of *them* too. Didn't you see the soldiers running five deep after one hungry little field rat? All right then, in a siege, my price for a giant capon is fifty hellers.

Cook: But we're not "in a siege," we're doing the besieging, it's the other side that's "in a siege," when will you get this into your head?

Mother Courage: A fat lot of difference that makes, *we* haven't got a thing to eat either. They took everything in the town with them before all this started, and now they've nothing to do but eat and drink, I hear. It's us I'm worried about. Look at the farmers round here, they haven't a thing.

Cook: Certainly they have. They hide it.

Mother Courage (*triumphant*). They have not! They're ruined, that's what. They're so hungry I've seen 'em digging up roots to eat. I could boil your leather belt and make their mouth water with it. That's how things are round here. And I'm expected to let a capon go for forty hellers!

Cook: Thirty. Not forty. I said thirty hellers.

Mother Courage: I say this is no ordinary capon. It was a talented animal, so I hear. It would only to feed to music—one march in particular was its favorite. It was so intelligent it could count. Forty hellers is too much for all this? I know *your* problem: if you don't find something to eat and quick, the Chief will—cut—your—fat—head—off!

Cook: All right, just watch. (*He takes a piece of beef and lays his knife on it.*) Here's a piece of beef, I'm going to roast it. I give you one more chance.

Mother Courage: Roast it, go ahead, it's only one year old.

Cook: One *day* old! Yesterday it was a cow. I saw it running around.

Mother Courage: In that case it must have started stinking before it died.

Cook: I don't care if I have to cook it five hours: I *must* know if it'll still be hard. (*He cuts into it.*)

Mother Courage: Put plenty of pepper in, so the Commander won't smell the smell.

[*The* SWEDISH COMMANDER, *a* CHAPLAIN, *and* EILIF *enter the tent.*]

Commander (*clapping* EILIF *on the shoulder*). In the Commander's tent with you, my son! Sit at my right hand, you happy warrior! You've played a hero's part, you've served the Lord in his own Holy War, *that's* the thing! And you'll get a gold bracelet out of it when we take the town if *I* have any say in the matter! We come to save their souls and what do they do, the filthy, irreligious sons of bitches? Drive their cattle away from us, while they stuff their priests with beef at both ends! But you showed 'em. So here's a can of red wine for you, we'll drink together! (*They do so.*) The chaplain gets the dregs, he's pious. Now what would you like for dinner, my hearty?

Eilif: How about a slice of meat?

Commander: Cook, meat!

Cook: Nothing to eat, so he brings company to eat it!

[MOTHER COURAGE *makes him stop talking, she wants to listen.*]

Eilif: Tires you out, skinning peasants. Gives you an appetite.

Mother Courage: Dear God, it's my Eilif!

Cook: Who?

Mother Courage: My eldest. It's two years since I saw him, he was stolen from me right off the street. He must be in high favor if the Commanders' invited him to dinner. And what do you have to eat? Nothing. You hear what the Commander's guest wants? Meat! Better take my advice, buy the capon. The price is one gilder.

Commander (*who has sat down with* EILIF *and the* CHAPLAIN, *roaring*). Cook! Dinner, you pig, or I'll have your head!

Cook: This is blackmail. Give me the damn thing!

Mother Courage: Paltry poultry like this?

Cook: You were right. Give it here. It's highway robbery, fifty hellers.

Mother Courage: I said one gilder. Nothing's too high for my eldest, the Commander's guest of honor.

Cook (*giving her the money*). Well, you might at least pluck it till I have a fire going.

Mother Courage (*sitting down to pluck the capon*). I can't wait to see his face when he sees me. This is my brave and clever son. I also have a stupid one but he's honest. The daughter is nothing. At least, she doesn't talk: we must be thankful for small mercies.

Commander: Have another glass, my son, it's my favorite Falernian. There's only one cask left—two at the most—but it's worth it to meet a soldier that still believes in God! The shepherd of our flock here just looks on, he only preaches, he hasn't a clue how anything gets done. So now, Eilif, my son, give us the details: tell us how you fixed the peasants and grabbed the twenty bullocks. And let's hope they'll soon be here.

Eilif: In one day's time. Two at most.

Mother Courage: Now that's considerate of Eilif—to bring the oxen tomorrow—otherwise my capon wouldn't have been so welcome today.

Eilif: Well, it was like this. I found out that the peasants had hidden their oxen and—on the sly and chiefly at night—had driven them into a certain wood. The people from the town were to pick them up there. I let them get their oxen in peace—they ought to know better than me where they are, I said to myself. Meanwhile I made my men crazy for meat. Their rations were short and I made sure they got shorter. Their mouths'd water at the sound of any word beginning with M, like mother.

Commander: Smart fella.

Eilif: Not bad. The rest was a walkover. Only the peasants had clubs and outnumbered us three to one and made a murderous attack on us. Four of them drove me into a clump of trees, knocked my good sword from my hand, and yelled, "Surrender!" What now, I said to myself, they'll make mincemeat of me.

Commander: What did you do?

Eilif: I laughed.

Commander: You what?

Eilif: I laughed. And so we got to talking. I came right down to business and said: "Twenty gilders an ox is too much, I bid fifteen." Like I wanted to buy. That foxed 'em. So while they were scratching their heads, I reached for my good sword and cut 'em to pieces. Necessity knows no law, huh?

Commander: What do *you* say, shepherd of the flock?

Chaplain: Strictly speaking, that saying is not in the Bible. Our Lord made five hundred loaves out of five so that no such necessity would arise. When he told men to love their neighbors, their bellies were full. Nowadays things are different.

Commander (*laughing*). Quite different. A swallow of wine for those wise words, you pharisee! (*To* EILIF) You cut 'em to pieces in a good cause, our chaps were hungry and you gave 'em to eat. Doesn't it say in the Bible "Whatsoever thou doest to the least of these my children, thou doest unto me"? And what *did* you do to 'em? You got 'em the best steak dinner they ever tasted. Moldy bread is not what they're used to. They always ate white bread, and drank wine in their helmets, before going out to fight for God.

Eilif: I reached for my good sword and cut 'em to pieces.

Commander: You have the makings of a Julius Caesar, why, you should be presented to the King!

Eilif: I've seen him—from a distance of course. He seemed to shed a light all around. I must try to be like him!

Commander: I think you're succeeding, my boy! Oh, Eilif, you don't know how I value a brave soldier like you! I treat such a chap as my very own son. (*He takes him to the map.*) Take a look at our position, Eilif, it isn't all it might be, is it?

Mother Courage (*who has been listening and is now plucking angrily at her capon*). He must be a very bad commander.

Cook: Just a greedy one. Why bad?

Mother Courage: Because he needs *brave* soldiers, that's why. If his plan of campaign was any good, why would he need *brave* soldiers, wouldn't plain, ordinary soldiers do? Whenever there are great virtues, it's a sure sign something's wrong.

Cook: You mean, it's a sure sign something's right.

Mother Courage: I mean what I say. Listen. When a general or a king is stupid and leads his soldiers into a trap, they need this virtue of courage. When he's tight-fisted and hasn't enough soldiers, the few he does have need the heroism of Hercules—another virtue. And if he's a sloven and doesn't give a damn about anything, they have to be wise as serpents or they're finished. Loyalty's another virtue and you need plenty of it if the king's always asking too much of you. All virtues which a well-regulated country with a good king or a good general wouldn't need. In a good country virtues wouldn't be necessary. Everybody could be quite ordinary, middling, and, for all I care, cowards.

Commander: I bet your father was a soldier.

Eilif: I've heard he was a great soldier. My mother warned me. I know a song about that.

Commander: Sing it to us. (*Roaring.*) Bring that meat!

Eilif: It's called "The Song of the Fishwife and the Soldier." (*He sings and at the same time does a war dance with his sabre.*)

To a soldier lad comes an old fishwife
 And this old fishwife, says she:
A gun will shoot, a knife will knife,
 You will drown if you fall in the sea.
Keep away from the ice if you want my advice,
 Says the old fishwife, says she.
The soldier laughs and loads his gun
Then grabs his knife and starts to run:
 It's the life of a hero for me!
From the north to the south I shall march through the land
With a knife at my side and a gun in my hand!
 Says the soldier lad, says he.

When the lad defies the fishwife's cries
 The old fishwife, says she:
The young are young, the old are wise,

You will drown if you fall in the sea.
Don't ignore what I say or you'll rue it one day!
Says the old fishwife, says she.
But gun in hand and knife at side
The soldier steps into the tide:
It's the life of a hero for me!
When the new moon is shining on shingle roofs white
We are all coming back, go and pray for that night!
Says the soldier lad, says he.

[MOTHER COURAGE *continues the song from her kitchen, beating on a pan with a spoon.*]

And the fishwife old does what she's told:
Down upon her knees drops she.
When the smoke is gone, the air is cold,
Your heroic deeds won't warm me!
See the smoke, how it goes! May God scatter his foes!
Down upon her knees drops she.

Eilif: What's that?

Mother Courage (*singing on*).

But gun in hand and knife at side
The lad is swept out by the tide:
He floats with the ice to the sea.
And the new moon is shining on shingle roofs white
But the lad and his laughter are lost in the night:
He floats with the ice to the sea.

Commander: What a kitchen I've got! There's no end to the liberties they take!

Eilif (*has entered the kitchen and embraced his mother*). To see you again! Where are the others?

Mother Courage (*in his arms*). Happy as ducks in a pond. Swiss Cheese is paymaster with the Second Regiment, so at least he isn't in the fighting. I couldn't keep him out altogether.

Eilif: Are your feet holding up?

Mother Courage: I've a bit of trouble getting my shoes on in the morning.

Commander (*who has come over*). So, you're his mother! I hope you have more sons for me like this chap.

Eilif: If I'm not the lucky one: you sit there in the kitchen and hear your son being feasted!

Mother Courage: Yes. I heard all right. (*Gives him a box on the ear.*)

Eilif (*his hand to his cheek*). Because I took the oxen?

Mother Courage: No. Because you didn't surrender when the four peasants let fly at you and tried to make mincemeat of you! Didn't I teach you to take care of yourself? You Finnish devil, you!

[*The* COMMANDER *and the* CHAPLAIN *stand laughing in the doorway.*]

SCENE III

[*Three years pass and* MOTHER COURAGE, *with parts of a Finnish regiment, is taken prisoner. Her daughter is saved, her wagon likewise, but her honest son dies.*]

[*A camp. The regimental flag is flying from a pole. Afternoon. All sorts of wares hanging on the wagon.* MOTHER COURAGE'S *clothes line is tied to the wagon at one end, to a cannon at the other. She and* KATTRIN *are folding the washing on the cannon. At the same time she is bargaining with an* ORDNANCE OFFICER *over a bag of bullets.* SWISS CHEESE, *in paymaster's uniform now, looks on.* YVETTE POTTIER, *a very good-looking young person, is sewing at a colored hat, a glass of brandy before her. She is in stocking feet. Her red boots are near by.*]

Officer: I'm letting you have the bullets for two gilders. Dirt cheap. 'Cause I need the money. The Colonel's been drinking with the officers for three days and we've run out of liquor.

Mother Courage: They're army property. If they find 'em on me, I'll be court-martialed. You sell your bullets, you bastards, and send your men out to fight with nothing to shoot with.

Officer: Oh, come on, if you scratch my back, I'll scratch yours.

Mother Courage: I won't take army stuff. Not at *that* price.

Officer: You can resell 'em for five gilders, maybe eight, to the Ordnance Officer of the Fourth Regiment. All you have to do is give him a receipt for twelve. He hasn't a bullet left.

Mother Courage: Why don't you do it yourself?

Officer: I don't trust him. We're friends.

Mother Courage (*takes the bag*). Give it here. (*To* KATTRIN.) Take it round the back and pay him a gilder and a half. (*As the* OFFICER *protests.*) I said a gilder and a half!

[KATTRIN *drags the bag away. The* OFFICER *follows.* MOTHER COURAGE *speaks to* SWISS CHEESE.]

Here's your underwear back, take care of it; it's October now, autumn may come at any time; I purposely don't say it must come, I've learnt from experience there's nothing that must come, not even the seasons. But your books *must* balance now you're the regimental paymaster. *Do* they balance?

Swiss Cheese: Yes, Mother.

Mother Courage: Don't forget they made you paymaster because you're honest and so simple you'd never think of running off with the cash. Don't lose that underwear.

Swiss Cheese: No, Mother. I'll put it under the mattress. (*He starts to go.*)

Officer: I'll go with you, paymaster.

Mother Courage: Don't teach him any hanky-panky.

[*Without a good-bye the* OFFICER *leaves with* SWISS CHEESE.]

Yvette (*waving to him*). You might at least say good-bye!

Mother Courage (*to* YVETTE). I don't like that. *He's* no sort of company for my Swiss Cheese. But the war's not making a bad start. Before all the different countries get into it, four or five years'll have gone by like nothing. If I look ahead and make no mistakes, business will be good. Don't you know you shouldn't drink in the morning with your illness?

Yvette: Who says I'm ill? That's libel!

Mother Courage: They all say so.

Yvette: They're all liars. I'm desperate, Mother Courage. They all avoid me like a stinking fish. Because of those lies. So what am I fixing my hat for? (*She throws it down.*) That's why I drink in the morning. I never used to, it gives you crow's feet. But now it's all one, every man in the regiment knows me. I should have stayed home when my first was unfaithful. But pride isn't for the likes of us, you eat dirt or down you go.

Mother Courage: Now don't you

start again with your friend Peter and how it all happened—in front of my innocent daughter.

Yvette: She's the one that should hear it. So she'll get hardened against love.

Mother Courage: That's something no one ever gets hardened against.

Yvette: I'll tell you about it, and get it off my chest. I grew up in Flanders' fields, that's where it starts, or I'd never even have caught sight of him and I wouldn't be here in Poland today. He was an army cook, blond, a Dutchman, but thin. Kattrin, beware of thin men! I didn't. I didn't even know he'd had another girl before me and she called him Peter Piper because he never took his pipe out of his mouth the whole time, it meant so little to him. (*She sings "The Fraternization Song."*)

Scarce seventeen was I when
The foe came to our land
And laid aside his sabre
And took me by the hand.
And we performed by day
The sacred rite of May
And we performed by night
Another sacred rite.
The regiment, well exercised,
Presented arms, then stood at ease,
Then took us off behind the trees
Where we fraternized.

Each of us had her foe and
A cook fell to my lot.
I hated him by daylight
But in the dark did not.
So we perform by day
The sacred rite of May
And we perform by night
That other sacred rite.
The regiment, well exercised,
Presents its arms, then stands at ease,
Then takes us off behind the trees
Where we fraternize.

Ecstasy filled my heart, O
My love seemed heaven-born!
But why were people saying
It was not love but scorn?
The springtime's soft amour
Through summer may endure
But swiftly comes the fall
And winter ends it all.
December came. All of the men
Filed past the trees where once we hid
Then quickly marched away and did
Not come back again.

I made the mistake of running after him, I never found him. It's ten years ago now. (*With swaying gait she goes behind the wagon.*)

Mother Courage: You're leaving your hat.

Yvette: For the birds.

Mother Courage: Let this be a lesson to you, Kattrin, never start anything with a soldier. Love does seem heaven-born, so watch out! Even with those who're not in the army life's no honey pot. He tells you he'd like to kiss the ground under your feet—did you wash 'em yesterday, while we're on the subject? And then if you don't look out, your number's up, you're his slave for life. Be glad you're dumb, Kattrin: you'll never contradict yourself, you'll never want to bite your tongue off because you spoke out of turn. Dumbness is a gift from God. Here comes the Commander's Cook, what's bothering *him?*

[*Enter the* COOK *and the* CHAPLAIN.]

Chaplain: I bring a message from your son Eilif. The Cook came with me. You've made, ahem, an impression on him.

Cook: I thought I'd get a little whiff of the balmy breeze.

Mother Courage: You're always welcome to that if you behave yourself and, even if you don't I think I can handle you. But what does Eilif want? I've no money to spare.

Chaplain: Actually, I have something to tell his brother, the paymaster.

Mother Courage: He isn't here. And he isn't anywhere else either. He's not his brother's paymaster and I won't have him led into temptation. Let Eilif try it on with someone else! (*She takes money from the purse at her belt.*) Give him this. It's a sin. He's speculating in mother love, he ought to be ashamed of himself.

Cook: Not for long. He has to go with his regiment now—to his death maybe. Send some more money, or you'll be sorry. You women are hard—and sorry afterwards. A glass of brandy wouldn't cost very much, but you refuse to provide it, and six feet under goes your man and you can't dig him up again.

Chaplain: All very touching, my dear Cook, but to fall in this war is not a misfortune, it's a blessing. This is a war of religion. Not just any old war but a special one, a religious one, and therefore pleasing unto God.

Cook: Correct. In one sense it's a war because there's fleecing, bribing, plundering, not to mention a little raping, but it's different from all other wars because it's a war of religion. That's clear. All the same, it makes you thirsty.

Chaplain (*to* MOTHER COURAGE, *pointing at the* COOK). I tried to hold him off but he said you'd bewitched him. He dreams about you.

Cook (*lighting a clay pipe*). Brandy from the fair hand of a lady, that's for me. And don't embarrass me any more: the stories the chaplain was telling on the way over still have me blushing.

Mother Courage: A man of his cloth! I must get you both something to drink or you'll be making improper advances out of sheer boredom.

Chaplain: That is indeed a temptation, said the Court Chaplain, and gave way to it. (*Turning toward* KATTRIN *as he walks.*) And who is this captivating young person?

Mother Courage: She's not a captivating young person, she's a respectable young person.

[*The* CHAPLAIN *and the* COOK *go with* MOTHER COURAGE *behind the cart, and one hears them talk politics.*]

Mother Courage: The trouble here in Poland is that the Poles *would* keep meddling. It's true our King moved in on them with man, beast and wagon, but instead of keeping the peace the Poles were always meddling in their own affairs. They attacked the Swedish King when he was in the act of peacefully withdrawing. So they were guilty of a breach of the peace and their blood is on their own heads.

Chaplain: Anyway, our King was thinking of nothing but freedom. The Kaiser enslaved them all, Poles and Germans alike, so our King *had* to liberate them.

Cook: Just what *I* think. Your health! Your brandy is first rate, I'm never mistaken in a face. (KATTRIN *looks after them, leaves the washing, and goes to the hat, picks it up, sits down, and takes up the red boots.*) And the war is a war of religion. (*Singing while* KATTRIN *puts the boots on.*) "A mighty fortress is our God . . ." (*He sings a verse or so of Luther's hymn.*) And talking of King

Gustavus, this freedom he tried to bring to Germany cost him a pretty penny. Back in Sweden he had to levy a salt tax, the poorer folks didn't like it a bit. Then, too, he had to lock up the Germans and even cut their heads off, they clung so to slavery and their Kaiser. Of course, if no one had *wanted* to be free, the King wouldn't have had any fun. First it was just Poland he tried to protect from bad men, specially the Kaiser, then his appetite grew with eating, and he ended up protecting Germany too. Now Germany put up a pretty decent fight. So the good King had nothing but worries in return for his outlay and his goodness, and of course he had to get his money back with taxes, which made bad blood, but he didn't shrink even from that. For he had one thing in his favor anyway, God's Holy Word, which was all to the good, because otherwise they could have said he did it for himself or for profit. That's how he kept his conscience clear. He always put conscience first.

Mother Courage: It's plain you're no Swede, or you'd speak differently of the Hero King.

Chaplain: What's more, you eat his bread.

Cook: I don't eat his bread. I bake his bread.

Mother Courage: He can never be conquered, and I'll tell you why: his men believe in him. (*Earnestly.*) To hear the big chaps talk, they wage the war from fear of God and for all things bright and beautiful, but just look into it, and you'll see they're not so silly: they want a good profit out of it, or else the little chaps like you and me wouldn't back 'em up.

Cook: That's right.

Chaplain: And as a Dutchman you'd do well to see which flag's flying here before you express an opinion!

Mother Courage: All good Protestants for ever!

Cook: A health!

[KATTRIN *has begun to strut around with* YVETTE'S *hat on, copying* YVETTE'S *sexy walk. Suddenly cannon and shots. Drums.* MOTHER COURAGE, *the* COOK, *and the* CHAPLAIN *rush round to the front of the cart, the two last with glasses in their hands. The* ORDNANCE OFFICER *and a* SOLDIER *come running to the cannon and try to push it along.*]

Mother Courage: What's the matter? Let me get my washing off that gun, you slobs! (*She tries to do so.*)

Officer: The Catholics! Surprise attack! We don't know if we can get away! (*To the* SOLDIER.) Get that gun! (*Runs off.*)

Cook: For heaven's sake! I must go to the Commander. Mother Courage, I'll be back in a day or two—for a short conversation. (*Rushes off.*)

Mother Courage: Hey, you've left your pipe!

Cook (*off*). Keep it for me, I'll need it!

Mother Courage: This *would* happen when we were just making money.

Chaplain: Well, I must be going too. Yes, if the enemy's so close, it can be dangerous. "Blessed are the peacemakers," a good slogan in wartime! If only I had a cloak.

Mother Courage: I'm lending no cloaks. Not even to save a life I'm not. I've had experience in that line.

Chaplain: But I'm in special danger. Because of my religion!

Mother Courage (*brings him a cloak*). It's against my better judgment. Now run!

Chaplain: I thank you, you're very generous, but maybe I'd better stay and sit here. If I run, I might attract the enemy's attention. I might arouse suspicion.

Mother Courage (*to the* SOLDIER). Let it alone, you dolt, who's going to pay you for this? It'll cost you your life, let me hold it for you.

Soldier (*running away*). You're my witness: I tried!

Mother Courage: I'll swear to it! (*Seeing* KATTRIN *with the hat.*) What on earth are you up to—with a whore's hat! Take it off this minute! Are you crazy? With the enemy coming? (*She tears the hat off her head.*) Do you want them to find you and make a whore of you? And she has the boots on too, straight from Babylon. I'll soon fix that. (*She tries to get them off.*) Oh God, Chaplain, help me with these boots, I'll be back straightaway. (*She runs to the wagon.*)

Yvette (*entering and powdering her face*). What's that you say: the Catholics are coming? Where's my hat? Who's been trampling on it? I can't run around in that, what will they think of me? And I've no mirror either. (*To the* CHAPLAIN.) How do I look—too much powder?

Chaplain: Just, er, right.

Yvette: And where are my red boots? (*She can't find them because* KATTRIN *is hiding her feet under her skirt.*) I left them here! Now I've got to go barefoot to my tent, it's a scandal! [*Exit.* SWISS CHEESE *comes running in carrying a cashbox.* MOTHER COURAGE *enters with her hands full of ashes. To* KATTRIN.] Ashes! (*To* SWISS CHEESE.) What have you got there?

Swiss Cheese: The regimental cashbox.

Mother Courage: Throw it away! Your paymastering days are over!

Swiss Cheese: It's a trust! (*He goes to the back.*)

Mother Courage (*to the* CHAPLAIN). Off with your pastor's coat, Chaplain, or they'll recognize you, cloak or no cloak. (*She is rubbing ashes into* KATTRIN'S *face.*) Keep still. A little dirt, and you're safe. A calamity! The sentries were drunk. Well, one must hide one's light under a bushel, as they say. When a soldier sees a clean face, there's one more whore in the world. Specially a Catholic soldier. For weeks on end, no grub. Then, when they get some by way of plunder, they jump on top of the womenfolk. That should do. Let me look at you. Not bad. Looks like you've been rolling in muck. Don't tremble. Nothing can happen to you now. (*To* SWISS CHEESE.) Where've you left the cashbox?

Swiss Cheese: I thought I'd just put it in the wagon.

Mother Courage (*horrified*). What!? In my wagon? God punish you for a prize idiot! If I just look away for a moment! They'll hang all three of us!

Swiss Cheese: Then I'll put it somewhere else. Or escape with it.

Mother Courage: You'll stay where you are. It's too late.

Chaplain (*still changing his clothes*). For Heaven's sake: the flag!

Mother Courage (*taking down the flag*). God in Heaven! I don't notice it any more. I've had it twenty-five years.

[*The thunder of cannon grows.*]

[*Three days later. Morning. The cannon is gone.* MOTHER COURAGE, KATTRIN, *the* CHAPLAIN *and* SWISS CHEESE *sit anxiously eating.*]

Swiss Cheese: This is the third day I've been sitting here doing nothing, and the Sergeant, who's always been patient with me, may be slowly beginning to ask, "Where on earth is Swiss Cheese with that cashbox?"

Mother Courage: Be glad they're not on the scent.

Chaplain: What about me? I can't hold service here or I'll be in hot water. It is written, "Out of the abundance of the heart, the tongue speaketh." But woe is me if *my* tongue speaketh!

Mother Courage: That's how it is. Here you sit—one with his religion, the other with his cashbox, I don't know which is more dangerous.

Chaplain: We're in God's hands now!

Mother Courage: I hope we're not as desperate as *that,* but it *is* hard to sleep at night. 'Course it'd be easier if *you* weren't here, Swiss Cheese, all the same I've not done badly. I told them I was against the Antichrist, who's a Swede with horns on his head. I told them I noticed his left horn's a bit threadbare. When they cross-questioned me, I always asked where I could buy holy candles a bit cheaper. I know these things because Swiss Cheese's father was a Catholic and made jokes about it. They didn't quite believe me but they needed a canteen, so they turned a blind eye. Maybe it's all for the best. We're prisoners. But so are lice in fur.

Chaplain: The milk is good. As far as quantity goes, we may have to reduce our Swedish appetites somewhat. We are defeated.

Mother Courage: Who's defeated? The defeats and victories of the chaps at the top aren't always defeats and victories for the chaps at the bottom. Not at all. There've been cases where a defeat is a victory for the chaps at the bottom, it's only their honor that's lost, nothing serious. In Livonia once, our Chief took such a knock from the enemy, in the confusion I got a fine gray mare out of the baggage train, it pulled my wagon seven months—till we won and inventory was taken. But in general both defeat and victory are a costly business for us that haven't got much. The best thing is for politics to kind of get stuck in the mud. (*To* SWISS CHEESE.) Eat!

Swiss Cheese: I don't like it. How will the Sergeant pay his men?

Mother Courage: Soldiers in flight don't get paid.

Swiss Cheese: Well, they could claim to be. No pay, no flight. They can refuse to budge.

Mother Courage: Swiss Cheese, your sense of duty worries me. I've brought you up to be honest because you're not very bright. But don't go too far! And now I'm going with the Chaplain to buy a Catholic flag and some meat. There's no one can hunt out meat like him, sure as a sleepwalker. He can tell a good piece of meat from the way his mouth waters. A good thing they let me stay in the business. In business you ask what price, not what religion. And Protestant trousers keep you just as warm.

Chaplain: As the mendicant monk said when there was talk of the Lutherans standing everything on its head in town and country: Beggars will *always* be needed. (MOTHER COURAGE *disappears into the wagon.*) She's worried about the cashbox. Up to now they've ignored us—as if we were part of the wagon—but can it last?

Swiss Cheese: I can get rid of it.

Chaplain: That's almost *more* dangerous. Suppose you're seen. They have spies. Yesterday morning one jumped out of the very hole I was relieving myself in. I was so off guard I almost broke out in prayer—*that* would have given me away all right! I believe their favorite way of finding a Protestant is smelling his, um, excrement. The spy was a little brute with a bandage over one eye.

Mother Courage (*clambering out of the wagon with a basket*). I've found you out, you shameless hussy! (*She holds up* YVETTE'S *red boots in triumph.*) Yvette's red boots! She just swiped them —because you went and told her she was a captivating person. (*She lays them in the basket.*) Stealing Yvette's boots! But *she* disgraces herself for money, *you* do it for nothing—for pleasure! I told you, you must wait for the peace. No soldiers! Save your proud, peacock ways for peacetime!

Chaplain: I don't find her proud.

Mother Courage: Prouder than she can afford to be. I like her when people say "I never noticed the poor thing." I like her when she's a stone in Dalarna where there's nothing but stones. (*To* SWISS CHEESE.) Leave the cashbox where it is, do you hear? And pay attention to your sister, she needs it. Between the two of you, you'll be the death of me yet. I'd rather take care of a bag of fleas.

[*She leaves with the* CHAPLAIN. KATTRIN *clears the dishes away.*]

Swiss Cheese: Not many days more when you can sit in the sun in your shirt sleeves. (KATTRIN *points to a tree.*) Yes, the leaves are yellow already. (*With gestures,* KATTRIN *asks if he wants a drink.*) I'm not drinking, I'm thinking. (*Pause.*) She says she can't sleep. So I should take the cashbox away. I've found a place for it. I'll keep it in the mole hole by the river till the time comes. I might get it tonight before sunrise and take it to the regiment. How far can they have fled in three days? The Sergeant's eyes'll pop out of his head. "You've disappointed me most pleasantly, Swiss Cheese," he'll say, "*I* trust you with the cashbox and *you* bring it back!" Yes, Kattrin, I *will* have a glass now!

[*When* KATTRIN *reappears behind the wagon two men confront her. One of them is a sergeant. The other doffs his hat and flourishes it in a showy greeting. He has a bandage over one eye.*]

The Man with the Bandage: Good morning, young lady. Have you seen a man from the Second Protestant Regiment?

[*Terrified,* KATTRIN *runs away, spilling her brandy. The two men look at each other and then withdraw after seeing* SWISS CHEESE.]

Swiss Cheese (*starting up from his reflection*). You're spilling it! What's the matter with you, can't you see where you're going? I don't understand you. Anyway, I must be off, I've decided it's the thing to do. (*He stands up. She does all she can to make him aware of the danger he is in. He only pushes her away.*) I'd like to know what you mean. I know you mean well, poor thing, you just can't get it out. And don't trouble yourself about the brandy, I'll live to drink so much of it, what's one glass? (*He takes the cashbox out of the wagon and puts it under his coat.*) I'll be back straightaway. But don't hold me up or I'll have to scold you. Yes, I know you mean well. If you could only speak!

[*When she tries to hold him back he kisses her and pulls himself free. Exit. She is desperate and runs up and down, emitting little sounds.* MOTHER COURAGE *and the* CHAPLAIN *return.* KATTRIN *rushes at her mother.*]

Mother Courage: What *is* it, what *is* it, Kattrin! Control yourself! Has someone done something to you? Where is Swiss Cheese? (*To the* CHAPLAIN.) Don't stand around, get that Catholic flag up! (*She takes a Catholic flag out of her basket and the* CHAPLAIN *runs it up the pole.*)

Chaplain (*bitterly*). All good Catholics forever!

Mother Courage: Now, Kattrin, calm down and tell me all about it, your mother understands. What, that little bastard of mine's taken the cashbox away? I'll box his ears for him, the rascal! Now take your time and don't try to talk, use your hands. I don't like it when you howl like a dog, what'll the Chaplain think of you? See how shocked he looks. A man with one eye was here?

Chaplain: That fellow with one eye is an informer! Have they caught Swiss Cheese? (KATTRIN *shakes her head, shrugs her shoulders.*) This is the end. (*Voices off. The two men bring in* SWISS CHEESE.)

Swiss Cheese: Let me go. I've nothing on me. You're breaking my shoulder! I am innocent.

Sergeant: This is where he comes from. These are his friends.

Mother Courage: Us? Since when?

Swiss Cheese: I don't even know 'em. I was just geting my lunch here. Ten hellers it cost me. Maybe you saw me sitting on that bench. It was too salty.

Sergeant: Who *are* you people, anyway?

Mother Courage: Law-abiding citizens! It's true what he says. He bought his lunch here. And it was too salty.

Sergeant: Are you pretending you don't know him?

Mother Courage: I can't know all of them, can I? *I don't ask,* "What's your name and are you a heathen?" If they pay up, they're not heathens to me. Are you a heathen?

Swiss Cheese: Oh, no!

Chaplain: He sat there like a law-abiding chap and never once opened his mouth. Except to eat. Which is necessary.

Sergeant: Who do you think *you* are?

Mother Courage: Oh, he's my barman. And you're thirsty, I'll bring you a glass of brandy. You must be footsore and weary!

Sergeant: No brandy on duty. (*To* SWISS CHEESE.) You were carrying something. You must have hidden it by the river. We saw the bulge in your shirt.

Mother Courage: Sure it was him?

Swiss Cheese: I think you mean another fellow. There *was* a fellow with something under his shirt, I saw him. I'm the wrong man.

Mother Courage: I think so too. It's a misunderstanding. Could happen to anyone. Oh, I know what people are like, I'm Mother Courage, you've heard of me, everyone knows about me, and I can tell you this: he looks honest.

Sergeant: We're after the regimental cashbox. And we know what the man looks like who's been keeping it. We've been looking for him two days. It's you.

Swiss Cheese: No, it's not!

Sergeant: And if you don't shell out, you're dead, see? Where is it?

Mother Courage (*urgently*). 'Course he'd give it to you to save his life. He'd up and say, I do have it, here it is, you're stronger than me. He's not *that* stupid. Speak, little stupid, the Sergeant's giving you a chance!

Swiss Cheese: What if I haven't got it?

Sergeant: Come with us. We'll get it out of you. (*They take him off.*)

Mother Courage (*shouting after them*). He'd tell you! He's not *that* stupid! And don't you break his shoulder blade! (*She runs after them.*)

[*The same evening. The* CHAPLAIN *and* KATTRIN *are rinsing glasses and polishing knives.*]

Chaplain: Cases of people getting caught like this are by no means unknown in the history of religion. I am reminded of the Passion of Our Lord and Saviour. There's an old song about it. (*He sings.*)

THE SONG OF THE HOURS

In the first hour of the day
Simple Jesus Christ was
Presented as a murderer
To the heathen Pilate.

Pilate found no fault in him
No cause to condemn him
So he sent the Lord away.
Let King Herod see him!

Hour the third: the Son of God
Was with scourges beaten
And they set a crown of thorns
On the head of Jesus

And they dressed him as a king
Joked and jested at him
And the cross to die upon
He himself must carry.

Six: they stripped Lord Jesus bare.
To the cross they nailed him.
When the blood came gushing, he
Prayed and loud lamented.

From their neighbour crosses, thieves
Mocked him like the others.
And the bright sun crept away
Not to see such doings.

Nine: Lord Jesus cried aloud
That he was forsaken!
In a sponge upon a pole
Vinegar was fed him.

Then the Lord gave up the ghost
And the earth did tremble.
Temple curtain split in twain.
Rocks fell in the ocean.

Evening: they broke the bones
Of the malefactors.
Then they took a spear and pierced
The side of gentle Jesus.

And the blood and water ran
And they laughed at Jesus.
Of this simple son of man
Such and more they tell us.

Mother Courage (*entering, excited*). It's life and death. But the Sergeant will still listen to us. The only thing is, he mustn't know it's our Swiss Cheese, or they'll say we helped him. It's only a matter of money, but where can *we* get money? Wasn't Yvette here? I met her on the way over. She's picked up a Colonel! Maybe he'll buy her a canteen business!

Chaplain: You'd sell the wagon, everything?

Mother Courage: Where else would I get the money for the Sergeant?

Chaplain: What are you to live off?

Mother Courage: That's just it.

[*Enter* YVETTE POTTIER *with a hoary old* COLONEL.]

Yvette (*embracing* MOTHER COURAGE). *Dear* Mistress Courage, we meet again! (*Whispering.*) He didn't say no. (*Aloud.*) This is my friend, my, um, business adviser. I happened to hear you might like to sell your wagon. Due to special circumstances, I'd like to think about it.

Mother Courage: I want to pawn it, not sell it. And nothing hasty. In war time you don't find another wagon like that so easy.

Yvette (*disappointed*). Only pawn it? I thought you wanted to sell, I don't know if I'm interested. (*To the* COLONEL.) What do *you* think, my dear?

Colonel: I quite agree with you, ducky.

Mother Courage: It's only for pawn.

Yvette: I thought you *had* to have the money.

Mother Courage (*firmly*). I do have to have it. But I'd rather wear my feet off looking for an offer than just sell. We live off the wagon. It's an opportunity for you, Yvette. Who knows when you'll have another such? Who knows when you'll find another . . . business adviser?

Colonel: Take it, take it!

Yvette: My friend thinks I should go ahead, but I'm not sure, if it's only for pawn. You think we should buy it outright, don't you?

Colonel: I do, ducky, I do!

Mother Courage: Then you must hunt up something that's for sale. Maybe you'll find it—if you have the time, and your friend goes with you, let's say in about a week, or two weeks, you may find the right thing.

Yvette: Yes, we can certainly look around for something. I love going around looking, I love going around with you, Poldy . . .

Colonel: Really? Do you?

Yvette: Oh, it's lovely! I could take two weeks of it!

Colonel: Really, could you?

Yvette: If you get the money, when are you thinking of paying it back?

Mother Courage: In two weeks. Maybe one.

Yvette: I can't make up my mind. Poldy, advise me, *chéri!* (*She takes the* COLONEL *to one side.*) She'll *have* to sell, don't worry. That lieutenant—the blond one—you know the one I mean—he'll lend me the money. He's *mad* about me, he says I remind him of someone. What do you advise?

Colonel: Oh, I have to warn you against *him.* He's no good. He'll exploit the situation. I told you, ducky, I told you *I'd* buy you something, didn't I tell you that?

Yvette: I simply can't let you!

Colonel: Oh, please, please!

Yvette: Well, if you think the lieutenant might exploit the situation I *will* let you!

Colonel: I do think so.

Yvette: So you advise me to?

Colonel: I do, ducky, I do!

Yvette (*returning to* MOTHER COURAGE). My friend says all right. Write me out a receipt saying the wagon's mine when the two weeks are up—with everything in it. I'll just run through it all now, the two hundred gilders can wait. (*To the* COLONEL.) You go on ahead to the camp, I'll follow, I must go over all this so nothing'll be missing later from *my* wagon!

Colonel: Wait, I'll help you up! (*He does so.*) Come soon, ducky-wucky!

[*Exit.*]

Mother Courage: Yvette, Yvette!

Yvette: There aren't many boots left!

Mother Courage: Yvette, this is no time to go through the wagon, yours or not yours. You promised you'd talk to the Sergeant about Swiss Cheese. There isn't a minute to lose. He's up before the court martial one hour from now.

Yvette: I just want to check through these shirts.

Mother Courage (*dragging her down the steps by the skirt*). You hyena, Swiss Cheese's life's at stake! And don't say who the money comes from. Pretend he's your sweetheart, for heaven's sake, or we'll all get it for helping him.

Yvette: I've arranged to meet One Eye in the bushes. He must be there by now.

Chaplain: And don't hand over all two hundred, a hundred and fifty's sure to be enough.

Mother Courage: Is it your money? I'll thank you to keep your nose out of this, I'm not doing *you* out of your porridge. Now run, and no haggling, remember his life's at stake. (*She pushes* YVETTE *off.*)

Chaplain: I didn't want to talk you into anything, but what are we going to live on? You have an unmarriageable daughter round your neck.

Mother Courage: I'm counting on that cashbox, smart alec. They'll pay his expenses out of it.

Chaplain: You think she can work it?

Mother Courage: It's to her interest: I pay the two hundred and she gets the wagon. She knows what she's doing, she won't have her colonel on the string forever. Kattrin, go and clean the knives, use pumice stone. And don't *you* stand around like Jesus in Gethsemane. Get a move on, wash those glasses. There'll be over fifty cavalrymen here tonight, and you'll be saying you're not used to running around, "oh my poor feet, in church I never had to run around like this!" I think they'll let us have him. Thanks be to God they're corruptible. They're not wolves, they're human and after money. God is merciful, and men are bribable, that's how His will is done on earth as it is in Heaven. Corruption is our only hope. As long as there's corruption, there'll be merciful judges and even the innocent may get off.

Yvette (*comes panting in*). They'll do it for two hundred if you make it snappy, these things change from one minute to the next. I'd better take One Eye to my colonel at once. He confessed he had the cashbox, they put the thumb screws on him. But he threw it in the river when he noticed them coming up behind him. So it's gone. Shall I run and get the money from my colonel?

Mother Courage: The cashbox gone? How'll I ever get my two hundred back?

Yvette: So you thought you could get it from the cashbox? I *would* have been sunk. Not a hope, Mother Courage. If you want your Swiss Cheese, you'll have to pay. Or should I let the whole thing drop, so you can keep your wagon?

Mother Courage: I wasn't reckoning on this. But you needn't hound me, you'll get the wagon, it's yours already, and it's been mine seventeen years. I need a minute to think it over, it's all so sudden. What can I do? I *can't* pay two hundred. I *should* have haggled with them. I must hold on to something, or any passer-by can kick me in the ditch. Go and say I'll pay a hundred and twenty or the deal's off. Even then I lose the wagon.

Yvette: I won't do it. And anyway, One Eye's in a hurry. He keeps looking over his shoulder all the time, he's so worked up. Hadn't I better give them the whole two hundred?

Mother Courage (*desperate*). I can't

pay it! I've been working thirty years. She's twenty-five and still no husband. I have her to think of. So leave me alone, I know what I'm doing. A hundred and twenty or no deal.

Yvette: You know best.

[*Runs off.* MOTHER COURAGE *turns away and slowly walks a few paces to the rear. Then she turns round, looks neither at the* CHAPLAIN *nor her daughter, and sits down to help* KATTRIN *polish the knives.*]

Mother Courage: Don't break the glasses, they're not ours. Watch what you're doing, you're cutting yourself. Swiss Cheese will be back, I'll give two hundred, if it's necessary. You'll get your brother back. With eighty gilders we could pack a hamper with goods and begin again. It wouldn't be the end of the world.

Chaplain: The Bible says: the Lord will provide.

Mother Courage: You should rub them dry, I said!

[*They clean the knives in silence. Suddenly* KATTRIN *runs sobbing behind the wagon.*]

Yvette (*comes running in*). They won't do it. I warned you. One Eye was going to drop it then and there. There's no point, he said. He said the drums would roll any second now and that's the sign a verdict has been pronounced. I offered a hundred and fifty, he didn't even shrug his shoulders. I could hardly get him to stay there while I came to you.

Mother Courage: Tell him I'll pay two hundred. Run! (YVETTE *runs.* MOTHER COURAGE *sits, silent. The* CHAPLAIN *has stopped doing the glasses.*) I believe—I've haggled too long. (*In the distance, a roll of drums. The* CHAPLAIN *stands up and walks toward the rear.* MOTHER COURAGE *remains seated. It grows dark. It gets light again.* MOTHER COURAGE *has not moved.*)

Yvette (*appears, pale*). Now you've done it—with your haggling. You can keep the wagon now. He got eleven bullets, that's what. I don't know why I still bother about you, you don't deserve it, but I just happened to learn they don't think the cashbox is really in the river. They suspect it's here, they think you have something to do with him. I think they mean to bring him here to see if you'll give yourself away when you see him. You'd better not know him or we're in for it. And I'd better tell you straight, they're just behind me. Shall I keep Kattrin away? (MOTHER COURAGE *shakes her head.*) Does she know? Maybe she never heard the drums or didn't understand.

Mother Courage: She knows. Bring her.

[YVETTE *brings* KATTRIN, *who walks over to her mother and stands by her.* MOTHER COURAGE *takes her hand. Two men come on with a stretcher; there is a sheet on it and something underneath. Beside them, the* SERGEANT. *They put the stretcher down.*]

Sergeant: Here's a man we don't know the name of. But he has to be registered to keep the records straight. He bought a meal from you. Look at him, see if you know him. (*He pulls back the sheet.*) Do you know him? (MOTHER COURAGE *shakes her head.*) What? You never saw him before he took that meal? (MOTHER COURAGE *shakes her head.*) Lift him up. Throw him on the junk heap. He has no one that knows him.

[*They carry him off.*]

SCENE IV

[MOTHER COURAGE *sings "The Song of the Great Capitulation."*]

[*Outside an officer's tent,* MOTHER COURAGE *waits. A* SCRIVENER *looks out of the tent.*]

Scrivener: I know you. You had a Protestant paymaster with you, he was hiding with you. Better make no complaint.

Mother Courage: I will too! I'm innocent and if I give up it'll look like I have a bad conscience. They cut everything in my wagon to ribbons with their sabres and then claimed a fine of five thalers for nothing and less than nothing.

Scrivener: For your own good, keep your trap shut. We haven't many canteens, so we let you stay in business, especially if you've a bad conscience and have to pay a fine now and then.

Mother Courage: I'm going to lodge a complaint.

Scrivener: As you wish. Wait here till the captain has time. (*Withdraws into the tent.*)

Young Soldier (*comes storming in*). Bugger the captain! Where *is* the son of a bitch? Swiping my reward, spending it on brandy for his whores, I'll rip his belly open!

Older Soldier (*coming after him*). Shut your hole, you'll wind up in the stocks.

Young Soldier: Come out, you thief, I'll make lamb chops out of you! I was the only one in the squad who swam the river and *he* grabs my money, I can't even buy myself a beer. Come on out! And let me slice you up!

Older Soldier: Holy Christ, he'll destroy himself!

Young Soldier: Let me go or I'll run *you* down too. This thing has got to be settled!

Older Soldier: Saved the colonel's horse and didn't get the reward. He's young, he hasn't been at it long.

Mother Courage: Let him go. He doesn't have to be chained, he's not a dog. Very reasonable to want a reward. Why else should he want to shine?

Young Soldier: He's in there pouring it down! You're all chickens. I've done something special, I want the reward!

Mother Courage: Young man, don't scream at *me,* I have my own troubles. And go easy on your voice, you may need it when the Captain comes. The Captain'll come and you'll be hoarse and can't make a sound, so he'll have to deny himself the pleasure of sticking you in the stocks till you pass out. The screamers don't scream long, only half an hour, after which they have to be sung to sleep, they're all in.

Young Soldier: I'm not all in, and sleep's out of the question. I'm hungry. They're making their bread out of acorns and hemp-seed, and not even much of that. He's whoring on my money, and I'm hungry. I'll murder him!

Mother Courage: I understand: you're hungry. Last year your Commander ordered you people out of the streets and into the fields. So the crops got trampled down. I could have got ten gilders for boots, if anyone'd had ten gilders, and if I'd had any boots. He didn't expect to be around this year, but he is, and there's famine. I understand: you're angry.

Young Soldier: It's no use you talking. I won't stand for injustice!

Mother Courage: You're quite right. But how long? How long won't you stand for injustice? One hour? Or two? You haven't asked yourself that, have you? And yet it's the main thing. It's pure misery to sit in the stocks. Especially if you leave it till then to decide you do stand for injustice.

Young Soldier: I don't know why I listen to you. Bugger that captain! Where is he?

Mother Courage: You listen because you know I'm right. Your rage has calmed down already. It was a short one and you'd need a long one. But where would you find it?

Young Soldier: Are you trying to say it's not right to ask for the money?

Mother Courage: Just the opposite. I only say, your rage won't last. You'll get nowhere with it, it's a pity. If your rage was a long one, I'd urge you on. Slice him up, I'd advise you. But what's the use if you *don't* slice him up because you can feel your tail between your legs? You stand there and the captain lets you have it.

Older Soldier: You're quite right, he's mad.

Young Soldier: All right, we'll see whether I slice him up or not. (*Draws his sword.*) When he comes out, I slice him up!

Scrivener (*looking out*). The captain will be out in a minute. (*In the tone of military command.*) Be seated! (*The* YOUNG SOLDIER *sits.*)

Mother Courage: And he *is* seated. What did I tell you? You are seated. They know us through and through. They know how they must work it. Be seated! And we sit. And in sitting there's no revolt. Better not stand up again—not the way you did before—don't stand up again. And don't be embarrassed in front of me, I'm no better, not a scrap. We don't stick our necks out, do we, and why not? It wouldn't be good for business. Let me tell you about the great capitulation. (*She sings "The Song of the Great Capitulation."*)

Long, long ago, a green beginner
  I thought myself a special case.
(None of your ordinary, run of the mill
    girls, with my looks and my talent
    and my love of the higher things!)
I picked a hair out of my dinner
  And put the waiter in his place.
(All or nothing. Anyway, never the sec-
    ond best. I am the master of my fate.
    I'll take no orders from no one.)
Then a little bird whispers!
  The bird says: "Wait a year or so
  And marching with the band you'll go
  Keeping in step, now fast, now slow,
  And piping out your little spiel.
  Then one day the battalions wheel
  And you go down upon your knees
  To God Almighty if you please!"

My friend, before that year was over
  I'd learned to drink their cup of tea.
(Two children round your neck and the
    price of bread and what all!)
When they were through with me, more-
    over,
  They had me where they wanted me.
(You must get well in with people. If
    you scratch my back, I'll scratch
    yours. Never stick your neck out!)
Then a little bird whispered!
  The bird says: "Scarce a year or so
  And marching with the band she'd go
  Keeping in step, now fast, now slow,

And piping out her little spiel.
Then one day the battalions wheel
And she goes down upon her knees
To God Almighty if you please!"

Our plans are big, our hopes colossal.
We hitch our wagon to a star.
(Where there's a will, there's a way.
You can't hold a good man down.)
"We can lift mountains," says the apostle.
And yet: how heavy one cigar!
(You must cut your coat according to your cloth.)
That little bird whispers!
The bird says: "Wait a year or so
And marching with the band we go
Keeping in step, now fast, now slow,
And piping out our little spiel.
Then one day the battalions wheel
And we go down upon our knees
To God Almighty if you please!"

And so I think you should stay here with your sword drawn if you're set on it and your anger is big enough. You have good cause, I admit. But if your anger is a short one, you'd better go.

Young Soldier: Oh, shove it up! (*He stumbles off, the other soldier following him.*)

Scrivener (*Sticks his head out*). The captain is here. You can lodge your complaint.

Mother Courage: I've thought better of it. I'm not complaining.

[*Exit. The* SCRIVENER *looks after her, shaking his head.*]

SCENE V

[*Two years have passed. The war covers wider and wider territory. Forever on the move the little wagon crosses Poland, Moravia, Bavaria, Italy, and again Bavaria. 1631. Tilly's victory at Magdeburg costs* MOTHER COURAGE *four officer shirts.*]

[*The wagon stands in a war-ruined village. Faint military music from the distance. Two soldiers are being served at a counter by* KATTRIN *and* MOTHER COURAGE. *One of them has a woman's fur coat about his shoulders.*]

Mother Courage: What, you can't pay? No money, no brandy! They can play victory marches, they should pay their men.

First Soldier: I want my brandy! I arrived too late for plunder. The Chief allowed one hour to plunder the town, it's a swindle. He's not inhuman, he says. So I suppose they bought him off.

Chaplain (*staggering in*). There are more in the farmhouse. A family of peasants. Help me someone. I need linen!

[*The* SECOND SOLDIER *goes with him.* KATTRIN *is getting very excited. She tries to get her mother to bring linen out.*]

Mother Courage: I have none. I sold all my bandages to the regiment. I'm not tearing up my officer's shirts for these people.

Chaplain (*calling over his shoulder*). I said I need linen!

Mother Courage (*stopping* KATTRIN

from entering the wagon). Not a thing! They have nothing and they pay nothing!

Chaplain (*to a woman he is carrying in*). Why did you stay out there in the line of fire?

Woman: Our farm—

Mother Courage: Think they'd ever let go of *anything?* And now I'm supposed to pay. Well, I won't!

First Soldier: They're Protestants, why should they be Protestants?

Mother Courage: Protestant, Catholic, what do *they* care? Their farm's gone, that's what.

Second Soldier They're not Protestants anyway, they're Catholics.

First Soldier: In a bombardment we can't pick and choose.

Peasant (*brought on by* CHAPLAIN). My arm's gone.

Chaplain: Where's that linen?

[*All look at* MOTHER COURAGE, *who doesn't budge.*]

Mother Courage: I can't give you any. With all I have to pay out—taxes, duties, bribes . . . (KATTRIN *takes up a board and threatens her mother with it, emitting gurgling sounds.*) Are you out of your mind? Put that board down or I'll fetch you one, you lunatic! I'm giving nothing, I daren't, I have myself to think of. (*The* CHAPLAIN *lifts her bodily off the steps of the wagon and sets her down on the ground. He takes out shirts from the wagon and tears them in strips.*) My shirts, my officer's shirts!

[*From the house comes the cry of a child in pain.*]

Peasant: The child's still in there!

[KATTRIN *runs in.*]

Chaplain (*to the woman*). Stay where you are. She's getting it for you.

Mother Courage: Hold her back, the roof may fall in!

Chaplain: I'm not going back in there!

Mother Courage (*pulled in both directions at once*). Go easy on my expensive linen.

[*The* SECOND SOLDIER *holds her back.* KATTRIN *brings a baby out of the ruins.*]

Mother Courage: Another baby to drag around, you must be pleased with yourself. Give it to its mother this minute! Or do I have to fight you again for hours till I get it from you? Are you deaf (*To the* SECOND SOLDIER.) Don't stand around gawking, go back there and tell 'em to stop that music, I can see their victory without it. I have nothing but losses from your victory!

Chaplain (*bandaging*). The blood's coming through.

[KATTRIN *is rocking the child and half-humming a lullaby.*]

Mother Courage: There she sits, happy as a lark in all this misery. Give the baby back, the mother is coming to! (*She sees the* FIRST SOLDIER. *He had been handling the drinks, and is now trying to make off with the bottle.*) God's blood! You beast! You want another victory, do you? Then pay for it!

First Soldier: I have nothing.

Mother Courage (*snatching the fur coat back*). Then leave this coat, it's stolen goods anyhow.

[KATTRIN *rocks the child and raises it high above her head.*]

SCENE VI

[*Before the City of Ingolstadt in Bavaria* MOTHER COURAGE *is present at the funeral of the fallen commander, Tilly. Conversations take place about war heroes and the duration of the war. The* CHAPLAIN *complains that his talents are lying fallow and* KATTRIN *gets the red boots. The year is 1632.*]

[*The inside of a canteen tent. The inner side of a counter at the rear. Rain. In the distance, drums and funeral music. The* CHAPLAIN *and the* REGIMENTAL CLERK *are playing checkers.* MOTHER COURAGE *and her daughter are taking inventory.*]

Chaplain: The funeral procession is just starting out.

Mother Courage: Pity about the Chief—twenty-two pairs of socks—getting killed that way. They say it was an accident. There was a fog over the fields that morning, and the fog was to blame. The Chief called up another regiment, told 'em to fight to the death, rode back again, missed his way in the fog, went forward instead of back, and ran smack into a bullet in the thick of the battle—only four lanterns left. (*A whistle from the rear. She goes to the counter. To a soldier.*) It's a disgrace the way you're all skipping your Commander's funeral! (*She pours a drink.*)

Scrivener: They shouldn't have handed the money out before the funeral. Now the men are all getting drunk instead of going to it.

Chaplain (*to the* SCRIVENER). Don't you have to be there?

Scrivener: I stayed away because of the rain.

Mother Courage: It's different for you, the rain might spoil your uniform. I hear they wanted to ring the bells for his funeral, which is natural, but it came out that the churches had been shot up by his orders, so the poor Commander won't be hearing any bells when they lower him in his grave. Instead, they will fire off three shots so the occasion won't be *too* sober—sixteen leather belts.

Voice from the Counter: Service! One brandy!

Mother Courage: Your money first. No, you *can't* come inside the tent, not with those boots on. You can drink outside, rain or no rain. I only let officers in here. (*To* SCRIVENER.) The Chief had his troubles lately, I hear. There was unrest in the Second Regiment because he didn't pay 'em but said it was a war of religion and they must fight it free of charge.

[*Funeral March. All look towards the rear.*]

Chaplain: Now they're filing past the body.

Mother Courage: I feel sorry for a commander or an emperor like that—when he might have had something special in mind, something they'd talk about in times to come, something they'd raise a statue to him for. The conquest of the world now, *that's* a goal for a commander, he couldn't do better than *that,* could he? . . . Lord, worms have got into the biscuits. . . . In short he works his hands to the bone and then it's all spoiled by the common riffraff that only wants a jug of beer or a bit of company, not the higher things in life. The finest plans have always been spoiled by the littleness of them that should carry them out. Even emperors can't do it all by themselves. They count on support from their soldiers and the people round about. Am I right?

Chaplain (*laughing*). You're right, Mother Courage, till you come to the soldiers. They do what they can. Those chaps outside, for example, drinking their brandy in the rain, I'd trust 'em to fight a hundred years, one war after another, two at a time if necessary. And I wasn't trained as a Commander.

Mother Courage: . . . Seventeen leather belts . . . Then you don't think the war might end?

Chaplain: Because a Commander's dead? Don't be childish, they're sixpence a dozen. There are always heroes.

Mother Courage: Well, I wasn't asking just for the sake of argument. I was wondering if I should buy up a lot of supplies. They happen to be cheap just now. But if the war ended, I might just as well throw them away.

Chaplain: I realize you are serious, Mother Courage. Well, there's always been people going around saying someday the war will end. I say, you can't be sure the war will *ever* end. Of course it may have to pause occasionally—for breath, as it were—it can even meet with an accident—nothing on this earth is perfect—a war of which we could say it left nothing to be desired will probably never exist. A war can come to a sudden halt—from unforeseen causes—you can't think of everything—a little oversight, and the war's in the hole, and someone's got to pull it out again! The someone is the Emperor or the King or the Pope. They're such friends in need, the war has really nothing to worry about, it can look forward to a prosperous future.

[*A* SOLDIER *sings at the counter.*]

Soldier:

One schnapps, mine host, be quick, make
haste!
A soldier's got no time to waste:
He must be shooting, shooting, shooting,
His Kaiser's enemies unrooting!
Make it a double. This is a holiday.

Mother Courage: If I was sure you're right . . .

Chaplain: Think it out for yourself: how *could* the war end?

Soldier:

Two breasts, my girl, be quick, make
haste!
A soldier's got no time to waste:
He must be hating, hating, hating,
He cannot keep his Kaiser waiting!

Scrivener (*suddenly*). What about peace? Yes, peace. I'm from Bohemia. I'd like to get home once in a while.

Chaplain: Oh, you would, would you? Dear old peace! What happens to the hole when the cheese is gone?

Soldier (*off stage*).

Your blessing, priest, be quick, make
haste!
A soldier's got no time to waste:
He must be dying, dying, dying,
His Kaiser's greatness glorifying!

Scrivener: In the long run you can't live without peace!

Chaplain: Well, I'd say there's peace even in war, war has its islands of peace. For war satisfies *all* needs, even those of peace, yes, they're provided for, or the war couldn't keep going. In war—as in the very thick of peace—you can empty your bowels, and between one battle and the next there's always a beer, and even on the march you can take a nap—on your elbow maybe, in a gutter—something can always be managed. Of course you can't play cards during an attack, but neither can you while plowing the fields in peacetime; it's when the victory's won that there are possibilities. You have your leg shot off, and at first you raise quite an outcry as if it *was* something, but soon you calm down or take a swig of brandy, and you end up hopping around, and the war is none the worse for your little misadventure. And can't you be fruitful and multiply in the thick of slaughter—behind a barn or somewhere? Nothing can keep you from it very long in any event. And so the war has your offspring and can carry on. War is like love, it always finds a way. Why *should* it end?

[KATTRIN *has stopped working. She stares at the* CHAPLAIN.]

Mother Courage: Then I *will* buy those supplies, I'll rely on you. (KATTRIN *suddenly bangs a basket of glasses down on the ground and runs out.* MOTHER COURAGE *laughs.*) Kattrin! Lord, Kattrin's still going to wait for peace. I promised her she'll get a husband—when it's peace. (*Runs after her.*)

Scrivener (*standing up*). I win. You were talking. You pay.

Mother Courage (*returning with* KATTRIN). Be sensible, the war'll go on a bit longer, and we'll make a bit more money, then peace'll be all the nicer. Now you go into the town, it's not ten minutes' walk, and bring the things from the Golden Lion, just the dearer ones, we can get the rest later in the wagon. It's all arranged, the clerk will go with you, most of the soldiers are at the Commander's funeral, nothing can happen to you. Do a good job, don't lose anything, Kattrin, think of your trousseau!

[KATTRIN *ties a cloth round her head and leaves with the* SCRIVENER.]

Chaplain: You don't mind her going with Scrivener?

Mother Courage: She's not so pretty anyone would want to ruin her.

Chaplain: The way you run your business and always come through is highly commendable, Mother Courage—I see how you got your name.

Mother Courage: The poor need courage. They're lost, that's why. That they even get up in the morning is something—in *their* plight. Or that they plow a field—in wartime. Even their bringing children into the world shows they have courage, for they have no prospects. They have to hang each other one by one and slaughter each other in the lump, so if they want to look each other in the face once in a while, well, it takes courage. That they put up with an Emperor and a Pope, that takes an unnatural amount of courage, for *they* cost you your life. (*She sits, takes a small pipe from her pocket and smokes it.*) You might chop me a bit of firewood.

Chaplain (*reluctantly taking his coat off and preparing to chop wood*). Properly speaking, I'm a pastor of souls, not a woodcutter.

Mother Courage: But I don't have a soul. And I do need wood.

Chaplain: What's that little pipe you've got there?

Mother Courage: Just a pipe.

Chaplain: I think it's a very particular pipe.

Mother Courage: Oh?

Chaplain: The cook's pipe in fact.

The cook from the Oxenstiern Regiment.

Mother Courage: If you know, why beat about the bush?

Chaplain: Because I don't know if you've been *aware* that's what you've been smoking. It was possible you just rummaged among your belongings and your fingers just lit on a pipe and you just took it. In pure absentmindedness.

Mother Courage: How do you know that's not it?

Chaplain: It isn't. You *are* aware of it. (*He brings the ax down on the block with a crash.*)

Mother Courage: What if I was?

Chaplain: I must give you a warning, Mother Courage, it's my duty. You are unlikely ever again to see the gentleman but that's no pity, you're in luck. Mother Courage, he did not impress me as trustworthy. On the contrary.

Mother Courage: Really? He was such a nice man.

Chaplain: Well! So that's what you call a nice man. I do not. (*The ax falls again.*) Far be it from me to wish him ill, but I cannot—cannot—describe him as nice. No, no, he's a Don Juan, a cunning Don Juan. Just look at that pipe if you don't believe me. You must admit it tells all.

Mother Courage: I see nothing special in it. It's been, um, used.

Chaplain: It's bitten half-way through! He's a man of great violence! It is the pipe of a man of great violence, you can see *that* if you've any judgment left! (*He deals the block a tremendous blow.*)

Mother Courage: Don't bite my chopping block halfway through!

Chaplain: I told you I had no training as a woodcutter. The care of souls was my field. Around here my gifts and capabilities are grossly misused. In physical labor my god-given talents find no—um—adequate expression—which is a sin. You haven't heard me preach. Why, I can put such spirit into a regiment with a single sermon that the enemy's a mere flock of sheep to them and their own lives no more than smelly old shoes to be thrown away at the thought of final victory! God has given me the gift of tongues. I can preach you out of your senses!

Mother Courage: I need my senses, what would I do without them?

Chaplain: Mother Courage, I have often thought that—under a veil of plain speech—you conceal a heart. You are human, you need warmth.

Mother Courage: The best way of warming this tent is to chop plenty of firewood.

Chaplain: You're changing the subject. Seriously, my dear Courage, I sometimes ask myself how it would be if our relationship should be somewhat more firmly cemented. I mean, now the wind of war has whirled us so strangely together.

Mother Courage: The cement's pretty firm already. I cook your meals. And you lend a hand—at chopping firewood, for instance.

Chaplain (*going over to her, gesturing with the ax*). You know what I mean by a close relationship. It has nothing to do with eating and woodcutting and such base necessities. Let your heart speak!

Mother Courage: Don't come at me like that with your ax, that'd be *too* close a relationship!

Chaplain: This is no laughing matter, I am in earnest. I've thought it all over.

Mother Courage: Dear Chaplain, be a sensible fellow. I like you, and I don't want to heap coals of fire on your head. All I'm after is to bring me and my children through in that wagon. It isn't just mine, the wagon, and anyway I've no mind to start having a private life. At the moment I'm taking quite a risk buying these things when the Commander's fallen and there's all this talk of peace. Where would you go, if I was ruined? See? You don't even know. Now chop some firewood and it'll be warm of an evening, which is quite a lot in times like these. What was that?

[*She stands up.* KATTRIN *enters, breathless, with a wound across the eye and forehead. She is dragging all sorts of articles, parcels, leather goods, a drum, etc.*]

Mother Courage: What is it, were you attacked? On the way back? She was attacked on the way back! I'll bet it was that soldier who got drunk on my liquor. I should never have let you go. Dump all that stuff! It's not bad, the wound is only a flesh wound. I'll bandage it for you, it'll be all healed up in a week. They're worse than animals. (*She bandages the wound.*)

Chaplain: I reproach them with nothing. At home they never did these shameful things. The men who start the wars are responsible, they bring out the worst in people.

Mother Courage: Didn't the Scrivener walk you back home? That's because you're a respectable girl, he thought they'd leave you alone. The wound's not at all deep, it will never show. There: all bandaged up. Now, I've got something for you, rest easy. A secret. I've been holding it, you'll see. (*She digs* YVETTE'S *red boots out of a bag.*) Well, what do you see? You always wanted them. Now you have them. Put them on quick, before I'm sorry I let you have them. (*She helps her to put the boots on.*) It will never show, though it wouldn't bother *me* if it did. The fate of the ones they like is the worst. They drag them around with them till they're through. A girl they don't care for they leave alone. I've seen so many girls, pretty as they come in the beginning, then all of a sudden they looked a fright—enough to scare a wolf. They can't even go behind a tree on the street without having something to fear from it. They lead a frightful life. Like with trees: the tall, straight ones are cut down for roof timber, and the crooked ones can enjoy life. So this wound here is really a piece of luck. The boots have kept well, I cleaned them good before I put them away.

[KATTRIN *leaves the boots and creeps into the wagon.*]

Chaplain (*when she's gone*). I hope she won't be disfigured?

Mother Courage: There'll be a scar. She needn't wait for peace now.

Chaplain: She didn't let them get any of the stuff away from her.

Mother Courage: Maybe I shouldn't have made such a point of it. If only I ever knew what went on inside her head. One time she stayed out all night, once in all the years. I could never get out of her what happened, I racked my brains for quite a while. (*She picks up the things* KATTRIN *spilled and sorts them angrily.*) This is war. A nice source of income, I must say!

[*Cannon shots.*]

Chaplain: Now they're lowering the Commander in his grave! A historic moment.

Mother Courage: It's a historic moment to me when they hit my daughter over the eye. She's all but finished now, she'll never get a husband, and she's so mad about children! Even her dumbness comes from the war. A soldier stuck something in her mouth when she was little. I'll not see Swiss Cheese again, and where my Eilif is the Good Lord knows. Curse the war!

SCENE VII

[MOTHER COURAGE *at the height of her business career.*]

[*A highway. The* CHAPLAIN, MOTHER COURAGE, *and her daughter* KATTRIN *pull the wagon, and new wares are hanging from it.* MOTHER COURAGE *wears a necklace: a chain of silver coins.*]

Mother Courage: I won't let you spoil my war for me. Destroys the weak, does it? Well, what does peace do for 'em, huh? War feeds its people better. (*She sings.*)

If war don't suit your disposition
When victory comes you will be dead.
War is a business proposition:
Not with cream-cheese but steel and lead.

And staying in one place won't help either. Those who stay home are the first to go. (*She sings.*)

Too many seek a bed to sleep in:
Each ditch is taken, and each cave,
And he who digs a hole to creep in
Finds he has dug an early grave.
And many a man spends many a minute
In hurrying toward some resting place.
You wonder, when at last he's in it,
Just why the fellow forced the pace.
(*The wagon proceeds.*)

SCENE VIII

[*1632. In this same year Gustavus Adolphus fell in the battle of Lützen. The peace threatens* MOTHER COURAGE *with ruin. Her brave son performs one heroic deed too many and comes to a shameful end.*]

[*A camp. A summer morning. In front of the wagon, an old woman and her son. The son is dragging a large bag of bedding.*]

Mother Courage (*from inside the wagon*). Must you come at the crack of dawn?

Young Man: We've been walking all night, twenty miles it was, we have to be back today.

Mother Courage (*still inside*). What do I want with bed feathers? People don't even have houses.

Young Man: At least wait till you see 'em.

Old Woman: Nothing doing here either, let's go.

Young Man: And let 'em sign away the roof over our heads for taxes? Maybe she'll pay three gilders if you throw in that bracelet. (*Bells start ringing.*) You hear, mother?

Voices (*from the rear*). It's peace! The King of Sweden's been killed!

Mother Courage (*Sticking her head out of the wagon. She hasn't done her hair yet.*) Bells! What are the bells for, middle of the week?

Chaplain (*crawling out from under the wagon*). What's that they're shouting?

Young Man: It's peace.

Chaplain: Peace?

Mother Courage: Don't tell me peace has broken out—when I've just gone and bought all these supplies!

Chaplain (*calling, toward the rear*). Is it peace?

Voice (*from a distance*). They say the war stopped three weeks ago, I've only just heard.

Chaplain (*to* MOTHER COURAGE). Or why would they ring the bells?

Voice: A great crowd of Lutherans have just arrived with wagons—they brought the news.

Young Man: It's peace, mother. (*The* OLD WOMAN *collapses.*) What's the matter?

Mother Courage (*back in the wagon*). Kattrin, it's peace! Put on your black dress, we're going to church, we owe it to Swiss Cheese! Can it be true?

Young Man: The people here say so too, the war's over. Can you stand up? (*The* OLD WOMAN *stands up, dazed.*) I'll get the harness shop going again now, I promise you. Everything'll be all right, father will get his bed back. . . . Can you walk? (*To the* CHAPLAIN.) She felt sick, it was the news. She didn't believe there'd ever be peace again. Father always said there would. We're going home.

[*They leave.*]

Mother Courage (*off*). Give her some brandy.

Chaplain: They've left already.

Mother Courage (*still off*). What's going on in the camp over there?

Chaplain: They're all getting together, I think I'll go over. Shall I put my pastor's clothes on again?

Mother Courage: Better get the exact news first, and not risk being taken for the Antichrist. I'm glad about the peace even though I'm ruined. At least I've got two of my children through the war. Now I'll see my Eilif again.

Chaplain: And who may this be coming down from the camp? Well, if it isn't our Swedish Commander's cook!

Cook (*somewhat bedraggled, carrying a bundle*). Who's here? The Chaplain!

Chaplain: Mother Courage, a visitor!

[MOTHER COURAGE *clambers out.*]

Cook: Well, I promised I'd come over for a brief conversation as soon as I had time. I didn't forget your brandy, Mrs. Fierling.

Mother Courage: Jesus, the Commander's cooks! After all these years! Where is Eilif, my eldest?

Cook: Isn't he here yet? He went on ahead yesterday, he was on his way over.

Chaplain: I *will* put my pastor's clothes on. I'll be back. (*He goes behind the wagon.*)

Mother Courage: He may be here any minute then. (*Calls toward the wagon.*) Kattrin, Eilif's coming! Bring a glass of brandy for the cook, Kattrin! (KATTRIN *doesn't come.*) Pull your hair over it and have done. Mr. Lamb is no stranger. (*She gets the brandy herself.*) She won't come out. Peace is nothing to her, it was too long coming. They hit her right over the eye. You can hardly see it now. But she thinks people stare at her.

Cook: Ah yes, war! (*He and* MOTHER COURAGE *sit.*)

Mother Courage: Cook, you come at a bad time: I'm ruined.

Cook: What? That's terrible!

Mother Courage: The peace has broken my neck. On the Chaplain's advice I've gone and bought a lot of supplies. Now everybody's leaving and I'm holding the baby.

Cook: How could you listen to the Chaplain? If I'd had time—but the Catholics were too quick for me—I'd have warned you against him. He's a windbag. Well, so now he's the big man round here!

Mother Courage: He's been doing the dishes for me and helping with the wagon.

Cook: With the wagon—him! And I'll bet he's told you a few of his jokes. He has a most unhealthy attitude to women. I tried to influence him but it was no good. He isn't sound.

Mother Courage: Are you sound?

Cook: If I'm nothing else, I'm sound. Your health!

Mother Courage: Sound! Only one person around here was ever sound, and I never had to slave as I did then. He sold the blankets off the children's beds in the spring, and he found my harmonica unchristian. You aren't recommending yourself if you *admit* you're sound.

Cook: You fight tooth and nail, don't you? I like that.

Mother Courage: Don't tell me you've been dreaming of my teeth and nails.

Cook: Well, here we sit, while the bells of peace do ring, and you pouring your famous brandy as only you know how!

Mother Courage: I don't think much of the bells of peace at the moment. I don't see how they can hand out all this pay that's in arrears. And then where shall I be with my famous brandy? Have you all been paid?

Cook (*hesitating*). Not exactly. That's why we disbanded. In the circumstances, I thought, why stay? For the time being, I'll look up a couple of friends. So here I sit—with you.

Mother Courage: In other words, you're broke.

Cook (*annoyed by the bells*). It's about time they stopped that racket! I'd like to set myself up in some business. I'm fed up with being their cook. I'm supposed to make do with tree roots and shoe leather, and then they throw the hot soup in my face. Being a cook nowadays is a dog's life. I'd sooner do war service, but of course it's peace now. (*As the* CHAPLAIN *turns up, wearing his old costume.*) We'll talk it over later.

Chaplain: The coat's pretty good. Just a few moth holes.

Cook: I don't know why you take the trouble. You won't find another job. Who could you incite now to earn an honorable wage or risk his life for a cause? Besides I have a bone to pick with you.

Chaplain: Have you?

Cook: I have. You advised a lady to buy superfluous goods on the pretext that the war would never end.

Chaplain (*hotly*). I'd like to know what business it is of yours?

Cook: It's unprincipled behavior! How can you give unwanted advice? And interfere with the conduct of other people's business?

Chaplain: Who's interfering now, I'd like to know? (*To* MOTHER COURAGE.)

I had no idea you were such a close friend of this gentleman and had to account to him for everything.

Mother Courage: Now don't get excited. The Cook's giving his personal opinion. You can't deny your war was a frost.

Chaplain: You mustn't take the name of peace in vain, Courage. Remember, you're a hyena of the battlefield!

Mother Courage: A what?

Cook: If you insult my girl friend, you'll have to reckon with me!

Chaplain: I am *not* speaking to you, your intentions are only too transparent! (*To* MOTHER COURAGE.) But when I see *you* take peace between finger and thumb like a snotty old hanky, my humanity rebels! It shows that you want war, not peace, for what you get out of it. But don't forget the proverb: he who sups with the devil must use a long spoon!

Mother Courage: Remember what one fox said to another that was caught in a trap? "If you stay there, you're just asking for trouble!" There isn't much love lost between me and the war. And when it comes to calling me a hyena, you and I part company.

Chaplain: Then why all this grumbling about the peace just as everyone's heaving a sigh of relief? Is it just for the junk in your wagon?

Mother Courage: My goods are not junk. I live off them. *You've* been living off them.

Chaplain: You live off war. Exactly.

Cook (*to the* CHAPLAIN). As a grown man, you should know better than to go around advising people. (*To* MOTHER COURAGE.) Now, in your situation you'd be wise to get rid of certain goods at once—before the prices sink to nothing. Get ready and get going, there isn't a moment to lose!

Mother Courage: That's sensible advice, I think I'll take it.

Chaplain: Because the Cook says so.

Mother Courage: Why didn't *you* say so? He's right, I must get to the market. (*She climbs into the wagon.*)

Cook: One up for me, Chaplain. You have no presence of mind. You should have said, "I gave you advice? Why, I was just talking politics!" And you shouldn't take me on as a rival. Cockfights are not becoming to your cloth.

Chaplain: If you don't shut your trap, I'll murder you, cloth or no cloth!

Cook (*taking his boots off and unwinding the wrappings on his feet*). If you hadn't degenerated into a godless tramp, you could easily get yourself a parsonage, now it's peace. Cooks won't be needed, there's nothing to cook, but there's still plenty to believe, and people are prepared to go right on believing it.

Chaplain: Mr. Lamb, please don't drive me out! Since I became a tramp, I'm a somewhat better man. I couldn't preach to 'em any more.

[YVETTE POTTIER *enters, decked out in black, with a stick. She is much older, fatter, and heavily powdered. Behind her, a servant.*]

Yvette: Hullo, everybody! Is this Mother Courage's establishment?

Chaplain: Quite right. And with whom have we the pleasure?

Yvette: I am Madame Colonel Starhemberg, good people. Where's Mother Courage?

Chaplain (*calling to the wagon*). Madame, Colonel Starhemberg wants to speak with you!

Mother Courage (*from inside*). Coming!

Yvette (*calling*). It's Yvette!

Mother Courage (*inside*). Yvette!

Yvette: Just to see how you're getting on! (*As the* COOK *turn around in horror.*) Peter!

Cook: Yvette!

Yvette: Of all things! How did *you* get here?

Cook: On a cart.

Chaplain: Well! You know each other? Intimately?

Yvette: Not half. (*Scrutinizing the* COOK.) You're fat.

Cook: For that matter, *you're* no beanpole.

Yvette: Anyway, nice meeting you, tramp. Now I can tell you what I think of you.

Chaplain: Do so, tell him all, but wait till Mother Courage comes out.

Cook: Now don't make a scene . . .

Mother Courage (*comes out, laden with goods*). Yvette! (*They embrace.*) But why are you in mourning?

Yvette: Doesn't it suit me? My husband, the colonel, died several years ago.

Mother Courage: The old fellow that nearly bought my wagon?

Yvette: His older brother.

Mother Courage: So you're not doing badly. Good to see one person who got somewhere in the war.

Yvette: I've had my ups and downs.

Mother Courage: Don't let's speak ill of Colonels. They make money like hay.

Chaplain (*to the* COOK). If I were you, I'd put my shoes on again. (*To* YVETTE.) You promised to give us your opinion of this gentleman.

Cook: Now, Yvette, don't make a stink!

Mother Courage: He's a friend of mine, Yvette.

Yvette: He's—Peter Piper, that's who.

Mother Courage: What!?

Cook: Cut the nicknames. My name's Lamb.

Mother Courage (*laughing*). Peter Piper? Who turned the women's heads? And I've been keeping your pipe for you.

Chaplain: And smoking it.

Yvette: Lucky I can warn you against him. He's a bad lot. You won't find a worse on the whole coast of Flanders. He got more girls in trouble than . . .

Cook: That's a long time ago, it isn't true any more.

Yvette: Stand up when you talk to a lady! Oh, how I loved that man! And all the time he was having a little bowlegged brunette. He got *her* in trouble too, of course.

Cook: I seem to have brought *you* luck!

Yvette: Shut your trap, you hoary ruin! And you take care, Mother Courage, this type is still dangerous even in decay!

Mother Courage (*to* YVETTE). Come with me, I must get rid of this stuff before the prices fall.

Yvette (*concentrating on* COOK). Miserable cur!

Mother Courage: Maybe you can help me at army headquarters, you have contacts.

Yvette: Damnable whore hunter!

Mother Courage (*shouting into the wagon*). Kattrin, church is all off, I'm going to market!

Yvette: Inveterate seducer!

Mother Courage (*still to* KATTRIN). When Eilif comes, give him something to drink!

Yvette: That a man of *his* ilk should have been able to turn me from the straight and narrow! I have only my own star to thank that I rose nonetheless to the heights! But I've put an end to your tricks, Peter Piper, and one day—in a better life than this—the Lord God will reward me! Come, Mother Courage! (*Leaves with* MOTHER COURAGE.)

Chaplain: As our text this morning let us take the saying, the mills of God grind slowly. And you complain of my jokes!

Cook: I never have any luck. I'll be frank, I was hoping for a good hot dinner, I'm starving. And now they'll be talking about me, and she'll get a completely wrong picture. I think I should go before she comes back.

Chaplain: I think so too.

Cook: Chaplain, peace makes me sick. Mankind must perish by fire and sword, we're born and bred in sin! Oh, how I wish I was roasting a great fat capon for the Commander—God knows where *he's* got to—with mustard sauce and those little yellow carrots . . .

Chaplain: Red cabbage—with capon, red cabbage.

Cook: You're right. But he always wanted yellow carrots.

Chaplain: He never understood a thing.

Cook: You always put plenty away.

Chaplain: Under protest.

Cook: Anyway, you must admit, those were the days.

Chaplain: Yes, that I might admit.

Cook: Now you've called her a hyena, there's not much future for you here either. What are you staring at?

Chaplain: It's Eilif! (*Followed by two soldiers with halberds,* EILIF *enters. His hands are fettered. He is white as chalk.*) What's happened to you?

Eilif: Where's mother?

Chaplain: Gone to town.

Eilif: They said she was here. I was allowed a last visit.

Cook (*to the soldiers*). Where are you taking him?

Soldier: For a ride.

[*The other soldier makes a gesture of throat cutting.*]

Chaplain: What has he done?

Soldier: He broke in on a peasant. The wife is dead.

Chaplain: Eilif, how could you?

Eilif: It's no different. It's what I did before.

Cook: That was in wartime.

Eilif: Shut your hole. Can I sit down till she comes?

Soldier: No.

Chaplain: It's true. In wartime they honored him for it. He sat at the Commander's right hand. It was bravery. Couldn't we speak with the provost?

Soldier: What's the use? Stealing cattle from a peasant, what's brave about that?

Cook: It was just stupid.

Eilif: If I'd been stupid, I'd have starved, clever dick.

Cook: So you were bright and paid for it.

Chaplain: At least we must bring Kattrin out.

Eilif: Let her alone. Just give me some brandy.

Soldier: No.

Chaplain: What shall we tell your mother?

Eilif: Tell her it was no different. Tell her it was the same. Oh, tell her nothing.

[*The soldiers take him away.*]

Chaplain: I'll come with you, I'll . . .
Eilif: I don't need a priest!
Chaplain: You don't know—yet.

[*Follows him.*]

Cook (*calling after him*). I'll have to tell her, she'll want to see him!
Chaplain: Better tell her nothing. Or maybe just that he was here, and he'll return, maybe tomorrow. Meantime I'll be back and can break the news.

[*Leaves quickly. The* COOK *looks after him, shakes his head, then walks uneasily around. Finally, he approaches the wagon.*]

Cook: Hi! Won't you come out? You want to sneak away from the peace, don't you? Well, so do I! I'm the Swedish Commander's cook, remember me? I was wondering if you've got anything to eat in there—while we're waiting for your mother. I wouldn't mind a bit of bacon—or even bread—just to pass the time. (*He looks in.*) She's got a blanket over her head.

[*The thunder of cannon.*]

Mother Courage (*running, out of breath, still carrying the goods*). Cook, the peace is over, the war's on again, has been for three days! I didn't get rid of this stuff after all, thank God! There's a shooting match in the town already—with the Lutherans. We must get away with the wagon. Pack, Kattrin! What's on *your* mind? Something the matter?
Cook: Nothing.
Mother Courage: But there is. I see it in your face.
Cook: Because the war's on again, most likely. May it last till tomorrow evening, so I can get something in my belly!
Mother Courage: You're not telling me.
Cook: Eilif was here. Only he had to go away again.
Mother Courage: He was here? Then we'll see him on the march. I'll be with our side this time. How'd he look?
Cook: The same.
Mother Courage: He'll *never* change. And the war couldn't get *him,* he's bright. Help me with the packing. (*She starts it.*) Did he tell you anything? Is he well in with the captain? Did he tell you about his heroic deeds?
Cook (*darkly*). He's done one of them again.
Mother Courage: Tell me about it later. (KATTRIN *appears.*) Kattrin, the peace is all through, we're on the move again. (*To the* COOK.) What *is* biting you?
Cook: I'll enlist.
Mother Courage: A good idea. Where's the Chaplain?
Cook: In the town. With Eilif.
Mother Courage: Stay with us a while, Lamb, I need a bit of help.
Cook: This matter of Yvette . . .
Mother Courage: Hasn't done you any harm at all in my eyes. Just the opposite. Where there's smoke, there's fire, they say. You'll come?
Cook: I may as well.
Mother Courage: The twelfth regiment's under way. Into harness with you! Maybe I'll see Eilif before the day is out, just think! That's what I like best. Well, it wasn't such a long peace, we can't grumble. Let's go! (*The* COOK *and* KATTRIN *are in harness.* MOTHER COURAGE *sings.*)

Up hill, down dale, past dome and steeple,
My wagon always moves ahead.
The war can care for all its people
So long as there is steel and lead.
Though steel and lead are stout supporters
A war needs human beings too.
Report today to your headquarters!
If it's to last, this war needs you!
Christians, awake! The winter's gone!
The snows depart, the dead sleep on.
And though you may not long survive
Get out of bed and look alive!

SCENE IX

[*The great war of religion has lasted sixteen years and Germany has lost half its inhabitants. Those who are spared in battle die by plague. Over once blooming countryside hunger rages. Towns are burned down. Wolves prowl the empty streets. In the autumn of 1634 we find* MOTHER COURAGE *in the Fichtelgebirge not far from the road the Swedish army is taking. Winter has come early and is hard. Business is bad. Only begging remains. The* COOK *receives a letter from Utrecht and is sent packing.*]

[*In front of a half-ruined parsonage. Early winter. A grey morning. Gusts of wind.* MOTHER COURAGE *and the* COOK *at the wagon in shabby clothes.*]

Cook: There are no lights on. No one's up.

Mother Courage: But it's a parsonage. The parson'll have to leave his feather bed and ring the bells. Then he'll have some hot soup.

Cook: Where'll he get it from? The whole village is starving.

Mother Courage: The house is lived in. There was a dog barking.

Cook: If the parson has anything, he'll stick to it.

Mother Courage: Maybe if we sang him something . . .

Cook: I've had enough. (*Suddenly.*) I didn't tell you, a letter came from Utrecht. My mother's died of cholera, the inn is mine. There's the letter, if you don't believe me. I'll show it to you, though my aunt's railing about me and my ups and downs is none of your business.

Mother Courage (*reading*). Lamb, I'm tired of wandering, too. I feel like a butcher's dog taking meat to my customers and getting none myself. I've nothing more to sell and people have nothing to pay with. In Saxony someone tried to saddle me with a chestful of books in return for two eggs. And in Württemberg they would have let me have their plough for a bag of salt. Nothing grows any more, only thorn bushes. I hear that in Pomerania the villagers have been eating their younger children. Nuns have been caught committing robbery.

Cook: The world's dying out.

Mother Courage: Sometimes I see myself driving through hell with this wagon and selling brimstone. And sometimes I'm driving through heaven handing out provisions to wandering souls! If only we could find a place where there's no shooting, me and my children—what's left of 'em—we might rest a while.

Cook: We could open this inn together. Think about it, Courage. *My* mind's made up. With or without you, I'm leaving for Utrecht. And today too.

Mother Courage: I must talk to Kattrin, it's a little bit sudden, and I don't like to make my decisions in the cold on an empty stomach. (KATTRIN *emerges from the wagon.*) Kattrin, I've something to tell you. The cook and I want to go to Utrecht, he's been left an inn. You'd be able to stay put and get to know some people. Many a man'd be prepared to take on a girl with a position. Looks aren't everything. I wouldn't mind it. I get on well with the Cook. I'll say this for him: he has a head for business. We'd be sure of our dinner, that would be all right, wouldn't it? You'd have your own bed, what do you think of *that?* In the long run, this is no life, on the road. You might be killed any time. You're already lousy. And we must decide now, because otherwise we go north with the Swedes. They must be over there somewhere. (*She points to the left.*) I think we'll decide to go, Kattrin.

Cook: Anna, I must have a word with you alone.

Mother Courage: Go back inside, Kattrin. (KATTRIN *does so.*)

Cook: I'm interrupting because there's a misunderstanding, Anna. I thought I wouldn't have to say it right out, but I see I must. If you're bringing *her,* it's all off. Do we understand each other? (KATTRIN *has her head out of the back of the wagon and is listening.*)

Mother Courage: You mean I leave Kattrin behind?

Cook: What do you think? There's no room in the inn, it isn't one of those places with three counters. If the two of us look lively we can earn a living, but three's too many. Let Kattrin keep your wagon.

Mother Courage: I was thinking we might find her a husband in Utrecht.

Cook: Don't make me laugh. With that scar? And old as she is? And dumb?

Mother Courage: Not so loud!

Cook: Loud or soft, what is, is. That's another reason I can't have her in the inn. Customers don't like having something like that always before their eyes. You can't blame them.

Mother Courage: Shut up. I told you not to talk so loud.

Cook: There's a light in the parsonage, we can sing now!

Mother Courage: Cook, how could she pull the wagon by herself? The war frightens her. She can't bear it. She has terrible dreams. I hear her groan at night, especially after battles. What she sees in her dreams I don't know. She suffers from pity. The other day I found a hedgehog with her that we'd run over.

Cook: The inn's too small. (*Calling.*) Worthy Sir, menials, and all within! We now present the song of Solomon, Julius Caesar, and other great souls who came to no good, so you can see we're law-abiding folk too, and have a hard time getting by, especially in winter. (*He sings "The Song of the Great Souls of This Earth."*)

You've heard of wise old Solomon
  You know his history.
He thought so little of this earth
He cursed the hour of his birth
  Declaring: all is vanity.
How very wise was Solomon!
  But ere night came and day did go
This fact was clear to everyone:
  It was his wisdom that had brought him
    low.
Better for you if you have none.

For the virtues are dangerous in this world, as our fine song tells. You're better off without, you have a nice life, breakfast included—some good hot soup maybe . . . I'm an example of a man who's not had any, and I'd like some, I'm a soldier, but what good did my bravery do me in all those battles? None at all. I might just as well have wet my pants like a poltroon and stayed home. For why?

And Julius Caesar, who was brave,
  You saw what came of him.
He sat like God on an altar-piece
  And yet they tore him limb from limb
While his prestige did still increase!
"Et tu, Brute, I am undone!"
  And ere night came and day did go
This fact was clear to everyone:
  It was his bravery that brought him low
Better for you if you have none.

(*Under his breath.*) They don't even look out. (*Aloud.*) Worthy Sir, menials, and all within! You should say, no, courage isn't the thing to fill a man's belly, try honesty, that should be worth a dinner, at any rate it must have *some* effect. Let's see.

You all know honest Socrates
  Who always spoke the truth.
They owed him thanks for that, you'd
    think,
Yet they put hemlock in his drink
  And swore that he was bad for youth.
How honest was the people's son!
  But ere night came and day did go
This fact was clear to everyone:
  It was his honesty that brought him low
Better for you if you have none.

Yes, we're told to be unselfish and share what we have, but what if we have nothing? And those who do share it don't have an easy time either, for what's left when you've finished sharing? Unselfishness is a very rare virtue—it doesn't pay.
Unselfish Martin could not bear
  His fellow creature's woes.
  He met a beggar in the snows
And gave him half his cloak to wear:
  So both of them fell down and froze.
What an unselfish paragon!
  But ere night came and day did go
This fact was clear to everyone:
  It was unselfishness that brought him
    low.
Better for you if you have none.

That's how it is with us. We're law-abiding folk, we keep to ourselves, don't steal, don't kill, don't burn the place down. And in this way we sink lower and lower and the song proves true and there's no soup going. And if we were different, if we were thieves and killers, maybe we could eat our fill! For virtues bring no reward, only vices. Such is the world, need it be so?

God's Ten Commandments we have kept
  And acted as we should.
  It has not done us any good.
O you who sit beside a fire
Please help us now: our need is dire!
Strict godliness we've always shown
  But ere night came and day did go
This fact was clear to everyone:
  It was our godliness that brought us
    low.
Better for you if you have none!

Voices (*from above*). You there! Come up! There's some soup here for you!

Mother Courage: Lamb, I couldn't swallow a thing. I don't say what you said is unreasonable, but was it your last word? We've always understood each other.

Cook: Yes, Anna. Think it over.

Mother Courage: There's nothing to think over. I'm not leaving her here.

Cook: You're going to be silly, but what can I do? I'm not inhuman, it's just that the inn's a small one. And now we must go up, or it'll be nothing doing here too, and we've been singing in the cold to no avail.

Mother Courage: I'll fetch Kattrin.

Cook: Better stick something in your pocket for her. If there are three of us, they'll get a shock.

[*Exeunt.* KATTRIN *clambers out of the wagon with a bundle. She makes sure they're both gone. Then, on a wagon wheel, she lays out a skirt of her mother's and a pair of the* COOK'S *trousers side by side and easy to see. She has just finished, and has picked up her bundle, when* MOTHER COURAGE *returns.*]

Mother Courage: (*with a plate of soup*). Kattrin! Stay where you are, Kattrin!
Where do you think you're going with that bundle? (*She examines the bundle.*) She's packed her things. Were you listening? I told him there was nothing doing, he can *have* Utrecht and his lousy inn, what would we want with a lousy inn? (*She sees the skirt and trousers.*) Oh, you're a stupid girl, Kattrin, what if I'd seen that and you gone? (*She takes hold of* KATTRIN, *who's trying to leave.*) And don't think I've sent him packing on your account. It was the wagon. You can't part us, I'm too used to it, *you* didn't come into it, it was the wagon. Now we're leaving, and we'll put the cook's things here where he'll find 'em, the stupid man. (*She clambers up and throws a couple of things down to go with the trousers.*) There! He's sacked! The last man I'll take into *this* business! Now let's be going, you and me. Get into harness. This winter'll pass—like all the others.

[*They harness themselves to the wagon, turn it around, and start out. A gust of wind. Enter the* COOK, *still chewing. He sees his things.*]

SCENE X

[*During the whole of 1635* MOTHER COURAGE *and* KATTRIN *pull the wagon along the roads of central Germany in the wake of the ever more ragged armies.*]

[*On the highway,* MOTHER COURAGE *and* KATTRIN *are pulling the wagon. They come to a prosperous farmhouse. Someone inside is singing "The Song of Shelter."*]

The Voice:

In March a tree we planted
　To make the garden gay.
In June we were enchanted:
A lovely rose was blooming
The balmy air perfuming!
　Blest of the gods are they
　Who have a garden gay!
In June we were enchanted.

When snow falls helter-skelter
　And loudly blows the storm
Our farmhouse gives us shelter.
The winter's in a hurry
But we've no cause to worry.
　Cosy are we and warm
　Though loudly blows the storm
Our farmhouse gives us shelter.

[MOTHER COURAGE *and* KATTRIN *have stopped to listen. Then they start out again.*]

SCENE XI

[*January, 1636. Catholic troops threaten the Protestant town of Halle. The stone begins to speak.* MOTHER COURAGE *loses her daughter and journeys onwards alone. The war is not yet near its end.*]

[*The wagon, very far gone now, stands near a farmhouse with a straw roof. It is night. Out of the wood come a* LIEUTENANT *and* THREE SOLDIERS *in full armor.*]

Lieutenant: And there mustn't be a sound. If anyone yells, cut him down.

First Soldier: But we'll have to knock —if we want a guide.

Lieutenant: Knocking's a natural noise, it's all right, could be a cow hitting the wall of the cowshed.

[*The* SOLDIERS *knock at the farmhouse door. An old* PEASANT WOMAN *opens. A hand is clapped over her mouth.* TWO SOLDIERS *enter.*]

Man's Voice: What is it?

[*The* SOLDIERS *bring out an old* PEASANT *and his* SON.]

Lieutenant (*pointing to the wagon on which* KATTRIN *has appeared*). There's one. (*A* SOLDIER *pulls her out.*) Is this everybody that lives here?

Peasants (*alternating*). That's our son. And that's a girl that can't talk. Her mother's in town buying up stocks because the shopkeepers are running away and selling cheap. They're canteen people.

Lieutenant: I'm warning you. Keep quiet. One sound and we'll crack you one with a pike. And I need someone to show us the path to the town. (*Points to the* YOUNG PEASANT.) You! Come here!

Young Peasant: I don't have any path!

Second Soldier (*grinning*). He don't know any path!

Young Peasant: I don't help Catholics.

Lieutenant (*to* SECOND SOLDIER). Let him feel your pike in his side.

Young Peasant (*forced to his knees, the pike at his throat*). I'd rather die!

Second Soldier (*again mimicking*). He'd rather die!

First Soldier: I know how to change his mind. (*Walks over to the cowshed.*) Two cows and a bull. Listen, you. If you aren't going to be reasonable, I'll sabre your cattle.

Young Peasant: Not the cattle!

Peasant Woman (*weeping*). Spare the cattle, captain, or we'll starve!

Lieutenant: If he must be pigheaded!

First Soldier: I think I'll start with the bull.

Young Peasant (*to the old one*). Do I have to? (*The* OLDER ONE *nods.*) I'll do it.

Peasant Woman: Thank you, thank you, captain, for sparing us, for ever and ever. Amen.

[*The* OLD MAN *stops her going on thanking him.*]

First Soldier: I knew the bull came first all right!

[*Led by the* PEASANT, *the* LIEUTENANT *and the* SOLDIERS *go on their way.*]

Old Peasant: I wish we knew what it was. Nothing good, I suppose.

Peasant Woman: Maybe they're just scouts. What are you doing?

Old Peasant (*setting a ladder against the roof and climbing up*). I'm seeing if they're alone. (*On the roof.*) Things are moving—all over. I can see armor. And a cannon. There must be more than a regiment. God have mercy on the town and all within!

Peasant Woman: Are there lights in the town?

Old Peasant: No, they're all asleep. (*He climbs down.*) There'll be an attack, and they'll all be slaughtered in their beds.

Peasant Woman: The watchman'll give warning.

Old Peasant: They must have killed the watchman in the tower on the hill or he'd have sounded his horn before this.

Peasant Woman: If there were more of us . . .

Old Peasant: But being that we're alone with that cripple . . .

Peasant Woman: There's nothing we can do, is there?

Old Peasant: Nothing.

Peasant Woman: We can't get down there. In the dark.

Old Peasant: The whole hillside's swarming with 'em.

Peasant Woman: We could give a sign?

Old Peasant: And be cut down for it?

Peasant Woman: No, there's nothing we can do. (*To* KATTRIN.) Pray, poor thing, pray! There's nothing we can do to stop this bloodshed, so even if you can't talk, at least pray! He hears, if no one else does. I'll help you. (*All kneel,* KATTRIN *behind.*) Our Father, which art in Heaven, hear our prayer, let not the town perish with all that lie therein asleep and fearing nothing. Wake them, that they rise and go to the walls and see the foe that comes with fire and sword in the night down the hill and across the fields. (*Back to* KATTRIN.) God protect our mother and make the watchman not sleep but wake ere it's too late. And save our son-in-law too, O God, he's there with his four children, let them not perish, they're innocent, they know nothing (*to* KATTRIN, *who groans*), one of them's not two years old, the eldest is seven. (KATTRIN *rises, troubled.*) Heavenly Father, hear us, only Thou canst help us or we die, for we are weak and have no sword nor nothing; we cannot thrust our own strength but only Thine, O Lord; we are in Thy hands, our cattle, our farm, and the town too, we're all in Thy hands, and the foe is nigh unto the walls with all his power. (KATTRIN *unperceived, has crept off to the wagon, has taken something out of it, put it under her apron, and has climbed up the ladder to the roof.*) Be mindful of the children in danger, especially the little ones, be mindful of the old folk who cannot move, and of all Christian souls, O Lord.

Old Peasant: And forgive us our trespasses as we forgive them that trespass against us. Amen.

[*Sitting on the roof,* KATTRIN *takes a drum from under her apron, and starts to beat it.*]

Peasant Woman: Heavens, what's she doing?

Old Peasant: She's out of her mind!

Peasant Woman: Bring her down, quick! (*The* OLD PEASANT *runs to the ladder but* KATTRIN *pulls it up on the roof.*) She'll get us in trouble.

Old Peasant: Stop it this minute, you silly cripple!

Peasant Woman: The soldiers'll come!

Old Peasant (*looking for stones*). I'll stone you!

Peasant Woman: Have you no pity, have you no heart? We have relations there too, four grandchildren, but there's nothing we can do. If they find us now, it's the end, they'll stab us to death! (KATTRIN *is staring into the far distance, toward the town. She goes on drumming.*)

Peasant Woman (*to the* PEASANT). I told you not to let that riffraff in your farm. What do *they* care if we lose our cattle?

Lieutenant (*running back with* SOLDIERS *and* YOUNG PEASANT). I'll cut you all to bits!

Peasant Woman: We're innocent, sir, there's nothing we can do. She did it, a stranger!

Lieutenant: Where's the ladder?

Old Peasant: On the roof.

Lieutenant (*calling*). Throw down the drum. I order you! (KATTRIN *goes on drumming.*) You're all in this, but you won't live to tell the tale.

Old Peasant: They've been cutting down fir trees around here. If we bring a tall enough trunk we can knock her off the roof . . .

First Soldier (*to the* LIEUTENANT). I beg leave to make a suggestion. (*He whispers something to the* LIEUTENANT, *who nods.*) Listen, you! We have an idea —for your own good. Come down and go with us to the town. Show us your mother and we'll spare her.

[KATTRIN *replies with more drumming.*]

Lieutenant (*pushing him away*). She doesn't trust you, no wonder with your face. (*He calls up to* KATTRIN.) Hey, you! Suppose I give you my word? I'm an officer, my word's my bond! (KATTRIN *drums louder.*) Nothing is sacred to her.

Young Peasant: Sir, it's not just because of her mother!

First Soldier: This can't go on, they'll hear it in the town as sure as hell.

Lieutenant: We must make another noise with something. Louder than that drum. What can we make a noise with?

First Soldier: But we mustn't make a noise!

Lieutenant: A harmless noise, fool, a peacetime noise!

Old Peasant: I could start chopping wood.

Lieutenant: That's it! (*The* PEASANT *brings his ax and chops away.*) Chop! Chop harder! Chop for your life! (KATTRIN *has been listening, beating her drum less hard. Very upset, and peering around, she now goes on drumming.*) It's not enough. (*To* FIRST SOLDIER.) You chop too!

Old Peasant: I've only one ax. (*He stops chopping.*)

Lieutenant: We must set fire to the farm. Smoke her out.

Old Peasant: That's no good, Captain, when they see fire from the town, they'll know everything.

[*During the drumming* KATTRIN *has been listening again. Now she laughs.*]

Lieutenant: She's laughing at us, that's too much. I'll have her guts if it's the last thing I do. Bring a musket!

[*Two* SOLDIERS *go off.* KATTRIN *goes on drumming.*]

Peasant Woman: I have it, Captain. That's their wagon over there, Captain. If we smash that, she'll stop. It's all they have, Captain.

Lieutenant (*to the* YOUNG PEASANT). Smash it! (*Calling.*) If you don't stop that noise, we'll smash your wagon!

[*The* YOUNG PEASANT *deals the wagon a couple of feeble blows with a board.*]

Peasant Woman (*to* KATTRIN). Stop, you little beast!

[KATTRIN *stares at the wagon and pauses. Noises of distress come out of her. But she goes on drumming.*]

Lieutenant: Where are those sons of bitches with that gun?

First Soldier: They can't have heard anything in the town or we'd hear their cannon.

Lieutenant (*calling*). They don't hear you. And now we're going to shoot you. I'll give you one more chance: throw down that drum!

Young Peasant (*dropping the board, screaming to* KATTRIN). Don't stop now! Or they're all done for. Go on, go on, go on . . .

[*The* SOLDIER *knocks him down and beats him with his pike.* KATTRIN *starts crying but goes on drumming.*]

Peasant Woman: Not in the back, you're killing him!

[*The* SOLDIERS *arrive with the musket.*]

Second Soldier: The Colonel's foaming at the mouth. We'll be courtmartialed.

Lieutenant: Set it up! Set it up! (*Calling while the musket is set up on forks.*) Once for all: stop that drumming!

[*Still crying,* KATTRIN *is drumming as hard as she can. The* SOLDIERS *fire.* KATTRIN *is hit. She gives the drum another feeble beat or two, then slowly collapses.*]

Lieutenant: That's an end to the noise.

[*But the last beats of the drum are lost in the din of cannon from the town. Mingled with the thunder of cannon, alarm bells are heard in the distance.*]

First Soldier: She did it.

SCENE XII

[*Toward morning. The drums and pipes of troops on the march, receding. In front of the wagon* MOTHER COURAGE *sits by* KATTRIN'S *body. The* PEASANTS *of the last scene are standing near.*]

Peasants: You must leave, ma'am. There's only one regiment to go. You can never get away by yourself.

Mother Courage: Maybe she's fallen asleep. (*She sings.*)

Lullay, lullay, what's that in the hay?
The neighbor's babes cry but mine are gay.
The neighbor's babes are dressed in dirt:
Your silks were cut from an angel's skirt.
They are all starving: you have a cake;
If it's too stale, you need but speak.
Lullay, lullay, what's rustling there?
One lad fell in Poland. The other is where?
You shouldn't have told her about the children.

Peasants: If you hadn't gone off to the town to get your cut, maybe it wouldn't have happened.

Mother Courage: She's asleep now.

Peasants: She's not asleep, it's time you realized. She's through. You must get away. There are wolves in these parts. And the bandits are worse.

Mother Courage: That's right (*She goes and fetches a piece of cloth from the wagon to cover the body.*)

Peasants: Have you no one now? Someone you can go to?

Mother Courage: There's one. My Eilif.

Peasants (*while* COURAGE *covers the body*). Leave *her* to us. We'll give her a proper burial. You needn't worry.

Mother Courage: Here's money for the expenses.

[*She pays the* PEASANT. *The* PEASANT *and his* SON *shake her hand and carry* KATTRIN *away.*]

Peasant Woman (*also taking her hand, and bowing, as she goes away*). Hurry!

Mother Courage (*harnessing herself to the wagon*). I hope I can pull the wagon by myself. Yes, I'll manage, there's not much in it now. I must start up again in business.

[*Another regiment passes at the rear with pipe and drum.*]

Mother Courage: Hey! Take me with you! (*She starts pulling the wagon. Soldiers are heard singing.*)

Dangers, surprises, devastations—
The war takes hold and will not quit.
But though it last three generations
We shall get nothing out of it.
Starvation, filth, and cold enslave us.
The army robs us of our pay.
Only a miracle can save us
And miracles have had their day.
Christians, awake! The winter's gone!
The snows depart. The dead sleep on.
And though you may not long survive
Get out of bed and look alive!

DISCUSSION QUESTIONS

Prologue

1. What is the ironic theme of Mother Courage's first song?

Scene I

1. What ironic comment on virtue is made in the opening dialogue between the Recruiting Officer and his Sergeant?
2. How is the way Mother Courage got her name ironic?
3. How do these ironies, particularly insofar as religion is concerned, help establish a sense of values?
4. What is the significance of the mixed, international parentage of Mother Courage's children?
5. How is the episode of the black crosses prophetic?
6. What conflict of values appears in Mother Courage's character?
7. What is the dramatic function of the tables of contents before each scene?

Scene II

1. How is Mother Courage characterized by her argument with the Cook?
2. How does Mother Courage's attack on courage ironically identify her with the pompous Commander?
3. What dubious qualities underly Eilif's bravery?
4. How does Eilif's song, "The Fishwife and the Soldier," foreshadow the outcome of his "bravery"?

Scene III

1. How is the transaction involving the bag of bullets related to the theme?
2. How is "The Camp Follower's Song," which Yvette sings, related to the theme?
3. What is the significance of Kattrin's muteness?
4. How do Yvette and Kattrin resemble and differ from one another?
5. How is Kattrin's imitation of Yvette by wearing her red boots and hat ironic?
6. How are the Chaplain's religion and Swiss Cheese's cashbox symbolic in similar ways?
7. How is Swiss Cheese, the "honest child," another victim of a dubious virtue?
8. How is Swiss Cheese's death Christ-like?
9. What other ironic parallels can be drawn between the Christ story and the situation as a whole?
10. How does Swiss Cheese's death result from his mother's dilemma?
11. How does Mother Courage's struggle to save her son involve suspense?
12. How does Mother Courage's denial of her son balance pathos with ruthless, pitiless exposure of her flaws?

Scene IV

1. What does the Young Soldier's failure to carry through his complaint suggest about the possibility of popular revolt against tyranny and injustice?
2. How does Mother Courage's "Song of the Great Capitulation" place her own past "adjustments" in a historical context?

Scene V

1. How is the report of "Tilly's Victory" ironic?
2. How does the action of the scene reveal Mother Courage as both victim and victimizer, sufferer and source of suffering?
3. What human virtue does Kattrin exemplify in this scene?
4. What is the significance of the wagon standing intact in the midst of the rubble of the ruined village?

Scene VI

1. What comment on war is implied by General Tilly's death?
2. How is Kattrin's mutilation symbolic?

3. How does the argument between the Chaplain and Courage place their attitudes in clearer perspective?

Scene VII

1. How has Courage's attitude toward the war changed since the previous scene?

Scene VIII

1. How does Mother Courage's reaction to the peace change our attitude toward her?
2. How is the conflict between the Cook and the Chaplain over Mother Courage significant?
3. How are Eilif's conviction and execution ironic?
4. How does Mother Courage's reaction to war at the end of the scene reveal the same trait which her reaction to peace at the beginning showed us?

Scene IX

1. What does Courage's choice between the Cook and Kattrin reveal about her character?
2. What ironic lesson does the Cook's "The Song of the Great Souls of This Earth" teach, especially since he himself is a rascal?
3. Is the Cook's song adapted in any way to the "virtues" of Mother Courage and her children?

Scene X

1. What is the significance of the song of shelter?

Scene XI

1. How does Brecht use conventional devices of alternation, transparency, and dramatic irony to achieve his dramatic purposes?
2. How do the episodic scenes and Chronicle-like texts expand rather than compress time, emerging naturally from the theme and atmosphere?
3. Does the death of each of Mother Courage's children, one after the other, emerge as a kind of formal, tripartite pattern?
4. Does Mother Courage bear responsibility for Kattrin's plight, as she had in the previous loss of her other two children?
5. How do Kattrin's motives and actions ironically reveal the flaws in more selfish, conventional concepts of virtue?
6. How has Kattrin's sacrifice been, ironically, in vain?
7. At the end, how is Mother Courage pathetic, heroic, and ironic?

Glossary

ANTICLIMAX An event occurring after the intended high point of the action which attempts to re-create dramatic tension, but which falls flat emotionally because of its weakness in comparison with the greater heightening and releasing of tension produced by the climax itself. Some critics have argued, for example, that Cordelia's death in *King Lear* is both anticlimactic and unnecessary. In comedy anticlimax may be used deliberately to achieve laughter, as in the final gossip scene in *The School for Scandal.*

ATMOSPHERE The feeling of "something in the air" which the playwright creates by his use of stage setting, imagery, costume, special effects, etc. to help motivate the action and condition its outcome. In *Heartbreak House* the odd behavior of Captain Shotover, the gravel pit outside, and the distant sound of drumming all create an atmosphere of potential disaster, which is finally realized by the dropping bombs in the last act.

CLIMAX The highest point in the action from the standpoint of dramatic tension and decisiveness for the outcome. It represents the termination of the protagonist's opportunity to choose; from this point on events progress to an inevitable catastrophe brought about by his decision at the climactic moment. In *Antigone,* for example, Creon's decision to imprison his niece in a tomb as prescribed by law leads to her death, Haimon's and his wife's, and his own tragic recognition of guilt and responsibility.

COMEDY A form of drama in which characters less than heroic are involved in conflicts and complications that are ultimately resolved successfully, that is, without the death of the protagonist or, if he dies, his death is brought about in some exaggerated, burlesque fashion. Even though the comic character may fancy himself a hero, he tends to act unheroically by valuing compromise and life over devotion to an ideal and the acceptance of death as a necessary price for getting what he wants. The ideal the comic hero pursues is often trivial or overvalued as judged by the standards of common sense. Instead of arousing pity and fear by presenting a man's self-caused downfall, as tragedy does, comedy arouses laughter and good will (or scorn, as in satire) by revealing the incongruity between the comic character's actions and the pattern of normal behavior. Great comedy acts as an antidote to great tragedy by permitting us to view things objectively. It exposes the follies of man in relation to his desires and goals, either amiably or critically, instead of delving into the moral order of the universe as tragedy does. Sometimes a character can be unintentionally comic when a playwright fails to create audience identification with the protagonist and the actions seem senseless rather than uncompromisingly heroic.

CONVENTIONS Stage techniques and conditions, varying from one age to another and from play to play, which are taken for granted by the audience. They govern the mode of presentation of the play and determine the extent to which reality is approximated.

One set of conventions may place a premium on literal reality, another on symbolism or imaginative reality. Conventions include such things as: devices to acquaint the audience with a character's thoughts (soliloquies, asides, interior monologues); the type of stage and theater used (an open-air theater with an altar-like stage, a modified inn yard with an elevated, bare platform for a stage, a three-walled box provided with multiple curtains and movable scenery); costumes, including stylized make-up and masks; language, which may be lofty or prosaic; and the observance or lack of observance of restrictions on time, place, and action, varying from the rigidity of the neoclassical "unities" to the complete freedom from such restrictions exercised by playwrights like Shakespeare and Brecht.

DENOUEMENT Literally the unraveling of the "skein" of conflicts and the complications that make up the plot. In *The Cherry Orchard* the entire last act with the departure of the inhabitants, the sound of axes striking the trees, and Firs' preparation for death represents the resolution or denouement of the action.

DRAMATIC IRONY Often called Sophoclean irony. A deliberate ambiguity of language or multiplicity of meaning which arises when a character says something that has an opposite or fuller meaning than he himself is aware of. When Lear says "Nothing will come of nothing," we suspect that the remark will be much more prophetic than he realizes at the moment.

EXPOSITION The providing of background information that gives the main action significance and a framework within which to operate. In *Heartbreak House* Ellie Dunn's description of her affair with Marcus Darnley provides us with background information that makes her escape from the illusion of happiness credible.

FARCE A form of comic action involving outlandish physical action and broadly suggestive language. Farce frequently relies on such devices as the confusion between physically identical characters; repeated beatings, usually unmerited and carried out with inappropriate weapons; loud vituperation; the use of stage props (collapsing chairs, trick clothes, animal characters, etc.). Pure farce bears the same relation to comedy that melodrama does to tragedy, that is, the emphasis is on action not on meaning. A serious dramatist may include farcical elements in his play to heighten the effect, as do Chekhov, Shaw, and Brecht in this collection.

FORESHADOWING The use of incidents, dialogue, symbols, characters, etc. to suggest what lies ahead in the action. In *Heartbreak House* Boss Mangan has a "presentiment" of death just before he is killed in the dynamite explosion.

MELODRAMA A form of serious drama that stresses action for its own sake and for the sake of the emotions it arouses, but which does not provide significant insight into the human condition. Usually a completely evil character, although not necessarily unattractive dramatically, works against a completely good person for the possession of something without spiritual significance. The counterplot in *Lear* contains a number of melodramatic elements in both action and characterization even though it is not pure melodrama. Chekhov toys with melodramatic possibilities in *The Cherry Orchard* but deliberately avoids developing them because he is interested in achieving a totally different effect.

MOTIVATION The forces—events, atmosphere, beliefs, background, personality, etc., —that impel a character to act as he does in the play. Lady Utterword objects to Ellie's use of the word "heartbreak" because she herself is too cold-hearted to experience such a change.

PARADOX A variety of irony in which a statement or event appears self-contradictory but yet is true in both its aspects. In *Lear* it is paradoxical that the old king should be both a greater and a lesser person when he is mad and half-naked on the heath than he was at the beginning of the play when he sat on his throne and exercised his regal powers.

PATHOS The quality of an occurrence or situation that arouses compassion or pity. Pathos, meaning suffering, is usually associated with the weak and helpless who face difficulties they cannot overcome and which destroy them. Gloucester in *Lear* is more of a pathetic figure than a tragic one because of his essentially weak and passive nature. A playwright may try to convey pathos when his characters and situation are trivial or exaggerated and fall into sentimentality or even farce; sometimes this effect may be deliberate. Or he may aim at tragedy, but, by failing to give his main character enough will or power to struggle, achieve only pathos instead.

PROBABILITY The logical movement of the play, given the characters and the situation at the beginning. The probable event is the most natural one, the one most likely to occur. In *The Cherry Orchard* it is probable that the improvident Madame Ranevsky and her equally impractical brother will do nothing constructive to save the orchard and that the practical, energetic Lopahin will purchase it and tear down the trees as he had advised them to do to turn the property into something of economic value.

PROBLEM PLAY A play concerned with some important social issue which the playwright is attempting to solve. In the hands of playwrights of small talent the form may degenerate into the dramatization of an outmoded platitude or a tired restatement of the golden rule. Skillful dramatists like Shaw and Brecht can take a social problem as the basis of their play and turn it into something far above mere didacticism as they do in *Heartbreak House* and *Mother Courage* respectively.

PROGRESSION The forward movement of the play; the development of the initial situation. Progression combines preparation, exposition, and action. In *The Cherry Orchard* we learn that Madame Ranevsky is returning from Paris and that the mortgage on the orchard is coming due soon. Her rejection of Lopahin's plan to save the orchard prepares us for its subsequent loss at auction and the total disintegration of the way of life represented by the Ranevskys.

REALISM Faithfulness to the facts of experience, which anyone in the audience might verify. Wilder disclaims realism in his use of imaginary newspapers to be tossed onto imaginary porches, household chairs for grave stones, ladders for stairs, etc. Ibsen, on the other hand, goes to great lengths to create an air of verisimilitude in his stage settings and directions for *An Enemy of the People.*

REVERSAL OF INTENTION An outcome that is exactly the opposite of what the character strived for and anticipated. In *Lear* the king divides his realm before his death to assure himself a peaceful old age; instead of this personal misery and civil war result.

REVERSAL OF SITUATION The protagonist's position changes from favorable to unfavorable or vice versa. In *Desire Under the Elms* the action of the play involves a reversal of situation in the relation of father and son to what they both want.

SYMBOL An object, situation, or even an entire plot that suggests or stands for something else. In *The Cherry Orchard* the beautiful but useless orchard is a symbol of the entire way of life of the Ranevskys. In the Brecht play Mother Courage's homeless, itinerant situation is symbolic of that of the human race in senseless wars of conquest.

THEME The general observation on life that the total play sets forth. In *The Cherry Orchard* Chekhov deals with the theme of the disintegration of a society that has outlived its usefulness but which cannot come to grips with the real situation confronting it because its members have been conditioned into attitudes and responses which are no longer viable.

TONE The general effect produced by the playwright's attitude toward his characters, conflicts, symbols, setting, and theme. *Tone* is a more inclusive term than *atmosphere* because it implies the purpose that lies behind atmosphere. By conditioning the audience to the total lack of materialistic common sense in the Ranevsky family, Chekhov establishes a tone of gentle and sadly comic irony which prepares for the loss and destruction of the cherry orchard. He creates an atmosphere of gradual but inevitably approaching twilight in the affairs of these childishly improvident feudal aristocrats through the ironic tone he employs in his choice of situation, language, action, and characterization.

TRAGEDY The term is so rich in its implications that a good short definition is virtually impossible without being cryptic. In *Lear,* a generally acknowledged great tragedy of a certain type, the protagonist is brought to degradation and ruin through his own folly and fatal error of judgment. Out of his despair, however, he emerges purged of his vanity and folly, and possessed of a sane set of values. He dies and so does Cordelia, but the old king has gained what he wanted most of all in life: the unselfish and total love of his child, in this case of his favorite one. His flaw has brought him and others to disaster, but there is a moral victory in physical defeat. Some of the characters in other plays in this collection fit this tragic pattern to a greater or lesser degree, e.g., Creon, Madame Ranevsky, Abbie, and Dr. Stockmann.

TRAGIC FLAW A term borrowed from the Greek philosopher Aristotle's short work on poetry. It means the error in judgment, the frailty, or human weakness that causes the misfortune of the tragic hero. In *Lear* the old king fails to realize that love cannot be measured by words and he reacts with rage and folly when his attempt to use this worthless criterion is foiled by Cordelia's uncompromising honesty and Goneril and Regan's opportunistic hypocrisy.

UNITIES Some followers of Aristotle argued that a play should conform to the "unities" of time, place, and action, that is, that the action should not take more than one day, that it should take place in one building or city, and that there should be a single plot. *Lear* violates all these restrictive demands: it has a main plot and a counterplot and a complex relationship between them; it moves about from one place to another and covers a period of several months. *The Cherry Orchard* confines its action to the single major event; all the action takes place on the Ranevsky estate, but the time covered is some six months or so. In *Desire Under the Elms* a single action takes place in a single setting, but the time is prolonged to a period of a year or so. *Our Town* and *Mother Courage* take the greatest liberty with time and space; *Antigone* observes all the unities to perfection.

WELL-MADE PLAY A form of drama, dominant in the nineteenth century and much used since then especially in popular drama, in which the highly realistic details of the action are worked out with special attention to cause and effect. It uses every scene, every character, every speech to lead to the inevitable climax. In its purest state it makes great use of inanimate objects as dramatic forces to provide progression and complication. It also remains quite faithful to the unities. In expressionist drama, which *Glass Menagerie* resembles in some ways, there is a revolt against the realism of the well-made play and every character and object in the play serves as a symbol of some social or psychological fact. Shaw uses some of the devices of the well-made play, like the dynamite and the gravel pit, but he uses them as expressions of his own dramatic idiosyncrasies instead of as mechanical elements in plot construction.

Selected Bibliography

Brecht

Brustein, Robert. "Bertolt Brecht," in *The Theatre of Revolt*. Boston, 1964.

Demetz, Peter. *Brecht: A Collection of Critical Essays*. Englewood Cliffs, N.J., 1962.

Esslin, Martin. *Brecht: The Man and his Work*. New York, 1960.

Gray, Ronald. *Bertolt Brecht*. New York, 1961.

Willett, John. *The Theatre of Bertolt Brecht*. New York, 1959.

Chekhov

Bruford, Walter H. *Anton Chekhov*. New Haven, 1957.

Deer, Irving. "Speech as Action in Chekhov's *The Cherry Orchard*," *Educational Theatre Journal*, 10:30-34.

Fergusson, Francis. "*Ghosts* and *The Cherry Orchard*," in *The Idea of a Theatre*. New York, 1955.

Gerould, D. C. "*The Cherry Orchard* as Comedy," *Journal of General Education*, 11:109-122.

Hingley, Ronald. *Chekhov: A Biographical and Critical Study*. London, 1950.

Latham, Jacqueline E. M. "*The Cherry Orchard* as Comedy," *Educational Theatre Journal*, 10:21-29.

Magarshack, Norman. "Chekhov's Comic Spirit and *The Cherry Orchard*," *Modern Drama*, 1:91-100.

Young, Stark. "Heartbreak Houses," in *Immortal Shadows*. New York, 1948.

Ibsen

Bradbrook, Muriel C. *Ibsen, the Norwegian, a Revaluation*. London, 1948.

Koht, Halvdon. *The Life of Ibsen*. Trans. R. L. McMahon. American-Scandinavian Foundation, 1931.

Lavrin, Janko. *Ibsen, an Approach*. London, 1950.

Lucas, F. L. *The Drama of Ibsen and Strindberg*. London, 1962.

McCarthy, Mary. "The Will and Testament of Ibsen," in *Sights and Spectacles*. New York, 1957.

McFarlane, J. W. *Ibsen and the Temper of Norwegian Literature*. London, 1960.

Muir, Kenneth. *Last Periods of Shakespeare, Racine, Ibsen*. Detroit, 1961.

Weigand, H. J. *The Modern Ibsen, a Reconsideration*. New York, 1960.

O'Neill

Alexander, Doris. *The Tempering of Eugene O'Neill*. New York, 1962.

Engel, Edwin A. *The Haunted Heroes of Eugene O'Neill*. Cambridge, Mass., 1953.

Falk, Doris V. *Eugene O'Neill and the Tragic Tension: An Interpretive Study of the Plays*. New Brunswick, N.J., 1959.

Gelb, Arthur and Barbara. *Eugene O'Neill*. New York, 1962.

Winther, Sophus K. "*Desire Under the Elms:* A Modern Tragedy," *Modern Drama*, 3:326-332.

Shakespeare

Baldwin, T. W. *William Shakespeare's Five-Act Structure*. Urbana, 1947.

Cairncross, A. "Quarto and Folio Text of *King Lear*," *English Studies*, 6:252-8, July 1955.

Craig, Hardin. *An Interpretation of Shakespeare*. New York, 1949.

Goddard, Harold, *The Meaning of Shakespeare*. Chicago, 1960.

Granville-Barker, Harley. *Prefaces to Shakespeare*. Princeton, 1946.

Kirschbaum, Leo. *The True Text of King Lear*. Baltimore, 1945.

Knight, G. Wilson. *The Wheel of Fire*. London, 1959.
McCarthy, D. "Shakespearean Criticism," *New Statesman* 20:236-238, November 1922.
Myers, Henry A. *Tragedy: A View of Life*. Ithaca, 1956.
Robertson, John M. *The State of Shakespearean Study: A Critical Conspectus*. London, 1931.
Spencer, Theodore. *Death and Elizabethan Tragedy*. New York, 1960.
Walker, A. "*King Lear*—The 1608 Quarto," *Modern Language Review*, 47:376-378. July 1952.

Shaw

Bentley, Eric. *Bernard Shaw*. New York, 1957.
Fergusson, Francis. "The Theatricality of Shaw and Pirandello," in *The Idea of a Theatre*. New York, 1955.
Henderson, Archibald. *George Bernard Shaw: Man of the Century*. New York, 1956.
McCarthy, Mary. "Shaw and Chekhov," in *Sights and Spectacles*. New York, 1957.
McDowell, Frederick. "Technique, Symbol and Theme in Heartbreak House," *PMLA* 68: 335-356, June 1953.
Nethercot, Arthur H. *Men and Supermen: The Shavian Portrait Gallery*. Cambridge, Mass., 1954.
Young, Stark. "Heartbreak Houses," in *Immortal Shadows*. New York, 1948.

Sheridan

Cove, J. W. *Sheridan, His Life and His Theatre*. New York, 1948.
Glasgow, Alice. *Sheridan of Drury Lane*. New York, 1940.
Jackson, J. R. deJ. "The Importance of Witty Dialogue in *The School for Scandal*," *Modern Language Notes*, 76:601-607, 1961.
Palmer, J. L. *The Comedy of Manners*. New *York*, 1962.
Sawyer, N. W. *The Comedy of Manners from Sheridan to Maugham*. Philadelphia, 1931.
Sherwin, Oscar. *Uncorking Old Sherry: The Life and Times of R. B. Sheridan*. New York, 1960.

Sophocles

Adams, S. M. *Sophocles, the Playwright*. Toronto, 1957.
Bowra, C. M. *Sophoclean Tragedy*. Oxford, 1944.
Goheen, Robert F. *The Imagery of Sophocles' Antigone*. Princeton, 1951.
Kitto, H. D. F. *Greek Tragedy*, Garden City, N.Y., 1950.
Whitman, C. H. *Sophocles: A Study of Heroic Humanism*. Cambridge, Mass., 1951.

Strindberg

Brustein, Robert. "Strindberg," in *The Theatre of Revolt*. Boston, 1962.
Dahlström, C. E. W. L. *Strindberg's Dramatic Expressionism* (2nd ed.). Ann Arbor, 1930. (Reissued 1965.)
Johnson, Walter. *Strindberg and the Historical Drama*. Seattle, 1963.
Lucas, F. L. *Ibsen and Strindberg*. New York. 1962.
Madsen, B. G. *Strindberg's Naturalistic Theatre: Its Relation to French Naturalism*. Seattle, 1962.
Valency, Maurice. *The Flower and the Castle: Ibsen and Strindberg*. New York, 1963.

Synge

Combs, William W. "J. M. Synge's *Riders to the Sea:* A Reading and Some Generalizations," *Publications of the Michigan Academy of Science, Art and Literature*, 50:599-607, 1965.
Gaskell, Ronald. "The Realism of J. M. Synge," *Critical Quarterly*, 5:242-248, 1963.
Greene, David H., and Edward M. Stephens. *J. M. Synge. 1871-1909*. New York. 1959.
Leyburn, Ellen D. "The Theme of Loneliness in the Plays of Synge," *Modern Drama*, 1:84-90, 1958.
Price, Alan. *Synge and Anglo-Irish Drama*. London, 1961.
Van Laan, Thomas F. "Form as Agent in Synge's *Riders to the Sea*," *Drama Survey*, 3:352-366, 1964.

Wilder

Brown, J. M. "Wilder: *Our Town*," *Saturday Review of Literature,* 32:33-34, August 6, 1938.

Burbank, Rex. *Thorton Wilder.* New York, 1961.

Scott, Winfield T. "*Our Town* and the Golden Veil," *Virginia Quarterly Review,* 29:103-117.

Stephens, George D. "*Our Town*—Great American Tragedy?" *Modern Drama* 1: 258-264.

McCarthy, Mary. "Class Angles and a Wilder Classic," *Sights and Spectacles.* New York, 1957.

Williams

Beaurline, Lester A. "*The Glass Menagerie:* From Story to Play," *Modern Drama,* 8:142-149, 1965.

Bluefarb, Sam. "*The Glass Menagerie:* Three Visions of Time," *College English,* 24:513-518, 1963.

Donahue, Francis. *The Dramatic World of Tennessee Williams.* New York, 1964.

Jackson, Esther M. *The Broken World of Tennessee Williams.* Madison, Wis., 1965.

Stein, Roger B. "*The Glass Menagerie* Revisited: Catastrophe Without Violence," *Western Humanities Review,* 28:141-153, 1964.

Tischler, Nancy M. *Tennessee Williams: Rebellious Puritan.* New York, 1961.

68 69 70 7 6 5 4 3 2 1